CLA®
REVIEW
MANUAL

Second Edition

D1300147

The West Paralegal Series

Your options keep growing with West Publishing.

Each year our list continues to offer you more options for every course, new or existing, and on-the-job reference materials. We now have over 140 titles from which to choose.

We are pleased to offer books in the following subject areas:

Administrative Law	Family Law
Alternative Dispute Resolution	Federal Taxation
Bankruptcy	Intellectual Property
Business Organizations/Corporations	Introduction to Law
Civil Litigation and Procedure	Introduction to Paralegalism
CLA Exam Preparation	Law Office Management
Client Accounting	Law Office Procedures
Computer in the Law Office	Legal Research, Writing, and Analysis
Constitutional Law	Legal Terminology
Contract Law	Paralegal Employment
Criminal Law and Procedure	Real Estate Law
Document Preparation	Reference Materials
Environmental Law	Torts and Personal Injury Law
Ethics	Will, Trusts, and Estate Administration

You will find unparalleled, practical teaching support.

Each text is enhanced by instructor and student supplements to ensure the best learning experience possible to prepare for this field. We also offer custom publishing and other benefits such as West's Student Achievement Award. In addition, our sales representatives are ready to provide you with needed and dependable service.

We want to hear from you.

The most important factor in improving the quality of our paralegal texts and teaching packages is active feedback from educators in the field. If you have a question, concern, or observation about any of our materials or you have written a proposal or manuscript, we want to hear from you. Please do not hesitate to contact your local representative or write us at the following address:

West Paralegal Series, 3 Columbia Circle, P.O. Box 15015, Albany, NY 12212-5015.

For additional information point your browser to
http://www.westpub.com/Educate and **http://www.delmar.com**

West Publishing — *Your Paralegal Publisher*
an imprint of Delmar Publishers

an International Thomson Publishing company I⟨T⟩P®

CLA®
REVIEW
MANUAL

Second Edition

A Practical Guide to CLA® Exam Preparation

Prepared by
Virginia Koerselman, J.D.
Metropolitan Community College
Omaha, Nebraska

In cooperation with
The National Association of Legal Assistants, Inc.
Tulsa, Oklahoma

WEST PUBLISHING

an International Thomson Publishing company I(T)P®

Albany • Bonn • Boston • Cincinnati • Detroit • London • Madrid
Melbourne • Mexico City • Minneapolis/St. Paul • New York • Pacific Grove
Paris • San Francisco • Singapore • Tokyo • Toronto • Washington

NOTICE TO THE READER

Delmar Staff

Publisher: Susan Simpfenderfer
Acquisitions Editor: Elizabeth Hannan
Developmental Editor: Rhonda Kreshover

Production Editor: Carolyn Miller
Production Manager: Wendy A. Troeger
Marketing Manager: Katherine M. Slezak

COPYRIGHT © 1998
By West Publishing
an imprint of Delmar Publishers
a division of International Thomson Publishing

The ITP logo is a trademark under license.

Printed in the United States of America

For more information, contact:

Delmar Publishers
3 Columbia Circle , Box 15015
Albany, New York 12212-5015

International Thomson Editores
Campos Eliseos 385,Piso 7
Col Polanco
11560 Mexico D F Mexico

International Thomson Publishing – Europe
Berkshire House
168-173 High Holborn
London, WC1V 7AA
England

International Thomson Publishing GmbH
Königswinterer Strasse 418
53227 Bonn
Germany

Thomas Nelson Australia
102 Dodds Street
South Melbourne, 3205
Victoria, Australia

International Thomson Publishing – Asia
221 Henderson Road
#05 -10 Henderson Building
Singapore 0315

Nelson Canada
1120 Birchmount Road
Scarborough, Ontario
Canada M1K 5G4

International Thomson Publishing – Japan
Hirakawacho Kyowa Building, 3F
2-2-1 Hirakawacho
Chiyoda-ku, Tokyo 102 Japan

3 4 5 6 7 8 9 10 XXX 03 02 01 00 99 98

Library of Congress Cataloging-in-Publication Data
Koerselman, Virginia.
    CLA review manual: a practical guide to CLA exam preparation/prepared by Virginia Koerselman in cooperation with the National Association of Legal Assistants, Inc. — 2nd ed.
        p. cm.
    Includes bibliographical references and index.
    ISBN 0-314-20621-3
    1. Legal assistants—Certification—United States. 2. Law examinations—United States. I. National Association of Legal Assistants. II. Title.
KF320.L4K64 1997
340'.076—dc21
                                                    97-31714
                                                        CIP

CONTENTS

CONTENTS

CONTENTS

CONTENTS

CONTENTS

DEDICATION

This CLA® Review Manual is dedicated to the memory of Virginia A. Bell, who supervised my first law office training with a firm hand and a marshmallow heart. She remained a formidable coach, cheerleader, and friend through law school and those lean first years of private practice. She is greatly missed.

PREFACE

When I took the CLA® certification examination in 1977, it occurred to me that someone ought to compile a comprehensive study manual to help people like me who were struggling to prepare for the exam. Law school and many years intervened, during which both NALA and I matured and grew larger; but there still was no national study manual for the CLA® examination.

At NALA's request and with its assistance, the *CLA® Review Manual* has become a reality. Although we hope it provides some degree of focus and direction for the study efforts of applicants everywhere, it is not designed to "teach the test" and should not be used as an applicant's sole reference source.

The *CLA® Review Manual* includes basic background information, general administrative policies, and an expanded outline for each section of the examination as they existed at the time of publication. Any administrative policy, any examination section, or the examination as a whole is subject to change at any time at the discretion of the NALA Certifying Board. Although every reasonable effort is made to keep the *Review Manual* current, there always will be some lag between the time of an examination or policy change and the ability to incorporate it into a publication of this type. Always check with NALA Headquarters to determine whether any changes have occurred.

The *CLA® Review Manual* contains tips for studying and for taking examinations in general. It also includes distilled and condensed topic coverage for each section and subsection of the examination as well as frequent examples, tables, and charts to aid the study effort. A self-test is provided at the end of each chapter.

We commend all those who undertake certification as a professional goal. To the extent that this *Manual* helps them to achieve that goal, we will have achieved ours.

ACKNOWLEDGEMENTS

The author gratefully acknowledges the contributions of the following individuals, each of whom provided invaluable assistance in compiling the *CLA® Review Manual*:

Robert W. Baker, M.B.A. Omaha, Nebraska	Elizabeth Hannan Minneapolis, Minnesota
Kirk Brumbaugh, J.D. Omaha, Nebraska	Kim Hawekotte, J.D. Omaha, Nebraska
Robert Francis Cryne, J.D. Omaha, Nebraska	Patricia Holt, M.S. Omaha, Nebraska
Marge Dover, CAE Tulsa, Oklahoma	Connie Kretchmer, CLAS Omaha, Nebraska
Karen M. Dunn, CLAS Vail, Colorado	Vicki Kunz, CLAS Bismarck, North Dakota
Marie Greninger Tulsa, Oklahoma	Karen Sanders-West, CLAS Wichita, Kansas

as well as the many students who have passed through my classroom over the years, leaving me significantly richer for the experience. She also thank the following legal assistants and paralegal educators who reviewed the manuscript and provided suggestions:

Leigh Anne Chavez Albuquerque Tech. Voc. Institute		Kimberly Houser Central PA Business School
Donna Coble, PLS, CLA Greeley, Colorado		Karen Jordan South Plains College
Patricia G. Elliott, CLAS Phoenix, Arizona		Stephanie K.W. Mark, CLAS Tulsa, Oklahoma
Kathleen J. Foos, CLAS North Palm Beach, Florida		Mark Milker, J.D. So. CA College of Business & Law
Toni Goss Hammerton, CLAS Broken Arrow, Oklahoma		Dorothy Moore Fort Lauderdale College
Amy J. Hill, CLAS Raleigh, North Carolina		Pamela Poole-Weber Seminole Community College
Susan A. Hines San Antonio Court Rptng. Instit.		

ABOUT THE AUTHOR

Virginia Koerselman, Attorney at Law, is a sole practitioner with emphasis in banking law and commmercial litigation. She is a professor at the Metropolitan Community College, Omaha, Nebraska, and became the director of its Legal Assistant Program in 1990. Ms. Koerselman is a graduate of the Creighton University School of Law (J.D. 1983) where she was a Lane Scholar and was a member of the Creighton Law Review (1981-83). She has worked in the Omaha legal community for over 30 years as a legal secretary, legal assistant, and attorney. Virginia received the first CLA certificate in Nebraska in 1978, is a former member of the NALA Certifying Board, and is a member of the Omaha Bar Association and the Nebraska State Bar Association. Ms. Koerselman was the editor of the latest edition of the *NALA Manual for Legal Assistants* (West Publishing Company), author of the accompanying instructor's manual, and currently serves on the faculty for NALA's CLA Short Course.

INTRODUCTION

Even if you're on the right track, you'll get run over if you just sit there.

—Will Rogers

CLA Certification
A Professional Goal

Certification bestows a measure of professional recognition to those who achieve significant competence in the field.

This opportunity for the legal assistant profession is provided by the National Association of Legal Assistants, Inc. (NALA), through its national certification program. The CLA® Certification Program consists of successful completion of a comprehensive two-day examination. Thereafter, evidence of continuing legal education must be submitted periodically to maintain the certification. The program is administered by the National Association of Legal Assistants through its Certifying Board, which is comprised of legal assistants who have attained the Certified Legal Assistant Specialist designation, attorneys, and legal assistant educators. From 1990 to 1997, the number of Certified Legal Assistants throughout the nation doubled over the preceding fifteen-year period. To date, legal assistants in 48 states, the District of Columbia, and the Virgin Islands have been certified by NALA.

Although the goal of becoming a Certified Legal Assistant is a voluntary commitment, the Certified Legal Assistant designation is recognized in the legal field as denoting high standards of professionalism and excellence. The legal community recognizes that the experience and knowledge of Certified Legal Assistants are not restricted to a few limited areas, but encompass a general knowledge and understanding of the entire profession and capabilities far exceeding minimal requirements.

The CLA® Certification Program involves successful completion of a two-day examination administered in the spring (the end of March or the beginning of April), in July, and in December. Details concerning specific testing sites are provided by NALA with the CLA® application forms. For additional information, contact:

NALA Headquarters
1516 South Boston Avenue, Suite 200
Tulsa, OK 74119
918-587-6828

The body of knowledge required to attain the Certified Legal Assistant designation is large. Although the NALA Certifying Board recognizes the expertise required of a legal assistant cannot be reduced to a formula, certain basic skills common to the profession are measurable: written communication skills, judgment and analytical abilities; and an understanding of ethics, human relations, legal terminology, and legal research. The examination covers these areas as well as substantive knowledge of law and procedures. The substantive law section requires each candidate to complete a section on the American legal system and to choose and complete four of eight sections: administrative law; bankruptcy; business organizations; contract law; criminal law; litigation; probate and estate planning; and real estate law. As a standardized national examination, all sections are on the federal level—no specific state laws or procedures are tested.

As with all NALA programs, the purpose of the examination program is to help the legal assistant profession by serving as a means of distinguishing and recognizing excellence among legal assistants and by serving as a stabilizing force and directional tool in the growth of the profession. The Certified Legal Assistant Program is not rigid; its foundation allows methodical and thoughtful change. It helps by attesting to the competency of certified legal assistants and by serving as a guideline for colleges and schools offering legal assistant programs. As the profession advances, the individuals within it must advance. Legal assistants are an integral part of the legal services team and must strive to improve the profession. NALA's voluntary certification program is one answer to those needs.

CLA® is a certification mark registered with the U.S. Patent and Trademark Office (No. 1131999). Any unauthorized use is strictly forbidden.

The Certified Legal Assistant Examination
Summary Outline

Each section of the examination contains objective questions that include multiple choice, true/false, and matching. In addition, both the Communications and the Judgment and Analytical Ability sections contain essay questions. The exact testing schedule is available upon request from NALA Headquarters.

Legal Terminology

The sections of this part deal with (1) Latin phrases, (2) legal phrases or terms in general, and (3) utilization and understanding of common legal terms. The questions involve legal terminology and procedures used in general practice.

Examination Time: 1.25 hours

Communications

This section of the Certified Legal Assistant examination covers the following areas of communications:

Word Usage	Rules of Composition
Punctuation	Concise Writing
Capitalization	Vocabulary
Grammar	Correspondence
	Nonverbal Communication

Examination Time: 2 hours

Ethics

This section deals with ethics in the legal assistant's contacts with employers, clients, co-workers, and the general public. Unauthorized practice, ethical rules, practice rules, and confidentiality are among the topics tested by this section.

Knowledge of the American Bar Association Model Rules of Professional Conduct and the National Association of Legal Assistants, Inc. Code of Ethics and Professional Responsibility is required for successful completion of this section.

Examination Time: 1 hour

Judgment and Analytical Ability

This section deals with (1) analysis and categorization of facts and evidence; (2) the legal assistant's relationship with the lawyer, the legal secretary, the client, the courts, and other law firms; (3) the legal assistant's response to specific situations; (4) handling telephone situations; and (5) reading comprehension, data interpretation, and preparation of documentation related to these areas.

Familiarity with the Model Rules of Professional Conduct of the American Bar Association and with the Code of Ethics and Professional Responsibility of the National Association of Legal Assistants, Inc. will be helpful. Knowledge of logical reasoning techniques and experience as a legal assistant are valuable assets.

Examination Time: 2.25 hours

Legal Research

It is important for the legal assistant to be able to use the most important tool of the legal profession—the law library. The purpose of the Legal Research section of the CLA® Certifying Examination is to test the applicant's knowledge of the use of state and federal codes, the statutes, the digests, case reports, various legal encyclopedias, court reports, Shepardizing, and research procedures.

The amount of study and practice that an applicant will need to pass this section of the examination will depend on his or her current knowledge and experience with legal research. One can gain excellent practice by researching various topics on one's own.

Examination Time: 1.25 hours

Human Relations and Interviewing Skills

The Human Relations portion encompasses professional and social contacts with employers, clients, and other office visitors; co-workers and subordinates; and persons outside the law office. For this reason, the legal assistant should be familiar with authorized practice, ethical rules, practice rules, delegation of authority, consequences of delegation, and confidentiality.

Interviewing Techniques covers basic principles, as agreed upon by most authors on the subject, definitions of terms and basic principles, and handling of specialized interviews. Subject areas included in this section of the examination are:

General considerations for the interview situation: courtesy, empathy, physical setting, and body language

Initial roadblocks: lapse of time, prejudice, and so forth

Form and manner of questions

Use of checklists for specific matters

Situations involving the very young, the elderly, and other persons who may require special handling

Both initial and subsequent interviews are included, as are interviews involving clients and other witnesses

Examination Time: 1.5 hours

Substantive Law

The substantive law section of the CLA® Certification Examination is divided into two parts:

PART I   General Law (including the American Legal System)

PART II   Select any *four:*
  • Administrative Law
  • Bankruptcy
  • Contract

- Business Organizations
- Criminal
- Family Law
- Litigation
- Probate and Estate Planning
- Real Estate

Each applicant is required to take the first part (General Law) and must select four of the remaining eight subsection tests at the time the original application is filed with NALA Headquarters.

Those who plan to take the examination, but who have not had formal law courses, will benefit from a study of one or more current textbooks in the area. A great deal of the material covered in this section of the examination is acquired through work experience in the legal field. The substantive law section of the examination is designed to test the legal assistant's general knowledge of various fields of law.

Examination Time: 2.25 hours combined

Grading and Retake Policy

A passing score of 70% is required for each of the examination sections. The substantive law section is graded as a whole. Of the total 500 points possible in the substantive law section, the applicant must achieve 350 points, regardless of how the points are distributed among the five subparts. Results are announced by the Certifying Board in writing to all applicants, generally six to eight weeks after the April and December tests are taken (eight to ten weeks after the July test is taken). Results are not available by telephone or by FAX.

Of the seven sections of the certification examination, four sections must be successfully completed in order to retake only those sections failed. Applicants in retake status may attend a maximum of five retake sessions within a three-year period. Applicants in retake status will be allowed to choose which sections will be retaken during any retake session. *Note: Subsections selected for Part II of the substantive law section cannot be changed while an applicant is in retake status.* Again, an applicant can attend a retake session only five times within a three-year period. The examination must be completed successfully within three years or credit for all passed sections is forfeited, and the applicant then must reapply for the full examination. If fewer than four sections are completed successfully at the initial testing, the applicant must reapply for the full examination.

Eligibility Requirements

An applicant for the Certified Legal Assistant examination must meet, at the time of filing the application, at least one of the three eligibility requirements shown below:

Category 1

Graduation from a legal assistant program that is:

a. Approved by the American Bar Association, or
b. An associate degree program, or
c. A post-baccalaureate certificate program in legal assistant studies, or
d. A bachelor's degree program in legal assistant studies, or
e. A legal assistant program that consists of a minimum of 60 semester (or equivalent quarter)* hours, of which at least 15 semester hours (or equivalent quarter hours)** are substantive law courses.

900 clock hours of a legal assistant program is equivalent to 60 semester hours. 90 quarter hours of a legal assistant program is equivalent to 60 semester hours.
**225 clock hours of substantive law courses is equivalent to 15 semester hours. 22½ quarter hours of substantive law courses is equivalent to 15 semester hours.*

Category 2

A bachelor's degree in any field plus one (1) year's experience as a legal assistant.*
Successful completion of at least 15 semester hours (or 22½ quarter hours or 225 clock hours) of substantive law courses is equivalent to one year's experience as a legal assistant.

Category 3

A high school diploma or equivalent plus seven (7) years' experience as a legal assistant under the direct supervision of a member of the Bar plus evidence of a minimum of twenty (20) hours of continuing legal education credit to have been completed within the two-year period immediately preceding the examination date. In connection with an application under this category, evidence of continuing education credit is documented by the attorney/employer attestation that must be signed to complete the application form. No further documentation is required.

Individuals currently serving a prison term are ineligible to sit for the Certification examination.

Application forms and information concerning testing sites for the Certified Legal Assistant examination are available from:

National Association of Legal Assistants, Inc.
1516 South Boston Avenue, Suite 200
Tulsa, OK 74119
(918) 587-6828

Maintaining the CLA® Designation

In recognition of the continuing change in laws and procedures that have a direct impact on the quality of work performed by legal assistants, Certified Legal Assistants are required to maintain their certified status by submitting proof of continuing education. The Certified Legal Assistant designation is conferred for a period of five years. If the Certified Legal Assistant submits to the Certifying Board proof of continuing education in accordance with the requirements of the Certifying Board, the designation is renewed for an additional five-year period. The continuing education requirement begins anew with each renewal period of the CLA® designation. Lifetime certification is not available.

The Certified Legal Assistant designation *may be revoked* for any one of the following reasons:

1.   Falsification of information on the application form.
2.   Subsequent conviction of the unauthorized practice of law.
3.   Failure to meet continuing legal education requirements established by the Certifying Board.
4.   Divulging the contents of any examination question or questions.
5.   Subsequent conviction of a felony.
6.   Violation of the NALA Code of Ethics and Professional Responsibility.

Preparation for the Examination

There is no simple or precise formula for successful completion of the CLA® Certification examination. The minimum requirements for success are embodied in the eligibility requirements themselves. However, nearly all applicants require additional, intensive study to prepare themselves adequately for the examination.

The form, method, and amount of study will vary from individual to individual. It is not possible to divulge the contents of the CLA® examination. Neither is it possible to disclose the precise format of the examination. There are, however, study methods that have proved successful for large numbers of applicants. Those are described here. In addition, this chapter contains suggestions on how to get the most from your study efforts, whether you study individually or as part of a study group, and how to approach the examination itself.

Individual Study

A major advantage of individual study is that it can be adapted very easily to suit your own needs in preparing for the exam. In fact, many applicants use individual study as the sole method of preparation.

There is no substitute for individual study, even though it requires substantial commitment and discipline. No one is equally good at everything. Each of us has an area where our skills are not used as much and are therefore not as sharp as we would like them to be; some of us have more than one such area. Individual study allows each applicant to assess what those weak points are and then to devote more study time to them, with less time spent on more familiar areas. The key to successful individual study is to give yourself enough time to prepare adequately, but not so much time that you tarry too long on the threshold of the study project.

What to Study   As with any major project, study for the CLA® examination requires planning. The first step is to inventory your present skills in relation to the requirements of the examination. You may have a good deal of experience with interviewing and drafting, with very little exposure to legal research. Or you may use your research and writing skills every day, with little or no exposure to clients. Everyone's situation is different, and you are the only one who can assess yours accurately.

Statistically, those parts of the examination that cause the most difficulty for most applicants are: (1) Communications, (2) Legal Research, (3) Substantive Law, and (4) Judgment and Analytical Ability.

Self-Assessment   Make a list of the sections of the examination that you must take, including the four substantive law subsections that you have selected.

Privately and realistically, evaluate yourself against each section, one at a time. Review the topic coverage of the section and gauge how you might do if you were to be rigorously tested right now. A checklist is provided to assist you.

Self-Assessment Checklist

_____

(name of section)

	Have you taken a formal course in this subject matter? Yes = 5 No = 0
	If you have taken a formal course, how long ago did you take it? less than 1 yr = 20 1 - 2 yrs = 16 2-3 yrs = 12 4-5 yrs = 8 5+ yrs = 4
	Rate your test-taking ability: easier than for others = 20 about the same = 10 harder than for others = 0
	% of monthly, billable hours spent using skills tested by this section: 61-80% = 40 41-60% = 32 21-40% = 24 11-20% - 16 10% or less = 8
	How familiar are you with the *details* of this section in the *Review Manual*? Extremely = 20 Very = 16 Moderately = 12 Somewhat = 8 Vaguely = 4
	Total Self-Assessment Points
	If there is more than a 20-point variance between the Self-Assessment and the Self-Test Scores, use the average of the two scores (add both scores and divide by two).

90 - 100%	Thorough review of this *Review Manual* may be sufficient
70 - 90%	Study of law summaries (Nutshell, Gilbert's, or Emanuel) + *Manual*
50 - 70%	Textbook study (see Bibliography) + law summary study + *Manual*
0 - 50%	Formal course may be advisable

Nutshell Series
West Publishing Company
610 Opperman Drive
St. Paul, MN 55164

Emanuel Law Outlines
481 Main Street
New Rochelle, NY 10801

Gilbert Law Summaries
Law Distributors
14415 South Main St.
Gardena, CA 90248

Give yourself an overall, pencil score for the section, using a percentile scale. Continue the process for each section, making the same type of evaluation and giving yourself a pencil score for each one. Even though the substantive law subsections (general law plus the four selected by you) are averaged together for examination purposes, you should consider each subsection separately in formulating your study plan.

This represents a conservative approach to gauge where you are now in relation to where you need to be by the time you sit for the examination.

When to Study

As is true of nearly everything connected with preparing for the CLA® examination, decisions about study schedules and when they should begin must be based upon individual needs. The self-assessment checklist may be helpful in gauging how much preparation is required. Unless formal course work is needed, three to six months of relatively intensive study is suggested. This assumes a legal assistant who is working full time and who has been away from a classroom for three to five years. It also assumes that this hypothetical legal assistant schedules two or three study periods of each week, with each study period lasting from two to four hours. During the four weeks immediately preceding the examination, study periods would increase to four each week, with each period lasting two to four hours. These are guidelines only. Each applicant must establish a realistic schedule based upon his or her own needs.

The only inflexible rule about establishing a study schedule is this: Do it. Every other decision can be based upon convenience or need. It is helpful, though, to schedule study periods on the same days and at the same times each week, such as Tuesday, Thursday, and Sunday evenings from 6:00 p.m. to 9:00 p.m. Changing the days and times of study periods from one week to the next invites ultimate abandonment of the schedule.

Once a study schedule has been established, it must be followed religiously. Otherwise, there is little point in having a schedule. Mark each study period on the calendar, just like any other planned event; then stick to it. Professional certification is a vital step in your career as a legal assistant. If it were not, you would not have purchased this *Review Manual* to help you prepare for it. You give vast amounts of time and energy to your employer, to your family, to volunteer organizations, and often to your community. Give this study time to yourself and be firm about it.

Those who have been away from a classroom for a time may have difficulty getting started, at least during the first few sessions. This is normal. The way to overcome such an obstacle is to persevere. Make yourself use the full time allotted for the study period, even if it does not seem to be especially productive. This circumstance makes it doubly important that no scheduled study period is missed. Studying is a skill like any other skill. The more you do it, the easier it gets.

Along with perseverance, developing good study skills requires the efficient use of the scheduled study period. There are a number of ways to maximize the productivity of your study time.

How to Study

Ultimately, everyone develops study methods that work best for him or her. If you have developed study methods that have proven themselves successful for you, use them. If not, the following suggestions are offered as methods that have worked for others, including this author. Use the ones that work for you; feel free to modify them to suit your particular situation and needs.

The Study Environment   The environment in which a person studies is critical in maximizing the study effort. Whether you live in a large house or in an efficiency apartment, you must have one special place for quiet study. It doesn't matter whether that special place is a den of your own or the kitchen table, as long as it is relatively quiet. Once you have selected a location, use it for every study session. Keep the following considerations in mind as well.

- Use good lighting to avoid eyestrain.

- Sit in a straight-back chair and work at a desk or a table. Do not sit on a sofa and try to write on the coffee table; do not lie on the floor or on a bed.

- Reduce the room temperature if possible. Cool (but not frigid) temperatures boost energy and improve concentration.

- Avoid distractions. Turn the television and music off. Do not take telephone calls; offer to call back later.

- Avoid unnecessary interruptions by keeping reference books and supplies near at hand.

The most important part of your study environment is you. In order to obtain maximum benefit from each study session, it is imperative that you be in good condition. Avoid unnecessary stress in every way that you can. This is not the time to go on a diet, to stop smoking, to move, to change jobs, or to undergo elective surgery. No less than a law student studying for the bar, you must be able, physically and mentally, to assume an increasingly rigorous study schedule as the examination date draws near. There are positive steps that you can take to assure your best performance at each study session.

- ▸ Wear loose, comfortable clothing when you study.

- ▸ Take a short break (five to ten minutes) once each hour. Leave the study area, do stretching exercises, move about, get a drink of water or a snack, and then return to work.

- ▸ If you snack, keep it light. Fresh vegetables, fresh fruit, or carbohydrates (without toppings) are best. Lightly salted, plain popcorn seems to be a favorite among students. Do not eat candy or snacks generally classified as junk food; they provide a very short burst of energy, followed by sleepiness.

- ▸ Unless there is a medical reason to avoid exercise, plan to exercise at least twenty minutes at a time, three times a week, throughout the three to six months of the study schedule. Regular aerobic exercise—walking, swimming, jogging, and so forth—releases tension; it also improves stamina and concentration. If you try it for a full three weeks and then skip a week, you will see a marked decline in your ability to study effectively. Exercise regularly.

- ▸ Record your progress as you move through the study schedule that you have established, and give yourself small rewards when you reach prescribed milestones. Have dinner with a supportive friend, see a good comedy show, or treat yourself to a massage.

As silly as some of these suggestions may seem at first glance, be assured that they are sound investments in your physical and mental well-being throughout the preparation and examination process. They work.

Study Aids Once you have estimated the depth of preparation needed for each section and subsection of the examination, you will need access to a suitable library of reference books and study aids. Refer to the section on self-assessment, *supra,* to determine whether you need a textbook, a law summary or outline, or some other study aid.

A list of reference books recommended by NALA's Certifying Board is shown in the Bibliography section of this *Review Manual.* This list, of course, is not intended to be exhaustive; neither is it intended as a limitation of the reference books that may be used. For instance, if you do not have access to any of the legal research texts shown in the Bibliography but do have a legal research text that is both thorough and current, use your text.

If you can borrow up-to-date textbooks and study aids from the library or from lawyers or from CLAs whom you know, this will reduce the expense of textbook acquisition substantially. You will want to avoid acquisition of materials in a way that violates copyright laws, such as photocopying. Aside from being against the law, photocopied material tends to be less legible and less durable than the original; more difficult to store; and almost as expensive as purchasing the reference yourself.

Whether you acquire reference materials by loan or by purchase, however, use discrimination in your selections. Don't try to obtain every textbook and study aid recommended to you. Notwithstanding the exorbitant cost of such an approach, it would be unreasonable to try to study all of them. The better course is to talk with several people who have passed the CLA® examination, compare their recommendations, and then select the study aids best suited to your needs. Regardless of the materials selected, assure yourself that they are up to date.

This *CLA® Review Manual* has been published specifically to provide a condensed, overall foundation for study. It is to a textbook or to a hornbook what *Readers Digest* is to a novel. The *NALA Manual for Legal Assistants*, Third Edition, addresses many of the subjects covered in the nonsubstantive sections of the examination and contains an excellent glossary of legal terms, which can be used as part of the preparation for the Legal Terminology section. Since the Certifying Board has adopted Strunk and White, *The Elements of Style*, Third Edition, as its primary composition and style reference, every applicant will be wise to obtain this text. It can be purchased in most bookstores at a very nominal cost.

Having obtained the reference books and study aids of your choice, you are ready to begin the study process.

Effective Study Methods   Study methods for the CLA® examination, like study methods in general, are as varied as the people who use them. While there is no single study method to ensure success, certain techniques emerge repeatedly when one analyzes the study patterns of successful students in general and of successful CLA applicants in particular.

- Use only up-to-date textbooks and reference materials.

- Limit your study to the national level. Since this is a national examination, no state-specific questions will be asked. General legal rules that are common to all states will be covered, however.

- Don't try to cram. Unless you have a photographic memory, cramming doesn't work; and it breeds unnecessary panic. Organize your study plan so that you have enough time to cover all of the topic areas, giving more time to those areas with which you are least familiar.

- When you encounter difficult or complex principles in your studies, read them aloud to improve clarity or to fix them more firmly in your mind.

- Obtain a large three-ring binder and make dividers for each section of the examination. Keep all of your outlines and notes in it for easy reference.

- Prepare basic outlines of the material to be tested in each section of the examination.

- After the basic outlines are completed, prepare detailed, annotated outlines for each section, using one or more of the reference books in your possession. State all important rules fully, together with any exceptions to those rules, and give examples of how the rules are applied. Include the source and page number from which the information was taken so that you can find it later if you need or want to do so.

- Create timelines or flow charts for technical areas. This method works especially well for substantive law areas. Use the flow chart or timeline to track a case from beginning to end, showing each of the steps involved along with any underlying statutory or procedural rules. *(See the Litigation chapter for a sample flow chart.)*

- Prepare and use flash cards (standard index cards work fine). This study method works especially well for legal terminology and is quite effective in studying legal research and substantive law areas.

In legal research, for example, use flash cards to learn the specific characteristics of a particular case reporter: identity of publisher; features (official or unofficial, type of cases reported, whether it reports all cases or only selected cases, contains a table of cases or a descriptive word index, and the like); how it is supplemented; and so forth. Prepare similar flash cards for each legal research reference tool.

- Do not use outlines, flash cards, or study aids created by others except for comparative reference. The act of creating your own is a critical part of the learning process. If you read the material *and* write it down, your chances of remembering it are doubled.

- Where feasible, create acronyms or mnemonics to help you remember especially troublesome phrases or lists. For instance, if you were trying to remember the elements needed to form a valid contract, you might create the acronym OACA:

> O-Offer
> A-Acceptance
> C-Consideration
> A-Absence of defenses.

Similarly, use a mnemonic to remember the common law felonies. Murder, rape, manslaughter, robbery, sodomy, larceny, arson, mayhem, and burglary become MR & MRS LAMB.

Used sparingly, this technique can be very helpful. If too may acronyms are created, however, remembering all of the acronyms can become a bigger problem than remembering what they were intended to signify in the first place.

- Take as many mock exams as you can find. The Self-Test portions of this *Review Manual* are good starting points. Mock exams are also available from NALA Affiliate Associations in a few states. For more information, contact:

National Association of Legal Assistants, Inc.
1516 South Boston Avenue, Suite 200
Tulsa, OK 74119
918-587-6828

- Without referring to your outlines, practice writing brief essays that require you to discuss or to compare the principles involved in any particular examination section. Mock exams or old tests from an instructor or a student of a legal assistant program are excellent sources. Otherwise, test yourself. One way is to put questions on slips of paper immediately after you have prepared a particular outline (or have someone do this for you), fold the question slips and put them into an envelope marked with the name of the section, and put the envelope away until you are ready to review.

  At review time, have someone select a question slip from each envelope or simply cover your eyes and select the question yourself. Write the essays without checking your outlines. When you have finished, compare them with the outlines to see whether you covered all points, covered them accurately, said too much, and so forth. Make the necessary corrections. This will reinforce the details you need to know for any given section.

- If possible, have someone else read your essays to be sure they make sense. The reviewer does not need a legal background to perform this function (no legal background may even be better). Otherwise, leave them for a day or so and read them again very critically—as if they were drafted by someone whom you do not like. Are the words precise? Are the thoughts concise? Are they stated as simply as possible? Are they crystal clear? Edit them until they meet these criteria.

These are suggestions only, designed to aid the working legal assistant who plans to study alone and who has been away from the classroom for some time. While they are known to produce the desired results, they require a substantial investment of time, effort, discipline, and commitment. Others have done it before you, and you can do it too. Visualize your name with the CLA designation following it; that should keep you going. Nothing worthwhile is ever easy.

For the successful CLA applicant, there is no way to avoid the rigors of individual study altogether. However, if suffering alone is not your cup of tea, organizing a study group may be a viable option.

Group Study

Group study has been used successfully by a number of CLA® applicants. It can be an excellent addition to the study schedules of most applicants, as long as its purposes, benefits, and limitations are understood.

A study group may be able to share some of the stresses associated with preparation for the examination; to provide a supportive, motivational network for study group members; or to reinforce the discipline needed to adhere to the study schedule. Using the theory that two heads are better than one, it may even serve as a filter or as a forum to refine members' understanding—or to expose misunderstanding—of principles likely to be covered on the examination. A study group cannot, however, serve as a substitute for individual study. Neither will it reduce the preparation effort of any individual. If anything, it is likely that a study group will increase the work load of its members.

So why join a study group if it means extra time and extra work? Because it is a good insurance policy. When applicants join a study group, it's because they believe that the extra work is a small price to pay for a support network, a sounding board, enforced discipline (albeit through guilt), and a cheering section—all rolled into one. The common goal of the group makes it easier for some applicants to persevere. Left to themselves, they may falter and then get too far behind. As a team member, however, they will be able to overcome almost any obstacle to fulfill their obligations to the team. This is neither good nor bad; it is simply a fact of human nature.

Since the NALA Certifying Board does not give extra points to those who do it the hard way, do whatever makes it easiest for you to be successful.

How To Organize A Study Group

If you choose to study with a group in addition to your individual study, let the experiences of others guide you. Many state and local NALA affiliates have first-hand experience in organizing study groups and are happy to share their wealth of information and suggestions. To find the NALA affiliate closest to you, contact:

National Association of Legal Assistants, Inc.
1516 South Boston Avenue, Suite 200
Tulsa, OK 74119
918-587-6828.

Keep these considerations in mind as you contemplate organizing a study group. They may provide a basis for discussion when you contact the NALA affiliate, together with any specific questions that you may have.

- Poll the participants to determine the substantive law sections for which each has registered. If no one has registered to take the bankruptcy section, for instance, there is no need to cover bankruptcy as part of the study group schedule.

- Select a group leader. Co-leaders are preferred by many, assuming that two qualified people are available. The CLAs in your geographic area may provide an excellent resource pool; they even may be able to obtain CLAE credits for recertification (check with NALA Headquarters for details). The CLA® group leader may not, however, divulge the contents or the specific format of exam questions.

- If no CLAs are available, locate other experts who can assist you—an English teacher or an attorney with superior writing skills for Communications, one or more attorneys for the substantive areas, and so forth.

- Establish a study schedule. Generally, the study group will meet once a week, leaving an additional week or two for individual review before the examination is taken.

- Take a mock exam prepared by one of the group members (possibly with the assistance of a group leader) at the beginning of each group session. This is generally a good way to get the discussion started. In fact, have group members prepare as much of the material as possible (coordinate with the group leader, of course). It's a good way to study and it takes some of the burden from the group leader.

- Decide how the expense of materials will be shared among the group members.

Taking the Examination

The ultimate goal of nearly everyone who may read this *Review Manual* is to pass the CLA® examination. That being so, and assuming that you have already qualified to take the examination, a few important observations should be made.

Based upon personal experience with both the CLA® exam and with the state bar exam, be assured that the CLA® exam was every bit as difficult within its realm of expertise as the bar exam was. The two examinations were comparable in other ways, the most prominent of which was the ever-mounting levels of stress associated with preparation for the exams and then with taking the exams themselves. By preparing for the stress, you will be in a much better position to manage it.

Some stress is good; it heightens performance. It is only when stress gets out of control and turns into panic that it becomes destructive. For stress management before the examination, refer to the suggestions on preparing for the examination. During the examination itself, there are some things that you can do to ease the stress and to ensure your best performance in an examination of this kind.

Prepare Yourself

- If possible, visit the testing site the day before the examination is to be taken. Determine the best route to take and estimate the time needed to arrive there. Allow for morning rush-hour traffic and plan to arrive 20 to 30 minutes ahead of time. Determine where you will park and how much it will cost. Familiarize yourself with the location of the testing room and of the other facilities located in the building, such as the restroom(s); snack bar or coffee shop, if any; and so forth.

- On the evening before the examination, review your outlines and notes one last time for the sections to be administered the next day. Then put them away.

- Get a good night's rest. You will need all of your energy when the test begins. Don't squander it by sitting up half the night, worrying about what will happen tomorrow or trying to cram. Cramming now will do nothing but cause confusion and panic. Don't do it.

- Relax. Immediately before the exam begins, panic can immobilize you unless you stay in control. Before entering the examination room, walk around and stretch your neck, shoulders, arms, hands, and legs. Don't just pace.

- In selecting your examination seat, sit where you can hear the examination administrator without being distracted by activity at or near his or her desk. If possible, avoid those seats located near air vents.

- Breathe deeply—breathe in through the nose, bring the air all the way down to the knees, and hold it for a count of five; then breathe out through the mouth *s-l-o-w-l-y* until all of the air is released. Continue this exercise until the air comes out slowly and smoothly.
- If you begin to panic (evidenced by the inability to think clearly: you see the words, but they don't register in your head) while taking the exam, stop and quietly perform the breathing exercise. As you breathe in, imagine yourself going down an elevator all the way to the lower sub-basement. Stay at that level for a count of five and then slowly breathe out as you return to ground level. Do it again. Then go back to work. This 30-second exercise is well worth the time invested.

Test Questions in General

- All test questions are designed within a national framework. Do not rely on the rules of a specific state when answering any of the questions.

- Answer all questions, even if you have to guess. Since there is no additional penalty for a wrong answer, guessing may result in a few extra points here and there. An unanswered question, however, never can be correct.

- Read the instructions for each group of questions *very carefully*. Be absolutely certain that you know what you are being asked to do before you begin.

- Be sure that you understand each question before you attempt to answer it. Read it twice if necessary. Fine-line distinctions are commonly drawn in examinations like this one. If you read a question too quickly, important words will be overlooked.

- Read the question as it is, not as you expected it to be. Don't try to help the question-writer by qualifying your answer. The question means exactly what it says.

- Pace yourself in relation to the length of the examination section. Answer the questions you know first. Write the page and question number of the others on your scratch paper and come back to them later. Don't spend too much time on any one question.

- Do not change your answers unless you are positive that you wrote the wrong answer the first time. If you read the question carefully, your first impulse is almost always right. If you second guess yourself, the second guess likely will be wrong.

- If you happen to finish the section before the allotted time has expired, stop. Do not go back through the questions, because second-guessing problems will arise (*see above*).

- Do not mark anything but the answers on the answer sheet. If you do change an answer, make sure the old (incorrect) answer is fully erased. Answer sheets for non-essay portions of the examination are scanned by computer. Stray marks, including incomplete erasures, may be treated as wrong answers.

- Use the break between each testing period effectively. Walk, stretch, relax, and mentally prepare yourself for the upcoming testing period. Do not squander this valuable time by dwelling on the section that you just finished. It is over. Move on.

- Resist the temptation to compare your answers with those of other applicants while on break, during lunch, or at the end of the day. Do not even listen to this type of discussion while sections remain to be taken. Politely excuse yourself if anyone else talks about specific answers. If any of their answers were different from yours (and some of them will be different), it will create unnecessary anxiety, which, in turn, will have a negative effect on your performance during the next testing period.

True-False Questions

- Be wary of true-false questions that contain the word "always" or "never." While there are occasional exceptions, few things in the law are "always true" or "never true."

- If any part of the statement is inaccurate or is incorrect, the entire statement is incorrect, in which case the answer is "false."

- The word "generally" or "may" in a true-false question often indicates that the answer is true. Once again, this is only a general rule; there are exceptions.

Multiple Choice Questions

- Read the questions carefully. Multiple choice questions generally will ask you to select the most correct answer or the best answer, but some will ask you to select the least correct answer or the worst answer. Watch for these.

- Beware of "none of the above" and "all of the above" selections. Certainly there are some questions for which "none" or "all" is the correct answer. As a general rule, these questions are few.

- If a question or a set of answers sounds totally foreign, leave that question and go on to those you can answer. Remember to write the page number and the question number on your scratch paper. If you return to the question and still do not know the answer, guess. There is no penalty for wrong answers, so there is no benefit in leaving any question unanswered.

Make an educated guess or use a process of elimination. Eliminate as many of the wrong selections as you can and then pick from the remaining selections. If your instincts point to one of them, choose it and move on to another question.

If you cannot make even an educated guess about the correct answer and if you have not already eliminated the "c" selection as being wrong, "c" is the best guess (based upon generic testing statistics). Although the "a" selection is sometimes the correct answer for a particular question, it is the worst guess statistically. Comparing statistics and educated guesses, your educated guess is always the better choice.

Matching Questions

- Read the instructions to determine whether items from either list can be used more than once. If not, the items can be matched through a process of elimination. Match those that you know are correct and select the others by eliminating those that you know are wrong.

- Matching questions tend to take more time than either true-false or multiple choice questions. Budget your time with this in mind.

Essay Questions

- Quickly skim the instructions and the question to get a feel for the material. Then read them again, very carefully this time. With this reading, underline any important points or items. This makes it easier to find things later, which saves time.

- Be absolutely sure you understand what it is that you are to do (whether it is to summarize, to compare, to discuss, and so forth).

- If you are asked to summarize material, condense it to the bare bones facts. Do not editorialize; do not change facts or add facts that are not clearly stated in the original material. In general, a summary should be no longer than one-fourth the length of the original material. Double-check to be certain that the names, places, times, and so forth in your summary coincide with the original material.

- If you are asked to compare one thing with another, limit the essay to comparison and contrast (similarities and differences). Don't engage in extraneous dissertations. For instance, do not explain how a particular concept or principle evolved historically when the question asks simply that you compare it with another specified concept or principle.

- When asked to explain or to discuss an issue, concept, term, or the like, do precisely that. At a minimum, the discussion must provide a concise definition. It may also include usage: when, how, and why it is used. Do not compare it with something else unless that is the only way to explain it, which rarely will be the case.

- Do not define terms by using those terms as part of the definition. In other words, do not say, "Criminal law is the law that defines criminal conduct." This is a circular statement. It defines nothing, and no points could be given for it.

- Do not ask rhetorical questions in an essay answer. For example, do not ask, "Why have the rule if it is not enforced?" Rephrase the thought into a declarative statement, such as: "The rule means nothing if it is not enforced."

- Plan to spend at least as much time thinking about and planning your answer as you spend writing it.

- Use the scratch paper provided to you to plan your answer completely before writing *anything* on the answer sheet. Do not merely begin to write, believing (or hoping) that you can clarify your thoughts as you progress. It almost never works.

- Get to the point. In planning your answer, write down the three or four (three is better) most important points to be made. Then put them in complete sentences; be sure they convey complete thoughts and make sense. Use abbreviations and brief forms of words to speed the process. Once you have done this, number them in the logical order in which they should be presented or discussed. Decide whether there are any subpoints that *must* be included for clarity. If so, jot a word or a phrase under the main point as a reminder. Unless the subpoint is absolutely necessary, leave it out.

- Formulate a brief, introductory sentence and draft the final answer. Stick to your planned outline. To the extent that you digress, your answer will appear disjointed and disorganized.

- Say what you need to say in as few words as possible and then stop. Refer to the Communications section of this *Review Manual* for more information.

- Double-check spelling, punctuation, grammar, and word usage. Make corrections as needed. Errors will result in lost points, particularly in the Communications section essays and in the Judgment and Analytical Ability section essays.

- Write the final essay legibly. Use care that the writing is large enough to be read easily. Discard calligraphic flourishes. If necessary, print the final essay answer to ensure its legibility.

- Do not attempt to divert the grader's attention by bluffing or by discussing peripheral issues at length. This technique does not work and can backfire in such a way that the resulting essay score is less than it would have been if the applicant had stopped at those things that were known and were relevant to the question.

- Do not try to be humorous; it generates no points. Likewise, do not write explanatory or apologetic notes to the grader. It's unprofessional.

After the Examination

Once the examination is finished, give yourself as much time as possible to unwind before you attempt to resume your normal schedule. If you plan to drive yourself to the testing site, do not plan to drive back home immediately. If your home is more than 30 or 40 miles away, it may be wise to drive home the following day. The CLA designation will have significantly less value to you if it must be awarded posthumously.

Nearly everyone experiences some degree of shell shock after the last testing period is concluded. Be prepared for the wide range of feelings that you will have if you are like most other applicants.

Stage One: Cessation of all discernable brain function (or so it will seem).

Stage Two: Relief that it is over, followed quickly by mild depression, followed by feelings of hopelessness. By now, you will have convinced yourself that you could not possibly have passed any section of the examination. This is not true, of course, but no one will be able to convince you otherwise.

Stage Three: Hope, fear, and dread, sometimes experienced all at once. First, you will hope that the notification letter arrives soon and will pray that you passed only four of the sections, because you don't ever want to take the whole exam again. Within a few weeks, you will feel a little better and will begin to hope that you passed *all* of it, because you don't want to take *any* of the sections again. At the same time, you will fear that you passed none of the sections; and for this reason, you will begin to experience both eagerness and dread about receiving the notification letter. Waiting will become torturous. Your patience will register on a minus scale, and everyone who is not at least as miserable as you are will irritate you.

All of these feelings are normal, but most of them are unfounded. They can be minimized by keeping the entire experience in perspective and by focusing on those parts of it that are important.

1.   Certification is a voluntary, professional goal. The fact that you have undertaken it says who you really are; attaining it is merely a question of docket control.

2.   All information about your application and your exam results is strictly confidential. No one will know that you are taking the exam (other than limited Headquarters staff) unless you elect to share this information. Not even the graders on the Certifying Board know whose examination is being graded.

3.   The worst that can happen is that you may fail *this time*. If you do, it will be either (1) because of inadequate preparation or (2) because of panic. You have the power to eliminate both obstacles; and once you become certified, no one will care how many times you—or anyone else—may have taken a particular section to pass it. Failure is not a reason for self-denigration; giving up is.

4.   Only those who are willing to risk failure ever succeed; only those who are satisfied with mediocrity never fail.

Expect the best, prepare for the worst, and capitalize on whatever happens. If you prepared and if you did not panic, you will pass the examination. In the meantime, save your outlines and notes and use those time periods previously reserved for study to pursue a favorite hobby while you wait for the results.

Chapter 1
LEGAL TERMINOLOGY

Diplomacy is the art of saying "Nice Doggie" until you can find a rock.

—Will Rogers

This section of the CLA® Certifying Examination tests the applicant's knowledge of (1) Latin phrases, (2) legal phrases or terms in general, and (3) utilization and understanding of common legal terms. The questions involve legal terminology and procedures used in general practice.

Preparation

The legal terms and procedures used in a general law practice typically are much more varied than they are in a legal specialty practice. A general practitioner does a little bit of everything, and applicants should keep this fact in mind as they prepare for this section of the examination.

Of those study suggestions found in the Introduction to the *CLA® Review Manual*, flash cards are particularly effective in learning and reinforcing terminology. Terminology flash cards can be purchased in most law school bookstores; however, customized flash cards are the ideal. A customized flash card is one which is prepared by hand (by you) on a 3 x 5 index card. Flash cards fit easily into a pocket, purse, or briefcase and can be reviewed during odd moments of free time in addition to the regularly scheduled study period.

Latin words and phrases are the most difficult for the greatest number of people, generally because they are used less frequently than are general legal terms. Spend extra time with Latin terms. There is no easy way to learn terminology, whether legal or Latin. It takes discipline, effort, and frequent review.

Latin Terms
—Reprinted in part by permission from the *NALA Manual for Legal Assistants, Second Edition* by the National Association of Legal Assistants, Inc.; Copyright ©1992 by West Publishing Company. All rights reserved.

a fortiori	with stronger reason
a priori	from what goes before; from the cause to the effect
ab initio	from the beginning
actiones in personam	personal actions
ad curiam	before the court, to the court
ad damnum clause	to the damage, clause of complaint which states plaintiff's monetary loss
ad faciendum	to do
ad hoc	for this purpose, for this occasion
ad litem	for the suit; for the litigation (a guardian ad litem, for example)
ad rem	to the thing at hand
ad valorem	according to the value (an ad valorem tax, for example)
adversus	against (defendant adv. plaintiff)

aggregatio menium	meeting of minds (relates to formation of contracts)
alias dictus	otherwise called, also known as (as in an assumed name)
alibi	in another place, elsewhere
aliunde	from another place, from without (as in evidence outside the document) see parol evidence
alter ego	the other self
amicus curiae	friend of the court (as an amicus curiae brief filed with an appellate court)
animo	with intention, disposition, design, will
animus	mind, intention
ante litem motam	before suit brought, before litigation is filed
arguendo	in the course of the argument, for the sake of argument
assumpsit	he undertook, he promised
bona fide	good faith
capias	take, arrest
capita	persons, heads
causa mortis	by reason of death
caveat	beware, a warning
caveat emptor	let the buyer beware
certiorari	send the pleadings up (from an inferior court to a superior court; U.S. Supreme

Court uses writ of certiorari to review most cases)

cestui	beneficiaries (pronounced "setty")
cestui que trust	beneficiaries of the trust
circa	in the area of, about, concerning
compos mentis	of sound mind
consortium	union of lots or chances; conjugal fellowship of husband and wife
contra	against
coram nobis	before us ourselves
corpus	body
corpus delicti	body of the offense; essence of the crime
cum testamento annexo	with the will annexed
datum (pl., *data*)	1. a thing given; information; 2. a date
de facto	in fact, in deed, actually
de jure	of right, lawful
de novo	anew, afresh
de son tort	of his own wrong
dies non	not a day
duces tecum	bring with you (as in subpoena duces tecum, whereby subpoenaed person must appear and bring records)
dum bene se gesserit	while he shall conduct himself, during good behavior

e converso	conversely, on the other hand
en banc	in the bench, all judges present (a three-judge panel sits individually or en banc)
eo instanti	upon the instant
erratum (pl., *errata*)	error
et alii	and others (as in Smith, et al. v. Jones)
et sequentia	and as follows (et seq.)
et ux	and wife
et vir	and husband
ex delicto	(arising) from a tort
ex gratia	as a matter of favor
ex officio	from office, by virtue of his office
ex parte	one side only, by or for one party only
ex post facto	after the fact
facto	in fact, in or by the law
felonice	feloniously
fiat	let it be done, a short order that a thing be done
fieri	to be made up, to become
fieri facias	cause to be made (writ directing sheriff to reduce judgment debtor's property to money [sell it] for the amount of the judgment)
flagrante delicto	in the very act of committing the crime

forum non conveniens	discretionary power of a court to decline jurisdiction over a case when the court believes it should be tried elsewhere for convenience of parties and witnesses
gravis	serious, of importance
habeas corpus	you have the body (writ directed to custodian of a person, commanding custodian to produce such person)
habendum clause	that part of deed which begins "to have and to hold"; defines extent of ownership
honorarium	honorary fee or gift; compensation from gratitude
idem	the same as above (id.)
idem sonans	having the same sound (as names sounding alike but spelled differently)
in curia	in court
in esse	in being, existence
in forma pauperis	permission given to a poor person to sue without liability for court costs
infra	beneath; below
in limine	at the beginning; threshold
in loco parentis	in place of a parent, one charged with a parent's rights and obligations
in pari delicto	in equal fault
in personam	personally, against the person
in praesenti	at once; now
in re	in the matter

in rem	proceedings against a thing (a bank account or real estate) distinguished from those against a person
in specie	in the same or in similar form
instanter	immediately
inter alia, inter alios	among other things, between other persons
inter se	among themselves
inter vivos	between the living, from one person to another
in toto	in the whole, completely
in transitu	in transit
intra	within, inside
ipse dixit	he himself said (it), as an assertion made but not proved
ipso facto	by the fact itself
ita est	so it is
jura personarum	right of a person, rights of persons
jura rerum	rights of things
jure divino	by divine right
jure uxoris	in his wife's right
jus (pl. *jura*)	law; right; laws collectively
jus ad rem	a right to a thing
jus commune	the common law, the common right

jus gentium	the law of nations, international law
just habendi	the right to have a thing
jus tertii	the right of a third party; the rights of another person
levari facias	cause to be levied, a writ of execution
lex	law
lex loci	law of the place where the cause of action arose
lis pendens	litigation pending, as in a lis pendens filed with real estate records to notify the world that the real estate is involved in litigation
locus delicti	the place of the crime or of the tort
locus sigilli (L.S.)	the place for the seal
mala	bad
mala fides	bad faith
mala in se	wrong in itself, an act which is morally wrong
mala praxis	malpractice
mala prohibita	acts declared as criminal by statute (failure to file a report), though not wrong in themselves (theft)
malo animo	with evil intent
mandamus	we command, a writ used to compel an official to perform an act which she is required to perform
manu forti	with a strong hand, forcible entry

mens rea	guilty mind, most crimes require the element of intent (mens rea)
nihil dicit	he says nothing, as in a default judgment against a defendant who does not raise a defense in the action
nil	nothing; of no account
nil debet	he owes nothing
nisi prius	unless before (used to distinguish the court where trial was held from the appellate court)
nolle prosequi	unwilling to prosecute (a crime), prosecutor's discretion not to file charges in a particular case
nolo contendere	I will not contest it
non	not
non assumpsit	plea in defense; that he did not promise
non compos mentis	not of sound mind
non est factum	it is not his deed
non obstante	notwithstanding
non sequitur	it does not follow
nota bene (N.B.)	note well; take notice
nudum pactum	nude pact, bare agreement which lacks the consideration to form a valid contract
nul tort	no wrong done
nulla bona	no goods (wording used on the return of a writ fieri facias)

nunc pro tunc	now for then, as in an order nunc pro tunc to correct clerical error in a previous order
obiter dictum	remark which is not central to the main issue
onus probandi	the burden of proof
opus (pl., *opera*)	work, labor
ore tenus	by word of mouth, orally, as in a motion ore tenus
pari delicto	in equal guilt
pari passu	by equal progress, ratably, equitably, without preference
pater familias	father of the family
peculium	private property
pendens	pending
pendente lite	pending the suit, during litigation
per annum	annual, by the year
per capita	by the head, equally shared
per contra	in opposition
per curiam	by the court
per diem	by the day
per se	by itself, taken alone
per stirpes	by representation, by the roots or stocks for purposes of inheritance
post	after, later

post-factum	after the fact, after the even
post-obit	to take effect after death
praecipe	writ commanding a person to do some act or to appear and show cause why she should not do so; order to clerk of court to issue a summons or execution on judgment already rendered
prima facie	at first sight, on the face of it
pro bono	free of charge, without cost
pro forma	as a matter of form
pro hac vice	for this occasion
pro rata	according to the rate or proportion
pro se	appearing for oneself; personally
pro tanto	for so much, to that extent
pro tempore	for the time being, temporarily
prochein ami	next friend
publici juris	of public right
pur autre vie	for or during the life of another
quaere	question, doubt
quantum	how much, the amount
quare	wherefore
quare clausum fregit	breaking the close, trespass
quasi	as if, as if it were

quid pro quo	what for what, something for something (as in consideration for a contract)
quo warranto	by what right or authority
res	thing, object, subject matter
res gestae	things done, excited utterance
res ipsa loquitur	the thing speaks for itself
res judicata	a thing (matter) adjudged
respondeat superior	let the master answer
scienter	knowledge, awareness
scilicet	to wit, that is to say, namely (SS or ss)
scintilla	a spark, the least particle
scire facias	cause to know, give notice (writ used to revive a judgment that has expired [dormant])
secundum	according to
se defendendo	in self-defense
semper	always
seriatim	severally, separately
sic	thus, so, in such manner (used to indicate an error in original, quoted material)
sigillum	a seal
sine	without
sine die	without a day, without a specific day assigned for a future meeting

sine qua non	that without which a thing cannot occur; indispensable condition or part
stare decisis	to abide by decided cases
status quo	state in which, present state
sua sponte	voluntarily, of his own will and motion
sub nomine	under the name of, in the name of, under the title of
sub silentio	under silence, without any notice being taken
sui generis	of its own kind or class, the only one of a kind, unique
sui juris	of his own right, having legal capacity to act for himself
supersedeas	superseding (as in the bond that accompanies a writ commanding a stay of proceedings pending appeal)
supra	above, cited in full above
tenere	to hold, to keep
terminus a quo	the starting point
ultra	beyond, in excess of, outside of
ultra vires	without power, beyond the powers of
venire facias	that you cause to come, a type of summons
versus	against (plaintiff v. defendant)
videlicet (viz.)	it is easy to see, that is to say, namely
vi et armis	by force and arms

vis-à-vis	one who (that which) is face to face with another
vivos	living
voir dire	to speak the truth, the process used to select jurors

Legal Terms

abatement	reduction, termination
abrogation	annulment of a former law by act of a legislative body, by constitutional authority, or by usage
acceptance	in contract law, consent to abide by the terms of an offer; taking or receiving a thing in good faith with the intention of retaining it
accession	that which increases the size or value of property
accommodation	arrangement made as a favor to another rather than for consideration received
acknowledgement	an admission, affirmation, or declaration
acquittal	release or discharge of an obligation or liability; in criminal law, a finding of not guilty

ademption	satisfaction of a legacy by gift prior to testator's death
adhesion contract	standardized contract form in which a party with little or no bargaining power is forced to accept its terms
adjudication	judgment or decision of a court
administrative law	body of rules and regulations having the force of law and promulgated by an administrative body created by Congress or a state legislature
adverse possession	acquiring title to real estate by hostile possession rather than by purchase
affiant	one who makes or swears to the truth of an affidavit
affidavit	sworn statement in writing taken before a notary public or other authorized officer
affirmative defense	allegation of a responsive pleading which, if it can be proved, negates the allegations of the complaint
agent	person authorized by another to act for him, one entrusted with another's business
agreement	meeting of the minds, preliminary to contract formation
allegation	assertion made but not proved
amortization	gradual extinction of a monetary obligation by periodic payments that usually includes interest
amnesty	sovereign forgetfulness of past acts, usually available for a limited time

ancillary	auxiliary, supplemental, subordinate
annotation	remark, note, or commentary intended to illustrate or explain
annul	cancel, make void, destroy
answer	written pleading by which a defendant responds to the plaintiff's complaint
antitrust laws	federal and state laws to prevent restraint of trade, price-fixing, price discrimination, monopolies, or other conduct detrimental to free commerce
appeal	review by a higher court
appellant	party who files an appeal
appellee	party who defends an appeal
appraisal	valuation or estimate of property value, made by qualified expert
arbitration	investigation and determination of dispute by neutral decision-maker; decision is binding on parties
arraignment	in criminal law, hearing at which accused pleads guilty or not guilty
assault	in tort, threat of imminent bodily harm accompanied by apparent ability to carry out the threat; in criminal law, often defined as the tort equivalent of battery (*see below*)
asset	real or personal property owned by an individual, estate, business corporation, or other entity
assignment	transfer of any right, title, or interest to another

attestation	act of witnessing the signing (execution) of a document
assumption of risk	doctrine under which a person cannot recovery for injuries received from a dangerous activity to which she voluntarily exposed herself
attachment	pre-judgment seizure of property based upon court order
attest	certify or affirm to be true or genuine
attorney-in-fact	one appointed by another to act in specific matters described in a power of attorney or in a letter of attorney
aver	assert, allege, claim
bailment	delivery of personal property to another to be held for a particular person and then returned
beneficiary	one who benefits from the act of another
bequest	gift of personal property by will
breach	failure (without legal justification) to perform when performance is due
brief	written argument of counsel concerning one or more legal issues in a case, sometimes called a memorandum of law
capacity	having legal authority or mental ability; being of sound mind
caption	that part of a pleading which states the name of the court, the name of the parties, the case number assigned, and the name of the pleading

cause of action	fact(s) giving rise to a legal remedy
chattel	personal property
choate	perfected; complete
chose in action	a personal right not yet reduced to judgment
civil code	collection of laws or statutes relating to private rights or remedies
civil law	laws which relate to private rights and remedies, distinguished from criminal law
CLA	abbreviation for Certified Legal Assistant, a professional designation earned through and awarded by the National Association of Legal Assistants to those legal assistants who successfully complete an extensive written examination of their general skills and their specific knowledge of substantive legal rules and procedure
Code Civil	law of the State of Louisiana consisting of a collection of statutes and based upon the Napoleonic Code, distinguished from common law
code	collection of laws or statutes
codicil	an addition or change to an original will
common law	law based upon custom, usage, and judicial decision, distinguished from statutory law
community property	property owned in common by husband and wife, each owning an undivided one-half interest as a result of their marital status

commutation	substitution of a lesser punishment for a greater one
condemnation	the process of taking private property for public use under a government's right of eminent domain
consideration	the lawful price, motive, cause, impelling influence, or inducement for a contract
contract	agreement between competent parties, supported by consideration, to do or to refrain from doing some lawful act
conversion	wrongful taking of personal property with intent to deprive its owner of it permanently
copyright	a right to reap the financial benefits of literary property
covenant	agreement or promise, often restricting the use of real estate
creditor	one to whom a debt or obligation is owed
criminal law	laws which control standards of conduct and which prescribe the punishments for disobedience
debenture	bond given as evidence of corporate debt
decree	the final order of an equity court
defamation	that which holds one up to contempt or ridicule; that which injures one's reputation
deponent	one who gives a deposition

deposition   sworn testimony given by question and answer in a non-courtroom setting, which is recorded and transcribed by a court reporter

devise   gift of real property by will

discharge   to release, liberate, annul, disencumber, dismiss

duress   unlawful constraint exercised upon a person, forcing her to do an act which she would not have done otherwise

enjoin   to prevent or forbid by injunction

equity   justice administered by principles of fairness, distinguished from strict rules of law

escheat   reversion of property to the state when there are no heirs to inherit the property at a person's death

estop   to stop, bar, prevent

estoppel   doctrine under which a person's acts or failure to act prevents her from seeking legal relief, although she would have been entitled to relief otherwise

eviction   to recover real estate (from a tenant) by legal process; to force out or remove from real property

evidentiary   constituting evidence or proof, having the quality of evidence

exemptions   immunity from a general burden, tax, or charge; in bankruptcy or in judgment executions, that portion of the debtor's property that cannot be liquidated and applied to her debts

felony	a crime for which the maximum possible punishment is death or imprisonment for one year or more in a penitentiary
fraud	any artifice used by one person to deceive another
general denial	a pleading in the form of an answer, which denies allegations made by the opposing party but which contains no affirmative defenses
grantee	one to whom real estate is conveyed; the buyer of real estate
grantor	one who conveys real estate; the seller of real estate
guarantor	one who agrees to undertake the (financial) obligation of another
guaranty	agreement to undertake the (financial) obligation of another
guardian	one charged with responsibility to manage the personal matters of another who is incompetent because of age, understanding, or lack of self-control
guardian ad litem	person appointed by a court to look after the interests of a child or incompetent during the pendency of a litigation
inchoate	unfinished, incomplete
indemnify	to secure against loss or damage
indictment	written accusation issued by a grand jury against a defendant in criminal law

indorsement	act of a payee, drawee, accommodation indorser, or holder of a bill, note, check, or other negotiable instrument, in writing his or her name upon the back of the instrument to assign or transfer the negotiable instrument to another
infant	one who has not reached the age of majority; a minor
information	written accusation issued by a prosecutor against a defendant in criminal law
injunction	an order issued by a court of equity, requiring a person to do or not to do a specific act
insolvent	condition of a person or entity that exists when total liabilities exceed total assets
interlocutory	provisional, interim, not final
interrogatories	series of formal, written questions addressed to a party for discovery purposes
intestate	without a will, one who dies without a will
judgment	final order of a court of law, based upon a jury verdict or upon findings of fact by the court
jurat	clause of a notary public or authorized officer attesting that a statement or document was sworn to by a specific person on a specific date
jurisdiction	power conferred on a court to hear a particular case and to render a final decision on the merits
jurisprudence	science of law; system of law

laches	a doctrine by which equitable relief is denied to one who has waited too long to seek relief
legal assistant	A distinguishable group of persons who assist attorneys in delivering legal services. Within this occupational category, some individuals are known as paralegals. Through formal education, training, and experience, legal assistants have knowledge and expertise regarding the legal system and substantive and procedural law that qualify them to do work of a legal nature under the supervision of an attorney.
lessee	one who possesses or uses the property of another; tenant
lessor	a title holder of property who contracts for its possession or use by another; landlord
liable	legally responsible
libel	written defamation
lien	a charge, security, or encumbrance on property
liquidated	property or claim that has been converted to its cash equivalent
litigation	contest in a court of law for the purpose of enforcing a right or seeking a remedy
magistrate	court officer with limited judicial authority; a public officer
malfeasance	evil doing; performance of an act with bad intent
malpractice	professional negligence or misconduct

mediation	arrangement to attempt settlement of a dispute by using a neutral party as the referee; unlike an arbitrator, a mediator does not issue a binding decision
memorandum of law	brief of law submitted to a court by the attorney for a party
memorandum opinion	very short opinion of a court
merger	absorption of one thing or right into another
metes and bounds	a method of describing real estate, using boundary lines with terminal points and angles
minor	person who is not an adult; child
misdemeanor	a criminal offense for which the maximum possible punishment is a fine or incarceration for a period less than one year
misfeasance	improper performance of an otherwise lawful act
mitigation	duty of parties to minimize damages after an injury is sustained or a breach occurs
mortgage	conditional conveyance of an interest in real estate, usually as security for a debt
mortgagee	one who receives a mortgage, usually a lender
mortgagor	an owner of real estate who gives a mortgage
motion	application (not a pleading) or request made to a court to obtain an interim ruling or order

motion in limine	application requesting a court to rule in advance that specific, unfairly prejudicial information will not be mentioned during trial
negligence	failure to use the care which a reasonable and prudent person would use in similar circumstances
notary public	public officer who administers oaths, attests and certifies documents, and takes acknowledgments
novation	substitution of a new contract, debt, or obligation for an existing one between the same or different parties
nuncupative	oral; not written
oath	solemn pledge attesting to the truth of a statement
offer	a promise; a commitment to do or to refrain from doing some specific act
offeree	one to whom an offer is made
offeror	one who makes an offer
option	a right supported by consideration to purchase property at an agreed price within a specified time
order	mandate, command, or direction authoritatively given; mandate of a court
ordinance	legislative enactment (law enacted) by a local government such as a county or a city
parol evidence	oral proof of contract terms which are not contained within the written contract document

parole	release from imprisonment upon specific conditions related to conduct or good behavior
patent	inventor's right to exclude others from making, using, or selling the invention for seventeen years
paternity	relationship of a father to a child
payee	one to whom payment is made
payor	one who makes payment
pecuniary	monetary; relating to money
perjury	false testimony given under oath
pleading	in federal court, complaint, answer to complaint, and reply to cross-claim (no other pleadings are allowed)
power of attorney	an instrument authorizing one to act as agent or attorney-in-fact for another as to those matters listed in the instrument
precedent	holding of a case which guides the decisions in future cases involving similar facts and similar legal issues
privileged communications	statements made by persons within specific, protected relationships for evidentiary purposes (husband-wife, attorney-client, priest-parishioner, and so forth)
probable cause	justification to believe that a crime was committed and that the accused is the person who committed it
probation	a sentence which releases a convicted person into the community under the supervision of a probation officer

promissory estoppel	a doctrine which prevents a party to a contract from denying that consideration was given for the contract
promissory note	a written promise to pay a specific sum of money at a future time
proximate cause	the last (negligent) act which leads to injury; legal cause
proxy	an instrument authorizing one to cast the votes of another at a corporate meeting
punitive damages	damages awarded over and above the amount of losses, which are awarded as punishment of the wrongdoer
quash	suppress; stop; cease; abate
quiet title action	action to determine clear title to real estate
quitclaim deed	deed without warranty, which passes only that title which the grantor has
recidivist	repeat offender
release	discharge of one party's obligation to another
replevin	action to recover possession of personal property
rescission	an equitable remedy which invalidates a contract on the basis of mutual mistake, fraud, impossibility, and so forth
restitution	restoration of a thing to its rightful owner; a measure of damages according to the defendant's gains rather than the plaintiff's losses

service of process	delivery of a writ, summons, subpoena to the person named therein
settlor	one who creates a trust, trustor
slander	spoken defamation
specific performance	equitable remedy in contract law which requires the breaching party to perform according to the specific terms of the contract
statute	legislative enactment (law enacted) by Congress or a state legislature
statute of limitations	statute which limits the time within which a cause of action may be filed
stipulation	agreement between parties to a lawsuit concerning matters related to the trial
subpoena	a writ commanding the named person to appear at a specific time and place
subpoena duces tecum	a writ commanding the named person to appear at a specific time and place and to bring specific records or documents with her
summons	document served upon a defendant to notify her that suit has been filed against her and directing her to answer or to otherwise appear in the case by a specific date
survey	process by which a tract of land is measured and its contents determined, with a map to scale created for it
temporary restraining order	an emergency injunctive remedy (order) of short duration to require or to forbid an act until a hearing can be held

testimonium clause	the clause of an instrument which begins "In witness whereof, . . . "
tickler system	reminder system used in law offices to supplement diaries and calendars in the overall docket control system
tort	a civil wrong such as negligence or trespass, as distinguished from a criminal offense (the same conduct may result in both tort liability and criminal liability)
trust account	account where client funds are kept separate from attorney funds
unconscionable	grossly unfair, unscrupulous, terms or conduct which shocks the conscience
usury	the excess over the lawful interest rate
vendee	the purchaser or buyer of property
vendor	the seller of property
venue	the location where an action is tried
verdict	finding(s) of fact by a jury in a civil or criminal trial
verification	confirmation of accuracy; sworn oath by an authorized person that certain statements are true to the best of his or her knowledge and belief
void	having no legal force or effect
voidable	that which is capable of being declared void but which is valid until such declaration is made
warranty	a promise to defend the truth of a fact

warranty deed

a deed conveying land which guarantees that the title is free of defects to marketability

with prejudice

a declaration (usually in connection with an order of dismissal) which ends the right to further relief; it prevents either party from filing future complaints based on the same claim or cause of action

without prejudice

a declaration (usually in connection with an order of dismissal) which preserves any rights or privileges that a party may have to file a future complaint based upon the same claim or cause of action

witness

one who has personal knowledge about facts related to a case; one who can testify about what she has seen, heard, or otherwise observed

writ of execution

order of a court after judgment commanding a court officer to seize property in satisfaction of the judgment

Legal Terminology Self-Test

Allow an uninterrupted thirty-minute period to answer all of the following questions. At the end of thirty minutes, check your answers against those in the Answer Key Section at the back of the Review Manual. Deduct two points for each incorrect answer (100 total possible points). Unanswered questions are counted as incorrect answers. Follow directions carefully and observe the time limit precisely to provide an accurate self-assessment.

Choose the most correct answer to the following questions unless you are instructed to do otherwise.

1. True or False.   An oral contract to purchase real estate is an example of a contract that is voidable.

2. True or False.   *Ad valorem* refers to a type of tax.

3. True or False.   If a court enters an order *sua sponte*, this indicates that the motion of counsel is granted immediately after it is made during a hearing or a trial.

4. True or False.   Acts performed outside the scope of authority of a public official are *ultra jure*.

5. An attorney involved in a case *ab initio* is one who was involved:

    a.   at the beginning of the case but is not involved now.
    b.   from the beginning of the case and continues now.
    c.   at that point in the case when litigation was initiated.
    d.   none of the above

6. A contract that is cancelled, as if it had never occurred, is said to have been:

    a.   vacated
    b.   rescinded
    c.   lapsed
    d.   abandoned

7.   Knowledge, sometimes known as "guilty knowledge," is:

   a.   carnal knowledge
   b.   mens rea
   c.   scienter
   d.   none of the above

8.   An order commanding a person to appear and to testify in a legal action:

   a.   subpoena
   b.   subpoena duces tecum
   c.   subpoena sub testimonium
   d.   summons

9.   One with authority to act for another is a(n):

   a.   agency
   b.   attorney in fact
   c.   principal
   d.   all of the above
   e.   none of the above

For the next group of questions, match each term in the first column with the word or phrase in the second column which most accurately defines it.

10.	_____ et vir	a.	notwithstanding the verdict
11.	_____ non obstante verdicto	b.	the right of a third party
12.	_____ a fortiori	c.	from the cause to the effect
13.	_____ jus tertii	d.	and husband
14.	_____ a priori	e.	for the sake of argument
		f.	and wife
		g.	with stronger reason

15.   True or False.   Conversion refers to the wrongful taking of personal property with the intent to deprive its owner of it permanently.

16. True or False.   *Pendente lite* refers to the jurisdiction acquired by a court over property involved in an action until a final judgment is entered.

17. True or False.   A verification is a sworn statement of the truth of the facts stated in an instrument, document, or pleading.

18. True or False.   *Nudum pactum* is a promise enforceable by law.

19. True or False.   *Res gestae* refers to a child in gestation for purposes of applying the Rule Against Perpetuities.

20. A court order directed to a public official, commanding her to do that which her office requires her to do, is called a(n):

    a. fiat
    b. mandamus
    c. quo warranto
    d. any one of the above
    e. none of the above

21. The temporary relinquishment of control over one's property to another is called a(n):

    a. assignment
    b. bailment
    c. accession
    d. none of the above

22. When a person dies without surviving heirs and without a will, the state may become the owner of the estate property by:

    a. reversion
    b. intestacy
    c. escheat
    d. none of the above

23. Disparaging statements that are published in The New York Times about another person may constitute:

    a. defamation
    b. slander
    c. liable
    d. libel

24. An order entered by a court without a hearing and with only one party represented is:

    a. ex parte
    b. ex officio
    c. ex delicto
    d. ex necessutate legus

For the next group of questions, match each term in the first column with the word or phrase in the second column which most accurately defines it.

25. _____ secundum   a.   the right to a thing

26. _____ liquidated   b.   second series

27. _____ corpus juris   c.   a legal fiction

28. _____ jus ad rem   d.   employer's liability for employee

29. _____ laches   e.   body of law

30. _____ constructive trust   f.   jurisdiction over a thing

31. _____ rescission   g.   auxiliary, in aid of

32. _____ settlor   h.   according to

33. _____ ancillary   i.   unreasonable delay in asserting a right

34. _____ respondeat superior   j.   converted to cash

                                     k.   trustor

                                     l.   termination before completion

35. True or False.   A supplemental provision for a will may be annexed by an addendum.

36. True or False.   That which increases the size or value of property is called an accession.

37. True or False.   Mediation is a type of non-judicial dispute resolution which is binding upon the parties.

38. That portion of a pleading which requests relief against the opposing party or parties is called the:

    a.   habendum clause
    b.   ad litem clause
    c.   ad damnum clause
    d.   ad respondendum clause

39. Once a claim between parties has been decided on its merits, it may not be relitigated between the same parties because of the doctrine of:

    a.   res gestae
    b.   res ipsa loquitur
    c.   res litigium
    d.   res judicata

40. When a testatrix includes a provision in her will to give $1,000 to each of her nieces and nephews and then pays $1,000 to each of them before she dies, this act is called an:

    a.   abatement
    b.   ademption
    c.   accrual
    d.   accretion

For the following group of questions, supply the most precise word or phrase for each of the definitions listed.

41. _____   a collection of legislative enactments

42. _____   a transfer of legal rights to another

43. _____   internal rules adopted by a corporation

44. _____   testamentary conveyance of real property

45. _____   habitual criminal

46. _____   tending to prove or disprove a fact in issue

47. _____   bond accompanying an order of stay

48. _____   averment

49. _____   performed without charge

50. _____   bond/note given as evidence of corporate debt

Chapter 2
COMMUNICATIONS

Only a mediocre writer is always at his best.

—Somerset Maugham

This section of the Certified Legal Assistant examination covers the following areas of communication:

Word Usage	Rules of Composition
Punctuation	Concise Writing
Capitalization	Vocabulary
Grammar	Correspondence
	Nonverbal Communication

Knowledge of communication rules and techniques is tested through true-false, multiple choice, matching, and essay questions.

Historically, the Communications section of the CLA® examination has caused great difficulty for applicants. This may lie in the fact that many legal assistants assume they know communication rules reasonably well. Consequently, they may allot less preparation time to this section than to some of the others. Do not fall into the trap created by this complacent view.

Recall, too, that the NALA Certifying Board has adopted Strunk and White, *The Elements of Style*, Third Edition, as its primary reference on the subject. It can be purchased in most retail bookstores. Where this text covers a particular topic, its rules control. Use the other texts listed in the Bibliography as supplemental references only.

The communication rules stated in the Strunk and White text are incorporated throughout the *CLA® Review Manual*. Where the Strunk and White text is silent about a particular rule, however, the *Review Manual* uses the following references: Fowler and Aaron, *The Little, Brown Handbook*; *Texas Law Review Manual on Style* (Texas Law Review Publications, Inc.), which is based upon both the Fowler and the Strunk and White texts; and Hollis Hurd, *Writing for Lawyers* (Journal Broadcasting & Communications).

Word Usage

The Word Usage portion of the Communications section tests the applicant's knowledge of how words are used in a particular context. These include words that are often confused, as well as words and phrases that are misused, by inexperienced writers.

In general, and in particular for examination purposes, avoid slang expressions and colloquialisms. The formal, concise expression of thought is preferred over the informal in legal writing. There may be the occasional situation when a lawyer or legal assistant purposely uses a slang expression or a colloquialism for a specific effect, perhaps in the preparation of a brief. However, this should happen rarely and certainly should not be taken as authority for poor writing generally.

Slang

Slang expressions are words or phrases that have been coined, usually by younger people, for use in a way that is inconsistent with their standard definitions. Slang is often regional and short-lived. While a legal assistant should be familiar with slang expressions in use at a particular time in his or her region, slang has no place in good writing. A few slang words and expressions to avoid are shown below. This list is not intended to include all of the slang words that exist.

bag, bag lady	dog, dog it	out of sight
bananas	drag	payoff
bomb, bomb out	flake off, flaky	peel out
bonkers	flunk, flunked	right on

bread	foxy lady	rip off
burned	gizmo	slick
bug off	gross, gross out	space cadet
bummed, bummer	hang-up	space off
chill, chill out	hooked	space out
cold	hooker	split
clobber	jacked up	stuff
cool, cool it	junk	turn off, turn on
cop, cops	make out	up tight

Colloquialisms

A colloquialism is a word or expression used in an informal, conversational setting. The term also may be used to indicate an expression of regional dialect. Colloquialisms are inappropriate in professional conversation. Their use is incorrect in legal writing, as well as in all other types of formal writing.

The italicized words and phrases in the following sentences are representative of the types of colloquialisms that should be avoided. A more appropriate expression is also shown.

I was ill but I am *alright* now.
I was ill but I am **all right** now.　　OR　　I was ill but I am **well** now.

I have *around* eight books in my library.
I have **approximately** eight books in my library.

She is regarded *as being* the best lawyer in the state.
She is regarded **as** the best lawyer in the state.

Let me know *as to whether* you plan to attend.
Let me know **whether** you plan to attend.

The judge has not arrived *as yet*.
The judge has not arrived **yet**.

I am *awfully* tired.
I am **extremely** tired.　　OR　　I am tired.

Joe *claimed* he saw the entire incident.
Joe **stated** he saw the entire incident.

I simply could not *cope*.
I simply could not **cope with the situation**.

We are no *different than* other people.
We are no **different from** other people.

There is no *doubt but* that you are a valued employee.
There is no **doubt** that you are a valued employee.

Jack was *enthused* about the wedding plans.
Jack was **enthusiastic** about the wedding plans.

I could not *help but notice* that the defendant was late.
I could not **help noticing** that the defendant was late.

Irregardless of anything else, I am determined to pass this test.
Regardless of anything else, I am determined to pass this test.

He *got sick* as soon as he retired.
He **became ill** as soon as he retired.

This part of the country is *kind of* pretty.
This part of the country is *sort of* pretty.
This part of the country is **rather** pretty.

It looks *like* it might snow.
It looks **as if** it might snow.

The cake tasted good, *like* homemade cake should.
The cake tasted good, **as** homemade cake should.

Lots of people have nightmares about public speaking.
Many people have nightmares about public speaking.

My raise was *nowhere near* as large as it should have been.
My raise was **not** as large as it should have been.

We were *plenty* worried.
We were **quite** worried.   OR   We were worried.

Your essay was *real* good.
Your essay was **very** good.

Do you *reckon* we can win?
Do you **think** we can win?

She *sure* is brilliant.
She is **surely** brilliant.   OR   She is **certainly** brilliant.

Be *sure and* edit your work.
Be **sure to** edit your work.

I am *terribly* worried about arriving on time.
I am worried about arriving on time.

Try and come home on time.
Try to come home on time.

The attorney *put across* her idea very well.
The attorney **expressed** her idea very well.

I *put in* many hours on the project.
I **spent** many hours on the project.

We *should of* spent more time researching the issues.
We **should have** spent more time researching the issues.

Words Confused and Misused

Write it right. As this statement demonstrates, some words (called homonyms) sound alike but have totally different meanings. Other words with similar meanings (called synonyms) sometimes are used as if they were interchangeable when the context of a sentence indicates that one is more accurate than the other. The CLA applicant is expected to recognize the most appropriate word to use in a given context.

Still other words are used incorrectly because the writer does not know their meaning and does not take the time to consult a dictionary. A complete list of confusing words is not feasible in a manual like this one. It may not be feasible in any kind of book other than a dictionary or a thesaurus. However, a list of those words most often confused (and therefore misused) has been included, along with definitions and examples for comparison.

accede (verb): *to agree, accept*
exceed (verb): *to go beyond*

> The supervisor acceded to all of our recommendations.
> We must use care not to exceed the authority given to us.

accept (verb): *to receive willingly*
except (preposition): *other than*

> I cannot accept gifts from clients.
> Everyone was there except the host.

access (noun): *admission*
excess (adjective): *surplus*

> How can we gain access to the rest of the information?
> The firm can contract the excess work to smaller companies.

adapt (verb): *adjust*
adept, used as *adept at* (adjective): *skillful*
adopt (verb): *to choose as one's own*

> You can adapt to the new management structure.
> Connie is adept at handling public relations problems.
> If I cannot have a child of my own, I would like to adopt one.
> I hope the Board of Directors will adopt my proposal.

advice (noun): *suggestion, recommendation*
advise (verb): *suggest, recommend*

> Legal assistants cannot give direct legal advice.
> Legal assistants may not advise clients by giving legal opinions.
> I advise you to heed my advice.

affect (verb): *to produce an effect, to influence*
effect (noun): *result, outcome*

> How will the new law affect you?
> What effect will the new law have on others?
> The new law may affect others, but it will have no effect on me.

aggravate (verb): *to make a bad situation worse*
irritate (verb): *to annoy, to vex*

> The neighbors' feud was aggravated by their children's fights.
> Pompous people irritate everyone.

all ready (adjective): *fully prepared*
already (adverb): *previously*

> The applicants were all ready to begin the examination.
> I tried to call but you already had left the office.

all right (adjective): *satisfactory, well*
all right (adverb): *well enough, very well*
alright: *incorrect* — use "all right" instead

> They were ill but they are all right now.
> She may not be a scholar, but she does all right in school.
> All right, let's go.

all together: *incorrect* — use "together" instead
altogether (adverb): *completely, wholly*

We want everyone to work together.
The proposal was altogether unsatisfactory.

allude (verb): *hint, indirect mention* **(not synonymous with refer)**
elude (verb): *evade, escape* **compare "illusion," infra**

Is it permissible to allude to the answers if we do not disclose them?
No matter how hard I try, athletic skills elude me.

among (preposition): *used to indicate three or more*
between (preposition): *used to indicate two*

It is difficult to choose among so many qualified candidates.
This dispute is between John and me.

amount (noun): *designates a quantity that is the whole*
number (noun): *designates a quantity divisible into units*

Judge Benson has an incredible amount of energy.
A number of members have expressed their dissatisfaction.

anxious (adjective): *apprehensive, uneasy*
eager (adjective): *marked by enthusiasm or impatience*

Nearly all students are anxious about their final grades.
I am eager to go on vacation this year.

any way (noun): *a possible way to do something*
anyway *(adverb): in any case, in any event*

Is there any way for us to resolve this situation?
I didn't want to be an actor anyway.

adverse (adjective): *unfavorable, opposite, hostile*
averse, used as **averse to** (adjective): *feeling of repugnance, abhorrence*

Adverse winds prevent us from sailing today.
We were disappointed with the adverse verdict.
I am averse to strenuous exercise only when it is my own.

bad (adjective): *unfavorable, severe, spoiled, disobedient*
badly (adverb): *poorly, disagreeably*

The applicant made a bad impression.
Alice has a bad cold.
The restaurant is known for its bad food.

There is no such thing as a bad child.
All children behave badly from time to time.
I felt bad because my head hurt too badly to attend the meeting.

born (verb): *brought into existence by birth*
borne (verb): *past participle of bear*

I was born in St. Louis, Missouri.
The cost of title insurance will be borne by the seller.

capital (noun): *assets calculated to produce income*
capitol (noun): *place where a legislative body meets*

Starting a business without enough capital is the formula for failure.
Springfield is the capitol of Illinois.

cite (verb): *to quote as authority, to name*
sight (noun): *vision*
site (noun): *location*

Remember to cite only those statutes that apply directly to the case.
Alice was cited for bravery during Desert Storm.
We watched the plane until it was no longer in sight.
Union leaders decided to picket the construction site.

composed [of] (verb): *include*
divided [into] (verb): *separated*

An orange is composed of skin, fruit, and seeds.
When peeled, an orange can be divided into sections.

comprise (verb): *include*
constitute (verb): *establish, make (create)*

A family comprises parents and one or more children.
Parents and children constitute a family.

conscience (noun): *internal distinction between right and wrong*
conscious (adjective): *alert, aware*

Your conscience would bother you if you were to lie.
After the surgery, he was barely conscious.

council (noun): *an official group*
counsel (verb): *advise*

counsel (noun): *advice or advisor, attorney*

> The town council meets on the first Monday of each month.
> How shall we counsel her?
> The elderly lawyer gave me sound counsel.
> I cannot discuss this matter on advice of counsel.

credible (adjective): *believable, trustworthy*
creditable (adjective): *worthy of praise*
credulous (adjective): *willing to take at face value, gullible*

> Our client's version of the facts was more credible than the plaintiff's.
> The litigation team's performance was creditable.
> The monitor was so credulous that he believed my excuse.

currently (adverb): *at this time*
presently (adverb): *in the very near future*

> | | The temperature is currently 87°. |
> | BETTER | The temperature is 87°. |
>
> | | The dinner guests will arrive presently. |
> | BETTER | The dinner guests will arrive soon. |

delusion (noun): *false belief about the self or about other people or things*
illusion (noun): *misleading image*

> Insecure people often have delusions of grandeur.
> Samuel appears self-confident, but this is an illusion.

device (noun): *object, vehicle*
devise (verb): *to give, as in a will or other testamentary document*

> A toaster is an electrical device.
> Upon my death, I devise all of my property to my bulldog.

disinterested (adjective): *impartial, unbiased*
uninterested (adjective): *lack of curiosity, not interested*

> A judge must be disinterested in the outcome of the case.
> I should learn more about cars but I am uninterested in grime.

eminent (adjective): *prominent in reference to a person*
imminent (adjective): *about to occur, threatening*

Oliver Wendell Holmes was an eminent legal scholar.
The black sky indicates that a storm is imminent.

expect (verb): *look forward to*
suspect (verb): *think probable or likely*

I expect to pass the certification examination next April.
I suspect that I will have to study hard between now and then.

farther (adverb): *distance*
further (adverb): *time, quantity*

I can hit the ball farther than anyone on the team.
We must investigate further before we reach any conclusions.

fewer (adjective): *reduced number*
less (adjective): *reduced extent or degree*

There are fewer students enrolled this year.
Anything less than full participation is unacceptable.

foreword (noun): *prefatory comments to a book, not by the author*
forward (adverb): *progressively toward the front, ahead*

In the foreword of the text, the editor reviewed the author's research.
We can accomplish nothing by standing still; we must move forward.

good (adjective): *suitable, satisfactory*
well (adjective): *healthy, desirable*
well (adverb): *suitably, satisfactorily*

This steak tastes good.
We believe our client has good title to the land.
I am very well, thank you.
It may be well for you to leave now.
Alice did well on the examination.
Ms. West spoke well of you.

imply (verb): *to suggest, to hint*
infer (verb): *to deduce, to draw a conclusion*

The instructor implied that I was doing well in class.
Based upon the instructor's words, I inferred that I would get an A.
Though I may imply that I am tired, do not infer that I need to sleep.

incredible (adjective): *unbelievable*
incredulous (adjective): *unwilling to take at face value, skeptical*

> It seemed obvious that the defendant had told some incredible lies.
> I am somewhat incredulous about being able to pass without study.

it's (contraction): *it is*
its (possessive pronoun): *belonging to it (a place or thing)*

> It's dangerous to jog when it's hot outdoors.
> A court must preserve its dignity.
> When problems arise, society must look to its members for solutions.

later (adverb): *at a subsequent time*
latter (adjective): *near the end, the last mentioned of the two*

> The Model Rules were adopted later than was the Model Code.
> I did not become tired until the latter part of the exercise.
> Given the choice of prestige or fulfillment, I would choose the latter.

lay, laying, laid, laid (verb): *to place a person or an object somewhere*
lie, lying, lay, lain (verb): *to be in or to take a reclining position*

> Please lay your glasses on the table.
> Laying cement is hard work.
> Yesterday, I laid the baby in his crib.
> I have laid my rings on the window sill every day of my adult life.
> I love to lie in the grass.
> My glasses are lying on the table.
> Yesterday, I lay in the grass for nearly an hour.
> My children have lain in the grass with me on a number of occasions.

lend (verb): *to relinquish temporarily*
loan (noun): *a thing given for the borrower's temporary use*

> Please lend me your textbook until tomorrow.
> If I ever buy a car, I will need to obtain a loan.

liable (adjective): *responsible or legally bound*
libel (noun): *defamatory statement in written form*

> You may be liable for damages if you cause an accident.
> It is sometimes easier to prove libel than it is to prove slander.

may be (verb): *might come to pass*
maybe (adverb): *perhaps, possibly*

If we find better cases, we may be able to overturn the decision.
If we don't find better cases, we may be in deep trouble.
Maybe we should search for more favorable cases.

nauseated (adjective): *affected by nausea (stomach distress)*
nauseous (adjective): *causing nausea*

I became nauseated by the smell.
I was nauseated.
The smell was nauseous.

*To say, "I was nauseous," is **incorrect**, unless you are certain that you affect other people that way.*

passed (verb): *past participle of "pass"*
past (noun or preposition): *previous time, beyond*

I passed the examination.
It is not good to live in the past.
Cars flew past me as if I were standing still.

percent (noun): *use with a specific number*
percentage (noun): *use when no specific number is stated*

Only 65 percent of the students complete the program of study.
A large percentage of our case load involves commercial litigation.

precede (verb): *to be, go, or come ahead or in front of*
proceed (verb): *go forward, continue*

Thunder generally precedes a rainstorm.
If negotiations fail, we can proceed with litigation.

principal (adjective or noun): *primary, leader of*
principle (noun): *rule*

Professional recognition is a principal reason for certification.
A corporate president is usually a principal in the business operation.
A child's worst fear is to be sent to the principal's office.
Karen believes in the principle of tradition.

suppose (verb): *assume, conjecture*
supposed (adjective): *alleged, expected*

I suppose that I can handle this matter, but I am not certain.

When did the supposed masked man appear?
Are you supposed to be here?

than (conjunction): *used in making a comparison*
then (adverb): *specifies when, used in describing time*

Pat is much brighter than I.
What did you do then?

that, who (pronoun): *introduces restrictive (essential) description*
which, who (pronoun): *introduces nonrestrictive (nonessential)
description*

The book that I want for Christmas is *Poor Richard's Almanac.*
The person who works hard likely will succeed.
My bicycle, which is broken, is in the attic.
Stevie Wonder, who is blind, is an outstanding musician.

their (possessive pronoun): *belonging to them*
there (adverb): *specifies where, used in describing a place*
they're (contraction): *they are*

People in London usually take their umbrellas to work.
Please put the book there.
They're going to miss the game if they don't get here soon.

to (preposition): *used as part of infinitives, connector in various idioms*
too (adverb): *also, in an excessive amount*

I find it difficult to think when I am tired.
To know me is to love me.
Jack will be there, and Jill may be there too.
Both of us were too tired to study.

use (verb): *utilize*
use (noun): *utilization*
used (adjective): *not new, accustomed*

Lawyers and legal assistants alike must know how to use a computer.
Perhaps you can find a use for these old textbooks.
I like used books better than new ones.
Legal assistants are used to hard work.

Punctuation

Punctuation is the use of standardized marks or signs in written material to clarify meaning and to separate structural units. Legal assistants must be able to punctuate their own work correctly and must be able to recognize incorrect punctuation when it is presented to them. Common punctuation marks include the apostrophe, the hyphen, the dash, the comma, the semicolon, the colon, the period, the question mark, the exclamation point, quotation marks, ellipses, parentheses, and brackets.

It has been said that no matter what the rules are concerning punctuation, they will change about every five years. That statement is not correct, at least not as it applies to formal writing. If legal writing is anything, it is formal. As they are used in legal writing, accepted rules of punctuation and grammar have changed very little through the years. Notice, for instance, that the Strunk & White *Elements of Style* text, which is the primary reference of the NALA Certifying Board and of numerous law reviews around the country, has been revised only twice since it was originally published in 1935. The last revision was published in 1972. It is incumbent upon lawyers and legal assistants alike to learn and to use punctuation rules correctly.

The proper use of punctuation marks will be tested in the objective portion of the exam, sometimes in very complicated sentence structures. For all essay questions (and for all writing in general), strive for simplicity in both writing style and punctuation.

The Apostrophe

The apostrophe is used to create possessive forms of some nouns, indefinite pronouns, abbreviations, and acronyms. It is also used to form contractions and to indicate a quotation within a quotation.

Singular Possessives Form the possessive of singular nouns, abbreviations, and acronyms by adding *'s* (Strunk Rule 1).[1]

a child's toys	a witch's broomstick
the boy's book	a month's notice
a dollar's worth	a year's accumulation
the group's decision	my mother-in-law's garden

---

[1]Reprinted with permission of Macmillan Publishing Company from THE ELEMENTS OF STYLE, Third Edition by William Strunk Jr. and E.B. White. Copyright © 1979 by Macmillan Publishing Company.

Bill Jones's farm
Alan Smith Jr.'s home
YWCA's charter
CPA's resume
Tess's son

one country's wealth
Susan's graduation
CEO's parking space
CLA's certificate
witness's statement

Plural Possessives

Forming the possessive of plural nouns, abbreviations, and acronyms is a two-step process: (1) correctly show the plural form of the word and (2) add **'s** unless the plural form already ends in **s** or the **s** sound. If the plural form of the word ends in **s** or the **s** sound, add only the apostrophe.

children's toys
the boys' books
ten dollars' worth
the groups' decisions
Bill and Mary Jones' farm
The Alan Smith Jrs.' home
YWCAs' charters
CPAs' resumes
Tesses' sons

witches' broomsticks
two months' notice
five years' accumulation
all mothers-in-law's gardens
many countries' wealth
Susan and Shiela's graduation
CEOs' parking spaces
CLAs' certificates
witnesses' statements

Possessive Form of Some Indefinite Pronouns

Personal pronouns and the relative pronoun *who* have possessive forms (*see section on Pronouns*) that eliminate the use of the apostrophe. Some indefinite pronouns, however, have possessive forms that require the use of **'s**.

another's ideas
everybody's nightmare
one's rights
someone else's problem

Contractions

A contraction is a shortened word group, formed by omitting a letter or sound. The omission is indicated by an apostrophe.

I would	I'd
I would not	I wouldn't
could not	couldn't
we are	we're
he is	he's
of the clock	o'clock
cannot*	can't

*Note that **cannot** is written as one word, not two words.*

The Hyphen

The hyphen is used to signal some, but not all, compound words. A compound word is a combination of words that are joined to express a single thought. While the rules that control compound words are almost as varied as the compound words themselves, some general patterns do emerge; and those rule patterns are stated below. When in doubt about a particular combination of words, consult a good dictionary.

Numbers   When writing numbers in words, use a hyphen to join the numbers *one* through *nine* to the base number (twenty, thirty, forty, and so forth).

> fifty-five
> nine hundred sixty-seven
> one thousand three hundred eighty-six dollars and seventy-nine cents

When a compound is created by combining a number and a noun and when that compound appears before the noun that it modifies, the number is always singular and the compound is hyphenated.

> four-way stop   second-class citizen
> one-horse town   five-drawer desk

Fractions   Use a hyphen to separate the numerator and the denominator of a fraction unless one of them already contains a hyphen.

> one-half
> four-fifths
> one and three-fourths
>
> BUT
>
> forty-five hundredths
> eighteen thirty-thirds
> thirty-seven forty-fifths

Dual Job Titles   When a person holds more than one job at the same time, a title may be formed by joining the two job titles with a hyphen.

> secretary-treasurer
> producer-director

Familial Relationships Compound words that begin with the prefix *great* are hyphenated. Compound words that begin with the prefix *grand* are not hyphenated.

> great-grandson   great-grandfather
> great-niece   great-aunt

BUT

granddaughter	grandmother
grandnephew	granduncle

Compound words describing in-laws are hyphenated.

mother-in-law	father-in-law
brother-in-law	sister-in-law

All, Ex, Self, Quasi, and Well Prefixes

Compound words created with the prefixes all, ex, self, quasi, and well are compound adjectives and are hyphenated when they precede the noun they modify.

all-American team	all-inclusive
ex-officio member	ex-husband
self-esteem	self-indulgent
quasi-contract	quasi-judicial
well-known fact	well-established rule

BUT

That fact is well known. *(no hyphen)*
The rule has been well established. *(no hyphen)*

Cross and Counter Prefixes

The prefixes *cross* and *counter* are hyphenated or not hypenated, depending on the specific word compound. Since there is no rule pattern that emerges for these words, writers simply must memorize the words that require a hyphen and the words that do not.

cross-petition	cross-claim
cross-examine	cross-referenced

BUT

crossroads

counterclaim	counteroffer
counterpart	counterattack

BUT

counter-petition	counter-clockwise

Prefixes That Are Not Hyphenated

The prefixes *anti, co, de, inter, intra, multi, non, para, post, pre, pro, re, semi, super,* and *un* are not hyphenated unless the second part of the word is capitalized, hyphenated, or a number or unless a hyphen is needed for clarity.

antidepressant	codefendant
devalue	interoffice memorandum
intracompany newsletter	multipurpose room

nonlawyer	paramedic
postoperative	preexistence
proactive	reconstruct
semimonthly	superimpose
unnecessary	

BUT

anti-American	non-Japanese
pre-1776	post-Revolutionary War
re-create*	de-emphasize

With the hyphen, this word means "to create again"; without the hyphen, it means "to engage in recreation."

Compound Adjectives   In general, a hyphen is used to join two or more words that function as a single adjective preceding a noun.

holier-than-thou attitude	cloak-and-dagger tactics
half-baked idea	tax-free earnings
seat-of-the-pants solution	soft-spoken judge
all-or-nothing proposal	part-time employee

BUT

Joe's idea was half baked.

Earnings on municipal bonds are usually tax free.
The trend is to hire employees part time.

It may help to remember that in general, compounds used as adjectives (modifying nouns, words used as nouns, pronouns, or other adjectives) are hyphenated, while compounds used as adverbs (modifying verbs or adjectives) are not hyphenated.

The Dash

Use a dash, sometimes known as the em dash, to set off a sudden break or interruption in thought. A dash also may be used to signal a summary of the idea that precedes it or to signal a long appositive. An appositive, which is a parenthetical or explanatory expression, also may be signaled by parentheses or by commas. Use a dash only when a more common punctuation mark, such as a comma or parentheses, is too weak to convey the writer's meaning.

We must condemn—we do condemn—the cruelties of war.

Life, liberty, and the pursuit of happiness—all constitutional goals—are the birthright of every American.

The halcyon days of youth—their challenges, their joys, their innocence—will be remembered for the rest of our lives.

POOR   My suspicions proved true—it was not me she liked—it was my vast library.

BETTER   My suspicions proved true. It was not me she liked; it was my vast library.

The Comma

The comma is the most overused, and therefore misused, punctuation mark in the English language. The purpose of the comma is to signal a slight pause to the reader, not to signal each pause or hesitation of the writer. Gradually longer pauses are signaled by semicolons and colons, respectively. A full stop is signaled by a period. Once writers understand the purpose of each of these punctuation marks, choosing among them in a given situation becomes simpler.

Of all the rules concerning commas in formal writing, the most important one is this: **When in doubt, leave it out**.

<u>In a Series</u>   Use a comma after each item—whether a word, phrase, or clause—except the last in a series of three or more items joined by a single conjunction (Strunk Rule 2).[2]

> coat, hat, and gloves
> He opened the mail, read it, and tossed it aside.
> I ordered wine, cheese, crackers, and so forth.

Semicolons are used in place of commas to separate a series of phrases or clauses in which commas (a series within a series) occur.

> The examination covered excise, income, and property taxes; personal, corporate, and private property law; and employment and labor relations law.

To see the logic of this rule, read the example with semicolons and then again with commas substituted for the semicolons. With semicolons, the reader is signaled to pause slightly longer after each group than after each item within the group. With all commas, the reader is signaled to pause equally after each item and each group. Such a reading is not only exhausting, it is also confusing.

<u>With Parenthetic Expressions</u>   Use a comma to enclose parenthetic expressions. A parenthetic expression is one that amplifies, explains, repeats in

---

[2]Reprinted with permission of Macmillan Publishing Company from THE ELEMENTS OF STYLE, Third Edition by William Strunk Jr. and E.B. White. Copyright © 1979 by Macmillan Publishing Company.

another way, or digresses from the passage into which it is inserted. As a part of speech, a parenthetic expression may be a nonrestrictive, nonessential phrase, which is always set off by commas. A nonrestrictive phrase or clause is one that does not identify or define the preceding noun and could be omitted entirely without detracting from the meaning of the rest of the sentence. **Hint:** Nonrestrictive clauses often are introduced by the word *which, who, when,* or *where.*

>Alice, however, was not interested in going to the opera.
>Marsha paid $75,000.00, her entire savings, for the house.
>St. Louis, which is my birthplace, has many tourist attractions.
>Synonyms, words with similar meanings, are covered on the test.
>Antique books, none of them mine, will be sold at the auction.

Restrictive (essential) phrases and clauses, on the other hand, are not parenthetic and are not set off by commas. Such phrases and clauses cannot be eliminated without affecting the meaning of the rest of the sentence. **Hint:** Restrictive clauses often are introduced by the word *who* or *that.*

>People who have poor vision should wear glasses.
>The car that hit me was a red convertible.
>My brother Fred drives a motorcycle to work.
>*(I have two brothers, making Fred's name essential for identity.)*

BUT

>My husband, who is a salesman, is on the golf course every weekend.
>Fred, my brother, drives a motorcycle to work.
>My father, Fred, retired last year.
>*(I have only one father; his name is not essential for identity.)*

Dashes and parentheses sometimes can be used to signal a parenthetic expression. In deciding whether to use parentheses, commas, or dashes, it may help to remember that parentheses whisper the expression, commas state the expression in a normal tone, and dashes emphasize the expression.

>Marsha paid $75,000.00 (her entire savings) for the house.
>St. Louis (which is my birthplace) has many tourist attractions.
>Synonyms—words with similar meanings—are covered on the test.
>Antique books—none of them mine—will be sold at the auction.

If the interruption created by the parenthetic expression is slight, however, the commas can be omitted.

>Jack was exhausted and was therefore irritable.

A noun of address is parenthetic and must be enclosed within commas unless it appears at the beginning or at the end of the sentence.

Wherever you go, Mary, your reputation goes with you.
Jack, please bring me the correspondence file.
I cannot find anything in this box of papers, Neal.

Dates generally contain parenthetic words or numbers and require commas.

Friday, June 5, 1992
April 19, 1994

BUT

19 April 1994

Use a comma to separate unrelated numbers.

In 1992, 328 legal assistants attended the refresher course.

Degrees and titles that follow a name are parenthetic and require commas.

Mary Fulbright, Ph.D., was elected to the Board.
The Reverend Nelson Kelly, S.J.
Kermit A. Brashear III, J.D.
William C. Ramsey, Attorney at Law

Although *Junior* and *Senior*, together with their respective abbreviations Jr. and Sr., have been regarded by some as parenthetic, logic dictates that both are restrictive (essential for identity), used to distinguish one person from the other. Used as restrictive parts of a name, they are not parenthetic and do not need a comma.

Fred Gerberding Jr.
Fred Gerberding Sr.

Before Conjunctions and Transitional Words

Use a comma before a conjunction that joins two independent clauses. A comma is not required when both independent clauses are very short and are closely connected in thought.

I have to be in court in an hour, and the tire on my car is flat.
The hour was late, and the judge became increasingly irritated.
The hour was late and I wanted to go home.

Similarly, use a comma before the second clause in a compound sentence when the second clause is introduced by any of these transitional words: *because, as* (meaning *because*), *for* (meaning *because*), *or, nor, since,* or *while* (meaning *at the same time*). Once again, it is permissible to omit the comma when the two clauses are very short and are closely connected in thought.

We will not add modems to our system, because we cannot find any.
Printers will be purchased, as they are essential to the system.

Use care wherever you go, for there is danger at every street corner.
Either do it right, or we will need to find someone who can.
Neither of us could find the theater, nor would anyone help us.

I could not help her, since I knew nothing about the case.
Jack prepared our dinner, while I went to the bakery.

BUT

Either you do it or I will.
I climbed the mountain because it was there.

When a sentence has a single subject with two verbs that are joined by the conjunction *but*, a comma may be used before the conjunction. On the other hand, when a sentence has a single subject with two verbs that are joined by the conjunction *and*, no comma is used. Since Strunk and White does not *require* a comma, however, it may be easier simply to omit the comma in both situations.

ALSO CORRECT

I wanted dessert, but could not eat another bite.
I wanted dessert but could not eat another bite.

ALSO CORRECT

We listened to his story, but were still unconvinced.
We listened to his story but were still unconvinced.

BUT

We listened to his story and were still unconvinced.

Do not join independent clauses with a comma; use a semicolon instead.

I don't want ham and eggs; I prefer doughnuts.

After Introductory Expressions   When any one of the following introductory expressions is used, it must be followed by a comma:

(1) Introductory infinitive or participial phrase

To become more knowledgeable, I took a course in the subject.
Having lost my glasses, I was unable to see the street signs.

(2) Introductory dependent clause

As I turned the corner, I saw my supervisor seated in my office.

(3) Introductory prepositional phrase

Until discovery is finished, we cannot discuss the case with anyone.

Note: Very short prepositional phrases do not require a comma.

> In 1992 the decision was reversed.
> After work I went directly home.

(4) Transitional expressions, such as those listed below

accordingly	besides
consequently	finally
first	for example
furthermore	however
meanwhile	moreover
namely	nevertheless
second	that is
therefore	

> Meanwhile, the band continued to play.
> Nevertheless, work proceeded on schedule.
> Therefore, we had no reason to continue with the deposition.

BUT

> We had no reason, therefore, to continue with the deposition.
> My family went, namely, my husband, my daughter, and my son.

(5) Introductory mild interjection

> Well, that must have been how it happened.
> Oh, go ahead and buy it.

Between Consecutive Adjectives

Use a comma to separate consecutive, coordinated adjectives that precede the noun they modify, but only when each adjective modifies the noun. When the first adjective modifies the second adjective (rather than the noun), no comma is required. *Hint:* One way to tell whether adjectives are coordinated is to substitute *and* for the comma. If the sentence still makes sense, the adjectives are coordinated, and a comma is required. Another way is to reverse the order of the adjectives; if they still make sense, a comma is required to separate them.

> She had a quiet, regal air. (She had a quiet and regal air. She had a regal, quiet air.)
> It was a dark, dreary day. (It was a dark and dreary day. It was a dreary, dark day.)
> She wore a mint green coat. (*Mint* modifies *green*, not coat.)
> He made a weak legal argument. (*Weak* modifies *legal,* not argument.)

With Informal Quotations

Use a comma to introduce or to conclude an informal, direct quotation.

> Uncle Harry always says, "Children are to be seen and not heard."
> "I wonder what time we will eat," Mary asked.

Formal quotations are introduced by a colon (see section on colons), while indirect quotations are paraphrased and do not use any specific punctuation mark.

> Thoreau said that civil disobedience is sometimes a good thing.

The Semicolon

The semicolon is used to signal a break that is stronger than the comma but not as strong as the colon within a phrase, independent clause, or sentence. The rules for use of semicolons are fewer than the rules for commas, because the semicolon is used much less often. As is true of all punctuation marks, do not use the semicolon unless there is a specific rule requiring it to be used.

In a Series   Use a semicolon to separate a series of phrases or clauses in which commas (signaling a series within a series) already occur.

> The examination covered excise, income, and property taxes; personal, corporate, and private property law; and employment and labor relations law.

To see the logic of this rule, read the example with semicolons and again with commas substituted for the semicolons. With semicolons, the reader is signaled to pause slightly longer after each group than after each item within the group. With only commas, the reader is signaled to pause equally after each item and each group. Such a reading is both exhausting and confusing.

Between Independent Clauses Without Conjunction   Use a semicolon to join two or more grammatically complete clauses that are not joined by a conjunction or connective word.

> We always vacation in New England; it's cooler there in July.
>
> The jury was sequestered for many hours; awaiting its decision was torturous.

When a conjunction or connective word is inserted, the proper punctuation mark is always a comma.

> We always vacation in New England, for it's cooler there in July.
> The jury was sequestered for many hours, and awaiting its decision was torturous.

Notice that each of the sentences in the first example group could have been written correctly as two separate sentences.

> We always vacation in New England. It's cooler there in July.
> The jury was sequestered for many hours. Awaiting its decision was torturous.

Between Independent Clauses With Conjunction

Use a semicolon to join two or more grammatically complete clauses that are joined by a conjunction when any one of the clauses contains a comma. Compare this rule with the rule stated immediately above. When neither of the independent clauses already contains a comma, however, the correct punctuation mark is a comma.

> No matter how I tried to follow the directions, I rarely hit the ball; and that angered me.
>
> As the day wore on without any end to the negotiations in sight, I became more and more tired; and all I wanted was to go home.

BUT

> I rarely hit the ball, and that angered me.
>
> I became more and more tired, and all I wanted was to go home.

The logic of this rule is similar to the logic of the rule requiring semicolons to separate a series in which commas already occur. The pause between the independent clauses (signaled by a semicolon) should be longer than the pause after the introductory phrase (signaled by a comma). If each the example sentences were punctuated with a second comma in place of the semicolon, the reader would pause equally at both commas, making the reader's job more difficult.

The Colon

The colon signals a pause that is longer than the pause required by either a comma or a semicolon. In formal writing, the colon is used most commonly to introduce a formal quotation or rule, a question, an antithesis, or a list. A colon should precede a list only when formal words of introduction—for example, *as follows* or *the following*—are used. Notice that when words of introduction are used, the first word following the colon is capitalized; otherwise, it is not.

> As we waited for the verdict, I was reminded of the words of Samuel Goldwyn: "A verbal contract isn't worth the paper it's written on."
>
> In reversing the decision, the Court said: "The case of *Roe v. Wade* involved the protection of privacy rights."

Of all the rules concerning punctuation, the most important one is this: When in doubt, leave it out.

There is just one thing that I want to know: How long have you had this information?

Someone wins: another loses. (*A semicolon is also proper.*)

To ensure success, legal assistants need the following characteristics: High intelligence, unflinching tenacity, and a great sense of humor.

Other Uses   The colon has a number of other uses, all of them related to separating different levels of the same item. The colon is used to separate:

•The title and subtitle of a literary work

Certification: A Professional Goal

•The page and line numbers in depositions and briefs

C. Kretchmer deposition, page 137, line 22   C. Kretchmer 137:22

•Chapter and verse numbers in Biblical references

chapter 23, verse 4 of the Book of Psalms   Psalms 23:4

•The differential in ratios or proportions

20 to 1   20:1

•Hour and minutes in expression of time

fifteen minutes before six a.m.   5:45 a.m.

•The salutation from the body of a formal business letter

Dear Mr. Smith:

The Period

The period is most frequently used to signal a complete stop at the end of a sentence. In addition, this punctuation mark is used to create abbreviations, decimals, outlines, and lists. Sentence termination and abbreviations are covered in this *Review Manual*.

At the End of a Sentence   The period is used at the end of a sentence to signal the reader to come to a complete stop. A sentence may be the simple, declarative kind (with both the subject and the verb shown) or it may be elliptical (one in which words are omitted but are understood).

> Amy arrived before Connie did.
> (you) Put the memorandum on the desk.
> (you) Stop that.
> (my answer is) No.

Never use a period when a comma is the required punctuation mark.

INCORRECT	I met him on an airplane many years ago. Coming home from San Francisco.
CORRECT	I met him on an airplane many years ago, coming home from San Francisco.
INCORRECT	He was fascinating. A person who had traveled the world and who told hilarious stories.
CORRECT	He was fascinating, a person who had traveled the world and who told hilarious stories.

With Abbreviations   Abbreviations should be used sparingly in formal writing or, for that matter, in any writing or conversation unless the abbreviation is defined for the reader or the listener first or unless the abbreviation is so common that no confusion can result from its use. The same is true of acronyms. Although it may be permissible to abbreviate common nouns in the business world, common nouns—account (acct.), amount (amt.), each (ea.), and so forth—are not abbreviated in formal writing.

Some abbreviations use periods; others do not. Learning the difference between the two is simply a matter of memorization and practice. Many abbreviations are already familiar to the experienced legal assistant.

Jane Terhune, CLAS	Bill Campbell, CPA	Dr. Jane Doe
Dale McHenry, Ph.D.	Oscar Wilde Jr.	St. Paul, MN
Mr. Alex Jones	Mrs. Kathy Janisch	Ms. Karen Dunn
1015 B.C.	1992 A.D.	12:40 a.m. EST
IBM	AT&T	U.S.A. or USA
USDA	SEC	IRS
Co.	Corp.	Inc.

The primary difference between an abbreviation and an acronym is pronunciation. Each is formed by using only the first letter(s) of each word comprising the abbreviation (*see above*) or the acronym (*see below*). Abbreviations are pronounced by saying each letter of the resulting combination of letters, while acronyms are pronounced phonetically. Acronyms are **not** punctuated with periods.

Mothers Against Drunk Drivers	MADD
National Association of Legal Assistants, Inc.	NALA
National Organization of Women	NOW
North Atlantic Treaty Organization	NATO
Zone Improvement Plan	ZIP
light amplification by stimulated emission of radiation	laser

Periods are placed inside quotation marks but are placed outside single quotation marks. When a quoted sentence appears within another independent sentence, use a comma instead of a period to punctuate the internal quotation.

Erin reported, "I have completed the deposition summaries."
The class was asked to define the term "common law."
The instructor said, "Please define the term 'common law'."
Mary said, "I cannot do this anymore," as she left the office.

When parentheses or brackets are used to enclose or to set off an independent sentence, the period is placed inside the final parenthesis or bracket. However, when parentheses or brackets are used to enclose other words, phrases, or clauses within an independent sentence, the period is placed outside the final parenthesis or bracket.

The client searched everywhere for the invoice. (It was never found.)
"I cannot find the document [it was never found] or the transmittal letter."
He could not find them (the document or the transmittal letter).
Heed this warning (if it applies to you).

When an abbreviation requiring a period appears at the end of the sentence (also requiring a period), only one period is used.

Send these interrogatories to our client at Acme & Co.
He works in the Legal Department of Thunderbird Enterprises, Inc.

The Question Mark

The question mark is used to indicate an independent inquiry (question) or an interrogative element (question) within a sentence. A sentence that is declarative in structure may become a question by substituting a question mark for the period.

How can we finish everything on time?
The form indicates that he was born in 1999 (?) and was married in 1924.
They reimbursed you?

Conversely, a request that is structured as a question should be punctuated with a period, not with a question mark. Indirect questions are punctuated with periods as well.

Please join me in welcoming our guest.
Will you take these documents to the courthouse.
The client wanted to know what he should do.
How to reconcile the two cases was the question before the court.

The question mark should be placed inside quotations, parentheses, or brackets only when it is part of the quoted or parenthetical material.

Allison inquired, "Where are the deposition summaries?"
When I found the client's file (where is it now?), I gave it to Richard.

BUT

Was she upset when she said, "I cannot condone this behavior"?
Why did you wait so long to call me (a whole week)?

The Exclamation Point

The exclamation point is used to signal strong emotion, such as surprise, disbelief, or enthusiasm. In order to preserve its effectiveness, the exclamation point should be used sparingly in all writing and even more sparingly in legal writing.

Oh, no!
How can you say that!

Like the question mark, the exclamation point should be placed inside quotation marks, parentheses, or brackets only when it is part of the quoted or parenthetical material. Otherwise, it should be placed outside.

"The boat is sinking!" he shouted.
Our young son told the cashier (we were so embarrassed!) that we starved him.

The Quotation Mark

Quotation marks are used to signal exact words that have been either spoken or written.

> On appeal the court held: "Where there is a right, there is a remedy."
> Jack said, "I can't hear the witness."

When a quotation appears within another quotation already enclosed between quotation marks, the inner quotation is enclosed between two apostrophes. Apostrophes used in this way are called single quotation marks.

> Harry said, "The article 'Contract as Right' is a favorite among lawyers."

When a quotation is fifty words or more in length, it is signaled by indenting it from both the left and right margins rather than by using quotation marks. When an inner quotation appears within an indented quotation, the inner quotation is signaled by quotation marks. Lengthy excerpts from court opinions demonstrate this method of quotation, such as this footnote from *Missouri v. Jenkins*, 109 S. Ct. 1463 (1989):

> *Amicus* National Association of Legal Assistants reports that 77 percent of 1,800 legal assistants responding to a survey of the association's membership stated that their law firms charged clients for paralegal work on an hourly billing basis. Brief for National Association of Legal Assistants as *Amicus Curiae* 11.
>
> Of course, purely clerical or secretarial tasks should not be billed at a paralegal rate, regardless of who performs them. What the court in *Johnson v. Georgia Highway Express, Inc.*, 488 F.2d 714, 717 (CA5 1974), said in regard to the work of attorneys is applicable by analogy to paralegals: "It is appropriate to distinguish between legal work in the strict sense, and investigation, clerical work, compilation of facts and statistics and other work which can often be accomplished by non-lawyers but which a lawyer may do because he has no other help available. Such non-legal work may command a lesser rate. Its dollar value is not enhanced just because a lawyer does it.

If the passage in the second paragraph were short enough to be shown between quotation marks, rather than indented, the inner quotation would appear between single quotation marks (the apostrophe).

Quotation marks are used to enclose any material introduced by these words and expressions: **endorsed, entitled, marked, signed, the term,** or **the word**.

> The class was asked to define the term "common law."
> The document marked "Exhibit A" was illegible.

When used with quotation marks, the comma and period are placed inside the quotation marks. Other punctuation marks are placed outside the quotation marks unless they are part of the quotation.

> We were asked to define the term "common law."
> We were asked to define the term "common law," but I could not do it.
> We were asked to define the term "common law"; I could not do it.

The Ellipsis

Ellipses (also called ellipsis points) are punctuation marks consisting of three spaced periods (. . .), which are used to indicate an omission within quoted material. When the omission occurs at the end of a quoted sentence, use the ellipses and then the period from the quoted sentence. When the omission occurs at the beginning of a quoted sentence (so that the first quoted word begins with a lower case letter in the original work), signal the omission with the ellipses and enclose the first letter of the next quoted word in brackets.

> "Plaintiff's claim involved lost wages, . . . medical expenses, and property damage.
>
> "Viewed in such a way, this is a case of first impression . . . ."
>
> ". . . [W]e affirm the superior court's ruling."

Parentheses

Parentheses are used to enclose material that explains, amplifies, or digresses from another element in the sentence; thus, the term "parenthetical expression." Remember that commas or dashes may be used to enclose parenthetical expressions as well. (*See the Comma section, supra, for examples of each.*)

> The National Association of Legal Assistants (NALA) offers the CLA exam.
> The black Cadillac (it's an Allante) is mine.
> I bought it as a repossession (at the wholesale price) from a client.

Parentheses may be used to enclose numbers or letters identifying separate elements of a list that is shown as part of a sentence.

> Parenthetical expressions may be signaled by (1) parentheses, (2) commas, or (3) hyphens.

When the parenthetical material is either a question or an exclamation, show the question mark or the exclamation mark before the final parenthesis. The period is not shown inside the parentheses unless the parenthetical material is a stand-alone, parenthetical sentence.

> Patricia Holt (do you know her?) is the WordPerfect expert at our office.
> Our young son told the cashier (we were so embarrassed!) that we starved him.
> The black Cadillac (it's an Allante) is mine.
> The black Cadillac is mine. (It's an Allante.)
> (This is a parenthetic sentence.)

Other, internal punctuation marks are shown outside the parentheses unless they are part of the parenthetical material.

> By waiting so long to call (a whole week), your case has been weakened.
> Decide what you want to do (press charges, sue, or settle); then call me.

The Bracket

Brackets are used to enclose editorial comments, corrections, or explanations within quoted material. They are also used to signal a parenthetic expression contained within another parenthetic expression.

> "Despite the damaging evidence [it was discovered by Sherlock Holmes], the defendant maintained his innocence."

> "The practice of lew [sic] by nonlawyers is prohibited."

> While young men, James and his brother (Andrew Ellis, who later discovered a new glue process [ustickum]) were demolition derby champions.

Capitalization

Capitalization is the practice established for the use of uppercase (capital) letters to identify or to emphasize. Capitalization of a word signals the reader to give more attention to it, signifying that it is more important than the words surrounding it. This *Review Manual* covers only the more common rules of capitalization, grouped according to the general categories to which they apply. Applicants will be wise to consult other references suggested in the Bibliography for detailed capitalization rules.

The First Word

Always capitalize the first word of a sentence. Capitalize the first word of a quoted sentence unless it flows into the underlying sentence structure.

> Simple sentences are best.
> The instructor said, "Simple sentences are best."
> The instructor said that "[s]imple sentences are best," and I believe him.

Capitalize the first word following a colon only if words of formal introduction are used, that is, if the words preceding the colon create an expectation that additional material will follow the colon.

> The most important punctuation rule is this one: When in doubt, leave it out.
> To pass the test, one must do the following: Prepare, prepare, and prepare.
>
> BUT
>
> Excellence in all that we do: that was the organization's motto.

Capitalize the first word of each item in a formal list, as well as the first word of each entry in an outline.

> 1. Dark shoes
> 2. Brown coat
> 3. Black tie
>
> I. First words
>   A. In a sentence
>   B. In a quotation
>   C. In a list

Personal Names

Capitalize names and initials of specific persons, as well as nicknames and fictitious names. Capitalize a foreign name according to the conventions of the language from which it derives.

> R. W. Williams   JFK   Suzy Q
> John Doe   Charles de Gaulle de Gaulle

Derivatives of Proper Names

Coined nouns and adjectives derived from personal or geographic names are capitalized unless they have become so commonly used (generic) that the capital letter is dropped. The names of nationalities and languages are always capitalized.

French	Spanish	English
American know-how	Native American history	Germans
Parkinson's disease	Canadian bacon	French cooking

BUT

india ink	manila envelope	french fries

Titles and Offices

When used as part of narrative text, capitalize titles when they precede a personal name, as part of the name. Do not capitalize titles when they are used as an appositive following the name or when no specific name is stated. When used to refer to the President of the United States, however, the title *President* may—but need not—be capitalized.

President Lincoln	Abraham Lincoln, president of the United States	the president
President Lincoln	Abraham Lincoln, President of the United States	the President
Governor Nelson	Ben Nelson, governor of the state of Nebraska	the governor
Chairman Benson	Robert Benson, chairman of the Finance Committee	the chairman
Dr. Ruth Ames	Ruth Ames, doctor of internal medicine	the doctor
Judge A. Richards	Ann Richards, judge of the Utah Supreme Court	the judge

When titles are shown following names in a formal list or as part of either the inside address or the signature block of business correspondence, the titles are capitalized. (*See the section on Correspondence, infra.*)

A title used alone, in place of a personal name, is capitalized in the context of a toast or an introduction. Likewise, titles used in place of names of direct address are capitalized.

Ladies and gentlemen, the Governor of New York.
Thank you, Mr. Chairman.
I would have objected, Your Honor, but I didn't hear the question.

BUT

Can you tell me, sir, where the law library is located?

A title of kinship begins with a lowercase letter when it is preceded by a modifier. When used before a proper name or when used alone, in place of the name, it is usually capitalized.

My father lives in Illinois.
The Williams sisters joined us for dinner.
Alice's brother is older than she.

BUT

My Uncle Ed cut a wide swath when he was young.
Let me go with you, Dad.
I remember that Mother always wore a hat to church.

Education and Academic Degrees   Academic degrees are capitalized following a personal name whether abbreviated or written in full. Academic degrees are not capitalized when they are not connected with a specific name.

> Nadine B. Trew, Juris Doctor
> Nadine B. Trew, J.D.
> One must have a juris doctor degree before taking most state bar exams.

The name of a specific course is capitalized; otherwise, courses are not capitalized unless they are required to be capitalized under some other rule (such as English, French, Spanish, and the like).

> I want to take more courses in accounting and in English composition.
> I have registered for Accounting 212 and English Composition 300 this term.

Geographic (Place) Names

Certain nouns and adjectives designating parts of the world or regions of a continent or country are generally (but not always) capitalized.

the Arctic Circle	the Arctic	arctic climate
the Eastern Seaboard	the East	east, eastern (direction or locality)
the Wild West	the Western world	western states

Note: compass points (north, south, east, and west) and their derivatives (northerly, southerly, and so forth) are never capitalized when they are used merely to indicate direction.

Topographic Names   Names of specific mountains rivers, oceans, and so forth are capitalized, including the generic terms *mountain, river,* or *ocean* when used as part of the specific names.

> Pacific Ocean   Mississippi River   Black Forest

Do not capitalize the generic terms when they are used descriptively, rather than as part of the specific name.

the coast of South Carolina	BUT	the East Coast (referring to region)
the Arizona desert	BUT	the Painted Desert
the Kansas prairie	BUT	the Prairie State

Buildings and Public Places   Names of specific buildings, monuments, and thoroughfares are capitalized. Generic terms like *avenue, boulevard, bridge,* *building, street,* and so forth are capitalized when they are part of the formal name. When they stand alone, they are not capitalized.

Fifth Avenue	BUT	the avenue where I live
Brooklyn Bridge	BUT	a bridge over the river

Government

Words designating political divisions or governmental units (country, state, city, and so forth) are capitalized when they follow the name and are an accepted part of it.

New York City	BUT	the city of New York
Harrison County	BUT	the county of Harrison
Washington State	BUT	the state of Washington
the state (referring to a government generally)		

Governmental Bodies   When the full name or the abbreviation of a legislative body or an administrative body is used, it is generally capitalized. When the name of the governmental body is paraphrased or when no specific governmental unit is named, do not capitalize. (See examples of exceptions below.)

General Assembly of Ohio
Ohio legislature
state legislature
state senate

St. Louis City Council
city council
council

Federal Bureau of Investigation (FBI)
the Bureau

Bureau of the Census
Census Bureau
the bureau

Although the following terms refer to governmental units, they generally are not capitalized:

federal government
national government
state government
church and state
the state

<u>Courts, Documents, and Parties</u>   Both the formal name and the paraphrased name of a specific court are capitalized. Standing alone, the word court is not capitalized unless it refers to the United States Supreme Court or unless it is used as a noun of address for a particular court.

> United States Supreme Court
> the Supreme Court
> the Court
>
> Colorado Supreme Court
> State Supreme Court (referring to a specific state supreme court)
> state supreme court (generally)
> the supreme court
> the court
>
> the Juvenile Court of Wade County
> Wade County Juvenile Court
> juvenile court

> The Court convenes on the first Tuesday in October. *(U.S. Supreme Court)*
> All state statutes are subject to review by that state's supreme court.
> COMES NOW the defendant and requests this Court to enter an order . . .
> The witness appeared under court order.
> The lower court found for the plaintiff in this case.

Do not capitalize terms referring to documents or pleadings unless they are included as part of the exact title of a document in existence. This is a common error among lawyers and legal assistants. Do not capitalize the word *appellant, appellee, defendant, movant, petitioner, plaintiff, defendant, respondent,* or the like unless it must be capitalized under another rule (such as the first word of a sentence or part of a document title or a pleading caption).

> Due process applies to states via the Fourteenth Amendment to the Constitution.
> Please refer to page 12 of the Brief for Petitioner Harris.
> The brief of the petitioner covered all salient points.
> The motion of plaintiff Collins was filed only yesterday.
> The purchase agreement was executed by Johnson Brothers, Ltd., the seller.

The term *state* is capitalized when it is used as a proper noun or as a proper adjective referring to a specific state or to "the State" as a party to litigation. Otherwise, it is treated as a generic term and is not capitalized.

> Applications must be filed with the State Department of Health.
> The state legislature adopted a new gun law during its last session.
> Nebraska is the only state with a unicameral legislature.
> Under Michigan state law, most contracts of minors are voidable.
> All witnesses for the State were sequestered during trial.
> The federal government is grounded in the separation of church and state.

Political Organizations

The names of national and international organizations and alliances are generally capitalized, as are members of a specific political party.

the Democratic Party	a Democrat	a democratic view	democracy
the Republican Party	a Republican	a republican view	republic
the Socialist Party	a Socialist	a socialistic philosophy	socialism

Other Names

Other nouns and adjectives may require capitalization, based upon their source or based upon the way in which they are used. As with all capitalization, the underlying rule is not to capitalize any word unless a specific rule requires its capitalization.

Associations, Companies, and Institutions

The full names of associations, companies, and institutions are capitalized, together with their departments and divisions. However, the words *association, company, society,* and the like are not capitalized when used alone.

National Association of Legal Assistants	NALA	the association
General Foods Corporation	General Foods	the corporation
Creighton University School of Law	Creighton Law School	the law school
Boy Scouts of America	a Boy Scout	a scout
New York Yankees	the Yankees	the team
Electrical Workers of America		the union

Historical Documents, Events, and Periods

The names of specific documents, events, and historical periods are capitalized.

the Magna Carta	the Boston Tea Party	the Roaring Twenties
the Constitution (U.S.)	the Vietnam War	the Middle Ages

BUT

the nineteenth century	the eighteen hundreds
the twenties	the 1920s

Calendar and Time Designations

Names of the twelve months of the year are capitalized, as are the names of the days of the week. The names of specific holidays are also capitalized.

January	June	Thursday
Lent	Independence Day	Halloween

BUT

election day	inauguration day	graduation day

A season of the year is not capitalized unless the term is personified (as in poetry) or is part of the title of either a literary work or a special event.

winter	summer solstice	spring break
O, Spring, how welcome!	the NALA Fall Seminar	The Winter of Discontent

Time zones are not capitalized when designated in words; time zone abbreviations are capitalized.

central standard time	CST
central daylight savings time	CDST

For further discussion of abbreviations and acronyms, see the section on punctuation (supra).

<u>Titles of Works</u> All words in the titles and subtitles of specific articles, books, periodicals, and newspapers are capitalized except (1) articles—a, an, the—unless the article is the first word of the title; (2) coordinating conjunctions—and, for, or, nor; and (3) prepositions, regardless of length, unless they are the first or last words of the title or subtitle.

The Winter of Our Discontent	Talk of the Town
the Wall Street Journal	A Man for All Seasons
A Miracle on Thirty-fourth Street	The French-American Connection
The Truth about a Cat in a Hat	Passages from a Stargazer's Notebook

Note: *The titles of complete works are underlined (or italicized), while articles and serial parts of an entire program or work are enclosed in quotation marks.*

Grammar

Questions within this category of the CLA® examination require the applicant to demonstrate knowledge of various parts of speech by recognizing their correct (or incorrect) use within the sentence structure. The words (parts of speech) used to construct a sentence generally can be categorized as nouns, pronouns, adjectives, verbs, adverbs, prepositions, conjunctions, articles, or interjections, with variations for each of these.

Every part of speech has a specific function within a sentence, each with rules that must be observed to assure cohesiveness of the thought being conveyed. Constructing a sentence is much like constructing a house. Large or small, fancy or plain, every good house must have a framework that matches on all sides; and the connecting points must be perfectly aligned. Without this precision, the house would be fairly drafty—if it could stand at all. Constructing a sentence is much the same. Long or short, elaborate or simple, its subject and all modifiers must match its verb (predicate) and all modifiers; and its mood, voice, and tense must be perfectly aligned. Without this balance and alignment, even the most eloquent of words will fall apart; and the thought will be buried in a heap of unintelligible terms.

Words are the essential stock in trade of lawyers and legal assistants, to be assembled into cohesive sentences. A mastery of the parts of speech and of the rules of sentence construction is critical to those who aspire to the CLA® designation.

Parts of Speech Defined

Every word in the English language can be categorized as a part of speech (noun, pronoun, verb, and so forth). Many words can fit into more than one category, defined by the way in which they are used, or can fit into more than one category by changing the form slightly. These words are classified according to their form and function within a particular sentence.

Noun A noun is the name of a person, a place, a thing, a concept, or a quality. Nouns are classified as common nouns *(child, river, book, patriotism, happiness)* or proper nouns *(Kenny, Mississippi River, Bible, World War II)*. Used as the subject of a sentence or clause, a noun answers the question: Who or what? Used as the direct object or indirect object of a sentence (or as the object of a phrase), a noun answers the question: What or whom? Nouns are the identifiers of actors and topics within a sentence.

Pronoun A pronoun is a word that substitutes for a noun *(I, me, you, he, she, it, him, her, they, them, themselves, everyone, myself, this, that, those, who, which,* and so forth). Pronouns are used in place of nouns and perform the same functions as nouns within a sentence.

Verb A verb can be either a word indicating action *(see, do, run, read, walk)* or a word of being *(am, is, are, was, were)*. The verb is the heart of every sentence. It sets the tone of the entire sentence by its tense (present, past, future); voice (active or passive); and its mood (indicative, imperative, or subjunctive).

Helping verbs *(can, could, did, do, does, has, have, may, might, must, shall, should, will, would)*, sometimes called auxiliary verbs, often combine with verbs to form a verb phrase. This verb phrase, together with its modifiers, is known as a predicate.

A verb preceded by the word "to" creates an infinitive. Infinitives function as nouns within a sentence.

Adjective   Adjectives are words that describe or modify nouns or pronouns *(tender, harmful, one, some, all)*. Adjectives answer the question: Which? what kind of? or how many? within the sentence structure.

Adverb   Adverbs describe or modify verbs, adjectives, other adverbs, or groups of words with these characteristics *(tenderly, simply, harmfully, nearly, almost, always, someday, somewhere, really, there)*. Adverbs answer the question: How? when? where? to what extent? or how often? within the sentence structure. Adverbs often (but not always) end in the letters *-ly*.

Preposition   Prepositions *(about, around, at, down, for, in, near, of, off, regarding, to, with, without)* are words that link nouns or pronouns to other words in the sentence structure. The applicant who has difficulty with prepositions may find it helpful to think of them as the "doghouse" words. They generally are not part of the main structure of the sentence and can be identified by saying: *around* the doghouse, *for* the doghouse, *regarding* the doghouse, *to* the doghouse, and so on. This method is not foolproof but it identifies the vast majority of prepositions.

Conjunction   Conjunctions are linking words. They link words, phrases, and clauses within the sentence structure. Coordinate conjunctions *(and, but, or, either . . . or, neither . . . nor, both . . . and, not only . . . but also)* link words, phrases, and clauses of equal value or importance within the sentence. Subordinate conjunctions *(although, because, if, whenever)* link subordinate clauses to the main sentence.

Article   Articles are easy. There are only three of them: *a, an,* and *the*. They precede nouns as well as words, phrases, and clauses used as nouns within the sentence structure.

Interjection   Interjections *(oh, hey, wow)* are words inserted to express feeling or to command attention. They can be used alone or as part of the sentence. When used alone, they usually are followed by an exclamation point. When used as part of the sentence, they usually are followed by a comma.

Defined by Function   Whether a word is categorized as one part of speech or as another depends upon its function within the sentence structure. The same word can have different functions in different sentences. Accordingly, one must know how a word functions within a particular sentence before it can be categorized as a noun, verb, or so on.

> The victims received medical **aid**. (*Aid* functions as a noun.)
> Physicians **aid** the sick. (*Aid* functions as a verb.)

A General Approach

This *Review Manual* is not intended as a substitute for an English grammar course but, rather, is intended to review common faults in grammar and sentence construction. Most faulty sentences could be avoided if the writer would use the simple exercise learned in elementary school: diagram sentences.

Diagram the sentence, whether mentally or on paper. Either draw or visualize the horizontal and vertical lines to separate the subject from the predicate (verb or verb phrase and its modifiers). If applicable, draw or visualize the backslash line after the predicate and put the direct object there. Show the indirect object if there is one. Then show the modifiers under the subject, predicate, or object to which they belong. Compare the diagram to the sentence. If the sentence is not grouped in the same basic way as the diagram, its construction is faulty; and it must be redrafted. This ritual is performed so often by good writers and becomes so automatic to them that they barely recognize it as diagramming the sentence.

For those who were not cursed with a Miss Tigner in elementary school, the skill of diagramming sentences can be acquired with thoughtful practice. While preparing for the CLA® examination, try this exercise with the sentences in your practice essay answers or with your drafting at the office. Diagram the sentences of others for additional practice.

- Draw a horizontal line and then draw two vertical lines to divide the horizontal line into thirds.

- Place the verb (main verb and any helping verbs) of the sentence inside the middle section of the horizontal line. Remember that the verb is the center of every sentence. No sentence can exist without a verb.

  > To find the main verb, look for either an action word (*run, grow, bring, give, help*) or a word of being (*be, become, is, was, seem*).

Include any helping verbs *(can, could, did, do, does, has, have, may, might, must, shall, should, will, would)* that complete the verb phrase.

- Place the subject on the left section of the horizontal line.

    To find the subject, use the verb to ask the question: Who or what ran? grew? brought? became? is? was? seemed? Remember that the subject is understood in some sentences but these are few. Remember, too, that the subject is the main actor (the predominant noun) in the sentence.

    Stop it.   =   (You) stop it.

    If there is no stated or understood word to answer the question, look for another verb for which the question: Who or what? can be answered. If there is no other verb, the word group is not a sentence and must be redrafted.

- Place the direct object (if there is one) on the right section of the horizontal line.

    To find the direct object, use the subject + the predicate to ask the question: What or whom? In the sample sentence above, for example, ask the question: (You) stop what or whom? The answer is the pronoun *it*. Therefore, the direct object of the sentence is *it*.

That's all there is to it. This simple diagram identifies the basic structure of the sentence. All other words, phrases, or clauses used in the sentence must modify one of the basic sentence parts shown in the main diagram. Modifiers should be placed on diagonal lines under the sentence part which they are intended to modify.

Diagram these examples:

1.   The tornado flattened the town.
2.   Mary saw Bill running from the murder scene.
3.   Joe will be running in the Olympic tryouts.
4.   The man who knows too much.

1.   There is only one action word (flattened); there is no word of being. The word *flattened* is the main verb. Who or what flattened? The answer is *tornado*. Tornado is the subject of the sentence. Tornado flattened what or whom? The answer is *town*. The word town is the direct object of the sentence.

2.   There are two action words (saw and running); there is no word of being. Bill was running, but Bill is not the main actor in the sentence; Mary is. Therefore, the verb *saw* is the main verb and *Mary* is the subject (main actor) of the sentence. Mary saw what or whom? The answer is *Bill*. Bill is the direct object, and the phrase "running from the accident scene" modifies Bill.

3. There is one action word (running); the words of being (will be) are helping verbs in this sentence, used to augment the main verb (running). The question is: Who or what will be running? The answer is *Joe*. Joe is the subject. Joe will be running what or whom? There is no answer; therefore, there is no direct object in this sentence. The phrase "in the Olympics" tells where Joe will be running; therefore, it is a prepositional phrase, used as an adverb to modify the verb phrase *will be running*.

4.   There is only one action word (knows); there is no word of being. The question is: Who or what knows? Because of the construction, the answer would have to be *who*, which cannot be correct. *Who* is not the main actor; *man* is. Therefore, this is not a sentence; it must be redrafted. Either of the following constructions solves the problem:

>   a.   *The man knows too much.* Striking the word *who* eliminates the construction problem.

>   b.   *The man who knows too much will make a poor juror.* In this sentence, the predicate is *will make*. Who or what will make? The answer is *man*, which is the subject of the sentence. Man will make what or whom? The answer is *juror*, which is the direct object. The word *poor* modifies juror. The phrase *who knows too much* modifies man.

Faulty grammar is nothing more than a failure to observe the rules of sentence construction. Every word of the sentence must have a specific function, and every word must coordinate with the words around it; there can be no words "left over." If the sentence is constructed in this way, correct grammar will follow. The first step, of course, is to identify the basic sentence structure (*see above*). Performing this exercise will eliminate many of the grammar problems that plague applicants on the CLA® examination. Once the basic sentence structure has been identified, the rules of correct grammar become easier to apply.

The Verb

Since the verb is the focal point of every sentence, it seems appropriate to begin the grammar review with the verb. A verb can be either a word indicating action (*see, do, run, read, walk)* or a word of being (*am, is are, was, were).* The verb is the heart of the sentence. It sets the tone of the sentence by its voice (active or passive); by its mood (indicative, imperative, subjunctive); and by its tense (present, present perfect, past, past perfect, future, future perfect).

The applicant must be able to recognize when any of these verb characteristics is used incorrectly within the context of a particular sentence and must be able to use verbs correctly in all essay answers.

<u>Active or Passive Voice</u>

If the subject of the sentence performs the action of the sentence, that is, directs the action toward an object, the active voice of the verb is used.

> Jane summarized the depositions.
> The jury deliberated for many hours.
> Dick mailed the notices of hearing to all parties.

> *Jane, the jury, and Dick performed the action indicated by their respective verbs.*

If, on the other hand, the subject of the sentence is acted upon, the passive voice of the verb is used.

> The depositions were summarized by Jane.
> The verdict was deliberated for many hours by the jury.
> The notices of hearing were mailed to all parties by Dick.

> *Depositions, the verdict, and the notices received the action indicated by the respective verbs.*

Nearly all authorities agree that the active voice is preferred over the passive voice. The active voice is the stronger, more interesting, and more persuasive of the two. Use the passive voice when the actor is unknown or when the intent is to minimize the actor's participation. Government agencies, for instance, tend to use the passive voice when discussing their actions, which leaves the impression that they are not directly responsible. Beyond these limited circumstances, use the active voice in all writing.

> The murder appears to have been committed by an intruder.
> The regulation was adopted by the IRS to prevent fraud by taxpayers.

Mood   A verb's mood indicates the attitude of the writer or of the speaker, as expressed by the verb. The verbal mood can be indicative, imperative, or subjunctive.

The indicative mood states a fact, expresses an opinion, or asks a question.

> The textbook was published in 1992. *(fact)*
> The text is an excellent reference tool. *(opinion)*
> Have you used this text? *(question)*

The imperative mood makes a request, states a command, or gives direction.

> Please call me after you have read the reports. *(request)*
> Review the discovery file right away. *(command)*
> Return all copies to me when you have finished. *(direction)*

The subjunctive mood states a suggestion or a requirement; expresses a desire or wish; or asserts conditions that are improbable, doubtful, or contrary to fact. Notice that the subjunctive mood uses distinctive verb forms.

> Dale should be told of your plans. *(suggestion)*
> Dale must be told of your plans. *(requirement)*
> I wish you would tell Dale of your plans. *(desire)*
> If I were you *(but I am not you)*, I would tell Dale.
> If you had your degree *(but you do not)*, you could apply for the job.
> George acted as if he were in charge. *(but he was not in charge)*
>
> BUT
>
> If Max was in Boston all week, he did not receive my letter. *(fact—indicative mood)*

Tense   The tense of the verb shows the time of the action or event. Based upon the time of the action or event, the correct verb tense is shown in the table below.

Table of Verb Tense Forms
Regular Verbs

	Past	Past Perfect	Present	Present Perfect	Future	Future Perfect
Time	started in the past and finished in the past	started and finished in the past, prior to some other past action	happening now	started in the past and continuing now	will happen in the future	will be finished in the future
Form	*add **d** or **ed** to base verb*	***had*** *+ past participle*	*base verb (add **s** to third person singular)*	***has*** *or **have** + past participle*	***shall** (first person) or **will** (all others) + base verb*	***shall** or **will** + **have** + past participle*
Samples	I helped you helped she helped he helped it helped we helped you helped they helped	I had helped you had helped she had helped he had helped it had helped we had helped you had helped they had helped	I help you help he helps she helps it helps we help you help they help	I have helped you have helped she has helped he has helped it has helped we have helped you have helped they have helped	I shall help you will help she will help he will help it will help we shall help you shall help they shall help	I shall have helped you will have helped she will have helped he will have helped it will have helped we shall have helped you will have helped they will have helped

I **helped** Gary with his homework. *(past)*
I **had read** many books by the time I **graduated**. *(both past, one before the other)*
Mother **helps** a great deal when she **visits** me. *(present)*
We **have helped** each other for many years. *(past, continuing now)*
She **will help** me with Gene's graduation party next month. *(future)*
I **shall have helped** many people by the time I leave. *(to be completed in the future)*

Irregular verbs vary their tense forms for present, past, future, and past participle forms. Consult a dictionary for tense formation of irregular verbs. If the verb's tenses are not shown, it is a regular verb and follows the conventions shown in the above table. Some of the more common irregular verbs are shown below, together with their past and past participle forms.

Common Irregular Verbs

Present	Past	Past Participle
am, are, is	was, were	been
become	became	become
begin	began	begun
bring	brought	brought
choose	chose	chosen
come	came	come
do	did	done
get	got	gotten
give	gave	given
go	went	gone
know	knew	known
lay	laid	laid (to put or place)
lie	lay	lain (to rest or recline)
make	made	made
run	ran	run
see	saw	seen
take	took	taken
write	wrote	written

Helping Verbs   Helping verbs *(can, could, did, do, does, has have, may, might, must, shall, should, will, would)*, sometimes called auxiliary verbs, often combine with verbs to "help" indicate voice or tense. The tense indicated by a helping verb shows whether something was happening (past progressive), had happened (past perfect), had been happening (past perfect progressive), is happening (present progressive), has happened (present perfect) has been happening (present perfect progressive), will have happened (future perfect), or will have been happening (future perfect progressive).

Agreement of Subject and Verb   The subject and verb of the sentence must agree in number. The number of the subject determines the number of the verb—whether singular or plural (Strunk Rule 9).[3] A singular subject requires a singular verb; a plural subject requires a plural verb.

> It **is** fascinating to wander through old courthouses.
> Old courthouses **are** fascinating.
> Bob Gronstal's name **was** mentioned among the acknowledgements.

---

[3]Reprinted with permission of Macmillan Publishing Company from THE ELEMENTS OF STYLE, Third Edition by William Strunk Jr. and E.B. White. Copyright © 1979 by Macmillan Publishing Company.

The Andersons' names **were** included on the guest list.

A verb with more than one subject (compound subject) is almost always plural. The exception is the compound subject, often a cliche, that is considered as a single unit.

> Bob and Judy Baker **have** a new granddaughter.
> A fool and his money **are** soon parted.
> Ian Jones and the woman who jogged across America, Jan Clark, **were** invited.

BUT

> Give and take **is** critical to a lasting relationship.
> Bread and butter **was** all that I could find to eat.

Use a singular verb when the subject is *anybody, anyone, each, each one, either, everybody, everyone, neither,* or *nobody* or when the subject is qualified by any of these words. **Hint:** When the subject of the sentence is *none* (meaning *no one* or *not one*), the verb is singular.

> Anyone who knows melons **knows** that this one is too ripe.
> Nobody **is** responsible.
> Each one of the applicants **was** prepared for the examination.
> Either of the candidates **is** qualified for the job.
> None of our children **was** permitted to chew tobacco.
> None of the legal assistants in our firm **is** ever late.
> None **is** so blind as he who refuses to see.

BUT

> None **are** so blind as those who refuse to see.

When the word *all* is used as a subject, a plural verb almost always is required.

> All **were** tested but only a few were qualified.
> All but one **have** the measles.
> All of the funds **were** spent on publicity.

BUT

> All of the money **was** spent on publicity.

Plural words that intervene between a singular subject and its verb do not change the singular number of the subject.

> Helen Dail, who has chaired many committees and workshops,
> **believes** this one is her best.

A singular subject remains singular even when other nouns are connected to it by words such as with, as well as, in addition to, except, together, and no less than.

> Her grammar as well as her spelling **was** poor.
> Scott, with all of his fine qualities, **is** not my first choice.
> Our neighbor as well as his cars **irritates** everyone on our block.

When compound subjects are joined by the words *either . . . or, neither . . . nor,* or *not only . . . but also,* the verb must agree in number with the subject closest to it.

> Neither the legal assistants nor their supervisor **was** ready to leave by 5:00 p.m.
> Either the attorney or her legal assistants **are** doing a creditable job.

Some nouns appear to be plural but are often treated as singular; these require a singular verb.

> Gymnastics **is** one sport that I will never master.
> NALA Headquarters **is** located in Tulsa, Oklahoma.
> Communications **causes** problems for most applicants.

BUT

> Calisthenics **are** good for sore muscles.
> My studies **require** more time than I had allotted.
> Communications **were** strained between us.

Group nouns (sometimes called collective nouns) require a singular verb when the members of the group act as one unit but require a plural verb when the members of the group act independently.

> The legal department **is** preparing to move to its new offices.
> The group **is** growing restless.

BUT

> The fish **were** swimming furiously upstream.
> The group **are** writing letters, calling volunteers, and drafting proposals.

The Pronoun

Pronouns cause more difficulty than any other, single part of speech. Sometimes the difficulty stems from a simple failure to **keep pronouns logistically close to their antecedents**. This failure creates confusion about the antecedent to which the pronoun refers.

INCORRECT — When *she* arrived at the office, Roger gave the letter to Joan; and Joan gave it to Ms. Wallace, the supervisor. *(Does **she** refer to Joan or to Ms. Wallace?)*

Roger gave the letter to **Joan** when **she** arrived at the office; and Joan gave it to Ms. Wallace, the supervisor.

EITHER MAY
BE CORRECT — Roger gave the letter to Joan; and Joan gave it to **Ms. Wallace**, the supervisor, when **she** arrived at the office.

Person, Number, and Gender   Pronouns and their antecedents—the words to which they refer—must agree in person (whether first, second, or third); in number (whether singular or plural); and in gender (whether masculine, feminine, or neuter). A common fault with **person agreement** of pronouns derives from the incorrect use of the pronoun *we*.

> How are *we* feeling today? *(This is incorrect when the speaker means: How are **you** feeling?)*
>
> I think that *we* shall have just a salad, thank you. *(This is incorrect when the speaker means: I shall have just a salad. As written, the sentence indicates that two or more people intend to share one salad.)*

INCORRECT   Congress gave *their* approval of the tax increase.
CORRECT   Congress gave **its** approval of the tax increase.

A **pronoun's number** depends upon the singular or plural status of its antecedent, using the same rules stated for agreement of subject and verb (see above). Separate but similar problems arise in **gender agreement** of pronouns with their antecedents. Nevertheless, the same rule applies: Refer to the number and gender of the antecedent to determine the number and gender of the pronoun.

> A civilized society resolves **its** disputes in courtrooms.
> Civilized societies resolve **their** disputes in courtrooms.
> The federation decided to disband **itself**.
> The jazz trio planned a special concert in honor of **its** reunion.

BUT

> The audience arose from **their** seats to cheer the actors.
> The old gang have gone **their** separate ways.

Notice, too, the distinctions in the following examples.

INCORRECT   The National Association of Legal Assistants (NALA) is a leader in the legal assistant profession. *Their* work with the American Bar Association has brought many positive changes to the field.

CORRECT   The National Association of Legal Assistants (NALA) is a leader in the legal assistant profession. **Its** work with the American Bar Association has brought many positive changes to the field. *(stressing the organization as a whole rather than its individual members)*

INCORRECT   Everyone in the car feared for *their* lives.

CORRECT   Everyone in the car feared for **his or her** life.

BETTER   All passengers in the car feared for **their** lives.

Pronoun Case   Misuse of **pronoun case** accounts for many errors on examinations. Because of this fact, pronoun case deserves careful attention in the applicant's review process. Pronoun case refers to how the pronoun functions within a sentence (whether subjective [nominative], objective, or possessive). The chart following the examples may be helpful in distinguishing among the three functions of pronouns.

INCORRECT	Please join Bill and *I* for dinner.
CORRECT	Please join Bill and **me** for dinner. *(used as object)*
INCORRECT	Bill and *me* want you to come with us.
CORRECT	Bill and **I** want you to come with us. *(used as subject)*
INCORRECT	This is *her* speaking.
CORRECT	This is **she** speaking. *(used as subject complement)*
INCORRECT	We can't hear anything above *him* talking.
CORRECT	We can't hear anything above **his** talking. *(used as possessive adjective)*
INCORRECT	I do not want to go with *he*.
CORRECT	I do not want to go with **him**. *(used as object of preposition)*
INCORRECT	*Us* Americans are independent people.
CORRECT	**We** Americans are independent people. *(used with the subject)*
INCORRECT	Give the job to *we* legal assistants.
CORRECT	Give the job to **us** legal assistants. *(used with object of preposition)*

PRONOUN CASE FORMS

Personal Pronouns	Subjective	Objective	Possessive
(Singular)			
First Person	I	me	my, mine
Second Person	you	you	your, yours
Third Person	he, she, it	him, her, it	his, her, hers, its
(Plural)			
First Person	we	us	our, ours
Second Person	you	you	your, yours
Third Person	they	them	their, theirs
Relative and Interrogative Pronouns			
	who	whom	whose
	whoever	whomever	—
	which that	which that	—

A pronoun must be used according to its case (function) in the sentence. Use the **subjective case** when the pronoun functions as one of the following:

●*Subject of a sentence (independent clause)*

> **She and I** will graduate in June.
> **They** ran to the courthouse in pouring rain.

●*Subject of a subordinate clause*

> Welfare laws often ignore the people **who** need their benefits most.
> The plaintiff offered all of the evidence that **he** had.
> Give the deposition project to **whoever** can finish it by tomorrow.

●*Subject of an understood verb*

> You have more tenacity than **they** (have).
> William is not as sophisticated as **she** (is).

•*Subject complement*

>It is **I**.
>Yes, this is **she**.
>The most pleasant guests were **she and he**.

•*Appositive identifying the subject of a sentence*

>Only two lawyers, **she and he**, have been with the firm longer than I.
>They are always together, **she and he**.

Use the **objective case** when the pronoun functions as one of the following:

•*Direct or indirect object of a verb*

>**Whom** shall I say is calling?
>We don't care **whom** the president selected for the post.

•*Object of a preposition*

>For **whom** shall we ask?
>Most of **us** were too busy to notice.

•*Object of a gerund, infinitive, or participle*

>Why not try singing **them** to sleep? *(gerund)*
>The chairperson tried to shout **her and me** into silence. *(infinitive)*
>Having seen **them**, Jane turned and raced across the street. *(participle)*

•*Appositive identifying the object of a clause or sentence.*

>The Board appointed two chairpersons, **her and him**.

Choosing between the pronouns *we* and *us* continues to perplex many applicants when the pronoun precedes a noun. Simply eliminate the noun and see which pronoun makes more sense. For the rule-minded, *we* is used with a noun subject; *us* is used with a noun object.

>**We** legal assistants want no part of this proposal. *(**We** want no part . . . .)*

>Just between **us** CLAs, the preparation was worth the time that it took. *(Just between **us**, the preparation was . . . .)*

The judge told **us** lawyers to try to settle the case. *(The judge told* **us** *to try . . . .)*

Regardless of what **we** quilters may think, it is not true that the person who dies with the most fabric wins. *(Regardless of what* **we** *may think, ...)*

A gerund usually is preceded by the **possessive case** of the noun or pronoun that modifies it.

The **judge's** singing startled all of us.
The judge disapproved of **our** singing with him.
Their singing was louder than ours.
My singing was the best of all.

Relative and Interrogative Pronouns

Relative and interrogative pronouns are sources of difficulty in both objective and essay questions. **Relative pronouns** (see chart above) are used to **relate** a subordinate clause to the main clause of the sentence. **Interrogative pronouns** are used to **ask questions** (interrogate).

(Interrogative - singular)
    Who is coming to dinner?   (**She** is coming to dinner.)
    To **whom** is the letter addressed?   (The letter is addressed to **her**.)

(Interrogative - plural)
    Who are coming to dinner?   (**They** are coming to dinner.)
    To **whom** are the letters addressed?   (The letters are addressed to **them**.)

(Relative - singular)
    Lee was the one **who** read the novel.   (**She** read the novel.)
    Terry, with **whom** I have worked, will do a good job.   (I have worked with **her**.)

(Relative - plural)
    Lee and Ann were the ones **who** read the novel.   (**They** read the novel.)
    Terry and Jo, with **whom** I have worked, will do a good job.   (I have worked with **them**.)

To tell whether to use the subjective case (who, whoever) or the objective case (whom, whomever), simply rephrase the sentence, substituting the pronouns *she* and *her* (*they* and *them* for plurals) to see which one makes more sense. If the pronoun *she* makes more sense, then use *who* or *whoever*; if the pronoun *her* makes more sense, then use *whom* or *whomever*.

Who is the president-elect? *(**She** is the president-elect.)*
Cora is the one **who** we think will do the job. *(We think Cora [**she**] will do the job.)*
She is the one **whom** we should elect. *(We should elect **her**.)*
Sarah is the one **who** everyone says will win. *(**She** will win.)*

Berniece is the one **whom** we respect. *(We respect **her**.)*
Whoever arrives first will get the job. *(**She** arrives first.)*
You may call upon **whomever** to assist you. *(You may call upon **them**.)*
Please give this to **whomever**. *(Please give this to **her**.)*

BUT

Please give this to **whoever** is in charge.

Here, the subjective case (whoever) must be used even though it is the object of the preposition "to." This is because the entire clause "whoever is in charge" is the object of the preposition, with "whoever" used as the subject of that clause.

When *than* and *as* are used to make comparisons, the clauses they introduce are sometimes incomplete. The subject and verb are understood in this type of sentence construction. In the first sentence below, the meaning is clear: Alice likes cola better than (she likes) coffee. The second sentence, however, may have one of two meanings.

Alice likes cola better than coffee.
Jack likes Jill more than Arthur.

As written, the sentence may mean that Jack likes Jill more than (he likes) Arthur. It also may mean that Jack likes Jill more than Arthur (likes Jill). When a pronoun is used in place of a noun, a specific meaning attaches to the pronoun, depending upon whether it is stated in the subjective case or in the objective case. Applicants must be familiar with the meaning implicit in using one case or the other; otherwise, the meaning intended may not be the same as the meaning conveyed.

Jack likes Jill more than **she**. *(more than she likes Jill)*
Jack likes Jill more than **her**. *(more than Jack likes her)*

Alice admires Doris more than **we**. *(more than we admire Doris)*
Alice admires Doris more than **us**. *(more than Alice admires us)*

Andrew cares for ice cream as much as **I**. *(as much as I care for ice cream)*
Andrew cares for ice cream as much as **me**. *(as much as Andrew cares for me)*

One way to eliminate the entire issue, at least for essay questions, is to state specifically what is meant. Don't leave words to be understood;[4] write all of the words needed to avoid misunderstanding (Strunk Rule 10).

Alice admires Doris more than we do.
Andrew cares for ice cream more than he cares for me.

---

[4]Reprinted with permission of Macmillan Publishing Company from THE ELEMENTS OF STYLE, Third Edition by William Strunk Jr. and E.B. White. Copyright © 1979 by Macmillan Publishing Company.

The relative pronouns *who, which,* and *that* cause problems for nearly everyone. Even seasoned grammarians have to think about which one is proper in certain situations. Since each of these relative pronouns relates a subordinate clause to the main sentence, many writers solve the dilemma by using this simplified, general formula:

who　　　*for all clauses related to people, whether restrictive or nonrestrictive*

which　　*for all nonrestrictive clauses related to non-people*

that　　　*for all restrictive clauses related to non-people*

> The man **who** helped us with directions was kind. *(restrictive)*
> Connie's mother, **who** sat next to you, is a physicist. *(nonrestrictive)*
> The art book, **which** I cannot find, belongs to Dr. McHenry. *(nonrestrictive)*
> The book **that** I borrowed from Dr. McHenry has been misplaced. *(restrictive)*

This formula works for essay answers, where applicants may select the pronouns that they will use. It even may work for some of the objective questions, but it is not sufficiently precise to work for all of them. The precise rule is:

who　　　*for clauses related to an individual or group of individuals, whether restrictive or nonrestrictive*

which　　*for clauses related to places, objects, and animals, whether restrictive or nonrestrictive, and to introduce a nonrestrictive clause*

that　　　*for clauses related to a class, species, or kind of person or group; for clauses related to objects or animals; or to introduce a restrictive clause*

The Gerund

A gerund is a verb form ending in **-*ing*** that functions as a noun. Gerunds may be used as subjects or as objects within the sentence structure.

> **Playing** the harmonica is Richard's favorite pastime. *(subject)*
> Ann went to the laundromat to do her **washing**. *(object of infinitive "to do")*
> The mayor disapproved of **picketing** after sunset. *(object of preposition)*

Do not confuse gerunds and present participles, both of which have the ***ing*** ending. The gerund functions as either a subject or an object, while the present participle functions as an adjective. (*See the section on participles below.*)

> Your **snoring** was too loud to ignore. *(gerund)*
> The entire congregation heard you **snoring**. *(participle)*

Teaching is demanding work. *(gerund)*
Joy hopes to earn a **teaching** degree. *(participle)*

The Infinitive

An infinitive is formed when a verb (usually first person singular) is preceded by the word *to*. Infinitives may function as nouns, adjectives, or adverbs.

Martin loves **to shop**. *(used as a noun, the object of this sentence)*
Richard is a sight **to see**. *(used as an adjective, modifying "sight")*
Canoeing is difficult **to do**. *(used as an adverb, modifying "do")*

Avoid "split infinitives" (an adverb inserted between *to* and the verb). For clarity, the adverb should be placed either before or after the infinitive.

INCORRECT   We need *to* carefully *proofread* the brief.
CORRECT   We need **to proofread** the brief carefully.

The **tense** of the infinitive is determined by the tense of the verb in the predicate. The **present infinitive** indicates action at the same time as or later than that of the verb.

I hope **to see** you soon. *(seeing will occur after the hope)*
I would have liked **to meet** you long ago. *(liking and meeting at the same past time)*

The (past) **perfect infinitive** indicates action earlier than that of the verb and is formed by combining the words *to have* with the past participle of the verb.

I would like **to have attended** Harvard. *(attended occurs before like)*
We believe the vote **to have been** secret. *(vote occurs before belief)*

Modifiers

A modifier is a word or group of words used to explain, limit, or qualify the meaning of another word or group of words. Modifiers include adjectives and adverbs, as well as those words, phrases, and clauses that function as adjectives or adverbs.

<u>Adjectives</u>   Adjectives are words that describe or modify nouns or pronouns. Adjectives answer the question: Which? what kind of? or how many? within the sentence structure.

The **downtown** office handles all of the computer equipment. *(which)*
Loose screws will ruin a car. *(what kind of)*
All students hope to earn an A in the course. *(how many)*

A group of words—a phrase or a subordinate clause—may function as an adjective within the sentence.

The man **in the yellow cap** came toward us. *(adjective phrase)*
Applicants **who plan for success** will have it. *(adjective clause)*

Adverbs   Adverbs are words that describe or modify verbs, adjectives, other adverbs, or groups of words that function as verbs, adjectives, or adverbs. Adverbs answer the question: How? when? where? to what extent? or how often? within the sentence structure. Adverbs often (but not always) end with the letters **-ly**.

The test was **extremely** long. *(how)*
Maurice will be here **tomorrow**. *(when)*
Please put the book **here**. *(where)*
I **nearly** lost my watch. *(to what extent)*
Ron **frequently** drives to Las Vegas. *(how often)*

A group of words—a phrase or a subordinate clause—may function as an adverb within the sentence.

At dawn the city comes to life. *(adverb phrase)*
The seminar was not as successful **as we had hoped**. *(adverb clause)*

Adjectives and Adverbs for Comparison   Adjectives and adverbs can be used to compare one person or thing to other people or things. The **comparative degree** is used to compare two people or things; the **superlative degree** is used to make comparisons among three or more people or things.

Who is **older**, Gene Autrey or Roy Rogers? *(comparative)*
Garnets are **less** expensive than rubies. *(comparative)*
The ink jet printer is **more** expensive than the dot matrix. *(comparative)*

Who is the **oldest** living cowboy? *(superlative)*
Crystals are the **least** expensive of all gemstones. *(superlative)*
The laser is the **most** expensive printer. *(superlative)*

Participles   Every verb has two participle forms: present and past. The **present participle** is formed by adding *-ing* to the present tense verb form (working, helping, knowing). The **past participle** is formed by adding -d or -ed to the present tense of regular verbs (worked, helped). Irregular verbs use their own past participle form (known). Both present and past participles function as adjectives to modify nouns and pronouns.

> **Working** mothers are busy people. *(present participle, modifies mothers)*
> Everyone needs a **helping** hand. *(present participle, modifies hand)*
> Ken gave us a **knowing** smile. *(present participle, modifies smile)*
>
> Having **worked** hard, Jill was promoted first. *(past participle, modifies hard)*
> Ben's story is **helped** by his sincerity. *(past participle, modifies story)*
> **Known** to be fair, Robert will make a good judge. *(past participle, modifies Robert)*

Nouns and Pronouns

Nouns can function as modifiers of other nouns in limited circumstances. Pronouns frequently are used as adjectives to modify nouns.

> **office** building   **sweat** shop   **slave** labor
>
> **Her** scores were higher than **his** scores.
> **This** paper has many errors.

Misplaced Modifiers

A misplaced modifier is one that seems to modify the wrong part of the sentence or that creates confusion about which part of the sentence it modifies. Misplaced modifiers can produce humorous results on occasion; more times than not, however, they are simply awkward and confusing. Nearly all problems with misplaced modifiers can be eliminated by following the rule stated at the beginning of the Grammar section: diagram the sentence to determine its basic structure. Then keep related words and word groups together.

INCORRECT	He barely died a month ago. *(Is he barely dead as a result?)*
CORRECT	He died barely a month ago.
INCORRECT	Adam served drinks to his guests in glasses. *(Those not wearing glasses went thirsty?)*
CORRECT	Adam served drinks in glasses to his guests.
INCORRECT	I knew that a crime had been committed by the smell of marijuana. *(Did the smell commit a crime?)*
CORRECT	I knew by the smell of marijuana that a crime had been committed.

A participial phrase placed at the beginning of a sentence must refer to the grammatical subject[5] of the sentence (Strunk Rule 11). In fact, this rule applies to most introductory phrases.

---

[5]Reprinted with permission of Macmillan Publishing Company from THE ELEMENTS OF STYLE, Third Edition by William Strunk Jr. and E.B. White. Copyright © 1979 by Macmillan Publishing Company.

Speeding down the street, we noticed two men in a red car.
In need of body work, Joe bought a car for a good price.
Just having had kittens, I was unable to coax Tabby from under the bed.

As written, the first sentence above indicates that *we* were speeding down the street. If the writer intends to say that the men were speeding down the street, the sentence must be rewritten. In the second sentence, it seems likely that the car needed body work—not Joe; the sentence must be rewritten. In the third sentence, surely it was Tabby who had kittens and not the writer; it, too, must be rewritten.

We noticed two men speeding down the street in a red car.
Joe bought a car in need of body work for a good price.
I was unable to coax Tabby, just having had kittens, from under the bed.

By keeping the basic parts of a sentence close to their modifiers, the vast majority of misplaced modifier problems can be avoided.

Dangling Modifiers

A dangling modifier is a misplaced modifier carried to its ultimate extreme; a dangling modifier does not modify anything in the sentence. Dangling modifiers often produce ludicrous sentences.

INCORRECT	Uncertain of what to do next, the doorbell rang.
CORRECT	Sam was uncertain of what do next when the doorbell rang.
INCORRECT	While in grammar school, my mother earned a college degree.
CORRECT	While I was in grammar school, my mother earned a college degree.
INCORRECT	At three years of age, both of Bill's parents died.
CORRECT	When Bill was three years old, both of his parents died.

To locate dangling modifiers, verify that the modifier describes the subject of the sentence. If it does not, it may be a dangling modifier. To avoid dangling modifiers, either rewrite the modifier and give it a subject of its own or change the sentence so that the modifier describes the right subject.

Conjunctions

A conjunction is a word that connects words, phrases, and clauses to form a cohesive sentence. Conjunctions may be coordinate, correlative, or subordinate. Applicants must be able to use conjunctions appropriately and to recognize their incorrect use within a given sentence.

Coordinate Conjunctions

A coordinate conjunction is one that connects words or groups of words that have equal grammatical value or rank. For instance, a coordinate conjunction may connect two nouns or may connect two independent clauses. The words *and, but, or, nor,* and *yet* are examples of coordinate conjunctions.

The conjunction *and* is used to connect words or groups of words to be given equal emphasis or to be considered as a single unit. The conjunctions *but* and *yet,* on the other hand, indicate contrast between two words or between two units. The conjunctions *or* and *nor* indicate that the connected words or groups of words should be considered individually, sometimes as a choice between the two. Use care to select that conjunction which is appropriate within the context of a particular sentence.

> It was the land of milk **and** honey.
> I had always longed to see it, **and** I am glad that we came.
> It has been a wonderful trip, **but** it's time to go home.
> Shall we travel by plane **or** by car?

Correlative Conjunctions

Correlative conjunctions are pairs of words used to connect words or word groups of equal grammatical rank. The most common correlative conjunctions are *either . . . or, neither . . . nor,* and *not only . . . but also.*

> I had hoped that **either** my parents **or** my sister would offer to house-sit.
> **Neither** my father **nor** my mother took the hint, however.
> Hiring a professional will be **not only** expensive, **but also** inconvenient.

Subordinate Conjunctions

A subordinate conjunction is a word used to connect a subordinate word or group of words to the main sentence. Examples of subordinate conjunctions include the words *after, although, as, because, if, though, when, whether,* and *while.* Subordinate conjunctions occasionally may be combined (*as if, as though*), but this should be done sparingly.

> I plan to return to work **after** I finish my dinner.
> It must be done, **although** I would prefer to watch television.
> I am working as quickly **as** I can.
> This task is important **because** it is the foundation for all that follows.
> I must hurry **if** I am to finish by Wednesday.
> There are corrections needed, **though** they are small.
> I hope to take a vacation **when** this project is finished.
> First, I need to see **whether** I can afford a vacation.
> Someone must care for our dog **while** we are away.
> Our dog acts **as if** he were in charge of our household.

Ambiguous and Misused Conjunctions

Most conjunctions indicate specific relationships between the words that they connect. For instance, the conjunction *because* signals that a cause or reason follows it. A few subordinate conjunctions, however, seem to create substantial confusion concerning their proper use. Among these, the words *as*, *while* and *like* are the primary offenders.

The subordinate conjunction **as** properly may be used to signal either time or comparison relationships to the main sentence.

> We arrived at the theater **as** the movie was beginning. *(time)*
> I am working as quickly **as** I can. *(comparison)*

When **as** is used as a conjunction to indicate reason or cause, it may cause confusion. The best solution is to use a more accurate conjunction as the connector.

UNCLEAR   *As* I was at the courthouse, I ordered the Smith land records. *(time or reason?)*

CLEAR   **Because** I was at the courthouse, I ordered the Smith land records. *(reason)*
CLEAR   **When** I was at the courthouse, I ordered the Smith land records. *(time)*

The subordinate conjunction **while** may be used to signal either time or concession. Unless this conjunction is used in such a way that its meaning is absolutely clear, choose a more precise conjunction as the connector.

UNCLEAR   *While* we were in trial, we did not see the witness enter. *(time or concession?)*

CLEAR   **When** we were in trial, we did not see the witness enter. *(time)*
CLEAR   **Although** we were in trial, we did not see the witness enter. *(concession)*

CLEAR   **While** I was working, Jim watched every movement that I made. *(time)*
CLEAR   **While** I do not agree with you, I understand your position. *(concession)*

Sometimes the subordinate conjunction **while** is used as if it were a coordinate conjunction. Notwithstanding the confusion to the reader, it is simply wrong.

INCORRECT   I want to go to Myrtle Beach, *while* Ken wants to go to San Diego.
CORRECT   I want to go to Myrtle Beach, **but** Ken wants to go to San Diego.

INCORRECT   Jack is studying medicine, *while* Ruth is studying law.
CORRECT   Jack is studying medicine, **and** Ruth is studying law.

Because the word **like** is misused so often as a subordinate conjunction, it warrants special mention. This word is a preposition that is generally used to indicate comparison. Never should it be used as a subordinate conjunction. The rule is simple: Never use **like** to connect a phrase or clause to the main sentence.

INCORRECT	This pie crust tastes *like* it was made from clay.
CORRECT	This pie crust tastes **as if** it were made from clay.
CORRECT	This pie crust tastes **like** clay.
CORRECT	This pie crust tastes **like** unseasoned clay.
INCORRECT	Jammo works *like* a caulking gun should.
CORRECT	Jammo works **as** a caulking gun should.
INCORRECT	It seems *like* I will never finish my work.
CORRECT	It seems **as though** I will never finish my work.
INCORRECT	It looks *like* it could rain any minute.
CORRECT	It looks **as if** it could rain any minute.

Rules of Composition

Once the basic grammar rules have been substantially mastered, composition rules become infinitely easier to understand and to use. Grammar rules deal with selection of the correct words or word groups for sentence construction; composition rules deal with the construction process itself. Using composition rules, the writer may construct sentences, paragraphs, sections, chapters, and entire books. Taken together, grammar rules and composition rules comprise writing style.

Writing is critical to the function of every lawyer and every legal assistant. The professional success enjoyed by these individuals often is tied directly to writing style. Although much has been written about writing style, certain truths or rules emerge consistently.

Rule 1: **Good writers read good writing.** Newspapers seldom fit the bill. Instead, periodically read and re-read the essays of Thoreau and Emerson; the poems of the Brownings and Poe; and the novels of Faulkner, Hemingway, and Mitchner. Aside from their aesthetic value, notice how these writers construct their sentences and paragraphs (or their prose). Diagram a few of them. This periodic exposure will improve writing skills—not by copying, but by unconscious emulation that approaches osmosis.

Rule 2: **Be precise, concise, simple, and clear.** Continually monitor the written product to ensure that these four principles are met. For the most part, writing is a slow process. It requires the writer to edit again and again until the product meets these four requirements. This process can be accelerated somewhat if the writer is willing to seek constructive criticism from more experienced writers. Accept their comments with an open mind and a positive attitude.

Rule 3: **Practice, practice, practice.** The writing done in the work environment is not enough. Keep a daily journal, offer to write articles for publication by associations to which you belong (or practice writing them as if you intend to offer them for publication), practice writing essay answers, and so forth. Write as much as you can, paying attention to grammar and composition rules. As is true of any skill, the effort, discipline, and frequency of practice have a direct bearing upon the ability to perform well.

Rule 4: **The best writing style is no style at all.** In other words, writing style is at its best when the reader doesn't notice it. The style stays in the background, as the foundation and facilitator of the thoughts being conveyed. If writers observe the basic rules of grammar and composition, their styles surface naturally.

A General Approach

Rules of composition are rules of construction, regardless of whether it is a simple sentence, a paragraph, an essay, a brief, or a book that is to be produced. All construction must start with a plan, whether it is a blueprint for building construction or an outline for composition.

An outline for composition is essential to achieve the intended result. The first step, then, is to determine what the result is to be. What is the goal of the finished product? To survey all known positions on the subject? To discuss and analyze known positions, reaching a conclusion as to those that are best or worst? To persuade the reader to adopt a particular conclusion? Fuzzy writing generally is the product of fuzzy thinking at the outline stage. Take the time to formulate the specific outline (plan) for the composition by deciding upon its intended goal and then listing those points which are essential in achieving that result. An outline can be modified if necessary; and it can be modified many times if necessary to reach the intended result.

After the intended result is determined and the outline has been prepared, the composition process can begin. Nearly every composition, regardless of its length, has three essential parts: the **introduction**, the **body**, and the **conclusion**. In a one-paragraph product, these parts are presented in the form of paragraph sentences. If the finished product is to be an essay or a longer work, the introduction, body, and conclusion generally are presented in the form of paragraphs, with transitional sentences used to shift the reader from one paragraph to another.

The Paragraph

The **paragraph is the primary unit** of composition. It may have a transitional sentence at its beginning or at its end or both, but it must be centered around a topic sentence. The **topic sentence** is that sentence which tells the reader what the paragraph's subject is, that is, why this particular paragraph is part of the composition. The topic sentence generally should be placed at the beginning or near the beginning of the paragraph, as a guidepost to tell the reader where the paragraph is headed. While it is possible to place the topic sentence at the end of the paragraph, this requires still greater attention to the remaining composition rules if the effect of its changed position is to be achieved.

Other sentences within the paragraph may amplify, limit, explain, argue, or question the subject raised by the topic sentence. Keep the reader in mind as these sentences are added, to be sure that they form a coherent, cohesive paragraph unit. If the reader must stop to wonder how a particular sentence (or a particular word) fits into the paragraph, the writer's objective is destroyed; and the paragraph should be revised. There are specific methods and techniques used by writers to ensure sound paragraph construction. The result of following these rules is strong, forceful writing that is a pleasure to read. That is, after all, the ultimate goal of every writer. The most common of these techniques and rules are discussed in the sections that follow.

Forceful Writing

Forceful writing combines the rules of grammar and composition in the sound construction of sentences and paragraphs. In this sense, forceful writing does not mean argumentative writing, though a particular composition may be argumentative by design. It means writing that is **unified, cohesive, clear,** and **concise**. It means writing that **flows smoothly**, with no stumbling blocks to distract the reader's attention from the thought being conveyed.

<u>**Use Verbs**</u>   Writing that uses active verbs is always more forceful and more interesting to read. Compare the following examples.

made a decision	decided
is binding upon	binds
have knowledge of	know
make a payment	pay

Split Verbs

Split Verbs   Splitting verb phrases (verbs and their helping words) interrupts the flow of the sentence and should be avoided. Similarly, avoid splitting subjects and their verbs with clauses and phrases that can be placed elsewhere.

POOR   The *plaintiff had*, at great expense to himself, *amassed* volumes of reference materials.

BETTER   At great expense to himself, the **plaintiff had amassed** volumes of reference materials.

POOR   The *lawyers*, who were preparing for trial, *had*, by working through the night, *completed* the trial brief.

BETTER   In preparing for trial, the **lawyers had completed** the trial brief by working through the night.

BETTER   The **lawyers worked** through the night to complete the trial brief.

Refer to the grammar rules concerning misplaced and dangling modifiers. Acquire the habit of keeping related words and word groups together and placing modifiers as close as possible to the words they modify.

Active Voice

Active Voice   As a general rule, use the active voice, rather than the passive voice. Recall that there are some justifiable exceptions to this rule (see prior discussion of active-passive voice in the Grammar section).

POOR   A more favorable climate *was hoped* to be created with the new rules.
BETTER   The agency **hoped** to create a more favorable climate with the new rules.

POOR   The question that *is proposed to be discussed* is compensation.
BETTER   We **will discuss** compensation.

POOR   The decision *was attempted* to be appealed to a higher court.
BETTER   The plaintiff **tried** to appeal the decision to a higher court.

Positive Statements

Positive Statements   State facts, propositions, and so forth in a positive, rather than in a negative, way.

did not remember	forgot
did not give consideration to	ignored
not important	trivial, minor
not very often	seldom

POOR   This provision *does not apply* to owners who do not live on their land.
BETTER   This provision **applies** only to owners who live on their land.

When writing about conduct of an opposing party, however, it may be more effective to say, for example, "the defendant did not remember" than to say simply "the defendant forgot." In this context, the writer may intend to cast the conduct in a negative light.

Parallel Construction   Construct similar parts of a sentence in a similar way, to the end that they parallel each other. This signals the reader that they belong together in thought. Use parallel construction when items are part of a series or a group to be considered as one, when items are compared or contrasted with each other, and when items are arranged in a list. When listing a series, such as in the first example below, place the most important word at the end for emphasis.

POOR	The defendant was convicted of robbery, murdering his victim, and rape.
BETTER	The defendant was convicted of robbery, murder, and rape.
BETTER	The defendant was convicted of robbery, rape, and murder.

POOR	American workers are disturbed about their prospects and economic plight.
BETTER	American workers are disturbed <u>about their prospects</u> and <u>about their economic plight</u>.

POOR	Not only does the act violate the commerce clause but also the due process clause.
BETTER	The act violates not only the commerce clause but also the due process clause.
BETTER	The act not only violates the commerce clause; it also violates the due process clause.

POOR	Legal assistants are capable of interviewing clients, performing research, and can implement discovery plans.
BETTER	Legal assistants are capable of interviewing clients, of performing research, and of implementing discovery plans.

In the same vein, cohesiveness of the paragraph is damaged by inappropriate shifts in person, number, and tense within the same sentence or from one sentence to another in the paragraph. Although a shift may be required because of meaning, it should be done judiciously and in a way that is consistent with the rest of the structure.

POOR	*This is a relatively new profession; they who enter it are blazing a trail for the ones that follow them. They must possess an insatiable curiosity, and you must have an eye for detail. The person who will be a good legal assistant could also be a good lawyer.*
BETTER	The legal assistant profession is relatively new; those who enter it are the trail blazers for all who follow. Legal assistants must have an insatiable curiosity and an eye for detail. Those who are good legal assistants possess the qualities to be good lawyers as well.

POOR
Law is not the field for everyone. It requires agility and patience at the same time. You must be able to speak in public and think of answers on their feet in all kinds of settings. They must be tenacious but patient, for the wheels of the legal system can be slow yet exasperating.

BETTER
Law is not for everyone. It requires both agility and patience. Its members must be able to speak in public and to think on their feet in all kinds of settings. They must be both tenacious and patient, for the wheels of the legal system can be both exasperating and slow.

Precision   Precision in writing means **choosing the right word or expression** to convey the thought intended. Mark Twain once said that the difference between the right word and the almost right word is the difference between lightning and the lightning bug.

Because legal writing is exposed to the scrutiny of opposing counsel and others so often, imprecise or ambiguous language can spring like a trap upon the unwary. Lawyers and legal assistants, more than others, must be able to say exactly what they mean. Their vocabularies must be extensive to select the precisely correct word from among all those words that could be used. The dictionary and the thesaurus are as much staples to them as statute books are. Though both words in the following sentence mean approximately the same thing, notice the different impressions that they convey.

Law *requires* both agility and patience.
Law *demands* both agility and patience.

The first rule of precision is: *Never use a word unless you know exactly what it means*. When in doubt, look it up. If a dictionary is unavailable (such as during examinations), don't use the questioned word. Select another one instead or the results could be disastrous. For instance, this phrase appeared in one student's factual summary: *the fence circumventing the premises* .... No instructor would be favorably impressed. Notice the precision problems in the following sentences as well.

INCORRECT   Traffic laws should be one *aura* of certainty from state to state.
CORRECT   Traffic laws should be one **area** of certainty from state to state.

INCORRECT   Your testimony is critical; without it, our case is extremely *tenable*.
CORRECT   Your testimony is critical; without it, our case is extremely **tenuous**.

The next rule of precision is: *It's okay to repeat the right word once you have found it*. It gives continuity to the writing. Trying to find a new word for the sake of variety can produce unintended results, such as this statement from a news article.

Two of the Democratic candidates are women; all of the Republican candidates are ladies. *(Does this mean the Democrats are not ladies?)*

Switching to a different word in legal writing creates the presumption that a different meaning is intended for each of the two words—a dangerous practice in legal documents. This is the stuff that lawsuits are made of.

When writing is precise, it generally is clear. Take the time to ensure that the writing says precisely what was intended. This means reading each sentence critically, trying to find words or expressions that may be misunderstood by others. If it can be misunderstood, rest assured that it will be. Redraft as many times as are necessary to remove all ambiguity. *(See section on misplaced modifiers.)*

The deceased consented to surgery. *(How could a corpse consent to anything?)*

The defendant stabbed the deceased when he thought he was about to shoot him. *(Does this mean the defendant stabbed a corpse in self-defense? Or does it mean that the defendant decided that it was better to stab the corpse than to shoot it?)*
The game warden filed a complaint, alleging illegal hunting in the Wade County Court. *(Does this mean that some hunting is legal at the courthouse?)*

Millions of children do not go to school in South America. *(Certainly, that includes all of the children who do not live there.)*

We arranged a meeting for small business people. *(Does this mean short business people or people who own small businesses?)*

Weasel Words   For all that has been said about precision in writing, legal writing sometimes must be seasoned lightly with ambiguity for the sake of accuracy. This is done with weasel words.

According to the Hurd text, weasel words allow the writer to "weasel out" of a hard-line statement by using terms like *appears, would appear to be, could reasonably be viewed as, could argue that, may be that,* and so forth. Legal writing, unlike other writing, sometimes requires qualifiers like these because the law itself is packed with qualifiers. We may argue that a rule should be interpreted this way or that, but we know that law is inherently imprecise. No one can predict results with 100% accuracy, so we qualify some of what we say with weasel words.[6]

Used in moderation, weasel words perform a necessary function in legal writing. They allow lawyers to take a defensive position without appearing to be defensive. They keep options open so that a position can be altered if the character of a case changes midstream. They provide maneuvering room when absolutes

---

[6]Reprinted with permission from Hurd, WRITING FOR LAWYERS. Copyright © 1982 Hollis T. Hurd.

would have to be filled with exceptions or when accurate generalizations would be too vague to be helpful. Weasel words have their place; the trick is to keep them in it.

Simplicity

The best writing is simple writing. **Never use a long word when a short one will do.** Never use a convoluted expression when a direct one says the same thing. Simple writing does not equate to simple ideas. Nor does it require the writer to patronize, as if the reader were someone of lower intelligence. The reader who finds it difficult to understand complicated legal jargon and ten-syllable words is not necessarily moronic. Most people can grasp even complex concepts if they are explained in simple English. If a writer does not understand an idea well enough to explain it in simple English, the writer does not understand it well enough.

The following passage, delivered by Franklin D. Roosevelt, is written in simple English. No word contains more than three syllables. Notice the parallelism, repetition, and rhythm of words. Other examples could be given, but this one says it all.

> I have seen war. I have seen war on land and sea. I have seen blood running from the wounded. I have seen men coughing out their gassed lungs. I have seen the dead in the mud. I have seen cities destroyed. I have seen two hundred limping, exhausted men come out of line—the survivors of a regiment of one thousand that went forward forty-eight hours before. I have seen children starving. I have seen the agony of mothers and wives. I hate war.

A Writer's Eye

Everyone who creates must acquire an eye for the aesthetic presentation of the final product. Actors use props and a stage, for instance. Artists use color and texture. No less than these, writers must have an eye for presentation. The final product must *look* interesting to read, first of all. Vary the length of paragraphs; occasionally use a single-sentence paragraph to make an important point; and never, ever create a paragraph longer than half a page. If the layout of the page looks interesting, readers will be more eager to read it.

Make the paragraphs themselves more interesting by varying length of sentences to pique the reader's interest and to maintain the reader's attention. Vary the structure, so that some sentences begin with transitional expressions and others do not. Occasionally, invert the order of subject, verb, and object to make important ideas stand out but never at the cost of rules of grammar and composition.

Concise Writing

Special emphasis is given to concise writing on the CLA® examination, perhaps because those connected with the law are prone to the disease of verbosity. The cure: **Never use two words when one word will do.** Brevity is the key.

Unnecessary words water down the necessary words. They clutter sentences and obscure ideas. Professor Strunk (Strunk & White's *Elements of Style*) maintained that the three most important rules of composition are these: Omit needless words, omit needless words, and omit needless words (Strunk Rule 17).[7]

After the first draft has been written, go back and do precisely that: omit needless words. Eliminate empty words and expressions such as these:

all things considered	—
as far as I am concerned	—
at the present time	now
at this point in time	now
by means of	by
by virtue of the fact that	because
due to the fact that	because
for all intents and purposes	—
for the purpose of	for
for the reason that	because
in my opinion	—
in the event that	if
in the nature of	like
until such time as	until

POOR   In my opinion, due to the fact that ongoing discrimination continues to exist in the field of law, women have not yet reached equality with men.

BETTER   Because of continuing discrimination in law, women have not yet reached equality with men.

POOR   I came to this college because of many factors, but most of all because of the fact that I want to be a legal assistant

BETTER   I came to this college mainly because I want to be a legal assistant.

---

[7]Reprinted with permission of Macmillan Publishing Company from THE ELEMENTS OF STYLE, Third Edition by William Strunk Jr. and E.B. White. Copyright © 1979 by Macmillan Publishing Company.

Redundant Words   As part of the editing process, check for redundant words and phrases. They add nothing to the meaning of the sentence, and they weaken the words that are important. Eliminate them.

basic essentials
circle *around*
consensus *of opinion*
continue *to remain*
cooperate *together*
definite decisions
few *in number*
final completion
frank *and honest* discussion
invisible *to the eye*
most unique
repeat *again*
return *again*
revert *back*
square *in shape*
surrounding circumstances
terribly important
true and correct
true facts
unexpected surprise
usual habits

POOR   He successfully resisted the temptation to have dessert.
BETTER   He resisted the temptation to have dessert.

POOR   The intention of the parties is found by looking to the contract to determine what was intended.
BETTER   The parties' intent is found in the terms of the contract.

The last rule of composition is to redraft as many times as are necessary. The ideal is to wait a day or two before editing. No one writes so well that he or she cannot find ways to write better. When we read our own writing critically, we can usually find ways to improve it. Perhaps the structure of a particular sentence needs to be changed. Perhaps there is a better word that could be used. Perhaps there is a more concise way to express an idea.

History tells us that Plato redrafted the first paragraph of The Republic about twelve times before he was satisfied with it. The Founding Fathers spent the better part of a summer redrafting the Constitution before they were satisfied with it. If those documents had to be rewritten again and again, surely ours could benefit from redrafting as well.

Vocabulary

Because writing is such a vital part of a legal assistant's job, every CLA is expected to have a strong vocabulary at his or her command. The best way to acquire vocabulary skills (plus the type of broad, general knowledge that every successful legal assistant must have) is to read—frequently and with an inquisitive mind. Read everything that you can find: newspapers, magazines, novels and poems by good authors, or legal opinions. If a word is unfamiliar, look it up in a dictionary right away. Write the meaning on paper or on a card and then draft a sentence or two of your own, using the new word. Dictionaries often include sample phrases that use the defined word. These will get you started. Look for ways to incorporate the new word into your spoken and written vocabulary. This helps to cement it into your mind.

An extensive vocabulary is acquired over a long period of time. There are no tricks to make the process easier or shorter. When you look up a word in the dictionary, notice its root word and the origin of the root word. More than half of the words in the English language come from Latin or Greek. Try to think of other words from the same root word. Keep your own mini dictionary of the words you look up, noting their root words; and you will see that there is similarity among many of the words we use.

Root Word	Source	Meaning	English Derivatives
aster, astsr	Greek	star	astrology, astronomy
audi	Latin	hear	audible, audience
bene	Latin	good, well	benefit, benevolent
bio	Greek	life	biology, biography
cir	Latin	around	circle, circumference
dict	Latin	speak	dictator, dictionary
fer	Latin	carry	refer, transfer
fin	Latin	end	finale, finite
fix	Latin	fasten	fix, prefix, suffix
geo	Greek	earth	geology, geography
graph	Greek	write	autograph, photograph
jur, jus	Latin	law	jury, justice
litera	Latin	letter	illiterate, literal
log, logue	Greek	word, speech	biology, catalog
luc	Latin	light	lucid, translucent
manu	Latin	hand	manual, manuscript
meter, metre	Greek	measure	barometer, metric
op, oper	Latin	work	operate, optimum
path	Greek	feeling	pathetic, sympathy

ped	Greek	child	pediatrics, pedophile
phil	Greek	love	philosophy, philander
phys	Greek	body, nature	physics, physician
scrib, script	Latin	write	scribble, transcript
tele	Greek	far off	telegraph, television
ter, terr	Latin	earth	terra cotta, territory
vac	Latin	empty	vacant, vacuum
verb	Latin	word	verbiage, verbose
vid, vis	Latin	to see	video, vision

See how many other root words and examples of English derivatives you can add to this list.

When you encounter a new word, whether on an examination or in your reading, try to guess its meaning by the context within which it is used. Sometimes the other words in the sentence will give clues about its meaning. Then look it up in the dictionary to see if you are correct. (This won't work on examinations, of course, until after the fact.) The study of words, their variations of form, and their uses can be fascinating, especially for those who work with words as much as legal assistants do.

The *audiogram* showed that Bill could benefit from a hearing aid.
Rejecting a *vacuous* lifestyle, the rich widow devoted herself to helping others.
Jack does not own any *mundane* ties, preferring bright colors and unusual patterns.

The following list provides examples of the type of words included on the exam but is not intended to be all-inclusive. Neither does it imply that any of the words on the list will be on the exam. It should be used as a starting point from which to build a more complete list.

aberrant	- deviant, abnormal	capacious	- spacious, vast
abrogate	- annul, revoke	capricious	- flighty, impulsive
abysmal	- endless, immense	cataclysm	- catastrophe
accretion	- addition, expansion	catharsis	- purging, venting
acolyte	- admirer, fan	cerulean	- as blue as the sky
acrimonious	- caustic, sarcastic	convivial	- festive, merry
adroit	- skillful, clever	copious	- voluminous, abundant
aeon	- infinitely long time	denigrate	- defame, slander
allegory	- symbolic story, parable	deprecate	- condemn, criticize
amulet	- charm, ornament	desecrate	- dishonor, contaminate
aperture	- opening, hole	desuetude	- period of disuse
arcane	- esoteric, obscure	diffident	- reserved, insecure
assay	- analyze	dilatory	- causing delay
aver	- allege, claim	doltish	- moronic
baleful	- evil, sinister	draconian	- cruel, harsh
banal	- ordinary, trite	ebullient	- effervescent, sparkling
berceuse	- lullaby, tranquil music	edifice	- building, structure

efface	- annul, erase	officious	- nosey, obtrusive
eleemosynary	- charitable	omniscient	- all-knowing
empirical	- pragmatic	ossify	- to become rigid
encomium	- praise, tribute	ostensible	- apparent
enervate	- to tire, to debilitate	panacea	- cure-all
epicurean	- connoisseur, gourmet	panoply	- ceremonial array
epithet	- a disparaging term	paradox	- contradiction
erudite	- learned, scholarly	pejorative	- belittle, make worse
esoteric	- confidential, obscure	percipient	- discerning
exacerbate	- worsen, intensify	peremptory	- unchallengeable
expiate	- make amends, repent	perspicuous	- clear
expository	- explanatory	perfunctory	- superficial, routine
fastuous	- arrogant, ostentatious	pique	- arouse, provoke
fatuous	- foolish, silly	platitude	- cliche´
ferret (out)	- to hunt (search) for	plebeian	- common, crude
flagellate	- to punish by whipping	plenary	- full, complete
fortuitous	- by luck, accidental	pleonastic	- redundant
gambol	- cavort, play	precipitous	- headlong, impulsive
garrulous	- talkative	proclivity	- inclination
halcyon	- golden, happy	profligate	- spendthrift
harbinger	- forerunner, herald	prognosticate	- predict
heterogeneous	- diverse, varied	propitious	- favorable
iconoclastic	- dissident	promulgate	- announce
ignominious	- degrading, shameful	pugnacious	- antagonistic
imbue	- to endow, to infuse	punctilious	- careful, by the rules
impugn	- attack	rapacious	- fierce, savage
indolent	- lazy	raze	- demolish
ineffable	- indescribable	rectitude	- righteousness
inertia	- failure to move	refraction	- deflection of light
innocuous	- harmless	relume	- rekindle
insipid	- dull, empty	remittent	- recurring
integral	- essential	remunerate	- compensate
intrinsic	- inherent	reparation	- indemnification
irascible	- cantankerous, ornery	replicate	- duplicate
lascivious	- lecherous, lustful	requite	- repay
loquacious	- talkative, verbose	reticulation	- network
lyceum	- hall for public lectures	rudimentary	- elementary, basic
magnanimous	- generous	riparian	- re natural waterway
malapropism	- misuse of a word	rhetoric	- discourse, oratory
mendacity	- lies (falsehoods)	ruminate	- ponder, reflect
mendicant	- a parasite, moocher	salubrious	- promoting health
metamorphosis	- transformation	sardonic	- mocking, sarcastic
metaphor	- symbol	sedulous	- diligent
morass	- quagmire	senescent	- aging, becoming old
myopic	- lacking foresight	servile	- subservient
neolithic	- outmoded	similitude	- counterpart
nemesis	- downfall, ruin	stellar	- star-like, outstanding
nescience	- ignorance	temerity	- audacity
nettle	- irritate	tenacious	- persistent, dogged
numinous	- mysterious, spiritual	tenets	- principles
obdurate	- stubborn	timorous	- mousy

umbrage	- shadows, hint
vapid	- boring, dull
veracity	- truthfulness
vicissitude	- changing fortunes
venal	- mercenary
venerate	- revere
veracity	- truthfulness
vicinal	- local
vilify	- defame
virulent	- deadly, toxic
visceral	- from deep within
vitiate	- to make faulty, debase
vituperate	- berate
vociferous	- boisterous
volatile	- explosive
voluble	- talkative
voracious	- insatiable

The vocabulary portion of the CLA® examination tests the mettle of the best wordsmiths. Approach it with the knowledge that it is only one small part of a larger Communications section and do the best you can.

Correspondence

Correspondence refers to business correspondence in the form of business letters and interoffice memoranda. Legal assistants should be sufficiently familiar with the essential parts of a business letter that they can replicate them, whether in an office setting or on an examination.

Business Letter Styles

The most widely used business letter styles are full block, modified block, and simplified.

Full Block: All lines begin at the left margin.

Modified Block with Block Paragraphs: All lines begin at the left margin except the date, complimentary close, and signature lines, all of which begin at the center of the page.

Modified Block with Indented Paragraphs: This style is identical to the modified block, except that the first word of each paragraph within the body of the letter is indented five to ten spaces. Additionally, the subject line may be either centered or indented five to ten spaces to match the paragraphs.

Simplified: All lines begin at the left margin. To *simplify* the keyboarding of this letter: the inside address is keyed in all capital letters; the salutation is omitted and is replaced by a subject line keyed in all caps; the complimentary close is omitted; and the writer's name and title are both keyed in all caps.

Business Letter Punctuation

Two punctuation styles are used in office correspondence:

Mixed Punctuation: This is the most widely used punctuation style. It requires a colon after the salutation and a comma after the complimentary close.

Open Punctuation: No punctuation is used after the salutation or the complimentary close.

Parts of a Business Letter

All business letters have certain basic elements. Other elements may or may not be included, depending upon the letter's requirements.

Required Business Letter Parts:

- Letterhead or return address of the writer
- Date
- Inside address
- Salutation (not used in simplified style)
- Body
- Complimentary close (not used in simplified style)
- Signature block (writer's name)
- Reference initials (writer and typist or typist only)

Optional Letter Parts:

- Mailing or special notations (air mail, confidential)
- Attention line
- Subject line
- Typed firm name
- Title of writer

- Enclosure notation
- Copy notation(s)
- Postscript

Full Block Style with Mixed Punctuation

Bilkum & Billum
123 Park Place
Timbuktu, Anywhere 00000
444-000-0000

July 15, 1992

PERSONAL

Mary Client, M.D.
466 North Forrest Drive
Anytown, AN 00000

Re: Client Deposition

Dear Dr. Client:

We have received a notice to take your deposition on Monday, August 31, 1992, at 11:00 a.m. The deposition is scheduled to be taken in Randy Popp's office, which is located in the Second National Bank Building downtown.

Please check your schedule to see if this date and time are convenient for you and then let me know. If you cannot have your deposition taken at that time, please provide me with three alternative dates when you could be deposed. We anticipate that the deposition will take approximately two hours.

Mr. Popp has not requested that you bring anything with you to the deposition, which should make things go much more smoothly. We will need to visit with you prior to the deposition, so that Ms. Bilkum can review the deposition coverage with you. We can arrange that time as well when you call.

I look forward to hearing from you within the next few days.

Sincerely,

Jane Doe, Legal Assistant

JD:mb

When drafting business letters, keep the reader in mind. Be concise. When a letter is longer than one page, the reader's attention diminishes by the time she reaches the second page. Avoid legalese as much as possible when writing to clients and to other nonlawyers. In addition, avoid archaic, meaningless expressions that are found too often in the business letters of lawyers and nonlawyers alike.

POOR   Enclosed please find our check in the amount (or in the sum) of $3,000.00.

BETTER	Enclosed is our check for $3,000.00.
BETTER	Our check for $3,000.00 is enclosed.
POOR	Please allow me to hear from you at your earliest convenience.
BETTER	I look forward to hearing from you within the next week.
POOR	Thanking you in advance for your kind consideration in this matter, I remain
BETTER	Thank you.

A letter is written to a specific person and should be written in such a way that it focuses on that person. In a one-on-one conversation, we would not say, for example, "In reply to your letter, . . ."; "we are in receipt of . . ."; or—the worst of all—"This is to acknowledge your letter of recent date, the contents of which have been duly received." That being so, we should not use such archaic expressions in letters. There are better ways for letters to begin, all of which get directly to the point and focus on the reader.

> The court has scheduled a trial date in your case . . .
> We have received interrogatories from the defendant's attorneys . . .
> The information that came with your letter . . .
> How soon will you be able to . . .
> Please send me . . .
> Please provide me with . . .
> Your concern about . . . is understandable.
> You are correct that . . .
> You will be glad to know that . . .

Use personal, rather than impersonal, language when writing letters, especially letters to clients or to those who are allies in the case.

POOR	A mortgage holder has the right to assign . . .
BETTER	You have the right to assign . . .
POOR	It will be observed from a reading of the first paragraph thereof . . .
BETTER	You will see by reading the first paragraph of the contract . . .

Nonverbal Communication

Nonverbal communication refers to the way in which we communicate, over and above the words we use. It is the image that we portray. Nonverbal communication includes office environment, physical appearance, and body language. A lawyer generally attempts to convey an image of trustworthiness, stability and conservatism through the office environment, including furnishings and decor. Regardless of how lavish or how spartan an office may be, however, the nonverbal communication skills of the lawyer and his or her legal assistant are critical to their effectiveness.

Nonverbal communication, sometimes called body language or demeanor, speaks as loudly as our voices. Time and time again, studies show that the things we do and the way in which we do them send messages that are just as powerful as the words we use. In fact, when the message is a negative one, it is more powerful than words. Keep the following points in mind to ensure that your verbal messages are consistent with your nonverbal messages.

- Be courteous. Regardless of the situation, courtesy costs nothing and pays dividends that will come back to you in all kinds of ways throughout your professional career.

- Use a conservative, understated manner of dress and appearance. This sends messages of professionalism, stability, and trustworthiness, which are critical to the work that legal assistants do.

- Crossing the arms sends mixed messages. It may mean that the person is closed to or disapproving of whatever is happening or it may signal a defensive position.

- When seated, crossed legs send mixed messages, neither of which is suitable in the office environment. Practice sitting with the ankles and knees aligned, since this indicates that the person is open or receptive.

- Stand and sit in an erect position; these make a person appear to be alert and interested. Slouching or leaning on objects indicates lack of energy, carelessness, and lack of interest.

- Maintain a reasonable distance between yourself and the person with whom you are speaking. Many people become uncomfortable when their personal space is invaded. Touching is usually taboo as well. Placing a hand on someone's shoulder outside a social setting may signal a superior-inferior relationship between the individuals—a message that the legal assistant does not want to send. Never touch a person with a pointed finger; this is a signal of attempted dominance and is certain to evoke a defensive, retaliatory reaction.

•Be careful of hand gestures. People who "talk with their hands," for instance, can be distracting in a one-on-one situation, so that the hand movements command more attention than the words.

•Maintain good eye contact during conversation. It indicates sincerity and interest. Conversely, no eye contact can indicate subservience or untruthfulness.

•Use facial expressions that indicate a positive attitude, interest, and professional concentration. Never display shock, disbelief, disapproval, or similar, negative expressions that are signaled by excessive frowning, raised brows, pursed lips, and the like.

As a corollary, the way we say things is just as important as what we say. Use correct pronunciation and good diction to ensure that words are clearly understood. Be mindful of voice tone and modulation to provide the right measure of calm reassurance that is so necessary for legal assistants. Voice inflection plays a significant role as well. Use care to ensure that the inflection is one that demonstrates a pleasant or at least a neutral attitude. This requires the ability to "shift into neutral" in stressful situations, so that impatience, disapproval, or other negative attitudes do not become apparent to others during a conversation.

This chapter, together with the Self-Test given below, should provide a basic review of the communication principles that may be encountered on the CLA® certifying examination. If the applicant is unfamiliar with any of the material covered, he or she is advised to consider close study of a relevant textbook or other study aid. *See the Bibliography for additional study references.*

Communications Self-Test

Allow an uninterrupted thirty-minute period to answer all questions. At the end of thirty minutes, check your answers against those in the Answer Key Section of this Manual. Deduct two points each for each incorrect answer (100 total possible points). Unanswered questions are counted as incorrect answers. Follow directions carefully and observe the time limit precisely to provide an accurate self-assessment.

Choose the more correct word by circling it.

1. Mary is (adverse) (averse) to air travel.

2. Invention is (borne) (born) of adversity.

3. We can do nothing without (him) (his) knowing about it.

4. A law library (comprises) (constitutes) books and periodicals.

5. We were (nauseated) (nauseous) by the time we left the restaurant.

6. (Regardless) (Irregardless) of the outcome, you did a superb job.

7. James felt (bad) (badly) about missing the party.

8. An association should screen (their) (its) membership applicants.

9. There are (less) (fewer) applicants for scholarships this year than ever before.

10. Please (lend) (loan) me a pen to finish the examination.

11. If Howard (was) (were) ill, he did not have time to complete the research.

12. Jack acts as if he (was) (were) infallible.

13. None of the computers (are) (is) working today.

In the following sentences, mark the underlined portions with "C" for Correct or "I" for Incorrect.

14. This file has been <u>lying</u> on your desk for more than a week.

15. <u>Between</u> the three of us, we should be able to think of one good idea.

16. It is <u>presently</u> 37° outdoors.

17. My knees hurt too <u>bad</u> to play tennis every week.

18. When I am in town, I always visit Jo; and she always visits me in Springfield.

19. <u>Us</u> legal assistants are a hearty breed.

20. Neither the teacher nor the children <u>were</u> ready to leave the playground.

21. All in the group <u>was</u> prepared for the examination.

22. To <u>insure</u> success, we must set goals for ourselves.

23. It seems <u>like</u> we still have so much to do.

Choose the best answer for each of the following questions.

24. Mark knows that we cannot win unless we work _____.

    a. all together
    b. altogether
    c. either is correct
    d. neither is correct

25. It is difficult to choose _____ the options available to us.

    a. between
    b. among
    c. either is correct
    d. neither is correct

26. Two legal assistants were appointed to the committee: _____.

    a. he and I
    b. him and me
    c. he and me
    d. him and I

27. Bill is the one _____ we selected for the job.

    a. that
    b. which
    c. who
    d. whom

28. Either of these could be _____.

    a.   Charleses' paper.
    b.   Charles' paper.
    c.   Charles's paper.
    d.   the paper of Charles.

29. Alexander is the one _____ we believe will be elected.

    a.   that
    b.   which
    c.   who
    d.   whom

30. _____ advice is received poorly by its beneficiaries throughout the world.

    a.   Mother's-in-law
    b.   Mother-in-law's
    c.   Mother-in-laws'
    d.   Mothers-in-law's

31. Mary ran quickly across the wet street and jumped clumsily into the rear seat of the moving car.

    a.   The sentence contains faulty punctuation.
    b.   The sentence contains faulty grammar.
    c.   The sentence is verbose.
    d.   The sentence is correct.

32. Thank you for your letter of January 7, the contents of which have been duly recorded.

    a.   The sentence contains faulty punctuation.
    b.   The sentence contains faulty grammar.
    c.   The sentence is verbose.
    d.   The sentence is correct.

33. Once she finished the brief, Ms. Avery congratulated Anne; and she passed it on to her legal assistant.

a. The sentence contains faulty punctuation.
b. The sentence contains faulty grammar.
c. The sentence is verbose.
d. The sentence is correct.

34. I cannot say that it was a complete fabrication, but it was the worst case of _____ that I have encountered recently.

a. acclaim
b. hyperbole
c. veracity
d. mendacity

35. We must eliminate the _____ that impede us before we can revitalize this organization.

a. falsehoods
b. principles
c. tenets
d. paradigms

36. The examination covered federal and state criminal law; contract, tort, and equitable remedies; and punctuation, grammar, and spelling.

a. The sentence contains faulty punctuation.
b. The sentence contains faulty grammar.
c. The sentence is verbose.
d. The sentence is correct.

37. I had studied the definition for the word "didactic", but I could not remember it.

a. The sentence contains faulty punctuation.
b. The sentence contains faulty grammar.
c. The sentence is verbose.
d. The sentence is correct.

38. To make matters worse, the instructor asked me to recite the first verse of "Desiderata"; and I was unable to recall any of it.

a. The sentence contains faulty punctuation.
b. The sentence contains faulty grammar.

c. The sentence is verbose.

d. The sentence is correct.

39. I wish I was a better writer.

a. The sentence contains faulty punctuation.

b. The sentence contains faulty grammar.

c. The sentence is verbose.

d. The sentence is correct.

40. This painting is the most unique piece of art that I have seen.

a. The sentence contains faulty punctuation.

b. The sentence contains faulty grammar.

c. The sentence is verbose.

d. The sentence is correct.

41. I recall my mother sewing every evening after dinner.

a. The sentence contains faulty punctuation.

b. The sentence contains faulty grammar.

c. The sentence is verbose.

d. The sentence is correct.

42. _____ arguments are unlikely to convince a court to modify existing rules.

a. Arcane

b. Erudite

c. Adroit

d. Eleemosynary

43. As far as I am concerned, Tort Law was the most interesting class that I took due to the fact that it was taught by an experienced personal injury lawyer who had a tremendous sense of humor.

a. The sentence contains faulty punctuation.

b. The sentence contains faulty grammar.

c. The sentence is verbose.

d. The sentence is correct.

44. The consensus of opinion is that grammar, punctuation, and spelling are the basic essentials for a successful legal assistant.

a. The sentence contains faulty punctuation.
b. The sentence contains faulty grammar.
c. The sentence is verbose.
d. The sentence is correct.

Match each word in the left column with the most correct definition from the right column.

45. _____ timorous   a. preachy

46. _____ vicissitude   b. demolish

47. _____ obdurate   c. trite

48. _____ banal   d. mousy

49. _____ temerity   e. inclination

50. _____ raze   f. audacity

                             g. changing fortunes

                             h. stubborn

Chapter 3
ETHICS

If you can dream it, you can do it.

—Walt Disney

This section deals with ethics in the legal assistant's contacts with employers, clients, coworkers, and the general public. Unauthorized practice, ethics rules, practice rules, and confidentiality are among the topics tested by this section.

Knowledge of the American Bar Association (ABA) Model Rules of Professional Conduct and the National Association of Legal Assistants, Inc. (NALA) Code of Ethics and Professional Responsibility is required for successful completion of this section. Familiarity with the NALA Model Standards and Guidelines for the Utilization of Legal Assistants also is helpful.

Ethics Defined

Ethics are those standards by which conduct is measured. Generally speaking, a professional is held to a higher ethical standard than is an average person. Professional ethics usually are governed by a set of written rules (a *code*) that establish the limits of permissible conduct in the professional's contacts with others as well as the manner in which the professional advances his or her practice. Most ethics rules seek to enhance the integrity of a profession by establishing the minimum levels of conduct required of its members.

In a nutshell, the objectives of professional ethics for legal assistants are twofold:

1.   *To maintain high levels of competence; and*

2.   *To refrain from the unauthorized practice of law.*

Implicit in both of these objectives is that the legal assistant possesses a level of personal integrity which is above reproach. Much like lawyers, legal assistants occupy positions of trust, which require them not only to observe the specific language of ethics rules, but also to embrace the spirit of those rules.

Competence   Competence means ability, capability, expertise, mastery, proficiency, or skill. Competence in any field requires the acquisition of sufficient knowledge, training, and experience to do the job.

Competence and education go hand in hand. Each is an ongoing process that cannot exist as a stagnant state of being. As soon as a person stops actively pursuing knowledge, his education begins to erode; and with that erosion, his competence is diminished. Highly competent professionals are the first to acknowledge that the more they learn about their fields of practice, the more they realize how much they have left to learn. Only by their perpetual search for more knowledge do they maintain personal levels of high competence.

Since legal assistants are expected to maintain high levels of competence, they must take advantage of educational opportunities whenever and wherever those opportunities arise. Education can occur in informal settings, such as a one-on-one exchange between a lawyer and a legal assistant while working on a client's case or the practice of reading professional literature from cover to cover. It also can occur in more formal settings, such as professional meetings, seminars, workshops, and college classrooms. A high level of competence exists only when it is perpetually evolving.

Unauthorized Practice of Law   Defining the unauthorized practice of law (UPL) is more difficult than defining competence, because there is no single, complete definition for the practice of law. Each state defines the practice of law by statute, and each state's statutes are slightly different. One thing they all have in common, however, is that violation of UPL statutes is a criminal offense.

Each state requires lawyers to be licensed before they can practice in that state. Before a license is issued, the applicant must demonstrate (1) good moral character; (2) graduation from an accredited law school; and (3) minimal competence by passing a state bar examination. California is the only state that does not require law school graduation as a prerequisite to taking the bar. Once issued, a license grants the holder the privilege to practice law—but only in the state where the license is issued.

In broad, general terms, the ***practice of law*** is any act that involves the giving of legal advice or opinions to others or involves representing others in legal matters. Generally speaking, legal assistants cannot:

- accept cases;
- set fees;
- give direct legal advice to clients;
- negotiate legal matters on behalf of clients; or
- represent clients in court settings.

Beyond these specific limitations, legal assistants ethically can perform virtually every other type of legal task imaginable on behalf of clients as long as three criteria are met:

1. The legal assistant's work is properly supervised by a licensed attorney;

2. The supervising attorney maintains a direct relationship with the client; and

3. The supervising attorney assumes full professional responsibility for the work product.

Any legal assistant who violates a UPL statute may incur one or more of the following sanctions:

- criminal prosecution;

- civil liability to any client damaged by the negligence of the legal assistant while engaging in unauthorized acts; and/or

- termination of employment.

In addition, the CLA® designation may be revoked permanently for this type of violation.

As serious as these sanctions are, they do not prevent the offender from obtaining other employment as a legal assistant—assuming that some other attorney is willing to hire him. The same is not true for the offender's supervising attorney who (1) can incur civil liability to any client damaged by the negligence of the legal assistant and/or (2) can be disbarred as a result of the misconduct of the legal assistant. If disbarment occurs, it is possible that the attorney may never practice law again.

Legal assistants are expected to distinguish between permissible and impermissible conduct in the UPL area. A few examples are illustrated by the problems presented below.

> Jane, an experienced and skilled legal assistant in the field of domestic relations, is dissatisfied with the fact that lawyers in her community have failed to provide low-cost legal services to the working poor. She believes that many litigants could handle their own uncontested divorces if they were provided with a procedure handbook and the necessary forms. Jane leaves her employment and compiles a procedure handbook with forms, which she sells in bookstores and by mail order for $50.00. Jane has no contact with purchasers. She does not represent herself as an attorney and, in fact, large notices are placed conspicuously and frequently throughout the handbook, urging that all questionable situations should be handled by a licensed attorney. The handbook gives no legal advice.

As presented, this situation does not violate the UPL statutes of most states. Members of the general public may purchase the handbook or not, as they choose; and, of course, a person always may represent himself in court proceedings if he chooses to do so.

> Continuing with the same problem, Jane discovers that purchasers of her handbook occasionally have difficulty in selecting the proper forms for their situations. A few others have encountered problems in putting the correct information in the correct blanks. For this reason, Jane decides to open an office where she can assist with these simple matters for a small, additional charge.

If she pursues this plan, Jane will have stepped over the line of permissible conduct and into the area of UPL. She cannot help people to select forms without advising them, and her advice constitutes the unauthorized practice of law in most states. Telling handbook purchasers what information goes into which blanks of the forms they have selected likewise requires advice, which is illegal.

By judicial decision, similar operations have been held in violation of UPL statutes. Included among them are typing services run by nonlawyers, where the nonlawyers provided advice on how to complete various legal documents; a credit counseling service that counseled in favor of bankruptcy for some clients and then helped them prepare their own bankruptcy petitions; a landlord's eviction service; and similar enterprises. In each case, the nonlawyer went beyond supplying forms.

> Joe is a legal assistant whose attorney-employer is away on a trip. Things have been particularly slow. A woman calls the office, saying she needs to see someone right away because her husband has filed for divorce. Joe visits with the woman to obtain details and tells her the office will take her case. Joe knows the attorney can use the business. Joe then calls the opposing counsel, pretending to be his employer, to see where things stand; and, before he realizes what is happening, he and the lawyer are discussing property settlement for the parties.

Based upon these facts, Joe has committed compound UPL violations. He was wrong to accept the case; wrong to impersonate his employer, regardless of the reason; and wrong to participate in negotiations with opposing counsel. Standing alone, any one of these three things may result in criminal charges, civil liability for damages incurred by the client, and termination of employment.

> Chris is a free-lance legal assistant who contracts her work to lawyers in the community. In addition, she represents clients independently in proceedings before the Social Security Administration. Her clients know that she is not a lawyer, and this is the only type of case that she handles without attorney supervision. When it is necessary to appeal cases beyond the agency level or when her clients require other types of legal services, she refers them to various young lawyers in the community, who are happy to get the work.

Nothing in these facts indicates a violation of UPL statutes. The rules and regulations of a number of federal administrative agencies permit both lawyers and nonlawyers to appear before them on behalf of others. Included among them are the Social Security Administration, the Internal Revenue Service, and the Immigration and Naturalization Service. Because the rules of the agency permit nonlawyer practice and because Chris's independent practice is limited to proceedings before that agency, there is no violation.

In a similar vein, a small number of courts allow a limited motion practice by nonlawyers who are either legal assistants or third-year law students. This is accomplished by a court rule, which generally allows the qualified nonlawyer to appear before the court to argue motions, provided the nonlawyer is sponsored by a licensed attorney. Even where this is permitted, the nonlawyer generally cannot sign pleadings alone or try a case alone. Other courts allow a limited motion practice by third-year law students but not by legal assistants. Still other courts allow only licensed attorneys to appear.

> Ben is a prison inmate who has become extremely proficient in post-sentencing matters related to his own incarceration. Before long, Ben finds himself devoting almost all of his free time to helping other inmates by doing legal research and by helping them prepare appropriate applications, petitions, and so forth to pursue earlier releases or lighter sentences.

Ben appears to have become what is known as a "jailhouse lawyer"—an inmate who has studied law and legal procedure on his own, usually in the prison library. Jailhouse lawyers are permitted to provide legal services to other inmates so long as (1) the other inmate requests it, (2) no other legal services are reasonably available, and (3) the legal services are related solely to post-sentencing matters. If an inmate commits a new crime while in prison, for example, the jailhouse lawyer cannot assist him for the trial or sentencing in that case. Neither can the jailhouse lawyer represent him in any civil proceeding, such as a divorce or a debt collection, that may arise while the inmate is in prison.

These examples are not intended to be comprehensive. The situations in which UPL issues can arise are as varied as the people governed by the statute. Additional examples are included in the Self-Test for this chapter.

Sources of Ethics Rules

Each state has adopted a set of ethics standards to govern the professional conduct and practices of licensed attorneys. These standards generally are based upon the UPL statute of that state plus the Model Rules or the Model Code adopted by the American Bar Association. As an employee of the attorney, the legal assistant likewise must be familiar with these ethics rules.

The most recent ethics standards of the ABA are incorporated in the Model Rules of Professional Conduct, which has been adopted in whole or in part by a majority of states. Some states, however, still follow the older Model Code of Professional Responsibility, also a product of the ABA. *All ethics questions on the CLA® exam are based upon the more recent **ABA Model Rules of Professional Conduct.***

Incorporating and supplementing the ABA standards, every member of NALA is governed by the NALA Code of Ethics and Professional Responsibility.

At the time of application, every Certified Legal Assistant (CLA) applicant agrees to be bound by the NALA Code of Ethics, whether or not the applicant is a member of NALA.

In addition to the ethics codes, NALA adopted its Model Standards and Guidelines for the Utilization of Legal Assistants, which subsequently has been adopted in substantial part by the American Bar Association and by a growing number of state bar associations. The Model Standards and Guidelines are designed to assist attorneys by delineating the proper uses of the legal assistant's skills.

The CLA applicant should be knowledgeable about all applicable ethics standards. Accordingly, summaries of portions of the ABA Model Rules of Professional Conduct are presented below. Applicants may benefit, however, from independent review of the complete Model Rules and comments. Immediately following the Model Rules summary, the NALA Code of Ethics and the NALA Standards and Guidelines are reprinted in their entirety.

American Bar Association
Summary of Model Rules of Professional Conduct[8]

> *Rule 1.1   A lawyer must provide competent representation to clients.*

This means that lawyers cannot accept representation in matters they know little or nothing about unless they are willing to undertake the study needed to become competent and unless that study can be completed in a reasonable time. If this cannot be done, it may be possible to affiliate with a lawyer who is knowledgeable, provided that the client consents and provided that the total fee is reasonable. All lawyers are required to participate in continuing education to remain competent in their respective fields of practice.

> *Rule 1.2   A lawyer must abide by a client's decision concerning representation, such as whether to accept a settlement or whether to enter a plea in a criminal case, whether to waive a jury trial, or whether the client will testify. A lawyer's representation may be limited to a specific matter. A lawyer cannot advise or assist a client to engage in fraudulent or criminal conduct; and if a client expects*

---

[8]1989 Edition Model Rules of Professional Conduct and Code of Judicial Conduct, copyright © 1989 by the American Bar Association. Reprinted by permission of the American Bar Association. Copies of this publication may be obtained from Order Fulfillment, American Bar Association, 750 North Lake Shore Drive, Chicago, IL 60611.

assistance not permitted by professional conduct rules, the lawyer must advise the client of the lawyer's ethical limitations.

This rule makes it clear that a lawyer is responsible for making decisions related to technical and legal strategy issues, but she must defer to the client about such things as acceptance of a settlement, incurring expenses, and concern for third persons who might be adversely affected. The rule strictly prohibits a lawyer from advising or assisting a client to destroy evidence, to commit a crime, or the like. Do not confuse this, however, with assisting a client to pursue a legal course of action that is unpopular but is not illegal.

> *Rule 1.3   A lawyer must exercise diligence in handling client matters.*

This means that a lawyer cannot procrastinate in handling cases. Legal assistants frequently assist with docketing deadlines, managing work loads, and ensuring that cases progress to conclusion within a reasonable time.

> *Rule 1.4   A lawyer must keep a client reasonably informed about the status of the client's case, must comply with a client's reasonable requests for information, and must explain things to the client so that the client can make informed decisions.*

A client has a right to know about events as they happen in her case. Legal assistants can assist the lawyer in this area by drafting status letters to clients and by helping to develop a system to ensure that all telephone calls and correspondence from clients receive prompt replies. Legal assistants frequently investigate facts and perform legal research, which the lawyer uses to advise clients concerning their rights and duties.

> *Rule 1.5   A lawyer's fee must be reasonable, considering such factors as the time and labor required; the difficulty of the legal issues involved; the time constraints to obtain a result; the results obtained; and the expertise, reputation, and experience of the lawyer(s) performing the service. Lawyers must advise clients right away of the rate that will be charged.*
>
> *Contingent fee arrangements must be in writing. Contingent fees cannot be charged in domestic relations cases when the contingency relates to obtaining a divorce or to the amount of alimony, child support, or property settlement awarded in the case. Contingent fees cannot be charged in criminal cases.*

Fees can be divided between lawyers in different firms only if the division is proportionate to the services provided or if each lawyer assumes joint responsibility for the representation; the client knows and does not object to the fee division; and the total fee is reasonable.

Contingency fees are prohibited in cases where a divorce will be granted or where support or property settlement will be awarded. However, when the objective is collection of support previously ordered and now in default because of nonpayment, contingency fees are permitted on much the same terms as any other case involving collection of a debt.

Retainer letters should be provided to all clients, whether the fee is contingent or not. If the fee is to be contingent, a retainer letter must be provided. In addition, clients should be told that legal assistants will be used and the rate that will be charged for the legal assistant's work on the case.

All discussions concerning fees are strictly the attorney's responsibility. A lawyer may require advance payment for all or a portion of the services to be performed, but she must return any unearned portion to the client. A lawyer may accept property or ownership interests in a business enterprise in payment of legal services but cannot accept a proprietary interest in the outcome of a case. This type of proprietary interest, called **champerty**, is forbidden.

Rule 1.6   A lawyer cannot disclose information concerning the representation of a client unless the client consents or unless the disclosure is necessary to carry out the representation.
This rule relates to client confidentiality and applies to legal assistants as well as to lawyers. It is intended to encourage clients to disclose all facts to their lawyers without fear that the lawyer may be required to divulge the information to others. It coordinates with the attorney-client privilege permitted by evidence rules but is not the same thing. If a lawyer is charged in a disciplinary proceeding for disclosing a client confidence, the charge will be based upon this rule and not upon the evidence rule.

Exceptions are made to the rule to allow a lawyer to disclose limited information to prevent a client from committing a criminal act that is likely to result in death or great bodily harm or to establish a defense for the lawyer against criminal charges or to establish a defense in a civil action between the lawyer and the client related to the lawyer's representation. A client's perjured testimony which is given without the attorney's prior knowledge also is excepted from the confidentiality protection.

The duty of confidentiality applies during the period of representation and continues after the attorney-client relationship has ended. Clearly, it prohibits the lawyer or the legal assistant from discussing either the client or the client's case in social settings outside the office. In addition, it prohibits such things as:

●Discussing the client or his case with others in the firm who have no specific need to know the information;

●Disclosing to opposing counsel or to others more about the client than is necessary to accomplish the required objective;

●Confirming to third parties that the client is represented by the firm unless that fact clearly is a matter of public record;

●Engaging in telephone conversations where the client's name or any identifiable information about the client or the case is mentioned within the hearing range of third parties (such as another client waiting in the firm's reception area);

●Permitting client files or papers to be in plain view where they can be seen by anyone who happens to pass by, such as on a receptionist's desk where visitors can see them or on any other desk where night cleaning staff or others can see them without so much as opening a file folder; or

●Inadvertently mailing information about a client's case to unintended persons, which can happen if multiple mailings are mishandled.

Where client confidentiality is concerned, the innocent intentions of the attorney or of the legal assistant may mitigate the sanctions imposed; but they cannot absolve the offender.

> *Rule 1.7   A lawyer cannot represent opposing parties in a legal matter unless (1) the lawyer reasonably believes that the representation will not affect either party adversely and (2) each party consents.*

This rule is directed at conflicts of interest. A single law firm cannot, for instance, represent both a debtor and a creditor in the same bankruptcy proceeding without adversely affecting the position of one or both of the parties. The conflict exists even if two different lawyers in the firm are involved. Because of this rule, law firms traditionally maintain an adverse party index that is checked before a new client is accepted by the firm. Similarly, legal assistants who free-lance by providing services to lawyers on a contract basis, as well as the lawyers for whom they perform these services, must be especially sensitive to potential conflict of interest problems that can arise.

When the interests of two clients are fundamentally antagonistic to each other (husband and wife seeking divorce), dual representation should be avoided. When a lawyer for an organization also sits on its board of directors, a potential conflict of interest exists.

The conflict-of-interest rule also applies to lawyers and to legal assistants who leave one firm to become employed by another. If the new firm represents parties adverse to those parties represented by the old firm, a conflict of interest exists. This difficulty may be resolved by isolating the lawyer or the legal assistant from all contacts with the conflicting case until it is concluded, sometimes referred to as a **Chinese Wall**. However, in at least one California case, a legal assistant was prevented (enjoined) from accepting employment at the new firm based upon this type of conflict of interest.

> *Rule 1.8   This rule lists a number of specific transactions by lawyers which are either prohibited or restricted. They include:*
>
> ►*Cannot enter into business ownership transactions with a client unless the terms are fair, client has a chance to seek independent legal advice, and client consents.*
>
> ►*Cannot prepare an instrument in which a client gives a lawyer or anyone related to the lawyer a gift, by will or otherwise, unless the client is related to the lawyer.*
>
> ►*Cannot negotiate or agree to give a lawyer media or literary rights to a portrayal based upon his or her representation in a case.*
>
> ►*Cannot provide financial assistance to a client in a pending claim except that court costs and expenses can be advanced in a contingency fee case and except that court costs and expenses can be paid for an indigent client.*
>
> ►*Cannot accept payment of fee from one other than the client unless the client consents, the lawyer remains independent of the third party, and client information remains confidential.*
>
> ►*Cannot settle a civil case for multiple clients or plea bargain for multiple criminal defendants unless all clients know all details of all other interests and consent to the multiple representation.*

▸*Cannot require client to agree prospectively to limit the lawyer's malpractice liability in a case.*

▸*Cannot assume representation when the opposing party is represented by counsel who is related to the lawyer unless client knows of the relationship and consents to representation.*

▸*Cannot acquire proprietary interest in litigation being handled for a client except by reasonable contingency fee contract or lawful attorney's lien to secure fees or expenses.*

. . .

Rule 1.14   When a client's ability to make adequately informed decisions in connection with the representation is impaired, the lawyer may seek appointment of a guardian or may take other action to protect the interests of the client.

If at all possible, the lawyer should represent such a client directly and should seek a guardian only if it clearly is in the client's best interests to do so. If a lawyer represents a guardian who is acting contrary to the ward's interests, the lawyer may be obliged to prevent or to rectify the guardian's misconduct.

Rule 1.15   A lawyer must hold property of clients or third parties separate from the lawyer's own property. Money must be held in a separate account located in the same state where the lawyer's office is located and complete records must be kept. Clients or third parties must be notified immediately when the lawyer receives money or property on their behalf; the money or property must be disbursed promptly; and a full accounting must be made by the lawyer.

This is the attorney trust account provision. Every law firm is required to maintain a trust account for clients and others in which no money of the lawyers can be commingled. Advance payment of fees from clients must be kept in the trust account until the lawyer performs work to earn the fees. Only that portion of the retainer which has been earned can be transferred to the lawyer's operating account. Legal assistants often deal with trust funds in the performance of their duties and must be familiar with the rules of conduct that govern this area.

Money held for a specific client in a lawyer's trust account may be subject to claims of creditors by proper garnishment proceedings or otherwise; however, the lawyer cannot unilaterally presume to serve as arbitrator between the client and a creditor.

Irregularities in a lawyer's trust account or in its management can result in extremely severe sanctions to the lawyer. The case law of some states indicates that when problems arise concerning a trust account, the lawyer should plan for disbarment without regard to the severity of, source, or reason for the problem.

> *Rule 1.16   A lawyer must not represent a client, or must withdraw from representation of a client, if the representation will result in a violation of the rules of professional conduct; if the lawyer's physical or mental condition materially impairs the ability to represent the client; or if the lawyer is discharged. If a court orders her to do so, the lawyer must continue the representation. If representation ends, the lawyer must give the client reasonable notice so that other counsel can be obtained and must cooperate with substitute counsel to protect the client's interests.*

If a client demands that a lawyer engage or assist in conduct that is illegal or that violates any rule of professional conduct, the lawyer should withdraw from the case. If a client makes such a demand of a legal assistant, it should be reported to the supervising attorney at once. Learning that a defendant in a criminal case is guilty, however, is not a valid basis for withdrawal from the case. Lawyers have a duty to protect the rights of all clients without regard to guilt or innocence.

If a lawyer is fired by a client, any property owned by the client should be returned except to the extent that the lawyer is permitted to retain papers and the like under existing law.

. . .

> *Rule 3.1   A lawyer must not file frivolous lawsuits or raise frivolous issues in a lawsuit.*

This simply means that lawyers cannot file lawsuits solely for the purpose of harassing or maliciously injuring another person.

> *Rule 3.2   A lawyer must take reasonable steps to expedite litigation consistent with the client's best interests.*

This rule prohibits dilatory strategies by lawyers. A lawyer's tactics during litigation must have some purpose other than mere delay. Realizing financial or other benefit from the delay or merely frustrating the opposing party is not a legitimate interest of the client and cannot justify an otherwise improper delay.

> *Rule 3.3   A lawyer cannot knowingly make a false statement of material fact to a tribunal or judge, cannot fail to disclose a material fact when disclosure is necessary to avoid assisting a fraudulent or criminal act by the client, cannot fail to disclose legal authority in the controlling jurisdiction even though it may be adverse to the position of the lawyer's client, and cannot knowingly offer false evidence, including perjured testimony.*

Many lawyers have philosophical difficulties with that part of the rule which requires a lawyer to disclose adverse legal authority which is not disclosed by opposing counsel. Nevertheless, this is the substance of the Model Rule; and it is supported by the concept that legal argument is a discussion which seeks to determine the proper legal principle to apply in the case at hand.

Legal assistants can become directly involved in situations that require application of one or more subparts of this rule and must work closely with their supervising attorneys to ensure that no part of the rule is violated.

> *Rule 3.4   A lawyer cannot unlawfully obstruct another party's access to evidence and cannot falsify, alter, destroy, or conceal material that may be used as evidence; neither can she advise or help anyone else to do any of these things. A lawyer cannot offer an illegal inducement to a witness for the witness's testimony. A lawyer cannot make a frivolous discovery request and must make a diligent effort to comply with all proper discovery requests made by the opposing party.*
>
> *A lawyer cannot counsel anyone other than a client to withhold information from the opposing party unless (1) that person is a relative, an employee, or other agent of a client <u>and</u> (2) the lawyer reasonably believes that no harm can come to the person by withholding the information.*
>
> *During trial, a lawyer cannot allude to any matter unless the lawyer reasonably believes it to be relevant. She cannot assert personal knowledge of facts except when testifying as a witness, and she cannot state a personal opinion about the justness of the cause, the credibility of a witness, or the guilt or innocence of a defendant accused of a crime.*

This rule is self-explanatory for the most part. Notice the provision concerning frivolous discovery requests, which has no counterpart in the older Model Code. Legal assistants typically work with discovery requests, both those transmitted and those received; this rule applies directly to the discovery function.

A fact witness generally can be paid a fixed statutory fee plus expenses, and an expert witness can be paid a reasonable fee within the parameters set by law. However, in most jurisdictions it is unlawful for an expert witness to receive a contingent fee for his testimony.

> *Rule 3.5   A lawyer cannot attempt to influence a judge, juror, or any other official. Neither can she communicate ex parte with any of these individuals except under circumstances clearly permitted by law.*

This rule prohibits a lawyer from attempting to bribe or to influence persons associated with a case.

> *Rule 3.6   A lawyer cannot make an out-of-court statement to the press if the statement could prejudicially affect a pending civil case triable to a jury or a pending criminal proceeding that could result in incarceration. Prejudicial statements are those that relate to the expected testimony, character, credibility, reputation, or criminal record of a party or a witness. Also included are statements about a person's guilt or innocence, confessions, pleas, results of a test, or a person's refusal to submit to a test. A lawyer can relate information concerning the general nature of a claim or defense, information contained in a public record, confirmation that an investigation is in progress, and the like.*

This rule attempts to strike a balance between a party's right to a fair trial and the public's right to free dissemination of information.

> *Rule 3.7   A lawyer cannot be an advocate in a case in which the lawyer likely will be a witness except (1) when the testimony relates to an uncontested matter, (2) when the testimony concerns the type and value of legal services rendered in a case, or (3) when disqualification of the lawyer would pose a substantial hardship to the client.*

When a lawyer combines the roles of advocate and witness, a conflict of interest can arise between the lawyer and the client or unfair prejudice can result to the opposing party. A witness testifies about personal knowledge, while an advocate explains or comments on evidence given by others. When a lawyer serves as both advocate and witness, it may be unclear whether her statements should be taken as proof or as an analysis of the proof. The problem can arise when the lawyer calls herself as a witness or when she is called as a witness by the opposing counsel. However, this rule does not prevent one lawyer in a firm from serving as advocate when another lawyer from the same firm will be called as a witness.

Rule 3.8   A criminal prosecutor must not file a charge when she knows it is not supported by probable cause and must not do anything else that might unfairly prejudice an accused.

This rule points out the primary role of a criminal prosecutor as one requiring her to see that justice is done, not to gain a conviction.

Rule 3.9   A lawyer appearing before a legislative body or an administrative agency in a nontrial setting must disclose that her appearance is on behalf of a client but need not identify the client if the matter relates to law reform generally.

Like courts, decision-making bodies are entitled to rely on the integrity of submissions made to them. Nonlawyer representatives generally are not held to this requirement; however, when the nonlawyer is a legal assistant employed by an attorney and when the legal assistant appears before an agency as permitted by the agency's rules on nonlawyer representation, the legal assistant should observe the same rules that apply to the attorney.

Rule 4.1   In the course of representing a client, a lawyer cannot make false statements about material facts or law to third persons and cannot withhold a material fact from a third person when disclosure is required to prevent a client from committing fraud or a crime.

This rule, which relates to truthfulness in relation to third parties, applies to legal assistants as well. The lawyer or legal assistant is not required to inform an opposing party of all facts he knows; however, facts cannot be misrepresented.

Rule 4.2   In representing a client, a lawyer cannot communicate with an opposing party directly or indirectly about the pending case when the lawyer knows that party is represented by counsel unless opposing counsel consents.

This means that a lawyer cannot have any contact with the opposing party about a pending case unless that party's counsel agrees to the contact in advance, which rarely will happen. However, the rule does not prevent a lawyer from communicating with the opposing party about matters unrelated to the pending case when no attorney represents the party in the unrelated matter. Because of his many contacts on a lawyer's behalf, the legal assistant should be particularly familiar with the application of this rule and must recognize that it applies to the lawyer and to the legal assistant alike.

Rule 4.3   While representing a client, a lawyer who comes into contact with an unrepresented person cannot do or say anything to lead that person to believe that the lawyer is disinterested. Additionally, when a lawyer knows or should know that an unrepresented person has misunderstood the lawyer's role, the lawyer must correct the misunderstanding.

A person who is not represented by counsel, especially one who is a novice to the legal system, can misunderstand the role of a lawyer as being one of a disinterested authority on the law. A lawyer never should give advice to an unrepresented person beyond the advice to obtain legal counsel.

Rule 4.4   While representing a client, a lawyer cannot use tactics that violate the legal rights of third persons or that have no purpose other than to embarrass, harass, or delay.

A lawyer owes her first loyalty to her client; however, this loyalty does not permit total disregard of the rights of others.

. . .

Rule 5.3   Lawyers who employ legal assistants and other nonlawyers are required to take reasonable measures to ensure that the legal assistant's conduct is compatible with the lawyer's professional obligations. Lawyers are responsible for any conduct of the legal assistant which violates the Rules of Professional Conduct.

Lawyers are expected to supply instruction concerning ethics rules and to supervise legal assistants and other nonlawyers concerning those rules. This applies to all areas of nonlawyer conduct and activities, including work product.

Rule 5.4   With limited exceptions, a lawyer cannot share fees with a nonlawyer and cannot enter a business relationship with a nonlawyer if any activities of the business involve the practice of law. In addition, when a person other than the client pays the lawyer's fee, that person cannot be permitted to interfere with the lawyer's independent judgment in providing legal services to the client.

This rule prevents lawyers from sharing fees with nonlawyers or from engaging in situations in which a nonlawyer has the right to direct or to control the professional judgment of the lawyer. It prevents paying bonuses to nonlawyers based upon the fee earned in a specific case.

The rule does not prevent the inclusion of nonlawyer employees in a retirement plan, even though the plan is based in whole or in part on a profit-sharing arrangement. In many jurisdictions, nonlawyer employees likewise may participate in year-end bonuses based upon overall profits for the preceding year or for a portion of the year. These types of bonuses may be paid either to all employees or only to some employees, as long as no part of the bonus is related to any specific case.

> *Rule 5.5   A lawyer cannot practice law in a jurisdiction where she is not authorized to do so. A lawyer cannot assist a nonlawyer to engage in the unauthorized practice of law in any jurisdiction.*

This rule is the basis for sanctions against a lawyer whose legal assistant employee engages in the unauthorized practice of law. It does not prevent a lawyer from delegating certain tasks to the legal assistant, so long as the lawyer supervises the delegated work and retains responsibility for the work product.

The rule does not prohibit a lawyer from providing counsel to a nonlawyer who wants to proceed *pro se* in his or her own case.

> *Rule 5.6   A lawyer cannot make an agreement that attempts to restrict another lawyer's right to practice. (Restrictive agreements concerning the provision of retirement benefits are permitted, however.)*

This rule generally would not apply to a legal assistant unless the legal assistant were asked to assist in drafting such an agreement.

> *Rule 6.1   A lawyer should provide pro bono or reduced-fee legal services to people of limited means or to charitable organizations or should provide financial support to organizations that provide legal services to people of limited means.*

Responsibility for providing legal services to those who are unable to pay for them, or who are unable to pay the full rate, ultimately rests with the individual lawyer. Every lawyer should devote a certain amount of time to providing legal services for this segment of the community. Similarly, legal assistants are encouraged to provide *pro bono* legal assistant services to lawyers representing clients of this type.

· · ·

> *Rule 7.1   A lawyer cannot make a false or misleading statement about either the lawyer or the lawyer's services. Statements are*

prohibited if they contain a material misrepresentation of fact or law, if they are likely to create unjustified expectations about what the lawyer can do, or if they compare a lawyer's services with the services provided by other lawyers unless the comparison can be substantiated.

This rule fosters honesty by lawyers when they market or advertise their services, whether to an individual or to the public at large. It generally prohibits advertising the results obtained for a client or the lawyer's record in obtaining successful verdicts, since either of these may create an unjustified expectation that similar results can be obtained for others without regard to specific facts. It also prohibits advertising divorces, for instance, for $100.00 when the fact is that only uncontested divorces of very short duration and with no children are provided at this price.

Rule 7.2   A lawyer is permitted to advertise his or her services through public media or through written or recorded communications, provided that the advertising does not violate any other ethics rule. The advertisement or communication must contain the name of at least one lawyer responsible for its content, and a copy of it must be kept for two years following its last dissemination. Lawyers cannot pay referral fees to private parties; however, the legitimate cost of advertising and the ordinary charges of nonprofit referral services are permitted.

This rule allows lawyers to advertise their services in telephone directories, newspapers, magazines, billboards, radio, and television, in addition to written or recorded advertising. Some jurisdictions limit advertising that goes beyond specific facts about the lawyer, limit television advertising, or limit "undignified" advertising. However, the Model Rules impose none of these limitations. Neither this rule nor the following rule prevents communications authorized by law, such as a notice to members of a class in class action litigation.

Rule 7.3   A lawyer cannot use direct contact (either in person or by live telephone) to solicit professional employment from those who have had no prior professional relationship with the lawyer or who have no family relationship to the lawyer.   All written or recorded communications soliciting employment from a prospective client known to be in need of legal services must include the term "Advertising Material" on the outside envelope or at the beginning and the end of recorded communications.

This is the "ambulance chasing" rule, which is intended to prevent a lawyer from taking advantage of a person who may be overwhelmed by the circumstances for which legal services are needed and may not be able to think clearly when confronted with an attorney soliciting his business, whether in person or on the telephone. The rule permits general mailings or autodial messages to prospective clients unless a particular prospective client has indicated that he does not wish to receive such information. Similarly, if a mailing or autodial message evokes no response from the prospective client, the lawyer may be prohibited from making any further contact.

Nothing in this rule prohibits a lawyer from participating in a prepaid or group legal services plan not owned or directed by the lawyer, even though in-person or telephone contacts are used by those who sponsor or manage the plan to solicit memberships.

> *Rule 7.4   A lawyer may communicate the fact that he does or does not practice in a particular field of law but can neither state nor imply that he is a specialist unless he is a patent attorney or is engaged in admiralty practice.*

This rule prohibits lawyers from portraying themselves as specialists in a particular area of legal practice. Although some states may permit communication of specialty practice, the rules of any specific state are not tested on the CLA® exam.

> *Rule 7.5   A lawyer cannot use a firm name, letterhead, or other professional designation that conveys false or misleading information. The name of a lawyer holding public office cannot be used in the name of the law firm during any period when the lawyer is not actively and regularly practicing with the firm. A lawyer cannot state or imply a partnership or other form of practice that does not exist.*

This rule does not prevent a firm from continuing to use the names of its deceased members as part of the firm name. It does, however, prohibit lawyers who merely share office facilities and personnel from representing themselves as a partnership by using a firm name such as "Jefferson and Davis" or the like.

A legal assistant may sign his name on law firm stationery if his nonlawyer status is clear and if the letter does not contain direct legal advice or otherwise violate an ethics rule. The best way to ensure that the author's nonlawyer status is clear is to include the title "Legal Assistant" or Legal Assistant to _____ " directly under the legal assistant's name in the signature block.

Under ABA Informal Opinion 89-1527, names of nonlawyer support staff may be printed on law firm stationery so long as the nonlawyer status is clear. Some states allow this practice; others do not.

Rules 8.1 through 8.5 deal with a lawyer's responsibilities in maintaining the integrity of the legal profession and cover topics ranging from making false statements on bar admission applications to reporting professional misconduct of other lawyers.

There is no blanket rule that requires a legal assistant to report (or that forbids a legal assistant from reporting) the professional misconduct of a lawyer. In the usual situation, the lawyer and the legal assistant work toward the same ethical goals. As team members, they provide support to each other for nearly all aspects of the case, including ethics. Most lawyers appreciate non-accusatory questions about potential ethics issues that may arise. They provide the basis for a thoughtful review and appraisal of the situation from all perspectives. However, close questions concerning the ethical implications of a particular course of action must be left for ultimate decision by the lawyer.

National Association of Legal Assistants, Inc.
Code of Ethics and Professional Responsibility

Preamble
A legal assistant must adhere strictly to the accepted standards of legal ethics and the general principles of proper conduct. The performance of the duties of the legal assistant shall be governed by specific canons as defined herein so that justice will be served and goals of the profession attained. (See NALA Model Standards and Guidelines for Utilization of Legal Assistants, Section II.) The canons of ethics set forth hereafter are adopted by the National Association of Legal Assistants, Inc. as a general guide intended to aid legal assistants and attorneys. The enumeration of these rules does not mean that there are not others of equal importance although not specifically mentioned. Court rules, agency rules, and statutes must be taken into consideration when interpreting the canons.

Definition
Legal assistants, also known as paralegals, are a distinguishable group of persons who assist attorneys in the delivery of legal services. Through formal education, training, and experience, legal assistants have knowledge and expertise regarding the legal system and substantive and procedural law which qualify them to do work of a legal nature under the supervision of an attorney.

Canon 1. A legal assistant must not perform any of the duties that lawyers only may perform nor take any actions that attorneys may not take.

Canon 2. A legal assistant may perform any task which is properly delegated and supervised by a lawyer, as long as the attorney is ultimately responsible to the client, maintains a direct relationship with the client, and assumes professional responsibility for the work product.

Canon 3. A legal assistant must not (see NALA Model Standards and Guidelines for Utilization of Legal Assistants, Sections IV and VI):

     A. Engage in, encourage, or contribute to any act which could constitute the unauthorized practice of law; or

     B. Establish attorney-client relationships, set fees, give legal opinions or advice, or represent a client before a court or agency unless so authorized by that court or agency; or

     C. Engage in conduct or take any action which would assist or involve the attorney in a violation of professional ethics or give the appearance of professional impropriety.

Canon 4. A legal assistant must use discretion and professional judgment commensurate with his or her knowledge and experience, but must not render independent legal judgment in place of an attorney. The services of an attorney are essential in the public interest whenever such legal judgment is required. (See NALA Model Standards and Guidelines for Utilization of Legal Assistants, Section VII.)

Canon 5. A legal assistant must disclose his or her status as a legal assistant at the outset of any professional relationship with a client, attorney, court or administrative agency or personnel thereof, or a member of the general public. A legal assistant must act prudently in determining the extent to which a client may be assisted without the presence of an attorney. (See NALA Model Standards and Guidelines for Utilization of Legal Assistants, Section V.)

Canon 6. A legal assistant must strive to maintain integrity and a high degree of competence through education and training with respect to professional responsibility, local rules and practice, and through continuing education in substantive areas of law to assist the legal profession in better fulfilling its duty to provide legal service.

Canon 7. A legal assistant must protect the confidence of a client and must not violate any rule or statute now in effect or hereafter enacted controlling the doctrine of privileged communications between a client and an attorney. (See NALA Model Standards and Guidelines for Utilization of Legal Assistants, Section V.)

Canon 8. A legal assistant must do all other things incidental, necessary, or expedient for the attainment of the ethics and responsibilities as defined by statute or rule of court.

Canon 9. A legal assistant's conduct is guided by bar associations' codes of professional responsibility and rules of professional conduct.

National Association of Legal Assistants, Inc.
Model Standards and Guidelines for Utilization of Legal Assistants

Preamble
Proper utilization of the services of legal assistants affects the efficient delivery of legal services. Legal assistants and the legal profession should be assured that some measures exist for identifying legal assistants and their role in assisting attorneys in the delivery of legal services. Therefore, the National Association of Legal Assistants, Inc., hereby adopts these Model Standards and Guidelines as an educational document for the benefit of legal assistants and the legal profession.

Definition
Legal assistants[9] are a distinguishable group of persons who assist attorneys in the delivery of legal services. Through formal education, training, and experience, legal assistants have knowledge and expertise regarding the legal system and substantive and procedural law which qualify them to do work of a legal nature under the supervision of an attorney.

Standards
A legal assistant should meet certain minimum qualifications. The following standards may be used to determine an individual's qualifications as a legal assistant:

1. Successful completion of the Certified Legal Assistant (CLA®) examination of the National Association of Legal Assistants, Inc.

2. Graduation from an ABA approved program of study for legal assistants.

3. Graduation from a course of study for legal assistants which is institutionally accredited but not ABA approved, and which requires not less than the equivalent of 60 semester hours of classroom study.

---

[9]Within this occupational category, some individuals are known as paralegals.

4. Graduation from a course of study for legal assistants, other than those set forth in (2) and (3) above, plus not less than six months of in-house training as a legal assistant.

5. A baccalaureate degree in any field, plus not less than six months of in-house training as a legal assistant.

6. A minimum of three years of law-related experience under the supervision of an attorney, including at least six months of in-house training as a legal assistant; or

7. Two years of in-house training as a legal assistant.

For purposes of these standards, "in-house training as a legal assistant" means attorney education of the employee concerning legal assistant duties and these guidelines. In addition to review and analysis of assignments, the legal assistant should receive a reasonable amount of instruction directly related to the duties and obligations of the legal assistant.

Guidelines

These guidelines relating to standards of performance and professional responsibility are intended to aid legal assistants and attorneys. The responsibility rests with an attorney who employs legal assistants to educate them with respect to the duties they are assigned and to supervise the manner in which such duties are accomplished.

Legal assistants should:

1. Disclose their status as legal assistants at the outset of any professional relationship with a client, other attorneys, a court or administrative agency or personnel thereof, or members of the general public.

2. Preserve the confidences and secrets of all clients; and

3. Understand the attorney's Code of Professional Responsibility and these guidelines in order to avoid any action which would involve the attorney in a violation of that Code, or give the appearance of professional impropriety.

Legal assistants should not:

1. Establish attorney-client relationships; set legal fees; give legal opinions or advice; or represent a client before a court; nor

2.   Engage in, encourage, or contribute to any act which would constitute the unauthorized practice of law.

Legal assistants may perform services for an attorney in the representation of a client, provided:

1.   The services performed by the legal assistant do not require the exercise of independent professional legal judgment.

2.   The attorney maintains a direct relationship with the client and maintains control of all client matters.

3.   The attorney supervises the legal assistant.

4.   The attorney remains professionally responsible for all work on behalf of the client, including any actions taken or not taken by the legal assistant in connection therewith; and

5.   The services performed supplement, merge with and become the attorney's work product.

In the supervision of a legal assistant, consideration should be given to:

1.   Designating work assignments that correspond to the legal assistant's abilities, knowledge, training and experience.

2.   Educating and training the legal assistant with respect to professional responsibility, local rules and practices, and firm policies;

3.   Monitoring the work and professional conduct of the legal assistant to ensure that the work is substantively correct and timely performed;

4.   Providing continuing education for the legal assistant in substantive matters through courses, institutes, workshops, seminars and in-house training; and

5.   Encouraging and supporting membership and active participation in professional organizations.

Except as otherwise provided by statute, court rule or decision, administrative rule or regulation, or the attorney's Code of Professional Responsibility, and within the preceding parameters and proscriptions, a legal assistant may perform any function delegated by an attorney, including, but not limited to the following:

1.   Conduct client interviews and maintain general contact with the client after the establishment of the attorney-client relationship, so long as the client is aware of the status and function of the legal assistant, and the client contact is under the supervision of the attorney.

2.   Locate and interview witnesses, so long as the witnesses are aware of the status and function of the legal assistant.

3.   Conduct investigations and statistical and documentary research for review by the attorney.

4.   Conduct legal research for review by the attorney.

5.   Draft legal documents for review by the attorney.

6.   Draft correspondence and pleadings for review by and signature of the attorney.

7.   Summarize depositions, interrogatories, and testimony for review by the attorney.

8.   Attend executions of wills, real estate closings, depositions, court or administrative hearings and trials with the attorney.

9.   Author and sign letters provided the legal assistant's status is clearly indicated and the correspondence does not contain independent legal opinions or legal advice.

Application of Ethics Rules

Like lawyers, legal assistants must be vigilant concerning ethics rules, both their specific terms and their intent. It is inexcusable for a lawyer or a legal assistant to run afoul of the rules based upon a lack of familiarity with them. The legal assistant should review applicable ethics rules routinely to refresh her memory concerning their specific provisions.

In addition to the rules themselves, informal opinions of bar associations concerning specific rules provide insight into their proper interpretation. Likewise, the body of judicial opinions related to ethics rules provides a practical framework by which to evaluate conduct that is governed by the rules. Both of these sources apply rules to specific factual situations. The more factual situations to which a legal assistant can relate, the more likely it is that he will be able to recognize potential ethics problems when they arise.

Presented below are a series of ethics questions involving legal assistants, each of which is followed by its probable resolution based upon current rules, ethics opinions, and case law. The questions are not intended to be all-inclusive. When considered with the rules, their comments, and the hypothetical situations presented in the Self-Test section for this chapter, however, the applicant is provided with a concise overview of the concepts that likely will appear on any ethics examination directed at legal assistants.

> Are business cards permissible for legal assistants employed by a law firm?

Yes, according to a substantial majority of states. Care must be taken, however, to ensure that the nonlawyer status of the cardholder is displayed prominently on the card. This helps to avoid any misunderstanding that the cardholder is an attorney.

> May a legal assistant's name appear on the law firm's stationery?

In many states, the answer is yes. The name must be set apart from the lawyers' names, and the legal assistant's title must be shown clearly. Some firms print lawyers' names on one side of the stationery and print legal assistants' names on the other.

> May a legal assistant sign letters prepared on firm stationery?

Yes, provided (1) the letter contains no direct legal advice or opinions and (2) the legal assistant's status is shown clearly. Even if the legal assistant's name and title are printed on the letterhead, the best practice is to include the title "Legal Assistant" or "Legal Assistant to _____" directly below the typed name in the signature block of the letter.

> May a legal assistant's name be shown on pleadings and briefs?

A few states permit a nonlawyer's name to appear on pleadings; most do not. More states allow the name of a nonlawyer (legal assistant or law clerk) to appears on briefs, provided that the nonlawyer made a significant contribution to its research and drafting. The name generally is shown immediately below the attorney's signature block, using language such as:

Jane Doe, Legal Assistant
Participating on Briefs.

Even where the legal assistant's name may be shown on pleadings or on briefs, the legal assistant never signs the pleading or the brief.

May a legal assistant's name be included in a firm's listing in public telephone directories or as part of the listing at a law firm's entrance?

Where these questions have been considered, the answer generally is no. Including legal assistants in these listings is more likely to lead the general public to believe that the legal assistant must be some type of lawyer.

May a legal assistant use the title "legal specialist," "legal aide," "legal technician," or the like?

These and similar titles may confuse or mislead the public about the legal assistant's status. It may lead one to believe that the legal assistant is a type of lawyer or that the legal assistant is one of those individuals engaging in illegal conduct by offering legal services directly to the public. For that reason, most jurisdictions frown upon their use.

The term "legal assistant" has a specific meaning that involves working under the direct supervision of a licensed attorney. Since there is a specific title for this occupational function, it should be used for the sake of simplicity and clarity.

How often and in what way must a legal assistant identify his or her nonlawyer status?

There is no single, correct way to identify the legal assistant's status. To keep things simple, just use the title "Legal Assistant" after the name. Telephone courtesy generally requires the caller to identify himself or herself at the beginning of the conversation in any event. It should be a simple matter to add the title "Legal Assistant" when placing telephone calls. Alternately, one might say, "Hello. This is Jack Samson, Bill Mitchell's legal assistant."

Neither is there a magic number of times at which the legal assistant must identify his status. It seems prudent to do so at the beginning of all telephone conversations and at the beginning of every initial conference with a client or witness. If it appears that the other party may believe the legal assistant to be a lawyer, that impression should be corrected right away. Any questions about the legal assistant's function should be answered in such a way that a statement is included to clarify that the legal assistant is not a lawyer. The issue is not how often identity must be clarified to comply with the rules; it is how often should identity be clarified to protect the legal assistant from charges related to the unauthorized practice of law.

May a legal assistant discuss fee ranges with a client on a preliminary basis, leaving the final discussion and decision to the supervising attorney?

All discussions related to fees must be deferred to the attorney. Even when a firm uses an internal fee schedule, it generally serves as a guideline only. It is solely the attorney's responsibility to measure the situation presented by each case and to set the fee.

Uniform fee schedules—the same fee schedule used by all attorneys within a specific regional area—are prohibited by judicial decision.

If a client relates information to a legal assistant in confidence, is the legal assistant required to keep the information to himself?

The answer is yes, except for the attorney handling the case. Other than the limitations related to giving legal advice and the like, the legal assistant is an extension of the attorney and cannot operate independently of the attorney where clients are concerned. The client should be informed that the legal assistant cannot withhold information from the attorney, preferably before the client relates the information. If the client then elects not to confide in the legal assistant, that fact also must be related to the attorney.

May a legal assistant accept gifts from clients?

Lawyers are prohibited from accepting gifts from clients, and the prohibition extends to legal assistants as well. A client occasionally may express thanks for a job well done by taking the lawyer or the legal assistant to lunch or to dinner or by sending flowers, a pair of theater tickets, or similar token of the client's appreciation. Small gifts such as these probably are permissible when they are infrequent, are not solicited, and are reported to the legal assistant's supervising attorney. If the attorney or the firm has a policy against accepting these types of small gifts, the legal assistant must adhere to that policy.

May a legal assistant counsel a close friend or a relative about a legal matter when the friend or relative knows that the legal assistant is not a lawyer and when the legal assistant is not paid for the advice?

Other than suggesting that the friend or relative see a lawyer of his or her own choice, the legal assistant cannot give advice or comment in any way that may be taken as a legal opinion. Whether the legal assistant is paid or not is irrelevant; legal advice cannot be given by the legal assistant under any circumstances.

The problem arises most frequently at family dinners, parties, and other social events. Friends and relatives can create an extremely uncomfortable situation, particularly when the legal matter appears to be a simple one and when the legal assistant is reasonably certain of the advice that probably would be given by most attorneys. However, the difficult situations are the ones most likely to backfire in catastrophic proportions.

It may be helpful to realize that responsible attorneys likewise will decline to offer legal opinions or advice in these settings. Rather than risk an erroneous opinion based upon incomplete, misperceived, or distilled facts related by the questioner, the attorney might say, "It sounds as if your situation may involve some fairly complicated legal issues. I think it might be better if you were to call the office tomorrow and make an appointment to explore it fully." *The questioner generally will not be offended by this type of approach—not very much, at least; and the attorney will have saved herself from rendering a shotgun opinion that could come back to haunt her.*

> May a legal assistant communicate with an opposing party in an emergency situation, such as when the opposing counsel cannot be reached?

The rule is absolute: A lawyer cannot communicate with an opposing party who is represented by counsel concerning the subject matter of the representation unless the opposing counsel gives his or her prior consent. Opposing counsel rarely will consent. If an act is forbidden for the attorney, whether by this or by any other rule, it is also forbidden for the legal assistant. There is no emergency that can justify violation of this rule.

> How much supervision is required under existing ethics rules for work delegated to a legal assistant?

The type and amount of supervision must vary according to the experience and capabilities of the legal assistant and according to the task(s) delegated to him or her. The attorney is the only person who is equipped to judge the precise level of supervision that is required. Inexperienced legal assistants, no matter how bright they are, never should be assigned major projects unless frequent progress checkpoints are also established. This is as much a principle of sound management as it is one of ethics. As the legal assistant matures in the position and builds a successful track record, less intensified supervision may be warranted. Refer to the NALA Model Standards and Guidelines for the Utilization of Legal Assistants, which is reprinted earlier in this chapter.

No matter how much experience or skill a legal assistant has, however, the attorney always is required to supervise tasks delegated to him or her. Ethics rules demand this. At a minimum, this means routine spot checks as a project is underway and careful review of the final work product. When an attorney fails to provide the proper level of supervision, she jeopardizes not only her own career but also the career of the legal assistant.

Legal assistants never should be asked to "cover" or to "fill in" for the lawyer by performing tasks that only a lawyer ethically may perform, such as accepting cases, setting fees, negotiating settlements, executing wills, appearing in court, and the like.

> May a legal assistant prepare a procedure manual in a specific area of law that is intended for use by new associates and law clerks?

Clearly, the answer is yes. A procedure manual is no different than any other document drafted under an attorney's supervision, and an experienced legal assistant may be the ideal person to undertake such a project. Within this context, "procedure" means the way in which a task is accomplished. It includes review and interpretation of statutes, administrative rules and regulations, court rules, and judicial decisions. All work of the legal assistant merges with and becomes the work product of the attorney who supervises the project.

> May a legal assistant prepare a discovery plan for a particular litigation case and then implement that plan?

For all of the same reasons mentioned in response to the immediately preceding question, the answer is yes. Once the legal issues have been established by the supervising attorney, a legal assistant experienced in litigation is capable of proposing a discovery plan directed at locating and documenting all relevant facts in a usable form from all available sources. When the discovery plan is approved by the supervising attorney, the task of implementing the plan by drafting interrogatories and similar discovery devices; scheduling depositions; monitoring discovery responses; and cataloging discovery results can be delegated to the legal assistant. Working under the attorney's supervision and at her direction, the legal assistant ethically may initiate nearly all phases of the discovery plan except signing discovery documents on behalf of the firm or asking questions during depositions.

> What is meant by "procedure" when it is said that a legal assistant ethically may answer client questions about procedural matters?

Within this context, the term "procedure" has the same meaning that is provided above: the way in which a task is done. It involves those matters which are fixed (meaning that they generally do not change according to changes in a client's factual situation) and which have been reviewed and confirmed previously with the supervising attorney. Client questions in this area may cover such things as (1) how long it will take to obtain a trial date or to process an appeal, (2) what must be filed with the Secretary of State to form a new corporation, or (3) how much it costs to obtain an authenticated copy of a court order. The legal assistant can be expected to recognize the difference between a certified copy and an authenticated copy, for example, and to provide accurate information to the client at the attorney's direction.

When a client asks a question about which the legal assistant is uncertain, she should provide the same answer that most attorneys provide when they find themselves in that situation—that she does not know but will check and then will contact the client with the answer. By the same token, if a particular attorney directs his or her legal assistant not to answer these types of client questions, the attorney's instructions must be followed.

Legal assistants may not answer client questions about substantive matters, of course. Substantive legal questions require either a legal opinion or legal advice, both of which constitute the practice of law and can be provided only by a licensed attorney. Although they can cover a wide range of topics, a few examples of substantive legal questions include (1) whether the client can sue her landlord for damages under a particular commercial lease, (2) whether the client can remove money from a joint account in view of a temporary restraining order that was just entered, or (3) what risks are involved if a case is appealed.

May a legal assistant's time be billed to clients for things such as organizing and photocopying exhibits for trial?

The answer is yes for organizing the exhibits, but no for photocopying them. The legal assistant's time can be billed to a client only when it constitutes the performance of legal services. In other words, it must be the type of service which an attorney would perform if the legal assistant were not available.

The same rule applies when the attorney organizes and photocopies exhibits for trial. She can bill the client for organizing the exhibits but not for making photocopies. Photocopying generally is a clerical function. It remains a clerical function, no matter who performs it and, therefore, cannot be billed to the client. The cost of clerical services presumably are built into the hourly fee rate charged for both the attorney's and the legal assistant's legal services.

Simple questions permit simple answers. For example, it is clear that a legal assistant is permitted to draft pleadings, documents, and instruments of all kinds for review and use by an attorney. It is also clear that a legal assistant cannot advise a client concerning rights and obligations in a substantive legal matter. The black-and-white situations are easy to resolve. More difficult are the varying shades of gray—those situations that fit somewhere between the two divergent examples given.

Ethics for legal assistants can involve complex circumstances, requiring thorough knowledge of the ABA Model Rules, the NALA Code of Ethics, and the NALA Standards and Guidelines, together with superior judgment and reasoning techniques and highly polished human relations skills. To illustrate, read the following ethics problems and the reasoning process used to resolve each of them.

> **Problem 1.** True or False. While working on a personal injury case for one of the firm's clients, Legal Assistant Bob Baker interviews Mary Wishbone. Ms. Wishbone was a witness to the accident and relates facts during the interview which, if they are true, place liability for the accident on the firm's client. After the case is filed, Ms. Wishbone suffers a stroke and dies without making any formal statements to anyone else concerning the accident. Opposing counsel has learned of her statement to Bob and now seeks either a copy of the statement or Bob's testimony concerning the statement. The statement cannot be provided to opposing counsel without violating the client's right to confidentiality.

The answer is *true* only if a client confidence would be violated by providing the statement. The ethics rules governing this issue are Canon 7 of the NALA Code of Ethics and the ABA Model Rule relating to confidentiality of client information, which is intended to encourage clients to tell their attorneys everything without fear of subsequent disclosure to others. To violate this rule, then, the information must have been obtained from the client. However, the information in the Wishbone statement was not obtained from the client; it was obtained from a non-client witness as part of the investigation in the client's case. Since it was not obtained from the client, the statement is not protected by the rule on client confidentiality. Therefore, *the correct answer is false*. (The attorney may try to block opposing counsel from obtaining the statement based upon something other than confidentiality, of course.)

> **Problem 2.** Approximately two months after the settlement of a lengthy litigation related to a corporate takeover, one of the directors of the corporate client returns to the attorney and confesses that he lied during his deposition testimony concerning key issues related to the case. Since then, his wife has filed for divorce and is blackmailing him concerning the perjured testimony. What should the attorney do?
>
> a.　Disclose the facts to the court.
> b.　Disclose the facts to the authorities.
> c.　Urge the director to make the disclosure.
> d.　Do nothing.

Among the four options, the third one presents the best choice; therefore, *c is the correct answer*. This problem raises a number of issues: the crime of perjury

(perjury can occur during a deposition as well as during trial); the ethics rule that excepts perjured testimony from the usual client confidentiality requirement; the attorney's responsibility as an officer of the court; and the attorney's potential conflict of interest if the interest of the director and the interest of the corporate client are different. If the director can be prompted to do the right thing on a voluntary basis, the attorney's dilemma is resolved without further action on her part.

The first option is the next best choice; if the director could not be urged to make the disclosure, the attorney would be well-advised to pursue this course of action. Since litigation was pending before the case was settled, there must have been a judge assigned to the case. If not, the chief judge of the court should be informed of the situation and allowed to participate in its resolution. Since perjured testimony is outside the scope of client confidentiality and since the attorney is an officer of the court, she has an obligation to disclose the perjury if the director does not do so. The second option also fulfills the attorney's obligation but suggests less sensitivity to the participation of others in resolving the problem (the director and the court). The final option—do nothing—is the worst choice of the four. Once the attorney becomes aware of the facts, she is obliged to do something to preserve the integrity of the legal system. Doing nothing cannot be justified based upon the facts provided.

Problem 3.   You are a free-lance legal assistant who contracts with the law firm of Billings & Munne to provide legal assistant services for a large probate estate. Ms. Munne is the supervising attorney. After the initial probate documents are filed with the court and as you begin the work needed to prepare the inventory, Ms. Munne compliments you on your fine work and states that she could not manage the case without you, since she never has worked in the probate area. Your best course of action is to:

a.   Discontinue work the case unless Ms. Munne agrees to upgrade her probate knowledge to the point where she can supervise you properly or agrees to affiliate with a probate attorney who can supervise you properly;

b.   Continue with the case because Ms. Munne needs your help more than a probate lawyer would need it.

c.   Continue with the case until you can obtain a ruling from the bar association's disciplinary agency concerning your proper course of action.

d.   Discontinue work on the case and do nothing.

Among the four options, the first one represents the best course of action; therefore, *a is the correct answer*. The issue here is adequate supervision of the legal assistant's work by the attorney. The supervision required for free-lance legal assistants is the same as that required for in-house legal assistants.

The second option implies that you could continue working on the case without adequate supervision; clearly, that is wrong, making this the worst option of the four. The third option is problematic for two reasons: (1) It requires you to continue working without adequate supervision until a ruling is made; and (2) It suggests that it is proper for a legal assistant to report a lawyer without discussing the underlying problem with the lawyer first. It may be that Ms. Munne's partner is experienced in probate matters or that affiliation with an unrelated probate lawyer can be accomplished without difficulty. Finally, if the first option were not provided, the fourth option would be the best of the remaining three. It is not an ideal solution, however. It appears from the facts that Ms. Munne does not recognize her duty to provide supervision. If you discontinue work on the case and do nothing, she may find a legal assistant to do the work who, like Ms. Munne, does not recognize the ethics problem.

The CLA applicant must be able to recognize a breach of ethics when it is presented, to determine how a breach can be avoided, and to resolve ethics problems in a variety of situations. This chapter, together with the following Self-Test, is designed to highlight the major ethics principles that legal assistants should know. *See the Bibliography for additional references.*

Ethics Self-Test

Allow an uninterrupted thirty-minute period to answer all questions. At the end of thirty minutes, check your answers against those in the Answer Key Section of this Manual. Deduct two points for each incorrect answer (100 total possible points). Unanswered questions are counted as incorrect answers. Follow directions carefully and observe the time limit precisely to provide an accurate self-assessment.

Choose the most correct answer to the following questions unless a specific question instructs you to do otherwise.

1. True or False. A legal assistant can form a partnership with a lawyer if none of the activities consists of the practice of law.

2. True or False. It is unethical for a law firm to advise a client's creditors of a settlement made in a case so that the creditor may attach the settlement.

3. True or False. A law firm may not be paid by a trust company to draft wills in which the trust company is named as trustee.

4. True or False. Under current ethics rules, a lawyer who is also a licensed insurance broker may join both business activities in the same office.

5. True or False. Karen is a legal assistant with the ABC Law Firm. Her supervisor has asked her to draft a type of document that she has never drafted before and that is not contained in the firm's form files. While searching some older files, she finds a document published and copyrighted by a real estate company which is exactly what she needs. Because the document comes from an old client file found in the law office, it is permissible for Karen to copy it as her own work product.

6. True or False. Allen is a legal assistant, newly hired to go to work for another law firm. Before starting the new job, the legal administrator at the new law firm wants to review the names of the files with which Allen has worked to avoid any potential conflict of interest in his new position. It is permissible for Allen to reveal this information.

7. True or False. Under current ethics rules, sanctions may be imposed upon the supervising attorney when his or her legal assistant drafts a frivolous discovery request.

8. True or False. When an attorney knows that her client has committed the criminal offense as charged, she should withdraw from the case because she cannot zealously defend one who is guilty.

9. True or False. A grateful client sends a diamond-studded pen holder to a legal assistant, as a way to say thanks for a job well done. It is permissible for the legal assistant to accept the pen holder.

10. True or False. A legal assistant cannot give a presentation of social security law at a senior citizens' center if any portion of the presentation will be devoted to answering specific questions from the audience.

11. True or False. Ruth is a legal assistant at Bill & Dunn. After working on a complex real estate case for nearly three years, the case is concluded successfully on behalf of Landsakes Realty. Isaac Landsakes arranges to have Super Bowl tickets sent to Ruth's father to show his appreciation for Ruth's fine work on the case. Ruth, upon learning about the tickets, which are nearly impossible to obtain and are quite expensive, must return them to Mr. Landsakes.

12. Jack is a legal assistant employed by William Walker. Jack's deposition is being taken concerning his investigation of an auto accident two years ago in which Mr. Walker represented one of the parties. When a particular question is asked, Mr. Walker objects on the basis of attorney work product and instructs Jack not to answer the question. The deposing attorney notes the objection for the record and demands that Jack answer the question. Under these circumstances, Jack's worst option is to:

    a.   Comply because the answer will not be admissible anyway.
    b.   Not answer the question based upon Mr. Walker's instructions.
    c.   Request a recess to discuss the situation with Mr. Walker.
    d.   Comply only if the answer can be given off the record.

13. A friend who is a legal assistant in another law firm calls you to ask if your firm has handled any recent litigation in federal court. There have been major changes in the rules of procedure in that court within the past six months, and your friend is uncertain about filing pleadings under the new rules. Your firm has just completed its first case under the new rules. What is your best course of action?

    a.   Decline to answer his questions because it would constitute the unauthorized practice of law.
    b.   Decline to answer his questions because he should figure it out for himself.
    c.   Answer any of the questions that you know concerning procedure.
    d.   Answer any of the questions that you know, provided that your friend promises not to divulge where he got the information.

14. Three months after the entry of the decree, a client in a divorce case returns to the attorney and confesses that he concealed assets while the divorce case was pending. Now his business partner is trying to blackmail him. What should the attorney do?

    a.   Disclose the facts to the court.
    b.   Disclose the facts to the authorities.
    c.   Urge the client to disclose the facts.
    d.   Do nothing.

15. After an initial client interview, the client asks you what the normal fee would be for the will. What is the best reply?

    a.   Legal assistants cannot quote fees.

(see next page)

b. The standard charge for a will is $100.

c. The charge probably will be between $50 and $200.

d. Attorney Smith must determine the charge, which can vary widely depending on the amount of time needed to draft the will.

16. Assume that Steve is a legal assistant and that he misappropriates client money from a trust account. What sanctions may be imposed upon Steve?

   a. termination of employment
   b. civil liability to the client
   c. criminal conviction
   d. all of the above
   e. none of the above

17. In the immediately preceding situation, what course of action may be imposed against Steve's employer as a result of Steve's conduct?

   a. criminal charges
   b. civil suit by the client
   c. disciplinary proceedings
   d. two of the above
   e. all of the above

18. Which of the following represent(s) ethical conduct by a legal assistant?

   a. Negotiating settlements within dollar limits established by the attorney.
   b. Obtaining a personal computer at 50% discount from a client who is a computer retailer.
   c. Performing ministerial acts at a real estate closing.
   d. Two of the above.
   e. All of the above.
   f. None of the above.

19. Which of the following represent(s) unethical conduct by a legal assistant?

   a. Drafting correspondence to a client to be signed by the legal assistant.
   b. Arranging a deposition with opposing counsel.
   c. Performing legal research.
   d. Two of the above.
   e. All of the above.
   f. None of the above.

20.   A retainer for legal services must be:

    a.   Agreed upon in advance.
    b.   Reasonable.
    c.   Deposited in a lawyer's trust account.
    d.   All of the above.
    e.   Two of the above.
    f.   None of the above.

21.   A legal assistant who discusses a client's case while at a friend's wedding violates the client's special right to privacy, which is called:

    a.   Attorney-client privilege.
    b.   Work product immunity.
    c.   Confidentiality.
    d.   None of the above.

22.   True or False.   When statements are sent to clients, the legal assistant's time may be billed at the same rate as the supervising attorney's, as long as the profit (the difference between the legal assistant's billing rate and the lawyer's billing rate) is donated to the client loss fund of the state bar association.

23.   True or False.   It is permissible for a legal assistant to give legal advice as part of his pro bono activities, as long as the recipient does not pay for the advice and the legal assistant makes his or her nonlawyer status clear.

24.   True or False.   If the rules of an administrative agency permit nonlawyer practice, a legal assistant may establish an independent practice which consists exclusively of representing clients before that administrative agency.

25.   True or False.   If the rules of an administrative agency permit nonlawyer practice, an attorney ethically may not restrict the right of a legal assistant employed by her to appear before that agency on behalf of the lawyer's clients.

26.   True or False.   It is unethical for a lawyer knowingly to offer evidence that is prejudicial.

27.   True or False.   It is permissible to discuss a case with an opposing party who is represented by counsel, so long as the opposing counsel consents.

28. True or False. It is permissible for a busy attorney to undertake representation of a client if she knows that she will not be able to do anything with the case for another nine months, so long as she discloses this fact to the client and so long as the client consents.

29. Of the following tasks, which ethically may not be performed by legal assistants under existing rules?

   a. Prepare answers to interrogatories.
   b. Prepare questions for a deposition.
   c. Assist a client in executing her will.
   d. Two of the above.
   e. All of the above.
   f. None of the above.

30. It would be unethical for a legal assistant to:

   a. Review a complaint and draft an answer to it.
   b. Explain appeal procedures to a client.
   c. Attend a deposition.
   d. Two of the above.
   e. All of the above.
   f. None of the above.

31. The NALA document which provides an outline for the proper use of legal assistants by attorneys is known as:

   a. NALA Model Rules of Professional Responsibility.
   b. NALA Model Standard and Guidelines for Utilization of Legal Assistants.
   c. NALA Code of Ethics and Professional Responsibility.
   d. None of the above.

32. Jane is a legal assistant for Bill Adams and is also a notary public. One morning Bill brings an affidavit to Jane, which already has been signed by Bill's client, Richard Johnson, and asks Jane to notarize the affidavit. Jane should:

   a. Notarize the signature if Bill swears that he saw Johnson sign it.
   b. Notarize the signature because Bill instructed her to do so.
   c. Not notarize the signature unless Johnson re-signs it in her presence.
   d. Not notarize the signature unless Johnson calls her and confirms that it is his signature.

33. Tom Decker is a legal assistant employed by Angela Carter, a solo practitioner. Angela's practice has become much busier over the last few months, and she is considering the addition of another attorney. In the meantime, however, it is very difficult for her to be in all of the places where she needs to be at the same time. Angela suggests to Tom that since nothing ever happens at pretrial hearings in county court except to set a trial date, perhaps Tom can cover these hearings until another lawyer is hired. Which of the following is correct?

   a. Tom's appearance would be unethical without a court rule that permits him to appear.
   b. Tom's appearance would be ethical as long as he handles procedural matters only.
   c. Tom's appearance would be ethical as long as the attorney and the client consent.
   d. None of these is correct.

34. Lawyers are required to segregate client funds from operating funds because of:

   a. Banking rules.
   b. Ethics rules.
   c. IRS rules.
   d. Two of the above.
   e. None of the above.

35. While at a professional meeting, Jane (who is a legal assistant with the ABC Law Firm) becomes involved in a conversation with Bill and Fred, both of whom are legal assistants in another law firm in the city. Fred, an obnoxious boor by anyone's standards, begins to relate courthouse rumors about Joe Carson's recent arrest and the pending criminal charges. Jane knows at least part of what Fred is saying to be untrue, because her firm represents Carson. Jane should:

   a. Correct Fred concerning those parts that she knows to be untrue.
   b. Inform Fred that he is incorrect but that she cannot discuss details because of client confidentiality.
   c. Report Fred to the district attorney for his breach of ethics.
   d. Say nothing.

36. It is permissible for legal assistants to perform work that otherwise would be performed by an attorney if:

   a. The attorney supervises the delegated work.
   b. The attorney maintains a direct relationship with the client.
   c. The attorney assumes full professional responsibility for the work product.
   d. Two of the above.
   e. All of the above.
   f. None of the above.

37. Which of the following represents ethical conduct by a legal assistant?

   a. Telling a prospective client that hers is the type of case the firm likes to handle.
   b. Drafting and signing status letters to clients where the nonlawyer status is shown clearly.
   c. Confirming that the firm once represented a particular client.
   d. Two are ethical.
   e. All are ethical.
   f. None are ethical.

38. True or False.   In John's capacity as a legal assistant over the last twenty years, he has seen innumerable people simply plead guilty or no contest to minor criminal charges because they earned too much to have appointed counsel but did not earn enough to hire a lawyer. Quite troubled by this situation, John prepares a brochure which outlines the steps of basic criminal procedure as well as the various options that a defendant may request when he appears in court. John wants to have the brochure distributed on the sidewalk outside the courthouse. There will be no charge for the brochure, and he plans to use volunteers for distribution. If John distributes the brochure as planned, he will be in violation of most states' UPL statutes.

39. True or False. Bill is a legal assistant for Lora Lawyer. While Lora is away from the office on April 15, Bill is contacted by one of Lora's divorce clients, who insists that he needs to know whether he can remove a portion of the funds from a joint savings account to pay federal income tax. In reviewing the temporary order entered by the court, it seems clear that the savings account can be used for joint obligations. It is permissible for Bill to relay this information to the client.

40. If Bill were uncertain about what to do in the immediately preceding question or in a similar situation, he should:

   a. Relay the information but document it for Lora's later approval.
   b. Try to imagine what Lora would say and then act accordingly.
   c. Do nothing until he talks with Lora.
   d. None of these is satisfactory.

41. True or False. Different ethics rules apply to legal assistants who offer their services only to licensed attorneys than to legal assistants who are employed full time by licensed attorneys.

42. True or False. It is permissible for a legal assistant to propose and to implement a discovery plan in a personal injury case.

43. True or False. While interviewing a witness in a personal injury case, the witness relays facts to the legal assistant which indicate that our client may have been the cause of the collision. If the legal assistant were deposed about this interview, she could refuse to answer questions based upon attorney-client privilege.

44. True or False. In an effort to resolve the situation without a hearing and at the instruction of the supervising attorney, it is permissible for a legal assistant to review with opposing counsel preliminary objections to answers to interrogatories submitted by that attorney's client.

45. True or False. If the supervising attorney instructs him to do so, a legal assistant ethically may contact opposing counsel and try to determine the possible range of settlement figures that the opposing party might be willing to accept, so long as the legal assistant identifies himself and so long as no specific amount is offered in settlement.

46. True or False. Under existing ethics rules, all contingent fee arrangements must be in writing.

47. True or False. It is never permissible for a lawyer to represent adverse parties in a case.

48. Mary is a legal assistant for Veronica Miles. While Ms. Miles is in Europe, Mary receives a notice that a probate hearing is scheduled at the end of next week. Ms. Miles is not scheduled to return to the office until after that time. Mary knows that a motion for continuance is needed to postpone the

hearing. Which of the following is the worst course of action for Mary to take in this situation?

    a.   mail the unsigned motion to the court for filing;

    b.   arrange to have the client sign the motion and file it with the court;

    c.   sign her name to the motion and show her legal assistant title; or

    d.   sign Ms. Miles name to the motion and place her initials under the signature.

49.   Carla is a licensed financial planner in her state. As part of her services to clients, she reviews their financial situations and recommends that combination of savings accounts, life insurance, and property ownership which she believes will best suit their needs. When they need a will or a trust, she refers them to a local law firm. Lawyers have been quite receptive to her referrals; and as a result, several of them have provided her with a series of standardized will and trust forms to use in advising her clients. Which of the following is most correct?

    a.   Carla may not recommend or select forms for her clients.

    b.   Carla may select and complete a form based upon its standard use.

    c.   Carla may select the form so long as the client completes it himself.

    d.   Carla may recommend a form but the client must complete it.

50.   Benjamin is a legal assistant for Bill Black, a licensed attorney. Bill and two of his law school classmates (Mary White and James Grey) decide to join forces by sharing the cost of a suite of offices, equipment, and personnel. Bill asks Benjamin to arrange to have a bronze plate bearing the name "Black, White, and Grey" placed on the office door. Which of the following is least correct?

    a.   The lawyers can use this name only if they are a partnership.

    b.   Benjamin may incur joint civil liability if he works for the lawyers.

    c.   The lawyers may incur joint civil liability if they use this name.

    d.   The lawyers cannot use the name unless all of them consent in advance.

Chapter 4
JUDGMENT AND ANALYTICAL ABILITY

The mind, stretched to a new idea, never goes back to its original dimension.
—Oliver Wendell Holmes

This section of the CLA® examination relates to (1) analysis and categorization of facts; (2) the legal assistant's relationship with the lawyer, the legal secretary, the client, the courts, and other law firms; (3) the legal assistant's reaction to specific situations; (4) handling telephone situations; and (5) reading comprehension and data interpretation.

Familiarity with the Model Rules of Professional Conduct of the American Bar Association, together with the NALA Code of Ethics and Professional Responsibility and its Model Standards and Guidelines for the Utilization of Legal Assistants, will be helpful to the applicant. *See Chapter 3 of this Review Manual for copies of the NALA Code of Ethics and of the NALA Model Standards and Guidelines for Utilization of Legal Assistants.*

Knowledge of logical reasoning techniques and experience as a legal assistant are invaluable assets in preparing for this section of the examination.

Judgment and analytical ability go hand in hand. One cannot make sound judgments if his analytical abilities are poor. By the same token, thorough analysis requires a full understanding of the judgment to be made, including all of its ramifications. For these reasons, it is difficult to separate judgment from analysis as if they were separate processes. As a practical matter, they are so closely tied to each other that it sometimes is hard to tell where one begins and the other one ends.

Judgment Defined   By definition, ***judgment*** is the process used to reach a decision or a conclusion. A particular judgment is good or bad, depending on its consequences. To exercise good judgment, one must:

- Know the ultimate outcome that is sought;

- Have a thorough understanding of the framework within which to work (chain of command, authority, deadline[s], and so forth);

- Use available resources (rules of law, applicable documents, and experience or knowledge gleaned from others) that may affect the outcome;

- Have a thorough understanding of the relevant facts;

- Exercise sound analytical techniques (*see below*); and

- Be sensitive to ethical obligations and to the public relations impact of any action(s) taken or omitted.

The person who develops a reputation for good judgment is the person who consistently takes the time to cultivate the skills outlined above. Acquiring good judgment skills is an evolutionary process that combines technical knowledge with experience. As a result, the legal assistant—like the lawyer—finds that challenging assignments increase in direct proportion to his or her demonstrated exercise of good judgment.

Analytical Ability Defined   ***Analytical ability*** is the process of sorting facts and related information into categories, separating that which is relevant from that which is not. To analyze is to break the whole into its parts and to determine the relationship of the parts (1) to each other and (2) to the whole, using logical reasoning techniques and the rules that govern the specific situation under analysis. ***Assume nothing.***

In its practical application within the legal environment, analytical ability requires some creativity and imagination. More important, however, it requires a disciplined, thorough, methodical, and painstakingly detailed approach to the project—whatever the project may be. Legal assistants must be able to understand, propose, and implement systems to manage factual analyses, including testimony and source information.

Effect of Ethics Rules   Ethical considerations, including both the spirit of ethics rules and the rules themselves, are so interwoven into judgment and analytical ability that it is impossible to discuss either without taking ethics into account. For instance, if logical reasoning techniques suggest options that are (or may be) unethical or that exceed the bounds of responsible conduct, those options must be eliminated. Similarly, if the range of possible judgments includes acts or omissions which are (or may be) unethical, those judgments cannot be implemented.

The type of success that sustains a professional career over an entire lifetime cannot be achieved by cutting ethical corners or by rationalizing ethics away. To believe otherwise is simply bad judgment.

Practical Judgment and Analysis by Legal Assistants

Regardless of his or her practice area, every legal assistant exercises some degree of judgment and analytical ability in daily job performance. For instance, legal assistants routinely document the instructions given to them for all assignments. This practice is an exercise of good judgment. It protects the legal assistant from failed memory, both his own and that of his supervising attorney. When a large project is assigned, good judgment requires the legal assistant to break it into phases and to get periodic feedback from the attorney concerning its progress. In this way, misperception can be corrected as it arises, before the legal assistant invests substantial time and energy—and personal identity—in the wrong direction.

Analytical processes are used to reach conclusions (judgments) about everything from obtaining proper supplies for a special project to avoiding conduct that may be interpreted as the unauthorized practice of law. Although it is not intended to be exhaustive, the following list illustrates areas in which legal assistants routinely make judgments.

■Range of authority within established rules of policy, whether written or unwritten:

●Know who supervises the legal assistant
●Understand the hierarchy of the office

●Know how and by whom office policy is established

■Fulfillment of professional duties within the delineated range of authority:

●Know and observe ethics rules
●Establish and adhere to deadlines
●Set priorities to complete assignments
●Assist with docket control for assigned cases
●Perform legal research as assigned or as needed for projects
●Know what resources are available and how to use them
●Locate, document, and manage witness information and evidence
●Interview clients and witnesses
●Organize and maintain trial notebooks, corporate books, etc.
●Assist in preparing questions for depositions and trial
●Assist in preparing clients/witnesses to give testimony
●Assist at trials, depositions, closings, or similar occurrences
●Institute procedures to keep clients informed of status of cases
●Formulate routine responses to clients and to others
●Recognize and respond appropriately to exceptional situations
●Cultivate positive, professional relationships at all levels
●Assist in training and supervising non-lawyer personnel

■Proper application of procedural rules for the most efficient administration of assigned cases and projects:

●Comply with procedural requirements set by statute and court rule
●Categorize facts, supporting documents, and other data based upon attorney's legal theories
●Summarize, index, manage, and retrieve case materials
●Anticipate and obtain authorizations as needed
●Obtain valuations and appraisals as required
●Implement systems to satisfy notice and publication requirements
●Implement and monitor discovery procedures
●Review objections to discovery requests
●Review and catalog data produced through discovery
●Draft pleadings, motions, orders, documents, inventories, notices, tax returns, correspondence, and the like
●Have subpoenas issued to non-party witnesses for trial

This list may be more or less expansive, depending on a particular legal assistant's level of experience; degree of expertise; and proven judgment capabilities. For the list to be more expansive, rather than less, the legal assistant must earn the trust of the supervising attorney by consistently demonstrating sound judgment in a panoply of situations. In fulfilling this need, the legal assistant is expected to analyze, categorize, summarize, and systematize all types of information from many different sources. The first step in any analysis is thorough comprehension of the data to be analyzed.

Comprehension of Data   All analysis begins with the review of instructions, applicable rules, basic facts, and other preliminary data. Implicit in the concept of review is the reviewer's ability to comprehend the data under review. Comprehension means understanding; it begins with a knowledge of what words mean, both literally and by reasonable inference.

To illustrate, read the following passage and circle the correct answers to the questions that follow it. Then place a check mark in front of those questions whose answers are implied by the passage but are not stated directly.

> Adults engage in sexual stereotyping when they encourage children to behave in ways that traditionally have been considered appropriate for males and females. For instance, when parents encourage a son to wrestle but discourage a daughter from wrestling, they set the pattern for all sexual stereotyping that follows.

1.   Parents engage in sexual stereotyping when they
    a.   encourage traditional behaviors.
    b.   write pornographic literature.
    c.   teach daughters to type.
    d.   discourage sons from wrestling.

2.   Parents engage in sexual stereotyping when they encourage
    a.   a girl to ride a bike.
    b.   a boy to care for a cat.
    c.   a girl to clean a house.
    d.   a boy to cook meals.

3.   Sexual stereotyping can be done by
    a.   relatives..
    b.   teachers.
    c.   ministers.
    d.   all of the above.

4.   Which of the following is not an example of sexual stereotyping?
    a.   telling a boy not to cry
    b.   teaching a girl to fight back
    c.   teaching a girl to be sweet
    d.   teaching a boy to fight back

You should have placed check marks in front of the second, third, and fourth questions. The answers are not stated in the passage; they are implied. Explanations of the correct answers follow.

1.   The answer, *a*, is stated in the first sentence; the answers to all other questions are not directly stated in the passage.

2.   The *c* answer is implied; you should have checked this question. Cleaning house and cooking traditionally have been considered more appropriate for females than for males. Riding bikes and caring for pets are not considered more appropriate for one sex than for the other; these activities usually are gender neutral.

3.   The *d* answer is implied; you should have checked this question. Sexual stereotyping can be done by any adult who influences a child's behavior, including parents, grandparents, aunts, uncles, teachers, and ministers.

4.   The *b* answer is implied; you should have checked this question. Fighting back traditionally has been considered more appropriate for males than for females. Boys traditionally have been encouraged not to cry, and girls traditionally have been encouraged to be sweet.

The distinction between a reasonable inference and an unreasonable assumption can be obscure at times. The legal assistant is expected to recognize that point at which obscurity begins and to exercise caution to remain within the bounds of reasonable inference.

For the legal assistant, a superior command of the English language and of specific legal terms is essential. If a legal assistant were assigned to help finalize existing drafts of a proposed contract between a wobblewonk manufacturing company and its widget supplier, for instance, the legal assistant could do very little without knowing the precise definitions of the terms *wobblewonk* and *widget*. Although terminology certainly is an appropriate starting point, comprehension involves much more than merely knowing textbook definitions.

The review of a series of corporate operating statements and balance sheets, for example, requires more than being able to recite dictionary definitions of the words found in those documents. The reviewer must be able to translate the terms and numbers from financial gobbledegook into plain English. This requires knowledge of how corporations work, knowledge of how corporations use operating statements and balance sheets in general (and how this corporation uses them in particular), and an understanding of generally accepted accounting principles and practices. Without this background, the reviewer cannot expect to comprehend the information contained in the operating statements.

Analysis of Facts   Thorough analysis demands a good memory and the ability to link specific facts to the legal issues or requirements of the case. As a corollary, conflicts and gaps in factual data must be noted and resolved.

Armed with the legal rules to be applied, the legal assistant analyzes facts and sorts them into categories according to their source and degree of relevance as they are gathered from available resources, including public records; private documents; witness statements; and interviews in various forms. The analytical methods used most generally are deductive reasoning and analogical reasoning, which often are used in combination with each other.

Deductive reasoning is an analytical process that uses a major premise and a minor premise to deduce a logical conclusion, also known as a syllogism.

MAJOR PREMISE:	All men have beards.
MINOR PREMISE:	Sam is a man.
CONCLUSION:	Sam has a beard.
MAJOR PREMISE:	Most men have beards.
MINOR PREMISE:	Sam is a man.
CONCLUSION:	Sam has a beard.

The conclusion is valid (logical) in the first example. If *all* men have beards and if Sam is a man, he is included in the same category as all other men. Therefore, logic dictates that Sam has a beard. The conclusion in the second example is not valid, however, since there is no way to know whether Sam is included in the same category as *most* men. He may be among the minority of men who do not have beards.

The conclusion reached through deductive reasoning is valid only if the major premise and the minor premise are themselves valid and only if they relate to similar things.

MAJOR PREMISE:	A foot is 12 inches long.
MINOR PREMISE:	William has two feet.
CONCLUSION:	William's feet total 24 inches in length.

Although each premise in the example is valid standing alone, neither is valid in context with the other. The term *foot* in the major premises implies a linear foot, while the term *feet* in the minor premise implies body parts. Therefore, the conclusion is invalid.

The analytical method that uses similarities and differences to categorize is called ***analogical reasoning***. The ability to recognize similarities and differences by analogy is found in many aptitude tests, including law school aptitude tests, using problems such as these:

1. Horse is to animal as _____ is to _____.
    a. cow; milk
    b. farm; pig
    c. tree; branch
    d. oak; wood

2. Thermometer is to temperature as _____ is to _____.
    a. telescope; astronomy
    b. clock; minutes
    c. scale; weight
    d. microscope; biologist

To solve the first problem, one would reason: "Horse is to animal as *blank* is to *blank*. A horse is an animal; it is a type or species of animal. Comparing cow and milk, a cow is not a type of milk; it produces milk. Comparing farm and pig, a farm is not a type of pig. Comparing tree and branch, a tree is not a type of branch; it contains branches. Comparing oak and wood, oak is a type of wood; this forms an analogy to the first pair of terms in the question. So the correct answer is *d, oak and wood.*"

To solve the second problem, one might reason: "Thermometer is to temperature as *blank* is to *blank*. A thermometer measures temperature. Comparing telescope and astronomy, a telescope does not measure astronomy. Eliminate this answer. Comparing clock and minutes, a clock measures minutes. This could be the answer. Comparing scale and weight, a scale measures weight. This could be the answer also. Comparing microscope and biologist, a microscope does not measure a biologist. Eliminate this answer. So, a thermometer measures temperature, a clock measures minutes, and a scale measures weight; but the word *minutes* is different from either *temperature* or *weight*. A clock measures time, not just minutes; minutes are units of time—just as degrees are units of temperature and pounds are units of weight. So the best answer is *c, scale; weight*. Temperature and weight are complete dimensions in themselves. A thermometer measures the dimension *temperature*, and a scale measures the dimension *weight*."

Analogical reasoning is the principal method used in *stare decisis*, which requires cases with like facts to be decided alike and cases with different facts to be decided differently—if the differences are important.

If legal research discloses a case reciting facts A, B, and C, *stare decisis* (analogical reasoning) requires all subsequent cases with facts A, B, and C to be decided in the same way as the first case. If a subsequent case contains facts A and B—but not fact C—the importance of fact C to the outcome of the original case must be analyzed. Similarly, if a subsequent case contains facts A, B, C, and D, the addition of fact D must be analyzed in light of the original case: Does it seem likely that the additional fact would have changed the outcome of the original case? If not, the original case retains its value as precedent and must be followed in the subsequent case. To illustrate:

CASE NO. 1   Fact A: Joe owns a prize bulldog.
                   Fact B: Susan steals the bulldog and sells it to Ken.
                   Fact C: Ken does not know the bulldog is stolen.
                   Result: Joe wins against Ken, because Ken acquires no better title than the thief.

CASE NO. 2   Fact A: Joe owns a prize bulldog.
                   Fact B: Susan buys the dog with an insufficient funds check.
                   Result: Joe wins against Susan, who has committed fraud.

CASE NO. 3   Fact A: Joe owns prize a bulldog.
                   Fact B: Susan buys the dog with a bad check and sells it to Ken.
                   Fact C: Ken does not know about the bad check.
                   Fact D: Ken has heard gossip that Susan "pulled a fast one" on Joe.
                   Result: Joe wins against Ken, because Ken knew something was amiss even though he did not know specifically what it was.

Regardless of the analytical method used, analysis of facts requires the legal assistant to read (or to listen to) facts critically to detect factual gaps and factual conflicts. *Factual gaps* occur when certain facts are missing or are unknown. Where possible, factual gaps must be supplied by other witnesses or other sources. *Factual conflicts* occur when the facts obtained from a single source are inconsistent with each other (*internal conflict*) or when they are inconsistent with those facts obtained from other sources (*external conflict*). Internal conflict may be more problematic, especially if the internal conflict occurs within a client's statement of the facts. This may indicate that the client does not know what happened or is not telling the truth about what happened. Either way, factual conflicts must be brought to the attorney's attention and must be resolved through other sources.

Segregation of Relevant Data

Along with their many other duties, legal assistants are information managers. In working with a particular case file, the legal assistant comes into contact with vast amounts of information or data. Some of it is relevant; some of it is not.

An important part of an attorney's expectation of the legal assistant involves the ability to separate relevant from irrelevant information. Using applicable statutes or rules—or legal theories supplied by the attorney—as the measuring stick, the legal assistant sifts through all of the facts to segregate those that are relevant and then categorizes them according to the issue or the element of an issue to which they relate. This applies both to facts that tend to support the client's claim and to facts that tend to refute it. The legal assistant who can perform this important task in a consistent and reliable manner, streamlining relevant facts and avoiding factual surprises, is invaluable to a busy attorney. To illustrate, the following exercise is provided.

Assume the following transcribed statement is handed to you by your supervising attorney after her initial conference with a potential client. The attorney tells you that the case involves a two-vehicle collision on an icy street and that no passengers were in either vehicle. She indicates that liability likely will be the major issue in the case and instructs you to start a new case file, to review the statement, and then to schedule a follow-up interview with the client.

My name is Nadine Kelly. I am a widow and have lived alone for ten years. I was on my way home late one night when this terrible accident happened. Let's see, I think it was January 12. That would be this year. Yes, this year; I am certain of that.

Anyway, it was pretty late. I'd say it was between 9:30 and 10:00 p.m. I was driving my truck west on Ames Avenue. I had just passed the stoplight at 52nd Street and was headed uphill on Ames when, all of a sudden, this yellow bus (maybe it was a yellow van) was in my lane and was headed straight for me.

I don't know how fast the guy was going, but it was too fast for me to get out of his way. I had just left the stoplight, so I couldn't have been driving very fast—maybe 10 or 15 m.p.h. Anyhow, when I saw that he was coming right for me, I tried to get out of his way. I hit the gas and headed for the curb, but I wasn't fast enough. He hit me almost head on. It broke out my headlight and smashed my fender into the tire on one side of the car, so that I couldn't drive it home. It had to be towed.

He got out of his car and started yelling that I was a crazy old bat, why didn't I watch where I was going, and stuff like that. I was real upset. It was pretty bad to be hit; but when he started yelling, that really upset me.

I don't remember a whole lot after that except that I think he must have been drunk—the way he was yelling and all. He was none too steady on his feet, either. He said his name was Earl or Darrell something-or-other. I have it written down on a piece of paper at home. I forgot to bring it with me.

A guy from the gas station came over to where we were. We all went back to the gas station to call the police, but they couldn't come because there were too many accidents that night. It was real icy and everything. The police said for us to give each other our names and the names of our insurance companies and then to file a police report the next day.

I guess I should have stayed at Pearl's house. She begged me to stay, but the roads didn't seem that bad then. The gas station guy towed my car and drove me home. I was still upset, but he was real nice about it.

Among the following statements, which are statements of fact? Indicate by writing the word "fact" in front of each such statement. Of the factual statements selected, which are relevant to the issue

*identified by the attorney? Indicate by placing a check mark in front
of them.*

1. ✓*fact* Mrs. Kelly is a widow.

2. Her husband died ten years ago.

3. The accident happened on January 12 of this year.

4. *fact* Mrs. Kelly was driving in a westerly direction. ✓

5. The accident happened at the intersection of 52nd Street and Ames
Avenue.

6. *fact* The other vehicle was driving in an easterly direction. ✓

7. *fact* The roads were icy. ✓

8. The other vehicle was speeding.

9. The other driver was drunk.

10. A gas station attendant witnessed the accident.

Answers

1. *Fact—irrelevant to the issue of liability, however.* ✓
2. *Assumption: Not all widows live alone; children or others may have lived with her.*
3. *Assumption: She only thinks the accident occurred on January 12.*
4. *Fact—relevant to the issue of liability.*
5. *Misstatement: She states she already had passed the intersection.*
6. *Fact—relevant to the issue of liability.*
7. *Fact—relevant to the issue of liability.*
8. *Conclusion of client; it may or may not be true.*
9. *Conclusion of client; it may or may not be true.*
10. *Assumption: No inference can be drawn about witnesses to the accident.*

Although substantially oversimplified, this exercise illustrates the type of filtering process that legal assistants use to segregate facts and to assess their relevancy. Where they may be relevant, the conclusions and assumptions suggested by the statement would be investigated and verified. In addition, the many factual gaps within the statement would be addressed in the legal assistant's investigation. Once gathered and verified, these facts likewise must be separated for relevancy and then must be categorized according to the issues to which they apply. A single fact may relate to more than one issue in the case.

Summarize Relevant Data   Once relevant facts and data have been segregated and placed within appropriate categories, summaries (or abstracts) generally are prepared. The form of the summary depends on the purpose for which it will be used. The summary of a particular witness's statement may be in a brief, narrative form for the attorney's working file or it may be summarized in a bullet format for the witness section of a trial notebook, similar to many of the lists used throughout this *Review Manual*. The same witness statement generally will be abstracted still further for purposes of indexing and cross-referencing evidence in preparation for trial.

Unless the attorney specifies a particular format, the legal assistant must know the purpose of the summary to determine which format will be most useful. Sound judgments must be made at the beginning of the case about indexing and retrieval systems to be used, as well as their formats. If the format (or the system) becomes unworkable, the financial costs to change the system can be substantial. The credibility cost to the legal assistant, however, is much greater. Working closely with the attorney, the legal assistant must make initial judgments about information management systems and the forms they should take. The system and system format selected should be the simplest ones available for the job.

Upon selection of an appropriate information management system, the legal assistant is responsible for summarizing all of the data that comprises it: witness statements, answers to interrogatories, depositions, answers to requests for admission, public records, relevant documents, legal memoranda, and so forth.

In preparing summaries, a good rule of thumb is to concentrate on subjects and verbs from an original witness statement, adding other information only if it is essential for clarity. Ordinarily, this is easier to accomplish with a bullet format than it is with a narrative. When a narrative is required, such as for the statement of a particular witness, it should be no longer than approximately one-fourth of the original (as a general rule). If it can be shortened further without sacrificing substance, do so. When summarizing depositions, the general rule of thumb is seven to ten pages of deposition testimony for each page of summary.

Interpretation of Procedural Matters

Legal assistants routinely interpret matters of procedure within the parameters established by law, ethics rules, and office policy. Within these parameters, the degree of procedural authority granted to a particular legal assistant is based upon his or her experience and the level of confidence engendered with the supervising attorney as that attorney's "good right arm." This type of confidence does not come quickly or easily; it is earned over a long period of time and is based upon a demonstrable history of good judgments by the legal assistant. As the attorney's confidence in a particular legal assistant grows, so does the delegation of procedural authority to that legal assistant.

Everything done by the legal assistant ultimately must be approved by the attorney, either expressly or tacitly, and incorporated into the attorney's final work product. Within this structure, however, legal assistants can and do make decisions about procedural matters related to client services, rule compliance, and case progression.

Experienced legal assistants routinely answer client questions regarding procedure: How much notice must be given to creditors? How long is the statutory waiting period for a particular type of case? They prepare and calculate inheritance tax, estate tax, and income tax returns. They prepare preliminary schedules and forms for probate, bankruptcy, and family law cases. They organize and maintain litigation files, including the trial notebook. They prepare preliminary drafts of pleadings, motions, notices, wills, trusts, and legal memoranda based upon legal research performed by them or by others. They conduct initial reviews of title binders and closing statements, draft deeds and related documents, and perform other ministerial tasks in real estate matters. At the attorney's direction, they communicate directly with clients (by letter, in person, and on the telephone) about the status of clients' cases.

Using guidelines set by the supervising attorney, legal assistants review statutes and court rules on a preliminary basis to determine procedural requirements; establish compliance checklists; and implement systems to comply with those requirements. They calculate deadlines (for example, hearings which must be set not sooner than 60 days and not later than 120 days after an occurrence; three-day notice requirement for hearing notices; and so forth), which requires them to know such things as whether a three-day notice includes the day of service; whether three days means three calendar days or three working days; and whether additional time is granted by a court when its deadline falls on a weekend or legal holiday. Legal assistants monitor all discovery, including that which is sent and that which is received, to assure compliance with applicable rules.

Legal assistants streamline case progression by implementing various forms of record searches and investigation at the instruction of the supervising attorney; by implementing and monitoring the discovery process in litigation matters; and by working closely with the attorney to ensure that cases move forward in an expeditious manner. Legal assistants play a vital role in maximizing the attorney's efficiency by providing higher quality legal service to clients at a lower cost.

In addition to their work on specific cases, legal assistants often provide assistance in administrative areas. Their superior organizational skills frequently are used in establishing systems of all kinds: training new personnel; library maintenance and acquisitions; general office procedures; filing systems; timekeeping systems; and billing systems. This systems list is not intended to be exhaustive, since the skills of a legal assistant can be used in any area where organization, attention to detail, and good judgment are required.

Good judgment in administrative areas demands a thorough familiarity with the system or project assigned, including its history; sensitivity to the office hierarchy; diplomacy in working with the personalities to be affected by any change that may be implemented; enough flexibility and self-confidence to be receptive to constructive criticism; and perseverance to see the project to successful completion.

Establish Priorities   Legal assistants with proven capabilities in matters requiring good judgment are blessed—and cursed—with ever-increasing responsibilities in the areas of case management and office administration. Since they do not receive ever-increasing amounts of time within which to accomplish these responsibilities, legal assistants must become adept at establishing and maintaining priorities.

Simply stated, establishing priorities means recognizing the difference between those things that can wait and those things that cannot (or should not) wait. The situation that involves being called away from a long-range project to complete an emergency assignment requested by the senior partner is an easy judgment call. If the project is one that must be completed before trial begins tomorrow morning, however, the judgment becomes more complex; and announcing it may require the most skilled judgment of all.

To establish reasonable priorities, the legal assistant must be able to distinguish between internal and external deadlines; must make an accurate assessment of the time required for any given project; must be willing to delegate responsibility wherever possible; and must take the priorities of others into account.

An internal deadline is one which is self-imposed or is imposed from within the law office, such as restructuring the trial brief file maintained by most litigation firms or drafting a modification to the personnel policy manual. An external deadline is one which is imposed by an outside source, such as the deadline to file an appellate brief with the court; a board of directors meeting scheduled by a corporate client; or a license renewal deadline for a client governed by an administrative agency.

As a general rule, external deadlines take priority over internal deadlines. The deadline for an appellate brief, for example, typically takes precedence over assignments connected with modifying a policy manual—even when the policy manual assignment comes from a senior partner. Missing a brief deadline may result in a malpractice claim; delaying the modification of an internal policy manual rarely does. In this situation, the legal assistant's good judgment should prompt him to enlist the aid of his immediate supervisor in gaining the senior firm member's support for the shift in priorities. Establishing priorities among conflicting external deadlines (two different appellate briefs due within a day or two of each other, for example) requires the full panoply of good judgment skills.

To ensure that all external deadlines are met, a legal assistant must assess accurately the time requirements for each project, recognizing that the tendency is to underestimate the time needed to do a thorough job. Most rush projects are needed yesterday. Since that deadline cannot be met in any event, the legal assistant must use care to make reasonable estimates of the time needed for completion. Otherwise, credibility with superiors is jeopardized when the deadline is not met. The delay wastes valuable time that could be used to obtain assistance from others or, if that is not possible, to obtain an extension of the deadline without the additional difficulty and stress associated with a last-minute request.

One generally knows ahead of time that there may be problems in meeting a deadline. As soon as that possibility appears, the experienced legal assistant prepares to meet it. This can be done in one of two ways: (1) Obtain the necessary help from others to meet the deadline; or (2) Delegate unrelated assignments to others if that will allow sufficient time to meet the deadline. Frequently, other legal assistants, associates, or law clerks can be reassigned to provide assistance until the priority project is completed. The inexperienced legal assistant sometimes tries to be superhuman and to do it all. The results of this type of judgment can be disastrous for the project and for the legal assistant.

Establishing priorities requires that the priorities of others be accommodated in every reasonable way. Assume, for example, that a case is unexpectedly moved forward on the court's trial docket. In what order should the legal assistant perform the following tasks: (1) Confer with his supervising attorney about final preparation for trial, as requested; (2) Call to cancel his dental appointment for the first morning of trial; and (3) Call to find out when the court reporter will have the final deposition transcribed so that it can be summarized and indexed?

First, call the court reporter. Until the legal assistant knows the reporter's transcription schedule, he does not have all necessary information to engage in a meaningful discussion with the attorney about final trial preparations. Moreover, the reporter's schedule may need to be rearranged to accommodate the earlier trial date. If so, the reporter should be informed as quickly as possible. **Second**, armed with all relevant information (including the date when the deposition will be completed), confer with the attorney as requested about final preparations for trial. If additional priority tasks emerge from this discussion which require the assistance of others, contact those individuals before attending to personal matters. Any unnecessary delay at this point seldom can be justified. **Third**, although it may take less than 60 seconds to call the dentist's office, this is the least important task and, therefore, the last one that should be undertaken. Imagine, for instance, the justifiable reaction of the trial lawyer who may enter the legal assistant's office as the dental call is being made. The better judgment, therefore, is to cancel the dental appointment later in the day, after trial preparations are underway.

Reaction to Specific Situations   There is no single rule to handle the wide array of situations encountered by a legal assistant. Rather, the legal assistant must draw upon his or her experience in handling a variety of procedural matters, in working with people in general and with clients in particular, and in working with a specific attorney.

The ideal professional relationship of the legal assistant and the attorney is one grounded in loyalty, trust, and mutual respect developed over a long period of time. To attain this ideal, the attorney must be willing to delegate tasks to the legal assistant in permissible areas and to serve as a professional mentor in developing the legal assistant's analytical and decision-making skills. The legal assistant must be willing and able to accept the responsibilities delegated to him or her in a reliable, professional way.

In any situation, the legal assistant should determine the objective to be reached within the parameters of office policy and sound ethics. Once the objective is known, the legal assistant's cautious common sense, analytical abilities, and diplomacy will go far in consistently exercising good judgment. A thorough understanding of office policy (both written and unwritten) and of legal ethics will assist the legal assistant in successfully managing situations such as these:

■Client questions about the merits of a case or about the course of action that he or she should take in the attorney's absence.

■The client who attempts to enlist the legal assistant's help—or silence—in providing inaccurate or incomplete information.

■Irate clients encountered in person and on the telephone, whether or not the supervising attorney may be a source of their irritation.

■The attorney who procrastinates about getting things done or who is inconsistent about returning telephone calls to clients and to others.

■The attorney who is lax about reviewing the legal assistant's work before incorporating it into his or her final work product.

■The attorney who works in spurts, making it virtually impossible to maintain an orderly work schedule.

■The attorney who shifts to the legal assistant blame which clearly rests with the attorney alone.

■The coworker who always needs help to meet deadlines.

■The coworker or the supervisor who persists in conduct that is unprofessional or that may be unethical.

■The supervisor who makes unreasonable demands or who finds some reason to criticize, no matter how quickly or how well a project is done.
■The supervisor who gives incomplete instructions.

■The supervisor who avoids utilizing the legal assistant's skills to their full potential.

Approach to Essay Questions

Essay questions for this section of the CLA® examination will require the applicant to demonstrate superior written communication skills, together with his or her analytical abilities and good judgment. For this section of the examination, more than for the others, practical experience is the applicant's most valuable asset. Those who are relatively new to the profession can substitute a rational and considered approach for practical experience.

In examinations of this type, questions dealing with analytical abilities may require a stated, hypothetical situation to be broken down, separating relevant from irrelevant data, with the relevant data to be accurately categorized or summarized or both. Questions dealing with judgment are designed to test the applicant's decision-making skills in specific, hypothetical situations which are outlined in the question. The applicant who possesses these skills will be able to demonstrate them to their best advantage by using the following approach:

•Quickly skim the question to get a feel for its general subject matter.

•Determine specifically what the question seeks: an analysis and recommendation; a listing or summary of relevant data; a survey of permissible options; a proposed plan of action; or other, stated objective.

•Reread the question, carefully this time, noting or highlighting words and phrases that may be important, given the subject matter of the question and the objective that it seeks.

•Unless the question directs otherwise, assume a hypothetical, average lawyer as the supervising attorney within the context of the question. Experienced legal assistants should visualize this hypothetical lawyer as a composite of all the lawyers with whom they have worked. In this way, the biases and idiosyncrasies of a particular lawyer are not injected into the answer.

•Use a definitive but conservative approach in answering the question. If more than one reasonable resolution or option is possible, touch upon each of them.

•Prepare an outline of the proposed answer first and use the outline to prepare the final answer.

•Review the suggestions for taking tests in general, which are found in the Introduction to this *CLA® Review Manual*.

A sample essay question is included as a separate Self-Test at the end of this chapter; a sample answer for that question is shown at the end of the Self-Test Answer Key.

Judgment and Analytical Ability Self-Test

Allow 30 minutes to answer all objective questions and 40 minutes to answer the essay question (70 minutes total). At the end of the time period, check your answers to the questions against those in the Answer Key Section of this Manual. Deduct two points each for incorrect answer (80 total possible points for objective questions). Unanswered questions are counted as incorrect answers. Add this score to the score from the essay question to determine the overall score for this section. Follow directions carefully and observe the time limit precisely to provide an accurate self-assessment.

Choose the most correct answer to the following questions unless you are instructed to do otherwise.

1. True or False.   A legal assistant is permitted to exercise independent judgment in procedural matters.

2. True or False.   Errors in judgment are to be expected of a legal assistant who is beginning a new job with a new law firm.

3. True or False.   A legal assistant assigned to reorganize the preprinted form files may assume that he has authority to charge the necessary supplies to complete the project.

4. True or False.   When a legal assistant hears office rumors concerning his supervising attorney, he should report them to his supervising attorney as soon as he is reasonably able to do so.

5. True or False.   When a client relates information about her case to a legal assistant in confidence, the legal assistant nevertheless should report the information to the supervising attorney.

6. _____ is to dollar as year is to _____.

    a.   money : calendar
    b.   dime : month
    c.   penny : century
    d.   savings : century

7. _____ is to liquid as ice is to _____.

    a.   flowing : solid
    b.   warm : cold
    c.   milk : cream
    d.   water : solid

8.   Tar is to _____ as coal is to _____ .

        a.   roofing : shovel
        b.   derived : heating
        c.   construction : heating
        d.   black : heating

9.   Fur is to bear as _____ is to _____ .

        a.   coat : man
        b.   warmth : animal
        c.   rug : floor
        d.   wool : sheep

10.   _____ is to cave as car is to _____ .

        a.   stone : steel
        b.   primitive : modern
        c.   apartment house : horse
        d.   modern : primitive

11.   Bill Evans is a legal assistant with Sochum & Howe. Mary Parks also is a legal assistant with the firm. Mary has acquired the habit of coming to Bill with questions and problems when they arise. Bill does not mind; he is glad to help. Recently, however, Mary has started to bring her personal problems to Bill as well. He now believes that he may have made a mistake in trying to help Mary with any of her difficulties, professional or personal. Which of the following is the least effective alternative for Bill to choose?

        a.   Invite Mary to a place away from the office and explain that he feels uncomfortable about becoming so involved in her personal life.
        b.   Meet with Mary at the office and explain that he feels uncomfortable about becoming so involved in her personal life.
        c.   Wait until the next time Mary asks him about a personal problem and tell her that he feels uncomfortable about getting involved.
        d.   Wait until the next time Mary asks him about a personal problem and feign puzzlement about what she should do.

12.   Susan Lewis has worked for attorney John Anderson for several years. More and more, Susan finds herself covering for him with clients and others when he fails to return telephone calls. Susan has come to resent being put in this position and wants it to end. What is the best thing for her to do at this point?

a. Visit with other legal assistants in the office about John and get their advice.

b. Visit with John and ask him if there is anything she can do to help him with returning calls more promptly.

c. Look for another job because John is unlikely to change old habits for very long if Mary is there to cover for him.

d. Seek intervention from the senior attorney to whom John reports.

13. Joan's supervising attorney recently undertook a very messy divorce case involving a prominent public official. One of the associate attorneys came into Joan's office while she was working on the file, asked what she was doing, and said, "Hey, let me see that. I bet there are things in there that would curl your hair." Joan's best course of action is:

a. Remind him that all client information is confidential and decline to show him the file.

b. Let him see the file because he is an attorney.

c. Let him see the file only if he insists, but inform her supervising attorney about the incident.

d. Tell him she can't show him the file because she needs it to finish her project, and the supervising attorney wants it back right away.

14. Roland has just been assigned several major projects involving a probate matter and is told that everything must be finished by the end of next week. Roland does not see how he can complete everything by that time, given the deadlines of his other work assignments. Roland should:

a. Determine specifically how much time the new projects will take and then visit with his supervising attorney about either reassigning a portion of them or changing deadlines on his current assignments.

b. Tell the attorney right away that the projects cannot be completed without either reassigning a portion of them or changing deadlines on his current assignments.

c. Check the offices of other legal assistants on his floor to see who is not doing anything important.

d. Be glad his supervising attorney has so much faith in him and do whatever is necessary to complete all projects on time.

15. As part of the investigation in a dog bite case, Karen's supervising attorney asked her to go to the address of the defendant and to take photographs of the dog in question if he happened to be in the yard. The address was in a bad neighborhood. When Karen arrived, she parked across the street; and as she was crossing the street to reach the defendant's yard, a huge dog raced

across the yard in her direction and began jumping ferociously at the chain-link fence. Startled by the dog and fumbling to focus the camera, she then noticed a small, wiry man emerge from the house. The man shouted at her to get off his property (she was on the city street) and began moving in her direction. Karen became completely unnerved, quickly got into her car, and drove away. When she related the incident to the attorney, he was visibly annoyed and said, "Well, if you hadn't given up so easily, you probably could have gotten at least one or two photos before you left." In retrospect, Karen should have:

a.   Remained calm and tried to snap at least one photograph before she left.
b.   Done nothing different.
c.   Described the man as being more threatening than he was.
d.   Returned at a different time to take the photos before giving up.

16.   Bill Jones works for Emily Kinder, a sole practitioner. James Buckley, one of the attorney's best clients, called Bill one afternoon in a state of panic. Mr. Buckley stated that he had to catch a plane to Boston in two hours and needed a trust deed to take with him to complete a real estate transaction there. At the attorney's direction, Bill has prepared a number of trust deeds for Mr. Buckley, who deals extensively in real estate matters all over the country. Bill told Mr. Buckley that Emily was expected to be in court for the rest of the day. The client became extremely agitated and said, "All I want is a simple form, and I need it right now. I can't wait all afternoon. If you don't give it to me, I will see that you are fired the first thing tomorrow morning; and don't think that I won't do it." Which of the following is Bill's best course of action?

a.   Offer to give the client a blank trust deed if the client agrees to absolve Bill of any liability if the attorney would have wanted form changed in any way.
b.   Offer to give the client the bailiff's telephone number at the courthouse so that he can contact Emily himself.
c.   Offer to call the bailiff to ask her to send a message in to Emily to contact the office right away.
d.   Offer to prepare the deed, have it approved by Emily when she returns, and fax it to Boston first thing in the morning.

17.   Everyone who is patriotic will vote in the presidential election. Ruth is patriotic. If both of these statements is true, it is correct to conclude that:

a. Ruth will vote in the presidential election.
b. Ruth may vote in the presidential election.
c. Ruth will not vote in the presidential election.
d. No conclusions can be made.

18. If a person uses a weapon during the commission of a crime, then he or she must be given an additional penalty. Raymond used a gun during the commission of a crime. Therefore:

a. Raymond must receive an additional penalty.
b. Raymond should receive an additional penalty.
c. Raymond should not receive an additional penalty.
d. Raymond will not receive an additional penalty.

19. A statute requires that a special meeting of shareholders cannot be held without three days' notice. If a notice of special meeting is mailed to all shareholders on Monday, November 30, the meeting should not be scheduled before:

a. December 2
b. December 3
c. December 4
d. December 5

20. Everyone who cares about workers will support the fair wage bill pending before the legislature. Senator Anderson supports the fair wage bill. If both of these statements is true, which the following conclusions is most correct?

a. Senator Anderson cares about workers.
b. Senator Anderson may or may not care about workers.
c. Senator Anderson does not care about workers.
d. The fair wage bill likely will be adopted.

21. Some snakes are amphibians. Some amphibians are intelligent. Some intelligent creatures are not snakes. Based upon these propositions, which of the following could be true?

a. No amphibians are intelligent.
b. Some snakes are intelligent.
c. No intelligent creatures are amphibians.
d. All amphibians are snakes.
e. All snakes are intelligent.

Read the following passage and answer the questions that follow it:
Ruth stopped at the supermarket one evening after work. Because she planned to be in the store only briefly, she hid the keys to the car under the sun visor. Matthew saw her do this. He waited until she was out of sight; then he started the car and drove away. Matthew was headed down Main Street at forty-five miles an hour, fifteen miles an hour faster than the posted speed limit for that road. As he approached the intersection of Poplar and Main, the light turned yellow. Matthew knew he would not be able to stop, so he accelerated in an attempt to drive through the intersection before the light changed. He was not successful. The side of the car driven by Matthew was struck by another car driven by Dehlia. Dehlia saw Matthew's car but was unable to stop in time because she had been drinking heavily. Had Dehlia been sober, she could have avoided the accident. Dehlia was killed.

22. A lawsuit by Dehlia's surviving relatives against Matthew is decided for Matthew on the following principle: *No damages may be awarded for injuries sustained as the result of the careless conduct of one person if the injured party, through his or her own carelessness, contributed to the accident.* Which of the following was the major factor in the court's disposition of the case?

    a.   Dehlia had the right of way when she entered the intersection.
    b.   Matthew had been driving substantially faster than the speed limit.
    c.   Dehlia was driving while under the influence of alcohol.
    d.   Matthew had attempted to beat the red light.

23. A lawsuit by Dehlia's surviving relatives is decided against Matthew on the following principle: *Conduct is careless per se and gives rise to damages without regard to the contributory carelessness of the injured party if the person causing the injury was violating a law passed to protect the injured party from the injury sustained.* Which of the following was the major factor in the court's disposition of the case?

    a.   Laws against car theft are passed to protect the property of the owner from theft, not to protect third parties from injuries in traffic accidents.
    b.   Matthew was violating the law against stealing cars at the time of the accident.
    c.   At the time of the accident, Matthew was violating the posted speed limit.
    d.   The accident could have been avoided if Dehlia had not been intoxicated.

24. A suit by Dehlia's relatives against Ruth is decided against Ruth on the following principle: *One who fails to take proper precautions to ensure that his automobile is not stolen is liable for any injuries that result if the automobile is stolen.* Which of the following was the major factor in the court's disposition of the case?

    a.   Ruth had left her keys in the car where they could be found easily.

    b.   Ruth planned to be in the store only for a brief time.

    c.   The accident was due primarily to Matthew's carelessness.

    d.   There was a one-in-a-million chance that someone would see Ruth put the keys under the visor.

25. In a criminal trial for murder, Matthew is found guilty on the following principle: *One who kills another during the course of commission of a crime classified as a felony is guilty of murder without regard to the usual elements of the crime.* Which of the following was the major factor in the court's disposition of the case?

    a.   Dehlia would not have been killed if Matthew had not been driving faster than the speed limit.

    b.   Dehlia was killed while Matthew was driving a stolen car.

    c.   If Matthew had not stolen the car, he would not have been in the area at the time of the accident.

    d.   Matthew did not intend to kill Dehlia.

26. A Supreme Court Justice once observed: "We are not the last word because we are infallible; we are infallible because we are the last word." Which of the following most closely parallels the logic of this statement?

    a.   Congressman: "Although I may make some mistakes, I always will use my best judgment to protect the interests of my constituents."

    b.   Doctor: "Doctors can ill afford to make errors when human lives are at stake, because they are the judges of life and death in our society."

    c.   Teacher: "I am the highest authority in the classroom because I am the teacher, not because I always know the right answer."

    d.   Lawyer: "I cannot assure my client of victory, because I cannot predict with certainty what it is that any court may do at any time."

27.   Democracy is the great leveler. The sentiment expressed in this statement is most closely paralleled by which of the following?

    a.   Birds of a feather flock together.
    b.   A bird in the hand is worth two in the bush.
    c.   The grazing herd eats the choicest stalks first.
    d.   Mediocrity tends toward gregariousness.

28.   An old man walked into a police station and confessed to having just killed his wife. The desk sergeant excused himself and left the room. When he returned, he explained to the old man: "We have no record of your wife's ever having been born. So, if she has not been born yet, she could not have died yet. Therefore, you have committed no crime." Which of the following best embodies the sergeant's way of thinking?

    a.   My mind is made up; don't confuse me with the facts.
    b.   Don't believe everything you read.
    c.   If it's not official, it doesn't exist.
    d.   The quality of mercy is not strained.
    e.   If all else fails, read the directions.

29.   Socrates: Is it raining?
Plato: Yes.
Socrates: Is that true?
Plato: No.
Which of the following best describes Plato's responses?

    a.   If his first response is true, then so is his second.
    b.   If his second response is true, then so is his first.
    c.   Plato knows very little about weather.
    d.   If his first response is false, then his second must be true.
    e.   If his first response if false, then his second must be false.

30.   No green products are manufactured in Orange County. All green products are made of plastic. All plastic products are fabricated in Orange County. If each of these statements is true, which of the following must be false?

    a.   John is pleased with his new plastic socks.
    b.   Margaret does not like John's plastic sink made in Orange County.
    c.   Raymond is delighted by his new green socks from Orange County.
    d.   Emily adores her Orange County plastic tub.
    e.   Morgan does not use his Orange County plastic table service.

31. Every taxicab that I have seen in Chicago is painted yellow; therefore, there must be a law that says cabs must be yellow. The logic of this statement is most similar to the logic contained in which of the following statements?

   a. Every time I have dropped a rock, it has fallen to the ground; therefore, there must be a law of gravity.
   b. Every dog I have seen in New York is on a leash; therefore, there must be a law that requires dogs to be on leashes.
   c. There is a law that requires all children under age 16 to be in school, which explains why I see no children on the street during school hours.
   d. Every drunk I have seen in New York has been micturating in the subway; therefore, there must be no law against it.
   e. Ever time I pass over the toll bridge, I pay the toll; therefore, there must ba a law requiring it.

32. Alice: All lawyers are shysters.
   Barry: That is not true. I know some doctors who would steal from their mothers.
   Barry's response shows that he understood Alice to mean:

   a. all lawyers are dishonest.
   b. some lawyers are dishonest.
   c. only lawyers are dishonest.
   d. lawyers generally are more dishonest than doctors.
   e. lawyers are more dishonest than any other profession.

33. Which is the most logical sequence of the following statements?

   I. Under such a view, there is but one alternative to majority rule: minority rule.
   II. As the great statesman Fromte once observed: "Democracy is not a very good form of government, but it is the best we have."
   III. Ultimately, democracy rests upon the simple proposition that every person has an equal right to make choices and that no single choice is right for all.
   IV. The danger of minority rule is obvious; for if humans are capable of incorrect choices, is not that danger magnified if the choice is that of the few?
   V. If everyone has an equal right to choose, then majority rule is the only way to take account of conflicting choices.

a. I, V, II, III, IV
b. V, I, IV, II, III
c. III, I, V, II, IV
d. III, I, V, IV, II
e. III, V, I, IV, II

Read this passage and answer the questions that follow it:
Ben was stopped on the street by a man in dark glasses. The man offered to sell Ben an Apex watch, which normally sells for $750, for only $50. Ben agreed and gave the man $50. Later that day, Ben learned that the watch was an Ampax, which normally retails for $19.95.

34. Which of the following is not an appropriate criticism of Ben's action?

a. You must look before you leap.
b. A fool and his money are soon parted.

c. There is a sucker born every minute.
d. The man who wants something for nothing is an easy mark.
e. Nothing ventured, nothing gained.

35. Which of the following could Ben best use in an effort to justify his action?

a. You cannot judge a book by its cover.
b. You must strike while the iron is hot.
c. Beware of Greeks bearing gifts.
d. A bird in the hand is worth two in the bush.
e. The guilty fleeth when no man pursueth.

36. Isn't it true that you and your wife had a bitter argument just before she was killed? The form and emphasis of this question is most closely paralleled by which of the following?

a. Did you leave the theater just before the fire broke out?
b. Were you aware that he had been siphoning funds for his own use?
c. Did you not, in fact, recognize the robber as your own brother?
d. Was your husband aware of the fact that you had decided to leave him?
e. Was your wife aware of the fact that you had decided to leave her?

37. Some of the cars driven in the city are equipped with anti-pollution devices. None of the cars driven outside the city are equipped with anti-pollution

devices. No car can be driven both in the city and outside the city. If each of these statements is true, which of the following conclusions must be true?

a. All cars driven in the city are equipped with anti-pollution devices.
b. Some anti-pollution devices may be found on cars driven outside of the city.
c. No car driven in the city lacks an anti-pollution device.
d. A car that is not driven outside the city does not have an anti-pollution device.
e. A car equipped with an anti-pollution device can be driven only inside the city.

Read this passage and answer the questions that follow it:
Alcohol has been labeled by safety experts as the number one medical factor in traffic accidents. A national medical panel funded by a government grant over the past two years finds alcohol to be a significant factor in a majority of personal injury cases related to driving. The panel recommended a sharp reduction in the amount of drinking tolerated in many states where a blood-alcohol blood level of .15 percent must be reached to be accepted as evidence of intoxication while driving. The panel reported that blood levels of .05 percent alcohol constitute medical impairment of a person's driving ability, and blood levels of .10 alcohol indicate intoxication. Doctors on the panel declined to interpret these findings in terms of how many drinks a person could consume before exceeding these different blood-alcohol levels. They said there are too many variables, including the weight of the drinker, the length of time over which the alcohol is consumed, and the potency of each drink consumed.

38. Of the following statements concerning the preceding passage, which is most correct?

a. Football players generally can tolerate more alcohol than marathon runners can tolerate.
b. Doctors say it is not alcohol but the weight of the drinker and other such variables that determine whether a person should drive after drinking.
c. A short, thin person will reach a .15 blood-alcohol level faster than will a tall, heavy person.
d. Thin people are less likely to be affected by alcohol consumption.

39. Of the following statements concerning the preceding passage, which is least correct?

a. Alcohol is a significant factor in traffic-related injuries.
b. A .15 blood-alcohol level is legal intoxication in most states.
c. Tolerable blood-alcohol levels vary from individual to individual.
d. Doctors believe that blood-alcohol levels above .10 should not be tolerated.

40. Based upon the preceding passage, which of the following conclusions is most valid?

a. Doctors will not be happy until all states adopt a .05 blood-alcohol level as evidence of intoxication for purposes of driving.
b. The findings of the panel are suspect, because the panel was funded by a government grant.
c. Laws should be adopted to prohibit drivers from drinking.
d. Alcohol is the most significant factor in accidents on streets and highways.

Allow 40 minutes to answer the following essay question. Follow the directions in the memorandum, analyzing the facts presented and using your judgment skills. Do not rely on any other authority or on your knowledge of the law. Use only the material presented with the question. Your answer should be in the form of a memorandum to the attorney, which will include the following: Facts, Issue(s), Discussion, and Conclusion. The memorandum must be well organized and concise.

At the end of 40 minutes, check your essay answer against the sample found at the end of the Answer Key Section of this Review Manual. Allocate ten points to style and ten points to content (20 total points), deducting a proportionate number of points for each error or omission. Add the score on the essay question to the score on the objective questions to determine the overall score for the Judgment Self-Test.

<u>Memorandum</u>

TO: Stanley Dorite, Legal Assistant

FROM: Wilma Wonka, Staff Attorney

DATE:

RE: Stewart Carr Disciplinary Proceeding

Stewart Carr is a sole practitioner and a long-time attorney in this city. One of this firm's senior partners, Edwin Tuttle, has been asked to work with the Counsel for Discipline of the Utopia State Bar Association as a special prosecutor in a matter regarding Mr. Carr. Mr. Tuttle promised the Counsel for Discipline that we would take a look at the case.

One of Carr's clients purchased a toy chest at an estate sale. Several years later, she found six series E United States savings bonds in the chest. The bonds had been issued to Hans and Louis Brinker as joint tenants. The client employed Carr to find the owners and to obtain a reward or a finder's fee. The client told Carr that she wanted a reward of one-third but would take less. She said that if she did not get a reward, she would light her fireplace with the bonds.

In December of last year, Carr located Dick Brinker, a grandson of the original owners, both of whom were deceased. Carr told Brinker that his client wanted a reward of one-third and would kindle her fireplace with the bonds if she did not get a reward. Brinker contacted Earl Ludlow, a lawyer practicing in a nearby city. After negotiations between Carr and Ludlow, Dick Brinker agreed to pay a finder's fee to the client.

Approximately one month later, Dick Brinker contacted another attorney, Steve Guenzel, and requested a second opinion about the arrangement made by Ludlow. Guenzel called Carr and, among other things, discussed Utopia Stat. § 35-514 with him. That statute provides:

> A person who comes into control of property of another that he knows to have been lost or mislaid commits theft if, with intent to deprive the owner thereof, he fails to take reasonable measures to restore the property to a person entitled to have it. Any person violating the

provisions of this section shall, upon conviction thereof, be punished by the penalty prescribed in the next lower classification below the value of the item lost or mislaid pursuant to section 38-518.

Carr responded to this discussion by repeating his demand for a reward; attorney Ludlow withdrew from the case.

Guenzel subsequently called Carr and retracted the Brinker's previous agreement.

Gladys Watson, Dick Brinker's sister, upon learning of the bonds' existence, filed a complaint against Carr with the Counsel for Discipline of the Utopia State Bar Association. Later, a police officer suggested to Watson that she call Carr and record the conversation.

Watson took the officer's advice and recorded the conversation. Instead of Stewart Carr, however, she spoke with Carr's legal assistant, Jack Fehrman. Fehrman related that Mr. Carr was out of the office, that they were no longer involved with the Brinker bonds, and that they had closed their file on the matter. Rather than discontinuing the conversation, however, Fehrman continued to talk to Watson. During that conversation, Fehrman said, "So, our client would rather light her fireplace with them if she doesn't get some money out of this . . . and if she decided to light her fireplace with it, I'm gonna applaud her. You people are so greedy that nobody wants to pay her anything."

The entire matter, including the recorded telephone conversation, has been referred to the Counsel for Discipline and is now the subject of a pending hearing before the Committee on Inquiry. Carr is being charged with violating Canon 7-102(A)(7), which states, "A lawyer must avoid the appearance of impropriety."

Upon his admission that he had the telephone conversation with Watson, Fehrman was fired by Carr. Carr believes he should not be held responsible for Fehrman's statements, which were made without his knowledge or consent.

Please prepare a memorandum which summarizes and discusses the relevant issues in this case in light of existing statutes, ethics rules, and case law. Then let's discuss the course of action that I will recommend to Mr. Tuttle.

Selected Case Law

STATE OF UTOPIA EX REL. UTOPIA STATE BAR ASSOCIATION,
RELATOR, v. ALEX M. KRIST
232 Utop. 445

Filed June 9, 1989   No. 87-546

Original action. Judgment of Disbarment.

The facts are that on or about April 30, 1986, the Counsel for Discipline received a written letter of complaint against the respondent by Mrs. Roy Butternut concerning respondent's handling of a bankruptcy matter. On May 1, 1986, the respondent received notice that he was the subject of a complaint made to the Counsel for Discipline, with an attached copy of Mrs. Butternut's complaint. He was further notified that he had fifteen (15) working days to respond. The letter from the Counsel for Discipline went on to state that if respondent failed to respond, "the Rules provide that this failure alone shall be grounds for discipline."

On or about February 21, 1986, the Counsel for Discipline received a written letter of complaint against the respondent by Ms. Judy Scriven on behalf of Scriven, Quill, and Scriven, a free-lance court reporting firm, asking for "help and/or advice" in collecting several accounts receivable. The Counsel for Discipline forwarded the complaint to respondent and stated, "In my opinion, [Scriven's] letter does not set forth sufficient facts to file a complaint against you. I would appreciate, however, a written response from you addressing the issues raised." On April 24, 1986, May 20, 1986, and June 11, 1986, the Counsel for Discipline again notified the respondent by letter that he was the subject of a complaint by Ms. Scriven and requested an immediate response.

In his first amended answer to formal charges, respondent affirmatively alleged that he had timely responded to any notices of complaints he received from and after February 21, 1986, and stated:

> 6.   For further defense, Respondent denies that violation of a duly imposed procedural rule of this Court states facts sufficient to constitute a cause of action for violation of a substantive Disciplinary Rule of the Canons of Ethics as adopted by the Court.

> 7.   For further defense, Respondent alleges that the Committee on Inquiry found that the failure to pay a disputed deposition bill did not form the basis of a substantive complaint against a member.

> 8. That such substantive complaint should have been dismissed if received by the Counsel on Discipline since such conduct, if true, has never been understood to form the basis of a disciplinary violation.

Respondent testified as to his personal problems, overwork, and extensive travel in 1986 and that he was not in his office on a daily basis commencing in May or June of that year. He became aware that his secretary, Ruth Johnson, often neglected to do the work he gave her and did not perform her duties while he was out of town, but he did not fire her because he did not want to train another secretary. Respondent also testified that Johnson took some of his files from the office while he was out of town after she had difficulty cashing one of her paychecks. Respondent testified that after Johnson quit in August 1986, a new secretary discovered a bundle of documents belonging to respondent, including his responses to the Butternut and Scriven complaints.

At the hearing before the referee, Betsy Boop, an attorney who shared an office with respondent, testified as to Johnson's general incompetence. Boop stated that she would not allow Johnson to do work for her. She also testified that after the new secretary was hired, they discovered old mail and notes which had been placed between two books on a table. Boop did not read the mail but noted that many of the items belonged to Krist.

Respondent was required to respond to the complaints pursuant to Utop. Ct. R. of Discipline 9(E) (rev. 1986). A reasonable attorney would understand that the type of conduct is prohibited and adversely reflects on his fitness to practice law. The record supports a finding that respondent violated the canons of ethics in this respect.

We note that respondent was not charged with failure to provide management, supervision, and control of his office staff and procedures. Respondent's own testimony suggested, however, that his failure to respond to the Butternut and Scriven complaints is the fault of his secretary, whom he knew to be incompetent.

Even though we conclude that the referee's finding that respondent violated the Canons of Ethics by failing to provide management, supervision, and control of his office staff and procedures was in error, respondent's reliance on his secretary's alleged incompetence as a defense is entirely misplaced. While respondent's failure to properly supervise his employee was not charged against the respondent, such conduct does not constitute a defense to the misconduct charged. A lawyer may not avoid responsibility for misconduct by hiding behind an employee's behavior and may not avoid a charge of unprofessional conduct by contending that his employees are incompetent.

The preliminary statement in the Canons of Ethics as adopted by this court states, "A lawyer should ultimately be responsible for the conduct of his employees and associates in the course of the professional representation of the client." "A lawyer also has responsibility to be aware at least of the major areas of responsibility and the actual work habits of employees and to exercise effective supervision." C. Wolfram on Modern Legal Ethics § 16.3.1 at 893 (West 1986).

In *State ex rel. USBA v. Statmore*, 218 Utop. 138, 356 E.W.2d 875 (1984), we said: "A lawyer's poor accounting procedures and sloppy office management are not excuses or mitigating circumstances in reference to commingled funds. (Citations omitted.) Similarly, "[a]n attorney may not escape responsibility to his clients by blithely saying that any shortcomings are solely the fault of his employee. He has a duty to supervise the conduct of his office." *Attorney Grievance Comm'n v. Goldberg*, 292 Md. 650, 441 A.2d 338 (1982). We hold that a lawyer is ultimately responsible for the conduct of his employees and associates in the course of the professional representation of the client.

Respondent's testimony shows only that his failure to supervise his employee directly contributed to his failure to timely respond to the Butternut and Scriven complaints. He may not use his secretary's alleged incompetence to shield him from the consequences of his unprofessional conduct.

The record clearly demonstrates that respondent has violated his oath of office and the disciplinary rules cited by the referee. We have no confidence that a public reprimand, or even a suspension, would serve to modify respondent's attitude or to protect the public. We recognize that disbarment is a harsh penalty. We conclude that in the circumstances of this case, a judgment of disbarment is appropriate.

JUDGMENT OF DISBARMENT.

Chapter 5
LEGAL RESEARCH

Every accomplishment starts with the decision to try.

—Anonymous

The legal assistant must be able to use the most important tool of the legal profession—the law library. The purpose of the Legal Research section of the CLA® Certifying Examination is to test the applicant's knowledge of the use of state and federal codes, statutes, digests, case reports, various legal encyclopedias, Shepardizing, and research procedures.

The amount of study and practice that an applicant will need to pass this section of the examination will depend on his or her current knowledge and experience with legal research. One can gain excellent practice by researching various topics on one's own.

The Objective of Legal Research

The objective of legal research is to find specific authorities (legal rules) that govern a specific factual issue. Like a seasoned traveler, the experienced researcher knows his or her ultimate destination and the quickest, simplest route to reach it. If a driver wanted to go to Timbuktu, Texas, she would not get into the car and simply start driving. Instead, she would use a map to plan the best route. That route likely would include some combination of federal or interstate expressways; state highways; and local streets or roads.

Similarly, to locate the specific legal authorities that govern a specific factual issue, one must plan ahead to determine:

- The type of system in which the factual issue arises (whether federal, state, or local);

- The type of substantive law involved (whether constitutional, statutory [civil or criminal], administrative, or case law [judicial decisions]); and

- The type of procedural law (which combination of statutes, rules of procedure [civil, criminal, or administrative], rules of evidence, and court rules) that must be followed to accomplish the desired result.

Until the researcher has determined which legal system and which type(s) of law may apply to a known set of facts, no legal research can be done.

The two major types of legal authorities are (1) those which are ***primary*** (mandatory) and (2) those which are ***secondary*** (persuasive).

Sources of Primary Law

Within the context of legal research, all legal authorities are categorized by system and type. Primary law includes—listed in the order of its general rank—constitutions, statutes, case law, rules of procedure, rules of evidence, administrative rules, court rules, executive orders, and so forth.

Primary law is ***mandatory***, which refers to amount of weight that it must be given in the decision-making process. Primary law carries the most weight; it must be followed within the legal system to which it applies. Whether federal, state, or local, each legal system has its own primary laws.

<u>**Types of Legal Systems**</u>   Ours is a nation of many legal systems. In addition to the federal system, there are fifty state systems and an indeterminate number of local systems. *(See the chapter on General Law for a more complete review of the summaries provided here.)*

Each system has its own areas of exclusive authority (jurisdiction) within its geographic boundary lines. For example, the federal government has exclusive authority to regulate interstate commerce; each state government has exclusive authority to regulate marriage and divorce, probate of estates, and intrastate commerce; and each local government has exclusive authority to regulate traffic laws within its boundaries.

In addition, areas of concurrent jurisdiction can and do exist. For example, both federal and state laws have been adopted to prohibit certain types of employment discrimination. Federal and state courts have equal authority to hear and to decide employment discrimination cases.

Each legal system (whether federal or state) is separated into a legislative, an executive, and a judicial branch *(separation of powers)*. Within each system, the legislative branch authorizes certain administrative agencies to exist and delegates limited powers to them. For these specified, limited areas only, agencies can adopt rules and regulations (quasi-legislative power) and can render decisions (quasi-judicial power).

The primary laws of each legal system are categorized according to their type, often determined by the branch of government from which they are issued. Then they are recorded and published so that citizens have notice of what the rules are. Legal research is the process of finding these rules.

Sometimes the rules are published by the issuing legislature, court, or agency; these are official publications. In addition, private companies often publish their own collections of statutes and case law that include additional aids and features to assist the legal researcher. The primary legal publishers in the United States are West Publishing Company and Lawyers Cooperative Publishing Company (formerly Bancroft-Whitney Publishing Company).

Types of Law (Substantive)   Substantive law establishes and defines the basic rights and duties that govern a society. Within the American legal system, it consists of constitutions, legislative enactments, common law (judicial decisions), and certain executive actions.

A.   Constitutional Law   A constitution exists for the federal system, as well as for each state system. A constitution embodies the government's authority to exist and serves as an outline for the exercise of governmental powers. At the local level, this authorizing document is called a charter. Within any legal system, constitutional rules carry the most weight and always will prevail when they conflict with other rules issued within that system.

B.   Statutory Law   A legislative enactment is called a *statute* at the federal and state levels; an *ordinance* at the local level. Statutes do not carry as much weight as a constitutional provision, but they carry more weight than an administrative rule or a prior judicial opinion.   Administrative rules and regulations adopted in the proper exercise of an administrative agency's quasi-legislative power carry slightly less weight than a statute or an ordinance but are given more weight in its limited area of expertise than a prior judicial decision on the same subject.

C.   Common Law   When identifying the categories of primary law, the term *common law* is used in its most narrow sense to mean case law or judicial opinions (as opposed to statutory law or constitutional law). In addition to articulating common law principles, judicial opinions are used to explain and to clarify existing constitutional and statutory law.   This is called judicial interpretation. Common law carries less weight than statutory law as a general principle; however, a particular judicial opinion can overrule a specific statute on constitutional grounds.

Case law (judicial opinions) articulates common law principles as they evolve. In this sense, the term *common law* has a much more expansive meaning based upon the way in which case law is used under the doctrine of stare decisis. ***Stare decisis*** is the process used to synthesize legal principles from all prior cases with similar facts and similar issues of law (called precedent) to arrive at a decision in a specific case. When a court has formulated a principle of law in a case, it then follows that principle by applying it to future cases where the facts and the legal issues are substantially the same.

A prior case is ***precedent*** within a particular jurisdiction if (1) its facts and legal issues were substantially similar to the facts of the case before the court, sometimes called the *instant case*; (2) it was decided by majority decision of a higher court of that jurisdiction; and (3) the case was reported (published). Thus, a case published by a particular federal court of appeals is precedent for all federal trial courts of that circuit. It is not precedent, however, for other federal courts of appeals. A case published by the United States Supreme Court is precedent for all state and federal courts. Although *stare decisis* and *precedent* have different technical meanings, the two terms frequently are used as if they were synonymous.

In exercising its quasi-judicial powers to decide whether its rules and regulations have been violated and the sanctions to be imposed for the violation, an administrative agency may decide administrative cases and publish administrative decisions affecting the party (or parties) brought before it. These decisions are precedent within that particular agency but have no precedential value outside the agency.

D.   Executive Action   Some types of executive action taken by the President (or by the governor of a state) have the force of law. Typical among these are:

> 1.   An *executive order* issued by the President under special authority granted by Congress. An executive order might direct the Justice Department to place emphasis on the enforcement of specific civil rights laws. An executive order is different from a Presidential Proclamation, which might be issued by the President to declare "National Legal Assistant's Day" on November 12 of a given year;

> 2.   A *treaty* (agreement made between the United States and one or more of the other sovereign nations of the world); and

> 3.   An *interstate compact* (agreement made by two or more states) concerning such things as disposal of radioactive waste or use of a common waterway.

<u>Types of Law (Procedural)</u>   Procedural law, sometimes called *adjective law*, prescribes the manner in which substantive laws must be enforced. The gist of most procedural rules is to assure parties of a fair and uniform adversary process, culminating in a fair hearing. Procedural rules can vary widely from jurisdiction to jurisdiction and can vary from court to court within a particular jurisdiction.

A.   Federal Procedural Law   Several distinct sets of procedural rules operate within trial courts of the federal jurisdiction. They are:

> 1.   The **Federal Rules of Criminal Procedure** govern the way in which a defendant is charged, tried, and sentenced for a federal crime.

> 2.   The **Federal Rules of Civil Procedure** govern how civil actions are handled, including rules that cover the complaint, summons, answer, discovery process, trial, and post-trial procedures.

> 3.   The **Federal Rules of Appellate Procedure** govern the form and procedure for appeals from the

U.S. District Court to the Court of Appeals within the federal system.

4. The **Federal Rules of Evidence** govern the types of evidence that are admissible in criminal and civil trials and, in some situations, the manner in which the evidence can be presented during trial.

5. **Local Court Rules**   In addition to the sets of procedural rules listed above, which govern all federal trial courts, each court typically adopts its own rules to govern things not covered by other procedural rules, such as management of the trial docket, how hearings are scheduled, and so forth. For example, the Federal Rules of Civil Procedure state that the first pleading to be filed in a case shall be called a complaint. Local court rules cannot change that rule by requiring the first pleading to be called a petition or an application, but a local court rule can require that all complaints be filed in duplicate.

B. **State Procedural Rules**   Many states have adopted procedural rules similar to those used at the federal level. They may be included as part of a state's statutory code or may be included as part of the court rules of a state's supreme court. Local court rules of state courts perform the same function as local court rules of federal courts. They augment—fill the gaps that may have been left by—a state statute or other procedural rule, but they cannot change the statutes or procedural rules adopted by the state.

How Primary Law is Recorded

At both the federal and state levels, primary law is recorded predominantly in constitutions, statutes, administrative rules and regulations, and court cases. The researcher must be familiar with how the recording process works, as well as with the forms that primary law takes as it evolves within that process.

<u>**Constitutions**</u>   Since the federal Constitution is the organizing document of the federal legal system, it does not undergo frequent change. It can be found at the front of the United States Code. An index of its articles and amendments have been included with the index to the United States Code.

Similarly, the constitution of each state generally is included with the state's statutory code and statutory index; a local government's charter may or may not be included with its ordinances.

Statutes   When a statute is adopted by a legislature, it is recorded in different forms at different stages of the legislative process. These differences are important when conducting a legislative history.

A **bill** is a proposed legislative measure. Until it is adopted by the legislature, it is not law. Once the bill is adopted, it becomes a **slip law**, meaning that it is printed singly rather than as a part of a group of laws.

At the close of each legislative session, all slip laws enacted during that session are arranged in chronological order according to date of enactment and are published as **session laws**. Because they are arranged chronologically, session laws can be difficult to use unless the researcher knows the exact date when the statute was adopted, together with the dates of any later modifications that may have been adopted. As a result, statutes generally are **codified** (collected into a statutory code) as well. The code arranges the statutes and their amendments by topic (subject matter). This arrangement makes statutes much easier to find.

A.   Federal   Federal session laws are published in the **Statutes at Large (Stat.)**. They are also codified and published in the **United States Code (U.S.C.)**. Because the codification of federal statutes is selective (not every statute is included), the Statutes at Large is the only complete collection of federal statutory law.

When an official body (Congress in this case) authorizes and directs the collection and publication of law, it is an **official** publication. An **unofficial** publication is one that is not specifically authorized or sanctioned by an official body but, rather, is compiled by a private publisher. Its status as an unofficial publication relates only to the source of the publication and not to its accuracy. Both the Statutes at Large and the United States Code are official publications.

In addition to the official publications for federal statutes, West Publishing Company (West) and Lawyers Cooperative Publishing Company (Lawyers Co-op) offer unofficial publications as well:

United States Code Annotated (U.S.C.A.) published by West; and
United States Code Service (U.S.C.S.) published by Lawyers Co-op.

The advantage of these unofficial publications is that each offers additional resources for the researcher in the form of explanatory notes, cases, and other helpful information relating to each code section.

U.S.C.A., like all West publications, uses the *key number system* to aid the researcher. Every topic and subtopic is assigned its own key number (a number displayed on the head of the familiar West key). The same key numbers are reserved to the same topics throughout all West publications, so that the researcher does not have to search for the topic alphabetically more than once. From that point forward, the researcher can use the key number so long as he or she is using a West publication.

U.S.C.S. contains the same distinguishing feature for which all Lawyers Co-op publications are known: extensive use of annotations. An *annotation* is an explanatory note. It may contain references to cases, but case references usually are more limited than in the West publications; the emphasis of the annotation is the explanatory material.

B.   State and Local   State legislatures typically publish their session laws at the close of each legislative session. In addition, most states either publish a codified version or rely upon a private company to publish the codified version. Some states have both, such as New Jersey Revised Statutes (official) and New Jersey Statutes Annotated (unofficial, published by West).

Local legislatures publish their ordinances, but the form of publication is much less consistent than it is for state statutes. Ordinances of larger cities sometimes are codified in a municipal code, but the practice varies from city to city.

Administrative Rules and Regulations   Within the federal system, the rules and regulations of administrative agencies are published chronologically in the **Federal Register (Fed. Reg.)** at the time of their adoption. In addition, they are codified (arranged by subject matter) in the **Code of Federal Regulations (C.F.R.)**. A complete set of rules and regulations for a particular agency generally can be obtained from the agency as well.

The rules and regulations of state administrative agencies often are codified; however, the rules and regulations of local administrative agencies seldom are codified.

Case Law   From the standpoint of volume alone, case law (sometimes called law reports, common law, court opinions, or court decisions) represents the bulk of recorded primary law. It consists of the opinions of reported cases, usually from appellate courts, of a particular jurisdiction. A reported case is one which is published. Reported cases are collected and published in case reporters, which may be either official or unofficial. Some jurisdictions have both.

Before reviewing specific case reporters, a brief summary of case law terminology is provided, followed by a table showing the elements typically found in a reported case. Even experienced researchers sometimes use the terms *court decision* and *court opinion* as if they were synonymous; they are not:

court decision	the court's ruling or disposition of the case (whether affirmed, reversed, remanded, or dismissed).
court opinion	the court's explanatory comments, which can include the holding, the rationale for the holding, and dicta.

A court's opinion may be one or more of the following types:

majority opinion	opinion issued by the majority of judges of the appellate court; the holding of this opinion may be cited as precedent if all other criteria are met (discussed *supra*). There is only one majority opinion in a case.
concurring opinion	opinion issued by one or more judges of the appellate court which agrees with the result reached by the majority but disagrees with the reasoning of the majority opinion. There can be more than one concurring opinion.
dissenting opinion	opinion issued by one or more judges of the appellate court which disagrees with both the result and the reasoning of the majority opinion. There can be more than one dissenting opinion.
per curiam opinion	opinion of the entire court (all judges who heard the case), as opposed to an opinion written by a specific judge.
en banc	the entire court participates rather than the permissible quorum. This does not mean that the entire court agrees on the outcome, however.
memorandum opinion	a very brief opinion; a cursory opinion; an opinion so abbreviated that it is hardly an opinion at all.

A single opinion may be a memorandum, *per curiam* opinion, reached by a court sitting *en banc*. This describes a very brief opinion written unanimously by the entire appellate court.

The review process used by an appellate court is determined by the form of appeal authorized for a particular type of case. The form of appeal changes according to the amount of deference the appellate court gives to the factual findings determined in the trial court:

de novo	anew, from the beginning; the case is tried in the appellate court as if it had not been tried previously, and witnesses are allowed to testify. The initial appeal from a small claims court to a district court or to a superior court, for instance, might be tried de novo.
de novo on the record	anew on the record; the appellate court must base its decision on the record (no new testimony can be received) but may reach an independent factual finding if the facts from the trial court are "clearly erroneous" based on the record as a whole. Appellate courts never defer to trial courts concerning issues of law.
on the record	the appellate court reviews the record for prejudicial legal errors committed in the trial court but gives great deference to the findings of fact; factual findings generally are reversed only when they are "arbitrary or capricious" (little or no factual basis). Appellate courts never defer to trial courts concerning issues of law. Appeals from administrative decisions are typical among those appealed on the record.

The *record* consists of the pleadings from the court file of the trial court (together with any motions or orders that may be part of the errors claimed on appeal) and the recorded transcript of the trial proceedings, including the exhibits offered during trial.

Elements of a Reported Case

CAPTION	Identifies the court issuing the opinion, the parties, and the docket number assigned to the case.
DATE OF DECISION	The date upon which the decision was rendered.
PARALLEL CITATION(S)	If the same case is published in another case reporter, the volume and page number of that reporter is shown.
HEADNOTE or SYLLABUS	Brief summary of a legal rule discussed in the opinion; headnotes are numbered. Key numbers are used in West publications.
STATEMENT OF FACTS	Brief summary of facts of case, including its procedural posture.
OPINION	Court's explanation; includes the holding, rationale, and dicta.
HOLDING	Rule of law for which the case is cited as precedent; it is the legal effect of the facts of the case.
RATIONALE	*Ratio decidendi*—court's reasoning or basis for its holding and decision.

DICTA

Obiter dictum—comments of the court about minor issues or concerns other than the specific holding, rationale, and decision. Dicta is never cited as precedent.

DECISION

Result or disposition of the case.

Federal Case Reporters   Within the federal system, cases are reported from the U.S. Supreme Court, the U.S. Courts of Appeals, and the U.S. District Courts.

When a federal court first decides a case, a ***slip opinion*** is issued. This is a single opinion of the court issued without headnotes and without indexing. Periodically, the slip opinions are collected and published in a softbound or looseleaf format called ***advance sheets*** (in advance of the next bound volume of the case reporter series). The page numbering used in advance sheets generally is the same as the page numbering that will appear in the case reporter volume when it is published in bound form.

In addition to the texts of reported cases, each case reporter volume usually includes a table of the cases contained in the volume, a table of statutes interpreted by the cases contained in that volume, a subject index or digest of the reported cases, and judicial definition of words and phrases used in the reported cases. Within a particular case reporter series, separate volumes may be devoted to the tables of cases, descriptive word index, or words and phrases contained in the entire reporter series or set.

Case reporters may cover a specific jurisdiction (United States Supreme Court), a specific geographical area (Arizona), or a specific subject (Bankruptcy Reporter). Cases within a particular reporter are arranged chronologically by the date of decision.

A.   United States Supreme Court   While the Court is in session, slip opinions are issued as cases are decided. These are collected periodically and published in two different sets of advance sheets: **United States Law Week (U.S.L.W.)** published by the Bureau of National Affairs and the **United States Supreme Court Bulletin** published by Commerce Clearing House. There are three case reporters for U.S. Supreme Court cases:

1. United States Reports, *cited* U.S.
2. Supreme Court Reporter, *cited* S. Ct.
3. United States Supreme Court Reports, Lawyers' Edition, *cited* L. Ed. or L. Ed. 2d

United States Reports is the official case reporter for the U.S. Supreme Court. The first ninety volumes of United States Reports originally were compiled by seven successive, private reporters (Dallas, Cranch, Wheaton, Peters, Howard, Black, and Wallace), which were cited, for example, 1 Dall. 233. The Court began using official reporters and its current numbering system in 1817. The original ninety volumes were reprinted later; but because the pagination was different in the reprinted versions, *star paging* was used to show where each new page number began in the original volume. Star paging is a star, asterisk, or insertion in the text of the opinion, followed by the page number.

Supreme Court Reporter is an unofficial case reporter, published by West. It does not contain decisions prior to 1882 but does contain star paging (*see example below*) to the official reporter, U.S. Reports. This allows a researcher to cite to the precise page of U.S. Reports even if he does not have access to U.S. Reports. Since it is a West publication, the Supreme Court Reporter incorporates the key numbering system.

It is undisputed that this contract falls within the coverage of the FAA, since it involves interstate commerce. The FAA contains no provision authorizing a stay of arbitration in the situation. Appellee, contends, however,	that §§ 3 and 4 of the FAA, which are the specific sections ⌐477 claimed to conflict with the California statute at issue here, are not applicable to this state-court proceeding and thus cannot be dispositive of the outcome of

—Reprinted by permission from SUPREME COURT REPORTER © by West Publishing Company. All rights reserved.

Supreme Court Reporter Lawyers Edition, another unofficial case reporter, is published by Lawyers Co-op. It likewise contains star paging to U.S. Reports. In addition, it includes a summary of each case (located before the headnotes). It is the only Supreme Court case reporter to include summaries of the briefs of counsel. Annotations, the distinctive feature of all Lawyers Co-op publications, are included for all cases beginning with volume 92 of the Lawyers Edition and for all cases in the Lawyers Edition Second Series.

B.   United States Courts of Appeals   The only case reporter for the federal courts of appeals (formerly circuit courts of appeals) is unofficial and is published by West. There is no official case reporter for these courts.

Federal Reporter, Third Series, *cited* F.3d	(1993 - present)
Federal Reporter, Second Series, *cited* F.2d	(1924 - 1993)
Federal Reporter, *cited* F.	(1880 - 1924)
Federal Cases, *cited* F. Cas.	(1789 - 1880)

C.   United States District Courts   Like the federal courts of appeals, the only case reporter for the federal district courts is unofficial and is published by West. There is no official case reporter. Reporting for federal trial courts is selective; not all cases are included.

Federal Supplement, *cited* F. Supp.   (1932 - present)
Federal Reporter, Second Series, *cited* F.2d   (1924 - 1932)
Federal Reporter, *cited* F.   (1880 - 1924)
Federal Cases, *cited* F. Cas.   (1789 - 1880)

Cases decided by the U.S. Court of International Trade (formerly U.S. Customs Court) are also reported selectively in the Federal Supplement.

D.   Federal Specialty Courts and Case Law   Areas of specialized federal law may be collected and reported in separate case reporters. For instance, cases related to federal rules of civil and criminal procedure are collected in the case reporter series called **Federal Rules Decisions**, *cited* F.R.D. Decisions of federal bankruptcy courts from 1979 forward are reported in the **Bankruptcy Reporter**, *cited* B.R.

Some federal specialty courts, such as the Tax Court, the Claims Court (formerly Court of Claims), and the Court of Military Appeals, publish their own opinions. The Court of International Trade was created in 1980 (formerly U. S. Customs Court) and has published its own decisions since that time; its decisions continue to be published selectively in the Federal Supplement.

A complete list of federal specialty courts and their case reporters can be found in the ***Uniform System of Citation*** (USOC), which is published by the Harvard Law Review Association, Gannett House, 1511 Massachusetts Avenue, Cambridge, MA 02138.

<u>**State Case Reporters**</u>   At the state level, cases are reported for a state's highest appellate court and intermediate appellate courts only. The exceptions are New York and California, which report lower court cases as well.

Like federal case reporters, state case reporters are preceded by slip opinions and then advance sheets. The page numbers of the advance sheets correspond to the page numbers that will appear in the bound volume of the case reporter.

A particular state may or may not publish an official case reporter; many states have abandoned the publication of an official reporter in favor of the unofficial reporter available through the National Reporter System.

The **National Reporter System** is the product of West Publishing Company. In addition to its federal case reporters *(see above)*, it divides the United States into seven geographical regions and reports the decisions of the highest appellate court of each state within that region. Some intermediate appellate court decisions are also reported. Because of the regional divisions, case reporters sometimes are referred to as **regional reporters**.

Atlantic Reporter, *cited* A. or A.2d	Connecticut, Delaware, District of Columbia (Court of Appeals), Maine, Maryland, New Hampshire, New Jersey, Pennsylvania, Rhode Island, and Vermont
North Eastern Reporter, *cited* N.E. or N.E.2d	Illinois, Indiana, Massachusetts, New York, and Ohio
North Western Reporter, *cited* N.W. or N.W.2d	Iowa, Michigan, Minnesota, Nebraska, North Dakota, South Dakota, and Wisconsin
Pacific Reporter, *cited* P. or P.2d	Alaska, Arizona, California, Colorado, Hawaii, Idaho, Kansas, Montana, Nevada, New Mexico, Oklahoma, Oregon, Utah, Washington, and Wyoming
South Eastern Reporter, *cited* S.E. or S.E.2d	Georgia, North Carolina, South Carolina, Virginia, and West Virginia
South Western Reporter, *cited* S.W. or S.W.2d	Arkansas, Kentucky, Missouri, Tennessee, Texas, and Indian Territories
Southern Reporter, *cited* So. or So.2d	Alabama, Florida, Louisiana, and Mississippi

Sources of Secondary Law

Secondary law consists of legal authorities which are persuasive but are not mandatory (binding) within a particular jurisdiction. Secondary law carries less weight than primary law but may be used effectively, depending upon its source, when primary law is not available or when a change in existing primary law is sought.

Law from other Jurisdictions

When an issue has not been decided previously within a particular jurisdiction (a case of first impression), case law from other jurisdictions may persuade or influence the court in reaching its decision. When one of the litigants seeks a change in existing law, case law from other jurisdictions may persuade a court to make the requested change.

Generally speaking, case law from neighboring jurisdictions is more persuasive to a court than is case law from distant jurisdictions.

Legal Encyclopedias   Legal encyclopedias are arranged alphabetically by subject matter and contain narrative, expository information on a variety of legal topics. They provide extensive background material in areas unfamiliar to the researcher, with footnotes to cases and other legal authorities on point. Like general encyclopedias, legal encyclopedias consist of a series of volumes. Legal encyclopedias are published both by West and by Lawyers Co-op.

West publishes **Corpus Juris Secundum**, *cited* C.J.S., which is tied to the key number system and is very heavily footnoted with legal authorities. It is so heavily footnoted, in fact, that it is common to find only one line of narrative text on a page and the rest of the page filled with footnotes. This, together with its use of key numbers, attracts many researchers to it.

Lawyers Co-op publishes **American Jurisprudence, Second Series**, *cited* Am. Jur. 2d, which contains more narrative and not as many footnotes. Many researchers prefer it when they want simply to obtain background information, because its uninterrupted text is easier to read. It also cites directly to Annotated Law Reports, another Lawyers Co-op research tool favored by many researchers.

Both sets of legal encyclopedias are kept current with periodic pocket parts inserted at the back of each volume of these multiple-volume collections.

American Law Reports   American Law Reports is the leading anotated law reproter. This secondary legal authority is published by Lawyers Co-op. It does not attempt to report every case or even to report most cases. Rather, it selects and publishes only those state appellate court cases which are significant. A case is significant to Lawyers Co-op editors if it indicates a change in the law or a new trend in legal thinking.

The distinguishing feature of this reporter is not the cases that it reports but, rather, the extensive editorial commentary (annotations) that follows each reported case. The annotations examine all sides of the issue; present general legal principles gleaned from the reported case and from other cases on the subject; and provide exceptions, distinctions, and qualifications of those legal principles. Cross-references to other, related annotations are also provided. To find annotations on a particular topic, one uses the *A.L.R. Quick Index* volumes that cover A.L.R.3d and A.L.R.4th. The A.L.R. series come in five parts:

A.L.R. (sometimes called A.L.R. First), supplemented by the *A.L.R. Blue Book of Supplemental Decisions*, which is kept current with a semi-annual supplement pamphlet;

A.L.R.2d, supplemented by the *A.L.R.2d Later Case Service*, which is kept current with a semi-annual supplement pamphlet;

A.L.R.3d, supplemented by an individual, cumulative pocket part found at the back of each volume in the series;

A.L.R.4th, supplemented by an individual, cumulative pocket part found at the back of each volume in the series; and

A.L.R. Fed., which reports only federal cases and is supplemented by an individual, cumulative pocket found at the back of each volume.

Whether an A.L.R. series annotation has been superseded (replaced by another annotation) can be determined by checking the Historical Table at the back of the *A.L.R. Quick Index*.

Restatements of Law　　　　Restatements of law have been published by the American Law Institute (A.L.I.) since 1923 on major legal topics (agency, conflict of laws, contracts, foreign relations, judgments, property, restitution, security, torts, and trusts). Restatements are persuasive legal authorities because they are compiled by committees of prominent legal scholars, all experts in the topic area of the restatement.

A restatement collects and distills the primary, general rules in a given legal topic area—what the rules are and sometimes what the committee believes they ought to be. It also provides explanations of the rules and gives examples of how they apply, using brief, hypothetical cases. Because legal rules are continually changing, however, a number of the Restatements have been rewritten as a Restatement Second.

Each Restatement has its own index. The second editions also contain cross-references to the key number digest system (West) and to the A.L.R. series (Lawyers Co-op).

Dictionaries　　　　Dictionaries, both legal and nonlegal, provide definitions of words and often provide illustrations of how they are used. Legal dictionaries frequently provide the case citation upon which the definition is based. **Black's Law Dictionary** and **Ballantine's Law Dictionary** are two of the law dictionaries available.

A nonlegal dictionary, such as *Webster's Collegiate Dictionary*, may be helpful when, for example, a contract term or some other word is the subject of dispute. Absent some specific, technical meaning for the word, it generally will be given its "ordinary meaning."

Treatises   Sometimes called a hornbook, a treatise is a single-volume text written by a legal scholar in a given topic area. A treatise usually provides more explanation than a legal encyclopedia but may be less critical than law review articles and other periodicals. *Prosser on Torts* and *Corbin on Contracts* are examples of treatises.

Periodicals   Periodicals, both legal and nonlegal, may provide persuasive authority in a given case and should not be overlooked as a research source. Law review articles, in particular, are very detailed and generally provide a critical analysis of the principles involved. The *Index to Legal Periodicals* can be used to access law review articles and other law publications in a specific topic area.

The Technical Skills of Legal Research

Legal research requires two different types of skills: technical and substantive. The researcher must be able to use research tools to find the most current legal authorities on a given point and must be able to cite the authorities correctly; these are technical skills. In addition, the researcher must be able to prepare case briefs and legal memoranda that summarize the legal authorities once they are found; these are substantive skills. This section covers technical skills, which include finding, updating, and citing legal authorities.

Finding the Law   After the relevant facts of a client's case are segregated and the legal issues are defined—at least tentatively—the researcher must find legal authorities that relate to the facts and issues (authorities on point). Finding the law means finding all applicable statutes and lines of cases, both favorable and unfavorable, together with any secondary authorities that apply. One cannot wear blinders by collecting only those authorities that seem favorable to a client's position. The attorney must be provided with a complete and accurate picture to evaluate the case properly.

The most difficult part of legal research for the inexperienced researcher is getting started or, more precisely, knowing where to start. There are several effective ways to begin.

   A.   Topic Method   When the researcher knows the topic area, this can provide the basis to locate primary and secondary authorities.

Case law, which represents the bulk of recorded law, can be located topically by using a digest. A *digest* is a finding tool, usually compiled by the publisher of the case reporter to which it relates. It reprints the headnote summaries of points of law found in reported cases and classifies them by subject, using pre-defined categories established by the publisher. A list of the categories which the publisher uses is located at the beginning of each digest volume.

There is a separate, multi-volume digest to accompany virtually every set of case reporters in existence, with a few notable exceptions. West uses a combined digest to access all federal courts, which is now in its third edition series (West's Federal Practice Digest 3d). There are two separate digests that access U. S. Supreme Court cases only: United States Supreme Court Digest (West) and United States Supreme Court Digest, Lawyers' Edition (Lawyers Co-op).

For state courts, West publishes separate digests for nearly every state plus the District of Columbia, as well as digests tied to five of its seven regional case reporters.

In addition, West publishes the American Digest System, a continuing digest series that collects headnote summaries from all federal and state courts (combined) during consecutive ten-year periods. The digest for each ten-year period is called a Decennial (sometimes, a Decennial Digest) except the digest for the current period, which is called the General Digest. At the end of each ten-year period, the General Digest accumulated to that point is published as a Decennial; and the General Digest continues for cases in the then current period.

Century Digest	1658 - 1896
First Decennial	1897 - 1906
Second Decennial	1906 - 1916
Third Decennial	1916 - 1926
Fourth Decennial	1926 - 1936
Fifth Decennial	1936 - 1946
Sixth Decennial	1946 - 1956
Seventh Decennial	1956 - 1966
Eighth Decennial	1966 - 1976
Ninth Decennial	1976 - 1986
General Digest	1986 -

All headnotes from reported state and federal cases are catalogued in the American Digest System, using West's key number system. This digest series is helpful when the researcher does not want to focus narrowly on one jurisdiction for applicable case law or when the researcher wants to compare the case law of various states, as well as federal case law, on a particular topic.

When a case has several different headnotes, each headnote is cataloged. This results in the case's appearance in several different places within the digest. Headnotes in the American Digest System are catalogued under topics and subtopics assigned to key numbers, using the TARP method:

T *Thing* or subject matter involved in the case, such as theater or bicycle;

A *Action* (cause of action) or ground for defense to an action, such as negligence or mandamus;

R *Relief* sought, such as restitution or damages; or

P *Parties*, meaning the legal relationship of parties, such as invitee or guardian.

In addition to headnote summaries, digests typically contain a *table of cases* listed by both plaintiff and defendant name and a *descriptive word index* to help the researcher find the correct topic area. Some digests contain a section called "Words and Phrases," which refers the researcher to those cases in the digest which interpret specific words and terms. In addition, West publishes a separate set of reference books called *Words and Phrases*, which is a finding tool devoted exclusively to the headnotes of court cases interpreting specific words and terms.

As helpful as digests are, one cannot rely upon their headnote summaries to state the exact principles contained in the case. They are guides only. Headnote summaries may miss a nuance or an element with significant impact on the facts being researched. A digest is a finding tool only. *Never cite a digest as legal authority for any purpose*.

Statutory law and constitutional law can be located by using the *general index* included in one or more volumes accompanying each statutory code, whether federal or state. For instance, there is a general index for U.S.C., for U.S.C.A., and for U.S.C.S. Statutory indexes are arranged alphabetically by topic or subject matter. Indexes, like digests, are finding tools; they are not legal authority for any purpose.

Similar to U.S.C.A. or U.S.C.S., many state statutory codes are annotated, which means that they contain notes and references to cases that have interpreted a particular statutory provision.

B. Case Method   There are occasions when the researcher has a case name or a complete case citation from which to begin the search for other authorities. When that occurs, the case method may be more efficient than the topical method.

With only the case name, a researcher can locate the entire citation. Each Decennial of the American Digest System contains an alphabetical table of cases by plaintiff. Each case listed gives the full citation, together with the topics and key numbers under which the case has been digested.

When only the popular name of the case is known, such as the "Dred Scott case," the best sources for finding the full citation are:

●*Shepard's Acts and Cases by Popular Name: Federal and State*

●The Sixth Decennial of the American Digest System contains a cumulative *List of Popular Name Titles*. This feature was discontinued in the Seventh Decennial.

●Most special digests contain a *Table of Cases by Popular Name*.

Once the researcher has the full citation for the case, he may use the appropriate set of *Shepard's Citations* to locate other cases and authorities that have mentioned the cited case, which indicates that the other cases and authorities pertain to the same topic area.

Shepard's Citations   The most comprehensive collection of legal citators is *Shepard's Citations*, published by Shepard's/McGraw-Hill. These citators are available in published volumes and by computer through WESTLAW and LEXIS *(discussed below)*. They list every published case in every state and federal case reporter, citation by citation, and show every subsequent case that has cited the case in question, as well as the treatment of the cited case by the subsequent case (whether affirmed, reversed, overruled, or modified in some other way). *Shepard's* also shows parallel citations for the cited case, if any, and its prior history, if any.

In addition to later case and treatment citations, *Shepard's* lists A.L.R. annotations, attorney general opinions, Restatements, and other authorities where the case is mentioned. These special features of *Shepard's Citations* make it useful for finding case law, as well as for updating the status of a particular case.

A separate set of *Shepard's Citations* is available for U. S. Supreme Court reporters, for federal court reporters, and for state and regional reporters. In addition, *Shepard's Citations* is available for federal and state constitutions and statutes, as well as for some court rules. *Shepard's* also publishes specialized citators, including *Shepard's Federal Law Citations in Selected Law Reviews* and *Shepard's Acts and Cases by Popular Name: Federal and State*.

Each set of *Shepard's Citations* includes one or two bound volumes. These are updated annually with a bright yellow paperback volume and approximately monthly with smaller, red paperback advance sheets. As a matter of practice, the researcher checks the red advance sheets first, since they are the most recent; then the yellow paperback; and finally, the bound volume(s).

Using a *Shepard's* citator is somewhat confusing for everyone at first; however, introductory pages in each citator volume explain its scope, format, and abbreviations. Shepard's publishes a teaching booklet entitled *How to Use Shepard's Citations*, which is available in most law libraries or directly from Shepard's/McGraw-Hill at a nominal cost. The best and quickest way to learn how to use *Shepard's Citations* is to have a knowledgeable researcher demonstrate its features, followed by practice and more practice.

Looseleaf Services   A looseleaf service consists of one or more looseleaf binders devoted to a specific topic of law. Pages can be removed and added with relative ease. As a result, changes in the law can be incorporated more quickly than in many other topical sources. Looseleaf services provide an excellent means to stay abreast of the newest developments in a specialty field.

Looseleaf services compile all relevant primary authority, regardless of its original source. When the researcher knows the general topic area, a looseleaf service can save substantial time in locating relevant federal and state statutes, federal and state cases, and federal and state administrative rules and decisions about the topic. Each looseleaf service contains its own topical index.

There is not a looseleaf service for every topic of law; rather, looseleaf services cover only selected topics. Examples of looseleaf services include *The United States Law Week, Criminal Law Reporter, Family Law Reporter*, and *Securities Regulation & Law Report*. Each of the named services is published by the Bureau of National Affairs (BNA). Another well-known looseleaf service publisher is Commerce Clearing House (CCH), whose publications include the *Congressional Index, Federal Securities Law Reporter, Standard Federal Tax Reports*, and *Trade Regulation Reporter*.

Computerized Search Tools   As they have done in every other area, computers have brought dramatic changes to the legal research process. Online databases are available to locate statutes and cases, as well as to locate any modifications that may have been made to those statutes and cases. The two predominant legal databases are:

WESTLAW, provided by West Publishing Company, and
LEXIS, provided by Mead Data Corporation.

A.   Benefits   Although WESTLAW and LEXIS use different
terminology, each database provides relatively quick access to federal and state
cases and statutes on a specific topic by using appropriate search words, called
search parameters. Access can be achieved by using a case citation as well. The
database allows the researcher to view the first page of a case (where headnotes are
located) to see if the case applies to the assigned topic area, to view the entire text
of a case, or simply to list citations for cases that may be related to the topic.

The computer database can limit the search in almost any way that a
researcher needs or wants. For instance, the search can be limited to court
opinions written by a specific judge or to court opinions issued during a specific
year, either of which would take substantial time to compile manually.

Both WESTLAW and LEXIS provide online access to *Shepard's Citations*
(*discussed above*), which allows the researcher to check for later treatment of cases
and statutes without leaving the database. Both systems provide services to verify
the accuracy of citations: *Insta-Cite* for WESTLAW and *Auto-Cite* for LEXIS.

Each system also provides software that performs various cite-checking
functions on all of the citations located in a brief or other document drafted by the
law office: *WestCheck* for WESTLAW and *CheckCite* for LEXIS. The software
checks the form of all citations that it finds in the document, dials the appropriate
system, accesses the needed services, and either downloads or prints a report for the
researcher to review.

B.   Drawbacks   The availability of computer databases to
aid the legal researcher is not a panacea. Cost is the most significant drawback of
computerized systems. Users pay a monthly service charge plus an additional fee
for each minute of online use. Therefore, it makes little economic sense to view an
entire case online when a bound set of case reporters is available. Although rates
are not as expensive as they once were, they remain prohibitive for many small law
firms and for most solo practitioners.

Another drawback is that the researcher who rarely uses the database
frequently has difficulty in narrowing the search enough to make it effective. For
example, even if the researcher wants only a list of cases on a topic—intending to
read the cases in the bound case reporters—the search parameter cannot be a term
as general as "court." It would take literally reams of paper to print all of the
citations to cases in which that word is used. The researcher who uses a computer
database, then, must think ahead to determine sufficiently narrow search

parameters, along with alternative parameters in case the first ones do not produce the desired results. If the researcher does not use the precise combination of words that are used in a particular court case, for instance, the system may not retrieve that case. If the case is an important one, the results can be devastating to the overall research project.

In addition, researchers (particularly those who had free access to a computerized system during law school) may come to rely too heavily on the system. As is true of digests, the database does not recognize nuances critical to a legal issue. A computer database cannot determine which cases are most important; neither can it distinguish between the holding and dicta.

As helpful as computer databases are, they should be used with these cautions in mind:

> *Computer databases should not be used by researchers until they are thoroughly familiar with and experienced in manual research methods. It's confusing, expensive, and risky.*

> *Databases are designed to be used as case-finding tools, not as reporters. They should be used only to locate, skim, and obtain citations and should represent only a part of the overall research plan.*

> *No citation obtained from the database ever should be used without reading the case thoroughly to ensure that it applies to the facts at hand. In the usual situation, cost constraints require that it be read from a bound case reporter.*

Computerized search tools can save substantial time for the researcher when they are used in their intended manner.

Updating the Law   Once relevant statutes and cases are found in the legal research process, the researcher must assure herself that the statute or case is still good law.

For statutes, updating means determining whether it has been (1) stricken as unconstitutional; (2) repealed; or (3) modified by amendment. All statutory codes are updated by *statutory supplements*. Some are published as separate, softbound volumes; others, as individual pocket parts for each volume in the code. If the statutory provision or section appears in the supplement, cite the supplement as the most recent version of the statute. If the section does not appear in the supplement, cite the bound volume. When a statute is stricken as unconstitutional by court decision, that fact may not appear in the statutory code. Use *Shepard's Citations for Statutes* to determine whether a statute was reviewed by a court.

For cases, updating means determining whether the case has been (1) reversed or modified on appeal or (2) overruled by a subsequent and different case. If the case has been reversed or overruled, it is not good law and cannot be cited at all. If the case has been diminished by a later modification, it may not be advisable to cite the case. The method used to determine whether a case still is good law is to check the citation in the appropriate set of *Shepard's Citations* (*discussed above*). This process is known as **Shepardizing**.

The procedure to locate statutes and constitutions is different from the procedure to locate cases. A summary of those procedures follows.

Statutes & Constitutions	Cases
•Use index to find statute section •Read the statutory section •Check supplements for status	•Use digest to find case references •Read the case in the reporter •Shepardize to determine status

Citing the Law

A **citation** is a reference to a legal authority, such as a constitution, statute, case, administrative rule, or other authority. Citations are included in briefs and legal memoranda to show the reader (often a judge or a supervising attorney) where the statute, case, or other authority can be found. In that sense, citations serve as road maps to a destination—the cited legal authority. Nothing can be worse than giving the wrong directions to reach the legal authority (wrong volume number, wrong page number of the reporter, or wrong statute section).

Precision in citation form is critical for a well-drafted presentation of legal principles or arguments. If the form of a citation is not correct, it sends a nonverbal message that the drafter is not careful. Taking that message to its logical conclusion, if the drafter is not careful about citation form, he probably is not careful about the substance of his research either. Proper citation form does not validate the substance of the research, of course; but it goes far in establishing preliminary credibility for the researcher.

The universally accepted authority on legal citations is *A Uniform System of Citation* (USOC), which is published jointly by the law reviews of Columbia,

Harvard, the University of Pennsylvania, and Yale Law Schools. USOC provides many, many technical rules about citation form as they apply in legal memoranda and briefs and in law review articles. However, this *Review Manual* limits its coverage to a summary of only those rules which relate to the Constitution, statutes, administrative rules, cases, procedural rules, legal encyclopedias, and law reviews as those rules apply to legal memoranda and briefs.

Caveat: *USOC rules may have been modified by local court rule or local rule of practice. For purposes of the CLA® examination, however, USOC rules are the standard.*

The most recent edition of USOC is essential to prepare for the CLA® examination. It can be ordered through bookstores or can be ordered by mail directly from:

Harvard Law Review Association
Gannett House
Harvard Law School
Cambridge, MA 02138

U.S. Constitution The United States Constitution consists of articles and various amendments. The citation form for an article and for an amendment follow.

U.S. Const. art. IV, § 2, cl. 3.

U.S. Const. amend. XIV, § 1.

Statutes Federal statutes are cited to the official publications, either the United States Code, cited as U.S.C. (which is the preferred citation reference), or to the Statutes at Large, cited as Stat. The popular name of the statute may, but need not be, included with the citation when citing to the United States Code; it is required when citing to the Statutes at Large.

●*The components of a* <u>*United States Code*</u> *citation are:*

①number of the Code title (*title* in the Code is analogous to chapter in state statutes);
②abbreviation for United States Code (U.S.C.);
③section symbol, followed by the number of the Code section; and
④date of the Code volume (date of supplement if applicable) in which the most recent version of the section can be found.

① ② ③ ④
15 U.S.C. § 7 (1988).

(optional)   ① ②   ③   ④
Robinson-Patman Act, 15 U.S.C. §§ 4-6 (1988).

●*The components of a* <u>*Statutes at Large*</u> *citation are:*

①name of the act (required);
②abbreviation for "Public Law" (Pub. L.) and the public law number;
③volume number of the Statutes at Large;
④abbreviation for Statutes at Large (Stat.);
⑤page number where the statute begins; and
⑥the year when the statute was passed as law.

①   ②   ③ ④ ⑤ ⑥
Health Care Act, Pub. L. 92-117, 83 Stat. 624 (1987).

Procedural Rules   The citation forms for various federal rules of procedure are shown below. Notice that each type of procedural rule follows the same citation format.

Fed. R. App. P. 2.	Rule 2 of the Federal Rules of Appellate Procedure
Fed. R. Civ. P. 12	Rule 12 of the Federal Rules of Civil Procedure
Fed. R. Crim. P. 42	Rule 42 of the Federal Rules of Criminal Procedure
Fed. R. Evid. 401	Rule 401 of the Federal Rules of Evidence

Cases   Federal and state case citations use similar citation form, regardless of which court issues the opinion.

Every case citation begins with the case name, identified by the names of the parties. Surnames are used for individual parties (<u>Watson v. Jones</u>). Omit initials in business names unless the initial is part of the widely recognized name (B.J. Hollis Corp. becomes Hollis Corp., but initials are retained for J.C. Penney Co.). Omit *Ltd., Inc.*, and similar terms if the party's name also contains *R.R., Co., Bros., Corp., Assn.*, or other, similar term to indicate clearly that the party is a business rather than an individual.

When the federal government is a party, it is identified as "United States" in the case name (do not abbreviate as U.S. or as U.S.A.). When a state government is a party, such as the plaintiff in a criminal case, it is identified in the case name simply as "State" (State v. Jones), because the identity of the state is apparent from the balance of the citation. When the Internal Revenue Service is a party, the term *Commissioner* is used to identify it (meaning Commissioner of the Internal Revenue Service); never use the abbreviation IRS. For all other administrative agencies, the abbreviation for the agency typically is used in the case name (FCC, SEC, and so forth).

The ***subsequent history*** of a cited case ***must be shown*** as part of the case citation. Prior history is shown only in the extraordinary situation where the prior history is necessary to explain the point for which the case is cited.

Parallel citations should not be used when citing to U. S. Supreme Court cases; cite to U.S. Reports only. A ***parallel citation*** is the same case published in more than one case reporter. For instance, citations to the same case published in U.S. Reports, Supreme Court Reporter, and U.S. Supreme Court Reports, Lawyers' Edition are parallel citations. Parallel citations for state cases must be cited if they exist *(discussed below)*.

Case names in legal memoranda and briefs must be either (1) underlined or (2) shown in italics. Both methods are shown in the examples.

●*The components of a standard case citation are:*

①case name (identified by names of parties);
②case reporter in which the case is published (include volume number, abbreviation of case reporter, and page where case begins);
③identity of court issuing the opinion unless the issuing court is apparent from the reporter abbreviation;
④year in which the decision was issued; and
⑤subsequent history, if any.

①   ②   ④
Avery v. Exxon Co., 397 U.S. 812 (1991).

①   ②   ③   ④
Smith v. Jones, 502 F.2d 233 (3d Cir. 1992).

①   ②   ③   ④
United States v. Central R.R., 436 F. Supp. 739 (N.D. Ill. 1990).

①   ② ③ ④
Commissioner v. J.C. Penney Co., 429 F. Supp. 57 (Neb. 1991),
aff'd, 509 F.2d 318 (8th Cir. 1992), *cert. denied* 417 U.S. 622 (1993).
⑤   ⑤

The final example shows a subsequent case history. If all of the opinions in this example had been decided in the same year, the year would have been shown only once (at the end of the entire citation).

When citing to information contained on a specific page of the opinion, rather than to the entire opinion, show the page as follows:

Parker v. United States, 402 U.S. 634, 639 (1991) (Stevens, J. dissenting)

This citation directs the reader to page 639 of the dissenting opinion in the case, rather than to the majority opinion; thus, the parenthetic reference at the end of the citation.

Once cited in full, any of the following short forms of the citation may be used when the case is subsequently cited in the memorandum or in the brief:

Parker, 402 U.S. at 640.
402 U.S. at 640.
Id. at 640.

The short form ***supra*** may not be used to refer to constitutions, statutes, or cases previously cited in full in legal memoranda and briefs; however, it may be so used in general text, in books like this one, and in law review articles. *Supra* may be used in legal memoranda and briefs only when referring to authorities other than constitutions, statutes, or cases (such as an A.L.R. annotation or a legal encyclopedia).

The researcher may use the short form ***infra*** to indicate that the full citation appears later in the memorandum, brief, or other work. This short form is not limited in the same way as the short form *supra*. The short form ***id.*** is used to indicate that the full citation appears immediately above, meaning that no other citations intervene between the full citation and the short form *id.*

Unlike the rule limiting the use of parallel citations for U.S. Supreme Court cases, the parallel citation for a state case cited in the state where the case was decided *must* be shown if a parallel citation exists. Parallel citations for out-of-state cases need not be cited; instead, cite only to the regional reporter. A citations to the same case appearing in both an official and an unofficial reporter is an example of a parallel citations.

<u>Sanders v. Keaton, Inc.</u>, 238 Kan. 376, 457 P.2d 609 (1992).
as cited in Kansas

<u>Sanders v. Keaton, Inc.</u>, 457 P.2d 609 (Kan. 1992).
as cited everywhere except Kansas

State v. Bryant, 388 Minn. 271, 439 N.W.2d 811 (1991).
as cited in Minnesota

<u>Chapin v. Brewster</u>, 357 N.E.2d 154 (Ind. 1992).
as cited in Indiana and elsewhere

Notice that no state identification is shown as parenthetic information at the end of the first and third citations, because the identity of the state is apparent in each of them. The second example is a Kansas case cited somewhere other than Kansas. The last example comes from a state that stopped publishing an official case reporter in 1981; therefore, the state must be identified as parenthetic information at the end of the citation regardless of where the case is cited (whether in Indiana or elsewhere).

Administrative Law   The rules and regulations of federal administrative agencies are cited either to the Code of Federal Regulations (arranged by topic and cited as C.F.R.) or to the Federal Register (arranged chronologically and cited as Fed. Reg.). The name of the regulation may be included but is not required.

●*The components of a <u>Code of Federal Regulations</u> citation are:*

①the title (chapter) number;
②abbreviation for Code of Federal Regulations (C.F.R.)
③section number symbol and the section number; and
④year of publication.

①   ②   ③   ④
22 C.F.R. § 145.6 (1992).

●*The components of a <u>Federal Register</u> citation are:*

①volume number of Fed. Reg. (volume number changes each calendar year);
②abbreviation for Federal Register (Fed. Reg.);
③page number where administrative rule begins; and
④year of publication.

① ② ③ ④

48 Fed. Reg. 37,315 (1983).

Secondary Authorities   Law review articles, annotations, legal encyclopedias, and dictionaries are cited as secondary authorities.

●*The components of a law review citation are:*

> ①full name of author;
> ②designation of type of article (required only if written by a student);
> ③title of article (underscored or in italics);
> ④volume number of law review;
> ⑤abbreviated name of law review (refer to USOC for complete list);
> ⑥page number where article begins; and
> ⑦year of publication unless it appears elsewhere in the citation.

①   ②   ③   ④

Virginia Koerselman, Comment, *Workmen's Compensation*, 15 Creighton L. Rev. 415 (1981).
      ⑤   ⑥   ⑦

①   ③   ④   ⑤   ⑥

William Benton, *Creation of Fetal Rights*, 29 Geo. L. J. 356 (1985).

Notice that the first example is a student article (it contains element no. 2); the second example is not.

●*The components of an A.L.R. citation are:*

> ①full name of author;
> ②the word "Annotation";
> ③title of annotation (underscored or in italics);
> ④volume number of A.L.R. series;
> ⑤abbreviation for Annotated Law Reports (A.L.R.) collection;
> ⑥page number where the annotation begins; and
> ⑦year of publication.

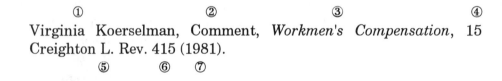

①   ②   ③

John Willis, Annotation, <u>Industrial Noise: Promoting an Unsafe Work Environment</u>, 76 A.L.R. Fed. 489 (1986).   ④   ⑤   ⑥
   ⑦

● *The components of a legal encyclopedia citation are:*

 ①volume number of encyclopedia;
 ②abbreviated name of encyclopedia (either Am. Jur. 2d or C.J.S.);
 ③title of article (underscored or in italics);
 ④section symbol and section number within the article;
 ⑤specific page within section (no page if citing to entire section); and
 ⑥date of publication.

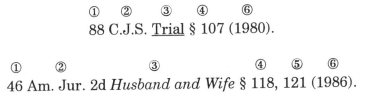

①   ②   ③   ④   ⑥
88 C.J.S. <u>Trial</u> § 107 (1980).

①   ②   ③   ④   ⑤   ⑥
46 Am. Jur. 2d *Husband and Wife* § 118, 121 (1986).

● *The components of a legal dictionary citation are:*

 ①full name of dictionary (do not abbreviate; no underscoring or italics);
 ②page where the term is defined; and
 ③edition of dictionary and year of publication.

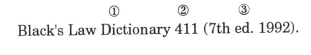

①   ②   ③
Black's Law Dictionary 411 (7th ed. 1992).

①   ②   ③
Ballantine's Law Dictionary 1078 (3d ed. 1969).

<u>Citation Signals</u>   Citations related to propositions made by the writer of a memorandum or brief are introduced by signals. Signals indicate how the writer of the memorandum (or brief) wants the reader to view the citation in relation to the proposition to which the citation relates. For example, the writer uses different signals to indicate that the cited authority either supports or contradicts the writer's proposition in the memorandum. If no signal is used, the writer's position is that the cited authority clearly states the same proposition as that stated by the writer.

Commonly used signals appear below. A full list of signals, together with their meanings and uses, appears at USOC Rule 1.2.

See generally	The cited authority presents helpful background information about the proposition.
See, e.g.,	The cited authority directly supports the proposition; other authorities also could have been cited but were not cited to avoid duplication.
Cf.	The cited authority states a proposition that is different from the proposition stated by the writer, but the proposition stated in the cited authority is sufficiently similar to lend support to the writer's proposition.
Contra	The cited authority contradicts the proposition stated in the memorandum.

Sequence of Citations Within Each Signal   When two or more citations follow a particular signal in a memorandum or brief, there is a prescribed sequence in which the citations should be listed. The sequence compares roughly to the weight or rank of the authority. For example, primary authorities are listed before secondary authorities; U.S. Supreme Court cases are listed before any other cases; and so on.

The sequence begins anew with each introductory signal. No signal is a signal for the purpose of sequential listing as well. In other words, if no signal is given to introduce an authority, the absence of a signal indicates that the writer believes the cited authority is directly on point.

If all of the authorities reviewed in this section on citation form were listed within one signal, they would be listed in the following order:

1. U.S. Constitutional provisions and amendments.
2. Federal statutes (most recent listed first).
3. Federal procedural rules.
4. Federal cases (U.S., F.3d, then F. Supp.).
5. State cases (official reporter first, then regional reporter).
6. Federal administrative rules and regulations.
7. Law review articles.
8. Annotations.
9. Legal encyclopedias.
10. Law dictionaries.

If there were two or more of the same type of authority (such as two U.S. Supreme Court cases), the most recent one would be listed first.

The Substantive Skills of Legal Research

The skillful legal researcher is one who has exercised patience and practice over a long period of time to acquire techniques that work for him or her in locating applicable legal rules. There is no right or wrong way to research, just as there is no right or wrong way to travel to Chicago. There are, however, processes generally used by experienced legal researchers to maximize their time:

- Obtain as much background information as needed.
- Identify the relevant facts.
- Frame the legal issues involved.
- Find legal authorities that apply to the facts and issues.
- Update the law through statutory supplements and *Shepard's* citators.
- Brief statutes and cases that are on point.
- Analogize the facts of the case with the statutes and cases found.
- Document the results in a memorandum to the supervising attorney.

Background Information   No one knows all of the law. Therefore, no judge, lawyer, or legal assistant exists who never needs to review background sources for information before tackling a research project. The fact is that the more knowledgeable a person is about the law, the more she recognizes how much more is left to be learned.

After evaluating the facts to determine the general legal topic involved (search and seizure, breach of an insurance contract, corporate director liability, or the like), the experienced researcher routinely reviews legal encyclopedias, A.L.R. indexes and annotations, treatises, and legal dictionaries to "brush up" on less familiar legal topic areas. Even if the researcher works with the subject matter every day, he nevertheless will conduct at least a scan to remind himself of each of the elements needed to prove—or to disprove—a legal theory or to remind himself to consider the peripheral legal issues that do not present themselves every day. This exercise helps in keeping the researcher's mind open to other theories and options during the balance of the research project.

Where pattern jury instructions exist for a particular state, they often provide an excellent starting point from which to create a checklist of elements that must be proved to support a particular legal theory. The table of contents of a legal encyclopedia may serve the same function.

Identify Relevant Facts   Using background sources and any legal theories supplied by the attorney, the researcher must evaluate all of the known facts in the case, separating those that are legally relevant from those that are not. For example:

> Mayor Roscoe Wiley slipped and fell on an icy sidewalk in front of
> BJ's Bingo Hall last Sunday, breaking his right arm and collarbone.
> He was hospitalized for ten days. Mayor Wiley and B. J. Hollis, the
> proprietor, have been political enemies for many years.

The fact that Wiley is a mayor may be relevant to the senior management of the firm, but it has no legal relevance. There are no legal rules for mayors who slip and fall that are different from the legal rules for other people who slip and fall. Likewise, the fact that Wiley and Hollis are political enemies has no legal relevance to the issue of liability. The remaining facts stated in the problem are (or may be) relevant to the researcher.

Frame the Legal Issues   All law is based upon classifications. Once the relevant facts are known, they are classified according to the legal rules that most accurately apply to them. These classifications are used as the basis to frame (phrase) the legal issues in relation to the facts of the case.

Framing legal issues and segregating relevant facts typically evolve at the same time, since one cannot frame all legal issues until the relevant facts are segregated. Yet, one cannot segregate all of the relevant facts until the legal issues are framed. The two functions generally are interdependent.

Based upon the abbreviated facts stated in the above example, one might frame the following legal issue: *Is a business proprietor liable to a plaintiff who slips and falls on an icy sidewalk in front of the proprietor's business location?* If background research indicates that liability may not be the same when the business is open as it is when the business is closed and if the researcher knows that bingo halls cannot operate on Sundays, the legal issue might be framed: *Is a business proprietor liable to a plaintiff who slips and falls on an icy sidewalk in front of the proprietor's business location during nonbusiness hours?* In other words, the issue is framed according to the legal classifications that can be drawn from the relevant facts.

Find and Update the Law   Using the facts of the case and the legal issues or legal theories suggested by those facts, the researcher must locate the legal rules that apply. She will use the finding tools (indexes for statutes, digests for cases) and the techniques (topic method, case method) described previously to accomplish this task. All major authorities should be searched—both favorable and unfavorable—and the results reported to the attorney.

Before the memorandum to the supervising attorney is prepared, the researcher must update those legal rules which are on point to determine (1) that the applicable statutes have not been stricken, repealed, or amended and (2) that the applicable cases have not been overruled, reversed, or modified. Statutory supplements and Shepard's citators are used for this purpose, both of which were described earlier in this chapter. Only the most recent version of the law can be used as legal authority.

Brief the Law   When the researcher locates relevant authorities (typically statutes and cases), briefing them is an efficient way to preserve their important points for later use. A brief is an abbreviated summary of the case (or statute), generally one page or less in length.

Statutes often contain lists of elements or requirements. When the statutory list is long or complex or both, its important parts usually can be pared down to a shorter or simpler list through the briefing process. To illustrate, an extract from the venue statute for the federal district court, cited as 28 U.S.C. § 1391 (1991), is shown immediately below and is followed by an example of one way in which the extract might be briefed.

(a)   A civil action wherein jurisdiction is founded only on diversity of citizenship may, except as otherwise provided by law, be brought only in (1) a judicial district where any defendant resides, if all defendants reside in the same state, (2) a judicial district in which a substantial part of the events or omissions giving rise to the claim occurred, or a substantial part of property that is subject to the action is situated, or (3) a judicial district in which the defendants are subject to personal jurisdiction at the time the action is commenced.

(b)   A civil action wherein jurisdiction is not founded solely on diversity of citizenship may, except as otherwise provided by law, be brought only in (1) a judicial district where any defendant resides, if all defendants reside in the same state, (2) a judicial district in which a substantial part of the events or omissions giving rise to the claim occurred, or a substantial part of property that is subject to the action is situated, or (3) a judicial district in which any defendant may be found, if there is no district in which the action may otherwise be brought.

(c)   For purposes of venue under this chapter, a defendant that is a corporation shall be deemed to reside in any judicial district in which it is subject to personal jurisdiction at the time the action is commenced. In a State which has more than one judicial district and in which a defendant that is a corporation is subject to personal jurisdiction at the time an action is commenced, such corporation shall be deemed to reside in any district in that State within which its contacts would be sufficient to subject it to personal jurisdiction if that district were a separate State, and, if there is no such district, the corporation shall be deemed to reside in the district within which it has the most significant contacts. . . .

VENUE FOR FEDERAL CIVIL ACTIONS:

(a) Actions based solely upon diversity of citizenship can be filed in district:

(1) Where any defendant resides if all defendants reside in the same state; or

(2) Where a substantial part of the claim arose or subject property is located; or

(3) With personal jurisdiction over all defendants when the action is commenced.

(b) Actions based upon federal questions and other cases can be filed in district:

(1) Where any defendant resides if all defendants reside in the same state; or

(2) Where a substantial part of the claim arose or subject property is located; or

(3) Where any defendant may be found if no other district has venue.

(c) For purposes of venue, a defendant corporation is deemed to reside in any district with personal jurisdiction over such defendant when the action is commenced.

●When a State has more than one district, the corporation is deemed to reside in that district which would have personal jurisdiction based upon minimum contacts if that district were a separate State; and

●If there is no such district, the corporation is deemed to reside in that district where it has the most significant contacts.

When the relevant statutes are few or when they are short, it may be more efficient simply to photocopy them and, using a colored marking pen, to highlight the key terms or the elements of the statute that apply to the facts of the client's case.

Court opinions, on the other hand, tend to be lengthy, making it impractical to photocopy every relevant case for the research file. Notwithstanding the time and expense, uncondensed photocopies of many cases are virtually useless when the time comes to organize and draft the memorandum of law. Briefing cases is awkward and confusing at first; but, as is true of all skills, it becomes easier with practice.

The components of a full case brief are:

■*Case Name and Citation*. Include the full name of the case and its complete citation, including parallel citations; they can be omitted in the memorandum if necessary.

■*Identity of court* issuing the opinion if it is not apparent from the citation.

■*Judicial history* or procedural posture. Knowing how the case arrived at the appellate court is helpful in understanding its facts and in evaluating the court's decision. For example: Where did the case originate and which other appellate courts, if any, have reviewed it? Was the original decision made at the pretrial stage (dismissal or summary judgment) or was it made after a full trial on the merits? Was it an interlocutory appeal, such as one based upon a disputed order to compel discovery? Many researchers prefer to include the procedural posture with the facts section of the case brief when that can be done reasonably.

■*Facts*. The researcher condenses the facts reported in the case, focusing on those which are directly relevant to the issue and stating them as succinctly as possible. Researchers often find it necessary to edit this section several times to strike the right balance between utility and brevity.

■*Issue*. This is the question decided by the court. The parties may present a number of questions for the court to decide; however, the appellate court selects the one (sometimes two) necessary to dispose of the case. This question is the issue. When a number of questions are raised by the parties, it sometimes is difficult to determine which one is the issue—even for an experienced researcher. When this happens, find the holding because it often suggests the issue.

■*Decision*. This is the disposition or result reached in the case (affirmed, reversed, remanded, or the like).

■*Holding*. The holding is the rule of law stated by the court which leads to or which supports the decision. The holding becomes precedent for all future cases with similar facts and similar issues that are decided by lower courts of the jurisdiction. It is the rule of law for which the case is cited. The holding is easy to locate when there is only one question presented for decision or when the court states, "This court holds that . . ." or "We hold that . . . ." Otherwise, the researcher may need to read the opinion several times to locate the holding. Use the court's language for the holding; do not paraphrase it.

■*Rationale*. The rationale represents the court's reasoning to support its holding in the case. As a general rule, the rationale is somewhere between one and three sentences in length. (It may be longer.) Use as much of the court's language as needed to retain the thrust of its reasoning.

All other statements in the opinion are dicta (comments unnecessary to the decision). Although dictum never can be cited as precedent, it may be helpful to the attorney in forming analogies and drafting arguments as part of the preparation for trial.

Not every case brief sets out each of the components separately. If an opinion is neither lengthy nor complex, the researcher properly may elect to combine two or more of the components into one or may elect to omit the issue component if it mirrors the holding precisely. To illustrate, read the following extracted case; then review the abbreviated case brief which follows it. Notice that each of the components is present, even though some of them are combined with others.

Just for practice, the applicant may want to prepare his or her own case brief before reviewing the sample case brief that has been supplied. If so, take particular care with the statement of facts to ensure that it is phrased as concisely as possible. Edit it several times if necessary and then compare it with the statement of facts in the sample brief.

E.I. Du Pont de Nemours & Co.
v. Christopher
431 F.2d 1012 (5th Cir. 1970)

Goldberg, Justice

This is a case of industrial espionage in which an airplane is the cloak and a camera the dagger. The defendants-appellants, Rolfe and Gary Christopher, are photographers in Beaumont, Texas. The Christophers were hired by an unknown third party to take aerial photographs of new construction at the Beaumont plant of E.I. Du Pont de Nemours & Company, Inc. Sixteen photographs of the Du Pont facility were taken from the air on March 19, 1969, and these photographs were later developed and delivered to the third party.

Du Pont employees apparently noticed the airplane on March 19 and immediately began an investigation to determine why the craft was circling over the plant. By that afternoon the investigation had disclosed that the craft was involved in a photographic expedition and that the Christophers were the photographers. Du Pont contacted the Christophers that same afternoon and asked them to reveal the name of the person or corporation requesting the photographs. The Christophers refused to disclose this information, giving as their reason the client's desire to remain anonymous.

Having reached a dead end in the investigation, Du Pont subsequently filed suit against the Christophers, alleging that the Christophers had wrongfully obtained photographs revealing Du Pont's trade secrets which they then sold to the undisclosed third party. Du Pont contended that it had developed a highly secret but unpatented process for producing methanol, a process that gave Du Pont a competitive advantage over other producers. This process, Du Pont alleged, was a trade secret developed after much expensive and time-consuming research, and a secret that the company had taken special precautions to safeguard. The area photographed by the Christophers was the plant designed to produce methanol by this secret process, and because the plant was still under construction parts of the process were exposed to view from directly above the construction area. Photographs of that area, Du

Pont alleged, would enable a skilled person to deduce the secret process for making methanol. Du Pont thus contended that the Christophers had wrongfully appropriated Du Pont trade secrets by taking the photographs and delivering them to the undisclosed third party. In its suit Du Pont asked for damages to cover the loss it had already sustained as a result of the wrongful disclosure of the trade secret and sought temporary and permanent injunctions prohibiting any further circulation of the photographs already taken and prohibiting any additional photographing of the methanol plant.

The Christophers answered with . . . [Rule 12(b) motions] to dismiss for lack of jurisdiction and failure to state a claim upon which relief could be granted. Depositions were taken during which the Christophers again refused to disclose the name of the person to whom they had delivered the photographs. Du Pont then filed a motion to compel an answer to the question and to all related questions.

On June 5, 1969, the trial court held a hearing on the pending motions . . . [and] granted Du Pont's motion to compel the Christophers to divulge the name of their client. . . . Agreeing with the trial court's determination that Du Pont had stated a valid claim, we affirm the decision of that court.

This is a case of first impression, for the Texas courts have not faced this precise factual issue, and sitting as a diversity court we must sensitize our *Erie* antennae to decide what Texas courts would do if such a situation were presented to them. The only question involved in this interlocutory appeal is whether Du

Pont has asserted a claim upon which relief can be granted. The Christophers argued both at trial and before this court that they committed no "actionable wrong" in photographing the Du Pont facility and passing these photographs on to their client because they conducted all of their activities in public airspace, violated no government aviation standard, did not breach any confidential relation, and did not engage in any fraudulent or illegal conduct. In short, the Christophers argue that for an appropriation of trade secrets to be wrong there must be a trespass, other illegal conduct, or breach of a confidential relationship. We disagree.

It is true, as the Christophers assert, that the previous trade secret cases have contained one or more of these elements. However, we do not think that the Texas courts would limit the trade secret protection exclusively to these elements. On the contrary, in *Hyde Corporation v. Huffines*, 1958, 314 S.W.2d 763, the Texas Supreme Court specifically adopted the rule found in the Restatement of Torts which provides:

One who discloses or uses another's trade secret, without privilege to do so, is liable to the other if

a. he discovered the secret by improper means, or

b. his disclosure or use constitutes breach of confidence reposed in him by the other in disclosing the secret to him....

Thus, although the previous cases have dealt with a breach of a confidential relationship, a trespass, or other illegal conduct, the rule is much broader than the cases heretofore encountered. Not limiting itself to specific wrongs, Texas adopted subsection (a) of the Restatement which recognizes a cause of action for the discovery of a trade secret by an "improper" means. . . .

The question remaining, therefore, is whether aerial photography of plant construction is an improper means of obtaining another's trade secret. We conclude that it is and that the Texas courts would so hold. The Supreme Court of that state had declared that "the undoubted tendency of the law has been to recognize and enforce higher standards of commercial morality in the business world." *Hyde Corporation v. Huffines*, at 773. That court has quoted with approval articles indicating that the proper means of gaining possession of a competitor's secret process is "through inspection and analysis" of the product in order to create a duplicate. Later another Texas court explained:

> The means by which the discovery is made may be obvious, and the experimentation leading from known factors to presently unknown results may be simple and lying in the public domain. But these facts do not destroy the value of the discovery and will not advantage a competitor who by unfair means obtains the knowledge without paying the price expended by the discoverer. (Brown v.

Fowler, 316 S.W.2d 111.)

We think, therefore, that the Texas rule is clear. One may use his competitor's secret process if he discovers the process by reverse engineering applied to the finished product; one may use a competitor's process if he discovers it by his own independent research; but one may not avoid these labors by taking the process from the discoverer without his permission at a time when he is taking reasonable precautions to maintain its secrecy. To obtain knowledge of a process without spending the time and money to discover it independently is improper unless the holder voluntarily discloses it or fails to take reasonable precautions to ensure its secrecy.

In the instant case the Christophers deliberately flew over the Du Pont plant to get pictures of a process which Du Pont had attempted to keep secret. The Christophers delivered their pictures to a third party who was certainly aware of the means by which they had been acquired and who may be planning to use the information contained therein to manufacture methanol by the Du Pont process. The third party has a right to use this process only if he obtains this knowledge through his own research efforts; but thus far all information indicates that the third party has gained this knowledge solely by taking it from Du Pont at a time when Du Pont was making reasonable efforts to preserve its secrecy. In such a situation Du Pont has a valid cause of action to prohibit the Christophers from improperly discovering its trade secret and to prohibit the undisclosed third party from using the improperly obtained information. . . .

In taking this position, we realize that industrial espionage of the sort here perpetrated has become a popular sport in some segments of our industrial community. However, our devotion to freewheeling industrial competition must not force us into accepting the law of the jungle as the standard of morality expected in our commercial relations. Our tolerance of the espionage game must cease when the protections required to prevent another's spying cost so much that the spirit of inventiveness is dampened. Commercial privacy must be protected from espionage that could not have been reasonably anticipated or prevented. We do not mean to imply, however, that everything not in plain view is within the protected vale, nor that all information obtained through every extra-optical extension is forbidden. Indeed, for our industrial competition to remain healthy there must be breathing room for observing a competing industrialist. A competitor can and must shop his competition for pricing and examine his products for quality, components, and methods of manufacture. Perhaps ordinary fences and roofs must be built to shut out incursive eyes; but we need not require the discoverer of a trade secret to guard against the unanticipated, the undetectable, or the unpreventable methods of espionage now available.

In the instant case Du Pont was in the midst of constructing a plant. Although after construction the finished plant would have protected much of the process from view, during the period of construction the trade secret was exposed to view from the air. To require Du Pont to put a roof over the unfinished plant to guard its secret would impose an enormous expense to prevent nothing more than

a schoolboy's trick. We introduce here no new or radical ethic, since our ethos has never given moral sanction to piracy. The marketplace must not deviate far from our mores. We should not require a person or a corporation to take unreasonable precautions to prevent another from doing that which he ought not to do in the first place. Reasonable precautions against predatory eyes we may require; but an impenetrable fortress is an unreasonable requirement, and we are not disposed to burden industrial inventors with such a duty in order to protect the fruits of their efforts. "Improper" will always be a word of many nuances, determined by time, place, and circumstances. We therefore need not proclaim a catalog of commercial improprieties. Clearly, however, one of its commandments does say, "Thou shalt not appropriate a trade secret through deviousness under circumstances in which countervailing defenses are not reasonably available."

Having concluded that aerial photography, from whatever altitude, is an improper method of discovering the trade secrets exposed during construction of the Du Pont plant, we need not worry about whether the flight pattern chosen by the Christophers violated any federal aviation regulations. Regardless of whether the flight was legal or illegal in that sense, the espionage was an improper means of discovering Du Pont's trade secret.

The decision of the trial court is affirmed and the case remanded to that court for further proceedings on the merits.

———————

SAMPLE CASE BRIEF

<u>Du Pont & Co. v. Christopher</u>, 431 F.2d 1012 (5th Cir. 1970)

<u>Facts</u>:   In this Texas case, Du Pont developed an unpatented process (trade secret) to manufacture methanol. While Du Pont's methanol plant was under construction, the Christopher brothers took 16 pictures of the manufacturing process from an airplane circling over the construction site. The Christophers refused to identify their client, and Du Pont sued for an injunction and damages. During discovery, the trial court ordered the Christophers to identify who hired them; they refused and filed an interlocutory appeal of the trial court's order.

<u>Issue</u>: Is aerial photography of a plant's construction site an improper means of obtaining another's trade secret?

<u>Holding</u>:   Aerial photography of a construction site is an improper means of obtaining trade secrets.

<u>Rationale</u>:   A trade secret properly may be obtained by reverse engineering or by discovering it through independent research, but one may not avoid these labors by taking it from the discoverer.

To obtain knowledge of a process without spending the time and money to discover it independently is improper unless the holder voluntarily discloses it or fails to take reasonable precautions to ensure its secrecy.

––––––––––––––

The researcher may vary the case brief format in any way that makes it a more useful tool for whoever will use it to draft the memorandum or the trial brief.

Analogize the Facts   A critical step in the research process is the comparison of the client's facts with the legal rules (usually statutes and cases) that the researcher finds. In this way, the researcher is able to evaluate whether the legal rule is on point (applies) or is not on point (does not apply). When the objective is a memorandum of law for the attorney's review and use, the researcher must use care to present all sides as objectively as possible.

In comparing a statutory list of what is required (or what is prohibited), the researcher evaluates the list, item by item, with the client's facts. For example, if a statute requires items A, B, and C, the researcher compares the client's facts to determine whether each item exists. If any item is missing or if its existence is questionable, one of two avenues may be pursued.

If A + B + C = benefit to client: Try to supply the missing item, if possible; otherwise, argue that it exists in the form of the questionable item. In this way, the statute properly applies; and the client may receive the benefit of the statute.

If A + B + C = burden to client: Argue that the statute does not apply unless all items exist; and since an item is missing, the client should be free of the statute's burden. If the legislature had intended to impose a burden for something less than A + B + C, it could have said so. Cases interpreting the statute or its legislative intent are helpful to the researcher in determining whether either of these arguments is likely to succeed.

The researcher evaluates case law by comparing the facts and issues of the case with the client's facts for similarities and differences. The more similarities that exist, the more likely that the case is on point and will apply to the client's facts. Conversely, the more differences that exist, the more likely that the case is not on point.

For example, a researcher working on Mayor Wiley's slip and fall case *(see sample problem above)* is unlikely to find many other cases where the plaintiff had slipped and fallen on an icy sidewalk in front of a bingo hall. In fact, there may be no cases found with these precise facts. The researcher, then, looks for cases with similar facts: Is an icy sidewalk in front of a bookstore sufficiently similar? A grocery store? A courthouse? An apartment complex? A private residence? Is a case related to a snow-covered sidewalk sufficiently similar? A wet sidewalk with large cracks? A dry sidewalk under construction? *A more complete discussion of analogical reasoning is provided with examples in the Judgment and Analytical Ability chapter of this Review Manual.*

Occasionally, a researcher locates a case "on all fours," which literally means that if the client's case were placed over the researched case, they would match on all four corners because the facts and issues are identical—or nearly identical—to each other. If a case is on point or is on all fours, it likely will be precedent in determining the outcome of the client's case.

Acknowledge Ambiguity

If legal research could produce clear answers in every case, there would be no reason for courts or trial attorneys to exist. Although research may provide definite answers to some questions, it is unlikely to provide definite answers to all of the questions raised by a particular client's facts. The more common situation is that statutes and case law merely narrow the legal issues that will be left for a judge to decide.

In researching statutes, ambiguity can occur when a legislature adopts a law that includes lists to deal with a specific type of problem. If the client's case is the same type as those addressed by the statute, but is not included in the statutory list, does this mean (1) that the legislature intended to exclude it or (2) that the legislature would have included it in the list if anyone had thought of it at the time? Statutory ambiguity also can occur when new technologies or new situations arise that were not, and could not have been, anticipated by the legislature (such as privacy rights attached to electronic mail or tort liability relating to AIDS exposure). Whether a particular statute is ambiguous is, of course, left to a court to decide.

Memoranda to Attorneys   Once the researcher is reasonably certain that he has located all of the major authorities dealing with the research assignment, he must organize and summarize them in a memorandum of law for the supervising attorney.

The first step is to know the purpose for which the memorandum will be used, whether to determine the procedure required to amend a corporation's bylaws, to draft a civil complaint, to draft an appellate brief, or for some other purpose. The intended use determines the focus of the memorandum, as well as how much technical detail to provide.

The format of the memorandum varies according to office policy and the preference of the supervising attorney. If no standard form is required by office policy, check the files for other memoranda prepared for or by the supervising attorney. Memoranda generally include (1) the heading, (2) date, (3) name of the attorney for whom the memorandum is written, (4) name of the writer, (5) client name or case name, (6) statement of facts, (7) question presented, (8) brief answer or brief summary of the conclusion, (9) discussion, and (10) conclusion. A researcher might prepare a memorandum of law for the attorney in the form shown on the following page.

MEMORANDUM

TO: Name of Attorney

DATE: Today's Date

FROM: Name of Writer

RE: Name of Client or Client File

Statement of Facts: Recite the relevant facts of the case or problem as you understand them to be. Be as concise as possible. A chronological presentation usually is best, although any form may be used if it is better suited.

Question Presented: State the issue or subject of the research assignment in question form (see section on framing the issue, discussed earlier in this chapter).

Brief Answer: Provide the short answer to the question, whether *yes, no,* or an abbreviated form of the conclusion.

Discussion: This section often begins with a statement of the general rule or principle that governs the subject matter, such as "The general rule is . . . ." or "The law of North Carolina and the general rule throughout the country is . . . ."

Relate applicable legal authority, both favorable and unfavorable (including citations), in a logical, narrative form. Exceptions to any general or specific rules are included as well. If more than one alternative or option is possible, each should be discussed.

Use a detailed outline to stay focused on the overall purpose of the research and redraft as many times as necessary to achieve the desired result.

Conclusion: The conclusion summarizes the major points of the discussion in one or two concise paragraphs (one is better). If the legal rules are unclear on a point, say so. It is correct to use words and phrases such as "appears," "seems to require," or "may be" if they are more appropriate than absolute statements.

It always makes sense to review the progress of the memorandum with the supervising attorney as it is being drafted. When the outline is completed, in particular, the attorney should review it to ensure that the project is on the right track. Before the memorandum is submitted as a final product, the researcher should review it with these questions in mind:

• *Could the memorandum be understood by someone who knows little or nothing about the case?*

• *Does the question presented in the memorandum focus accurately on the central issue? Could it be stated more precisely?*

• *Are the facts of cited cases given in enough detail to show their relevance?*

• *Do the cited authorities adequately support the conclusion(s) stated?*

• *Does the memorandum provide enough information to allow the attorney to take the next required step without asking further questions and without performing additional research?*

Legal research can be challenging and rewarding to the researcher who takes the time to master its technical and substantive skills. A skilled researcher provides an invaluable service to the attorney and to the profession in the delivery of quality legal services at a reasonable cost. The materials in this chapter, together with the following Self-Test, are designed to highlight the major principles of legal research. *See the Bibliography for additional references.*

Legal Research Self-Test

Allow an uninterrupted thirty-minute period to answer all questions. At the end of thirty minutes, check your answers against those in the Answer Key Section of this Manual. Deduct two points for each incorrect answer (100 total possible points). Unanswered questions are counted as incorrect answers. Follow directions carefully and observe the time limit precisely to provide an accurate self-assessment.

Choose the most correct answer to the following questions unless a specific question directs you to do otherwise.

1. Which reporter of Supreme Court decisions contains summaries of the briefs of counsel?

    a.   United States Reports
    b.   Supreme Court Reporter
    c.   United States Supreme Court Reports, Lawyers' Edition
    d.   All of the above.
    e.   None of the above.

2. Which of the following is most correct?

    a.   Freedom of Information Act, 46 U.S.C. § 89 (1976).
    b.   Freedom of Information Act, 46 U.S.C.A. § 89 (1976).
    c.   Freedom of Information Act, 197 Stat. 230 (1976).
    d.   46 U.S.C. § 89 (1976).

3. Which of the following is the most correct citation form?

    a.   <u>Montana v. United States</u>, 440 U.S. 147 (1979).
    b.   <u>Montana v. United States</u>, 440 U.S. 147, 99 S. Ct. 970 (1979).
    c.   <u>Montana v. United States</u>, 440 U.S. 147, 59 L. Ed. 2d 210, 99 S. Ct. 970 (1979).
    d.   <u>Montana v. United States</u>, 440 U.S. 147, 99 S. Ct. 970, 59 L. Ed. 2d 210 (1979).

4. Which of the following statements best describes the term *star paging*?

    a.   Signal used to indicate page numbers in another reporter.
    b.   Signal used to indicate original paging when a reporter is reprinted.

(see next page)

    c.   Signal used to indicate page where the court's holding is found.

    d.   None of these is correct.

5.   Star paging is used in

    a.   All volumes of United States Reports.

    b.   First 90 volumes of Unites States Reports plus all unofficial reporters of Supreme Court decisions.

    c.   All volumes of all official and unofficial Supreme Court reporters.

    d.   All volumes of all federal reporters.

6.   What is the primary difference between the Statutes at Large and the United States Code?

    a.   The Statutes at Large are compiled by topic; the Code, chronologically.

    b.   The Statutes at Large contains state statutes; the Code, federal.

    c.   The Statutes at Large contains federal statutes; the Code, state.

    d.   The Statutes at Large are compiled chronologically; the Code, by topic.

7.   Identify the reporter in which federal trial court opinions are contained.

_____

8.   True or False. The United States Code contains all federal statutory law enacted by Congress.

9.   True or False. The signal *supra* is used in legal memoranda and briefs to refer to a case that has been cited in full previously.

10.   True or False. The typical case reporter contains either a separate section or a separate volume devoted to a table of cases and a descriptive word index.

11.   True or False. Each state has both an official and an unofficial reporter series for the opinions of its highest state court.

12.   To update the status of a particular case, what research tool is used?

    a.   Federal Digest

    b.   Supplement volumes or pocket part supplements

(see next page)

    c.   Shepard's Citations

    d.   None of these is correct

13.   Identify the two legal encyclopedias in existence today:

    a.   American Jurisprudence Second and Corpus Jurisdiction Second

    b.   American Jurisprudence and Corpus Jurisdiction

    c.   American Jurisprudence Second and Corpus Juris Secundum

    d.   American Jurisprudence and Corpus Juris.

14.   If one reporter citation of a case is known, its parallel citation(s) can be determined by using:

    a.   Shepard's Citations

    b.   Table of Cases

    c.   West's National Reporter Blue Book

    d.   Any one of the above

15.   To update the status of a particular statute, what research tool should be used?

    a.   Federal Digest

    b.   Supplement volumes or pocket part supplements

    c.   American Law Reports

    d.   None of these is correct

16.   True or False. Parallel citations for an appellate court opinion may include citations to the trial court reporter series where the trial court opinion is published.

17.   True or False.   Parallel citations generally are not provided for federal cases, but they are required for home state cases when parallel citations exist.

18.   True or False.   Within the Shepard's Citator volumes, the citations appearing in parentheses indicate other cases which have overruled the case being researched.

19.   True or False. Federal statutes are arranged topically in the Statutes at Large.

20. True or False. The signal *infra* is used in legal memoranda and briefs to indicate the full citation for the case follows at a later point in the memorandum or brief.

21. True or False.   The signal *supra* is used in law review articles and other textual material (but not in legal memoranda and not in briefs) to indicate that the full citation for the case was given previously.

22. True or False. Digests are compilations of case law for a particular reporter or a particular group of reporters.

23. True or False. The case summaries found in digests may be cited as primary authority.

24. True or False.   The case summaries found in digests may be cited as secondary authority.

25. When a researcher is unfamiliar with the subject matter to be researched, what tool may be consulted to provide background information?

    a.   United States Code
    b.   Case digests
    c.   Legal encyclopedias
    d.   Federal Reporter

26. The principles stated in opinions of judges, to be followed in future cases, are called:

    a.   res judicata
    b.   precedent
    c.   case law
    d.   jurisprudence

27. A type of secondary authority which is not the law itself but is, rather, a persuasive presentation by legal scholars of what the law is or what it should be in a particular topic area, is called:

    a.   encyclopedia
    b.   restatement
    c.   treatise
    d.   none is correct

28. Which legal publisher is noted for its extensive use of annotations?

    a.   West Publishing Co.
    b.   Lawyers-Cooperative Publishing Co.
    c.   Bureau of National Affairs
    d.   Commerce Clearing House

29. True or False. The American Digest System indexes and classifies all case law, both state and federal.

30. True or False. Secondary authorities are those that contain a general commentary on or explanation of the subject.

31. True or False. Digests summarize judicial decisions, while indexes summarize statute topics.

32. True or False. The American Digest System is sometimes called the Decennial Digest and uses the key number system.

33. True or False. When researching a particular federal statute, the United States Code is the most useful source because it is an official publication.

34. Compilations of cases and historical matters dealing with various aspects of a code or statute, which contain short summaries of other cases, both for and against, are called:

    a.   annotations
    b.   restatements
    c.   encyclopedias
    d.   digests

35. If a researcher knows the date when a federal statute was adopted, which of the following will provide the most direct access to the text of that statute?

    a.   Code of Federal Regulations
    b.   Congressional Record
    c.   United States Code
    d.   Federal Rules Decisions

36. When an appellate judge disagrees with the result and with the reasoning of the majority opinion, but disagrees with the reasoning of the dissenting opinion as well, she may write:

      a.   a concurring opinion
      b.   an abstaining opinion
      c.   a partial dissenting opinion
      d.   a dissenting opinion

37. Which of the following represents the correct citation to a term found at the 15th line of column 1, page 41 of the Third Edition of Ballantine's Law Dictionary, which was published in 1969?

      a.   Ballantine 41 (3rd ed. 1969).
      b.   Ballantine's Law Dictionary 41 (3rd ed. 1969).
      c.   Ballantine's Law Dictionary 41 (3d ed. 1969).
      d.   Ballentine at 41-1-15 (3d ed. 1969).

38. True or False. When a state's highest court elects to publish an official reporter, it must publish all cases decided by that court.

39. True or False. When a case has been affirmed, reversed, or modified on appeal, the subsequent history of the cited case must be included in the citation.

40. True or False. A memorandum opinion is an opinion of the entire court, rather than an opinion written by a specific judge.

41. True or False. In a petition for writ of certiorari to the United States Supreme Court, the name of the appellant appears first in the case caption, regardless of how the caption may have been shown in lower courts.

42. True or False. Indexing is the accepted process for checking the status of specific cases, while Shepardizing is used for checking the status of statutes.

43. True or False. Cases decided by the U.S. Court of International Trade (formerly the U.S. Customs Court) are reported selectively in the Federal Supplement.

44. Which is the correct citation for an article entitled *Nocturnal Crimes*, written by Professor Willard Weitz and published in the 20th volume of the Brooklyn Law Review in 1992. The article appears at page 180.

      a.   W. Weitz, <u>Nocturnal Crimes</u>, 20 Brooklyn L. Rev. 180 (1992).
      b.   W. Weitz, <u>Nocturnal Crimes</u>, Brooklyn L. Rev. 20-180 (1992).
      c.   W. Weitz, *Nocturnal Crimes*, 20 Brooklyn L. Rev. 180 (1992).
      d.   Willard Weitz, <u>Nocturnal Crimes</u>, 20 Brooklyn L. Rev. 180 (1992).

45. Which is the correct citation for a case in which Ralph Ritches Jr. is the plaintiff and Won Handy Li is the defendant, decided by the federal trial court in the eastern district of Pennsylvania on October 15, 1991 and published in the appropriate reporter series at volume 658, page 139 on October 28, 1991.

    a.   Ritches Jr. v. Li, 658 F. Supp. 139 (E.D.Pa. 1991).
    b.   Ritches v. Li, 658 F. Supp. 139 (E.D. Pa. 1991).
    c.   Ritches v. Won Handy Li, 658 F. Supp. 139 (E.D. Pa. 1991).
    d.   Ritches v. Won Handy Li, 658 F.2d 139 (E.D. Pa. 1991).

46. Which is the correct citation for an appeal by the defendant in the preceding question to the Court of Appeals for the Third Circuit, decided on August 28, 1992 and published in the appropriate reporter series at volume 597, page 843 on September 12, 1992.

    a.   Ritches v. Won Handy Li, 597 F.2d 843 (3d Cir. 1992).
    b.   Ritches v. Won Handy Li, 597 F.2d 843 (3rd Cir. 1992).
    c.   Ritches v. Li, 597 F. Supp. 843 (3d Cir. 1992).
    d.   Ritches Jr. v. Li, 597 F.2d 843 (3rd Cir. 1992).

47. Which is the correct citation for a petition for certiorari by the defendant in the preceding question to the United States Supreme Court, where the petition was denied on December 28, 1992 and reported at volume 636 of the United States Reports on page 322, which was published on January 7, 1993.

    a.   *Won Handy Li v. Ritches*, 636 U.S. 322 (1993).
    b.   *Li v. Ritches Jr.*, 636 U. S. 322 (1993).
    c.   *Won Handy Li v. Ritches*, 636 U.S. 322 (1-7-93).
    d.   *Won Handy Li v. Ritches*, 636 U.S. 322 (1992).

48. Which of the following case names is correctly cited?

    a.   State of Colorado v. James Wonka
    b.   Colorado v. Wonka
    c.   State v. Wonka
    d.   In Re State v. Wonka

49.   Which of the following case names is correctly cited?

    a.   *Internal Revenue Service v. Jackson*
    b.   *IRS v. Jackson*
    c.   *Commissioner v. Jackson*
    d.   *IRS Commissioner v. Jackson*

50.   Which of the following case names is correctly cited?

    a.   John Brown Company v. Archer Industries, Ltd.
    b.   John Brown Co. v. Archer Industries, Ltd.
    c.   Brown Co. v. Archer Industries
    d.   Brown Co. v. Archer Industries, Ltd.

Chapter 6
HUMAN RELATIONS
and
INTERVIEWING TECHNIQUES

If you aren't fired with enthusiasm, you will be fired with enthusiasm.

—Vince Lombardi

The human relations portion of the CLA® examination encompasses professional contacts with employers, clients, and other office visitors; co-workers and subordinates; and persons outside the law office. For this reason, the legal assistant should be familiar with unauthorized practice of law prohibitions, ethics rules, practice rules, delegation of authority, consequences of delegation, and confidentiality. Principles from the chapters on Communications, Ethics, and Judgment and Analytical Ability within this *Review Manual* will be helpful in preparing for the human relations portion of the examination. In addition, the *NALA Manual for Legal Assistants, Second Edition* contains a comprehensive chapter on interviewing techniques.

The interviewing techniques portion of the examination covers basic interviewing procedures, as agreed upon by most authors on the subject; definitions of terms and basic principles; and handling of specialized interviews. Subject areas included in this section of the examination are:

●General considerations for the interview situation: courtesy, empathy, physical setting, and body language;

●Initial roadblocks: lapse of time, prejudice, and so forth;

●Form and manner of questions;

●Use of checklists for specific matters; and

●Situations involving the very young, the elderly, and other persons who may require special handling.

Both initial and subsequent interviews are covered, as are interviews involving clients and other witnesses.

Human Relations

The topic of human relations involves a wide range of associations between individuals, both positive and negative. Legal assistants must deal with all types of people in all types of situations, which demands superior human relations skills. The successful legal assistant is one (1) who has mastered the technical skills of his craft and (2) who can relate to and can work well with people from all walks of life.

Human relations skills are measured by the legal assistant's ability to deal with others in a positive way. Those who possess this ability have several things in common: They genuinely like themselves, like what they are doing, and like people in general. They are interested in the well-being of others; they are compassionate without gushing. They practice courtesy and common sense in their professional relationships.

The successful legal assistant is the one who observes ethics rules and office policies enthusiastically, who can be firm without being overly aggressive, and who is flexible enough to compromise or to try new approaches when situations warrant them. He strives to be a team player in relation to his employer and co-workers. He always is courteous in contacts with persons outside the office, realizing that he is an emissary for his employer. He protects client confidences and willingly assumes additional responsibilities connected with his position. He respects the contributions of others on the legal services team (lawyers, legal secretaries, law clerks, and messengers) and does not view himself as the most important contributor. A sincere interest in others and the ability to generate empathetic understanding from them are key ingredients in building the trust and confidence which engender positive human relations.

Contacts Outside the Office

The legal assistant frequently comes into contact with individuals outside the office in person, by letter, or by telephone as part of her responsibilities. These situations provide opportunities to foster long-term relationships based upon honesty, mutual respect, and professional cooperation. The legal assistant should strive to be congenial without being too familiar.

When requests are made of others, provide sufficient lead time for them to comply. No one likes to be pushed with last-minute requests for information. When little lead time is possible, however, the clerk, court reporter, or other person is more likely to comply with a rush request when it is the exception rather than the rule. Convey appropriate thanks for a job well done. Better still, express appreciation to the person's immediate supervisor or employer.

From time to time, every lawyer and legal assistant encounters a public official who is uncooperative or difficult in general (a court clerk, for example). Rather than further alienate such a person by demanding that he do his job, the experienced lawyer or legal assistant strives to gain his support. Ask how he prefers to have documents submitted or what is the best way to go about a certain task, even if you already know. Thank him for his time and for his help. Acknowledge him in the courthouse hall. Ask about his family and take the time to remember his wife's name if you happen to learn it. It may take several months, but even the most surly court clerk can be converted to an ally over time. Having an ally in a position such as this can be an invaluable asset.

When the legal assistant must contact a legal assistant, attorney, or other person aligned with the opposing party, she should avoid power games or tricks of one-upsmanship. In the long run, these tactics are counterproductive and can result in retaliatory actions which cause additional harm or expense to this or to a future client. When power tactics are used by the opposing side, the best advice is to sidestep and ignore them as much as possible without harm to the client—as difficult as this is to do at times. Power games are a ploy of insecure people, and nothing is more frustrating to an insecure person than to be ignored.

Office Politics

The only way to avoid office politics is not to work in an office. Office politics exist wherever there are two or more people working together in an office setting. Although office politics often carry a negative connotation, they provide the vehicle for beneficial changes as well.

When a legal assistant is new to any law office, he is wise to form no firm alliances until he has had time to assess the "lay of the land" by determining where the power centers are. The power centers may or may not correspond with the firm's official hierarchy. For instance, if the senior partner's legal secretary carries great influence with the senior partner, the legal secretary (rather than the senior partner) may be a power center. An assistant to the administrator (rather than the administrator) may be the true power center in allocating assignments and general work loads. By the same token, an alliance formed too soon may be difficult to overcome.

> Bill is a new legal assistant at Samson & Woodward and knows no one except Jane Mitchell, the attorney who hired him. Another legal assistant in the firm, Betsy Barnes, invites Bill to join her for lunch on his first day. He accepts and also accepts two other invitations later in the same week. After about a month, Bill discovers that Betsy is regarded by nearly everyone in the firm as a gossip and a general troublemaker.

Bill may have difficulty extricating himself from the perceived alliance with Betsy, which can create unnecessary obstacles for a person without a proven track record of his own.

Knowledge of the political structure of a particular law office is necessary to effect change when change is either necessary or desirable. (*See the chapter on Judgment.*)

Although office politics certainly have a role in developing and maintaining rapport within the law office, one seldom can go wrong by being a courteous, cooperative, and competent member of the legal services team.

Personal Recognition

Everyone needs recognition for his or her contributions. This may come as part of a formal evaluation process, by informal evaluation, or through feedback from the supervising attorney on a specific project.

The first step in receiving recognition for a job well done is to do a good job, no matter how menial or insignificant that job may seem. As a general rule, one who can do a superior job of photocopying and marking voluminous exhibits will be given more challenging tasks in the natural scheme of things. If that does not happen within a reasonable time and if the legal assistant is certain that past and current tasks have been performed well and on time, she can ask to assist with a specific project which she knows is pending. Alternately, she might try her hand at drafting interrogatories or answers to interrogatories based upon information already in the file and then take the draft to the attorney for review. Most lawyers recognize the value of a self-motivated individual and, if the drafting job is done reasonably well, are quite willing to delegate other tasks to such a person.

The legal assistant should keep track of major projects that he has completed and should review those prior to formal, scheduled performance evaluations. An appointment diary or calendar can be used for this purpose. Unless the project is recorded, it may be forgotten or overlooked—especially if it was completed early in the evaluation period.

If formal evaluations are not performed regularly (which may be true in a very small law office), the legal assistant can visit informally with the supervising attorney concerning job performance and future goals. The exact approach may vary from one attorney to another, but most are willing to discuss these matters if the legal assistant asks to talk about them and specifically schedules a time to do so. Try to select a time that is likely to be more quiet than other times—if there is such a thing—based upon the lawyer's usual court and appointment schedules. Although it is a good idea to ask for the lawyer's advice or input concerning increased responsibilities, the legal assistant must have specific goals in mind as well. The attorney's needs and the legal assistant's goals generally can be combined in a way that benefits both of them.

One of the best ways to receive deserved recognition is to give recognition when and where it is due. The person who is willing to share the limelight often finds it is reciprocated by others. Do not overlook legal secretaries and other key support staff members. Mutual respect, support, and good will between a legal assistant and a legal secretary can be invaluable in the success of future projects.

A thorough analysis of all aspects of human relations skills required of legal assistants is beyond the scope of this *Review Manual*. The CLA applicant will be well served, however, by reviewing the materials from other chapters as they relate to ethics, judgment, and communications and by reviewing the human relations perspectives of the interviewing materials discussed immediately below.

Interviewing

Legal interviewing involves the exchange of information between individuals, the objective of which is to elicit relevant facts based on personal knowledge, leads to other witnesses who may possess relevant facts, and corroboration of facts.

Interviews typically are conducted either in person or by telephone. The interviewer controls the process, assisted by checklists to facilitate collection of information and to keep the dialogue focused. A question-and-answer approach is used to obtain maximum details from the person interviewed, to separate facts from beliefs, and to provide clues to other sources that can be used to corroborate the facts supplied by the client or by the witness.

Although checklists and forms can expedite the interview, no two legal interviews are exactly the same. Throughout the interview process, the interviewer must be sensitive and responsive to the reactions, attitude, and emotions of the client or the witness. This frequently puts the interviewer's best human relations skills to the test.

The interview process requires preparation and flexibility from the interviewer. The facts and information obtained during the interview are collected and summarized in a memorandum or witness statement, which is essential in the lawyer's legal analysis of the case.

Types of Interviews

As a general rule, an interview is conducted with either a client or a non-client witness and may be conducted either in person or by telephone. Each situation presents different considerations and requires different techniques for interview management, although common themes do emerge.

Client Interviews　　　　　　The client usually is the lawyer's first source of information, and the initial client interview should be conducted in person if at all possible. Because one interview may not provide the depth of information needed, subsequent interviews—either in person or by telephone—may be required before the attorney can complete a full analysis of the facts and legal issues of a particular case.

The details of ascertainable facts must be complete, their accuracy must be verified, and resulting inconsistencies must be reported to the attorney. Probing the factual details of sensitive matters requires tact and diplomacy. An intense, confrontational interrogation is certain to escalate the client's discomfort.

Depending on the sensitivity of the client and the subject matter, an interviewer can damage the attorney-client relationship irreparably. Should this occur, the fact that the interviewer obtained a complete factual account is of little value.

The lawyer or legal assistant should explain the investigative process to the client as well as how each step lays the foundation for the next. The client needs to know that the legal assistant will interview others to corroborate the client's facts and to obtain additional facts. Not explaining the importance of corroborating evidence can strain the client relationship. If a client does not understand the process, she may infer that other people are being interviewed because the lawyer or the legal assistant did not believe her.

Witness Interviews   In addition to the corroboration provided through documentary evidence (reports, contracts, leases, invoices, and so forth), personal interviews of witnesses often are used to verify factual details and to corroborate the client's allegations. A witness can be anyone with personal knowledge of facts related to the case. Witnesses generally are classified according to their relationship to the client or to matters involved in the client's case.

A.   The Neutral Witness   The neutral witness is one who has personal knowledge of facts relevant to the case but who has no relationship with either the client or the opposing party. Neutral witnesses with favorable facts are the most desirable, of course. Neutral witnesses might include a disinterested bystander to an assault or a driver who witnessed an accident while she was stopped nearby.

B.   The Friendly Witness   This witness generally shares the same perspective, business interests, or career as that of the client. He may be a social acquaintance of the client. The friendly witness often is willing to speak freely but may offer a slightly different perspective than the client. This witness, however, generally corroborates the client's claims; and his statement is used for comparison with statements made by the opposing party's witnesses.

C.   The Official Witness   A person is an official witness because of employment or because of a position held through election or affiliation with an organization. For instance, a police officer, a tax assessor, a city planning director, and a court clerk are official witnesses. In theory, official witnesses are impartial to both sides of a controversy. They generally provide factual background which neither advances nor restricts either side's legal theories in any dramatic way.

D.   The Expert Witness   An expert witness may be either friendly or hostile. As a practical matter, this may be influenced—at least in part—by which party retains the expert's services. An expert witness should be interviewed at length to determine his depth of expertise, his presentation skills, and his preparation abilities. An expert witness must have the ability to cope calmly with attacks on his general credibility and on the thoroughness of his conclusions. Examples of expert witnesses include real estate appraisers, architects, engineers, doctors, and other individuals with substantial training and experience in a technical area.

      E.   The Hostile Witness   A hostile witness is not necessarily one who exhibits hostility. Rather, it is one who is unwilling to divulge information. A hostile witness may have knowledge of facts that support either side of the case but is reluctant to volunteer the information. Thus, an individual can be a hostile witness even though she supports the client's position in the case. Such a person technically is an objectively hostile witness, although the term *hostile witness* is used more commonly.

      As the term ordinarily is used, a hostile witness may be reluctant to provide information because of inconvenience to herself or because of uncooperativeness in general—not because of a personality clash between the witness and the client or between the witness and the interviewer.

      Less frequently, the term *hostile witness* is used to describe a witness who displays personal distaste for the client or for the interviewer. If the interviewer believes the hostility is directed toward him (rather than toward the client) and if adjustments in the interviewer's approach prove ineffective, someone else should interview the witness. Acknowledging a personality conflict early in the interview can save time and effort. Having another interviewer conclude the interview is not a failure of the initial interviewer; rather, it indicates maturity and strength in having recognized the incompatibility.

      All interviewers encounter personal hostility from a witness on occasion. If this situation occurs more frequently, however, the interviewer must re-evaluate his interviewing style thoroughly and thoughtfully and must make constructive changes.

Personal Interviews   Personal interviews are those conducted face to face between the interviewer and the client or the witness. The law office generally is the most conducive location for personal interviews, because the environment is more easily controlled by the interviewer. Client interviews, especially initial client interviews, generally are conducted in the law office; witness interviews, however, frequently are conducted at the witness's place of employment or home. These types of interviews are called ***field interviews***.

When the legal assistant or the attorney must travel to the witness to conduct a personal interview (field interview), adapting to the witness's environment is critical in establishing rapport. This is where the flexibility of the interviewer pays its greatest dividends. Because the environment is foreign to the interviewer, using a prepared outline and planning the questions to ask create a measure of confidence that will benefit both the interviewer and the witness.

The primary advantage of a personal interview is that it facilitates more personal interaction than a telephone interview does. The relationship of trust and confidence between the attorney and her client is fostered by personal contact. A personal interview allows the legal assistant or attorney to use all of her senses to evaluate the client (or the witness) and the facts related by him. Unusual physical characteristics, body language, and physical mannerisms are important in assessing credibility and the way in which the client or witness likely will be perceived by a jury. None of these things can be determined in a telephone interview.

Telephone Interviews　　　　　　When a personal interview cannot be arranged, a telephone interview may be the next best option. At the beginning of every telephone interview of a witness, state the purpose of the interview and obtain permission to conduct the interview. In addition, clarify who the parties are in the case and who it is that the law firm represents.

The legal assistant's telephone skills are tested regularly when dealing with individuals who are reluctant to divulge information. Making a simple inquiry such as, "Can you help me?" followed with an explanation of what information is needed, often opens the conversation. People usually want to help, and they certainly like to be asked.

Although a telephone interview may not be the most desirable interview method, it is efficient and economical. Many individuals and agencies can be contacted by telephone in a short time, without great expense to the client. Those who have personal knowledge about the case can be scheduled for personal interviews. Even if an individual has little or no personal knowledge about the matter, she may provide leads to others who do have helpful information. Also, contacting a witness early in the case—even by telephone—may generate a psychological alignment of that witness with the client rather than with the opposing party.

A major disadvantage of the telephone interview is the inability to see the witness. Being unable to observe the reaction and body language of the witness is an obstacle for the interviewer. The witness's reaction to questions can be revealing in evaluating the information provided by him. Nervousness, fidgeting, twitching, lack of eye contact, or similar conduct may indicate a problem with credibility; however, these exhibitions cannot be detected in a telephone interview.

The decision to tape-record or not to tape-record a telephone interview is left to the supervising attorney. If the attorney approves the use of a tape recorder, the legal assistant must seek permission of the witness to tape-record before any recording takes place. If permission is given, the legal assistant must follow the same rules that apply when tape-recording a personal interview (*see below*).

The Interviewer's Role

Creating rapport and building trust throughout the interview are the responsibility of the interviewer, whether the interviewer is the legal assistant or the lawyer. Treating clients and witnesses with respect goes far in establishing and maintaining the requisite level of trust.

Attitude   The legal assistant often has significant contact with the client and with witnesses during the investigation period of a case. Thus, the legal assistant is a public relations representative for the firm; she has great impact on these important people. Courtesy, truthfulness, and discretion throughout this process are critical to the credibility of the legal assistant and of the firm. *The legal assistant **never** expresses personal opinions, **never** patronizes a client or a witness, and **never** is condescending.*

On very rare occasion, one encounters a legal assistant or a lawyer who assumes an attitude of superiority, particularly when dealing with a client or witness with less education or with a lower economic position. This approach assumes that education or money equate to intelligence. Frequently, the exact opposite is true; and the fact that an educated person ever could make such an assumption proves the assumption wrong. The interviewer who views herself as superior to a client or witness cannot possibly hope to be successful in eliciting full cooperation from that person; her attitude will come across in a negative way no matter how much she tries to hide it. These types of interviewers seldom are found in private law offices for the simple reason that they cannot sustain themselves as effective members of the legal services team for very long.

Concern   For a client more than for a witness, a visit to the law office frequently is triggered by some traumatic event. Divorce, personal injury, death, rape, criminal charges, or business failure can produce intense stress. Although the situation may be minor, routine, or "old hat" to the interviewer, the client's perception is quite different. His problem is unique and traumatic for him, making it essential for the interviewer to exercise patience, understanding, and sensitivity to the client's plight. Generating a feeling of empathy exhibits true concern for the client.

Sensitivity to the client's situation provides countless benefits in establishing a solid attorney-client relationship. Studies indicate that it is not the lawyer's win-loss ratio which retains clients or which prompts them to refer others to a particular lawyer. Rather, it is the respect and genuine concern shown by the lawyer and the lawyer's staff. Despite all of the marketing techniques now available to lawyers, repeat and referral business ultimately make the difference between a lawyer who is successful and one who is not.

Courtesy   Courtesy always is a correct approach to dealing with people, no matter what the situation is. Extending small courtesies to a client or to a witness pays huge dividends. An open, communicative environment begins with common courtesy. For example, greet the client in the reception area and personally escort him to the conference room or to your office; this is a simple but essential client development technique. Remember and mention significant occasions previously referred to by the client (an anniversary, a birthday); this demonstrates personal interest. When the interview is over, escort the client back to the reception area as a common courtesy. It can be both embarrassing and awkward for the client to try to find his way out of the office unescorted. Every client wants to be assured that he is important to the law firm, and personal attention from the lawyer and from the legal assistant symbolizes a client's importance.

During the interview and throughout the progress of the case, a simple way to demonstrate genuine interest in the client is to listen closely to what he has to say, whether in person or by telephone. People generally like to talk if they have an audience and will reveal information readily to a courteous, interested listener. This approach allows the legal assistant to hear what the client says, to relate the information to data gathered previously, and to formulate relevant questions at the appropriate time. The courtesy of listening is a powerful tool for building the attorney-client relationship.

Return the client's telephone calls promptly. Although information may not be the positive news hoped for, the client expects and deserves to know all information related to her case. Delaying calls sends a negative message about the lawyer, which can extend to the legal assistant as well.

Send courtesy copies of correspondence and periodic status reports to the client. These simple communications keep clients informed and happy. Lack of communication sends a negative message. Lack of communication is the most frequent criticism of lawyers. Inundating the client with relevant information is essential for maintaining a positive professional relationship.

Avoid Legal Jargon   Avoid technical legal terms as much as possible during an interview. Using a foreign vocabulary of legal jargon will not impress any client. More likely than not, it will be a source of genuine frustration, which can shatter all previous efforts to establish rapport with that client. Asking questions in plain English generally is one of the things that legal assistants do best; the interview process allows them to capitalize on this asset.

If, on the other hand, the client uses technical terms connected with his expertise or profession, the legal assistant should seek precise definitions for those terms to ensure that she uses them in the same context as the client uses them. It is helpful for the legal assistant to adapt to the jargon of the client, but is unrealistic to expect the client to adapt to the jargon of the law office. To understand the technical terminology of a case better, the legal assistant should review available documents or materials as well as the attorney's notes prior to the interview. This will provide some familiarity with the terminology and will prepare the legal assistant to ask appropriate questions for clarification during the interview.

Personal Opinions   The legal assistant never expresses his personal opinions or personal judgments about the case, the opposing party, the opposing party's lawyer, or anyone else connected with the client's case—not even if his opinions concur with those expressed by the client and not even if his motive is to show support for the client. Find some other way to show support.

Limiting personal opinion during the fact-gathering process does not mean the legal assistant is not allowed to express personal feelings about any topic. It is appropriate to identify with a client's joy or frustration, as the case may be, as long as the legal assistant does not lose his objectivity. It would be insensitive, for example, not to show pleasure if the client relates that she has won a $30,000 lottery.

False Expectations   Never should the lawyer or the legal assistant give the impression that a client's case is a sure winner. Letting the client know that the law firm will work diligently on the client's behalf is the best message.

Keep the Client Involved   Describing the legal process and explaining the steps involved are basic to the client's understanding of her legal matter. The lawyer also should give the client a realistic explanation of the range of anticipated results, and the client should be involved in any decisions affecting the outcome of the case. With the lawyer sharing authority with the client, the end result often is more positive for both.

Whenever possible, involve the client in the fact-gathering process. In some situations, only the client can obtain privileged records. If the client is cost conscience (who is not these days?), she will feel she is contributing to the cost containment of her case. Keeping her involved by asking her to obtain some of the records and documents needed for the case produces a cooperative spirit between the client, on the one hand, and the lawyer and her staff, on the other.

Ethical Limitations The lawyer should explain the legal assistant's function and role in the overall case management. If the lawyer has not explained the legal assistant's role, the legal assistant must explain her status to the client and the purpose of her involvement. The client must be informed, for example, that the legal assistant is not a lawyer and cannot offer legal advice, represent the client in court, or discuss fees. With these limitations, the legal assistant will be involved in all phases of the case and will work closely with the lawyer throughout the case.

Any information conveyed to the legal assistant by the client is confidential, just the same as if the information had been conveyed directly to the lawyer. The legal assistant has a responsibility to furnish all information she obtains to the lawyer, even if the client requests that specific information be withheld. Everything must be shared with the lawyer. If a client asks the legal assistant not to tell the lawyer about a particular fact or situation, she should try to stop the client before he divulges the information and should remind the client of her ethical obligation to deliver all information to the lawyer. The client then can decide whether to provide the information or not. If the client elects not to discuss the matter, the legal assistant also has an obligation to inform the lawyer of the client's reluctance to share specific information.

The Interview Environment

The setting of the interview should be conducive to the fact-gathering process. Ideally, this means a private interview in a controlled environment. Interviews conducted in the law office usually meet this criterion; field interviews seldom do.

Office Interviews The interview should be conducted in a location which is completely private, orderly, and conservatively furnished. A private conference room is ideal if one is available. To avoid potential distractions, remove all other files and materials not associated with the client's case from the room.

Anticipate any needs that the client or witness may have (beverages, tissues, ashtrays, and so forth) and bring those items to the conference room.

If a conference room is unavailable, the legal assistant may conduct the interview in his office as long as his desk is clear and the office is neat. All files and loose papers other than those related to the client should be removed from sight. Nothing other than the client's materials and a note pad should be on the desk. This conveys the message that the client's case is the most important thing on the legal assistant's agenda.

If the legal assistant's office is used for interviewing, the decor should be aesthetic as possible; any art work, conservative; and the color scheme, muted. Male interviewers may find it helpful to incorporate a few plants or photographs of children into the decor; this indicates his nurturing side. Female interviewers should avoid having more than one plant in the office for the same but opposite reason. Females may benefit from a decor which incorporates a framed Bill of Rights, Gettysburg address, or similar items. Hopefully, sexual stereotyping is on its way to becoming an archaic social blunder. In the meantime, however, the legal assistant cannot ignore its impact—particularly when dealing with older people who are not ready for radical social changes.

A.   Privacy   Privacy is the most important environmental characteristic of a successful interview. When clients are interviewed, privacy underscores client confidentiality, which is critical to free exchange of information between the client and the legal assistant.

Let the receptionist know when an interview begins and arrange for the telephone to be answered during the interview conference. Making these arrangements emphasizes to the client that her case is important and is taken seriously by the interviewer. As a practical matter, the information from the client will flow more easily if distractions and interruptions are held to a minimum.

B.   Image   First impressions count and frequently are difficult to displace. Just as the office setting creates a first impression, the appearance of the legal assistant leaves a distinct and lasting impression on the client.

Clients and witnesses expect lawyers and those associated with lawyers to look professional; they should not be disappointed. Conservative, tailored business attire creates a favorable impression. Simple jewelry (no excessive number of rings, no gaudy tie tacks), conservative hairstyles, and only the most subtle perfumes or colognes (if any at all) likewise should advance the client's first impression of a conservative professional.

C. Seating Arrangements The seating arrangement is important to the interview process. For example, a particularly gregarious client or witness may need to be kept at a distance (such as across the desk) as an unspoken reminder that the legal assistant is in charge.

In interviewing a shy client, it may be better for the interviewer to move her chair to the side of the desk (to minimize the authority symbol of the desk) to promote the client's sense that she and the legal assistant are much the same. Using an excuse of poor hearing or some other pretext, the interviewer even may move to a chair located on the same side of the desk as the client's chair, using care not to move so close as to invade the client's personal space—especially during a first interview.

Many lawyers use a small, round table; a small sofa; or overstuffed chairs located away from the desk area, sometimes in the corner of the office, to create an impression of intimacy that is similar to a home environment. This frequently puts people at ease and helps to build trust and confidence with the client or witness. The more comfortable a person feels, the more information the interviewer will obtain.

Field Interviews The environment in which a field interview is conducted is difficult for the interviewer to control. The interview may be conducted at a construction site, in a manufacturing plant, or at the home or office of the witness. Each of these locations is approached differently by the interviewer.

It may be necessary, for example, to interview a witness at a construction site with heavy equipment operating in the background or at a manufacturing plant with assembly-line noise. The interviewer's ability to adapt calmly to these types of environments helps to establish trust and confidence with the witness.

The legal assistant may be required to wear protective clothing, a helmet, or goggles in some field settings. At a construction site, a male legal assistant may elect to loosen or to remove his tie or to roll up his sleeves to bridge the identity gap with the witness more quickly. A female legal assistant in the same setting may want to wear flat shoes and a simple, open-collared blouse—perhaps with a denim skirt or jumper—that day. It will be easier for a witness to identify with an interviewer whose appearance in the field is somewhat similar to his own. The more information the interviewer can glean from the witness and from observing applicable procedures or processes at the field site, the better prepared the case will be for settlement or trial.

If manufacturing procedures or processes are not an issue in the case, the field interview should be conducted in a private location, preferably one that is quiet enough to permit normal conversation. Avoid high-traffic areas, such as a lunchroom or a loading dock, where the curiosity of other workers may be aroused. More information will be obtained if the witness is comfortable that he will not be overheard by others. If no other quiet place is available to conduct the interview, an automobile may provide some privacy. Another option may be to invite the witness to lunch at a nearby restaurant or diner. Field interviews often test the interviewer's creativity as well as the soundness of her interviewing skills.

Preparing for the Interview

A well-executed interview cannot occur without thoughtful preparation. In addition to planning the interview's general direction ahead of time, the legal assistant must gather all necessary files, paperwork, and equipment for the interview. This may include authorization or release forms, checklists, business cards, note pads, and recording devices (if appropriate). If copies of documents will be distributed during the interview, extra sets of these documents should be available. The organization and efficiency of the interviewer create a favorable impression in any interview setting.

Review Relevant Data   Well before the scheduled interview, the legal assistant should review carefully any information about the case and the client or the witness that may be available. This should include at least a brief conference with the supervising attorney to obtain her preliminary evaluation, analysis, and instructions.

When it is possible to do so, initial interviews with clients should be preceded by a review of any applicable statutes and case law. This helps to define the legal issues as well as the elements of proof required in a particular type of case, which, in turn, helps to focus the direction of the interview.

Checklists   Select the appropriate checklists and related forms prior to the interview. Use checklists to help stay on track and to obtain the information needed but do not be slave to them. Recognize that every interview flows differently because the person interviewed is different; the checklist should facilitate—not obstruct—the interview process.

Each practice area typically generates its own checklist, which should be revised frequently to hone the procedures and the interview style of the interviewer. Used appropriately, a checklist improves the interviewer's efficiency and effectiveness. It allows the interviewer to concentrate on what the client is saying rather than on the next item of information that the interviewer needs to obtain.

Forms   Determine whether any preprinted forms may be needed in connection with the client's matter and gather all such forms prior to the interview.

If the interview relates to a personal injury claim, for example, authorizations or releases usually are required to investigate the claim. Several authorization or release forms should be signed during the interview. The signed forms then are presented to doctors, hospitals, insurance companies, and others to obtain privileged information.

Each area of the law typically requires its own standardized forms for authorization or release of pertinent information. For instance, estate planning or probate administration requires releases to obtain financial information from various institutions; labor law requires signed forms to acquire personnel records; and real estate mortgage companies require releases from individuals before financial information is relinquished. Anticipating what forms may be necessary will save contacting the client again merely to sign forms.

Note Pad   Use a note pad to record the client's or the witness's comments during the interview process. The legal assistant never should allow note-taking to impede the flow of the interview. Notes must be sufficient to allow the legal assistant to prepare a detailed memorandum or witness statement of the facts related to him. At the same time, however, the interviewer must be attentive to the client (or to the witness) by using frequent eye contact and other active listening techniques. This reassures the client that the legal assistant is listening and is interested.

Over time, most interviewers develop their own codes to record notes efficiently during the interview. Studies indicate that significant rapport is lost when answers are recorded by the longhand method while the client or witness sits quietly, waiting for the next question. Using a shorthand or speed writing method to take notes maintains spontaneity and rapport. Immediately after the interview, the legal assistant should dictate or otherwise prepare the memorandum—while the notes still are fresh (*see below*).

A note pad also comes in handy if a field witness is willing to sign a written statement. When the witness agrees to sign a written statement during the interview, it is best to obtain his signature before returning to the office. In this situation, the statement ordinarily is written in longhand. After the interview is over, witnesses sometimes decline to sign statements. The lapse of time occasionally causes people to question their involvement or to be influenced negatively by the opinions of others. Some interviewers make it a practice to use the signed, handwritten statement to prepare a typewritten statement, which then is delivered to the witness for signature. This may seem less threatening, because the witness already will have signed one statement (the handwritten one) and can compare the two statements to be certain that nothing has been changed. *Additional information on witness statements is covered later in the chapter.*

Recording Devices   Lawyers differ in their views about tape- recording interviews. Some lawyers believe that tape-recording inhibits the client or witness, making her more concerned about how sentences are structured than about telling what she knows. Some witnesses feel uncomfortable about being involved if their every word is recorded at the first interview. (Taped interviews of witnesses can be a disadvantage if the information is more beneficial to the opposing party than it is to the client.)

Other lawyers believe that the benefits of a tape recording outweigh the disadvantages. A tape recording keeps the witness honest by providing a irrefutable record of the facts and events related by the witness; the witness becomes committed to that version of the facts contained in the recording; and subsequent, contradictory statements are minimized. A tape-recorded interview occasionally is so convincing that it can be used as leverage to negotiate a favorable settlement for a client. Another advantage of a tape-recorded witness statement is that it accurately reflects voice inflection and mood, which notes cannot do.

If tape-recording occurs, certain formalities must be observed.

- The interviewer states his name, date, and the purpose and site of the interview.

- The witness is introduced and is asked for permission to record the interview, and a statement is made or acknowledged by the witness that the interview is given voluntarily.

- All persons in the room are identified, together with their connection to the litigation and their reason for appearance.

- Any interruption is identified by time, date, and reason for the interruption. When recording recommences, the time, date, and those present are announced once again.

- Some jurisdictions require that the witness receive a copy of the transcribed statement or of the taped interview.

- The conclusion of the recording includes a statement that the recorded interview was given freely and that the witness was given the opportunity to make any changes.

An indirect benefit of recording an interview is that it allows the interviewer to assess his own performance. This is particularly helpful for an apprentice interviewer. Allowing him to evaluate his interviewing style and verbal skills provides a means to improve his interviewing technique.

Photocopy Equipment   Photocopy equipment should be accessible at the interview site. If a witness brings useful information to the interview and is willing to share it, copies of everything should be made immediately. After the interview is concluded, the witness may misplace the information or may not feel as cooperative as he did during the interview.

Before a field interview takes place, determine where the nearest photocopy machine is located. Timely access to valuable information through photocopies can affect the strategy of the case. Until a comprehensive analysis of the facts and legal issues is performed, all information potentially is relevant.

Preparation for Field Interviews   The preparation for a field interview proceeds in much the same way as preparation for an interview in the law office. One additional consideration in a field interview is transporting the interview items (file, forms, documents, tapes, recording devices, and business cards) to the interview site. A good leather briefcase is a status symbol in the corporate world and serves the legal assistant well, particularly in conducting field interviews. It enhances the legal assistant's professional image and solves the problem of transporting equipment and supplies.

A business card identifies the interviewer to unfamiliar witnesses in the field. If a letter was mailed to the witness to arrange the field interview, show a copy of the letter to the witness to establish further identification. Provide as much information as is necessary to make the witness comfortable with the legal assistant's identity.

Conducting the Interview

A successful interview requires planning, effective use of equipment and resources, and superior human relations skills of the interviewer. The ultimate purpose of an interview is to obtain the facts within the personal knowledge of the client or the witness. The way in which facts are gathered sets the climate and the tone of the interview; it directly affects the quality and quantity of facts that a client or witness may be willing to share. A successful interview depends on:

- the interviewer's demeanor or "bedside manner";
- the client's (or witness's) impression of the interviewer;
- the interviewer's method of seeking information;
- the interviewer's comprehension of the facts related by the client;
- the client's expectations of the outcome of the case; and
- the interviewer's ability to address the client's (or witness') apprehensions.

Interviewing skills are used in both litigation and nonlitigation matters. Preparing for litigation requires considerable client and witness interviewing. With proper discovery work and thorough investigation of facts before and during litigation, a case often can be settled without trial. This saves time and effort for the lawyer and saves money for the client.

In addition, client interviewing is used extensively in the (i) corporate area to create new businesses, for mergers, consolidations and acquisitions; (ii) estate administration area to create estate plans and administer probates; (iii) labor relations area to investigate discrimination matters and union/management disputes; (iv) bankruptcy area to gather financial data and to investigate financial records; and (v) real estate area in relation to closings and other transactions.

Once the lawyer determines that she may be interested in accepting the case, the fact-gathering process begins.

The time of the interview must be convenient for the client or the witness. Allocating sufficient time is essential to the interview's success, although planning around the schedules of professional people can be challenging. The interviewer's sensitivity to schedule demands will gain the cooperation of these busy people. To be effective, interviews should not be sandwiched too tightly between other appointments for either the interviewer or the client. Otherwise, needless time pressures and stress can result.

Introductions   Proper introductions are essential to establish the credibility and the roles of all those involved in the interview process. Especially in connection with an initial client interview, the lawyer should introduce the legal assistant formally to the client—either during or immediately following the lawyer's preliminary conference with the client. The lawyer should use the introduction as an opportunity to explain the involvement of the legal assistant to reassure the client of the legal assistant's competence and expertise.

For example, the lawyer might call the legal assistant into her office and say, *"This is Chris Baker, my legal assistant, who works closely with me on several of my cases. I have asked him to assist me with your case as well. Feel free to discuss anything with Chris that you would discuss with me. If ever you need to reach me and if I am not available, do not hesitate to get in touch with Chris. He usually can locate me within a very short time and will be able to answer many of the questions that you might have. Since Chris is not a lawyer, your overall attorney fees will be reduced if we use him. Chris is extremely capable; and, fortunately, he has some time to help me with your case."*

If the legal assistant is not introduced at the initial conference but meets with the client alone at a later time, he must describe his role clearly and must explain that he is not a lawyer. At any subsequent meeting with the client, the legal assistant should be aware of how the client refers to him. Any confusion concerning the legal assistant's status should be corrected immediately. The client must understand that the legal assistant **cannot**:

- *offer direct legal advice or interpret the law;*
- *accept a case;*
- *represent individuals before a court; or*
- *set or adjust fees.*

Any inquiries concerning these subjects must be referred to the lawyer for response.

Getting Started   In the ideal situation, the lawyer will have introduced the legal assistant to the client (*see above*). After introductions are made, the legal assistant should escort the client to the location where the interview will take place, whether in a conference room or in the legal assistant's office.

Offer to do something personal for the client (or the witness), such as getting a cup of coffee or a cold beverage. The interviewer should not ask someone else to do this but, rather, should do it himself. This small gesture often puts a nervous client more at ease, particularly when the client is a private person rather than a large corporation being interviewed through an officer or other representative. Even if the client is not nervous, everyone likes to receive special, personal attention. The process of building rapport begins the moment the legal assistant meets the client or the witness, and personal courtesies extended by the legal assistant will speed the process.

On the way to the interview site, make small talk about whether the client was able to find the office easily, parking, the weather, travel conditions, or a newsworthy event of the day. This exchange allows the legal assistant to begin her assessment of the client's attitude and communication style. It also allows the client to size up the legal assistant and to become comfortable with the law office atmosphere (if that is the interview site).

Explain the Process   Early in the interview, explain the interview process to the client, including the fact that notes will be taken to record the information which the client provides. Also explain that questions will be asked to clarify facts. This type of explanation prepares the client or witness for those events when they occur.

Because a lawsuit generates a winner and a loser, the environment of the client's interview can become strained when the legal assistant begins to probe for specific details. Questioning must be used to establish the factual basis for the client's claims or defenses. Nevertheless, an unintentional confrontation can arise if the client has not been prepared properly for extensive inquiries. Without a full explanation of the process and proper handling by the legal assistant, a client may regard extensive questioning as an affront to her integrity or to her powers of recollection. If the client knows what is going to happen, she will be more at ease during the interview.

Framing the Questions   The question-and-answer segment may begin with routine matters such as personal background information about the client. Background information is necessary for a complete factual picture, and this type of questioning allows both the client and the legal assistant to ease into the more substantive—and possibly more difficult—questioning that lies ahead. Background information generally includes the client's full name, address, telephone number, date of birth, social security number, place of employment, length of employment, job title, marital status, and so forth.

Once the client's personal background information is recorded, the interview can move to the substantive facts related to the client's case. Ideally, varied questioning techniques are employed by the legal assistant during the interview, with most of the following types of questions being used:

- ***Open Questions***   An open question is one designed to elicit a narrative response. This type of question is particularly effective at the beginning of an interview but may be used at any time that a narrative description or explanation is sought. Examples of open questions include:

  ▸*Starting from the beginning, what do you remember about the accident?*

▸*Tell me something about* _____ (your business, your marriage, your son's problems at school, the way you want your property divided after your death).

▸*How did you happen to be in Cincinnati that weekend?*

- **Closed Questions**   A closed question is one which seeks a specific, narrow answer. Closed questions generally are used in combination with open questions—and much more sparingly—to obtain specific details or to verify details previously provided by the client. Examples of closed questions include:

  ▸*What color was the traffic light when you first noticed it?*

  ▸*Have you and your wife ever seen a marriage counselor?*

  ▸*Were you in Cincinnati on business?*

- **Leading Questions**   A leading question is one which either (1) suggests the answer desired by the questioner or (2) suggests a fact not stated previously by the client. Leading questions may be used to good effect during cross-examination of a witness at a deposition or at a trial. However, their utility is limited in a client or witness interview, where the objective is to elicit facts and information. Examples of leading questions include:

  ▸*Of course, you were wearing your seat belt at the time of the accident, weren't you?*

  ▸*Surely you don't believe that your wife is having an affair, do you?*

  ▸*Where did you and your girlfriend stay while you were in Cincinnati?* (The client did not say that he had a girlfriend or that anyone accompanied him to Cincinnati.)

- **Silent Questions**   A silent question is not a question at all; rather, it is a questioning technique by which the interviewer maintains an extended, expectant silence after an answer is given. The implication is that the interviewer is waiting for the rest of the answer. Faced with this situation, a client or a witness often will supply further details or explanation without being asked a specific question. This technique can be extremely effective in the right circumstance; however, because it creates some anxiety, it should be used judiciously.

Of all the questioning techniques described, open questions generally are the best method to obtain the most details about those facts known to the client.

A.   Flexibility   A successful interviewer adapts to the communication style of the client or witness as much as possible. The sensory terms used by the client during conversation reveal his communication style. For example, if he uses the phrase "I see what you mean," he probably is a visual communicator. The most effective questions for this type of individual are those phrased in terms of vision, such as *"When you recall the accident, describe what you see."* If a person uses a phrase such as "I hear what you say," the interviewer should try to ask questions in auditory terms whenever possible, for example, *"Did you hear anything unusual in the way he spoke?"* or *"What sounds did the pump make before it stopped operating?"* Imitating the communication style of the client or witness minimizes misunderstanding of both the questions asked and the answers provided. A person is more comfortable and open with an interviewer when they both use the same communication style.

Flexibility also includes a recognition that the words of a question can mean different things to different people. The legal assistant must be able to tailor questions to the background, cultural circumstances, and vocabulary of the client or of the witness. For example, a witness may not have *perceived* anything, even though he saw the entire incident. He may have no *acquaintances*; however, he may know many people.

The questions should be phrased simply and clearly. Avoid multiple-part questions and limit those questions which can be answered by a "yes" or "no" or by a single word. Above all, beware of using leading questions.

Leading questions can turn a credible, honest person into an untrustworthy witness. Questions such as *"You did see John Blackhart deliberately crash into the department store window, didn't you?"* or *"You saw John's pals looting merchandise from the store, right?"* create an obligation to agree with the questioner rather than to provide an answer based on personal knowledge. Leading questions such as these plant ideas in the client's mind and put words into his mouth. The end result is that the interviewer supplies the facts, and the client merely agrees. The better practice is to use open questions as much as possible to obtain facts during the interview.

Open questions produce narrative answers, which include fact details known by the client. The more details that are obtained, the more successful the interview and the easier it is to secure corroboration from other witnesses and sources.

Finally, prepare for the unexpected. Although ultimate control of the interview rests with the legal assistant, she should allow the interview to take a natural course. This flexibility sometimes produces unanticipated, revealing information with tremendous impact on the case.

B. Seeking Sensitive Information   As valuable as tact is to an interviewer, legal assistants and lawyers alike sometimes take this attribute too far when dealing with topics such as death, suicide, or sexual activities. Taken to its most extreme level, tact becomes evasion. An evasive question indicates the interviewer is uncomfortable with the subject matter or that the topic cannot be discussed candidly. Moreover, the most typical response to an evasive question is an evasive answer, which does nothing to advance the purpose of the interview.

To illustrate, it is more direct to ask, "*How do you want your assets distributed at your death?*" than it is to ask, "*If you should pass on, how should your property be distributed?*" It is apparent that everyone will die one day. The client would not visit an attorney to discuss his estate plan unless he knew this to be true. The more direct question reinforces the client's perceived need for legal services and paves the way for a frank discussion of his specific situation.

Direct questions are most effective when they are combined with the interviewer's sensitivity to a particular client's emotional state. The topic of death, for example, evokes a very different emotional reaction when a client discusses his own death in relation to an estate plan than it does when he discusses the situation which led to the death of his child. The death of a child is a traumatic experience. When a person has difficulty describing a traumatic experience, acknowledge the difficulty and move to a more neutral topic until the person regains enough composure to return to the difficult—but necessary—topic of the interview. It may be necessary to take one or more breaks during an interview related to a traumatic experience or to conduct the full interview in more than one session. The best way to gauge a particular client's emotional state during the interview process is to let the client talk.

C. Let the Client Talk   Every individual has her own chain of beliefs concerning facts and events as well as her own, unique way of describing them. Allowing a client to describe a sequence of events freely and without interruption is an efficient way to measure her testimony in terms of both substance and style of presentation.

It also permits a client to tell her story, very possibly for the first time, to someone who she is reasonably certain will be on her side. Many people are reluctant to discuss their most personal affairs or their financial situations even with close friends for fear of criticism, ridicule, or rejection. This may be especially true if they believe that they may be at fault in some way or if they believe that they have an obligation to protect someone close to them.

While the client tells her story, listen for and note those facts that require further clarification or verification. Encourage the client or witness to continue her narrative with active listening techniques (*see below*), with additional open questions, and with supportive comments such as, "*Please go on*," "*That must have been difficult for you*," or "*Anyone would have been worried at that point*."

A narrative allows the legal assistant to evaluate the client and her testimony style in a way that cannot be done with a series of closed questions. The legal assistant should assess the client's familiarity with details and her level of articulation: logical or rambling, composed or nervous, self-assured or shy, and so forth.

Note any extraordinary physical characteristics (stuttering, a noticeable birthmark, a limp, excessively long hair on a man) or mannerisms (popping of knuckles, tugging at an ear, fidgeting) that may distract a juror from the client's testimony during a trial or that may create unfavorable bias or prejudice in a juror. These types of features generally are noticed when the lawyer or legal assistant first meets a client but are overlooked and quickly forgotten after a very short time. Noting them tactfully in the interview memorandum (*discussed below*) ensures that whoever prepares the case for trial will be reminded to address them during jury selection or during the opening statement.

Long hair can be cut; but if the client stutters, for example, a jury is certain to notice it at trial—just as the legal assistant notices it during the initial interview. Some jurors may be so distracted by it that they will not hear the substance of her testimony. To avoid this result, a trial attorney might mention during jury selection, "*My client, Mary Jones, is very embarrassed about this—and she probably will be a little upset with me for mentioning it—but Mary sometimes stutters when she gets nervous. I just want Mary to be reassured that you could render a fair verdict without being affected by her stuttering if it happens. Do you think her stuttering would affect your final verdict in the case?*" Of course, no one will answer "yes"; but the real advantage is that the jurors will expect Mary to stutter, will not be distracted by it, and may be even more supportive of her as a result of the explanation. If her stutter is not included as part of the original interview memorandum, it might be overlooked in the trial preparation.

D.   Who, What, When, Where, How, and Why   Encourage the client or witness to supply details through supportive questioning. After the initial story is told fully, questions are phrased to authenticate the details of the narrative. Brusque, interrogation-type questioning likely will result in brusque answers. Even if a witness is aligned with the opposing party, there is no justification to alienate the witness further by terse questions or by an argumentative style. Tactful, carefully phrased questions will produce more information and a more cooperative spirit. After a case has been concluded, adverse witnesses—and sometimes adverse parties—have been known to seek assistance from the lawyer's office where they were treated well as adversaries rather than return to the lawyer who represented them originally.

Questions phrased in terms of who, what, when, where, how, and why are more likely to produce detailed, narrative answers. This type of question encourages a storytelling atmosphere: *"Who delivered the box to the Trade Center?"; "What was the messenger wearing when the box was delivered?"; "Where were you when you first noticed the messenger?"; "How would you describe the messenger?"; or "Why were you at the Trade Center that day?"* This form of question also may be used to ask follow-up questions to verify some previous answer.

If statements seem to conflict, ask the client's help in resolving the misunderstanding. The client or witness never should have the sense that the legal assistant believes he is lying. Asking for clarification because of the legal assistant's (not the client's) confusion likely will produce the needed information. If the client senses that his integrity is being questioned, an opposite result can occur: he may recoil quietly or he may become obstinate and refuse to answer further questions.

Use Checklists to Stay on Track   Checklists should be designed and used to facilitate, not inhibit, the interview process. Used correctly, they serve as a map to a specific destination, allowing frequent side trips along the way. The legal assistant should be flexible enough to ask pertinent questions not listed on the checklist as the dialogue progresses. If the client or the witness wanders too far from the subject, however, the checklist provides focus to put the interview back on track.

Forms or questionnaires completed by the client sometimes provide an efficient method to gather facts. They work best, however, after the working relationship already has been established between the lawyer and the client. A prospective client who has no previous working relationship with the law office understandably may be offended by forms or questionnaires sent to her for completion before the initial client interview. In this situation, the prospective client justifiably may conclude that she will be just another form in a vast sea of forms located somewhere in the lawyer's office. Each client prefers to believe her case is the most interesting one that the lawyer has, and she expects the lawyer and the legal assistant to feel the same way. A pre-interview questionnaire makes this belief difficult to maintain.

If a follow-up form or questionnaire is given or sent to a client for completion after the client relationship has been established, it should be client friendly. It should be constructed simply, with ample "white space" to provide answers. Questions should be phrased in a clear and concise way and should be couched in terms which demonstrate sensitivity to the typical situation addressed by the form. A bankruptcy questionnaire, for example, might include the following:

POOR   List the name and address of each creditor holding a disputed, contingent, or non-liquidated claim against the debtor's estate:

BETTER   Give the name and address of anyone who claims you owe money if you think the claim is wrong (1) because you do not owe the money or (2) because you do not owe as much as the creditor says you owe (do not include claims that are part of a past or present lawsuit):

POOR   List all debts for which you have defaulted in payments:

BETTER   List each of the bills for which payments are not current:

The second question in each group is better, because it states the instruction in simple English and because it avoids words that imply the client is to blame for his situation.

Corroboration of Facts   All relevant facts obtained during a client or witness interview must be corroborated. Corroboration is the process used to substantiate or to verify the accuracy of a particular fact. It assures the attorney of the client's (or witness') credibility; it also provides supporting evidence which can be used during trial to assure the jury of the credibility of a particular witness or of the justness of the overall claim or defense raised by the client.

After any interview, the legal assistant must verify the information gathered, distinguishing facts of personal knowledge from conjecture, opinion, or gossip. Clients and witnesses frequently are confused or mistaken about dates, times, events, distances, and other specific details (unless they are among those rare individuals who record everything that happens during the course of a day). Investigate outside sources for corroborating evidence to substantiate the client's recollection of facts and the lawyer's legal theory. Corroboration is essential for every factual statement made during the interview.

A.   Identity of People   Obtaining the complete name, address, telephone number, and place of employment of any person mentioned during a client or witness interview is important to the investigative process. For example, if a client relates that her neighbor was present when the defendant threatened her, the legal assistant must obtain as much identifying information about the neighbor as possible. After the interview, the neighbor is contacted to corroborate the client's story.

A witness interview may reveal that a particular witness has little or no firsthand knowledge about the case. Although a witness may not offer the strong statement hoped for, she may be able to provide leads to others who have relevant information.

Every lead must be checked. The person thought least likely to have relevant information may become the star witness in a case. In conducting the investigation, the legal assistant should determine why a particular person was in the area at the time of the event or incident, whether he frequented the area, how he may know the client, the person's relationship (if any) to the client or any witness, and whether he has given this or similar information to others. If a person seems to have useful information, a background check should be conducted to assure his credibility and reliability. Careful scrutiny of witnesses eliminates surprises at trial.

B.   Identity of Documents   The client generally is the first source of documents connected with a case, which he often brings with him to the initial interview. If there are other documents which may be relevant to the case but which the client does not have, the legal assistant must obtain as many details as possible about those documents from the client, including their location and the identity of the person who has them.

If geography, weather conditions, technical structure, or similar conditions are relevant to an issue in the case, the legal assistant may need to obtain plat drawings from the city or county engineers, weather maps from the weather service, evaluation reports from technical engineers, or other documentation from appropriate specialists. If there is a charge for any of the information, authorization must be obtained from the supervising attorney.

Keep documents produced by the opposing party separate from those supplied by the client. Compare documents in the two groups to determine if there is a "smoking gun" among the documents which may be detrimental to the client's case.

Listen   The legal assistant or lawyer must listen actively throughout the interview, which means more than simply hearing and recording the facts. Gathering facts is only one small part of active listening.

Active listening requires the legal assistant to visualize the situation as the client relates it. This means being quiet and letting the client speak; it also means being actively engaged with the storyteller. An active listener places himself into the story and imagines being there as the events are described. This sometimes is called imaginative listening or *empathy*. An active listener feels what the client feels, and he is able to express those feelings in objective terms.

The way to understand the meaning of words and the feeling behind them is to listen closely to the client. The client's story is central to the fact-gathering process. It delineates the experiences and expectations of the client. By allowing the client to talk freely, the legal assistant is able to see the situation or the problem from the client's vantage point.

Equally important to active listening is the client's nonverbal communication (body language). The way she presents herself (relaxed or nervous, pleasant or angry) frequently communicates messages much more loudly than her words. If the client appears wary, distrustful, or guarded, the legal assistant needs to work harder at gaining the trust necessary for a good working relationship. Recognizing the client's unwillingness to talk or unwillingness to talk about a particular subject requires the legal assistant to be flexible enough to discuss more neutral topics until the client is ready to move back to the issues at hand.

Active listening results in signals from the interviewer to indicate that she hears and understands what the client or witness is saying and that she wants to hear more. The signals include an attentive posture, the proper amount of eye contact, approving nods, and supportive comments such as *"please go on," "I see," "of course," "it must have been very hard for you,"* and so forth.

A.   Is That a Fact?   As part of the interview process, the legal assistant records information, sorting it into broad categories according to whether it is a fact or not. Clients frequently inject opinions, speculation, conjecture, or assumptions as they relate facts. Without interrupting the natural flow of the narrative, the legal assistant segregates the facts and obtains as many details as possible about those facts during subsequent questioning.

A *fact* is a situation, event, or occurrence which is within the personal knowledge of the client or witness. With the exception of an expert witness, clients and most other witnesses are permitted to testify about only those things they know personally; they cannot testify about their opinions, impressions, or assumptions. This distinguishes fact witnesses from expert witnesses. For example, a fact witness could not testify at trial that a particular thing tasted like dirt without first establishing that he had tasted dirt. Likewise, a fact witness generally could not testify that the defendant was intoxicated, because few fact witnesses are experts in the area of intoxication. The witness could testify about only what he saw, heard, smelled, and the like. He could testify that the defendant was unsteady on his feet (the witness could see this), that the defendant's speech was slurred (the witness could hear this), or that the defendant reeked of alcohol (the witness could smell this). Although it may be profitable to pursue a client's opinion statements during an interview to determine their factual basis, the legal assistant's ultimate objective is to obtain as many facts and details about facts as possible from the interview.

A more complete discussion of segregation of facts is contained in Chapter 4, Judgment and Analytical Ability, in this *Review Manual*.

B. Does it Make Sense? Active listening means listening critically to what the client or witness says to determine if it makes sense. Sometimes people simply make errors or misstate the facts when they relate them (*see below*). Frequently, however, people determine ahead of time what it is that they think the interviewer needs to know; and that is the narrative they give. Generally speaking, facts obtained through this type of filtering must be explored by the legal assistant to ensure that all facts are exposed and to evaluate credibility of the facts provided based on principles of logic.

Understanding the client's communication style is helpful in recognizing her pattern of logic. During an interview, answers fall into a pattern which tends to reveal more than their factual content. If the client talks in circles, the message may be that she is reluctant to face the issue. For example, a driver who hits a child pedestrian may have difficulty describing the sequence of events because of guilt feelings, even though the accident was not his fault. A battered woman who explains in detail how she acquired bruises through her clumsiness may not even mention her abusive husband's behavior toward her. The facts must be pieced together carefully to re-create an accurate chain of events. This is particularly important for jury trials, where the jury must be able to relate to a logical sequence of events. Showing how the pieces fit together is the lawyer's job, with the help of the client and the witnesses.

Every interviewer has an obligation to practice active listening techniques. Devoting less than full attention to the dialogue is a disservice to the client. Attentive listening exposes not only the facts, but also groundless beliefs, false interpretations, misconceptions, and fears. When several people are interviewed about the same incident, their stories may contain inconsistencies even though all of them point to the same ultimate conclusion. All inconsistencies must be investigated to determine the true details and sequence of events.

Contradictory Statements   Stories filled with contradictions or inconsistencies present challenges to the legal assistant. The legal assistant must (1) recognize the inconsistency and (2) analyze the motive of the client or witness who is telling the story. Some inconsistencies may be simple misunderstandings or misperceptions; others may be deliberate deceptions.

A.   Error   Clients and witnesses frequently become confused about specific details of facts and events unless they can identify the event with a special occurrence. The confusion leads to errors or to misstatements of fact. For example, a client may be certain of the date of an accident because it happened on his birthday; his recollection that the day was a Wednesday may be wrong, however. The interviewer always should ask if there is anything special about the date that causes the client to remember it. If there is no special reason to remember it, be skeptical about details related to dates, times, and so forth. Most people cannot remember what they had for lunch last Wednesday unless there is a special reason to remember. They become confused and then convince themselves that it must have happened on a particular day or in a particular way.

Interviews conducted soon after an incident provide the most accurate information. Memories fail after a period of time—the longer the time between the incident and the interview, the weaker the recollection of the witness. If the witness cannot remember the facts surrounding an incident or if he knew only part (but not all) of the facts in the first place, he may engage in presumption and conjecture about what he thinks must have happened rather than report only what he knows to be the fact. It is more difficult for the legal assistant to separate fact from conjecture when statements are taken long after the incident because by then, the witness will have convinced himself that all of it is fact.

A corollary to this problem is the witness who knows only a few facts and fills in the gaps with information that he thinks the interviewer wants to hear or that he thinks make his story more believable. This sometimes is called *confabulation*. Faced with a thorough and tactful interviewer, this witness may be able to back away from the fictional parts of his statement without losing face. This type of witness generally is somewhat easier to deal with than one who has become convinced that his conjecture is fact (*see above*).

B.   Misperception   Misperception and differences in perception sometimes occur because people perceive things differently. The differences in what two different people perceive may stem from the fact that each was located at a different vantage point when the incident occurred. If two different witnesses were standing on opposite corners of an intersection, for example, a comparison of their statements likely would show inconsistencies or contradictions. What each witness saw genuinely could be different, because each saw a different side of the accident scene.

Even if both witnesses were standing on the same street corner, they may give different accounts of the accident. A classic illustration of how this phenomenon works is used in evidence classes across the country. Shortly after the class begins, an unidentified person darts into the room, grabs something from the professor's podium or desk, and darts out again. Everyone is startled except the professor, who arranged for the incident to occur. The professor asks the students to write a description of the thief. None of the students has any reason to misrepresent the facts (who would not want to get a good grade?); yet, if there are fifteen students in the class, there will be fifteen different descriptions of the thief. He might be described variously as wearing a blue jacket, a black jacket, a navy blue jacket, or no jacket at all. The balance of the thief's description will be just as diverse as the information reported about his jacket. When the "thief" returns to the classroom for inspection, students generally are astounded to see for themselves how inaccurate most of their descriptions are.

This type of inconsistency or contradiction occurs all the time, particularly in connection with a startling event. It has nothing to do with lying; different people simply perceive things in different ways.

C. **Deception** Occasionally, a legal assistant encounters a witness who misrepresents facts and events intentionally. The best efforts to establish rapport with a witness may not prevent her from telling distortions and lies. Probing with diplomatic questions will not accomplish much if the witness is intent on concealing the truth. The motive for such behavior may never be known, but this witness should not be dismissed lightly. An unscrupulous witness may align himself with the opposing party and can create havoc, at least for a short time. When such a witness is discovered in the investigation of a case, a second interview may be warranted—preferably conducted by the attorney and conducted with recording equipment.

If it is becomes clear during an initial interview that a client or witness deliberately is lying, the legal assistant should excuse himself tactfully and advise the lawyer immediately. If the lawyer is not available, the alternative is to end the interview on some pretext and to advise the lawyer when she returns.

Verify Accuracy Factual contradictions and inconsistencies can arise through error, misperception, or deception. Because of this, every factual account must be verified. Those factual accounts provided by clients must, in addition, be corroborated through written documentation and the testimony of witnesses.

A.   During the Interview   During the interview and after the client has concluded her initial narrative, the legal assistant asks questions designed to verify what the client said and to fill the factual gaps left by the narrative. Empathetic questioning, rather than showmanship, reaps the greatest rewards in this process. For example, a question that begins, "*Isn't it true that . . .?*" is the worst way to obtain additional information. This type of leading question may be appropriate in a cross-examination during trial, but it serves no beneficial purpose in the interview process. If it is asked during an interview, the client or witness may become defensive and refuse to provide helpful information or may refuse to provide further information of any kind.

Instead, phrase the question as a request for help or clarification. For example, questions that begin with "*Let me see if I understand . . .*" or "*I am confused about . . .*" are less intimidating and are more likely to be answered freely. Questioning has two purposes: (1) to obtain specific information and (2) to guide the discussion to meaningful details concerning that information. The client or witness usually is more willing to cooperate by helping if the interviewer is confused than if the interviewer seems to think that he (the client or witness) is confused or—even worse—that he is lying.

The process of verifying facts and details with the client or the witness during the interview sometimes is called ***internal verification***. In addition to probing gently for further facts to verify details previously supplied, the legal assistant may misstate a detail purposely. This gives the client an opportunity to correct the error, which tells the legal assistant how certain the client is about the facts. This technique is quite effective if it is used in moderation. Overused, the client may infer that the legal assistant was not paying attention at all while he was relating his problem.

B.   After the Interview   Once the interview is concluded, the legal assistant prepares a list of potential documents to acquire as well as a list of agencies, companies, and other witnesses to contact for supplemental information and documentation. In addition, ***external verification*** is used to check outside sources to verify the facts obtained from the client or witness.

Accounts reported by newspapers and other media may verify or corroborate the client's claims. Other sources might include hospital records, photographs, police reports, employment records, business records, school records, military records, driving records, court records, and vital statistics records. If a case involves a personal injury claim related to employment, investigation of the employment background of the claimant may reveal a history of job-related personal injury claims. Investigation of the claimant's medical records for similar injuries previously sustained also may be useful. Even if these sources are not accessible early in the case because the claimant is the opposing party, anyone can check the records of those courts where prior cases would have been filed. If this type of information exists, the lawyer certainly will want to have it as early in the case as possible, without regard to which side she represents.

The public also has access to weather maps, geography maps, demographics of a city, census information, engineer plats and surveys, real estate records, and similar types of official records. Depending on the issues involved in a particular case, this type of documentation can be helpful.

Obtaining official records from a government agency or from a private organization can test the patience and perseverance of the most experienced legal assistant. Writing or telephoning the agency and asking for the record is the most direct approach. However, because some records are privileged, it may be necessary to obtain signed authorizations or releases from the client. Even with the client's written authorization, some information may not be available to the law office. Certain government agencies will release documents and information to the client only. One such agency is the Social Security Administration.

Obtaining public and private records has its price. Agencies normally charge a fee for information. Always check with the supervising attorney first to determine if the record's benefit to the case justifies its cost. Clients generally are not happy about being charged to stockpile useless documents.

Any individual named by the client or the witness should be contacted to learn what information this person has. Each lead needs to be thoroughly checked because the next lead could produce a key witness in the case. Some leads will be dead ends; a few will be worthwhile pursuing.

The legal assistant searches for verification (whether internal or external) of every factual detail related to him. Gentle probing of the client or witness is necessary to seek additional information or to raise the client's awareness to remember other details and other witnesses. During the questioning and at the conclusion of the interview, the issues raised by the client or the witness are separated between personal knowledge and conjecture. The legal assistant has the responsibility to confirm (corroborate) those items of personal knowledge through witnesses and documentation.

Complete All Required Forms

Before the client leaves an interview, the legal assistant should have any appropriate forms available for the client's signature. Bringing anticipated forms to the initial interview reflects the organization, efficiency, and professionalism of the lawyer and her staff. These forms might include medical authorization forms, powers of attorney for tax information, or releases to obtain financial information from banking institutions. If the required forms are signed right away, work on the client's case can begin more quickly.

Conclude the Interview   The legal assistant should end the interview cordially, outlining any responsibility that either she or the client has to furnish supplemental data. An agreed deadline is set so that each knows the time frame, and the date is recorded on the calendar. If the client is to bring or to send additional documents to the law office, list them on a separate sheet of paper so the client can take the list with her when she leaves the office.

If a deadline cannot be met, the legal assistant should inform the lawyer as soon as that fact is known. An explanation also may be necessary to the client if she is involved. Keeping the client informed and involved throughout the case is important in maintaining a positive attorney-client relationship.

When the interview is over, accompany the client or witness back to the reception area of the law office. Abandoning visitors in the hallway is a poor practice (*see above*).

Document the Interview

Immediately following the interview, the legal assistant must summarize the interview and record the facts obtained, based on her interview notes. The less time that elapses between the conclusion of the interview and its documentation, the more accurate the documentation will be. All relevant information (whether it is helpful or is damaging) is included in a written memorandum, which is provided to the lawyer, with a copy placed in the client file.

Notes and Memorandum   In addition to a neatly typed file memorandum to summarize the interview, all handwritten notes are preserved in the client file. The file memorandum should follow a standardized format established by office policy, which typically includes: heading, personal data, stated assignment, chronology of facts, and conclusion. A sample memorandum is shown on the following page.

MEMORANDUM

TO: Virginia Koerselman, Staff Attorney

FROM: Susan Lewis, CLA, Legal Assistant

DATE: July 3, 1998

RE: Clyde Client v. ABC Corporation
File 98-345, Personal Injury

WITNESS: I.C. Awl (witness at scene of accident)

INTERVIEW DATE: July 3, 1998

****

Personal Data

Name and Address: I.C. Awl
1234 Main Street
Anywhere, D.C. 12345

Telephone: 101-333-3333 (Home)
101-333-0000 (Work)

Marital Status   Single

Employer   Wacky Widgets, Inc.
333 LaSalle Street
Anywhere, D.C. 12347

****

Assignment

Interview I.C. Awl, witness to a personal injury accident on January 1, 1998, to obtain information about the accident scene, to identify who was at the scene and location of vehicles before and after the accident, weather conditions, and other relevant details.

Chronology of Facts

On January 1, 1998, I.C. Awl was driving to a friend's house located at 100 Murphy Drive, Nowhere, D.C. to attend a New Year's Day football party. On his way to the party, I.C. Awl witnessed an accident involving our client, Clyde Client.

The remainder of the chronology section lists the sequence of events and the details reported by the witness. Every relevant detail is included in logical, chronological order for further investigation. The chronology is presented in a narrative paragraph format, similar to that of a story.

Conclusion

Summarize the major points of the chronology, together with the interviewer's evaluation of the witness, his knowledge of the facts, and his believability. These are important considerations to the lawyer in the management of the case. In addition, the conclusion may include a list of additional investigative steps to be taken by the legal assistant or a list of documents or other items to be produced by the witness.

Recorded Interviews   Whether to tape-record an interview is a decision made by the attorney (*see above*). If the attorney elects to record an interview, the recording is transcribed and the original tape, preserved. The transcription should reflect exactly what was recorded, grammatical errors and all.

It is not uncommon after the initial interview of a witness that a second interview is necessary to clarify inconsistent statements or details of events. When this occurs, a recorded interview may be advisable, not only to provide clarity but also to determine the basis or motivation for the inconsistent or contradictory facts provided. A witness usually is eager to correct the record, particularly if he knows the information will be used in a court proceeding.

Witness Statements   Witness statements may take various forms:

- Handwritten statement;

- Typewritten statement;

- Questionnaire completed by the witness;

- Tape-recorded statement in a question-answer format; and

- Statement recorded and transcribed by a court reporter in a question-answer format.

The purpose of a witness statement is to memorialize the exact events recalled by a witness in a form which may be used in court, without violating evidence rules related to hearsay and privilege. A witness statement is a different document than the interview memorandum prepared by the legal assistant. Both types of documentation can result from a single witness interview.

A witness statement should identify the witness, the date and place of the interview, and the interviewer. Additional information may include the address of the witness, her place of employment, or any other identifying information.

The interviewer may guide the witness to present the events in sequential order and to give the statement focus and organization. However, the words should be those of the witness. At its end, a witness statement should contain specific language to show that the witness made the statement voluntarily.

A handwritten statement may be prepared either by the interviewer or by the witness. The important factors are to record the information accurately as the witness stated it to be and to have the witness review and sign the handwritten statement. If the interviewer handwrites the statement, he may make an intentional error of fact so that when the witness reviews the statement, the error is discovered, corrected, and initialed by the witness. The initials and correction in the handwriting of the witness show that the witness reviewed the statement.

In a typewritten statement, everything is transcribed exactly as the witness stated. An impartial investigator (someone other than the legal assistant) may seek some insignificant information so the witness has an opportunity to make unfavorable statements about the client. This reinforces the investigator's objectivity.

At the conclusion of a typewritten statement, a sentence similar to the following should be included: *I have read ___ pages of this statement, and the information recorded is correct to the best of my knowledge.* Asking the witness to initial each page provides further evidence that she had the opportunity to review the entire document and that no pages were substituted. The witness signs the statement and is provided with a signed copy.

Taking witness statements soon after an incident is the best practice. Recollection of events is clearer and usually is more accurate at that time. During trial, properly recorded witness statements may be used as a source for refreshing the memory of the witness.

Special Interview Challenges

Because each interview is unique, it can present a unique set of challenges to the interview process. Among the challenges encountered by legal assistants with some frequency are clients or witnesses with special communication needs. Interviewing foreign-born individuals, persons with disabilities, very young children, or persons of advanced age requires special accommodation and consideration.

<u>Foreign-Born Persons</u> A client or a witness who does not speak English (or who does not speak English as her first language) may require an interpreter to translate information during the interview. A friend or family member may not be the best choice if the case involves an estate plan, a proposed guardianship, relinquishment of parental rights, or similar matter. If an independent interpreter is arranged, use care to ensure that his or her reputation for reliability is above reproach. If the firm has not used an independent interpreter in the past, an immigration lawyer in the community may be able to provide possible sources.

If the person speaks enough English to communicate in an interview setting, special care must be taken to ensure that she understands fully the questions asked of her and that the legal assistant understands the answers provided. An interview with this type of individual usually requires more time and planning than the typical client interview.

Disabled Persons   The client (or witness) with a physical or mental disability affecting her sight, speech, hearing, or level of comprehension presents a special set of challenges. This individual may require a sign interpreter, a braille expert, or special equipment to communicate. The legal assistant must make arrangements prior to the interview to accommodate the person's special communication needs.

The legal assistant must be especially sensitive to this person's situation in planning and in conducting the interview.

Young Children   When a child is interviewed, the permission of at least one parent is required to conduct the interview.

The best situation is to interview the child without a parent in the room if he is old enough to engage in an interview on that basis. With or without a parent, additional time generally is required to gain a child's trust before the substantive portion of the interview begins—how much time depends on the age of the child and the interviewer's expertise in working with children. Because a young child's attention span is extremely short, it may be necessary to schedule more than one session to complete the interview.

If the child is too young to be interviewed effectively without his parent, arrange the seating so that the parent is nearby but the child cannot see the parent during the interview (perhaps by seating the parent in a chair next to the child's chair but placed slightly back). If the child cannot see his parent's reaction to the questions, he is more likely to give his own account of the events. Otherwise, he may rely on the parent's facial expression to respond in whatever way he thinks will please the parent.

Elderly Persons   Clients and witnesses of advanced age may present an entirely different set of challenges. As much as possible, the legal assistant should determine this client's general physical and mental condition well before the interview. It may be that no special accommodation is required. If that is not the case, however, the interview should be planned in whatever way best accommodates the client or witness.

As a general rule, an elderly person tires more easily; his attention span is relatively brief; and his powers of concentration are not as sharp as those of a younger individual. Interviews scheduled in the middle of the morning are more successful than those scheduled in the late afternoon or evening. These factors must be taken into account in planning an interview with an elderly client.

If the client is hospitalized or if he resides in a nursing home, a field interview may be the only type of interview that is possible. Even if an elderly client is ambulatory, a field interview nevertheless may be advisable. Traveling to the law office can be an exhausting endeavor, which reduces the amount of energy left for the interview itself.

A client who is hospitalized (whether aged or not) frequently is taking some type of prescribed medication. If it is a type which substantially impairs mental clarity, the interview should be postponed if that can be done reasonably.

Even in the very best of circumstances, interviewing is an inherently imperfect art which has many styles. The objective of each interview is to find the truth. The legal assistant who enjoys people, challenges, and changes will find interviewing gratifying. *See the Bibliography for additional study references.*

Human Relations & Interviewing Self-Test

Allow an uninterrupted thirty-minute period to answer all questions. At the end of thirty minutes, check your answers against those in the Answer Key Section of this Manual. Deduct two points for each incorrect answer (100 total possible points). Unanswered questions are counted as incorrect answers. Follow directions carefully and observe the time limit precisely to provide an accurate self-assessment.

Choose the most correct answer to the following questions unless a specific question instructs you to do otherwise.

1. True or False.   Listening is the most passive part of the interview process.

2. True or False.   Statements concerning size or distance may be verified by personal examination of the interviewer.

3. True or False. Generally speaking, legal assistants should not conduct extensive investigations of background facts; instead, this type of investigation should be done by a private investigator.

4. True or False. When a legal assistant prepares a statement for the signature of the witness who provided the facts for the statement, the legal assistant must take special care to ensure an error-free document before it is submitted to the witness for review and signature.

5. True or False. The first documentation in a client's file, usually made after the initial interview, is a memorandum.

6. Which of the following witnesses generally are the least reliable?

    a. expert witnesses
    b. friendly witnesses
    c. hostile witnesses
    d. official witnesses

7. Collaboration occurs when:

    a. the testimony of a witness is supported by another witness.
    b. the testimony of a witness is supported by an independent source.
    c. two or more people work together on a project.
    d. none of these is correct.

8. If the legal assistant has reason to believe that a witness is lying during an interview, the legal assistant should:

    a. Discontinue the interview and notify the supervising attorney.
    b. Point out the inconsistencies to the witness and allow him to offer an explanation if he can.
    c. Continue the interview, noting the inconsistencies as the interview progresses.
    d. Continue the interview to see how far the witness will take the fabrication.

9. Ideally, interviews with very small children should be conducted:

    a. with a parent present, who should be seated along side the interviewer.
    b. with a parent present, who should be seated along side the child.

(see next page)

    c.   with a parent present, who is seated slightly behind the child.

    d.   without a parent present.

10.   Which of the following witness statements should be verified?

    a.   Before he died, he told me many times when we were alone that I would inherit the farm upon his death.

    b.   It was so foggy that I could not see more than four feet ahead.

    c.   I want to place my child for adoption.

    d.   It was extremely embarrassing for me.

11.   True or False.   Part of the interview summary should relate to the interviewer's observations concerning the apparent credibility of the witness and the information upon which the interviewer's conclusions are based.

12.   True or False.   Once the legal assistant has been introduced to a new client, he should reiterate his nonlawyer status to the client before the interview begins.

13.   True or False.   If the legal assistant suspects that a client would prefer to be interviewed by a lawyer, it is acceptable to resolve the issue by simply asking the client.

14.   True or False.   When it is apparent that a client is upset with the opposing party in the case, the legal assistant should show agreement with and support for the client by agreeing with her negative statements.

15.   True or False.   Generally speaking, the interviewer may rely on a witness' recollection of details related to times and dates.

16.   Which of the following witness statements requires corroboration?

    a.   I was furious.

    b.   Amy punched me in the stomach.

    c.   I cannot remember.

    d.   None requires corroboration.

17.   As a general rule, an interview should be tape recorded:

    a.   Always.

    b.   Never.

    c.   Only when instructed by the attorney.

    d.   Except when instructed otherwise by the attorney.

18. The capacity of a witness to manufacture details to make known facts more believable is called:

    a.   confabulation
    b.   corroboration
    c.   configuration
    d.   fabrication

19. Which of the following represents the type of supportive comment that may be made by a legal assistant during an interview to gain the trust of the witness?

    a.   Don't worry about a thing; (name of lawyer) never loses a case.
    b.   I'm sure it was difficult for you.
    c.   You can rest assured that (name of lawyer) is a tiger in the courtroom.
    d.   Trust me.

20. Which of the following witness statements relates a fact?

    a.   I left the restaurant between 10:00 p.m. and 10:30 p.m.
    b.   I don't know when Bill left.
    c.   Bill was extremely drunk, even before dinner was served.
    d.   He may have been drinking before I arrived.

21. True or False. One acceptable way to verify details during the interview is to misstate them purposely to see if the witness corrects the interviewer.

22. True of False. If a witness seems unusually anxious during the interview, the interviewer should ask leading questions about the central facts until the witness relaxes enough to provide narrative information.

23. True or False. A witness who is uncooperative during an interview generally is classified as a hostile witness.

24. True or False. The ideal client interview is one in which the client relates events in his or her own words.

25. True or False. When interviewing, the legal assistant should stick closely to the interview checklist to avoid wasting time on extraneous information.

26. Which of the following interview questions is most likely to elicit further narrative explanation from a witness?

   a. Please state your complete name and address.
   b. How long have you been employed by the defendant?
   c. How did you happen to get into this line of work?
   d. Where were you at 3:00 p.m. on the day of the murder?

27. Which of the following witness statements requires documentary verification?

   a. We sold our house on June 1.
   b. Bill was severely depressed after he lost his job.
   c. Ken is incapable of harming anyone.
   d. None requires documentary verification.

28. Which of the following statements requires corroboration of some type?

   a. I hated to sell the house.
   b. Bill was severely depressed for nearly a year.
   c. Ken is incapable of such a cruel act.
   d. None requires corroboration.

29. Which of the following is the best way to handle a client who has dissolved into uncontrolled tears during the initial interview?

   a. Take a break.
   b. Offer tissues, sit quietly, and wait.
   c. Ask the client not to cry.
   d. Tell the client to be strong and continue with the interview.

30. A witness who is known to oppose the client's position is a(n):

   a. Opposing party
   b. Negative witness
   c. Negative party
   d. Hostile witness

31. True or False.   An expert witness generally may be classified as an official witness as well.

32. True or False.   When large numbers of witnesses must be interviewed, the legal assistant should endeavor to schedule group interviews of three or more witnesses each to save time.

33. True or False.   With experience, a legal assistant is able to acclimate to witnesses who have attention problems, language barriers, or similar difficulties in the traditional interview setting.

34. True or False.   A legal assistant should not take photographs of accident scenes or of visible injuries of victims, because the legal assistant's position prevents him or her from providing the foundation testimony needed to admit the photographs at trial.

35. True or False.   The most successful interviewer is one who can demonstrate surprise, approval, disbelief, and disapproval by facial expression alone during the interview.

36. When a witness uses a slang word that the legal assistant does not understand during an interview, the legal assistant should:

    a.   Stop the witness and seek an explanation of the word.
    b.   Ask the witness about the word later in the interview.
    c.   Make note of the word and ask the attorney after the interview.
    d.   None of these is satisfactory.

37. Judicious use of frowns by the legal assistant during the interview process indicates to the witness:

    a.   That the legal assistant accepts the witness' statements as true.
    b.   That the legal assistant is concentrating on the witness' words.
    c.   That the legal assistant is concerned for the witness' well being.
    d.   None of these is indicated.

38. When a witness is reluctant to talk with the legal assistant during a field interview, the legal assistant's best course of action is to:

    a.   Advise the witness that if he does not talk voluntarily, he can be deposed.
    b.   Offer to come back at another time.
    c.   Get the witness to talk about unrelated things, hoping to come back to the reason for the interview.
    d.   See if the witness knows anyone else who might have relevant information.

39. The ideal client interview is one in which:

    a.   The client controls the interview process.
    b.   The checklist controls the interview process.
    c.   The legal assistant controls the interview process.
    d.   The process moves forward in its own direction and at its own pace.

40. True or False.   Witnesses tend to be inhibited by the use of checklists and by note taking of the interviewer during the interview process.

41. True or False.   Witnesses tend to be inhibited by the use of a tape recording device during the interview process.

42. True or False.   When a legal assistant records a telephone interview, he or she first must obtain the consent of the witness and should refer to the recording at several points during the telephone interview.

43. True or False.   When two different witnesses give two different versions of the facts of an incident, the legal assistant can be reasonably certain that one of them is lying.

44. True or False.   Because witnesses want to be believed, they generally relate facts in such a way that they can be reasonably certain of accomplishing this result.

45. True or False.   To conduct an effective interview, the legal assistant must control the pace, purpose, and direction of the dialogue.

46. True or False.   When conflicts arise in information supplied by a witness, the legal assistant may assume that the witness is either lying or mistaken.

47. Among the following items, the best corroboration for a client's statement that the other party caused the client's injuries is:

    a.   The other party's admission under oath.
    b.   A favorable police report.
    c.   A favorable eye witness.
    d.   Skid marks from the other party's vehicle.

48.   Which of the following is (are) closed questions?

      a.   What happened next?
      b.   Where did you go after that happened?
      c.   What leads you to say that?
      d.   How long have you known the plaintiff?
      e.   Two of the above
      f.   None of the above

49.   True or False. When conducting an interview, the legal assistant should not pursue any of the statements made unless they are directly relevant to the issues in the case.

50.   True or False. When a legal assistant interviews a witness who seems uncooperative, the legal assistant should re-evaluate his own conduct and mannerisms and should alter them if necessary to relate better to the witness.

Page left
intentionally
blank.

Page left
intentionally
blank.

Chapter 7
GENERAL LAW

Our capacity for justice makes democracy possible; it is our inclination to injustice that makes democracy necessary.

—Reinhold Niebuhr

All applicants are required to take the General Law subsection of the CLA® certifying examination. This chapter highlights and summarizes general legal history, sources, structure, terminology, principles, and concepts, with special emphasis on the American legal system.

Every legal assistant must be able to articulate the American legal structure and the general legal principles which have evolved, and which continue to evolve, within it. The concepts reviewed in this chapter—and those tested on the certifying examination—provide the foundation for every legal practice area that exists, no matter how specialized it is. Advocating the importance of these concepts to legal assistants who are preparing for the CLA® examination may be similar to preaching to the choir; nevertheless, it is difficult to imagine that their importance could be overstated.

Law Defined

There are many definitions of the word *law* within the context of the practice of law, not to mention the system which is served by law practitioners. Black's Law Dictionary devotes an entire page to defining the word. Each definition provides a slightly different perspective or nuance, but all of them seem to boil down to this:

> *Law is a system of enforceable rules adopted by a controlling body to govern the conduct of a society.*

Every society or group of people—from the smallest family unit to the largest nation—lives by rules. Because an ordered society cannot exist (not yet, at least) if everyone in the society makes his or her own rules, the rules or laws must emanate from a controlling body. The controlling body might include parents in a family unit or a dictator of a world nation. Finally, to ensure their enforceability, rules generally impose sanctions upon those who disobey, which can range from denial of a privilege to capital punishment.

The above definition can be applied to any economic, social, or political unit in the world, including the United States. The characteristic of American law which distinguishes it from the law of other nations is the structure of its controlling body—a government of the people, by the people, and for the people. Our democratic structure was unique at its inception, as was the legal system that was fashioned to meet its needs.

One could devote a lifetime to memorizing the multitude of legal rules that have evolved within the American legal system. It is a poor member of that legal community, however, who acquires only a technical knowledge of the rules. Both technical knowledge and historical understanding are crucial to comprehend the framework of the legal system.

Historical Background

To understand how and why the American legal system has developed the way that has (and is structured the way that it is), we have to look farther back in history than the adoption of the U.S. Constitution and even farther back than the Revolutionary War. We have to look back to the colonists who settled in America, to the legal systems from which they came, and to the legal philosophies they brought with them.

The English Influence   Although American colonists came from several different European countries, the vast majority of them came from England at a time when the king and the Church of England had comprised the controlling body of English law for centuries. England's court system reflected these two controlling forces.

Only specific types of legal actions were authorized to resolve disputes among English commoners. They were heard by the king's court, which became known as the *king's court of common pleas* or, stated more generally, the law court. The forms of action depended on the issuance of writs and were very technical. Litigants frequently lost cases because of noncompliance with a technical rule. The rigidity of law court actions and their perceived unfairness eventually prompted the king to establish an additional court, the **Court of Chancery**. This court handled cases for which the law court could not provide relief, that is, when the equities of the case indicated that some type of relief should be granted. Staffed by high-ranking clergy, the idea was that the Court of Chancery could decide cases based on principles of fairness rather than on technical rules.

Parliament had been established as an advisory body to the king, but it had no power to make laws. (The shift of power from the king to Parliament did not occur until long after the Revolutionary War.) The ranks of the king's army and navy were maintained in high numbers through a hated conscription (compulsory draft), which allowed Great Britain to establish colonies in many parts of the world, including America.

America was not a land of milk and honey in its earliest days. Survival was grueling, and many colonists died. Once colonies initially were founded, only the most adventurous or the most desperate came voluntarily. The rest, primarily political radicals and social misfits, arrived on the point of a sword. Whether they came through banishment or through flight, early colonists considered themselves British subjects; and many dreamed of going home one day.

Although the king generally ignored them, the colonies endured. Because of the problems that caused them to leave England in the first place, colonists persisted in their mistrust of military force. They relied instead on voluntary militia for protection. They mistrusted lawyers and judges even more than they mistrusted the military. The laws they established were of English common law origin, but did not follow English law precisely. The colonists retained those parts of England's common law which suited their needs, modified other parts as they believed necessary (or as they could remember them), and ignored the rest. They retained both the law court and the equity court (originally the Court of Chancery). A law library, if it existed at all, consisted only of *Blackstone's Commentaries* brought from England. This four-volume set fit easily into a lawyer's saddlebags as he traveled from town to town. More often, there was no *Blackstone's*; and even if a set had been available, few would have been able to read it.

The state of American law continued in this way as the colonies began to flourish. The British-Americans cultivated more land, grew more crops, and prospered. Some even were able to educate their sons in England, and the king finally took notice. As the writings of John Locke on natural law (and other legal philosophers) were read and debated by the educated, the king looked more and more to the colonies for commodities (such as lumber) and tax revenues.

Having begun as radicals and misfits and having become self-sufficient in their years of relative isolation, it should have come as no surprise when the British-Americans requested—and then demanded—to be represented in Parliament, the king's advisory body. Their demands were dismissed summarily. The hated British army appeared in increasing numbers, colonists were required to board the soldiers in their homes, taxes continued to escalate, and the Revolutionary War erupted.

From the end of the Revolutionary War until the Constitutional Convention in 1787, the American government operated under the **Articles of Confederation**. Each state elected delegates to Congress, who, in turn, elected a president from their own ranks. This system was ineffective. There was no enforcement power for any of Congress' decisions, and there was no money to support an army or to provide the needs of government. The United States Constitution subsequently replaced the Articles of Confederation.

Both the Declaration of Independence and the United States Constitution were influenced strongly by John Locke's natural rights theories. Americans were accustomed to tinkering with the law to make it fit their situation, so it was natural that they would debate and modify Locke's theories as they thought necessary "to form a more perfect government."

The American System The framers of the Constitution were divided concerning how much power should be given to a federal government, but they finally agreed that each state should retain its sovereign status even if a federal government were established. They did not want any single part of the federal government to hold too much power, so they divided it into three branches (legislative, executive, and judicial) to provide a system of checks and balances. Congress was created with two houses to ensure fair representation of the states.

The system created by the Constitution was unique. It had never been tried before anywhere in the world, and many believed it could not work. When it became clear that some states were reluctant to ratify the Constitution's draft, a group of ten amendments (the Bill of Rights) was added to list specifically what an individual's rights were. Thomas Jefferson was the most vocal of those who thought it was unnecessary to write individual rights into the Constitution. He and others believed these rights to be so obvious that surely they never could be questioned by anyone. Nevertheless, by adding the Bill of Rights—as redundant as it was thought to be—the Constitution was ratified. It is ironic that the Bill of Rights, which was only an afterthought, has become the soul of constitutional law in protecting individual freedoms.

Understanding legal history gives life and fire to the Constitution. Legal history helps to understand why the Boston Tea Party happened, why the South believed in the justness of its secession from the Union, why we accept civil disobedience as a valid form of protest, and why generation after generation grows up committed to the belief that each of us has basic rights which no one can take away. Legal history also helps to understand why lawyers and judges always have been mistrusted by the public in general; but when a specific individual's rights are threatened, a lawyer is the first person he contacts.

Philosophies of American Law

A legal philosophy is a school of thought (method of reasoning) concerning the purpose of law and how it should operate. Several different legal philosophies are intertwined in the American legal system. Although they evolved at various points in history, they continue to impact the way in which our laws operate. The most prominent legal philosophies are summarized here.

Natural law, sometimes called the natural rights theory, is a philosophy which emphasizes the individual's right to make personal choices as long as those choices do not interfere with another's right to make personal choices. The freedom of choice is a birthright; it is not conferred by anyone, and it cannot be taken away by anyone—not even if everyone else in the world believes the choice is stupid. Thomas Jefferson stated the principles of natural law in the Declaration of Independence: *We hold these truths to be self-evident, that all men are created equal; that they are endowed by their creator with certain inalienable rights; that among these are life, liberty, and the pursuit of happiness.*

Legal positivism is a philosophy which emphasizes the institutional rule of law and which distinguishes law from morality. If the process used to adopt a particular rule is just (fair) and if no other rule exists to carve out an exception to that rule, the legal positivist adheres to the rule—even if it leads to a questionable result in a particular case. Legal positivism is reflected in the maxim: *Hard cases make bad law.*

Sociological jurisprudence is a philosophy which promotes society's values as the measuring stick for right and wrong; it evaluates a legal rule by looking at its social effect. If the effect is bad, the legal sociologist favors getting rid of the rule, changing it, or simply ignoring it this time. Law is seen as a tool for *social engineering*. A drawback of sociological jurisprudence—recognized even by its supporters—is that the legal system moves too slowly to respond to needed social change. Roscoe Pound was a strong advocate of sociological jurisprudence.

Legal realism is a philosophy which determines what reasonable people would do in a given situation and then sanctions that conduct. Legal realists treat legal rules as little more than rebuttable presumptions. They look at the underlying policy of the rule and measure conduct according to the policy. This philosophy often gives great weight to economic analysis (a "Brandeis brief," for example) in showing the effect of a legal rule. In short, legal realism took social engineering one step farther, resulting in the doctrine of *economic waste* and similar concepts. Oliver Wendell Holmes and Karl Lewellyn led the cause for legal realism.

Different methods of legal reasoning can (but do not always) lead to different results. Therefore, we look not only at the controlling rule of law stated in a judicial opinion (the holding), but also at the reasoning (rationale) used to support the stated rule. Strains of each of the above philosophies are evident in current judicial opinions, although other philosophies seem to be operating as well.

Legal history, legal structure, and legal philosophies are the dynamics which have brought the American legal system to its present state. Against that background, increasingly complex legal rules have evolved to serve an increasingly complex society.

Classifications of Law

All legal rules can be grouped into broad categories according to their type (classification). A rule's classification tells us the situations to which it applies and how it applies in relation to other rules. For example, all law is classified as either criminal or civil.

This section defines the basic classifications of law and reviews their relationship to each other. The chart on the following page may help to visualize where the classifications fit in relation to each other.

CLASSIFICATIONS OF LAW

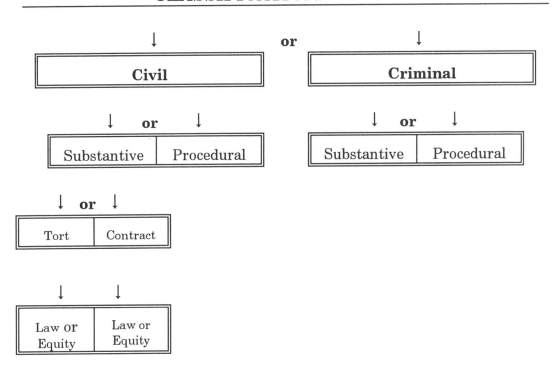

Substantive or Procedural Law   All law is either substantive or procedural. A ***substantive law*** is a legal rule which creates or defines rights and duties. For every right, there is a corresponding duty. For example, if Bob owns land, he has a ***right*** to its exclusive possession. Bob's right imposes a ***duty*** on the rest of the world not to enter the land without his permission.

Examples of substantive law are the constitutional provision establishing Congress, an administrative regulation requiring the registration of publicly traded securities, a state statute limiting the speed of vehicles, or a court opinion interpreting the terms of a contract or further refining common law rules of negligence.

Every substantive law can be classified as either public or private, either criminal or civil (*discussed below*).

Procedural law, sometimes called ***adjective law***, complements substantive law by providing the mechanisms to enforce substantive rights and duties. As it relates to courts and administrative agencies, procedural law typically includes the method for initiating an action, serving a summons, making motions, conducting discovery and trial, and appealing the final judgment. As it relates to a legislative body, procedural law includes the steps required to enact a law or a rule (notice, hearing, quorum, majority vote) and the way in which those steps must be performed. Every rule of substantive law can be associated with one or more groups of procedural rules to provide a way of enforcement.

Examples of procedural law are the Federal Rules of Civil Procedure, the Federal Rules of Criminal Procedure, the Federal Rules of Evidence, and the Federal Rules of Appellate Procedure, together with any local court rules adopted for use in connection with them. States also adopt rules of procedure which are similar to the federal rules, sometimes in a separate set of rules and sometimes incorporated with that state's statutes.

A local court rule is a rule adopted by the court in which the case is pending; it supplements the procedural rules mentioned above. It may be more easily conceptualized as a forum court rule. Every federal court and every state court has its own set of local court rules. The local court rules of the U. S. District Court for the Southern District of Iowa may vary slightly from the local court rules of the Northern District of Iowa, for example.

The purpose of local court rules is to augment or to fill the gaps left by the procedural rules mentioned in the preceding paragraph. For example, the Federal Rules of Civil Procedure state that every case is commenced by filing a complaint. Local court rules cannot change the rule of procedure by requiring that cases be commenced by filing an application (instead of a complaint), but local court rules can require that all complaints be filed in duplicate, be filed on letter-size paper, be double-spaced, and so forth.

A. **Public or Private Law** All substantive law is either public or private. ***Public law*** consists of rules which involve the relationship of government to society as a whole. Constitutional law, administrative law, and criminal law are examples of public law.

Private law consists of rules which involve the relationship of private individuals to each other. Most civil law is private law, including tort law, contract law, and most property law.

Criminal Law All substantive law is either criminal or civil. Criminal law consists of rules designed to protect society by providing minimum standards of conduct which must be observed by each of its members. Penal sanctions (punishments) are imposed on those who fail to observe the minimum standards. Crimes generally are defined by statute (federal or state) or by ordinance (local), although common law crimes are still recognized in the District of Columbia. Crimes are further classified as treason, felonies, or misdemeanors.

Treason is an attempt to overthrow the government as defined by Article III, § 3 of the U.S. Constitution.

A *felony* is a crime for which the maximum *possible* punishment is either death or imprisonment for one year or more. The classification focuses on the maximum punishment that *could* be imposed, not on the punishment that is actually imposed.

A *misdemeanor* is a crime for which the maximum *possible* punishment is either a fine or imprisonment for less than one year. *Refer to the chapter on Criminal Law for a more thorough review.*

Civil Law   Civil law consists of those legal rules which focus on the rights and duties of individuals in relation to each other. In contrast to criminal law, which imposes penal sanctions, civil law sanctions are remedial; they grant a remedy (provide relief) to enforce a right.

American civil law is based upon common law principles and traditionally is classified according to (1) the basis of the right or duty to be enforced, whether in tort or in contract, and (2) the type of remedy sought, whether legal or equitable.

A *tort* is a wrongful act (other than breach of a contract) for which the law provides a remedy, typically in the form of money damages. Torts are based upon rules of conduct to which each member of society is expected to conform. Examples of torts include assault, battery, conversion, false imprisonment, negligence, and trespass. A tort may be *intentional* (assault, battery, conversion, trespass); *unintentional* (negligence); or based upon *strict liability* (defective product sold to public).

Conduct which creates civil liability in tort may also create criminal liability, depending on the criminal statutes of a particular location. For instance, if Jane punches Ruth in the nose, Ruth could file a civil action against her for the tort of battery. The standard of proof would be *a preponderance of the evidence* (more likely than not that Jane is responsible). Based on the same incident, the state could prosecute Jane for the crime of assault. The standard of proof would be *beyond a reasonable doubt* (very nearly certain that Jane is guilty).

In this situation, the result in the criminal case has no effect whatsoever on the result in the civil case. Neither does the result in the civil case have any effect on the result in the criminal case. They are completely separate. Jane could be found guilty in the criminal case, even though she is held not liable in the civil case.

A **contract** is an enforceable agreement between two or more parties (comprised of an offer, an acceptance, and consideration which are not subject to any defenses). The contract is the agreement, not the paper on which the agreement is written. When any party does not perform as agreed, a breach occurs; and the nonbreaching party is entitled to the benefit of her bargain. Her remedy may take the form of money damages or equitable relief, including specific performance if the proper circumstances exist.

A contract can be oral or written; it can be express (specifically stated) or implied in fact or in law from conduct of the parties. *Refer to the chapter on Contracts for a more thorough review.*

The remedies available in a civil suit are either legal or equitable. A **remedy at law** typically seeks damages (money). If money cannot compensate the plaintiff adequately for her losses, she may be able to obtain equitable relief. A **remedy in equity** typically requests some specific act, such as an injunction or the rescission, reformation, or specific performance of a contract. *(Legal and equitable remedies are discussed in greater detail below.)*

Institutional Sources of Law

Under a democratic form of government, the people are the sovereign. They are the source of all power, including the power to establish law, which they exercise through elected representatives.

There are at least 51 legal systems operating simultaneously in the United States: the federal legal system and the legal systems of 50 sovereign states. Within this setting, the institutional sources of substantive law are constitutions, statutes enacted by legislative bodies, rules and regulations adopted by administrative agencies, and the common law.

Constitution A constitution is a written document which provides the fundamental source of law within a particular geographic region. It establishes the basic principles and the structure under which a government must operate.

The United States Constitution is the written agreement which unites the states as one cohesive nation. It incorporates the doctrine of **separation of powers** by dividing all governmental power among three branches (legislative, executive, and judicial), which allows each branch to serve as a check and balance on the other two.

Each state has its own constitution, generally with provisions similar to those of the federal Constitution.

Statutes The second institutional source of substantive law is statutory law. A statute is a written law enacted either by Congress or by a state legislature. Both federal and state statutes must comply with the federal Constitution. In addition, the statutes of each state must comply with that state's constitution. Both state and federal statutes are subject to review and interpretation by courts.

Since the federal government is one of limited powers, federal statutes may be enacted only in those areas specifically delegated to Congress in the United States Constitution. State statutes, on the other hand, may be enacted in nearly any area except those which are prohibited to states by the United States Constitution (*see below*).

Statutes are collected and published in a code. Federal statutes are published selectively in the United States Code. Each state has its own code of state statutes.

A. Administrative Rules and Regulations Legislatures create administrative agencies, boards, and commissions to assist them when the legislature lacks expertise in an area that requires (1) special knowledge and (2) more supervision than the legislature can provide directly. An agency of this type is created by an ***enabling act***, which authorizes the agency to exist and which lists the specific areas to be administered by it.

Administrative agencies have become so pervasive that they often are referred to as the *fourth branch of government*. Examples of administrative agencies are the Internal Revenue Service (IRS), the Immigration and Naturalization Service (INS), the Social Security Administration (SSA), the Securities and Exchange Commission (SEC), the Federal Communications Commission (FCC), the Equal Employment Opportunity Commission (EEOC), the Food and Drug Administration (FDA), and the Environmental Protection Agency (EPA). There are many, many others.

Subject to some limitations, a legislature may delegate a special form of legislative authority to the agency, which permits the agency to make rules and regulations to clarify or explain statutes within its authorized area of expertise. This *rulemaking power* is an exercise of the agency's ***quasi-legislative*** function. Although they are not quite on the same level as statutes, administrative rules and regulations carry the same force of law as statutes.

In addition, an administrative agency has authority to investigate, to enforce, and to interpret its own rules and regulations. An administrative law judge or a hearing officer (neither of whom is required to be a lawyer by many administrative agencies) presides over hearings that are similar to trials. This is permitted as part of the agency's *quasi-judicial function*. If a violation is found to have occurred, the agency may impose civil sanctions. *No one can be incarcerated by an administrative agency.* When criminal action is warranted, the case is referred to the Justice Department (federal) or to the appropriate state attorney general or equivalent for prosecution.

All federal agencies must comply with the Administrative Procedure Act (APA) when exercising their rulemaking and decision-making functions. Both (1) the rules and regulations and (2) the decisions of an administrative agency are subject to review and interpretation by courts. Before judicial review is granted, however, the appellant or petitioner must demonstrate that he has exhausted all of his administrative remedies. This means that he must have utilized all of the procedures and remedies at the administrative level before he can seek judicial relief.

In general, judicial review of the acts of an administrative agency boils down to two questions: (1) Does the agency have the power to do what it did (based upon its enabling act)? and if it does, (2) Did the agency use the power fairly (due process)? *Refer to the chapter on Administrative Law for a more thorough review.*

B.   Uniform State Laws and Model Acts

Because each state has inherent power to enact statutes as it thinks appropriate, the statutes on a single topic can vary widely from state to state. If the topic is one of local interest only, the variations make little difference outside a particular state. With ever-increasing interstate activities by businesses and by citizens, however, inconsistent state laws became a significant obstacle by the turn of the century.

The *National Conference of Commissioners on Uniform State Laws* was organized in 1915 to resolve this problem. Each state, the District of Columbia, and Puerto Rico appoint at least one commissioner to this organization. The commissioners consider those areas of law requiring uniformity and draft model legislation in the form of *uniform codes*, *uniform acts*, or *uniform laws*; and they encourage their adoption by each of the states.

Each state legislature considers the uniform code or act in the same way that it considers any other proposed legislation. The legislature may adopt it, adopt it with modifications, adopt only part of it, or adopt none of it—as the legislature chooses. (If substantial changes are made, however, the purpose of a uniform law is destroyed.) If the uniform code or act is adopted, it becomes a part of the state's other statutes and is incorporated into the state code.

The National Conference of Commissioners has drafted more than 250 acts, including the Uniform Commercial Code, the Uniform Partnership Act, the Uniform Limited Partnership Act, the Uniform Fraudulent Conveyance Act, the Uniform Probate Code, and the Uniform Reciprocal Support Enforcement Act.

Other organizations also draft model acts, though not in the same volume as the National Conference. For example, the American Law Institute is responsible for the Model Penal Code. The American Bar Association drafted both the Model Business Corporation Act and the Revised Model Business Corporation Act.

Common Law   The third institutional source of substantive law is common law. In its most narrow sense, common law means the *rule of law announced as the holding in a judicial opinion*. (Judicial opinions sometimes are called ***case law***).

In a broader sense, common law means the collection of legal rules extracted from judicial opinions in a particular area of law. For instance, there are common law rules of contract, common law rules of employment relationships, common law rules of negligence, and so forth. To the extent that the common law rules have not been replaced by statutes—which often restate the common law rules in statutory form—the common law rules still are used either alone or to supplement existing statutes. As the term is used in this sense, however, it applies to state law only. Federal law comes only from the federal Constitution, federal statutes, and rules and regulations of federal administrative agencies. The rule is well-established since the ***Erie* doctrine** was announced: *There is no federal common law.*

In its broadest sense, common law refers to the judicial decision-making process which is the foundation of the American legal system. Common law is based on the doctrine of *stare decisis*. ***Stare decisis*** is the *process* used by judges to analyze past cases to determine if any exist which had similar facts and similar legal issues as the present case (the one being decided now). If one or more such cases are found, the holding of the past case is ***precedent*** in the present case, which means that the present case must be decided in the same way.

Following precedent in judicial decision-making gives stability and certainty to the law. It allows people to predict the outcome of specific conduct or events, which, in turn, makes them better able to plan their lives. It provides order to a society.

Common law principles do not require judges to follow precedent slavishly or to wear blinders when they decide cases, however. Implicit in the concept of common law is its ability to reflect the mores of society as they exist at any given time. For instance, extra-marital relationships are almost universally more acceptable in today's society than they were, say, fifty years ago. The common law should reflect that fact.

Judges are reluctant to overturn past decisions, because it injects an element of instability into the system. However, as technological developments and society's needs change over a long period of time, past decisions must be overruled occasionally. At the turn of the century, for example, industrial development was encouraged; and the courts generally took a *laissez-faire* approach to working conditions and disposal of industrial waste. This is not so today. Although many of the changes have resulted from legislation, a review of judicial opinions shows a stop-and-start change in judicial attitude, which resulted in some past cases being overruled.

Judicial application of common law principles is covered in the section on judicial decision making (*see below*).

Having reviewed the legal system and the institutional sources of law in general, the remaining sections provide a more detailed review of those areas of special concern to legal assistants, including principles of constitutional law and due process, court systems, judicial decision making, and alternative dispute resolution.

Constitutional Law

By its own declaration in Article VI, the United States Constitution is the supreme law of the land. The Constitution consists of seven articles and twenty-six amendments, and it serves three important functions in the legal system:

1. It limits the powers of the states;

2. It enumerates the powers granted to the federal government by the states; and

3. It guarantees certain fundamental rights to the people of the United States.

Limitation of State Powers   Since each state is a sovereign, it has inherent power to enact its own laws. The federal Constitution restricts that power, however, by making state law subordinate to federal law under the Supremacy Clause of Article VI. What this means is that when a state law directly conflicts with a federal law on the same subject, federal law controls. This is known as the doctrine of *federalism*.

In addition to the Supremacy Clause, other provisions of the Constitution restrict state powers in specific areas. For example, states cannot form treaties with foreign nations, cannot tax imports or exports, cannot coin money, and cannot impair contractual obligations. If the federal government preempts a field, such as post offices, no state or private person may enter the same field. This means that a private person could establish an express parcel service, but she could not establish a post office because of the *preemption* doctrine.

Aside from those areas covered by the doctrines of federalism and preemption, a state has inherent and nearly unfettered power to regulate people and activities within its borders. If a power has not been given specifically to the federal government, that power is held by the state. For example, Congress has been granted the specific power to regulate interstate commerce; but if the commerce is purely *intra*state (wholly within state boundaries), Congress has no power to regulate it.

Each state holds a general *police power* which allows it to regulate in any area affecting the *general health, safety, and welfare* of its citizens. The federal government has no similar power. A state can regulate such things as marriage, divorce, abortion, probate, and most crimes as long as it does not violate any constitutional provision in doing so. When a state law violates a provision of the Constitution, the law may be stricken by the U.S. Supreme Court in an appropriate appeal.

Enumerated Federal Powers

Unlike the states, the federal government is one of limited powers. It has no inherent powers; it possesses only those which have been delegated to it by the states. All other powers are reserved to the states.

Article I of the Constitution establishes Congress (consisting of the House of Representatives and the Senate) as the legislative branch of government and lists the powers of Congress. For example, Congress is given the power to impose taxes, to borrow money, to regulate interstate commerce and commerce with foreign countries, to control bankruptcy laws, to issue currency, to appropriate money, to punish the counterfeiting of money, to establish post offices, to control patents and copyrights, to create inferior federal courts, (inferior to the Supreme Court), to declare war, to provide for national defense, to serve as the legislature for District of Columbia, and to make all laws which are necessary and proper to carry out the powers of Congress. Congress exercises its powers by enacting federal statutes.

Article I forbids Congress from suspending the writ of *habeas corpus* except during rebellion or invasion. A **writ of habeas corpus** is an order to "deliver the body" of one held in custody; it typically is used to secure the release of a prisoner who is wrongfully held by authorities. Article I further prohibits Congress from passing any bill of attainder or any *ex post facto* law. A **bill of attainder** is a law directed against a specific person or against a specific group. An **ex post facto law** is one which defines conduct as a crime after the fact (after the act had been committed).

> A law which provides that no lawyer may serve as a member of Congress is a bill of attainder. It is directed at a specific group and is unconstitutional.

> A law passed on March 1 provides that any person who gains ten pounds or more between January 1 and March 1 of (the same year) shall be subject to a fine of not less than $100. This is an *ex post facto* law; to be subject to the fine, the weight gain must already have occurred by the time the law is passed. The law is unconstitutional.

As a check on the executive and judicial branches, Congress controls the purse strings of the nation. In addition, the House of Representatives has the power to impeach judicial and executive officers, and the Senate has the power to try all impeachments.

Article II vests executive power in the president, who appoints executive officers, including a cabinet, to assist with executive duties. In addition to enforcing federal laws, the president serves as commander-in-chief of the armed forces. The president has the power, with the advice and consent of the Senate, to make treaties with foreign nations; to appoint ambassadors; and to appoint judges to the Supreme Court. As a check on the legislative branch, the president has the power to veto acts of Congress. Congress, in turn, may override the veto by a two-thirds vote of both houses.

Article III grants judicial power to the United States Supreme Court and to such other, inferior federal courts as Congress may establish. Federal courts can hear only limited types of cases (*discussed below*).

The framers of the Constitution viewed the judiciary as the "least dangerous branch" of the three. The Supreme Court was given original jurisdiction in certain cases (*see below*) and was also given the power to review acts of the legislative and executive branches to ensure their compliance with the Constitution. Those acts which do not comply with the Constitution are invalidated by the Supreme Court.

In the landmark case of *Marbury v. Madison*, 5 U.S. 137 (1805), Chief Justice Marshall asserted the doctrine of *judicial review* in a situation in which the Court could have exercised original, concurrent jurisdiction. This decision permanently established the Supreme Court as the court of final review. Thus evolved the expression, "The Supreme Court is not the last because it is always right; it is always right because it is the last."

Guarantee of Individual Rights   In addition to limiting the power of states and enumerating the powers of the federal government, those fundamental rights which are guaranteed to the people are listed in the first ten amendments to the Constitution, called the *Bill of Rights*. In capsule form, these rights include:

1.   Freedom of religion, speech, and press; the right to assemble; and the right to petition the government.

2.   Right to bear arms.

3.   No soldiers quartered in private homes in time of peace.

4.   No unreasonable searches or seizures.

5.   No double jeopardy or self-incrimination in criminal cases; guarantees due process of law; guarantees just compensation when private property is taken.

6.   Right of accused to speedy trial and to assistance of counsel.

7.   Right to a jury trial in civil cases over $20.

8.   No excessive bail or fines; no cruel or unusual punishment.

9.   Constitutional powers do not diminish rights retained by the people.

10.   States retain powers not delegated under the Constitution and not prohibited by it to the States.

The *Fourteenth Amendment* prohibits states from making or enforcing any laws which diminish the privileges and immunities of any citizen of the United States. It further requires states to provide *due process* of law and the *equal protection* of laws to all people within their respective jurisdictions. This Amendment is sometimes called the *Equal Protection Clause*.

In addition to these protections, the Supreme Court has defined a fundamental *right of privacy* which is guaranteed to all people. Privacy is not mentioned specifically in the Constitution or in the Bill of Rights; rather, the Supreme Court found it in the *penumbras* of the Constitution, as part of the Necessary and Proper Clause of Article I, § 8(18).

When faced with competing claims to fundamental rights (freedom of the press and privacy, for example), the Supreme Court balances (weighs) the rights and attempts to give effect to each.

Due Process

The due process clause of the Fifth Amendment provides that "no person shall be deprived of life, liberty, or property without due process of law" by the federal government. The Fourteenth Amendment provides: ". . . nor shall any state deprive a person of life, liberty, or property without due process of law."

Due process of law means *fundamental fairness*. The concept of fundamental fairness, however, can vary according to the type of right involved as well as according to the language and effect of a particular statute or rule. As a result, courts review due process claims on a case-by-case basis. Case law produces some common themes, which are discussed here.

Due process is not an issue unless state action is present. In this context, *state action* includes acts of either the federal or state government or any of its agents. If the government is not involved, there is no state action. When a statute or rule is adopted, state action clearly is present. When a sole proprietor of a private business adopts a rule, no state action is present unless the business has some governmental tie—a government contract or some type of governmental grant or subsidy, for example—which permits a court to find that state involvement, and therefore state action, exists.

Once state action is found, due process is classified as either substantive due process or procedural due process.

Substantive Due Process
Substantive due process requires fundamental fairness in the *content* of the statute or rule.

The content is fundamentally unfair if it *shocks the conscience* or if it is *unreasonable, arbitrary, or capricious*. For example, a statute limiting the number of children that any one woman could bear would be unconstitutional on substantive due process grounds.

The content of a statute is fundamentally unfair when it is overly broad. When faced with this type of statute, courts frequently quip that "*it paints with too broad a brush.*" **Overbreadth** is a form of arbitrariness that occurs when the state has a legitimate purpose for the legislation, but the language of the statute is not sufficiently tailored to the purpose.

Suppose, for example, that a legislature has determined through investigative hearings that males are significantly more likely than females to drive after drinking. If, in response to the overwhelming statistics, the legislature were to pass a law granting driving privileges only to women, the statute would be overly broad and, therefore, unconstitutional on substantive due process grounds. The statute is overly broad, because it restricts males who do not drink and drive as well as those who do. At the same time, it fails to restrict those females who drink and drive, which leaves a gap between the purpose and the means.

Finally, the content of a statute is fundamentally unfair when it is too vague. A vague statute leads to arbitrary enforcement and is objectionable on that basis. **Vagueness** occurs when a person of normal intelligence cannot tell from the statute's language what conduct is prohibited (or is required). For instance, if a legislature were to pass a statute prohibiting "undesirable elements" from seeking political office, the statute would be too vague and would be unconstitutional on substantive due process grounds. Similarly, a high school disciplinary rule would be too vague if it were to provide that "any student may be expelled if he or she is found to be a bad influence on fellow students." In either example, a person of ordinary intelligence could not tell what conduct causes one to be an undesirable element or a bad influence. The prohibited conduct could be anything that an enforcement official wants it to be.

Vagrancy ordinances of many cities have been repealed by legislative bodies or have been stricken by courts on vagueness grounds. The following language was typical among those which levied criminal penalties on persons who fit into any of its statutory categories:

> . . . rogues and vagabonds, or dissolute persons who go about begging, common gamblers, persons who use juggling or unlawful games or plays, common drunkards, common night walkers, thieves, pilferers, or pickpockets, traders in stolen property, lewd, wanton and lascivious persons, keepers of gambling places, common railers and brawlers, persons wandering or strolling from place to place without any lawful purpose, disorderly persons, persons neglecting all lawful business and habitually spending their time by frequenting houses of ill fame, gaming houses, or places where alcoholic beverages are sold or served, or persons able to work but habitually living upon the earnings of their wives or minor children.

Procedural Due Process   Procedural due process requires fundamental fairness in terms of (1) notice and (2) an opportunity to be heard.

Notice is fundamentally fair if a person is informed of the nature of the charges or claims against her. The *Miranda* warnings in criminal cases are based on procedural due process requirements. In certain situations, notice may also require that she be informed of the general factual basis for the charges and the time limit for defensive action. For example, a notice of criminal prosecution is insufficient if the charges are for "felonious criminal activity." Similarly, a notice of civil suit is insufficient if the complaint alleges "damages for tortious acts."

An opportunity to be heard generally means that a hearing of some type must be held so that the accused can defend herself if she wishes to do so. The fundamental fairness of the hearing varies according to the circumstances. For example, one who is charged with murder or homicide is entitled to every procedural safeguard available, including assistance of counsel, trial by jury, and formal rules of evidence. One who is charged with jaywalking, by contrast, is entitled to a trial of some type, but generally is not entitled a full-blown jury trial or to the assistance of a public defender unless a conviction could result in incarceration.

Military personnel and students usually receive less in the way of a hearing than those who are charged for similar conduct in other arenas. However, this general rule can vary with the gravity of the offense. If a student were suspended from school for three days, for example, she may not be entitled to anything more than an informal hearing in the school principal's office; formal rules of evidence will not apply; and the hearing even may be held after the three-day suspension period has ended. If the same student were expelled for the balance of the school term, however, the hearing would have to be held either before expulsion takes effect or very shortly afterward. Otherwise, her right to an education could be impaired unfairly if, for example, the hearing did not occur for thirty days and if the basis for the expulsion were shown to be insufficient.

Regardless of the type of hearing required in a given situation, the hearing process must be fair. A hearing is not fair if the judge or hearing officer asks, "Do you have any more witnesses to present before I find you guilty?"

The rules of procedure, whatever they are, must treat both sides evenly. For example, an administrative rule is unconstitutional on its face if it permits the agency to cross-examine witnesses but does not permit the defendant or respondent to do the same.

Equally unfair is a rule which is applied unfairly. Assume that a rule states: "No motor vehicle operator's license may be suspended without a prior hearing." The rule itself may be fair; but if the practice is for the arresting officer to impound the license until the hearing date, the rule is unfair as applied.

The Judicial System

Although the legal assistant must be familiar with all aspects of the American legal system, the practice of law typically revolves around the judicial branch. The function of the judicial branch is to apply law to facts in resolving disputes between adversaries, which is accomplished through the trial and appellate processes.

Each legal system (federal and state) has its own judicial branch, which operates through a system of courts. A court is classified by the system in which it operates (either federal or state) and by the types of cases which it is authorized to hear. These classifications are part of a court's jurisdiction. *Jurisdiction is the power or authority of a court to hear a specific case.* Both subject matter jurisdiction and personal jurisdiction must exist before a court can decide the merits of a particular case.

Subject Matter Jurisdiction

Congress

Within the federal system, the United States Supreme Court is created by Article III of the Constitution. All other federal courts are created by federal statute. The highest court of a state system usually is created by state constitution, and all other state courts typically are created by state statute. Whether it is constitutional or statutory, the law that creates a court is the same law that defines its subject matter jurisdiction. **Subject matter jurisdiction** *relates to the type of case which a court is authorized to hear.*

If a court does not have subject matter jurisdiction, it lacks the power to decide the merits of the case. In that situation, any action taken by it is void; it has no effect whatsoever. Because it relates to a court's power to act, *subject matter jurisdiction never can be waived.* Moreover, it can be raised by anyone (including the judge) at any point in the litigation process, including the appeal.

Constitutions and statutes use special terms to confer jurisdiction. For example, a provision may state that a court has concurrent, original jurisdiction of certain types of cases and also has appellate jurisdiction of other types of cases. The terms help to understand how subject matter jurisdiction works.

Every court is either a court of limited jurisdiction or a court of general jurisdiction. No court can be both. **Limited jurisdiction** means that the court cannot hear every type of case presented to it; it can hear only those types of cases which are listed in its creating constitutional provision or statute. Because the federal government is one of limited powers, every federal court (including the United States Supreme Court) is a court of limited jurisdiction.

By contrast, **general jurisdiction** means that the court can hear any type of case presented to it unless exclusive jurisdiction has been granted to some other court for a particular type of case (*see below*). Every state has at least one court of general jurisdiction, sometimes called a district court or a superior court.

Every court is either a court of original jurisdiction or a court of appellate jurisdiction, but some courts are both. **Original jurisdiction** means that actions are commenced in this court for particular types of cases. A court of original jurisdiction is the trial court for those types of cases specified in its creating constitutional provision or statute.

Appellate jurisdiction means that the court is authorized to review decisions of an inferior court (either a trial court or a lower appellate court) in certain types of cases. A single court, however, may have original jurisdiction in one type of case and appellate jurisdiction in another type of case. Such a court wears two hats: it is a superior court when it exercises its appellate jurisdiction in one type of case, and it is an inferior court when it exercises its original jurisdiction in another type of case.

In relation to a particular type of case, a court is granted either exclusive jurisdiction or concurrent jurisdiction. **Exclusive jurisdiction** means that no other court has the power to hear this type of case—not even a court of general jurisdiction. For example, the federal courts have exclusive jurisdiction of all bankruptcy cases. In a state court system, exclusive, original jurisdiction of all probate cases typically is given to one court.

Concurrent jurisdiction means that more than one court is authorized to hear a specific type of case. This allows a plaintiff to choose between (or among) those courts having concurrent jurisdiction of the subject matter of her case. For example, a small claims court typically has concurrent, original jurisdiction of civil cases under a certain dollar amount, say, $1,500. A plaintiff with a civil claim of $1,000 has the option to file it in the small claims court or in any other state court having jurisdiction. At a minimum, her other options will include that state's court of general jurisdiction, which can hear any type of case except those for which exclusive jurisdiction has been granted to another court.

Personal Jurisdiction

A court must have both subject matter jurisdiction and personal jurisdiction (sometimes called *in personam* jurisdiction) before it can hear and decide the merits of a particular case. ***Personal jurisdiction*** *refers to the court's power or authority over the parties to the litigation.*

A court acquires personal jurisdiction over a plaintiff when he files his complaint or petition. Personal jurisdiction over a defendant usually can be acquired in one of several ways:

- Defendant's consent;
- Defendant's domicile in the same state where the action is filed; or
- Long-arm statutes (for out-of-state defendants).

To satisfy constitutional requirements, an out-of-state defendant must have ***minimum contacts*** with the forum state before any court of that state can exercise jurisdiction over him. Minimum contacts exist if the defendant has engaged in some voluntary act in relation to the forum state. Examples of voluntary acts are doing business there, soliciting business, or visiting it. At least one court has found that flying over the forum state may be sufficient to establish minimum contacts.

If a defendant is subject to a state's long-arm statute, he generally has performed acts sufficient to satisfy the minimum contacts requirement. A ***long-arm statute*** allows a court to reach outside its state boundary lines to reach a defendant and to require him to defend himself in the forum state. Long-arm statutes are designed to reach out-of-state defendants who have caused injury within the forum state. *(A more detailed review of personal jurisdiction is included in the chapter on Litigation.)*

In Rem Jurisdiction

In rem literally means "in relation to the thing." A court has *in rem* jurisdiction when the subject matter of the suit relates directly to property located within the court's geographic boundary lines. The property, or thing, is the ***res***.

A court always has jurisdiction of property located within its geographic boundaries. When any claim arises concerning such property, the court with subject matter jurisdiction in that location has *in rem* jurisdiction, without regard to whether it has personal jurisdiction over the defendant or not.

Benson lives in Brazil and owns real estate in Marshall County, Iowa. Thomas, who lives in Oregon, lends money to Benson and

> receives a mortgage on the Iowa land as security for the loan. Benson defaults in his payments and Thomas wants to foreclose the mortgage.

Unless Benson consents, no American court can acquire personal jurisdiction over him while he remains in Brazil—not even with a long-arm statute. Because of *in rem* jurisdiction, however, Thomas can file his foreclosure action in the court having subject matter jurisdiction of mortgage foreclosures in Marshall County, Iowa. That court has the power to deal with the property with or without personal jurisdiction over Benson.

The result would be the same even if Benson and Thomas both lived in Oregon. It would be pointless for Thomas to file his mortgage foreclosure action in Oregon, because no Oregon court would foreclose a mortgage against Iowa real estate.

Quasi In Rem Jurisdiction

Quasi in rem jurisdiction arises when the subject matter of the suit does not relate to property in the court's jurisdiction, but the defendant has property in the court's jurisdiction which may be used to satisfy the judgment. Again, the court's jurisdiction exists whether or not it has personal jurisdiction over the defendant.

> Same facts as above, except that Benson gives Thomas a promissory note (no mortgage on the Iowa land).

Thomas still can file suit in Iowa. The Iowa court does not have *in rem* jurisdiction, because the subject of the suit does not relate to any Iowa property. However, since Benson owns property in Iowa, *quasi in rem* jurisdiction operates "as if" the Iowa property were the subject of the suit.

In the second example, Thomas also may elect to file suit in an Oregon court on the promissory note; obtain a judgment; and register the Oregon judgment as a foreign judgment in the Iowa court where the property is located. After the foreign judgment is registered in Iowa, he can enforce it against Benson's Iowa property. This is possible because of the Full Faith and Credit Clause of the Constitution (*discussed below*).

Venue

Venue refers to the place of trial or, more specifically, to the location within a particular jurisdiction where trial should take place.

Venue for a criminal trial generally is the place where the crime was committed. A defendant may be able to request a change of venue if pretrial publicity or public sentiment about the case will make it impossible to obtain a fair and impartial jury where the crime was committed.

Venue for a civil trial generally is the place where the claim arose (or property is located); where the defendant resides; or where the defendant has either a place or business or an agent. In federal civil trials, the forum court may decline to hear the case if *forum non conveniens* is found to exist (the court is inconvenient for witnesses, for obtaining evidence, and so forth). *A more thorough review of venue is contained in the chapter on Litigation.*

Federal Courts

The federal court system includes the United States Supreme Court, a court of appeals divided into 13 regions (one for each circuit); a district court divided into more than 90 federal district trial courts (one for each district, and a series of specialty courts (Tax Court, Court of Claims, Court of International Trade, and so forth).

All federal courts are courts of limited jurisdiction. They have authority to hear only those types of cases specifically authorized by constitutional provision (for the U.S. Supreme Court) or by federal statute (for all other federal courts).

Article III of the Constitution establishes the United States Supreme Court and authorizes Congress to establish lower federal courts, which Congress has done (United States District Court and United States Court of Appeals). These are constitutional courts, and their judges serve life terms subject to good behavior. The salaries of judges of constitutional courts cannot be decreased.

Legislative courts are established by Congress under Article I of the Constitution. Their judges have fixed terms. Legislative courts are the specialty courts (Tax Court, Court of Claims, and so forth).

United States Supreme Court   The United States Supreme Court is the court of last resort in the American legal system. It is the highest-ranking appellate court in the federal court system. The Supreme Court is comprised of nine justices (one chief justice and eight associate justices), who function as the final authority on—and protectors of—the Constitution.

Of all federal courts, the Supreme Court's jurisdiction is the only one specifically defined in Article III of the Constitution. It cannot be increased or decreased by Congress.

A.   **Original Jurisdiction**   The Supreme Court has original jurisdiction in the following types of cases:

•Disputes between two or more states (*exclusive*);

•Actions in which ambassadors, public ministers, or foreign consuls are parties;

•Disputes between the United States and a state; and

•Actions by a state against citizens of another state or against aliens.

Of these, only the first (disputes between states) is exclusive; all others are concurrent, original jurisdiction, which means that lower federal courts also have original jurisdiction in these areas. As a practical matter, then, the only original action that must be heard by the Supreme Court is one involving a dispute between two or more states.

B.   Appellate Jurisdiction   The Supreme Court has appellate jurisdiction of all appeals from (1) the United States Court of Appeals and from (2) the highest appellate court of each state—but only if the state appeal presents an issue concerning federal law.

Beginning in 1988, appellate cases have reached the Supreme Court almost exclusively by *writ of certiorari*. To obtain the writ, an appellant from the court of appeals must file a petition for writ of *certiorari* with the Supreme Court, asking the Court to hear the appeal. Granting the writ is discretionary. The Court generally grants a writ only when the justices believe that the case has sufficient national importance to warrant the Court's attention.

The writ of certiorari also is used to resolve issues within the federal court of appeals when there is serious conflict among the circuits.

United States Court of Appeals   The U.S. Court of Appeals is the intermediate appellate court in the federal court system. It is divided into 13 circuits: 11 circuits numbered according to their respective regions of the country, the Court of Appeals for the District of Columbia, and the Court of Appeals for the Federal Circuit.

The Court of Appeals for the Federal Circuit has exclusive appellate jurisdiction over all cases involving copyright, patent, trademark, and plant variety protection. It also has exclusive appellate jurisdiction over decisions of the U.S. Claims Court, U.S. Court of International Trade, and the U.S. Court of Veterans Appeals.

The Court of Appeals has appellate jurisdiction over all appeals taken from final decisions of the United States District Court except those involving cases within the exclusive appellate jurisdiction of the Court of Appeals for the Federal

Circuit (*see above*). It also has appellate jurisdiction of some (but not all) final decisions appealed from federal administrative agencies.

United States District Court   The U.S. District Court is the trial court in the federal court system. There are more than 90 districts across the United States. Each state and territory has at least one district.   The U.S. District Court has original jurisdiction in a number of areas, the most prominent of which are (1) federal question cases and (2) diversity of citizenship cases.

> A *federal question* case is an action arising under the Constitution, laws, or treaties of the United States.

> A *diversity of citizenship* case is a civil action between the citizens of different states where the matter in controversy exceeds $50,000, exclusive of interest and costs.

The U.S. District Court has original jurisdiction in these additional areas:

- Admiralty, maritime, and prize cases *(exclusive)*;

- Suits brought by the United States, its agencies, or officers *(exclusive)*;

- Suits against the United States or its officers (concurrent with U.S. Claims Court up to $10,000);

- Suits to compel officers of the United States to perform their duty (plaintiff seeks a writ of *mandamus*);

- Removal of suits against federal officers in state courts;

- Suits in bankruptcy *(exclusive)*;

- Suits in copyright, patent, trademark, and plant variety protection *(exclusive)*;

- Suits involving improper collection of Internal Revenue and customs duties;

- Suits involving civil rights; and

- Suits affecting ambassadors and other public ministers and consuls (*exclusive* as a practical matter, even though it is concurrent with U.S. Supreme Court).

A defendant may remove a case from state court to the federal court in the same district as the state court if (1) the defendant is not a resident of that state; (2) if the case could have been filed in federal court originally; (3) if the state court from which the case is removed has jurisdiction; and (4) in diversity cases only, if there was complete diversity between plaintiffs and defendants both at the time the case was filed in state court and at the time it is removed to federal court. *See the chapter on Litigation for a more detailed review.*

When the U.S. District Court exercises its jurisdiction in diversity of citizenship cases, it applies state substantive law to decide the case. *Refer to section on judicial decision-making later in this chapter and to the chapter on Litigation for more details.*

The U.S. District Court has appellate jurisdiction of some (but not all) final decisions taken on appeal from federal administrative agencies.

Federal Specialty Courts   Congress has established a number of courts under Article I of the Constitution. These are legislative courts, sometimes called federal specialty courts. Judges of federal specialty courts have specified terms, typically 15 years. Unlike the judges of constitutional courts, their salaries are not protected from congressional decreases. The most prominent federal specialty courts are listed here.

> •*United States Court of International Trade.* Hears disputes between citizens and the government based upon import and export matters.

> •*United States Claims Court.* Hears claims of citizens against the government based upon federal law or contracts; concurrent jurisdiction with U. S. District Court for taxpayer claims against IRS for improperly collected taxes.

> •*United States Tax Court.*   Hears taxpayer challenges to tax deficiency determinations issued by the IRS.

> •*United States Court of Military Appeals.*   Hears appeals from the Courts of Military Review.

> •*United States Court of Veterans Appeals.*   Reviews decisions of the Board of Veterans Appeals.

In addition, two Article I courts have been created and annexed to the U.S. District Court (an Article III court). They are:

●*Federal Magistrate Court.* Assists the U.S. District Court in areas such as hearing minor cases if the parties consent, conducting preliminary hearings in federal criminal cases, and conducting pretrial conferences in federal civil cases.

●*Bankruptcy Court.* Original jurisdiction (by referral from U.S. District Court) in all bankruptcy matters and in some civil or criminal matters related to debtors.

State Court Systems

State court systems vary from state to state; however, most of them follow an organizational structure which is similar to the federal court system. In the typical state court system, there is a supreme court, one or more intermediate appellate courts, a court of general jurisdiction, a county court, a small claims court, and a variety of specialty courts. Specialty courts may include a probate court, a family court, a juvenile court, a traffic court, and other courts as the state legislature may authorize.

State courts have concurrent jurisdiction with federal courts in all matters except those which are exclusively within federal jurisdiction, such as bankruptcy.

If a state case involves a federal question or issue, the case may be appealed to the U.S. Supreme Court following an unfavorable ruling by the state's highest court. The federal issue must be raised at the trial stage or it is waived. Matters which are purely of state interest (probate, divorce, adoption, and the like) cannot be appealed into the federal court system unless they also involve a federal issue (estate tax, due process, or equal protection, for example).

Judicial Decision Making

The decision makers in the trial process are the judge and the jury. The jury decides the facts of the case; the judge decides the law. When a case is tried without a jury (a bench trial), the judge fulfills a dual role by deciding both the facts and the law to be applied to those facts. At the appeal stage, the appellate judge reviews the accuracy of trial judge's decisions on the law. This section of the *Review Manual* reviews only the judge's role in deciding the law.

Law carries different weight in the decision-making process, depending on whether it is primary law or secondary law. ***Primary law*** carries the greatest weight in the decision-making process. In a state case, primary law includes the constitution, statutes, administrative rules and regulations, and case law of the state as well as the federal Constitution and any federal statutes (if there is a direct conflict between the two jurisdictions). Primary law is **mandatory law**; to the extent that it relates to the facts and issues of the pending case, it must be followed in the pending case. Procedural rules are primary law as well.

Secondary law includes the constitution, statutes, and case law of other states. The jurisdictions of other states are of equal level, unlike the federal jurisdiction (*see above*). Also included as secondary law are legal encyclopedias, annotations, restatements, and treatises. Secondary law is **persuasive law**; it may assist a court in reaching a decision in the pending case, but it need not be followed if the court does not wish to do so.

The judge has many substantive and procedural rules to consider at every stage of the trial. Much of the judicial decision-making process relates to proper interpretation and application of substantive law in the form of constitutional provisions, statutes, and common law. Common law is applied only in state cases (other than Louisiana) and in federal diversity cases.

Constitutions and Statutes   When a constitutional provision or a statute of the jurisdiction applies in a case, it takes precedence over all other legal rules. In this situation, it is mandatory law and must be followed to reach the decision.

Unless a particular statute violates some constitutional provision (constitutions carry more weight than statutes), the court's job is to determine the meaning of the statute and then to apply it to the facts of the case to determine the result. A judge cannot ignore the statute just because she does not like it; neither can she interpret it to mean something other than what the legislature says. If the statute passes constitutional requirements, the court must apply it as it stands.

Courts generally read (construe) statutes in criminal cases more narrowly or strictly to give every advantage to the defendant, while still complying with what the statute says. If a statute says that "a motorist *may* come to a complete stop at any intersection," a court is unlikely to allow anyone to be convicted under the statute. The word *may* indicates that stopping is optional.

The words used in statutes are given their ordinary meaning. If the words of a statute are ambiguous, a court is permitted to consider the statute's legislative history in determining what purpose the statute was intended to accomplish.

Common Law   If no constitutional or statutory provision applies or if its application leaves gaps in the final decision, state courts—and federal courts hearing diversity cases—supply the appropriate legal rules through common law principles.

Once an issue is decided by a court, the holding (rule of law) stated in that case is followed by that court and by lower courts of the same jurisdiction in all future cases involving similar facts and issues. The holding is precedent for all such future cases. The process of reviewing past cases is called **stare decisis** (*discussed above*). When a past case is found which has similar facts and similar issues, the holding of that case may be a **precedent** for the current case. If a precedent, it is **mandatory law** and must be followed in deciding the current case.

The holding of a past case is precedent only if:

- it is found in a case decided by the present court or by a higher court;

- the prior case was recorded (published); and

- it is contained in the majority opinion of that court.

If all of these requirements are met, the holding of the case is precedent; and it is followed. If the facts or issues of the past case and the current case are sufficiently different or if one of the above requirements is missing, the holding is not precedent.

Recall that even if the prior case is precedent in the current case, a court is free to consider the surrounding circumstances and the societal changes since the prior case was decided to determine if the rule still fits. If it does not, common law principles are flexible enough to allow those adjustments which may be necessary to fit the rules to the current case.

If there are no applicable statutes and no precedents in the case law of the jurisdiction, the court is presented with a **case of first impression**. In a civil law system (one based substantially on codified statutes) or in the federal system (based only on the Constitution and federal statutes), the court's hands would be tied. Without a statute covering the subject, such a court could do little. In a common law system, a case of first impression is handled by looking to other jurisdictions for a similar case to provide guidance. If none are found or if they are unsatisfactory, a common law court can draw analogies from existing case law and statutes.

For instance, if a company manufactures a new product called a skymobile and if no statutes yet exist to regulate its use, a common law court can decide whether the skymobile is more like an airplane or is more like an automobile. Depending on the outcome of that analysis, the court can apply common law rules applicable either to airplanes or to automobiles. If the legislature does not agree with the court's decision concerning the skymobile—or does not agree with the court's decision in any other area—the legislature is free to enact statutes to deal with the matter.

Federal courts sitting in diversity must apply the same state substantive law (including common law) that a state court of that district would apply. This is the only situation in which federal courts use common law principles. Even when a state's common law applies as the substantive law in a federal diversity case, the federal court applies its own rules of procedure (Federal Rules of Civil Procedure), not the rules of procedure of the state court.

Conflicts of Law   Because the substantive laws of one state can vary widely from the substantive laws of another state, a conflict of law can arise: (1) when the facts of a case occur in a state other than the forum state; or (2) when the facts of a case occur in more than one state. Conflicts of law questions sometimes are referred to as *choice of law* questions.

When either of these situations occurs, the forum court may be uncertain about whether to apply the substantive law of its own state or whether to apply the substantive law of the foreign state. A federal court sitting in diversity can encounter the same situation. To alleviate this problem, each state has developed a set of conflicts-of-law rules to help courts decide if and when to apply the substantive law of a foreign state. The forum court always follows its own procedural rules, no matter which state's substantive law is followed.

Issues involving conflicts of law can become highly complex. The material in this section provides only an overview of basic terminology and concepts. More detailed information is outside the intended scope of this *Review Manual*.

In tort cases, the traditional approach to a conflict of law is to apply the law of the state where the wrong was committed (*lex loci delicti commissi*). The current trend of cases, however, is to replace the traditional rule with the significant relationship rule. Using the *significant relationship rule*, the court applies the substantive law of the place having the most significant contacts with the occurrence or event. As a practical matter, this frequently is the state where the wrong was committed.

In contract cases, the rules are different than in tort cases. Courts traditionally have used several different approaches:

●*lex fori*	the law of the state where the suit is filed;
●*lex loci solutionis*	the law of the state where the contract was to have been performed;
●*lex loci contractus*	the law of the state where the last act occurred which was required to create a binding contract;

●the law of the state agreed to by the parties as part of their contract; or

●the law of the state having the most significant contacts with the events and the parties (*significant relationship* rule).

The Uniform Commercial Code (UCC), which applies to the sale of goods, uses a rule similar to the significant relationship rule when parties fail to specify a choice of law. The UCC provides no assistance, however, when the subject of the contract is employment, services, construction, or real estate.

Full Faith and Credit   Article IV of the U.S. Constitution requires that "full faith and credit shall be given in each state to the public acts, records, and judicial proceedings of every other state."

This provision requires each state to enforce the final judgments of all other states, without regard to the differences in substantive law and public policy from state to state. The only basis for refusing to enforce a final judgment of another state is when the issuing state did not follow constitutional requirements in obtaining the judgment, such as notice and an opportunity to be heard. If the defendant had the requisite minimum contacts with the issuing state and if the state properly exercised its long-arm statute, procedural due process requirements likely were met; and the resulting final judgment must be honored.

Thus, if loan sharking is legal in State A but not in State B and if State A obtains a valid final judgment against a defendant, State B must enforce the judgment—even when the source of the underlying debt is repugnant to the public policy of State B. Article IV does not make judgments self-executing, however. The party who seeks enforcement still must initiate action in State B according to State B's judgment enforcement procedures.

Article IV applies only to states. Federal courts are held to the same requirement, however, by federal statute.

Comity   Comity relates to the recognition of the public acts (legislative, executive, or judicial) of one nation by another nation. Comity is a matter of courtesy; no international law requires it.

American courts ordinarily honor the judgments of foreign countries unless it would be repugnant to public policy or prejudicial to citizens' interests in general to do so. A Canadian judgment on a defaulted promissory note, for example, likely would be honored by American courts under the doctrine of comity.

Limitations in Judicial Decision Making

Not every case can be decided by a court, even if jurisdictional requirements are met. Other factors may preclude parties from bringing their dispute before the court. Non-jurisdictional obstacles are reviewed in this section.

Case or Controversy   Article III, § 2 of the U.S. Constitution requires that there be a case or controversy before parties can maintain legal action. In general, this means that *no advisory opinions* will be issued by the federal courts. An advisory opinion is one rendered on the basis of hypothetical facts. Some states allow their courts to issue advisory opinions; others do not.

Because of the case or controversy requirement, *no collusive suits* are permitted. A collusive suit is one based on a friendly agreement to litigate an issue, just to see how it comes out or—even worse—to influence the result in a certain direction by agreeing that one party will not put up a genuine struggle. A genuine case or controversy requires true adversaries to litigate the issues fully.

Parties to the suit must have *standing*, which means that their rights must be personally and immediately affected by the issues in the suit. One who is denied a medical treatment because of a state statute, for instance, has standing to challenge the statute. His physician does not.

The issue in the case must be *ripe* for judicial decision. It cannot be based upon something that might happen in the future. There must be an actual, full-blown dispute. For example, if a college official tells a student that the student's admission application will be denied if it is submitted, a lawsuit by the student probably would be dismissed if it were filed. The dispute is not ripe for decision, because the student's application has not been denied. It may very well be that the application will be accepted, notwithstanding what the official says now.

A very narrow distinction from the ripeness doctrine is the declaratory judgment action, which may be an appropriate remedy when a case is on the verge of becoming a full-blown dispute (*see below*).

The issue in the case cannot be moot. **Moot** is the opposite of ripe. An issue is moot if it has become irrelevant or academic at any stage of the proceeding, including the appeal. Courts will not decide moot cases, because the decision will not affect the litigants one way or the other. For example, if the student in the above example applies to college and is refused admission for discriminatory reasons, she could file suit and receive an injunction ordering her admission for the duration of the case. If she graduates before the case is concluded, the case is moot; and it will be dismissed. No matter what the court decides at that point, it will not affect the student.

Bar   Litigation may be barred (prohibited) from being litigated for several reasons, the two most common of which are (1) statute of limitations and (2) the doctrine of *res judicata*.

A **statute of limitations** is set by the legislature and requires that a civil action in a certain type of case must be filed within a fixed time after the cause of action first arises. The time limit varies from state to state; it also varies according to the type of case. For example, a state may set a four-year limitation on oral contracts; a five-year limitation on written contracts; and a two-year limitation on malpractice claims. If the complaint or petition is not filed within that time period, it is barred. The plaintiff loses the right to sue after the time limit expires.

Most statutes of limitation are **tolled** (put on hold) by infancy (being a minor), insanity, imprisonment, court order, fraudulent concealment by a fiduciary, and so forth. Every state is slightly different. If the statute is tolled because of infancy, for example, the minor usually has a reasonable time after becoming an adult in which to file the action. Whether a particular amount of time is reasonable usually depends on the circumstances.

If final judgment has been rendered in a case, the doctrine of **res judicata** prevents the same facts from being litigated again between the same parties. *Res judicata* literally means "the thing decided." The doctrine applies to a final judgment on the merits, to a motion for summary judgment, and to a dismissal with prejudice to future action. For *res judicata* to apply, (1) the parties must be the same or must be in privity with the original parties; and (2) the factual basis must be the same as the first suit. For example, if a plaintiff loses a case in a small claims court, she cannot file another case against the same defendant under a different legal theory if the underlying facts are the same. Neither can she file part of her claim, wait to see if she wins, and then file another claim if both claims are against the same defendant and are based on the same facts.

Immunity   Certain defendants are immune from civil prosecution for tort liability. For varying reasons, they are protected from potential liability.

Sovereign immunity insulates a government from tort liability on the premise that the "king can do no wrong." Sovereign immunity applies to any governmental unit (federal, state, or local). A military hospital, a prison, and a public school are immune from tort actions because of sovereign immunity.

A government may waive its sovereign immunity in whole or in part. The federal government, for example, waived a portion of its sovereign immunity when it enacted the Federal Tort Claims Act in 1946. Tort actions now may be brought against the federal government except for discretionary acts of government employees or for acts of the military in time of war.

Sovereign immunity does not apply when government assumes a non-governmental role, such as sponsoring rock concerts for profit, owning a horse racing track, or engaging in other commercial enterprises.

Sovereign immunity extends to government officials so long as the official acts within the scope of her authority and in the discharge of her official duties. Immunity is very strong for high-ranking government officials who exercise many discretionary powers, such as judges. The immunity does not apply, however, when the official steps outside the powers of her office and invades the constitutional rights of others. For example, if a judge discharges a female deputy sheriff because the judge thinks a male deputy presents a better image in the courtroom, there is no immunity for the judge's decision.

Nonprofit organizations traditionally have been provided with a *charitable immunity* from tort actions. Many states have restricted this type of immunity, simply because many charitable organizations have become huge business operations and can afford to purchase insurance protection, the same as any other business.

Most states allow a limited *parental immunity* from suit by unemancipated children in the areas of child-rearing and discipline. The immunity does not apply when a parent is abusive to a child.

Many states recognize a limited *contractual immunity* by allowing enforcement of an *exculpatory clause* on a case-by-case basis. The court looks at the subject matter of the contract, the clause itself, the relation of the parties, and the relative bargaining power of the parties. Such a clause may not be enforceable by a slum landlord against a poor tenant who does not read or write English. On the other hand, such a clause may be enforceable by a ski resort against a college student who rents a pair of skis for the day but does not take the time to read the rental agreement.

Judicial Remedies

In addition to its function of applying applicable law to cases, a court also must decide the type of relief that the winning party is entitled to receive in a civil case. A basic maxim of law is, *"For every right, there is a remedy."* To some extent, selection of a proper remedy depends on what the litigant requests. If the remedy is damages, deciding the amount is within the province of the jury up to a certain point. The judge ensures that the remedy is one which is permitted by the substantive laws of the state.

The court's goal is to put the injured party in the same position where she would have been if the injury had not occurred. To the extent that a statute addresses the issue of remedies, the statute must be followed. In the absence of a statute, however, the court applies common law principles to establish the type and amount of relief that a party may receive. Those decisions initially are based upon whether the case is (1) at law or (2) in equity.

Law and Equity   The concept of law courts and equity courts in America has existed since the first English colonists settled in this country. Historically, if a case involved both legal issues and equity issues, the litigant had to file two actions in two separate courts—and have two separate trials. Physical separation of the two courts continued until the early 1900s, when they were merged. Although the merger streamlined many of the procedures connected with dual law-and-equity cases, the distinctions between the two forms of action (and the relief that can be obtained) continue to be significant.

1. Identification of the parties often is different. In law actions, parties are identified as the plaintiff and the defendant. In equity actions, they typically are identified as the petitioner and the respondent.

2. Parties in law actions generally are entitled to a jury trial. No juries are allowed in equity actions.

3. The final order in a law action is a judgment; the final order in an equity action is a decree.

4. In the usual case, a judgment in a law action simply declares that Party A owes money to Party B. If Party A does not pay, there is no special penalty. No matter what happens, Party A cannot go to jail for simple nonpayment of a debt.

However, a decree is a personal order of the court to do (or to refrain from doing) some specific act. If Party A does not obey, she is in contempt of court and may be penalized accordingly. The punishment for civil contempt in most states can be as severe as incarceration for a period of months or until the party obeys.

When legal and equitable issues exist in a single case, the jury determines the facts concerning the legal issues; the judge decides everything concerning the equity issues. If it is necessary to try legal issues separately (at a different time) from equitable issues, the process is called a *bifurcated trial*.

Remedies at Law   Only a few legal remedies remain as carryovers from the early common law writ system:

•*Replevin*, which requires return of specific personal property in the defendant's possession; and

•*Ejectment*, which requires return of specific real property in the defendant's possession.

With these exceptions, remedies at law take the form of money (called damages). *Damages* always result in the payment of money. However, the basis or purpose for awarding damages determines how much money is awarded. The purpose of damages always is to make the plaintiff whole, but making the plaintiff whole means different things in different situations.

Damages must have been *foreseeable* at the time a contract is made or at the time the tort occurs. Damages which are too far removed from the contract (or the tort) are not foreseeable and cannot be awarded. In addition, the plaintiff has a duty to *mitigate* his damages. In other words, he must take reasonable steps to minimize his losses. If he fails to mitigate, his damage award is reduced by the amount of loss that could have been prevented through mitigation. Both compensatory damages and restitution must be proved with a "reasonable degree of certainty" at the time of trial. This means the plaintiff must provide evidence of his losses when he seeks either compensatory damages or restitution.

A.   Compensatory Damages   Compensatory damages focus on the plaintiff's losses. Compensatory damages are further classified as either general damages or special damages. Special damages may be called consequential damages in some jurisdictions. By black-letter definition, *general damages* are those losses which anyone in the plaintiff's situation would incur. *Special damages* are those losses which are special (unique) to this particular plaintiff.

The goals of general damages and special damages are the same in both contract and tort cases; however, because the basis for the losses are different, the damages may seem to be different. They are not.

> Bill agreed to build a house for Dan for $100,000 on an existing foundation. Bill broke his arm and could not do the job. Dan had to pay $200.00 for plastic sheeting to re-cover the foundation while he found another contractor. He had to pay the second contractor $115,000 to build the house.

In this contract case, Dan lost the benefit of his bargain when he had to pay the second contractor $15,000 more than he originally had agreed to pay Bill. The benefit of his bargain ($15,000 in this case) is Dan's general damage. He also incurred $200 in special damages.

Had Bill started to work on the house before he broke his arm, he might be able to receive payment or credit for the value of his work. This is called *quantum meruit*, which is awarded on a quasi-contract theory.

> Judy was injured in an automobile accident. She was driving a car that was a gift from her parents when she graduated from high school. Both of her parents since have died, and the car means a great deal to her (although it is worth only $4,000). The accident was the fault of Betty, who was the driver of the other car. Judy was in the hospital three weeks and could not return to work for two months.

Judy's general damages are her pain and suffering as a result of her physical injuries and $4,000 for the value of her car. The jury decides the dollar value of Judy's physical pain and suffering. Her special damages are her medical bills and lost wages. The law does not compensate for the sentimental value of her car.

B. Punitive Damages

Sometimes called exemplary damages, the purpose of punitive damages is to punish the defendant for outrageous conduct, such as causing injury while driving under the influence of alcohol or a controlled substance. An employer who fails to pay earned wages may be required to pay punitive damages in addition to compensatory damages (the wages).

Punitive damages are not allowed in some states. Where they are allowed, they serve the purpose of teaching a lesson to the defendant. They also deter others from engaging in the same conduct by making an example of the defendant.

C.   Nominal Damages   The purpose of nominal damages is to vindicate a right which has been violated when no monetary loss has occurred. A court typically awards a trivial amount plus court costs in that situation.

> Karen grows prize roses for a hobby. She owns a corner lot, which neighborhood children use as a shortcut on their way to and from school.

> Same facts, except that one little girl tramples a new rosebush, which is valued at $10.

In the first example, Karen is entitled to be vindicated for the trespass. A judge might award $1 and court costs, $10 and court costs, or some other trivial amount as nominal damages. In the second example, Karen is entitled to compensatory damages of $10. Even though the amount is small, it represents compensation for an actual loss. It cannot be termed nominal damages when an actual loss has occurred.

Nominal damages may be awarded in either contract or tort cases.

D.   Liquidated Damages   Liquidated damages arise in contract cases only. They are damages agreed to by the parties at the time the contract is made, and they represent the parties' reasonable estimate of losses in the event of breach. A liquidated damages provision is appropriate when damages are difficult to determine, such as lost profits for a new business.

Unless a liquidated damages provision is excessive or unless the parties occupy grossly disproportionate bargaining positions, courts are inclined to enforce a provision for liquidated damages.

Equitable Remedies   Equitable remedies are fashioned by courts to achieve fairness when legal remedies are inadequate for that purpose. Therefore, a plaintiff's threshold objective is to demonstrate to the court that he has ***no adequate remedy at law***. That is, he must show that money cannot compensate for his injury.

In addition, a petitioner who seeks equitable relief must be blameless in the matter or equity will not intervene. Thus, the maxim: *He who comes into equity must come with clean hands.*

A.   Restitution   Restitution focuses on the defendant's gains rather than on the plaintiff's losses (*see above*). Restitution serves a different purpose than compensatory damages; it prevents defendants from profiting by their wrongful conduct.

> Mary steals stock certificates valued at $40,000 from Joe. She cashes in the certificates and spends the money on trips and clothes.

> Same facts, except that Mary sells the stock at a premium price of $50,000 to a person who wants them for a special purpose.

In both examples, Joe's losses are the value of the stock certificates: $40,000. If compensatory damages were his only option, Mary would have to repay that amount; and she would keep $10,000 profit. Restitution prevents Mary from being unjustly enriched by allowing Joe to reach Mary's ill-gotten gains. The court uses the legal fiction that Mary has created a ***constructive trust*** for Joe's benefit, with Mary as the trustee. By using the doctrine of ***tracing***, the court is able to "trace" the stock certificates to the cash. Mary, then, would be required to make an ***accounting*** for the profits she received.

If Mary had made a down payment on real estate with the proceeds, tracing could have been used to protect Joe's interest by placing an ***equitable lien*** of $50,000 on the real estate. The equitable lien then can be foreclosed in the same way that any other lien on real estate is foreclosed.

Yet another form of restitution is ***subrogation***. Subrogation applies when a person (other than an intermeddler) pays the debt of another. An insurance contract typically contains a subrogation clause.

> Wayne is injured through the negligence of George. Wayne's insurance carrier pays the medical bills. In a suit against George, Wayne subrogates his claim for medical bills to the insurance carrier. If Wayne wins, the carrier is reimbursed for the medical bills; and Wayne receives the balance of the judgment.

Restitution may be awarded in either contract or tort cases.

B.   Injunction   An injunction is a personal order to a respondent to do (or to refrain from doing) a specific act. An injunction, therefore, may be *mandatory* or *preventive*. The rules to obtain an injunction vary slightly from state to state, but they generally are similar to the format described here.

The petitioner who seeks injunctive relief often needs interim intervention to keep matters at a status quo pending trial. For example, if the petitioner claims ownership of trees on a boundary line and wants to prevent the respondent from chopping them down, the trees likely will be gone by the time a full hearing can be scheduled; and injunctive relief will have become moot.

At the beginning of her suit (or at any later time), the petitioner may seek a ***temporary restraining order*** (TRO). The initial TRO hearing often is ***ex parte***, which means that only one party (the petitioner) is heard on the matter. She must, by motion and sworn affidavit, demonstrate that she has no adequate remedy at law and that she will suffer irreparable harm if the TRO is not granted, compared with little or no harm to the respondent if it is granted. In addition, the judge must be convinced that the petitioner has a reasonable chance to win on the ultimate issues of the case.

If the judge grants the TRO, the petitioner ordinarily must post a bond to cover the respondent's damages in case the petitioner ultimately loses; and a copy of the TRO must be served on the respondent personally before it has any effect. If the judge does not grant the TRO (the trees are cut down), the lawsuit often becomes moot.

A temporary hearing is scheduled within a very short time, perhaps within seven or ten days. At the temporary hearing, both parties are present and have an opportunity to present their sides in a setting which is substantially less formal than a trial. After hearing the evidence, the judge issues a ***temporary injunction*** if it still appears that the petitioner may win ultimately and that the status quo should be maintained until trial. On the other hand, the judge dissolves the TRO if it appears to have been granted improvidently. In this circumstance, petitioners frequently do not pursue the case further.

At the trial of the case, a ***permanent injunction*** is issued if the petitioner wins. Unlike other litigation, the trial of an injunction case often is anti-climactic. One who is successful in obtaining a TRO and is also successful in obtaining a temporary injunction seldom will lose at the trial.

NOTE: *Libel or slander cannot be* ~~enjoined~~ prevented by injunction *or restrained because of First Amendment speech protections. After the fact, the injured plaintiff can seek damages, however.*

C. **Declaratory Judgment** A declaratory judgment action is a suit which asks the court to declare the rights of parties in an impending dispute. The dispute must be imminent (ready to happen) and not merely a probability. In addition, one or both of the parties must be in danger of facing personal peril (prosecution under a criminal statute) or a great financial burden (tearing down a whole building) if the dispute actually occurs.

> The State of Utopia recently enacted a statute which makes it unlawful to operate a commercial bingo hall after dusk but which permits nonprofit bingo halls to operate after dusk. William operates commercial bingo halls all around the state, and most of his business is after dusk. William believes the statute is unconstitutional. The statute goes into effect on January 1.

In the example, if William operates his bingo halls after January 1, he will be subject to criminal prosecution. If he stops operating the bingo halls while he sues to challenge the statute, he will face financial ruin; and his case likely will become moot. A declaratory judgment may resolve the dilemma.

If William can obtain a declaratory judgment after the statute is passed but before it takes effect, his rights may be determined before he takes irreversible action one way or the other. Similarly, if the statute becomes effective right away, William may be able to combine the declaratory judgment action with a request for injunctive relief, pending the outcome of the case.

A declaratory judgment can be obtained in nearly every type of case (contract, tort, civil rights, and so forth).

D.   Rescission   Rescission is an equitable remedy available only in contract cases (one cannot rescind a tort). When rescission is granted, the underlying contract is cancelled and made void—as if it never existed. Where money has already changed hands in furtherance of the contract, rescission and restitution frequently are granted at the same time.

A contract may be rescinded as a remedy for fraud, misrepresentation, unconscionability, duress, or certain types of mistakes.

E.   Reformation   Like rescission, reformation is an equitable remedy available only in contract cases (one cannot reform a tort). Reformation typically is sought to correct errors in the document evidencing a contract or in a deed of conveyance when the document (or the deed) does not reflect the parties' agreement accurately.

Recall that the contract is the parties' underlying agreement. The document labeled "Contract" is merely evidence of that contract. Reformation can change (correct) only the document evidencing the contract; it cannot change the contract terms themselves.

> Pam agrees to purchase a pasture from Carla at $100 an acre; both parties believe the pasture contains ten acres of land. They execute a purchase agreement to satisfy the Statute of Frauds. At the

closing, Carla provides a warranty deed to Pam for ten acres at $100 an acre; and Pam pays $1,000. Pam then discovers that the pasture contains 9.4 acres.

In this example, reformation may be used to correct the deed so that it reflects the parties' true agreement, which was to purchase and sell a 9.4-acre pasture.

Although not connected directly to the remedy of reformation, Pam also may be entitled to abate (reduce) the purchase price if the parties' agreement was to buy pasture at $100 an acre. At $100 an acre, Pam received only $940 in value; $60 should be returned to her. If, however, the parties' agreement was to purchase this particular pasture for $1000 and if the language "10 acres at $100 an acre" was merely a convenient way to describe the pasture, Pam received the benefit of her bargain (the pasture she wanted). Abatement would not be appropriate in the latter situation.

F.   Specific Performance   Specific performance, too, is an equitable remedy available only in contract cases (one would not demand specific performance of a tort). This remedy may be available when the subject matter of the contract is unique, such as an original Renoir painting. The only way to make the disappointed buyer whole is to award her the Renoir. Money frequently is inadequate when unique property is in dispute.

Alternative Dispute Resolution   Alternative dispute resolution (ADR) is precisely what the name implies. It provides a way to settle parties' claims without the expense and delay of a full-blown trial through (1) a pretrial procedure designed to evaluate the parties' claims and to effect settlement, (2) arbitration, or (3) mediation. The Rules of Professional Conduct of some states require attorneys to advise their clients of ADR options.

A.   Court-Annexed ADR   An experimental, court-annexed arbitration program was initiated in ten federal district courts under the Judicial Improvements and Access to Justice Act of 1988. In addition, approximately half of the states have some form of court-annexed ADR, whether authorized by state statute or by local court rule. With only minor exception, the federal experiment and the state ADR programs appear to be successful so far.

In a court-annexed program, parties are required to submit to a type of pretrial arbitration or pretrial conference before their cases are docketed for trial. A court-appointed arbitrator, hearing officer, or magistrate conducts the proceeding. This individual may be a lawyer (such as the magistrate), but the programs of many state courts permit nonlawyers (including legal assistants) to serve as the arbitrator or hearing officer for certain types of cases.

The presiding officer assists the parties in laying all the issues on the table, with the goals of disposing of non-issues and of bringing the parties to a compromise position. In some situations, the presiding officer may inform the parties of results of recent cases similar to theirs and may assist them in predicting the probable outcome of their case. Court-annexed programs may take the form of an arbitration proceeding or may take the form of a mediation conference.

Parties who are unable to resolve their disputes through a court-annexed program are entitled to proceed to trial, although they frequently find that the results at trial are strikingly similar to the results predicted during the ADR proceeding.

B.   Arbitration   Arbitration has existed for many years in the business world as a voluntary method of resolving disputes without litigation. An impartial arbitrator, usually a person with expertise in the area of the parties' dispute, listens to evidence presented by both sides and renders a decision. As part of the agreement to arbitrate, the parties agree that the arbitrator's decision will be binding.

If either party is dissatisfied with the decision (believes that errors were made by the arbitrator), the decision can be appealed into the court system.

Panels of impartial arbitrators can be identified through the American Arbitration Association, the Center for Public Resources, or the Federal Conciliation and Mediation Service. The Better Business Bureau, which operates in most major cities, can supply contact information for these organizations.

C.   Mediation   Mediation is also a voluntary method of dispute resolution. The primary distinction between arbitration and mediation is that mediation is not binding on the parties.

In a mediation conference, an impartial third party presides over the conference and attempts to help the parties reach an agreement. This may be done in a variety of ways; but the objective is to identify areas of common ground and to present viable options to resolve those areas of genuine dispute. A mediation conference is much less structured than an arbitration proceeding. Labor union negotiators traditionally have turned to mediation when they were unable to reach a compromise. Mediation is a particularly useful alternative in family law cases as well.

A mediator sometimes makes recommendations but never makes decisions. Therefore, unsuccessful mediation participants are free to proceed through the judicial processes if they choose to do so.

This chapter, together with the remaining chapters on substantive law and with the accompanying self-tests, should provide a basic review of the principles and procedures that may be encountered on the certifying examination. If the applicant is unfamiliar with any of the material covered, he or she is advised to consider close study of a relevant textbook or other study aid as well as the applicable Rules and statutes. *See the Bibliography for additional study references.*

General Law Self-Test

Allow an uninterrupted thirty-minute period to answer all questions. At the end of thirty minutes, check your answers against those in the Answer Key Section of this Manual. Deduct two points for each incorrect answer (100 total possible points). Unanswered questions are counted as incorrect answers. Follow directions carefully and observe the time limit precisely to provide an accurate self-assessment.

Choose the most correct answer to the following questions unless a specific question instructs you to do otherwise.

1.   If a case were filed by 50 women, none of whom is pregnant, to challenge a state's abortion statute, the case most likely would be:

      a.   dismissed for lack of standing.
      b.   dismissed under the standards doctrine.
      c.   dismissed under the mootness doctrine.
      d.   dismissed under the overbreadth doctrine.

2. Which of the following courts is authorized to exercise original jurisdiction in certain types of cases?

   a. United States Supreme Court.
   b. United States District Court.
   c. State District (or Superior) Court.
   d. All of the above.
   e. None of the above.

3. As it relates to court systems, concurrent jurisdiction means:

   a. more than one court has the power to hear a case.
   b. two courts have the power to hear a case.
   c. more than two courts have the power to hear a case .
   d. none of the above.

4. The United States Court of International Trade formerly was known as:

   a. U.S. Court of Customs.
   b. U.S. Court of Claims.
   c. U.S. Court of Customs and Patent Appeals.
   d. none of the above.

5. True or False. The United States Supreme Court decides questions based upon stipulated facts that have been certified to it by lower courts.

6. True or False. When federal constitutional issues are involved, the United States Supreme Court is required to hear the case.

7. True or False. Laws relating to contracts are examples of private laws.

8. True or False. Laws relating to rules of evidence are examples of procedural laws.

9. True or False. Federal courts of appeals properly may be referred to as circuit courts of appeals.

10. True or False. The United States Supreme Court is known as the supreme law of the land.

11. True or False. Those who participate in mediation proceedings are bound by the decision of the mediator.

12. True or False.   The power of a state's legislative body to enact laws in areas relating to the health, safety, and welfare of its citizens is known as its welfare power.

13. The federal intermediate courts of appeals are established by:

    a.   federal statute.
    a.   United States Constitution.
    b.   United States Supreme Court.
    d.   None of the above.

14. A law that describes how a defendant must be served with summons in a case is an example of:

    a. substantive law.
    b. secondary law.
    c. adjective law.
    d. none of the above.

15. The Bill of Rights is found:

    a.   in the first fourteen amendments to the U.S. Constitution.
    b.   in the first ten amendments to the U.S. Constitution.
    c.   in the First and Fourteenth Amendments to the U.S. Constitution.
    d.   in all of the amendments to the U.S. Constitution.

16. Generally speaking, a case is appealed to the United States Supreme Court by filing:

    a.   a petition for writ of certiorari.
    b.   a writ of certiorari.
    c.   a writ of habeas corpus.
    d.   none of the above.

17. True or False.   Since there is no federal common law, federal courts do not have jurisdiction to decide contract cases.

18. True or False.   The doctrine under which powers are divided between the federal government and the states is known as federalism.

19. True or False.   Congress could expand the jurisdiction of the United States District Courts by vesting in them jurisdiction of all cases including local and state matters.

20. True or False.   Personal jurisdiction of federal courts generally is determined under the principle of maximum contacts.

21. Two sources of primary law are:

    a.   legal references and judges.
    b.   decisions of courts and enactments of legislative bodies.
    c.   United States Supreme Court and case law.
    d.   legislation and statutory law.

22. Stare decisis is:

    a.   a writ first issued.
    b.   legislation last issued.
    c.   guiding principle whereby a court is bound by prior cases.
    d.   declaratory legislation.

23. A law providing that no legal assistants may serve on boards of directors of national banks would be a(n):

    a.   ex post facto law. → *after the fact*
    b.   bill of attainder. → *specific person or specific group*
    c.   ipso facto law.
    d.   none of these is correct.

For each of the following definitions, supply the correct legal term or phrase.

24. _____*acknowlegement*_____ sworn declaration that the execution of an instrument is voluntary

25. _____*ad damnum*_____ clause of pleading that asks for damages

26. _____*nunc pro tunc*_____ now for then

27. _____*witness*_____ one with personal knowledge of a fact

28. _____*ex post facto*_____ law making conduct illegal after the fact

29. _____appellee_____ party defending an appeal

30. _____Venue_____ geographic location of trial

31. _____chattel_____ an article of personal property

32. _____mandatory~~Primary law~~_____ constitutions, statutes, and case law

33. _____writ of mandamus_____ order commanding a public official to do that which the law requires her to do

34. True or False. A uniform law is one adopted by Congress as a proposal to states, which each state is free to adopt in its entirety, adopt with modifications, or not adopt at all.

35. True or False. The federal government has preempted several areas of regulation, including interstate commerce and the postal service.

36. True or False. When rights of citizens conflict with each other, the courts choose the rights that are more important and uphold those, which means that the less important rights are no longer recognized.

37. True or False. A single court can be authorized to exercise both original and appellate jurisdiction.

38. True or False. When both a criminal charge and a civil action arise from the same set of facts, a guilty verdict for the criminal charge means the defendant will be found liable in the civil action as well.

39. The Model Penal Code was drafted by:

a. American Law Institute.
b. American Bar Association.
c. National Conference of Commissioners on Uniform State Laws.
d. None of the above.

40. Today's equity court descends from the:

a. king's court.
b. queen's court.
c. court of champerty.

(see next page)

d.   court of chancery.
e.   none of the above.

41.   True or False.   Stare decisis and precedent mean the same thing.

42.   True of False.   The federal Constitution grants exclusive power to Congress to establish and to operate a post office.

43.   True or False.   Article II of the Constitution grants the President the exclusive right to declare war on behalf of the United States.

44.   True or False.   Article I of the Constitution grants Congress the exclusive right to control intrastate commerce.

45.   The prohibition against mandatory self-incrimination in criminal cases is guaranteed by the:

a.   First Amendment.
b.   Fifth Amendment.
c.   Sixth Amendment.
d.   Eighth Amendment.
e.   None of the above.

46.   According to the Seventh Amendment, persons are entitled to a jury trial in civil cases where the amount in controversy exceeds:

a. $20.
b. $20,000.
c. $50,000.
d.   None of the above

47.   Neither a court nor the parties ever can waive:

a.   concurrent jurisdiction.
b.   personal jurisdiction.
c.   subject matter jurisdiction.
d.   none of the above.

48.   The United States Supreme Court consists of how many justices?

a.   three
b.   seven

(see next page)

       c.   nine

       d.   eleven

49.   True or False.   Disputes between two of more states may be heard either by the United States Supreme Court or by the United States District Court.

50.   True or False.   The power of all federal judges derives from Article III of the Constitution.

Chapter 8
ADMINISTRATIVE LAW

You must do the thing you think you cannot do.

—Eleanor Roosevelt

Administrative agencies exist at all levels of government; however, because of its national scope, this subsection of the CLA® Certifying Examination necessarily emphasizes federal administrative agencies. Administrative law is a law practice specialty area which deals with those legal rules that create, affect, and are generated by administrative agencies. At the federal level, those legal rules emanate from the federal Constitution; federal statutes (such as enabling acts, the Administrative Procedure Act, and the Freedom of Information Act); and the rules, regulations, and decisions generated by the agencies themselves. Administrative law centers around the powers granted to administrative agencies, on the one hand, and the limitations placed on those powers, on the other. It is a highly specialized form of procedural law.

References to specific case law are provided throughout this chapter for resource purposes only. Applicants are not expected to cite specific cases as part of the examination process.

Background

An administrative agency is a governmental unit charged with responsibility to implement and administer statutes adopted by a legislative body (Congress, at the federal level).

Federal administrative agencies have existed almost as long as the federal government has existed. The first administrative agency was created by Congress in 1790 to regulate patents. Federal administrative agencies did not come into their own, however, until late in the nineteenth century, when industrialization with its related social and economic problems brought the concept of administrative agencies to the foreground. The Interstate Commerce Commission was the first agency created during that era. Since then, administrative agencies—and the rules they generate—have proliferated and have become so pervasive that it is difficult to find anyone whose business or personal life is not touched by at least one federal administrative agency on a daily basis.

Administrative agencies are designed to provide assistance in those areas requiring more expertise and closer supervision than Congress or the other branches of government can provide. Agency actions involve a blend of delegated powers which carry some characteristics of the legislative, executive, and judicial branches of government simultaneously. However, the vast majority of administrative agencies function separately from any of those branches; and, as a result, administrative agencies frequently are referred to as the *fourth branch of government*. Many of the principles governing federal agencies apply similarly to state agencies.

Organization and Classification

We are accustomed to explaining our legal system by classifying its parts according to the characteristics of structure and function that distinguish one part from another. For example, trial courts typically have a different structure and function than appellate courts. If one knows the structure of a court, it is possible to classify it as either a trial court or an appellate court; its structure is a distinguishing feature. The same classification techniques are used in various areas of substantive law. Lawyers and legal assistants are familiar with classification techniques and apply them in nearly everything they do. They work well much of the time—but not in classifying administrative agencies.

The general rule in classifying administrative agencies by structure, function, or type is: *There are no general rules*. Certain structural and functional characteristics tend to exist in certain types of agencies, but there are too many exceptions to formulate reliable general rules. It may be helpful to remember that administrative agencies—like tax laws—are created largely by Congress, which often is affected more by political exigencies than by logical consistency.

Classifications do exist but must be approached cautiously. They are not always helpful in identifying the actual structure or function of an agency. Fortunately, once an agency's "classification" threshold is hurdled, agency powers and functions are fairly uniform—no matter which agency exercises them. In other words, informal rulemaking procedures operate essentially in the same way from one agency to another.

Federal administrative agencies are classified by type, either as independent agencies (sometimes called legislative agencies) or as executive agencies. Executive agencies far outnumber independent (legislative) agencies. In addition, federal administrative agencies are classified by function, either as regulatory agencies or as non-regulatory agencies.

Independent or Executive

Independent agencies, designed to function without excessive political pressures, are created by Congress and are governed by a commission or board appointed by the President, subject to confirmation by the Senate. The commissioners or board members serve fixed terms in office and cannot be removed except for cause. Examples of independent administrative agencies are the Interstate Commerce Commission, the Securities Exchange Commission, the Federal Trade Commission, the Federal Reserve Board, the Federal Communications Commission, the Federal Energy Regulatory Commission, and the National Labor Relations Board.

Most independent agencies are stand-alone units, which means they do not report to anyone in the President's Cabinet. However, Congress has made some exceptions by placing several "independent" agencies within the executive branch, such as the Federal Energy Regulatory Commission (FERC) housed within the Department of Energy.

By definition, *executive agencies* are units within the executive branch of government. They typically are headed by one individual, who is appointed by the President; and, although some appointments require Senate approval, many serve at the pleasure of the President. Executive agencies generally have more restricted powers than independent agencies, and the scope of their authority frequently is more narrow or is limited to one industry. Yet, some executive agencies, such as the Internal Revenue Service and the Social Security Administration, wield tremendous administrative power.

Most executive agencies are located within Cabinet departments. For example, the Social Security Administration, the Food and Drug Administration, and the Veterans Administration are located within the Department of Health and Human Services; the Internal Revenue Service is located within the Treasury Department; the Immigration and Naturalization Service is located within the Department of Justice; the Small Business Administration is located within the Department of Commerce; and the Occupational Safety and Health Administration is located within the Department of Labor. The Environmental Protection Agency is the only executive agency which is not located within a Cabinet department.

Although few executive agencies were created by Congress directly, federal statutes enacted by Congress impose duties and responsibilities on executive agencies or their administrators, making them nearly indistinguishable from independent agencies in the application of administrative law principles.

Most executive agencies are subject to E.O. 12291, an executive order which prohibits agencies from promulgating regulations unless their benefits exceed their costs, and it names the Office of Management and Budget (OMB) to enforce compliance. President Reagan exempted those agencies whose administrators he could not fire except for cause (all independent agencies and some executive agencies), and Congress has forbidden a cost-benefit analysis from being applied to the regulations of a few other executive agencies. Some independent agencies comply voluntarily with the executive order, however.

Regulatory or Nonregulatory   A *regulatory agency* usually is given comprehensive authority to oversee a wide spectrum of economic activities of a specific industry. The ICC was created by Congress in 1887 as the first independent, regulatory agency. Since that time, Congress has used the ICC model to create several major agencies. The FTC was created in 1914. Five major regulatory agencies were created after the Depression: the Federal Power Commission (FPC), FCC, SEC, NLRB, and Civil Aeronautics Board (CAB). Collectively, the *big seven* still regulate the major industries of the United States economy: communications, transportation, and energy.

Note, however, that the responsibilities of the FPC were transferred to the Federal Energy Regulatory Commission in 1977. The responsibilities of the CAB were transferred to the Department of Transportation in 1985.

Economic regulation can be divided into three categories:

1.   *Licensing*   Most regulatory agencies regulate entry into the affected industry by issuing certificates of "public convenience and necessity" to successful applicants;

2. *Ratemaking*   Many regulatory agencies establish the minimum and maximum rates that can be charged to consumers for products offered by the regulated industry; and

3. *Business Practices*   Many regulatory agencies have comprehensive jurisdiction over a variety of corporate activities of the regulated industries, including purchases, mergers, consolidations, interlocking boards of directors, issuance and sale of stock, and antitrust.

Although nearly all independent agencies hold regulatory powers, several executive agencies hold regulatory powers as well (such as the Department of Agriculture).

More recently, regulatory agencies have been created to supervise non-economic behaviors of business enterprises, including the Occupational Safety and Health Administration (OSHA) and the Environmental Protection Agency (EPA). Safety, health, and environmental regulations are designed to force businesses to internalize the costs of public interest protections.

Nonregulatory agencies typically—but not always—dispense money to promote social and economic welfare in the form of government insurance and pensions. Examples include social security benefits, unemployment compensation, welfare benefits, and veterans' assistance.

Source of Agency Powers

A legislature (Congress or a state legislature) establishes an administrative agency by passing a statute called an ***enabling act***, which creates the agency and, at the same time, determines its structure, functions, powers, and operational standards. Alternatively, the statute may authorize entry of an executive order to create the agency. The statute that creates an agency also defines the powers that it possesses (whether rulemaking, investigative, or adjudicative). Courts look to a particular agency's enabling act (and resulting executive order, if applicable) to determine whether the agency has acted within the scope of powers delegated to it.

Courts and legal scholars always have been uneasy about delegating too much power to administrative agencies, particularly legislative powers. Article I of the federal Constitution provides that all legislative power is vested in the Congress. Administrative agencies are not specifically authorized by the Constitution; however, Congress is authorized to "make all laws which shall be necessary and proper" in carrying out the powers granted to it. This language, taken with both the overall structure of the Constitution and the benefits provided by administrative agencies, resulted in the delegation doctrine. The ***delegation doctrine*** is a judicially enforced principle which reflects the type and degree of legislative power that Congress may delegate.

Despite a speckled early history, the delegation doctrine has not been used to strike a federal statute on delegation grounds since 1936. Early cases spoke of delegation in terms of Congress' setting sufficient standards for the agency to follow. Modern cases permit Congress to set ***intelligible standards*** and policies, with administrative agencies adopting the specific rules to carry out those standards and policies. Two substantive limitations are placed on Congress' power to delegate:

1. *Congress cannot delegate its power to decide who and what to tax; and*

2. *Congress cannot delegate its power to private persons.*

With these two exceptions, congressional delegation likely will be upheld as long as there are sufficient ***safeguards*** in place (controls such as procedural due process, adoption of standards by the agency, and judicial review) to protect against abuse or oppression by the administrative agency.

Part of the system of safeguards or controls against abuses of power by an administrative agency is the federal ***Administrative Procedure Act*** (APA) adopted in 1946. This Act controls much of the administrative process by establishing the procedures that must be followed when an agency engages in its quasi-legislative function (rulemaking) or in its quasi-judicial function (adjudication). It also regulates dissemination of information gathered by an administrative agency as part of its investigation powers. Many states have adopted APAs which are similar to the federal APA.

Overview of Agency Powers

An overview of agency powers is provided here. The procedures connected with each of these powers is discussed in more detail later in the chapter.

Congress has given most—but not all—administrative agencies three types of powers: investigation, rulemaking, and adjudication. If an agency is authorized to compel persons to turn over information in their possession to the agency, the agency is authorized to engage in ***investigation***. If an agency is authorized to promulgate regulations to supplement or to clarify its statutory mandate, it is authorized to engage in ***rulemaking***. If an agency is authorized to determine (judge) whether a party is in compliance with the agency's statutory mandate or with its regulations, it is authorized to engage in **_adjudication_**.

Investigation Powers

Agencies with investigation powers can compel the disclosure of evidence or testimony. Most agencies use investigation powers to develop information, which they use in rulemaking or adjudication decisions. Accordingly, they typically are granted the power to subpoena documents, to compel depositions, and to inspect premises. The agency's use of investigative tools is subject to judicial review to ensure compliance with constitutional requirements.

Rulemaking Powers

Agencies with rulemaking powers can promulgate regulations (if they comply with the procedural requirements); regulations have the force of law. The rulemaking power is a quasi-legislative power. Unlike Congress, an agency cannot enact regulations about any subject permitted by the Constitution. Although the agency's rules and regulations have nearly the same force of law as a federal statute, the agency's authority to adopt rules and regulations is limited to those powers specified in the agency's enabling act.

The agency usually starts the rulemaking process on its own initiative or occasionally in response to a petition from an interested party requesting that a regulation be adopted. Rulemaking may be informal, hybrid, or formal.

1. *Informal Rulemaking* Most agencies use the "notice and comment" procedures, called informal rulemaking, found in the Administrative Procedure Act. The agency must announce the proposed rule and give interested parties an opportunity to file written comments. No hearings are required, but the agency may hold hearings if it wishes to do so.

2. *Hybrid Rulemaking* A few agencies use hybrid rulemaking, which includes all of the procedures of informal rulemaking plus additional procedures required by the agency's enabling act, such as a hearing at which interested parties may appear.

3. *Formal Rulemaking* A few agencies use formal (trial-type) rulemaking, which includes a hearing similar to an adjudication at which interested parties not only may appear but also may cross-examine witnesses. An agency is required to use formal rulemaking only if its enabling act specifies that it must be used. Because so many procedures are involved in

formal rulemaking, Congress generally has avoided requiring it.

Persons affected by a particular rule or regulation arising from the rulemaking process ordinarily can seek judicial review.

Adjudication Powers Agencies that have been granted adjudication powers can make decisions which have nearly the same force of law as decisions of a federal court (if they comply with the procedural requirements). This is a quasi-judicial power. Although an agency decision carries the force of law, it is limited to those areas of power specified in the agency's enabling act.

Some agencies (FTC, for example) use their adjudication powers to determine whether a party must pay a civil penalty for violation of a law or regulation. Others (Social Security Administration) use adjudication to determine whether a party is eligible to receive a government benefit, such as monetary assistance to those who are disabled and cannot work. Still others (Department of Education) use adjudication to determine whether state and local governments or persons are eligible for government grants or awards under applicable statutes and regulations, such as guaranteed student loans to college students. Agencies may use either formal or informal adjudication procedures.

At some agencies, Congress requires the use of *formal adjudication*, which consists of procedures that are nearly identical to those used in a civil trial. The losing party typically may appeal the decision to the commission or to the administrator in charge of the agency, which resembles the appellate procedure in a civil court system; no new trial is held.

Other agencies use *informal adjudication*, which means either that (1) Congress has not created any procedural requirements for adjudication or that (2) Congress requires only a few procedures, such as the review of a grant application by a committee. Even when Congress does not so specify in a particular agency's enabling act, courts require agencies to observe procedures sufficient to satisfy constitutional due process standards (*see below*).

Political Oversight of Agency Actions

Despite the broad powers that have been delegated to administrative agencies, they remain subject to control by all three branches of government. This structure permits each of the three branches to oversee agency conduct, which helps to reduce or to eliminate abuse of power or oppression by a particular agency.

Executive Oversight   The President has the power to appoint or to remove the heads of many executive administrative agencies. The President also appoints the commissioners who head independent agencies, subject to confirmation by the Senate. However, commissioners cannot be removed by the President; instead, the commissioner's term generally must expire before a new commissioner can be appointed. A commissioner can be removed for cause, however.

The executive branch exercises additional oversight of agencies through the budget process. Before submitting budgets to Congress, appropriations for administrative agencies are reviewed and may be revised by the OMB, which is under the President's control. Although Congress is not required to adopt OMB's budget, OMB does influence congressional allocations. The scope of an agency's activities, of course, is determined in large part by the funding that it receives.

E.O. 12291, discussed previously, impacts some executive agencies by forbidding them to adopt regulations whose costs exceed their benefits.

Another source of executive oversight is the President's power to control litigation that affects agencies through the Department of Justice. Because of their enabling act powers, many—but not all—agencies lack the authority to litigate on their own behalf. Those agencies must secure representation from the Department of Justice. If the Department of Justice refuses to prosecute or to defend a particular agency regulation, the regulation becomes meaningless.

An example of this oversight power came in a slightly different vein when the Attorney General issued a letter to all executive departments and agencies during the Carter administration concerning disclosure of information under the Freedom of Information Act. The letter advised them that the government would not defend an agency in suits to compel disclosure of information, even if it were exempt, unless the agency could show that the disclosure was "demonstrably harmful." The directive facilitated the President's policy of a more open government.

Legislative Oversight   Congress creates administrative agencies, and Congress retains the power to eliminate them. Congress rarely exercises this power due, in large part, to political pressures. However, Congress has shown that it is not averse to major restructuring and reassignment of agency powers. During the 1970s, Congress reassigned the public relations powers of the Atomic Energy Commission to the Department of Energy and restructured the Atomic Energy Commission into what became the Nuclear Regulatory Commission (NRC). Congress can also expand or restrict the powers delegated to an administrative agency without restructuring it.

For several years, Congress exercised what was called a *legislative veto*. Under this procedure, agency regulations could be vetoed by one or both houses of Congress. The practice ended in <u>INS v. Chada</u>, 462 U.S. 919 (1983), when the House of Representatives vetoed a decision of the Attorney General to suspend Chada, an alien, from deportation. The Supreme Court held that the veto was a legislative act and could not be effective unless it was approved by both houses of Congress and signed by the President.

Legislative vetoes no longer exist; however, a particular agency rule can be nullified as to future applications by enacting a statute on the same topic; statutes override administrative rules. (Statutes generally cannot reach past applications of a regulation because of the *ex post facto* and bill of attainder prohibitions of the Constitution.)

Congress can limit appropriations to a particular agency, which is very effective in curtailing agency activities. In addition, "watchdog" committees oversee various government functions, including those of administrative agencies.

Congress also retains some control over personnel through the requirement that appointment of some agency heads and commissioners be approved by the Senate.

Another idea in the area of regulatory reform was a statutory plan known as **sunset laws**. When a sunset law was appended to an agency's enabling act, that agency would cease to exist after a period of time unless Congress re-enacted its statutory authority. The concept was that legislators would be forced to re-examine the need for the agency in the overall governmental structure. Many states still use the sunset concept, but it seems no longer to be in vogue at the federal level.

Judicial Oversight　　　　　Judicial oversight of the actions of administrative agencies provides a third form of control. However, unlike the political oversight of either the executive or legislative branches, judicial oversight takes the form of judicial review to determine the validity of agency action under the Constitution, existing statutes, and the agency's own regulations. Judicial review is discussed more thoroughly at a later point in this chapter.

Investigation

Administrative agencies gather information in the process of rulemaking and adjudication; however, they compile and disseminate information for other purposes as well. The information may be used to inform the public, to advise Congress, to monitor conduct, or to aid in an agency's efforts to educate itself.

Lawyers who specialize in administrative law spend a great deal of time complying with administrative requests for information and preparing required reports. Business clients especially dislike providing information to the government. Because of legislation such as the Freedom of Information Act (*see below*), disclosure to the government may mean disclosure to the general public, including competitors.

Early case law sought to avoid administrative fishing expeditions and required an agency to demonstrate some ground (probable cause) for requesting information supposedly within its area of supervision. Those early cases were rejected in the mid-1940s. Agencies now have almost total freedom to compel access to information. The methods of compelling obedience to a request for information vary, and each has slightly different rules concerning its use.

- Those who deal with an agency on a regular basis may comply with requests to foster cooperation between themselves and the agency.

- An agency may encourage compliance by informal methods, such as refusal to accept an application for either a license or a benefit.

- Many agencies are authorized to issue subpoenas; ***administrative subpoenas*** must be enforced by courts when they are properly issued.

- The Internal Revenue Service may issue an ***administrative summons*** for information, which raises some of the same enforcement issues as administrative subpoenas.

- An agency may seek physical access to ***inspect private premises***, but this method may require a warrant.

- An agency may require compilation and submission of ***required reports***, which may be enforced by a fine or by nonrenewal of a license for noncompliance.

The Subpoena and Other Compulsory Devices

An agency may be granted subpoena power or some other compulsory device, such as the IRS summons, to obtain information. Administrative subpoenas may need to be enforced against the subpoenaed person (called the respondent) in a judicial proceeding; and if the respondent disobeys, she may be held in civil contempt of court. If the agency possesses subpoena powers, agency rules typically provide the method for obtaining the subpoena and also provide the limitations on that power.

A private person, particularly one who is involved in an adjudication with the agency, generally has the same opportunity to compulsory process (subpoena or summons). APA § 555(d). However, the devices for obtaining information are not available in all situations. For example, only a party to the adjudication may require the agency to issue a subpoena. This allows an agency to obtain information from nonparties to the adjudication or from those who are not the subject of a formal adjudication without granting such nonparties a similar right to compulsory process directed at the agency.

Before any subpoena can be issued, there must be some showing of general relevance and reasonable scope of the evidence sought. APA § 555(d). The respondent usually can file a *motion to quash* with the agency, requesting the agency to limit or to nullify the subpoena. If a judicial enforcement proceeding ensues, the respondent again may challenge the issuance of the subpoena. However, Supreme Court opinions have upheld administrative subpoenas when they were authorized and germane; issued in good faith; not incomprehensibly vague or offensively burdensome; not privileged; and issued in proper form by one who is authorized to issue subpoenas.

Premises Inspections   An agency's demand for inspection (physical access) may be scrutinized more closely than other requests for information. An agency may be required to obtain a search warrant before conducting an inspection; however, there are well-recognized exceptions to the warrant requirement.

In other areas of law, the requesting official must demonstrate probable cause before a warrant is issued. However, probable cause is not a strong limitation on administrative authority to information; and a general inspection warrant frequently is acceptable in an administrative context.

There are four recognized exceptions to the warrant requirement; administrative inspections may be conducted without a warrant in these circumstances.

1. *Emergency Searches*   Emergency searches have been upheld in various situations: seizure of unwholesome food, destruction of diseased animals, and health quarantines. Entry to fight a fire requires no warrant; once in the building, officials may remain to determine the cause of the fire. However, any additional investigation must meet warrant requirements.

2. *Consent*   Consent does not have to be as clear for an administrative search as it does for a criminal search.

However, consent cannot be obtained by unconstitutional means, such as forcing a person to waive his constitutional protection from warrantless searches in order to obtain a government benefit.

3. *Public View*   An official may conduct a warrantless inspection of any public area, which can include aerial photographs taken of a visible area—even if the area is one that ordinarily would be considered part of the curtilage of a private dwelling or of a private place of business.

4. *Closely Regulated Businesses*   One who engages in a heavily regulated business enterprise impliedly may have consented to certain types of inspections. Examples of these types of businesses may include a meat packing plant, a radio broadcasting station, or a junkyard.

Administrative search warrants are relatively easy to obtain, and the Supreme Court has reinforced the agency's obligation to obtain a warrant unless the inspection clearly falls within one of the categories of exceptions.

Required Reports   An effective method for developing information in support of policy formulation, enforcement, informing the public, and other administrative functions is to require those controlled by the agency to compile the information and to report it to the agency. Organizations and businesses can claim virtually no protection, even if the reports serve no purpose other than to satisfy official curiosity. Only individuals are protected by the Fifth Amendment; therefore, organizations are not protected against self-incrimination caused by required reports.

Individuals have slightly more protection because of the Fifth Amendment; however, the protection does not cover government access to those records which an individual is required by law to compile. A wholesale grocer, for example, was required to turn over incriminating sales records under the Price Control Act. Shapiro v. United States, 335 U.S. 1 (1948). However, the Supreme Court refused to uphold required reports to the IRS in connection with a gambling tax, because the tax records were not the type that customarily would be kept and because the records were inherently related to criminal activities. Marchetti v. United States, 390 U.S. 39 (1968).

The Fourth Amendment provides very little protection for individual information, and documents in the physical possession of a third party generally cannot be protected at all.

The Paperwork Reduction Act of 1980 was enacted to eliminate redundant and costly required reports. All reporting requirements must be approved by the Office of Management and Budget (OMB); however, OMB supervision (called oversight) may be reduced if an agency regulates its own required reports through the rulemaking process.

Dissemination of Information An agency may release information—even adverse information—as a method of enforcing its laws or as a means of preventing law violations by others. An agency can, for example, issue press releases to announce the recall of a defective product.

In addition, a number of statutes enacted from the late 1960s forward opened government information to greater public scrutiny. They are:

●Freedom of Information Act (FOIA), 5 U.S.C. § 552, which requires disclosure of all governmental information unless exempted by the Act;

●Privacy Act, 5 U.S.C. § 552(a), which requires an agency to divulge any record to a person that is filed for purposes of retrieval under that person's name;

●Sunshine Act (Government in the Sunshine Act), 5 U.S.C. § 552(b), which requires any agency headed by a multiple-member commission to meet in public; and

●Federal Advisory Committee Act (FACA), 5 U.S.C. app., which requires federal advisory committees to meet in open session.

A. **Freedom of Information Act** The FOIA requires agencies to disclose adjudicatory opinions, nonpublished agency policy, interpretive statements, staff manuals and instructions, and requested records unless an exemption applies. From this list, all items but "requested records" must be disclosed without exception; Congress has been clear that it does not want agencies operating according to secret laws that are unavailable to the persons who are subject to them. Requested records may or may not be exempt from disclosure.

The government's refusal to disclose information raises three issues:

(1) Is the government unit which possesses the documents an "agency" subject to the FOIA;

(2)   Are the requested documents "records" or are they other materials that must be disclosed (*see above*); and

(3)   If they are records, does an exemption apply?

To obtain a record, a person must file with the agency a reasonable description of the information sought. If the agency denies the request, or fails to act within the statutory time limit of ten working days (a ten-day extension can be granted in unusual circumstances), the requestor can seek a federal district court order to compel disclosure. The agency has the burden of establishing that it is entitled to an exemption, and the court uses a *de novo* scope of review to resolve the agency's claim. An agency typically will attempt to justify the exemption by filing detailed affidavits. The requestor, who has not seen the documents and has little basis for challenging the agency, may ask the court to order a **Vaughn index** that summarizes each record withheld, states the statutory basis on which it is withheld, and cites the affidavits which explain why the exemption should apply. The *Vaughn* index comes from the case <u>Vaughn v. Rosen</u>, 484 F.2d 820 (D.C. Cir. 1973), where the index was first used. To resolve the agency's claims, the FOIA authorizes a court to examine the contents of agency records in camera (in chambers, privately). 5 U.S.C. § 552(a)(4)(B).

Although most government units fall within the statute's broad definition of "agency," a unit is not an agency if its sole function is to advise the President (national security advisor or council of economic advisors). Neither is a private entity an agency, even though the government has authority over records held by it (such as a government contractor).

A document is a record if it is generated or used by the agency and is within its possession and control. For example, a weekly tax service compiled by an agency is an agency record that can be made available to a litigant, even though the same information is available through another public source. <u>Department of Justice v. Tax Analysts</u>, 109 S.Ct. 2841 (1989).

Exemptions (those records that do not have to be disclosed) must fit into one of the nine subsections of APA § 552(b). The exemptions often are referred to by their subsection numbers, so that an exemption claimed under § 552(b)(1) commonly is referred to as Exemption 1. Listed in summary form, they are:

Exemption 1   *Secrecy*   Exempts classified records that must be kept secret in the interest of national defense and foreign policy and which are classified as secret by executive order. § 552(b)(1).

Exemption 2	*Personnel* Exempts internal personnel rules and practices to protect the personal privacy of agency employees and to shield the agency from excessive harassment. § 552(b)(2).
Exemption 3	*Statutory Nondisclosure* Exempts documents for which another statute specifically forbids disclosure (very narrow exemption). § 553(b)(3).
Exemption 4	*Private Business Information* Information is confidential if its disclosure is likely to harm the competitive position of the one who filed it or if its release would impair the agency's ability to obtain similar information in the future. Trade secrets and commercial or financial information, as well as privileged or confidential communications, are included in this exemption. § 553(b)(4).
Exemption 5	*Agency Memoranda* Exempts inter-agency memoranda to protect the candor of discussions within an agency. § 553(b)(5).
Exemption 6	*Personal Privacy* Exempts personnel files, medical files, and so forth, the disclosure of which clearly would constitute an unwarranted invasion of personal privacy. § 553(b)(6).
Exemption 7	*Investigation Records* Exempts information that might interfere with enforcement proceedings, deprive a defendant of a fair trial, disclose the identity of a confidential source, or the like. § 553(b)(7).
Exemption 8	*Financial Institutions* Exempts records that relate to examination or supervision of financial institutions. § 553(b)(8).
Exemption 9	*Geological Exploration* Exempts maps and geophysical information concerning the location and drilling of wells. § 553(b)(9).

If one of the nine exemptions applies to only a portion of a record, the remaining portions must be provided to the requestor if they can be segregated reasonably.

Several corporations have filed *reverse-FOIA suits* against the government, attempting to block the government's release of information concerning the corporation to others. When the information involves trade secrets or similar, privileged data, the agency does not have discretion to release the information. Chrysler Corp. v. Brown, 441 U.S. 281 (1979).

Even though the exemptions remove substantial numbers of documents from disclosure, the FOIA remains a very powerful tool for inspection of government records.

B.   Privacy Act   The Privacy Act works as the mirror image of the FOIA. It *forbids disclosure* of records under an agency's control which are retrievable by an individual's name unless the records are one of the eleven categories mandating disclosure. The Act defines an agency's obligation to acquire and to maintain accurate records; it forbids disclosure of the records unless the information fits within one of eleven categories.

In general, disclosure is permitted: (1) when disclosure is required by the FOIA; (2) when disclosure is requested by another agency; or (3) when disclosure is requested by the individual to whom the record relates.

One of the exemptions under the Privacy Act authorizes disclosure of documents under the FOIA if no FOIA exemption applies. However, if an FOIA exemption applies, the agency *must* withhold the record.

C.   Sunshine Act   The Sunshine Act requires agencies headed by collegial (multiple-member) bodies to give notice and to hold open meetings when the body or a subcommittee of the body has formal authority to make agency decisions. Notice of both the meeting and its agenda must be provided unless the body votes to close the meeting because of a likelihood that exempt information will be disclosed.   Exempt information includes most of the FOIA exemptions, accusations that a person committed a crime, or information likely to concern matters of litigation strategy. The Sunshine Act has been modified somewhat by court decisions, which allow the body to meet privately on certain important matters when the meeting is not arranged by the agency's commission or board.

D.   Federal Advisory Committee Act   The Federal Advisory Committee Act (FACA) was established to minimize the number of citizens' advisory committees that are used and to ensure that the public is aware of committee activities. Advisory committees must provide advance notice of their meetings and must open them to the public unless the President—or the administrator to whom the committee reports—determines that the meeting may be closed under the Sunshine Act.

Formulation of Administrative Law

Acting under the authority of their respective enabling acts, administrative agencies formulate rules and decisions (which have the force of law) through their rulemaking and adjudication functions. Various characteristics of those functions have been referred to in preceding sections of this chapter; however, the characteristics are collected here to provide a unified picture of the rulemaking and adjudication powers.

Terminology

When an administrative agency exercises the powers granted by its enabling act, it engages in decisions which raise one or more issues concerning facts, law and policy, procedure, and discretion. Before reviewing the details of an agency's decisionmaking processes, it may be helpful to define terminology as it is used in the context of administrative decisions.

1. *Adjudicative facts* are those things which can be proved by objective evidence and which concern individuals (or businesses) in relation to what they did or in relation to what happened to them; they answer the questions of who did what, when, where, why, and how.

2. *Legislative facts* are those things which can be proved by objective evidence and which resolve broad, social questions such as what factors produce economic growth; how dangerous is a particular practice in the workplace; or why the glass ceiling persists in relation to female executives in corporations.

3. *Legal issue*, as that term is used in administrative law, means a rule based upon a social choice made by a source outside the administrative process (Constitution or statutes).

4. *Policy issue*, as the term is used in administrative law, means a rule based upon a social choice made by sources inside the administrative process (administrative officials) in carrying out their mandate. Policy is "agency-made" law.

5.   *Procedural issues* relate to the rules which dictate the methods or steps used to reach an administrative decision. The sources of procedural requirements encompass the Constitution, statutes, an agency's regulations, and an agency's past practices or tradition.

6.   *Discretion* relates to the freedom of an administrator or of an administrative board or commission to make decisions; the freedom can be unbridled or can be carefully confined, depending on the degree of authority granted (or the substantive constraints imposed) by an agency's enabling act. The amount of discretion given to an administrator frequently is an important issue in administrative law cases.

The Administrative Process

Action by an administrative agency usually concerns either investigation (*discussed above*) or making decisions. The decisions of an administrative agency involve either rulemaking or adjudication processes. Rulemaking (quasi-legislative) results in decisions similar to those of a legislature, and the procedures may be similar to those of a legislative committee hearing. Adjudication (quasi-judicial) results in decisions similar to those of a court, and the procedures sometimes—but not always—are similar to those of a trial.

Agency decisions may be further classified as formal or informal. Rulemaking may be either informal or formal; likewise, adjudication may be either informal or formal. A formal proceeding has many of the same characteristics of a trial; an informal proceeding may have only a few of those characteristics or it may have none. A recurring issue in administrative law is how trial-like a particular proceeding must be.

Analysis of the Internal Process   The first step in analyzing the action of an administrative agency is to determine whether the process calls for rulemaking or adjudication.

Adjudication is used to decide individual rights and duties. It focuses on a specific controversy; it develops specific facts (adjudicative facts) about individuals or organizations and applies the statute or agency-made law to those facts. Adjudications usually are adversarial, but the term *adjudication* does not necessarily mean a proceeding resembling a trial. Many adjudications have very few of the elements of a judicial proceeding. The term *hearing* means any method that permits participation by individuals or organizations; it does not necessarily mean a trial-like proceeding. The result of an adjudication is an order, which may require a party to take some action or to come into compliance with the law. An order also may be used to grant a benefit or to issue a license.

Rulemaking is used to develop policy and results in a rule or a regulation which is prospective (applies to future action) in regard to a defined group. Rulemaking sets general standards to be followed. Proposed rules are published, and interested persons are permitted to participate in rulemaking through proceedings that may resemble a trial or through proceedings that merely call for filing written comments.

To support the development of policy, rulemaking focuses on general facts (legislative facts) about groups or issues; adjudication focuses on specific facts (adjudicative facts) about an individual or an organization. Administrative agencies may choose between adjudication and rulemaking; the choice raises one of two issues: (1) whether the agency may decide individual rights or duties in the context of rulemaking; or (2) whether the agency may decide policy in an adjudication. The Supreme Court has upheld an agency's power to formulate policy on a case-by-case basis through adjudication, as well as through rulemaking. SEC v. Chenery Corp., 332 U.S. 194 (1947). The Court also has held that an agency has nearly absolute discretion in its choice between developing policy through rulemaking or through adjudication. NLRB v. Bell-Aerospace, 416 U.S. 267 (1974).

State courts have not been this accepting, however. Many have developed case law which requires rulemaking for policy decisions, and the 1981 Model State Administrative Procedure Act provides for a "required rulemaking."

The degree of formality required in either adjudication or rulemaking (how trial-like the proceeding must be) depends on the Due Process Clause and on statutory requirements.

Due Process Requirements   The Due Process Clause of the Constitution provides that the government cannot deprive any person of life, liberty, or property without due process of law. Where administrative agencies are concerned, the "property" concept extends to *entitlements* as well, such as welfare benefits. Goldberg v. Kelly, 397 U.S. 254 (1970). The Due Process Clause covers only government action (called state action) and covers only that state action which deprives one of a protected interest in the context of an affirmative abuse of power. Negligence alone is not enough.

Once a due process interest is found, the next question is: "How much process is due?" Due process requires *some kind of hearing*, but it may not require a trial-type hearing. The type of hearing required must fit the right involved. Courts have adopted a *balancing test* to determine whether a particular hearing fits the right involved by weighing the individual's interest, the value of the procedure, and the government's (public's) interest. A three-day suspension of a student, followed by a brief "hearing" at which the student was allowed to present his side of the story, satisfied due process requirements in <u>Goss v. Lopez</u>, 419 U.S. 565 (1975). If the student were expelled without a hearing until thirty days after the expulsion, due process likely would have required a different result.

Statutory Requirements   Statutes also guarantee an opportunity to be heard in the administrative process. Typically, these statutes include the federal ***Administrative Procedure Act*** (APA), the agency's enabling act, or some combination of the two. The federal APA was enacted in 1946 and governs the internal procedures of all federal agencies. 5 U.S.C. § 551 et seq. The term "agency" excludes only Congress, the courts, the governments of the District of Columbia and territories, military authorities, and a few miscellaneous government functions.

Most states have their own APAs, and their coverages vary. Also in 1946, the National Conference of Commissioners on Uniform State Laws adopted a Model State Administrative Procedure Act (MSAPA), which was revised in 1961 and again in 1981. Because it was a model act, and not a uniform act, individual state enactments may include significant modification of the model act provisions.

The federal APA recognizes the distinction among formal adjudication, informal adjudication, formal rulemaking, and informal rulemaking. However, it does not prescribe procedures for informal adjudication, which leaves them to be governed by due process principles.

Despite the inherent flexibility of the administrative process, the procedures required in many administrative programs have become much like trial-type proceedings; and many agencies have started to look for *alternative dispute resolution* (ADR) methods, including mediation or written hearings. Some agencies avoid long, drawn-out rulemaking hearings through an alternative procedure called *negotiated rulemaking*. Both ADR and negotiated rulemaking have been incorporated into the federal APA.

The federal APA provides the procedures and controls for certain types of administrative decisionmaking when those areas are not covered specifically by an agency's enabling act.

General Requirements of Policy Formulation Under the APA

Agency Method	Formal	Hybrid	Informal
Rulemaking	5 U.S.C. §§ 553, 556, 557	not covered	5 U.S.C. § 553 or § 556(d)
Adjudication	5 U.S.C. §§ 554, 556, 557	not covered	not covered
Interpretive, Procedural, & Housekeeping Rules - 5 U.S.C. § 553(b)(A) and (B)	does not apply	does not apply	does not apply

Integrity of the Process Administrative law has developed some general prohibitions against *bias and prejudgment*. However, the prohibitions are very narrow, because the incorporation of certain types of bias and prejudgment (institutional bias) is the goal of most administrative programs. For example, the President may select FCC commissioners because of their biases against X-rated programming. Personal bias or prejudgment on an issue of specific fact, however, is prohibited. The tests for personal bias in a rulemaking context are less stringent than in an adjudicative context. To prove personal bias in an adjudicative context requires a showing that the decisionmaker has a personal monetary interest in the outcome of a specific case or that criticism by the decisionmaker has biased the decision. For instance, if an agency head were to give a newspaper interview prior to adjudication in which she vowed to make a particular person sorry to have been born, personal bias probably could be shown. In this situation, even the appearance of personal bias would be sufficient to disqualify the decisionmaker.

In addition to personal bias, various types of *conflict of interest* are prohibited by statute. The *Ethics in Government Act*, for example, seeks to prevent government employees from performing their official duties in such a way as to enhance their opportunity for private employment when their terms are ended. This Act prevents former high-level officials from engaging in private employment related to activities over which they exercised authority during their appointments. Government lawyers also have special professional responsibility standards. They represent the agency (the people) and not agency officials, which may require them to question illegal activity by a particular official; yet, they may not disclose confidential government information simply because they disagree with the agency's policy decisions.

Administrative agencies often combine several functions. The doctrine of **separation of functions** prohibits only those combinations that create bias in the performance of adjudication functions. Unless there is a showing of actual bias, a combination of prosecutorial and decisionmaking functions does not violate due process. However, an individual who performs investigative and prosecutorial functions in a case is prohibited from advising or participating in the decision for that case or for a factually related case. APA § 554(d). The agency or "a member or members of the body comprising the agency" is exempt from this provision, which means that an agency head (1) may decide whether a case should be filed and then (2) may participate in the adjudication's decision.

The doctrine of separation of functions does not apply to rulemaking.

Ex parte communication between agency decisionmakers and "interested persons," both inside and outside the agency generally are prohibited; but the prohibition is much more rigid in adjudication than it is in rulemaking. An *ex parte* communication is one made with the decisionmaker outside the presence of the other person(s) interested in the controversy.

Once an adjudication proceeding is initiated, the decisionmaker cannot consult with staff members who are involved directly with the adjudication. The *ex parte* doctrine allows her to consult with staff members who are not involved in the case; however, under no circumstances, may the staff provide facts which are not in the adjudication record.

In general, all communication with the individual presiding at the hearing (whether a hearing examiner or an Administrative Law Judge) must be on the record. Thus, the presiding officer must avoid communications concerning the case outside the record with all members of the staff, whether interested or not.

Ex parte communication with persons outside the agency in adjudication proceedings is covered by APA § 557(d) and is defined as:

- With an "interested person" (the requisite interest is defined broadly and need not be monetary);

- For other than a "status report"; and

- Must be "relevant to the merits of the proceeding."

Violations of this rule generally can be cured by placing the *ex parte* communication on the public record. In the most egregious situations, the violating party may have to show why his claim or interest should not be dismissed, denied, disregarded, or otherwise adversely affected because of the violation. APA § 557(d)(1)(C).

To avoid the problems of adjudicative bias, Congress separated the adjudicative process in at least one agency when it created the Occupational Safety and Health Review Commission to adjudicate OSHA violations independent of the Department of Labor (which makes OSHA policy and prosecutes violators). This is an exception and not the general rule.

Rulemaking

An agency may develop policy on a case-by-case basis through adjudication if it chooses to do so, and courts have upheld this method of policy development even when Congress' intent appeared to have been for the agency to develop rules first. However, rulemaking is considered the superior method of developing policy; it has the advantage of compiling general facts and soliciting the views of various interested persons and groups.

APA § 551(4) defines a rule as any "agency statement of general . . . and future effect designed to implement, interpret, or prescribe law or policy" or to describe procedures. (By this definition, a rule cannot have retroactive effect.) Moreover, the Supreme Court has ruled that a presumption exists against the retroactive applicability of a rule.

<u>**Types of Rules**</u>   Agency rules vary in their purpose and effect. Some have the force of law and are binding on courts as well as on the agency; others are mere announcements, with only an advisory effect. A ***legislative rule***, sometimes called a substantive rule or agency-made law, is made according to an agency's delegated authority to make quasi-legislative rules. The delegation may be either general or specific. In some situations, courts have upheld legislative rulemaking even when there was no statutory rulemaking authority, because rulemaking was necessary to carry out the administrative scheme. Legislative rules have the *force and effect of law* and may preempt state statutes and regulations because of the Supremacy Clause. Judicial review of legislative rules is very limited; rules generally will be upheld unless they are arbitrary, capricious, or were adopted without complying with all procedural requirements.

Non-legislative rules carry a variety of labels: *interpretations, policy statements, guidelines,* and *rulings*. They do not have the force of law but may be persuasive. They are not "controlling upon the courts by reason of their authority, [but] do constitute a body of experience and informed judgment to which courts and litigants may properly resort for guidance." <u>Skidmore v. Swift & Co.</u>, 323 U.S. 134

(1944). A non-legislative rule is not made by delegated rulemaking authority; rather, it is accepted as a power necessary to carry out the administrative function. If the agency has no statutory authority for its rule, the rule is non-legislative. Although an agency's characterization of the rule as legislative or non-legislative is important, courts make independent judgments as to whether particular rules are legislative or not.

APA § 553 exempts certain types of rules from public notice and comment requirements. They include interpretive rules, general statements of policy, procedural rules, and rules for which "good cause" is shown. This means that in addition to interpretations, announcements, and policy statements, an agency's rules of practice and procedure are exempt from the public notice and comment requirement. "Good cause" justifications to bypass public notice and comment might include a showing that it is *impracticable* (because of an emergency situation), *unnecessary* (no public interest, such as editorial changes), or *contrary to public interest* (cases have cited this only in connection with an emergency situation already found).

A subject matter exception also exists. Rules relating to certain subject matter such as military, foreign affairs, management, personnel, contracts, and benefits (sometimes called housekeeping rules) are not subject to rulemaking procedures. An agency can waive these exceptions, of course, or Congress can require notice and comment rulemaking for an agency with jurisdiction over one of these subjects.

Rulemaking Procedures Rulemaking is the agency process which focuses on development of general facts and makes policy for future application. Because it is quasi-legislative, rulemaking procedures have evolved from the methods used to develop legislation. However, rulemaking procedures can vary from (1) the trial-type procedures of formal rulemaking to (2) informal notice and comment procedures similar to those used by legislative committees to (3) little or no public participation. Of these, informal notice and comment procedures are the most common.

The decision to institute rulemaking may be motivated by internal sources, external sources, or a combination of the two. An agency may recognize a problem as appropriate for rulemaking during the course of individual adjudications, after an investigation, or based on staff recommendation. APA § 553(e) allows interested persons to petition for rulemaking and requires the agency to state its reasons if it denies the petition. As a practical matter, however, there is very little review of an agency's decision not to undertake rulemaking.

Informal Rulemaking   The usual form of rulemaking is informal (notice and comment). APA § 553 requires informal rulemaking to include (1) notice, (2) an opportunity to comment, (3) statement of reasons, and (4) publication.

Notice must be adequate to elicit informed comment. Notice is either published in the *Federal Register* or personally served on interested persons (publication is more typical). APA § 553(b) requires that the notice contain the time and place of the public rulemaking proceeding and a proposed rule (or a description of the subject and issues involved).

Courts, however, may require more. Specifically, a court may require notice of technical information or types of studies leading to the proposed rule, a preliminary cost-benefit analysis, or a regulatory impact statement (RIS). Raw data need not be a part of the notice but may become part of the rulemaking record.

In addition, E.O. 12498 requires each *executive* agency to perform a regulatory impact statement (RIS) and to publish a "regulatory agenda" twice a year, which lists proposed regulations under consideration. In addition to the regulatory impact statement, E.O. 12291 forbids agencies from promulgating rules if their costs exceed their benefits; this executive order applies only to executive agencies and only if it does not violate their statutory mandate (Congress has exempted some executive agencies). Independent agencies are exempt as well, although several of them participate voluntarily.

Because rulemaking is an information gathering process, the opportunity to comment should be free and open to reap the full benefit of public participation. The opportunity to comment may be either oral or in writing. APA § 553(c). Many agencies use a legislative-type oral hearing, along with the opportunity to file written comments.

All information critical to development of the rule must be included in the rulemaking record; otherwise, the rule may be found arbitrary or capricious on judicial review. It is the duty of the agency to assure itself that all major interests are represented. If an important interest does not participate in the rulemaking, the agency should assure that the viewpoints of that interest are represented in the records. However, courts sometimes will dismiss a challenge to the rule based upon a failure to exhaust administrative remedies if the challenger does not participate in the rulemaking proceeding.

Negotiated rulemaking may be used to expedite rulemaking if the major interests are represented and are willing to negotiate a rule to accommodate others. Negotiated rulemaking works best when the major interests are concentrated only in two or three power sources, when they are convinced that unilateral agency action would be undesirable, and when they are under pressure to resolve the matter. The *Negotiated Rulemaking Act of 1990* establishes a statutory framework to conduct negotiated rulemaking and is incorporated into the APA.

Public comments, transcripts of any oral hearing, results of agency investigations, and *such other information as the agency may find useful* constitute the rulemaking record, which lacks the strict admissibility requirements ordinarily ascribed to a trial record. The **rulemaking record** is the information which the agency actually considered in formulating the rule.

APA § 553(c) provides that the "agency shall incorporate in the rules adopted a concise general statement of their basis and purpose." Courts generally ignore the words "concise" and "general"; instead, they expect the statement to contain a full and comprehensive justification for the rule or rules.

The rule must be published in the *Federal Register* 30 days before it takes effect. APA §§ 552(a)(1)(D) and 553(d). Courts will invalidate an unpublished rule. In addition, permanent rules of the agency are codified and published in the *Code of Federal Regulations*.

Formal Rulemaking   APA § 553(c) requires formal rulemaking under §§ 556 and 557 when the agency's enabling act requires that its rules be "made on the record after opportunity for an agency hearing." Because the Supreme Court has construed the word "hearing" very narrowly in the rulemaking context (contrasted with adjudications), Congress must use the precise term **hearing on the record** if it intends to require formal rulemaking to be used by an administrative agency.

Formal rulemaking is a trial-type proceeding at which interested persons are permitted to appear and to cross-examine witnesses.

Assume, for example, that citizens in a particular city want more radio or television channels available for assignment. The Federal Communications Commission must use formal rulemaking procedures to allocate or to re-allocate broadcast frequencies for this purpose. Under formal rulemaking procedures, the FCC publishes notice in the *Federal Register* as well as in the newspaper of the locations to be affected for several weeks. Radio or television stations may be required to broadcast notice of the proposal as well.

Written comments are solicited by the publications (and broadcasts, if applicable) for a period that can range from three to six months. In the meantime, the FCC must conduct engineering studies to show the proposal's impact on existing aviation facilities and the broadcast frequencies used by them, existing transmission facilities (towers), and existing broadcast frequencies used by other licensed broadcasters in the area as well as by businesses and ham operators. If the frequency is to be moved from another community, similar solicitation of comments and similar studies must be undertaken in that community also.

Public hearings are scheduled, and all interested persons are invited to attend. Those testifying on behalf of themselves or through legal counsel are provided the opportunity to ask limited questions of others who testify. It is easy to imagine the controversies that can arise when one community wants a particular broadcast frequency and another community does not want to lose it.

At the close of hearings, the FCC must assimilate all of the information and reach a decision based on public need, engineering impact of the proposed change, and a host of other criteria. The entire process can take anywhere from two to five years to complete. The final decision can be challenged (appealed) by those who are affected adversely by it, which adds more years to the process.

Because it is so cumbersome, time-consuming, and expensive, Congress ordinarily does not require formal rulemaking.

Hybrid Rulemaking   The concept of hybrid rulemaking was developed in lower federal courts to augment the "notice and comment" procedures of informal rulemaking by requiring that some additional procedures, such as limited cross-examination, be imposed. The Supreme Court abruptly ended judicial development of hybrid rulemaking in <u>Vermont Yankee Nuclear Power v. NRDC</u>, 435 U.S. 519 (1978) by holding that if Congress did not prescribe trial-type procedures, courts could not impose them.

Congress subsequently incorporated hybrid rulemaking in a few enabling acts, including the FTC Improvement Act, but the trend ended after only a few such provisions had been enacted. Because of these statutory provisions, hybrid rulemaking does exist; but it is rare. The APA does not provide procedures for hybrid rulemaking. Instead, they come entirely from the enabling act and due process requirements.

Rule Content   Judicial review of the substantive content of administrative rules is very limited. Even less effort is made to monitor drafting; however, a final rule cannot be substantially different from the proposed rule contained in the original notice. This simply means that a rule does not have to be re-published for additional comments when modifications are made before its adoption, as long as the modifications are minor.

Amendment, Repeal, and Waiver   APA § 553(e) allows an agency to amend or to repeal a rule after its adoption, either on its own motion or on petition from interested persons. The procedure to amend or to repeal a particular rule is the same as the procedure used to adopt the rule. If informal rulemaking (notice and comment) procedures were used to adopt the rule, the same type of notice and comment procedures may be used to amend it or to repeal it.

Disputes arise when the agency claims that its statement about the rule is not an amendment but, rather, is an interpretation which does not require public procedures (*see above*).

Waiver or variance is one method to assure individual justice in the context of a general rule. Fairness requires some opportunity to seek a waiver based on individual circumstances, which is accomplished by filing a petition for waiver. The difficulty lies in the fact that filing a waiver petition does not create a right to a formal hearing on the matter.

Adjudication

Adjudication is used to determine individual rights and duties, contrasted with determinations of group rights and duties of the type found in rulemaking. Adjudication proceedings may have all or most of the elements of a trial; these proceedings are called *formal adjudications*. If the proceeding determines individual rights and duties but has few, if any, identifiable elements of a trial, it is called an *informal adjudication*.

An adjudication results in an *order*. The federal APA defines an order as *any disposition that is not a rule*. APA § 551(6).

Commencement of the Case   Adjudication may be commenced when an agency begins an enforcement proceeding to address a possible violation of the law entrusted to it. Similar to the authority to initiate investigations, administrative agencies have almost unbridled authority to decide whether to undertake an enforcement proceeding in a particular case. Like criminal prosecutors, agency officials may engage in selective enforcement in deciding which violators to pursue. After an internal investigation, the staff of an agency recommends that an administrative complaint be issued.

Adjudication also may be commenced when a private party requests a government grant (license, rate increase, welfare benefit, or a public service); in this context, an agency may not decline to undertake the requisite adjudication. Many adjudications of this type provide for a staff member to make an initial ruling or determination on the application. If the ruling is unfavorable, the claimant moves to the adjudication process by challenging the initial ruling. Due process (or a particular statute) provides the private party with the right to "some kind of hearing." Informal adjudication is not covered by the APA.

Presiding Officer   A referee, hearing officer, or an administrative law judge (ALJ) is assigned to a particular case and presides over the adjudication hearing. The more formal the adjudication proceeding, the more likely that an ALJ will be used. Administrative law judges act much like typical judges, but they are not members of the federal judiciary. Their status, role, and function are unique to administrative adjudication.

Presiding officers are expected to be experts, not "general" judges. They generally are more active in the hearing process than judges are; they are responsible for ensuring a complete record.

APA § 557(b) provides that the presiding officer issues an *initial decision*. The initial decision becomes the decision of the agency unless it is appealed to a higher agency authority. In some systems, the presiding officer issues a *recommended decision* only; this type of decision does not become final until it is adopted by the agency. APA § 557(b) provides that in lieu of an initial decision, the agency may adopt a rule that presiding officers merely *certify the record*, leaving the entire decisionmaking responsibility to the agency head, governing board, or commission.

Prehearing Practice   Before the hearing occurs, an administrative adjudication may involve prehearing practice, including prehearing conferences, motions, discovery, and settlement negotiations.

Motions similar to those in a judicial proceeding may be filed in formal adjudications, and the ALJ rules on the motions in much the same way as a judge would do. Administrative discovery in the form of subpoenas, depositions, and FOIA requests may be available to private parties involved in the adjudication (*discussed previously*).   An ALJ may schedule a prehearing conference to narrow the issues, to limit discovery, and to explore settlement, particularly in a complex case.

The prehearing procedures may involve settlement negotiations. An applicant for a rate increase, for example, may agree to a lesser rate in lieu of spending the time and money involved to complete the hearing process. A respondent in an enforcement proceeding may agree to a consent decree, to a consent order, or to a cease-and-desist order (*see below*).

Hearing Procedures   The hearing itself can vary from a conference before a hearing officer or a referee (informal adjudication) to a full trial-type proceeding before an ALJ (formal adjudication). Most fall somewhere between these two poles. However, there is almost always an adversary character to the hearing, with some type of opportunity to confront adverse arguments and evidence. Direct evidence may be very similar to testimony given at a trial, but some agencies rely on direct testimony in written form.

One has the right to confront adverse evidence presented at the hearing, though not always through cross-examination. In an informal hearing, the right of confrontation may be limited to an opportunity to tell the other side of the story or to present rebuttal evidence. Due process does not necessarily require cross-examination in this setting. In a formal adjudication, a party has some right to cross-examination; however, cross-examination may be more limited than it is in either a civil or criminal trial. APA § 556(d).

A private person or organization does not necessarily have the right to an attorney (counsel) in an administrative hearing. In settings where discipline is important (a prison or a school), representation may be limited. In other settings, however, APA § 555(b) provides that a party is entitled to appear in person or by or with counsel or other qualified person. Those compelled to appear (by subpoena, for example) may be accompanied by counsel; but unlike a party, they cannot appear by counsel (counsel cannot appear in their place). A few agencies permit nonlawyer representatives to appear on behalf of others, including the Social Security Administration, the Immigration and Naturalization Service, and the Internal Revenue Service.

A person does not have the right to be provided with appointed counsel in administrative adjudications.

Rules of Evidence   Due process does not require adherence to the rules of evidence, nor does it require that a decision be based on evidence that would be admissible in a civil or criminal trial. An agency may rely solely on hearsay evidence, for example, in reaching its decision.

Statutes have given agencies great latitude to fashion individual sets of evidence rules to suit their needs. There are as many sets of evidence rules as there are types of agency adjudications. However, they seem to fit within one of three broad categories. Some agencies have adopted the wide open standard of admissibility of APA § 556(d), by which all evidence is admissible in a formal hearing. An agency may—but is not required to—exclude "irrelevant, immaterial, or unduly repetitious evidence." Other agencies have incorporated the Federal

Rules on a selective basis. Still other agencies have adopted evidence rules which follow the Federal Rules "so far as practicable."

A significant variance from court trials is the fact that evidence at an administrative hearing frequently is in written form.

Much like judicial notice, administrative decisionmakers may take **official notice** of certain types of facts developed outside the adjudication process and may incorporate them into the ultimate decision in the case. When official notice is taken of an adjudicative fact, the APA requires that the parties be advised of the intent to take official notice and requires that they be given an opportunity to comment. APA § 556(e). However, the APA does not cover official notice of legislative facts (those general facts used to support legislation). The result is that a decisionmaker may take official notice of a legislative fact without giving the parties notice and without providing an opportunity to comment. Although it is criticized by many, this remains the rule in administrative adjudications.

Standard of Proof   A standard of proof tells the decisionmakers how much evidence they need to reach a particular conclusion. For example, a preponderance of the evidence requires the result or conclusion to be supported by a majority of the evidence in terms of weight. Other standards, such as "clear and convincing" or "beyond a reasonable doubt" require progressively more proof in terms of weight to support the ultimate conclusion. Note that the standard of proof is different from the standard of review (judicial review) used by a court to review an agency decision (*see below*).

APA § 556(d) requires that a decision be supported by "reliable, probative, and *substantial* evidence." Courts interpret this to mean a **preponderance** of the evidence. As a practical matter, however, if there is any fact in the record of the adjudicative proceedings to support a particular result, a reviewing court is not likely to overturn an agency decision based upon standard of proof. This is because of the agency's special expertise—and a court's lack of special expertise—in the area governed by the agency.

The proponent of the administrative action bears the burden of proof (burden of establishing the required standard of proof). APA § 556(d). The FTC bears the burden of proof in an enforcement proceeding, for example; but an SSA claimant bears the burden of proof in establishing his or her entitlement to the grant of a government benefit. However, if the SSA seeks to discontinue an existing SSA benefit (one previously granted by it), the SSA becomes the proponent and bears the burden of proof.

The Order   Adjudication results in an order, which either compels compliance with the law or grants (or denies) a benefit. The order must be reasonably related to the violations found during adjudication of an enforcement proceeding, for example.

Both due process and the APA require findings of fact and reasons to support an adjudicative decision. APA § 557(c). This serves several purposes: it provides the basis for judicial review, it informs the parties, and it forces the decisionmaker to consider the decision carefully. Due process generally does not require *detailed* findings of fact, however.

The record of a trial has identifiable boundaries, defined by the admissibility of evidence. By contrast, the administrative record is much less structured, even in formal adjudications. In formal adjudications, APA § 556(e) provides that the evidence developed in the formal hearing is the "exclusive record" upon which a decision may be reached. Defining the record in an informal adjudication may be substantially more difficult because of the lack of structure in informal hearings.

A particular adjudicative decision is not limited by concepts of *stare decisis* and precedent. However, administrative decisionmakers must act consistently with their prior decisions, which requires them to justify any deviation from prior agency law. Some agencies have a ***non-acquiescence policy***, which means they will not acquiesce in a judicial decision. The agency will comply with the court's order in a particular case, of course; but it will not change its general policy in relation to other, similar cases. This policy is defended on the basis of the agency's superior expertise and the agency's need to have a national policy that does not change from one judicial region to the next.

Sanctions   When a party in an enforcement proceeding is found to have violated a statute or regulation, the agency may impose sanctions to redress the violation. The sanctions that may be imposed are found among the delegated powers in the agency's enabling act, and they can be as diverse as the powers delegated to the various agencies. All administrative sanctions, however, share one common limitation based on constitutional prohibitions: *No administrative sanction can include imprisonment.*

Unlike an agency, Congress can provide in the enabling act that violation of a regulation is punishable as a criminal offense. When violation occurs, however, the violator is prosecuted in the federal courts for the criminal act—not before an administrative agency. One practical reason for the limitation is that persons accused of criminal acts are entitled to a trial by jury. Juries are not authorized in the structure of administrative agencies.

An administrative sanction generally takes the form of a **penalty**. The penalty may be a fine, denial of a license or other privilege, revocation of a license or privilege previously granted, injunctive relief, or any one of the myriad of civil penalties that have been fashioned by legislative bodies.

The practice in many federal agencies is to issue a cease-and-desist order as a preliminary measure. A **cease-and-desist** order is a type of official warning; it allows the violator to discontinue offending conduct or practices before more serious sanctions are imposed. In some situations, a consent decree may be entered by negotiation and settlement between the agency and the offender. A **consent decree** serves essentially the same purpose as a stipulated judgment in civil court cases or as a plea bargain in criminal court cases.

Intra-agency Appeal   Most administrative agency processes include at least one level of administrative appeal to an administrative review board or authority. Often the board or commission that heads the agency acts as an intra-agency appellate authority, much like an appellate court. In some agencies, the head of the agency appoints a special staff, sometimes an **appellate review board**, to handle administrative appeals within the agency.

In some agencies, the administrative appellate review board has plenary power to substitute its judgment on findings of fact, as well as on law and policy, unless a specific statute denies that power. In other agencies, the appellate review board has only limited review powers, similar to those exercised by a reviewing court.

Unless a claimant or respondent avails herself of all intra-agency appellate reviews that are provided (exhausts her administrative remedies), she cannot obtain judicial review of the agency's decision.

Judicial Review

An action by an administrative agency generally can be challenged in court. An agency's action in regard to obtaining information can be challenged by filing a motion to quash the offending summons, deposition, or subpoena. Challenging dissemination of information by an agency can be achieved through a declaratory judgment action, possibly accompanied by a request for injunctive relief (temporary restraining order). One also can obtain judicial review of a final regulation (rulemaking) or of a final order (adjudication) if certain preliminary requirements are met.

Parties sometimes seek judicial review of agency decisions in which they have no real stake. They also may seek judicial review too soon, which can frustrate and delay the administrative process and can waste judicial resources. To avoid these kinds of problems, courts have developed doctrines on standing, exhaustion of administrative remedies, and unreviewability.

Statutory Review   Judicial review of an agency's decisions is established by the same enabling act which creates the agency. Most provide that a final decision may be appealed by filing a *petition for review* in a federal court of appeals. A few enabling acts, such as the Social Security Act, provide for review by the federal district court.

The appellate court (or district court) court reviews the administrative record to determine whether the agency violated any constitutional, statutory, or regulatory provision in reaching its decision. If not, the decision is affirmed. If a violation is found, the reviewing court may vacate the decision or may remand it to the agency for further proceedings.

The standard of review varies according to whether the agency proceeding was formal or informal and according to the burden of proof required for a particular type of proceeding (*see below*).

Nonstatutory Review   Nonstatutory review arises (1) when Congress has failed to provide a statutory procedure in the enabling act for review of an agency's decision or (2) when the prescribed procedure cannot provide adequate relief.

One nonstatutory basis for review is mandamus. A *mandamus* action seeks to compel an official to perform a duty that is owed to the complaining party. Mandamus can be used only when the agency's decision is ministerial, which means nondiscretionary. Nondiscretionary acts are fairly limited.

Another basis may be the general *federal question* jurisdiction of federal courts to hear any case "arising under" the Constitution or the laws of the United States. The complaining party may be able to use federal question jurisdiction to seek a declaratory judgment or injunctive relief or both.

Unreviewable Agency Decisions   Although judicial review is available for nearly all agency decisions, APA § 701 provides two exceptions when judicial review is not available: (1) to the extent that statutes preclude judicial review; and (2) to the extent that the action is committed (left) to agency discretion.

There is a presumption that judicial review is available for any agency decision. The statute clearly must preclude judicial review to overcome this presumption; and even then, many courts have found ways around the preclusion to provide a limited review of certain aspects of the decision.

Courts cannot review agency decisions which are "committed to agency discretion," which may include decisions related to such things as national defense, foreign policy, or when the administrator is required to act in a managerial capacity. Within this context, managerial capacity means supervising a succession of small decisions that may require an administrator to use her best judgment, hunch, or intuition. For example, when an administrator must monitor rents charged by private landlords in subsidized housing, agency discretion may prevent review of each, separate decision.

Even where parts of a decision may be unreviewable under one of these two bases, a court is free to review the remaining parts for errors that may have been committed at the agency level. In many situations, courts have treated unreviewable discretion cases as being subject to a limited judicial review of their nondiscretionary parts.

Standing   Before seeking review of an agency's decision, the complaining party must establish that he, she, or it has standing to sue. Standing exists if the party has sustained actual injury by an agency decision and is "arguably within the zone of interests to be protected or regulated by the statute or constitutional guarantee in question."

The standing requirement ensures that a legitimate controversy exists and prevents suits by those who disagree with agency decisions on purely political or philosophical grounds.

Exhaustion of Remedies   In addition to standing requirements, courts also require a complaining party to exhaust all administrative remedies before seeking judicial intervention. This is administrative law's version of the ripeness doctrine. The purpose of this requirement is to limit judicial review to only those issues which have been considered thoroughly by the agency and to final orders which accurately reflect the final ruling of the agency.

Thus, a party must take advantage of all levels and methods of appeal provided by the agency before petitioning for review by a court. For example, if an application for Social Security disability benefits is denied at the initial determination level, the applicant must challenge the decision within the agency by requesting a redetermination hearing. If she loses at that stage, she must seek review by the agency's appellate review board and, ultimately, by the head of the Social Security Administration. Because it is possible that the applicant may prevail at any one of these stages, a court will not review any decisions except those which represent the final word of the agency.

Scope of Judicial Review

When judicial review is available, the next question is how much authority a court may exercise over a particular administrative regulation or administrative order. Judicial review is designed to maintain minimum standards, not to ensure perfect decisions. Courts frequently defer to agencies on certain matters to ensure that Congress' intent is carried out in relation to the powers delegated to administrative agencies.

The degree of authority to review administrative decisions is established by word formulas called *standards of review*. To understand the various standards of review, it may be helpful to remember the steps used by the agency in reaching a particular decision. In general, the agency (1) *interprets the law* assigned by its statutory mandate; it (2) *finds facts* in relation of a specific situation; and it (3) *uses discretion* in applying the law to the factual situation found to exist.

APA § 706 covers the standards of review to be used by courts in reviewing agency decisions; § 706(2) lists those grounds that can be used to reverse a particular decision. The APA does not provide the jurisdictional basis for review; it only covers the standard of review to be used once the reviewing court has acquired jurisdiction by other means (whether statutory or nonstatutory). The grounds—and the standards of review—can be grouped roughly in the same way as the steps used by the agency to reach its decision:

Questions of Law   1.   Whether the agency has committed a procedural error § 706(2);

Specific procedures may be required by the enabling act, by the APA, by the Due Process Clause, or by the agency's own rules.

2.   Whether the Constitution has been violated § 706(2)(B); and

Constitutional violations can occur in relation to the Due Process Clause or any other provision of the Constitution.

3.   Whether the agency has exceeded its statutory authority § 706(2)(C).

Look to the agency's enabling act and any addenda to it.

Questions of Fact

1.   Whether there is "substantial evidence" in the record to support the result § 706(2)(E);

The substantial evidence test is used most often for a trial-type hearing in rulemaking or adjudication. It often involves the issue of whether the agency prepared a sufficient explanation of its decision to allow a court to understand its rationale; and if it did, the court will uphold the decision as long as it is reasonable.

2.   Whether the decision is arbitrary, capricious, or an abuse of discretion § 706(2)(A); or

A decision is arbitrary if it is wholly unsupported by the facts developed in the record; it is capricious if deviates radically from past practices or rules without any justification for the change. The "arbitrary or capricious" test is used most often in reviewing informal rulemaking or adjudication.

3.   *De novo* review, where permitted § 706(2)(F).

When de novo fact review is permitted—which is rare—the reviewing court determines whether it agrees with the findings of fact made by the agency. Recall that judicial review of agency refusals to provide FOIA information is de novo by the federal district court.

Discretion

1.   Whether the decision is arbitrary, capricious, or an abuse of discretion § 706(2)(A).

Abuse of discretion is a slippery concept but may be defined as one which shocks the conscience or one which is equivalent to extreme arbitrariness or to extreme capriciousness. The agency is given much more latitude and deference in its discretionary decisions, but the discretion may not be limitless if a reviewing court genuinely believes that it was carried too far in a particular case.

In relation to adjudication, a general rule of thumb for scope of review is that a reviewing court will give less deference to an agency's conclusions on questions of law than to its conclusions on factual or discretionary issues.

Where rulemaking is concerned, courts typically look to see (1) whether the regulation is within the authority delegated to the agency by Congress and (2) whether all of the procedural requirements were met in the rulemaking process.

If an agency adopts a rule that exceeds its delegated authority, the rule is *ultra vires* (beyond the agency's power) and is void. Because Congress typically delegates such broad authority to administrative agencies, courts rarely find a rule to be *ultra vires*. Most judicial review of agency rulemaking, therefore, concerns due process requirements: proper notice of the proposed rule or amendment, obtaining comments from those segments of the public whose interests are affected by the rule, publication thirty days before the effective date of the rule, and so forth.

Enabling Act Addendum

To conclude this chapter, an abbreviated list is provided of federal enabling acts, together with the administrative agencies created by them and their general function. A complete list of federal administrative agencies and of the acronyms typically used in administrative law is available in the *United States Government Manual*, which can be obtained through many government offices or through any member of Congress.

Enabling Act	Agency	Function
Interstate Commerce Act of 1887	Interstate Commerce Commission	Regulate transportation that affects interstate commerce; restraint of trade; price-fixing
Federal Trade Commission Act of 1914	Federal Trade Commission	Regulate antitrust laws; monopolies; unfair competition; deceptive advertising practices; truth in lending
Wagner Act	National Labor Relations Board	Monitor unfair labor practices in relation to unions; determine bargaining units for unions

Food, Drug and Cosmetic Act	Food and Drug Administration	Regulate food and drug contents, packaging, and safety
Securities Exchange Act of 1934	Securities and Exchange Commission	Regulate interstate trading in securities (stocks & bonds)
Social Security Act	Social Security Administration	Administer government benefits to retired and disabled workers; death benefits to families of workers
Civil Rights Act of 1964 (Title VII)	Equal Employment Opportunity Commission	Eliminate employment discrimination based on race, color, national origin, sex, or religion
Occupational Safety and Health Act	Occupational Safety and Health Administration	Regulate safety and health standards in the workplace
Executive Order (reorganization)	Environmental Protection Agency	Regulate pollution of air, water, and land caused by industrial waste

This chapter, together with the following Self-Test, should provide a basic review of the principles and procedures that may be encountered on the certifying examination. If the applicant is unfamiliar with any of the material covered, he or she is advised to consider close study of a relevant textbook or other study aid as well as the applicable APA provisions. *See the Bibliography for additional study references.*

Administrative Law Self-Test

Allow an uninterrupted thirty-minute period to answer all questions. At the end of thirty minutes, check your answers against those in the Answer Key Section of this Manual. Deduct two points for each incorrect answer (100 total possible points). Unanswered questions are counted as incorrect answers. Follow directions carefully and observe the time limit precisely to provide an accurate self-assessment.

Choose the most correct answer to each of the following questions unless a specific question instructs you to do otherwise.

1. Federal administrative agencies receive their authority to act from:

    a. the Constitution.
    b. Congress.
    c. their respective enabling statutes.
    d. none of the above.

2. When constitutional objections are raised within an administrative proceeding concerning an agency's rules or procedures, that issue will be decided initially by:

    a. the administrative agency.
    b. the appellate court.
    c. the U.S. Supreme Court.
    d. none of these is correct.

3. The rule-making proceedings of a federal administrative agency cannot be reviewed *per se* by the U.S. Supreme Court because:

    a. rule-making proceedings do not generate a record to review.
    b. rule-making proceedings are established by Congress.
    c. rule-making proceedings are purely discretionary with the agency.
    d. rule-making proceedings are reviewed de novo.

4. True or False.   If a federal agency elects to prosecute some violators of its regulations and not to prosecute others, such a decision likely will be found arbitrary and capricious by a reviewing court.

5. True or False.   When quasi-judicial decisions arise as issues of fact, rather than as issues of law, within an agency's area of expertise, courts are less likely to reconsider the evidence in such a way as to second-guess the agency.

6. True or False.   Administrative hearing officers generally must have the same qualifications as federal judges.

7. True or False.   Damages may be awarded under the Federal Tort Claims Act for false imprisonment by federal law enforcement officers.

8. True or False.   All federal administrative agencies are governed by the APA in addition to their own rules and regulations.

9. True or False.   The APA requires a federal agency to include in its rules a statement of the bases and purposes of the rules.

10. True or False.   EXACTA, a federal agency charged with enforcing employment regulations, makes rules concerning employment that will bring heavy financial burdens to businesses. If ABC Fruit Company charges that the regulations will force it to declare bankruptcy, the agency must provide a trial-type hearing and must allow cross-examination of its experts in connection with adoption of the regulations.

11. True or False.   In the immediately preceding situation, EXACTA announces that it will permit only written comments, with no opportunity for ABC Fruit Company or anyone else to make oral arguments. If ABC files suit to contest this procedure, it will not prevail.

12. True or False.   Nonlawyers are permitted to represent persons appearing before all federal administrative agencies governed by the APA.

13. True or False.   An agency may impose criminal sanctions against a named defendant or respondent.

14. True or False.   If an agency relies upon its own expertise in reaching an adjudication in a specific case, it must enter such expert opinion(s) as part of the record in a particular hearing.

15. True or False.   As a general rule, an administrative law judge may not consult with a nonwitness concerning an issue of fact without first providing notice and an opportunity for all other parties to participate.

16. True or False.   Eviction from public housing is a sufficient invasion of privacy interests by the evicting administrative agency that it requires a trial-type hearing.

17. True or False.   Raising the rent of a public housing tenant is a sufficient invasion of privacy interests by the supervisory administrative agency that it requires a trial-type hearing.

18. True or False.   A federal administrative agency may institute new policy either by rulemaking proceedings or by adjudication.

19. True or False.   Review of agency decisions by appellate courts is based upon the record made at the administrative hearing.

20. True or False.   Appellate review of administrative agency decisions generally are similar in scope to appellate review of a trial court's decision.

21. True or False.   One generally can tell whether a federal administrative agency is an independent agency or is an executive agency by its name.

22. Which of the following agency decisions may be reviewed by a court of law?

    a. Admission of aliens
    b. Military decisions
    c. Enforcement and prosecution decisions
    d. Suspension of licenses previously granted
    e. Rate suspensions

23. Appellate review of an administrative agency decision will result in affirmance of the agency's decision if the record shows that the decision was based upon:

    a. a preponderance of the evidence.
    b. significant evidence.
    c. substantial evidence.
    d. clear and convincing evidence.

24. The rulemaking function of most administrative agencies requires:

    a. notice only.
    b. notice and comment.
    c. notice and hearing.
    d. none of these is correct.

25.   A sunset law is one which:

    a.   suspends an agency's authority after a stated period of time.
    b.   requires that no advisory committee can meet after sunset.
    c.   terminates an agency's authority on a stated date.
    d.   terminates an agency's authority after a stated period of time unless Congress re-adopts the agency's enabling act.

26.   True or False.   As part of an agency's authority, Congress may include a provision which makes certain administrative acts subject to legislative veto.

27.   True or False.   An federal agency may refuse to issue or to renew licenses for failure to provide requested information.

28.   True or False.   Administrative agencies may obtain information from private citizens or from businesses through the Freedom of Information Act.

29.   True or False.   Under the Privacy Act, agency disclosure of records retrievable by a person's name is forbidden to anyone other than the person to whom the records relate.

30.   True or False.   As a general rule, memoranda between agency officials are not required to be disclosed under the FOIA.

31.   The Sunshine Act requires:

    a.   federal advisory committees to meet in open session.
    b.   agencies headed by a commission or board to meet in public.
    c.   federal agencies to meet in open session.
    d.   none is correct.

32.   A federal agency may obtain information through:

    a.   summons.
    b.   subpoena.
    c.   warrant.
    d.   two of the above.
    e.   all of the above.
    f.   none of the above.

33.   Unless an extension is granted, how long does a federal agency have to comply with an FOIA request?

a.   ten days
b.   fourteen days
c.   twenty days
d.   none is correct

34.   If the petitioner is successful in a reverse-FOIA suit, the result is that:

a.   the petitioner does not have to provide specific information to the agency.
b.   the agency does not have to provide specific information to the petitioner.
c.   the agency is enjoined from supplying specific information to others.
d.   the petitioner is enjoined from supplying specific information to others.
e.   none of these is correct.

35.   True or False.   Reviewing courts typically give great deference to the legal issues decided by an administrative agency as part of its quasi-judicial function.

36.   True or False.   The APA requires certain formalities for formal, hybrid, and informal rulemaking.

37.   True or False.   The doctrine of separation of functions in administrative law applies to an agency's adjudication proceedings but does not apply to its rulemaking proceedings.

38.   True or False.   E.O. 12991 requires all administrative agencies to perform a cost-benefit analysis before adopting any rule or regulation.

39.   True or False.   Under the APA, an individual who performs a prosecutorial function in an adjudication proceeding generally may not participate in the decision reached by the administrative agency.

40.   An agency may formulate administrative law by:

a.   adopting rules and regulations.
b.   adjudication.
c.   adopting internal guidelines.
d.   two of the above.
e.   all of the above.
f.   none of the above.

41.   Before an agency rule is given the force of law, the agency must:

      a.   publish the rule before it is adopted.
      b.   allow opportunity for public comment.
      c.   publish the rule after it is adopted.
      d.   two of the above.
      e.   all of the above.
      f.   none of the above.

42.   When publication of a rule or regulation is required, the publication must appear in:

      a.   the Federal Register.
      b.   the Congressional Record.
      c.   the agency's advance sheets.
      d.   all of the above.
      e.   none of the above.

43.   Agency rulemaking may be:

      a.   formal.
      b.   informal.
      c.   hybrid.
      d.   negotiated.
      e.   three of the above.
      f.   all of the above.
      g.   none of the above.

44.   Which of the following terms is required in an enabling act before a reviewing court will enforce formal rulemaking procedures?

      a.   public hearing
      b.   formal rulemaking
      c.   hearing on the record
      d.   two of the above
      e.   all of the above
      f.   none of the above

45.   Before a person may appeal the decision of an administrative agency, she must be able to demonstrate to the reviewing court that she has:

a. published notice.
b. exhausted all administrative remedies.
c. been unfairly prejudiced by the agency decision.
d. two of the above.
e. all of the above.
f. none of the above.

46. True or False.   Independent agencies typically possess both quasi-legislative and quasi-judicial functions.

47. True or False.   Federal administrative agencies typically follow the same rules of evidence in adjudication proceedings as federal courts follow in trials.

48. True or False.   Even though a reviewing court reverses an administrative action in a particular case, that judicial decision may not change the agency's general policies in relation to future cases.

49. True or False.   The decisions of most administrative agencies are reviewed *de novo* on the record.

50. True or False.   By authority of Congress, the President may create an administrative agency by executive order.

Chapter 9
BANKRUPTCY LAW

*If you want to know what God thinks of money, just look
at the people She gives it to.*

—modified Yiddish proverb

Success on this portion of the CLA® examination requires a thorough knowledge
of the Bankruptcy Code, together with its terminology and procedures in light of
its ultimate goals. The successful CLA applicant must know and understand
terminology as it is used within the context of the Bankruptcy Code and must
develop a firm concept of the organizational structure of the Code, the kinds of
relief available under each of the applicable chapters, and the interrelationship of
various sections of different chapters. Familiarity with specific Bankruptcy Code
sections is critical.

Chapter 9 of the Bankruptcy Code, which relates to reorganization of
municipalities, is not covered in any depth on the CLA® examination and is not
included in this *Review Manual*.

Background and Goals of Bankruptcy Law

Some form of debt relief has existed almost as long as people have. The Old
Testament, for instance, refers to the practice of forgiving debts every seven years.

At one time or another, nearly every bankruptcy lawyer has seized upon this piece of history as evidence that he or is is doing the Lord's work.

In Europe during the fourteenth century, merchants lined the town square with their benches and worked there while they sold their crafts. When a merchant was unable to pay his debts, his creditors smashed his bench as a symbol for all to see. From this practice came the word *bankruptcy*, which means literally "broken bench."

In that era, England favored more severe punishment of insolvent debtors after their debts had been forgiven. English debtors often found themselves in a debtors' prison or indentured as servants and transported to America to work. In 1898 Congress passed the Bankruptcy Act, which was the first legislation to provide a form of relief for debtors that is somewhat similar to the relief provided under today's Bankruptcy Code.

The Bankruptcy Act was amended substantially in 1938 and was replaced by the Bankruptcy Code on October 1, 1979. Amendments were adopted in 1984 to correct jurisdictional defects. In 1986, further amendments permitted the appointment of additional bankruptcy judges, created the Chapter 12 reorganization for family farmers, and established the United States Trustee as a permanent officer within the bankruptcy structure. The most recent amendments to the Code were enacted in 1994.

The overriding goal of the Bankruptcy Code is to relieve the honest debtor of his or her debts and to provide the opportunity for a financial *fresh start*. At the same time, the Code strives to ensure fair treatment of creditors and to maximize the bankruptcy estate for distribution to unsecured creditors.

Organization of Bankruptcy Code

Bankruptcy law is based upon federal statutes found in Title 11 of the United States Code (The Bankruptcy Code). Title 11 is divided into chapters, with each chapter covering a specific area of bankruptcy law.

Chapter 1:	General Provisions, Definitions, and Rules of Construction
Chapter 2:	The Trustee
Chapter 3:	Case Administration

Chapter 5:   Creditors, the Debtor, and the Estate

> *Note: The provisions of Chapters 1, 3, and 5 apply to all bankruptcy proceedings unless otherwise specified.*

Chapter 7:   Liquidation

Chapter 9:   Adjustment of Debts of Municipality

Chapter 11:   Reorganization

Chapter 12:   Reorganization of Family Farmer

Chapter 13:   Debt Adjustment of Individual with Regular Income

Within each chapter, the sections begin with the same number as the chapter number where they are located. For instance, § 102 is located in Chapter 1 *(Definitions and General Rules)*; § 722 is located in Chapter 7 *(Liquidation)*; and § 1106 is located in Chapter 11 *(Reorganization)*. Thus, the section number is an instant indicator of the overall chapter coverage of any particular section.

In addition to the substantive law sections found in the Bankruptcy Code, bankruptcy practice is governed by the Bankruptcy Rules adopted by the United States Supreme Court. The Bankruptcy Rules, not the Federal Rules of Civil Procedure, govern all proceedings conducted in the Bankruptcy Court. Part VII of the Bankruptcy Rules is devoted to adversary proceedings and substantially incorporates the Federal Rules of Civil Procedure into its provisions.

Once again, the rule number indicates the overall topic coverage of the rule. For instance, Bankruptcy Rule 7004 relates to adversary proceedings and incorporates Rule 4 of the Federal Rules of Civil Procedure. Bankruptcy Rules 7026 through 7037 relate to adversary proceedings and incorporate Rules 26 through 37 (discovery) of the Federal Rules of Civil Procedure.

The rules of individual bankruptcy courts (local court rules) also may affect bankruptcy practice. *See the section on General Law for further discussion of local court rules.*

Participants and Terminology

Some terms appear frequently throughout the Bankruptcy Code (the Code). An understanding of their bankruptcy definition is necessary to understand the other provisions of the Code.

After Notice and Hearing When this language appears in the Code, it means appropriate notice under the circumstances and an opportunity for hearing. A number of situations can exist where no actual hearing is held, such as when no hearing is requested by a party in interest. § 102(1).

Claim A right to payment, even though it is unliquidated, unmatured, disputed, or contingent. The definition of a claim is important in determining which debts are discharged and who shares in distribution. § 101(4).

Consumer Debt A debt incurred by an individual primarily for a personal, family, or household purpose. § 101(7).

Creditors' Committee In a Chapter 11 proceeding, a committee of those unsecured creditors holding the seven largest claims against the debtor; a creditors' committee is appointed by the United States Trustee. §§ 1102, 1103. A creditors' committee may be appointed in a Chapter 7 proceeding (but usually is not). § 705.

Debt A "liability on a claim"; the discharge of debts in bankruptcy is the method by which debtors are given a fresh start.

Debtor The person who seeks relief under the Bankruptcy Code (formerly known as the "bankrupt" under the Bankruptcy Act). § 101(12).

Debtor in Possession In proceedings under Chapters 11, 12, or 13, the debtor is known as a "debtor in possession" of the estate unless a trustee has been appointed. §§ 1101(1), 1203. Within this *Review Manual*, the acronym DIP is used routinely to refer to the debtor in possession.

Equity Security Holder A holder of a share or similar security in a debtor corporation, a holder of the right to buy or sell a security in a debtor corporation, or a limited partner in a limited partnership debtor. §§ 101(15), (16).

Entity   A more comprehensive term than "person" under the Code, entity includes persons and trusts, estates, governmental units, and the United States Trustee. § 101(14).

Family Farmer   Individual or individual and spouse engaged in farming operations whose total debt (exclusive of personal residence) is not more than $1,500,000 (total of secured and unsecured), at least 80% of which arises from farming operations and at least 50% of whose gross income was derived from farming operations in the tax year immediately before the year in which the petition for relief is filed. § 101(18)(A).

A corporation may be a family farmer if, in addition to the above, at least 50% of the outstanding stock is held by family members engaged in farming, the stock is not publicly traded, and at least 80% of the corporation's assets are related to farming. § 101(18)(B).

Insider   How the term "insider" is defined depends on whether the debtor is an individual, a corporation, or a partnership. § 101(30).

Individual debtor   As to an individual debtor, the following are insiders: relatives; general partners, relatives of general partners, a partnership where the debtor is a general partner, and a corporation where the debtor is an officer, director, or person in control. §§ 101(30)(A), (39).

Corporate debtor   As to a corporate debtor, the following are insiders: directors, officers, persons in control, relatives of any of these, and a partnership where the debtor is a general partner. § 101(30)(B).

Partnership debtor   As to a partnership debtor, the following are insiders: general partners in or of the debtor, persons in control, relatives of any of these, and a partnership where the debtor is a general partner. § 101(30)(C).

Insolvent   An entity is insolvent when its debts are more than the total value of all of its property (excluding exempt property and fraudulent transfers). As to a partnership, the excess of nonexempt personal assets of each general partner over his or her nonpartnership debts is included in the partnership assets.

Order for Relief   Occurs automatically upon the filing of a voluntary petition; occurs after trial in an involuntary proceeding when the court determines that a debtor generally is not paying his or her debts as they become due. §§ 102(6), 301, 302(a).

Person   An individual, a corporation, or a partnership is a person under the Code (governmental units are not persons). § 101(35).

Professional Persons   Include attorneys, accountants, appraisers, auctioneers, and so forth employed by the trustee, the debtor, or a creditors' committee.   Their employment and compensation must be approved by the court. §§ 327-331.

Secured Creditor   An entity holding a claim against the debtor that is secured by a lien on property of the estate or that is subject to setoff. § 506(a).

Transfer   Voluntary or involuntary disposition of property or an interest in property. Includes conveyance of security interest or mortgage, judicial lien, or foreclosure sale.

Trustee   The official representative of the estate; exercises statutory powers primarily for the benefit of unsecured creditors. § 323(a).

United States Trustee   Appointed by the Attorney General for a term of five years; assumes many of the administrative responsibilities previously performed by the court. 28 U.S.C. § 581.

Unsecured Creditor   An entity holding a claim against the debtor that is not secured by collateral.

Bankruptcy Jurisdiction

The bankruptcy court is a distinct unit or arm of the federal district court in each federal judicial district. It is authorized to hear cases by referral from the federal district court; bankruptcy cases receive a blanket referral to the bankruptcy court.

Judges of the bankruptcy courts are appointed to 14-year terms by the United States courts of appeals. Each bankruptcy judge is authorized to implement the provisions of the Bankruptcy Code by issuing necessary or appropriate orders or judgments and is expressly authorized to take action on the court's own motion *(sua sponte)* to enforce bankruptcy court orders.

Bankruptcy Rule 9020 authorizes a bankruptcy judge to enter civil or criminal contempt orders in appropriate cases. If an objection is made within ten days of its issuance, however, the contempt order is reviewed *de novo* by the federal district court. § 105(a).

Personal Jurisdiction   A bankruptcy court may exercise personal jurisdiction anywhere in the geographical United States by first-class, prepaid mail. Unlike litigation generally, minimum contacts with the forum are not required. Bankruptcy Rule 7004.

Subject Matter Jurisdiction   The U.S. district courts have original, exclusive jurisdiction over all cases arising under the Bankruptcy Code. They also have original, exclusive *in rem* jurisdiction over the debtor's property as of the date when the debtor's petition for relief is filed and over all property of the estate, wherever it is located. The federal district court's jurisdiction in these areas preempts any state court jurisdiction that might apply otherwise. 28 U.S.C. § 1334.

Other than the trial of personal injury and wrongful death claims, nearly all cases and core proceedings pertaining to bankruptcy matters are referred by the federal district court to the bankruptcy court for disposition. Bankruptcy judges can hear all referred cases and core proceedings and can issue final orders and judgments, which are appealable to the appropriate federal district courts. In non-core proceedings, however, a bankruptcy judge may (but is not required to) hear the matter but must submit proposed findings of fact and conclusions of law to the district court for final disposition, including entry of any orders that may be required.

A.   Core Proceedings   Examples of core proceedings are those matters related to administration of the debtor's estate, allowance of exemptions and of creditors' claims, claims of the estate against others, the automatic stay, fraudulent transfers, preferences, and sale or lease of estate property. Core proceedings also include matters affecting liquidation of estate assets or affecting debtor-creditor adjustments.

Although federal district courts have issued a blanket referral of all core proceedings to the bankruptcy court, the federal district court may withdraw the referral of a particular case or proceeding for cause. This withdrawal may be on the court's own motion or upon the motion of a party.

The federal district court must withdraw a proceeding if it requires "substantial consideration" of both the Bankruptcy Code and a federal non-bankruptcy statute regulating organizations involved in interstate commerce. An order of withdrawal issued by the federal district court is not subject to appeal.

B.   Non-Core Proceedings   Non-core proceedings (also known as related proceedings) include causes of action that the debtor could have filed in state court or in federal court if no bankruptcy proceeding had been filed. Examples of non-core proceedings include enforcement of a pre-petition contract right, eviction, or a property damage claim.

Although a bankruptcy judge may hear non-core matters, he or she cannot enter a final order unless all parties consent. Absent this consent, the proposed findings of fact are submitted to the federal district court for final disposition. Claims related to personal injury or to wrongful death *must* be heard by the federal district court; these claims cannot be heard by the bankruptcy court, not even with the consent of all parties.

Whether a matter is core or non-core is determined by the bankruptcy court judge, whose decision is subject to appeal.

Abstention   The federal district court (including the bankruptcy court unit) *may* abstain from hearing a particular proceeding, whether core or non-core, when justice, comity, or respect for state law favors resolution in state court.

Upon motion properly made, the federal court *must* abstain from hearing a non-core proceeding if it involves an action based upon state law related to the bankruptcy proceeding (but not arising from the bankruptcy proceeding or under the Bankruptcy Code) and if the action:

1.   could not have been brought in federal court without the bankruptcy proceeding;

2.   has already been filed in state court; and

3.   is capable of timely adjudication in the state court.

Venue   Venue for filing a bankruptcy proceeding rests with the federal district court where the debtor has maintained her residence, domicile, principal place of business, or assets for the longest portion of the 180 days immediately preceding the filing of the case.

Once a bankruptcy petition has been filed, venue rests generally with the federal court where the case is pending with these exceptions:

A.   Proceedings initiated by a bankruptcy trustee to recover money or property worth less than $1,000 or to recover a consumer debt under $5,000 must be filed where the defendant resides.

B.   Post-petition actions initiated by a trustee and arising from the operation of a debtor's business can be filed only where the action could have been filed under applicable nonbankruptcy rules of venue.

C.   Actions against the trustee and arising from the post-petition operation of a debtor's business can be filed in the district where the bankruptcy proceeding is pending or where the action could have been brought under applicable nonbankruptcy rules of venue.

Appeal   Appeal from a decision of the bankruptcy court is made to the federal district court—except in the Ninth Circuit, where appeal is made to a bankruptcy appellate court.

The party who wishes to appeal (the appellant) must file a notice of appeal with the clerk of the bankruptcy court within ten days of the entry of the order or judgment being appealed.   Upon appeal, the district court applies a "clearly erroneous" standard of review. Unless the decision of the bankruptcy court was clearly erroneous, it will be affirmed by the district court.

A ruling concerning relief from the automatic stay is a final order for purposes of appeal. Where a debtor wishes to appeal an order of relief from the automatic stay, the debtor also must obtain a stay pending the appeal. Without a stay, the appeal will become moot if a foreclosure sale occurs while the debtor's appeal is pending.

Officers of the Estate

The officers of a bankruptcy estate consist of the United States Trustee and the trustee assigned to the case. In addition, a particular estate may require the appointment of an examiner and professionals (usually attorneys and accountants) as needed to administer the estate properly.

United States Trustee   Under the supervision of the Attorney General, the United States Trustee serves as an administrator of the bankruptcy system in his or her region. The United States Trustee is responsible for establishing a panel of private trustees for Chapter 7 cases and for appointing trustees to a particular case. He or she also convenes and presides at § 341 meetings and supervises the administration of bankruptcy cases via appointed trustees.

Under the Bankruptcy Code, the United States Trustee has standing to appear and to be heard on any issue in any bankruptcy case but cannot file a reorganization plan under Chapter 11.

Trustee The trustee is the official representative of the estate and, as such, can sue or be sued. The trustee has a variety of administrative powers and a number of administrative duties, which vary with the chapter under which he or she serves.

In general, the trustee must be a disinterested, competent person or corporation. In Chapter 7, 12, and 13 cases, the trustee must reside or have an office in the judicial district where the case is pending or in the adjacent judicial district. If necessary, the United States Trustee may serve as the trustee in a Chapter 7, 12, or 13 case, but may not serve as the trustee in a Chapter 11 case.

The term "disinterested" precludes the debtor's creditors, equity security holders, insiders, directors, officers, employees, investment bankers, or any other person with materially adverse interests from serving as the trustee in a particular case.

A. Selection The method of selecting the trustee varies from chapter to chapter.

1. Chapter 7 The Chapter 7 trustee is chosen from a panel of private trustees maintained by the United States trustee. A disinterested panel member is appointed as the interim trustee until the § 341 meeting, after which the interim trustee becomes the permanent trustee unless a different trustee is elected by the creditors.

2. Chapter 11 Ordinarily the Chapter 11 debtor remains in possession of estate property and continues to manage the business, so that appointment of a trustee is not necessary. However, the court may order that a trustee be appointed for cause or in the interest of creditors. "Cause" for appointment of a trustee may include one of the following acts of the current management: fraud, dishonesty, incompetence, or gross mismanagement.

3.   Chapters 12 and 13   In regions where there are many cases filed under Chapter 12, the United States trustee generally appoints a standing trustee for all of the cases under that chapter; otherwise, a disinterested person or the United States trustee serves as the trustee. The same procedure applies to Chapter 13 cases. Under both chapters, the debtor ordinarily retains possession of estate property.

B.   Authority   As the official representative of the estate, a trustee is vested with a wide range of authority in connection with the case. Included among them are the powers to:

- File a proof of claim on behalf of a creditor who has not timely filed a claim. U.S.C. § 501(c).

- Operate the debtor's business:

    —unless otherwise ordered in Chapter 11 cases. U.S.C. § 1108.

    —if the court permits, for a short time before liquidation in a Chapter 7 case. U.S.C. § 721.

    —only if the debtor in possession has been removed in a Chapter 12 case.   U.S.C. §§ 1202(b)(5), 1203.

- Deposit or invest money of the estate. U.S.C. § 345.

- Employ professional persons (such as attorney, accountants, auctioneers, appraisers) but *only with prior court approval*. U.S.C. § 327(a).

- Avoid certain transfers and liens (*see trustee's avoiding powers below*) in order to enlarge the estate for the benefit of creditors. The Trustee has the status of a judgment lien creditor without priority, allowing the trustee to defeat unsecured creditors as well as secured, unperfected creditors. U.S.C. §§ 544-551, 553.

- Use, sell, or lease property of the estate. U.S.C. § 363.

- Obtain credit. U.S.C. § 364.

- Assume or reject executory contracts or unexpired leases. U.S.C. § 365.

- Demand utility services for the estate. U.S.C. § 366.

- Abandon property of the estate. U.S.C. § 554.

1.   Sale of Co-owned Property   Sections 363(g)-(j) allow the trustee to sell property free and clear of spousal interests, community property interests, or other co-ownership interests, including joint tenancy, tenancy by the entirety, and tenancy in common where four conditions are met:

- Partition of the property is impracticable;
- Sale of the estate's interest alone would result in significantly less money to the estate;
- The benefit to the estate outweighs the harm to the co-owner; and
- The property is not used to produce, transmit, or distribute electricity or gas for heat, light, or power.

Assuming that all four conditions are met and that a buyer is found, the trustee can sell the property free and clear of the co-owner's claim but must first give the co-owner the opportunity to buy the property at the proposed sale price. The proceeds of sale are to be paid in the following order: first, to the expenses of the sale; second, to the co-owner in his or her proportionate ownership interest; and third, to the estate.

2.   Abandonment of Property   Not all property of the estate has value. In some situations, the property has more liens against it than its value; in others, the cost of maintaining and selling a particular item is more than the property item is worth. When this occurs, § 554(a) allows the trustee to abandon the property.

Generally, abandonment is accomplished by the trustee, who files a notice of proposed abandonment of the property. Creditors and other parties in interest have 15 days to file an objection. If objections are filed, a hearing is scheduled. If no objection is filed, there is no hearing and no specific order is issued. The property is deemed abandoned. This procedure may vary among jurisdictions because of local court rules.

Property also can be abandoned by specific court order (based upon a creditor's motion to require the trustee to abandon) or by closing the estate without having administered all of the property listed on the debtor's schedules. If the debtor does not list the property, however, it remains property of the estate even though the estate has been closed.

C.   Duties   The duties of the trustee vary according to the chapter under which the trustee is appointed; however, many of the trustee's duties overlap from chapter to chapter. The duties of a Chapter 12 trustee are outlined in § 1202(b) of the Code and are similar to the duties of a Chapter 13 trustee as long as the debtor continues as the debtor in possession. If a Chapter 12 debtor is removed from possession, however, the trustee assumes many of the same duties as a Chapter 11 trustee appointed for cause, including the duty to operate the debtor's farm.

As a fiduciary, the trustee may be held personally liable for either an intentional or an unintentional (negligent) breach of duty. A trustee must file a bond with the court before assuming office.

A trustee may be removed for cause (misconduct, incompetence, conflict of interest). Notice and a hearing are required.

The table on the following page lists the trustee's duties under Chapters 7, 11 (appointed for cause), and 13. Where the trustee's duties are the same among the three chapters, those particular duties are shown on the same line all the way across the table.

Trustee Duties

Chapter 7 11 U.S.C. § 704	Chapter 11 11 U.S.C. § 1106(a)	Chapter 13 11 U.S.C. § 1302(b)
●Locate and take possession of estate property ●Convert the property to cash ●Make distributions to claimants in the order prescribed by the Code Close the estate expeditiously	●Make § 521 filings (list of creditors, assets and liabilities, statement of debtor's financial affairs, etc.) if not already filed by debtor ●Prepare and file Chapter 11 Plan (also periodic reports if plan is confirmed) or recommend conversion to another chapter	●Testify at hearings on valuation of property, confirmation of Chapter 13 Plan, or post-confirmation matters ●Provide nonlegal advice to debtor and assist debtor in implementing Plan ●Ensure that debtor begins making payments within 30 days after Plan is filed
Other Duties: ●Account for all property received ●Monitor debtor's intentions regarding collateral securing consumer debt ●Investigate debtor's financial affairs	●Account for all property received	●Disburse money to creditors under a confirmed Plan ●Account for all property received ●Monitor debtor's intentions regarding collateral securing consumer debt ●Investigate debtor's financial affairs
	●Investigate debtor's conduct, finances, and advisability of continuing debtor's business; file report and send copy to creditors' committee re fraud, dishonesty, mismanagement, etc.	●(If debtor operates a business) Investigate debtor's conduct, finances, and advisability of continuing debtor's business; file report re fraud, dishonesty, mismanagement, etc.
	●Examine proofs of claim and object to improper claims	●Examine proofs of claim and object to improper claims
●Object to debtor's discharge if warranted		●Object to debtor's discharge if warranted
●Provide information about estate as requested by parties in interest	●Provide information about estate as requested by parties in interest	●Provide information about estate as requested by parties in interest
●File periodic financial reports with the court and U.S. Trustee. If operating debtor's business, file returns with taxing authorities	●File periodic financial reports with the court, U.S. Trustee, and proper taxing authorities + tax information for any year when debtor failed to file a return	●File periodic financial reports with the court and U.S. Trustee.
●Prepare and file final report and accounting with the court and the U.S. Trustee	●Prepare and file final report and accounting with the court and the U.S. Trustee	●Prepare and file final report and accounting with the court and the U.S. Trustee

Examiner   If a trustee has not been appointed, an examiner may be appointed prior to confirmation of a plan in a Chapter 11 case to investigate any charges of fraud, dishonesty, incompetence, or gross mismanagement by the debtor's present or former management. An examiner also may be appointed if the court determines that it is in the best interests of the creditors and shareholders to do so.

Once appointed, the examiner's duties are:

- To investigate the debtor's conduct, financial condition, business operations, and advisability of continuing the debtor's business.

- To file a report of the investigation, relating any facts evidencing fraud, dishonesty, incompetence, misconduct, or gross mismanagement, and to send a copy of the report to any creditors' committee or equity holders' committee in existence.

- Any other responsibilities of a trustee that the court directs the debtor in possession not to perform.

An examiner in a particular Chapter 11 case cannot serve as the trustee (if one is appointed) and cannot be employed as a professional person by the trustee in that case.

Commencement of the Case

A bankruptcy case is commenced by filing a petition for relief under one of the chapters of the Bankruptcy Code. Regardless of whether the petition is voluntary or involuntary, the debtor must be one who is eligible for relief under a particular chapter of the Code.

Eligibility   Only a person residing or having a domicile, a place of business, or property in the United States is eligible to be a debtor. A person need not be insolvent to qualify for relief. § 109.

A person may be an individual, a partnership, or a corporation. The bankruptcy definition of corporation includes business trusts (trusts engaged in an active business other than preservation of assets), labor unions, and most companies or associations with corporate attributes. A limited partnership or a probate estate is not included in the definition.

*An individual or a family farmer is ineligible under **any** chapter if he or she has been a debtor in a case dismissed within the preceding 180 days either (1) because of intentional failure to obey court orders or (2) because of a voluntary dismissal following a party's request for relief from the automatic stay.*

Not every person is eligible for relief under every chapter of the Code. A particular debtor may be ineligible for relief under Chapter 13, for instance, but is eligible under Chapter 11.

A.   Chapter 7—Liquidation   Chapter 7 relief is available to any person **except** railroads, domestic and foreign savings institutions (including banks and credit unions), and insurance companies. Stockbrokers can file under special provisions of Chapter 7.

B.   Chapter 11—Reorganization   Only a person eligible for relief under Chapter 7 may be a debtor under Chapter 11 **except** stockbrokers, who can file *only* under Chapter 7. Railroads can file under special provisions of Chapter 11. Although Chapter 11 is designed primarily for business reorganizations, a few jurisdictions permit consumer debtors to file under this chapter. Chapter 11 also provides for liquidation of a debtor without the need to convert the case to Chapter 7.

C.   Chapter 12—Family Farmer   A family farmer with regular annual income (sufficiently stable to fund a reorganization plan) is eligible for relief under Chapter 12. An individual, a husband and wife, a corporation, or a partnership may qualify under this definition. Family farmer cases can be commenced only by voluntary petition.

D.   Chapter 13—Individual with Regular Income   Chapter 13 relief is available **only** to an individual who has regular income (sufficiently stable to fund a payment plan), whose total unsecured debts are less than $250,000, and whose total secured debts are less than $750,000 as of the date the petition for relief is filed. Stockbrokers, partnerships, and corporations cannot file under Chapter 13. This is sometimes called the consumer bankruptcy or wage earner plan and, like the family farmer case, can be commenced only by voluntary petition.

> Don Debtor is a sole proprietor of a business. He owns a home with a mortgage of $300,000 and has other secured debt of $50,000. His unsecured debts total $79,000. *Don is ineligible to file under Chapter 13, because his secured debt is not "less than $350,000."* However, on these facts, Don is eligible to file under either Chapter 7 or Chapter 11.

The "regular income" requirement is ordinarily satisfied with a salary or wages, but it can be satisfied with regular interest income, regular income from a business, rental income, a pension, trust income, social security benefits, or welfare benefits. The key is whether it constitutes regular, stable income to the debtor.

Voluntary Petition   A voluntary case is commenced when an eligible debtor files a petition for relief under Chapter 7, 11, 12, or 13 and pays the required filing fee. Upon application to the court, the filing fee can be paid in installments under special circumstances. No payment can be made to any party (including the debtor's attorney) until the filing fee is paid in full. Individuals who are married to each other may file a joint petition and pay a single filing fee.

Before filing, individuals with primarily consumer debts must be advised of each chapter under which they are qualified to file. Filing the petition automatically constitutes an order for relief, together with the automatic order of stay, under the Code.

A corporation must authorize filing the petition for relief by a resolution adopted by its Board of Directors. One or more general partners may file on behalf of a partnership but must obtain the consent of all other general partners; otherwise, the petition will be treated as involuntary.

A.   Schedules Required   In addition to the bankruptcy petition itself, a debtor must file a list of creditors and their addresses. Either with the petition or within 15 days after filing the petition, debtors must file a schedule of assets and liabilities; a schedule of current income and expenses; and a statement of the debtor's financial affairs. § 521. In a Chapter 7 or a Chapter 11 case, the debtor also must file a list of executory contracts.

1.   Chapter 7—Consumer Debtor   In addition to the schedules, a debtor with primarily consumer debts must include a statement with the Chapter 7 petition, showing that he or she knows that filing can occur under Chapter 7, (11 if applicable), 12, or 13. The attorney for the debtor must file a similar statement, certifying that the debtor has been advised of his or her eligibility and the relief available under Chapter 7, (11 if applicable), 12, or 13.

In addition, under both Chapters 7 and 13, a consumer debtor must file a statement of intentions concerning secured collateral (whether the debtor intends to retain it, to redeem it, or to surrender it).

2. **Chapter 11** In addition to the schedules, a debtor in a Chapter 11 case also must file a separate list disclosing the names and addresses of the creditors holding the twenty largest unsecured claims (excluding insiders) and the amounts of their claims, together with a detailed list of the debtor's equity security holders.

3. **Chapter 13** In addition to the schedules, a debtor in a Chapter 13 case also must file a proposed plan of repayment, a Chapter 13 statement, and (if the debtor is engaged in business) a statement of financial affairs for a debtor engaged in business. Similar to Chapter 7, the Chapter 13 debtor must file a statement of intentions concerning secured collateral (whether the debtor intends to retain, redeem, or surrender the collateral). Payments under the proposed plan are to commence within 30 days after the plan is filed regardless of confirmation. § 1326.

4. **Partnerships** In addition to the schedules, general partners may be required to file a statement of personal assets and liabilities by specific court order, with the time for filing fixed by the order.

Involuntary Petition An involuntary petition may be filed only in Chapter 7 or Chapter 11 cases and only against a person who qualifies as a debtor under one of those chapters. An involuntary petition cannot be filed against a bank, for instance, because a bank cannot qualify as a debtor under Chapter 7 or under Chapter 11.

An involuntary petition may not be filed under Chapter 12 or Chapter 13. Moreover, an involuntary petition may not be filed against a farmer, a family farmer, or a nonprofit (charitable) corporation.

An involuntary petition is filed to force the debtor into bankruptcy. If the debtor has twelve or more creditors, three or more of them must join in filing the involuntary petition. If the debtor has fewer than twelve creditors, only one is required to file the involuntary petition. Insiders, employees, and those holding avoidable transfers of the debtor's property are excluded when the number of creditors is computed.

Whether one or three or more, the petitioning creditors must (1) hold claims that total at least $10,000 in unsecured (or under-secured), noncontingent, undisputed debt and (2) must show that the debtor generally is not paying debts as they become due or that a custodian was appointed to take possession of the debtor's property within 120 days before the petition was filed. As with voluntary petitions, it is not necessary that the debtor be insolvent.

When an involuntary petition is filed, the case is commenced and the automatic stay goes into effect; but there is no order of relief until a hearing is held. Creditors can move for an order restricting the debtor's activities from the time of filing until the time of hearing. If granted, the order may appoint a trustee or, alternately, may prohibit the debtor from making transfers outside the ordinary course of business until the hearing is held.

The debtor must be served with a copy of the petition and a summons. He or she has twenty days to answer (contest) the involuntary petition. If the debtor does nothing, an order for relief will be entered by default. From this point forward, the case will proceed as if it were based upon a voluntary petition. If it is a Chapter 7 case, a trustee will be appointed. If it is a Chapter 11 case, the debtor will become a debtor in possession.

If the debtor contests the involuntary petition, it will be handled as an adversary proceeding. If the court finds in favor of the creditors at trial, an order for relief will be granted. If the court finds in favor of the debtor, the petition will be denied and damages may be granted to the debtor, including costs and attorney fees.

Once an order for relief is entered (whether by consent, default, or following a trial), the debtor may elect to convert the case to any other chapter under which he or she is qualified as a debtor.

> Creditors of Jack Jones dba Jones Company file an involuntary petition under Chapter 7. Jones consents to the order for relief but wants to convert to Chapter 13. He may do so, assuming that he has a regular source of income and assuming further that his total secured debt is less than $350,000 and his total unsecured debt is less than $100,000.

The Bankruptcy Estate

When an order for relief is entered (the date of filing for voluntary petitions), a bankruptcy estate is created automatically. It includes a wide range of property interests and property rights, regardless of where the property is located or who possesses it, as well as various claims and causes of action belonging to the debtor at the moment of filing.

The estate also includes certain types of property that the debtor acquires (or becomes entitled to acquire) within 180 days after the order of relief, such as an inheritance, divorce decree or settlement, life insurance proceeds, and property or funds generated or produced by existing property of the estate. The definition of estate property is so expansive that it may be easier to remember the **exclusions**:

●*Post-petition wages:* Wages earned by the debtor for personal services after filing the petition are excluded from Chapter 7 and Chapter 11 estates. (Compare Chapter 13, where post-petition, disposable income funds the Chapter 13 plan.)

●*Power held for third party:* A power or right held by the debtor but exercisable only for the benefit of a third party, such as the power of appointment in a will.

●*Interest in expired nonresidential lease:* Any interest held by the debtor in a nonresidential lease that expired before the debtor filed for relief is not estate property.

●*Property in which the debtor holds bare legal title:* When the debtor holds bare legal title and no equitable interest in property, it is property of the estate only to the extent of the legal title; the estate gains no equitable interest in the property.

> Debtor sells land to Buyer and carries a second mortgage for the down payment. Three years before filing for bankruptcy relief, Debtor sells (assigns) the second mortgage to Tom Tuffit for a small yacht. Although Debtor is the record mortgagee, Debtor holds no equity in the mortgage; and no equity passes to the estate. If the Debtor still owns the yacht, that property interest passes to the trustee.

●*Property (including money) acquired by fraud* or other tort is excluded from the estate.

●*Money paid into an employer-held pension plan.*

●*Property claimed as exempt* under U.S.C. § 522.

Exemptions Both the Bankruptcy Code and state law recognize that some property interests are so basic to survival, they should be protected from the reach of creditors. These property interests are known as exemptions under both state law and the Code and cannot be liquidated by creditors (or by the trustee in bankruptcy) unless the debtor is compensated for her exempt interest.

> Doris Debtor owns a car worth $4,000. The bank holds a purchase money security interest in the car, with a balance of $2,000 due on the loan. The allowable exemption for a vehicle is $1,200. The trustee in a Chapter 7 case could sell the car and pay the bank $2,000; pay Doris $1,200; and retain the balance of the sale price as estate property.

Section 522(d) of the Bankruptcy Code contains a list of allowable federal exemptions. Unless a particular state has "opted out" of the federal exemption schedule, the debtor may claim either federal or state exemptions, whichever are higher. *A list of the federal exemptions under § 522(d) is shown below.*

A majority of states have "opted out" of the federal exemptions, which means the debtor is limited to those exemptions created by state law and cannot claim the federal exemptions. Those states are: Alabama, Arizona, Arkansas, California, Colorado, Delaware, Florida, Georgia, Idaho, Illinois, Indiana, Iowa, Kansas, Kentucky, Louisiana, Maine, Maryland, Missouri, Montana, Nebraska, Nevada, New Hampshire, New York, North Carolina, North Dakota, Ohio, Oklahoma, Oregon, South Carolina, South Dakota, Tennessee, Utah, Virginia, West Virginia, and Wyoming.

When both spouses file for relief in a state which has opted out of the federal exemptions, most states require that the exemptions be shared between them. In states where federal exemptions are allowed, each spouse may claim the federal exemptions (U.S.C. § 522[m]) separately to the extent that they have total property interests (equity) in those amounts. However, U.S.C. § 522(b) prevents one spouse from claiming state exemptions, while the other claims federal exemptions. Even though many states have "opted out" of the federal exemptions, the CLA applicant nevertheless should know what the federal exemptions are.

FEDERAL EXEMPTIONS UNDER § 522(d)

Exempt Property Classification	Description
(1) Homestead	Maximum $15,000 in real or personal property (i.e., mobile home) which the debtor or a dependent uses as a resident or intends to use as a burial plot.
(2) Motor Vehicle	Maximum $2,400 in one motor vehicle.
(3) Household Goods	Maximum $8,000 in household furnishings, household goods, clothing, animals, books, crops, and musical instruments for the personal, family, or household use of the debtor or a dependent ($400 maximum for any single item).

| (4) | Jewelry | Maximum $1,000 in jewelry held primarily for personal, family, or household use of the debtor or a dependent. |

| (5) | General Exemption | Maximum $800 in any personal property item + maximum $7,500 of any unused portion of homestead exemption in (1) above. This exemption may be called the wild card exemption or the grubstake exemption. The debtor who rents (has no homestead exemption) may claim a maximum of $8,300 under this exemption. |

| (6) | Tools of the Trade | Maximum $1,500 in implements, professional books, or tools of the trade of the debtor or a dependent. |

| (7) | Life Insurance | Any unmatured life insurance contract owned by the debtor (other than credit life insurance). |

| (8) | Life Insurance Loan Value | Maximum $8,000 in accrued dividends, interest, or loan value of any unmatured life insurance contract if the insured is the debtor is a person upon whom the debtor is dependent. |

| (9) | Health Aids | Professionally prescribed health aids for the debtor or for a dependent |

| (10) | Benefits Similar to Earnings | Social Security; unemployment; public assistance; veteran's benefits; disability or illness benefit; alimony or support to the extent necessary for support of debtor or dependent; stock bonus, pension, profitsharing, or annuity due to illness, disability, age, retirement, or death to the extent necessary for support of debtor or dependent (with some exceptions for insiders). |

| (11) | Compensation for Losses | Crime victim's reparation award; wrongful death award for person upon whom debtor was dependent to the extent necessary for support; insurance payments for person upon whom debtor is dependent for support; maximum $15,000 for personal injury of debtor (other than pain and suffering and actual monetary losses) awarded to debtor or to a person upon whom the debtor is dependent; and payment for loss of future earnings to the extent necessary for support. |

Liens on Exempt Property   Section 522(f) of the Bankruptcy Code allows a debtor to avoid some types of liens that otherwise would impair exempt property, thus allowing the debtor to keep the property for a fresh start. They are:

(1)   Judicial liens; and

(2)   Nonpossessory, nonpurchase money security interests in:

■(2)(A):   household goods and furnishings, wearing apparel, appliances, books, animals, crops, musical instruments, or jewelry held primarily for personal, family, or household use of debtor or debtor's dependent;

■(2)(B):   implements, professional books, or tools of trade of debtor or debtor's dependent; and

■(2)(C):   professionally prescribed health aids of debtor or debtor's dependent.

A judicial lien is one obtained by judgment, levy, or other legal process. It does not include statutory liens, such as tax liens, mechanic's liens, and so forth. A judicial lien is avoidable on all types of property that the debtor may claim as exempt.

Conversely, a consensual nonpossessory, nonpurchase money security interest is avoidable only on the types of property specified in the statute (see above). A nonpossessory, nonpurchase money security interest on a vehicle, for instance, is *not avoidable* because vehicles are not among the listed property, even though a vehicle may be claimed as exempt under the federal exemptions (and under most state exemptions). A security interest given to secure the loan to purchase a refrigerator likewise is *not avoidable*, because it is a purchase money security interest.

A qualified lien can be avoided only to the extent that it impairs the exemption allowed to the debtor.

> Debtor is a professional writer. She owns a computer and monitor valued at $500 and a laser printer valued at $1,500, for a total value of $2,000. A judicial lien of $1,000 has attached to the equipment. Debtor files for bankruptcy relief. Exemption statutes in Debtor's state allow the Debtor to claim up to $500 in implements, professional books, and tools of the trade as exempt property. Since the Debtor's state has "opted out" of the federal exemptions, state exemption statutes apply in bankruptcy.

The debtor in this example cannot avoid the judicial lien on all of the computer equipment because her allowable exemption is only $500. That leaves $1,500 to satisfy a $1,000 judgment; the debtor's exemption is not impaired. The Debtor could, however, claim the computer and monitor as exempt property and could avoid the judicial lien as an impairment of the exemption for those two items.

Redemption   If exempt property is secured by a valid lien, U.S.C. § 722 allows a Chapter 7 debtor to redeem (purchase) the property from the secured creditor by paying its fair market value, even though the fair market value may be less than the amount owed. By paying the fair market value, the debtor obtains a release of the lien, without regard to the amount of the underlying debt.

In order to exercise the right of redemption, the property must be claimed as exempt or must be abandoned by the trustee; it must be personal property intended primarily for personal, family, or household use; and the redemption price must be paid to the secured creditor in one lump sum. (If the debtor and secured creditor agree to payment in installments, the procedure for reaffirmation agreements must be used.)

The intention to redeem property should be included with the statement of intentions that is filed with the debtor's schedules and accompanied by a motion to redeem property, since the debtor must perform her intention (redeem the property) within 45 days after the statement of intentions is filed.

Discrimination Prohibited   Debtors often are concerned that seeking bankruptcy relief will cause them to lose their jobs. Section 525 of the Code specifically prohibits such a result by forbidding governmental agencies and private employers from discriminating against a debtor solely because the debtor files a bankruptcy proceeding or does not pay a discharged debt.

The type of discrimination forbidden to governmental agencies is found in *Perez v. Campbell*, 402 U.S. 637 (1971), where the U.S. Supreme Court held that a state could not refuse to renew a driver's license because the debtor had not paid a discharged judgment. A debtor who believes that § 525 has been violated by a governmental agency or by an employer may commence an adversary proceeding under B.R. 7001.

The Code does not prohibit a lender from denying new credit or additional credit to a particular debtor when the denial is based upon the lender's determination that a bankruptcy filing indicates a poor credit risk.

Creditor's Right of Setoff   A creditor who is entitled to the right of setoff under state law may set off a debt owed to the debtor against a claim that she owes to the debtor, if both the claim and the debt are mutual and if both arose prior to the time the bankruptcy case was filed.

The trustee may avoid a setoff made by a creditor within 90 days prior to the filing of the petition to the extent that the creditor (often a bank) has improved its position. *(See trustee's avoiding powers below.)*

Trustee's Avoiding Powers

The trustee must identify, locate, and take possession of all estate property, with the goal of maximizing the distribution to creditors. To maximize the estate, the trustee is given a number of avoiding powers in relation to certain types of pre-petition and post-petition transfers. The trustee has the authority to exercise these avoiding powers and to pull property back into the estate, which, in turn, provides a larger pot for division among creditors.

Statutory Liens   Statutory liens are defined in U.S.C. § 101(47) as those liens arising solely by force of a statute. Examples might include a mechanic's lien, a materialman's lien, an artisan's lien, and so forth. Statutory liens do not include security interests consensually given by the debtor; neither do they include liens arising from enforcement of a judgment.

Section 545 of the Bankruptcy Code provides that the trustee can avoid a statutory lien if it is the type that becomes effective at the following times:

- At the commencement of the bankruptcy case or other insolvency proceeding.

- When a custodian is appointed.

- When the debtor becomes insolvent or fails to meet a particular financial standard.

- When another party levies on the debtor's property.

A statutory lien is also avoidable if a good faith purchaser could buy the property free and clear of the lien, such as a federal tax lien that has not yet been filed of record. Statutory liens for rent are avoidable by the trustee as well.

The trustee may avoid a statutory lien by filing a complaint to begin an adversary proceeding, which usually requests recovery of the property or its value in addition to relief to avoid the lien.

Fraudulent Transfers   A trustee has the power to avoid fraudulent transfers (and to disallow fraudulent obligations) that occurred *within one year* immediately before the petition was filed. U.S.C. § 548.

The first type of fraudulent transfer that can be avoided is one in which there was actual intent to hinder, delay, or defraud a present or future creditor. For instance, if a cattle breeder were to transfer all of his assets to a corporation and then file for personal bankruptcy relief six months later, the transfer may qualify as a fraudulent transfer. Because intent is difficult to prove unless the debtor admits this was his intent, many courts will infer actual fraud if the circumstances indicate that there could be no other, reasonable motivation.

The second type of fraudulent transfer that can be avoided is one in which the debtor received less than fair market value for the property transferred or for the obligation incurred *plus one* of the following elements:

●The debtor was insolvent at the time of the transfer or obligation (or became insolvent as a result of the transfer or obligation).

●The transfer or obligation left the debtor with unreasonably small capital to conduct his business or transactions.

●The debtor intended to incur (or believed that he would incur) debts beyond his abilities to repay.

> Joe Debtor's business was doing poorly, and he became concerned that his family home may be in jeopardy if creditors began to file suit. Joe conveyed the home to his mother for $10 plus love and affection, and his mother paid $10. Joe filed for bankruptcy relief six months later.

Even if the trustee could not prove intent in this example (which she probably could), the transaction nevertheless would qualify as a fraudulent conveyance of the second type. The transfer was for less than fair market value, and Joe was insolvent at the time.

To set aside the transfer and bring the property back into the estate, the trustee must commence an adversary proceeding by filing a complaint.

As a Successor Creditor

Section 544(b) of the Bankruptcy Code allows the trustee to stand in the shoes of an existing, unsecured creditor to avoid a transfer of property or to avoid the creation of a debt if the unsecured creditor would have been able to do so under state law.

In the immediately preceding example, for instance, if Joe had waited two years before seeking bankruptcy relief, the trustee could not set aside the transfer because of § 548's one-year limitation. The fraudulent conveyance statute under state law, however, generally provides a much longer limitation period. Assuming that the limitation period is two years or more, § 544(b) allows the trustee to "stand in the shoes" of an existing, unsecured creditor and seek to have the conveyance set aside. As a general rule, it is not difficult to find an unsecured creditor in the case who has not yet been paid.

As with fraudulent transfers, the trustee in this situation must file a complaint to begin an adversary proceeding.

As a Hypothetical Creditor

Section 544(a) of the Bankruptcy Code gives the trustee the hypothetical status—and the rights and powers—of (1) a judicial lien creditor, (2) a creditor with an unsatisfied execution, and (3) a bona fide purchaser of real property. Because of the powers granted under this section, it is sometimes called the trustee's "strong arm clause." With these powers, the trustee can avoid any transfer of the debtor's property that any of the three types of hypothetical creditors could avoid. It does not matter whether any such creditor actually exists in relation to a particular debtor.

As a hypothetical judicial lien creditor, for instance, the trustee is given the rights and powers of a hypothetical creditor who provides credit to a debtor at the time the bankruptcy case begins and who simultaneously acquires a judicial lien on as much of the debtor's property as may be permitted by applicable state law.

> On August 15, Doris Debtor borrows $2,000 to repair her car from Fast Finance Company, giving Fast Finance a security interest in the rare coin collection that she inherited from her uncle. On October 1, Doris files for bankruptcy relief. Fast Finance has not yet perfected its security interest. Since a judicial lien has priority over an unperfected security interest under the Uniform Commercial Code, the trustee's hypothetical judicial lien as of the date of filing will prevail over Fast Finance's unperfected security interest in the coin collection.
>
> On September 23, Doris Debtor obtains $500 from Fast Finance Company to buy a new refrigerator, which is purchased and delivered to her the same day. On October 1, Doris files for bankruptcy relief; on October 1, Fast Finance perfects its security

interest. Because of the ten-day grace period allowed under the
U.C.C. to perfect a purchase money security interest, the trustee's
hypothetical status as a judicial lien creditor cannot defeat Fast
Finance's purchase money lien status. If Fast Finance did not
perfect the lien until after the ten-day grace period had lapsed, the
trustee would prevail.

If a state's laws give more rights to a creditor whose execution has been returned
unsatisfied than to a judicial lienholder who has not yet tried to execute on the lien,
the trustee may exercise the rights of a hypothetical creditor whose execution has
been returned unsatisfied.

If there is any interest as of the date of filing that could be defeated by a
bona fide purchaser of real property (such as an unrecorded mortgage), the trustee
is given the same status as the hypothetical bona fide purchaser and likewise can
defeat the unrecorded mortgage.

If the trustee can use any hypothetical status provided in U.S.C. § 544(a) to
enlarge the bankruptcy estate, the proper procedure is for the trustee to file a
complaint to begin an adversary proceeding.

Preferences   Section 547 of the Bankruptcy Code authorizes the
trustee to avoid certain transfers made within 90 days before the petition was filed
when those transfers allow one unsecured creditor to benefit at the expense of all
other unsecured creditors. Recall that an under-secured creditor is an unsecured
creditor to the extent that the value of the collateral is less than the amount of the
debt.

Section 547(a) lists six elements, all of which must be present for a
preferential transfer to exist:

●A transfer of property of the debtor must be made.

●The transfer must be to or for the benefit of a creditor.

●It must be on account of an antecedent debt owed by the debtor.

●It must be made while the debtor is insolvent.

●It must be made within 90 days before the petition was filed (within
one year if the transferee was an insider).

●It must enable the transferee to receive more than it would have
received in a Chapter 7 liquidation if the transfer had not been made.

The term *transfer* is defined broadly and includes nearly every imaginable way of disposing of a property interest, whether voluntary or involuntary. It specifically includes the granting of a security interest that, if the other elements are present, could be avoided as a preference. The transfer must be of the *debtor's property*. If a third party pays a creditor, there is no preference because the debtor's property is not transferred.

The element of *to or for the benefit of a creditor* is met easily, as a general rule. A payment to a creditor is not a preference, however, unless it is for an antecedent debt owed by the debtor. A pre-payment or a payment made contemporaneously with delivery of goods is not on account of antecedent debt.

The transfer must have been made while the debtor was *insolvent* (assets less than liabilities). Although a debtor need not be insolvent to seek bankruptcy relief, most debtors are. In addition, there is a rebuttable presumption of insolvency during the *90 days* immediately before the petition is filed.

The transfer must give the creditor more than she would have received under a hypothetical Chapter 7 liquidation. If all creditors could be paid in full under a liquidation, there can be no preference.

A.   Exceptions   Section 547(b) lists seven types of transfers that may not be avoided by the trustee, even though they contain all elements required for a preferential transfer. They are:

- A substantially contemporaneous exchange for new value.

- A payment made and received in the ordinary course of business.

- A security interest given to a lender whose loan enabled the debtor to obtain the collateral given as security and which is perfected within ten days.

- A transfer where the transferee subsequently gave new value to the debtor (such as a pre-payment).

- A transfer to an account receivable or to an inventory financier whose position did not improve during the preference period.

- Any statutory lien that cannot be attacked successfully under § 545.

- A transfer by a consumer debtor that does not exceed $600.

The most commonly used preference exception is for ordinary course of business transactions. To qualify within this exception, the transaction must have been routine in the debtor's business, in the creditor's business, and in the course of dealing between the debtor and the creditor. The determination of what is ordinary varies from case to case. If a particular debtor has a history of paying a particular creditor's invoices within 30 days, a payment within 30 days is probably ordinary. If a particular payment is not made until the 42nd day, however, it may be a preferential transfer.

Post-Petition Transactions   The trustee may avoid transfers of estate property that occur after the petition is filed unless the transfer is specifically authorized by the Bankruptcy Code, is approved by the court, or falls within one of the following categories.

  A. **No Knowledge or Notice**   If the transferor has not received notice and has no knowledge of the bankruptcy proceeding, she is not liable for a post-petition transfer (such as a bank honoring the debtor's check). However, the post-petition payment may be subject to the trustee's avoiding powers.

  B. **Value Given**   The trustee may avoid a transfer made during the gap period (between date of filing and date of order for relief) in an involuntary case except to the extent that ***post-petition value*** is given (either goods or services) to the debtor.

  C. **Bona Fide Purchase of Real Estate**   If notice of the bankruptcy proceeding has not been filed in the recording office of the county where real estate is located, the trustee may not avoid a transfer to a bona fide purchaser of the real estate who does not know of the bankruptcy proceeding and who has paid present and fair equivalent value for the real estate.

Limitations on Trustee's Avoiding Powers   Most of the trustee's avoiding powers are subject to the limitation that the trustee file an action to avoid a transfer before (1) ***two years*** following permanent appointment of the trustee ***or*** (2) the time of ***closing or dismissal*** of the case.

  In addition, the Bankruptcy Code recognizes a seller's statutory (state law) or common law right to ***reclaim goods*** from an insolvent buyer when all of the following elements are present:

  •The property sought to be reclaimed is goods.

  •The sale was in the ordinary course of the seller's business.

● The debtor received the goods while the debtor was insolvent.

● The seller made written demand for reclamation within ten days after the debtor received the goods.

The right prevails over a trustee's power to avoid various transfers. In extraordinary situations, a court may deny reclamation; in that event, the seller of goods must be given either a lien securing her claim or an administrative expense priority. The Code's reclamation provision also recognizes a seller's state law right to stop goods in transit upon discovery of the debtor's insolvency. U.S.C. §§ 546(c)(2), 503(b).

Administration

In addition to the provisions within particular chapters, administration of all bankruptcy estates is governed generally by §§ 341-366 of the Bankruptcy Code. Regardless of the chapter under which a debtor's petition is filed, for example, all debtors are required to attend a meeting of creditors. In addition, there are certain rules governing all debtors in relation to the automatic stay, adequate protection, sale and use of estate property, executory contracts, utility service, obtaining credit, and the like.

Automatic Stay   The automatic stay provided in § 362 of the Bankruptcy Code is one of the most important benefits to the debtor. It is a type of injunction that applies to all entities (including governmental units) and takes effect at the time of filing the petition. The purpose of the automatic stay is to provide a respite for the debtor and to permit the orderly administration of the bankruptcy case. The automatic stay protects the debtor, property of the debtor, and property of the estate from certain types of creditor actions while the case is being administered.

A.   Acts Stayed by § 362

1.   Commencement or continuation of most types of legal proceeding against the debtor.

2.   All attempts to collect existing judgments against the debtor or the property of the debtor.

3.   All acts to obtain property of the estate or property over which the debtor has possession or control.

4.   All acts to create, to perfect, or to enforce liens against property of the estate.

5.   All acts to impose or to enforce liens against the debtor's property.

6.   All attempts to collect debt created before the filing of the petition.

7.   Setoff of debts due to the debtor against claims due from the debtor.

8.   Proceedings in the U.S. Tax Court concerning the debtor.

B.   Acts Not Stayed by § 362

1.   Commencement or continuation of criminal proceedings against the debtor.

2.   Collection of alimony, maintenance, or support from property that is not part of the bankruptcy estate (such as exempt property or post-petition income).

3.   Perfection of security interests in property if the Code provides that the trustee takes the property subject to those security interests.

4.   Actions by governmental units to enforce police or regulatory powers, such as environmental controls, consumer safety regulations, or anti-fraud measures.

5.   Enforcement of restraining orders and injunctions obtained by governmental units to enforce police or regulatory powers.

6.   Issuance of tax deficiency notices to the debtor by a governmental unit.

7.   Eviction of the debtor from nonresidential real estate under an expired lease.

8.   Presentation of negotiable instruments (such as checks) for payment and protest of the nonpayment of such negotiable instruments.

9.   *Chapter 11 Only:* Foreclosures by Secretary of Transportation or by the Secretary of Commerce of certain ship or vessel security interests after 90 days have expired following the filing of the Chapter 11 petition.

10.   *Chapter 11 Only:* Repossession of certain aircraft, aircraft equipment, and vessels by lessors, conditional vendors, or secured creditors with purchase-money security interests (with some limitations).

Since the automatic stay is for the benefit of the debtor, the property of the debtor, and the property of the bankruptcy estate, its protection generally does not extend to others. The exception is in a Chapter 13 case, which provides a co-debtor stay.

> Joe and his father are co-signers on a loan at Second National Bank. The loan is in default. Joe files for relief under Chapter 7. Second National Bank may proceed against Joe's father, even though the automatic stay prevents the Bank from proceeding against Joe. *(If Joe had filed under Chapter 13, the stay would have extended to his father as well.)*

> Joe dba Joe's Lawn Service has a business account with Frank's Fertilizer Co. Joe's father is the guarantor for that account, which is past due. Joe files for relief under Chapter 11. The automatic stay protects Joe but not his father. *(If Joe had filed under Chapter 13, the stay would have extended to his father as well.)*

Relief from the Automatic Stay   The automatic stay enjoins acts against estate property from the time the petition is filed until the property is no longer part of the estate (such as when it is abandoned by the trustee). It enjoins all other acts until (1) the debtor is discharged or (2) relief from the stay is granted by court order.

Relief from the automatic stay may be granted for cause, upon request to the court, after notice and hearing. Generally, the request for relief is made by a secured creditor as to specific property in which it holds a security interest. For relief to be granted, the creditor must show:

●the debtor has no equity in the property; and

•the property is not necessary for an effective reorganization (debtor cannot reorganize successfully in a reasonable period of time).

In a Chapter 7 case, reorganization is not an issue; thus, the debtor's equity in the property often becomes the central issue.

As it applies to relief from the automatic stay, **cause** can include such things as **bad faith** on the part of the debtor, either in the debtor's conduct after the petition is filed or in seeking bankruptcy relief at all (in some situations).

The party requesting relief (usually a creditor) has the burden of proof on the issue of the debtor's equity in the property; the party opposing relief (usually the debtor) has the burden of proof on all other issues, including the issue of adequate protection (see below).

When the court decides that relief should be granted to the creditor, the court can terminate the stay; annul the stay (effective as of the date when the bankruptcy petition was originally filed); modify the stay; or place conditions on the stay.

Adequate Protection   Another basis for obtaining relief from the automatic stay is **lack of adequate protection.** In other words, the creditor claims that the value of the secured property is being depleted in the hands of debtor to such an extent that the creditor's security is impaired. Once a creditor raises the issue of lack of adequate protection, the debtor must show that the creditor's value in the secured property is adequately protected. This can be done in a number of different ways:

•*Payments* (periodic or lump sum) to compensate for any depletion of the collateral.

•Lien on other property, that is, the trustee may provide the creditor with an *additional or replacement lien* on other collateral in which the estate has equity.

•If the trustee or debtor provides a creditor with the *indubitable equivalent* of its secured position, the creditor is adequately protected. The indubitable equivalent standard is purposely vague to give the flexibility needed to fashion whatever protection may be necessary in a particular situation.

•*Guaranty* by another, assuming that a suitable and willing guarantor can be found.

•*Equity cushion* in the collateral, which is available in situations where the creditor is over-secured.

Use, Sale, or Lease of Property   Issues related to the use, sale, or lease of property arise most often in Chapter 11 cases (business reorganizations) and Chapter 12 cases (family farmer). Section 363(c)(1), together with Bankruptcy Rule 1107 (B.R. 1206 for family farmers), authorizes the debtor in possession to use, sell, or lease property of the estate without court approval as long as the use, sale, or lease is in the ordinary course of business. Any use, sale, or lease of property outside the ordinary course of business, however, requires either the consent of the creditor holding a lien on the property or court approval.

Property of the estate often includes ***cash collateral***, since many creditors obtain security interests in cash accounts, deposit accounts, and the like in exchange for extending credit to the debtor. For cash to be cash collateral, it must be subject to a creditor's lien. Cash from other sources is not subject to the restrictions placed on cash collateral. Typical examples of cash collateral might include cash from the sale of crops; sale of a delivery van; cash from the sale of inventory; or rents received from an office building. If a creditor holds a valid lien in property and its proceeds, the proceeds are the creditor's cash collateral.

Since cash flow is the lifeline of most businesses, the debtor in possession who wants to use cash collateral has two choices: (1) obtain the consent of each creditor having a security interest in the cash collateral or (2) obtain a court order approving its use. Subject to the accounting and reports required of debtors in possession throughout the bankruptcy reorganization, creditors often will stipulate to a structured, restricted use of cash collateral in order to preserve their overall security interests. This may be done by stipulation between the debtor and the creditor, but the stipulation also must be approved by the court.

Debtors in possession (and/or their attorneys) who use cash collateral without the consent of secured creditors or without an appropriate court order may be required to compensate for the expended cash from their personal funds.

Executory Contracts and Unexpired Leases   With the court's approval, the trustee (or debtor in possession under Chapters 11 and 12) may assume or reject an executory contract or an unexpired lease.

To qualify as an executory contract, there must be sufficient performance remaining on both sides so that if there were a breach by one party, it would excuse the other party from performing.

> A property management contract is executory. If the owner fails to pay the management fee, the manager will be excused from performing further management duties.
>
> An installment sale contract is not executory. The seller has already delivered possession of the goods; there is nothing left for the seller to do but to collect the monthly payments from the buyer.

To qualify as an unexpired lease, the transaction must be a true lease, not just a secured transaction that is called a lease.

> A lease of a photocopy machine, under which the lessee makes monthly lease payments and then pays $1.00 (or other nominal amount) at the end of the lease term to own the machine, is not a true lease. It is a secured transaction.

A.   Rejection   When considering a request to reject an executory contract or an unexpired lease, courts apply the business judgment rule and approve the trustee's request unless bad faith or gross abuse of discretion is shown. Good business judgment is demonstrated when the trustee can show a financial savings by rejecting the present contract and (1) entering into a less expensive contract or (2) entering into no contract at all.

Generally, rejection constitutes a breach of the contract or lease, giving the nonbreaching party the right to file a claim for damages but not for specific performance. If a claim for damages is filed with the estate, it will be treated as a pre-petition claim and will be paid on the same basis as all other pre-petition claims against the estate.

Specialized and more stringent standards for rejection apply to certain types of contracts where it would be inequitable to allow a trustee or a debtor in possession to reject. These include executory contracts where the debtor is the seller or is the landlord of real property; is the licensor of rights to intellectual property; has entered into a collective bargaining agreement; or puts the medical, accident, or death benefits of retired employees at risk (pension plans). In these situations, the nondebtor party to the executory contract is given greater protections than nondebtor parties to other types of executory contracts. As to a collective bargaining agreement, for instance, the trustee or debtor in possession must demonstrate a good faith attempt to work out a modification of the collective bargaining agreement before rejection will be allowed.

B.   Assumption   Some executory contracts cannot be assumed without the other party's consent. They include:

- Personal services contracts (contract to hire a nanny or contract to paint a portrait);

- Contracts to lend money or to make other types of financial accommodations to the debtor; and

- Contracts to issue the securities for the debtor (stocks, bonds, debentures, and so forth).

Some contracts and leases contain provisions that the agreement will terminate upon the debtor's insolvency or upon the commencement of a bankruptcy proceeding. These provisions are called *ipso facto clauses* and are unenforceable. They do not prevent the trustee or the debtor in possession from assuming the contract when there is good reason to assume it (such as financial benefit or gain to the estate).

The rules for assumption are more stringent than the rules for rejection. If a contract or lease is assumable and if the trustee or debtor in possession wants to assume it, certain conditions must be met by the trustee or debtor in possession at the time of the assumption for the court to give its approval:

- Cure all defaults (other than those created by ipso facto clauses) or give adequate assurance that the defaults will be cured promptly.

- Compensate the other party for losses incurred as a result of the debtor's breach or give adequate assurance of compensation.

- Provide adequate assurance that the contract or the lease will be fully performed by the debtor in the future.

C.   Assignment   If a contract or a lease has monetary value, it may be beneficial to the estate for the trustee or the debtor in possession to assign (sell) the rights to a third party.

> The debtor may have a contract right to purchase equipment that it can no longer use in its business operation. If the equipment is worth $16,000 and if the debtor (now the estate) has the right to purchase the equipment for only $11,000, the estate may be able to assign that right to a third party for $4,000.   Under this

> arrangement, the equipment seller would receive the full $11,000 contract price; the third party would save $1,000 on the market price by paying $4,000 to the estate and $11,000 to the seller; and the estate would gain $4,000.

To assign a contract or a lease, the trustee or debtor in possession must first assume it from the debtor. The assumption and the assignment often are completed at the same time, with adequate assurance of performance given by the third party. Like ipso facto clauses, restrictions on assignment in the contract or in the lease are unenforceable.

Once the contract or lease has been assigned, the estate has no further liability in the event of breach.

D.   Time Limitations   In a Chapter 7 case, assumption or rejection of executory contracts or unexpired leases for personal property or for residential real estate must occur within 60 days after the order for relief under U.S.C. § 365(d). The date of the order of relief will vary, depending upon whether the petition was voluntary or involuntary. In a Chapter 11, 12, or 13 case, the time for assumption or rejection can be any time prior to confirmation of the plan, with the exact date set by the court.

Assumption or rejection of unexpired leases for nonresidential (commercial) real estate under any chapter generally must occur within 60 days after the order for relief, and the trustee or debtor in possession must timely perform all obligations required by the lease from the time of the order for relief until the time of assumption or rejection.

Utility Service   A debtor's utility service may not be discontinued, altered, or refused due to the filing of a petition for relief in bankruptcy or due to a failure to timely pay a utility bill for services furnished before the order for relief. Utility services may be discontinued, altered, or refused, however, if the trustee or the debtor in possession fails to pay a deposit or other security within 20 days after the order for relief. This deposit provides assurance to the utility company that it will be paid for services provided after the date of the order for relief.

Obtaining Credit   When a business operation is part of the bankruptcy estate, the trustee or debtor in possession may obtain credit or incur debt without prior court approval in the ordinary course of business (trade accounts, supplies, and so forth used routinely in the business). To encourage creditors to deal with businesses in this situation, the Bankruptcy Code gives this type of post-petition debt an administrative expense priority.

Debt or credit obtained out of the ordinary course of business (such as an operating loan) requires prior court approval to be treated as an administrative expense. If prior approval is not obtained, the lender will be treated as a general, unsecured creditor.

Prospective post-petition lenders may not be satisfied with an administrative expense priority, even though this is the first level of unsecured claims to be paid. In these situations, after notice and hearing, the court may authorize credit to be acquired or debt to be incurred on one of the following bases:

Super-superpriority: The court may authorize a super-superpriority claim to be paid before all administrative expense claims and before all superpriority claims. *Superpriority claims are those paid to give adequate protection to secured creditors whose collateral is being depleted or diminished by its continued use.*

Lien on Unencumbered Property: The court may authorize secured debt or credit by granting a lien on all or part of the unencumbered property of the estate.

Junior Lien on Unencumbered Property: The court may authorize secured debt or credit by granting a junior lien on property of the estate that is already encumbered.

Debtor's Duties

Implicit in all conduct of the debtor is the obligation to act in good faith in all dealings with the court, its officers and representatives, and others.

In addition to filing the required schedules and fulfilling other procedural requirements, the debtor must cooperate with the trustee, must relinquish estate property and all relevant records, and must appear at the discharge hearing (individuals only) if one is held. Many local court rules dispense with attendance at the discharge hearing if no objection to discharge has been filed and if no reaffirmation agreement requires the court's approval.

In a Chapter 7 case, an individual debtor with secured consumer debts must file a statement of intention either to retain or to surrender collateral and then must perform the stated intention in a timely manner.

Section 341 Meeting of Creditors

Within 20 to 40 days after the order for relief, a § 341 meeting of creditors is held. (Under the prior Bankruptcy

Act, this meeting was called the first meeting of creditors.) § 341. The debtor must attend in person. Since the meeting is not a judicial hearing, the United States Trustee or an assistant presides.

The purpose of the meeting of creditors is to permit creditors, the trustee, or the United States Trustee to examine the debtor under oath about issues related to the case. The examination might include questions related to the schedules or statement of affairs filed in connection with the debtor's petition for relief, valuations of property listed on the schedules, or facts that may indicate bad faith on the part of the debtor.

The clerk of the court provides notice by mail to all parties in interest (including all creditors) at least 20 days prior to the meeting of creditors. If notice by mail is impracticable, notice may be accomplished by publication. In addition to the time and place of the meeting of creditors, the notice ordinarily includes identity of the debtor's attorney, notice of the order for relief, and final dates for filing proofs of claim, objections to dischargeability of a particular debt, and objections to the debtor's discharge.

Conversion

No matter how carefully the decision to file under a particular chapter was made originally, events can occur that make proceeding under another chapter more advantageous. Switching from one chapter to another is accomplished by converting the case to the new chapter. The rules for conversion vary from chapter to chapter, but the one universal rule is that a debtor can convert only to those chapters under which the debtor could have filed originally.

> Ruth owns Rent-It-All, a residential property management company, which provides her only source of income. She originally filed for relief under Chapter 11 but is finding it too cumbersome for her small business. Ruth wants to convert to a different chapter. Since Ruth qualified to file under Chapter 7, 11, or 13 at the time of the original filing, she may convert either to Chapter 7 or 13. She cannot convert to Chapter 12 because she was not qualified originally to file under that chapter.

When a case is converted from one chapter to another, the conversion constitutes an order for relief under the new chapter but generally does not change the date of the commencement of the case, which remains the date of the original order of relief. If this were not so, debtors could avoid the consequences of preferences or of fraudulent transfers simply by converting a case to a different chapter.

Other deadlines and requirements may be affected by the transfer, however. If a case is converted from Chapter 13 to Chapter 7, for instance, the deadline for filing a complaint to determine dischargeability of a particular debt is different in Chapter 7 than it was in Chapter 13. If a case is converted from Chapter 11 to Chapter 7, the requirement for filing proofs of claim will be different. If the claim is accurately listed in the Chapter 11 schedules, no proof of claim is required. Unless a proof of claim is filed in a Chapter 7 case, however, the creditor will not share in distribution in most jurisdictions.

When a case is converted to Chapter 7 from either Chapter 11 or Chapter 13, a new time period begins for purposes of filing § 523 complaints to determine dischargeability of a particular debt. B.R. 1019(3). This rule does not apply, however, if the case is being reconverted and if the original period expired in the original Chapter 7 proceeding.

Chapter 7 Conversion

Because Congress favors reorganization over liquidation, § 706(a) of the Code allows a debtor to convert a Chapter 7 case to Chapter 11, 12, or 13 at any time, as a matter of right. No court approval is needed unless the case was previously converted to Chapter 7 from a different chapter. In the latter event, the court must approve the conversion upon notice to creditors and hearing.

A party in interest (such as the trustee) can request that a Chapter 7 case be converted to Chapter 11 but not as a matter of right. The nondebtor making this request must file a motion, giving 20 days' notice of the hearing to creditors. B.R. 2002(a), B.R. 9014. Unlike Chapter 11, Chapters 12 and 13 can be initiated only by voluntary petition; the court cannot require a debtor to convert to either of these chapters.

Chapter 11 Conversion

If a Chapter 11 case was started voluntarily and if the debtor in possession retains custody of estate property (rather than a court-appointed trustee), the *debtor in possession* may convert to Chapter 7 as *a matter of right*. However, if the case was commenced by involuntary petition, if the case was previously converted to Chapter 11 by a nondebtor, or if a trustee was appointed to replace the debtor in possession, the debtor cannot convert to Chapter 7 without court approval.

When creditors or other *parties in interest* want a Chapter 11 case converted to Chapter 7 liquidation, conversion can occur only upon motion and hearing and *only for cause*. Cause for conversion may be based upon fraud or gross mismanagement by the debtor in possession or may be based upon one or more of the occurrences listed in § 1112(b):

●Continuing losses or diminution of the estate, with no reasonable likelihood of rehabilitation.

●Inability to effectuate a plan of reorganization.

●Unreasonable and prejudicial delay to creditors.

●Debtor's failure to propose a plan.

●The court's denial or revocation of confirmation of a plan.

●Debtor's inability to substantially consummate the plan or debtor's material default under the provisions of the plan.

●Termination of the plan due to the failure to meet a specific condition of the plan.

Chapter 13 Conversion   The debtor has an absolute right to convert a Chapter 13 case to Chapter 7 at any time. If a party in interest other than the debtor wants to convert the case to Chapter 7, the request must be made by motion; and the court may convert the case if cause is shown. (The Bankruptcy Rules do not provide for any specific notice or hearing in this situation.) Examples of *cause* are found in B.R. 1307(c):

●Debtor's unreasonable and prejudicial delay

●Debtor's nonpayment of fees and charges assessed under the Bankruptcy Code

●Debtor's failure to file a plan on time or failure to commence timely payments under the plan

●The court's denial of confirmation of a plan or revocation of a previously confirmed plan

●Occurrence of a material default in the provisions of a plan or termination of the plan

Conversion of a Chapter 13 case to Chapter 11 is solely within the court's discretion. If conversion is to occur, it must be requested by a party in interest (the debtor, the trustee, a creditor) and approved by the court prior to the time that a plan is confirmed.

Chapter 12 Conversion   Section 1208 of the Code governs conversion of Chapter 12 and, similar to debtors under Chapters 11 and 13, a family farmer may convert to Chapter 7 at any time, as a matter of right.

It is virtually impossible for anyone other than the debtor in possession (family farmer) to force a conversion to any other chapter. An interested party may request conversion to Chapter 7 by motion, but the court may convert the case only if the family farmer has committed fraud in connection with the bankruptcy case. A nondebtor party in interest may be able to have the case dismissed for cause, such as failure to file a timely plan, but cannot force a liquidation under any chapter (absent fraud) because involuntary petitions cannot be filed against family farmers.

Dismissal

The reasons for dismissing a bankruptcy case are as varied as the participants in the bankruptcy process. A debtor may want to dismiss the case if she no longer needs the bankruptcy protections or if bankruptcy is not the panacea that she thought it would be. A creditor may want to dismiss the case if it believes the case was filed in bad faith and wants to pursue its remedies under state law. The trustee may want to dismiss the case if the debtor refuses to cooperate. The court may want to dismiss the case if the debtor fails to pay an installment of the filing fee. The requirements for dismissal vary from chapter to chapter.

If a case is dismissed without prejudice, the debtor may refile at any time. If it is dismissed with prejudice, however, the debtor must wait 180 days. § 109(f). Upon dismissal, liens, pending lawsuits, and so forth revert to their pre-petition status; and creditors may proceed with any remedies available to them under state law.

Chapter 7 Dismissal   Dismissal of a Chapter 7 case requires a finding of cause by the court, after notice and hearing. § 707(a).

Chapter 11 Dismissal   Dismissal of a Chapter 11 case requires the court's approval, upon a finding of cause. In deciding whether to dismiss a case under Chapter 11 or to convert it to another chapter, the court is required to do whatever is in the best interests of the creditors and of the estate, regardless of whether it is in the best interests of the debtor.

Chapter 12 Dismissal The debtor in a Chapter 12 case has an absolute right to dismiss the case unless it has been previously converted from another chapter, in which event dismissal can occur only with the court's approval. In addition, § 1208(c) provides that upon request of a party in interest, after notice and hearing, the court may dismiss a Chapter 12 case for cause. That section defines cause in essentially the same way as cause is defined under a Chapter 11 case, including (in part): unreasonable delay or gross mismanagement; nonpayment of fees and costs; failure to file a timely plan or to make timely payments under a confirmed plan; denial of confirmation; or continuing loss to or diminution of the estate, with no reasonable likelihood of rehabilitation.

Chapter 13 Dismissal Like Chapter 12, a Chapter 13 debtor has an absolute right to dismiss the case unless it has been previously converted from another chapter, in which event the court's approval must be obtained. In addition, a party in interest may request dismissal for cause, defined in the same way as cause is defined for purposes of involuntary conversion. Section 1307(c) requires the court to do whatever is in the best interest of the creditors and the estate, without regard to the best interest of the debtor.

Claims of Creditors

In the process of administering a bankruptcy estate, the claims of creditors are reviewed, categorized, and paid (or not paid) based upon the assets in the estate and the category into which a particular creditor fits. Creditor claims may be classified as priority, secured, or unsecured.

Filing Proofs of Claims Other than a Chapter 11 creditor, each creditor is required to file a proof of claim within 90 days after the first date set for the § 341 meeting of creditors. If this deadline is missed, the claim is barred.

A Chapter 11 creditor need not file a proof of claim unless the debt is listed incorrectly on the debtor's schedules or unless the case is converted to another chapter. Cautious practitioners generally file proofs of claims in all cases so that Chapter 11 conversions do not catch them off guard. When a Chapter 11 case is converted, the creditor who has already filed a proof of claim is not required to file another one in the converted case.

If a claim cannot be filed within the filing period (such as claims arising from adversary proceedings or claims based upon executory contracts that are rejected after the deadline has passed), those claims must be filed within the time specially set by the court.

Claim forms can be obtained from the court or from a legal stationer; they are self-explanatory for the most part. Creditors are required to state whether the claim is priority (giving details to support the priority), secured (attaching proof of the security interest), or unsecured.

If a creditor does not file a claim, the trustee or the debtor may do so to ensure that the claim is discharged when the estate is closed.

Allowance of Claims

Unless the debtor, trustee, or other party in interest objects to a particular claim, the claim will be allowed (recognized by the court as a valid claim). This does not ensure that the claim will be paid, however.

Following objection, a particular claim may be disallowed or may be disallowed in part for any one of the many reasons listed in § 502(b), including existence of any valid nonbankruptcy defense (statute of limitations, failure of consideration, and so on), post-petition interest claimed for an unsecured debt, unmatured alimony or child support, and so forth.

Administrative Expenses

Those expenses incurred in the administration of the bankruptcy estate are called administrative expenses and are entitled to priority status in the distribution of estate assets (after creditors with valid liens on estate property are paid). U.S.C. §§ 503, 507(a)(1). Some of these are:

- *Post-petition credit obtained to continue operation of a business during administration;*
- *Post-petition costs of preserving the estate;*
- *Post-petition taxes of the estate;*
- *Compensation of trustee, examiner, debtor's attorney, and other professional persons;*
- *Expenses connected with filing an involuntary petition; and*
- *Expenses of a pre-petition custodian (receiver, trustee, or the like).*

Priority Claims

Priority claims are unsecured claims that are given priority over general, unsecured claims for purposes of payment. When such a claim is allowed, it is paid according to its level of priority. The priority level of claims, ranked in their order of payment, are:

SUPER-SUPERPRIORITY   *Post-petition credit* granted to the trustee or debtor in possession (with court approval) when post-petition credit cannot be obtained with only an administrative expense priority.

SUPERPRIORITY   *Adequate protection* given to a creditor whose secured lien position is diminished, for instance, by debtor's continued use of the collateral during administration of the estate.

FIRST PRIORITY   *Administrative expenses* (*see above*).

SECOND PRIORITY   Allowed claims of *gap creditors* in an involuntary case (claims incurred during the gap between filing the involuntary petition and granting the order of relief).

THIRD PRIORITY   *Wages*, salaries, or commissions earned by an individual *within 90 days* before bankruptcy or cessation of debtor's business, whichever is earlier. Limitation: $4,000 maximum for each claimant.

FOURTH PRIORITY   Contributions to *employee benefit plans* for services rendered *within 180 days* before bankruptcy or cessation of debtor's business, whichever is earlier. Limitation: Number of employees covered by the plan x $4,000 minus total amount paid to such employees as third priority claims.

FIFTH PRIORITY   Claims of *grain farmers and U.S. fishermen* against debtor who owns or operates grain (or fish) storage or processing facilities. Limitation: $4,000 for each claimant.

SIXTH PRIORITY   *Consumer claims* for prepayment or deposit of money with the debtor for goods or services intended for personal, family, or household use of claimant ("*layaway*" provision). Limitation: $1,800 for each claimant.

SEVENTH PRIORITY   Unsecured, *pre-petition tax claims*, including income tax for three years prior to bankruptcy; property tax; trust fund tax (employee withholding taxes); employment tax; excise tax; customs duties; and penalties on seventh priority tax claims.

Payment of Claims

After exemptions allowed to the debtor, the claims of creditors are paid according to (1) their class or category (whether secured, priority, or unsecured) and (2) their level within that class (applies only to priority claims).

All secured creditors are paid first, based upon the value of the collateral at the time the bankruptcy petition was filed. If the debt is more than the value of the collateral, the deficiency is treated as a general, unsecured claim; and the deficiency is paid only to the extent that all other general (unsecured) creditors are paid.

Priority creditors are paid next, according to their level of priority. If there is enough money to pay all allowed claims within the highest level of priority claims in full, the trustee pays those claims and then moves down to the next level. The trustee continues in this manner until all priority claims at all levels are paid in full. If the money runs out at any level, allowed claims within that level are paid on a pro-rata basis; and the remaining levels of priority claims, if any, are not paid.

If all priority claims are paid in full, the trustee pays the balance (if any) to general, unsecured creditors on a pro-rata basis. Assuming that all creditors within this class are fully paid from estate assets, the remaining assets are returned to the debtor.

> Second Bank files a proof of claim for $1000, secured by collateral valued at $800. The debtor continues to use the collateral in her business during administration of the estate. Second Bank requests adequate protection and receives a superpriority lien that amounts to $300, the difference between $800 and the value of the collateral at the time it is ultimately sold. Second Bank's claim falls into three classes:
>
> $500   secured by collateral (paid first, from sale of collateral)
> 300   priority, superpriority level
> 200   general, unsecured

Discharge

In exchange for giving up all non-exempt property to the trustee in a Chapter 7 case or making payments as required under the plan (Chapter 11, 12, or 13), the individual debtor receives a discharge or a complete forgiveness of most debts. Corporations cannot receive a discharge *per se*; but since the corporation will have no assets left at the end of the bankruptcy proceeding (exemptions are available only to individuals), the effect will be the same.

Discharge generally bars any future collection against the debtor for those debts incurred before the petition for relief was filed. There are situations through which the debtor can lose the right to discharge and, with it, most of the benefits of bankruptcy. In other situations, the debtor may lose the right to discharge a particular debt. Even if the debtor fully complies with all rules and completes the bankruptcy case, some types of debts will survive the bankruptcy case. In other words, some debts are simply nondischargeable.

<u>Denial of Discharge</u>   By engaging in what Congress had declared to be bad conduct in § 727 of the Code, a debtor may be denied a discharge. This conduct includes:

●The debtor transferred, destroyed, or concealed property within one year before the petition was filed or transferred, destroyed, or concealed post-petition property with the intent to defraud a creditor or the trustee.

●The debtor unjustifiably concealed, destroyed, falsified, or failed to keep or preserve the books and records necessary to determine the debtor's financial affairs, condition, or business transactions.

●In connection with the bankruptcy case, the debtor knowingly and fraudulently made a false oath; presented a false claim; gave, offered, received, or attempted to obtain money, property, or unfair advantage for acting or for forbearance to act; or withheld books and records related to the debtor's property or financial affairs from the trustee.

Without regard to bad conduct, a debtor will be denied a discharge if:

●The debtor is not an individual.

●The debtor received a discharge in a Chapter 7 or Chapter 11 case filed within six years before the date when the pending petition for relief was filed (measured from filing date to filing date).

●The debtor received a discharge in a Chapter 12 or Chapter 13 case filed within six years before the date when the pending petition for relief was filed (measured from filing date to filing date) unless payments under the plan in the previous case totaled at least:

    1.   100% of all of the allowed, unsecured claims in that case; or

    2.   70% of such claims and the plan was proposed in good faith and was the debtor's best effort; or

    3.   The court approves a written waiver of discharge executed by the debtor after the order for relief in the present case.

If requirement 1, 2, or 3 (*above*) can be met, the effect is to permit discharge of a Chapter 12 or 13 debtor more often than once every six years.

Objection to Discharge   If the trustee, a creditor, or other interested party opposes a debtor's discharge under § 727, the opponent must file a complaint within 60 days of the § 341 meeting of creditors. Filing of the complaint begins an adversary proceeding. R. 4004.

Revocation of Discharge   Section 727(d) allows a creditor, the trustee, or the United States Trustee to attempt to revoke a discharge previously granted if any of the following occurs:

- The discharge was obtained by fraud of the debtor and the creditor (or the trustee) was unaware of the fraud when the discharge was granted.

- The debtor acquired (or became entitled to acquire) property of the estate but knowingly and fraudulently failed to report it or to deliver the property to the trustee.

- The debtor engaged in one of the incidents of bad conduct described previously (see *denial of discharge, infra*).

The complaint for revocation must be filed within one year after the discharge was granted or within one year after the case was closed, whichever is later. If the discharge was obtained by fraud, the complaint must be filed within one year after the discharge was granted.

Nondischargeable Debts   Some debts cannot be discharged for any debtor as a matter of policy determined by Congress. They are listed in § 523 of the Bankruptcy Code and survive a discharge without any requirement that the creditor do anything. Once the case is closed, creditors holding these types of claims are free to pursue the debtor for their collection. They are:

- Taxes (essentially those incurred within three years before filing for bankruptcy relief), as well as all taxes for which the debtor failed to file a return or filed a fraudulent return;

- Debts that were not listed on the schedules filed with the petition for relief, where the creditor did not have knowledge of the bankruptcy case in time to file a proof of claim or to take action to contest the dischargeability of the debt.

- Alimony, maintenance, and child support.

- Student loans in repayment less than five years (unless it would be an "undue hardship" on the debtor or the debtor's dependents to exempt the loan from discharge).

- Fines, penalties, and forfeitures payable to a governmental unit.

•Debts arising from a judgment or consent order based upon liability as a result of the debtor's drunk driving.

•Debts that existed but were not discharged in any previous bankruptcy case of the debtor.

Nondischargeability of a Particular Debt   Other, individual debts cannot be discharged because of bad conduct in which the debtor engaged pertaining to that debt. If a particular creditor believes that the debtor engaged in any of the bad conduct described below concerning that creditor's debt, the creditor may file a complaint to determine the dischargeability of a particular debt within 60 days following the date of the § 341 meeting of creditors. The complaint is handled as an adversary proceeding. At the time of trial, the creditor must be able to prove one of the following acts by the debtor:

•The debtor obtained money, property, services, or an extension, renewal, or refinancing of credit (from the complaining creditor) by fraud.

•The debtor used a materially false financial statement with the intent to deceive and upon which the creditor reasonably relied.

•The debtor incurred debt of more than $1,000 for "luxury goods or services" within 60 days before the bankruptcy case was commenced.

•The debtor obtained cash advances of more than $1,000 under a consumer credit plan, such as a credit card, within 60 days before the bankruptcy case was commenced.

•The debtor committed fraud or defalcation while acting in a fiduciary capacity or committed embezzlement or larceny.

•The debtor willfully and maliciously injured another or the property of another.

If the creditor loses on her complaint to determine dischargeability of her debt, she ordinarily is required to pay the debtor's attorney fees and costs, as well as her own. U.S.C. § 523(d).

Reaffirmation Agreements   Once a debtor is granted a discharge, all unsecured pre-petition debt and all deficiencies incurred by under-secured debts are uncollectible. However, a debtor may want to repay a certain debt (even though she is not required to do so) because of moral obligation or because of practical concerns (such as preventing the creditor from pursuing a guarantor of the debt).

A debtor's promise to pay a discharged debt is enforceable only when the debtor has reaffirmed the debt formally. Reaffirmation requires a written agreement between the debtor and the creditor, which the debtor must file with the court (together with a motion to reaffirm) before the discharge is granted. If the debtor is represented by an attorney, the attorney must file a declaration that the debtor is fully informed of the consequences of reaffirmation; that it is voluntarily done; and that it will not impose undue hardship on the debtor or upon the debtor's dependents.

If the reaffirmation agreement is approved by the court prior to discharge, the debtor still has 60 days from discharge or from filing of the reaffirmation agreement (whichever is later [5524(c)]) to rescind the agreement. Rescission is accomplished merely by giving notice to the creditor. The Code requires that the debtor's right to rescind be stated in the reaffirmation agreement itself and that it be "clear and conspicuous." This means that simple language must be used and that it must be written in typeface that is capitalized, bold, underlined, or the like.

If the debtor fails to rescind the reaffirmation agreement within the 60-day period, it becomes a fully enforceable contract.

Chapter 7 Liquidation

The statutory scheme of Chapter 7 is liquidation. Sometimes called a straight bankruptcy, liquidation is the most straightforward form of debt relief available under the Code. Nearly everyone can qualify to be a Chapter 7 debtor except railroads, insurance companies, and banking institutions.

When the petition for relief is filed under Chapter 7, an estate is created automatically. In theory, the debtor turns over all of her assets to a bankruptcy trustee. In the typical case, there are few assets to administer (the no-asset bankruptcy); but when there are assets, the trustee administers them by collecting, liquidating, and distributing them to creditors. The trustee attempts to maximize the estate by recovering fraudulent conveyances and preferences; by overriding any unperfected security interests that may exist; and by collecting debts owed to the estate by third parties. At the same time, the debtor is protected from creditor actions by an automatic stay that ordinarily continues throughout the balance of the case unless relief from the stay is granted to a specific creditor by court order.

Other than the exempt property carved out by statute and retained for the debtor's fresh start and other than that the debtor may have redeemed, the property of the estate is liquidated (converted to cash) by the trustee, using special powers of sale, assumption, and assignment granted under the Code. Property with little or no monetary value is abandoned by returning it to the debtor, along with the debtor's exempt property.

To the extent that there are proceeds, they are distributed to creditors according to the status of the creditor (whether secured, priority, or unsecured), and final reports are filed with the court. Except for the types of debts that cannot be discharged (such as alimony, child support, and other § 523 nondischargeable debts), the debtor is discharged in the typical case; and the case is closed.

Chapter 11 Reorganization

Designed for business debtors, the goal of Chapter 11 is to reorganize, not to liquidate, so that a viable business can continue its operations during and after the bankruptcy proceeding. The business owner remains in possession of the business assets (rather than a trustee) and is called a debtor in possession (DIP). The debtor will remain the DIP unless she is guilty of fraud, incompetence, or gross mismanagement, in which event a trustee will be appointed to reorganize the business.

The DIP is given many of the powers of a trustee, including the power to avoid preferences and certain liens on estate property. In addition, the DIP must file periodic reports of business activities throughout the bankruptcy's term. As with Chapter 7, collateral can be sold free and clear of liens; but if the sale is out of the ordinary course of business, sale can occur only with the secured creditor's consent unless the secured creditor receives all sale proceeds.

Generally, creditors play a more active role in the Chapter 11 case than they do in Chapter 7. A creditors' committee is formed, consisting of those seven creditors with the largest unsecured claims. The creditors' committee functions as a watch dog on behalf of the other creditors. It can employ its own attorneys and accountants (with prior court approval), and it can appear before the court on any issue concerning the reorganization.

The Chapter 11 process culminates in a plan of reorganization that is approved by unsecured creditors or is confirmed by the court as being in the creditors' best interests. During the first 120 days after a voluntary petition is filed and assuming that no trustee has been appointed, the DIP has the exclusive right to propose a plan of reorganization. After that time, other parties in interest, including the creditors' committee, may propose a plan.

The plan generally divides creditors into different classes, based upon the types of claims that they hold. For instance, a very simple plan could provide for four classes of creditors:

Class 1:   Priority Claims
Class 2:   Secured Claims
Class 3:   Nonpriority, Unsecured Claims
Class 4:   Shareholders

All creditors within a particular class must be treated the same as all other creditors within that class. Unless they consent otherwise, each senior class must be paid in full before any junior class can receive payment under the plan. The plan might provide that all Class 1 creditors would be paid in full when the plan is confirmed. Class 2 creditors would retain their liens in the debtor's property and would receive the monthly installment payments called for in their contracts with the debtor. Class 3 creditors would receive quarterly, pro-rata payments from the debtor's net profits over the next five years, together with all or part of the debtor's stock, which would equal seventy percent of their claims. Since Class 3 creditors will not be paid in full, Class 4 creditors can receive nothing under the plan.

Most plans provide for either liquidation and distribution of all of the debtor's assets or a variation of the basic plan described above. Although no two plans are exactly alike, the Code requires that all plans contain certain provisions.

■The plan must designate the classes of claims to be included, and the claims within each class must be substantially similar.

■The plan must identify those classes of creditors whose rights are not impaired (altered) under the plan. A secured creditor is impaired if he will not be paid in full, will not be paid on time, or will receive substitute collateral under the plan. An unsecured creditor is impaired if she will not be paid in full under the plan.

■The plan must state how impaired classes of creditors will be treated.

■The plan must treat each member of a particular class the same.

■The plan must state specifically how it will be carried out.

■The plan must identify the debtor's post-confirmation management personnel and must state how management will be chosen in the future.

In addition to the required provisions, the plan may contain any other provisions that are consistent with the mandatory provisions. The Code itself suggests some optional provisions:

■The plan may impair the rights of creditors and equity holders (shareholders and others).

■The plan may provide for the assumption or rejection of executory contracts and leases.

■The plan may provide for the settlement of one or more claims against the estate.

■The plan may provide for liquidation of all or substantially all of the property of the estate.

The reorganization plan must be accompanied by a **_written disclosure statement_** that contains adequate information for creditors to make an intelligent decision in voting for or against the plan. **_Adequate information_** is defined by the Code as information about the nature and history of the debtor and the condition of the debtor's books and records that would enable a hypothetical, reasonable investor to make an informed judgment about the plan. In other words, the disclosure statement is similar to a prospectus that might be sent to a would-be shareholder, so that creditors can make an intelligent decision in voting for or against the plan.

A hearing is held to determine whether the disclosure statement contains adequate information. If the disclosure statement is approved by the court, a hearing is scheduled to confirm the plan. The plan's proponent (whether the DIP or another party in interest) then mails the proposed plan, the disclosure statement, and a ballot to creditors and equity security holders. Creditors who are impaired by the proposed plan may vote to accept or to reject the plan by returning the ballot to the plan's proponent. Creditors who are unimpaired by the plan are not entitled to vote.

The proposed plan will not be confirmed unless each class of creditors or equity security holders votes to accept it or unless the plan is crammed down. For the plan to be accepted by a particular class of impaired creditors, class members representing at least two-thirds of the total dollars and at least one-half of the total claims within the class must vote to accept it. If a particular class of creditors fails to accept the plan, the Code's **_cram down_** provisions allow the court to approve the plan anyway if:

1. The plan does not unfairly discriminate; and
2. The plan is fair and equitable to the class that rejected it.

That is to say, the nonconsenting class must be paid in full before any junior class can be paid anything.

For any class of secured creditors to be crammed down, the plan must provide:

- The secured creditors must retain their security interests until they have received payments equal to the value of their collateral; *or*

- The collateral is sold with the liens attached to the proceeds of sale; *or*

- The creditors must receive the *indubitable equivalent* of their claims.

The term "indubitable equivalent" in relation to a creditor generally means that the creditor must receive her contract interests (the benefit of the bargain). For a secured creditor, this may be interest paid on the value of collateral.

In confirming a particular plan of reorganization, the court must find specifically that:

> ☐ *The plan complies with Chapter 11 of the Bankruptcy Code.*
> ☐ *The plan proponent has complied with Chapter 11 of the Bankruptcy Code.*
> ☐ *The plan has been proposed in good faith and not by means forbidden by law.* ☐ *All payments made or promised in connection with the bankruptcy case and the plan have been disclosed.*
> ☐ *The identities of management (officers and directors) have been disclosed.*
> ☐ *All necessary regulatory approval has been obtained.*
> ☐ *Unless they agree otherwise, the plan provides more to all creditors and equity security holders than they would receive in a Chapter 7 liquidation.*
> ☐ *Unless they agree otherwise, all priority classes are paid in full on the effective date of the plan.*
> ☐ *At least one class of creditors has accepted the plan.*
> ☐ *The plan is feasible and likely will not be followed by the need for liquidation or for further reorganization.*

Once the plan is confirmed, it binds the DIP and all creditors. Any debts that are not paid or are not paid in full by the plan are unenforceable. Unless the plan provides otherwise, the DIP is no longer subject to the scrutiny of the court or of the United States trustee. The bankruptcy case is closed when the plan is fully executed.

Chapter 13 Individual Reorganization

Chapter 13 is commonly known as the wage earner plan. It gives individual debtors, including sole proprietors much the same kind of relief as that given to corporate debtors under Chapter 11. Stockbrokers and commodities brokers cannot file under Chapter 13; they can file only under Chapter 7. Although nothing prohibits a sole proprietor from filing under Chapter 11, sole proprietors often prefer Chapter 13 because it costs less; imposes fewer burdens on the debtor; and ordinarily takes less time to approve a plan.

Chapter 13 relief is available only to individuals (1) who have regular income and (2) who have unsecured debts of less than $250,000 and secured debts of less than $750,000. When married persons file for relief, the debt limitations apply to them jointly, as if they were filing as a single debtor. The regular income requirement may be satisfied with social security benefits, welfare payments, or other income that is sufficiently stable to fund regular payments to creditors under an approved plan. It is not necessary that the debtor be employed. When married persons file jointly, only one of them is required to have regular income.

Under Chapter 13, the automatic stay protects not only the debtor during administration of the case but also protects any co-debtor who may be liable on a particular debt (assuming the debtor received the consideration for the debt). This is different from Chapters 7 and 11, where the automatic stay applies only the debtor.

A Chapter 13 debtor is viewed as a debtor in possession (DIP) for many purposes and—similar to the Chapter 11 DIP—can avoid certain types of liens, can assume or reject executory contracts and leases, and can operate a business. A Chapter 13 DIP is entitled to claim exempt property and to avoid liens that impair the exempt property, similar to the Chapter 7 debtor; however, the trustee in a Chapter 13 case does not administer the DIP's property or take control of it in any way (unlike a Chapter 7 trustee). Like a Chapter 7 debtor, the Chapter 13 may redeem property; unlike a Chapter 7 debtor, however, the redemption can be made in installment payments under the reorganization plan rather than in a lump sum.

The trustee may be a Chapter 13 standing trustee or may come from the panel of trustees maintained by the U.S. Trustee, depending upon the district. The duties of the trustee are to conduct the meeting of creditors, to examine the DIP's plan of reorganization, to collect payments from the DIP to fund the plan, and to distribute the payments to creditors as required by the plan.

Only the DIP may propose a plan of reorganization under Chapter 13; neither the creditors nor the trustee may do so. The plan must be filed within 15 days after the filing of the petition for relief. Chapter 13 plans are not as complex as the plans in Chapter 11 cases, no disclosure statement is required, and creditors do not vote on the plan. If a creditor objects to the plan, the debtor must show that all disposable income is being used to fund the plan. The Code's mandatory requirements for a plan of reorganization under Chapter 13 are relatively few.

■The plan must pay enough of the debtor's regular income to fund the payments provided under the plan.

■The plan must provide that certain priority claims (trustee fee, attorney fee, taxes, and so forth) be paid in full.

■The plan must provide for equal treatment of all claims in the same class.

■The plan must pay secured creditors an amount equal to the value of their collateral as of the date when the petition for relief was filed.

■The plan must pay unsecured creditors at least as much as they would have received if the debtor had filed a Chapter 7 case. *(If unsecured creditors would have received nothing under a Chapter 7 liquidation, it is permissible for them to be paid nothing under the Chapter 13 plan.)*

In addition, the Code permits optional provisions as follows:

●The plan may divide claims into different classes, as long as the claims in a particular class are substantially similar to each other.

●The plan may provide a different treatment for each class of claims.

●The plan may modify the rights of secured creditors by extending the due date of the last payment or by paying less than the full debt if the collateral is worth less than the debt. ***Exception:*** *The plan may not modify the claim of a mortgage holder on the debtor's residence. If the debtor wants to keep her home, all payments due after the petition is filed must be paid, although any amounts in default when the case began may be paid over the term of the plan.*

●The plan may provide that all creditors be paid simultaneously, without regard to their class. Unlike a Chapter 11 plan, secured creditors and priority creditors do not have to be paid in full first.

●The plan may provide for payment of post-petition claims over the term of the plan; however, all post-petition claims must be paid in full.

Payments to the trustee under the reorganization plan may be approved for a term of three years; with the court's approval and for good cause shown, the term may be extended to five years. The court does not have authority to approve a plan for longer than five years total.

A hearing to confirm the plan of reorganization is scheduled approximately 45 days after the petition is filed. In confirming a particular plan, the court must find specifically that:

☐ *The plan complies with all requirements of Chapter 13 of the Bankruptcy Code.*
☐ *The debtor has paid all fees and charges (such as the filing fee).*
☐ *The plan has been proposed in good faith and not by any means forbidden by law.*

Once the debtor has performed all requirements of the confirmed plan, she is granted a discharge of any debts not paid in full under the plan. A Chapter 13 discharge also discharges the debtor from claims based upon fraud, defalcation, embezzlement, and so forth (unlike Chapter 7, in which these claims are nondischargeable). The only types of claims that are not dischargeable under Chapter 13 are alimony and child support, long-term debts where the final payment is due after the completion date of the plan, post-petition claims, and claims that the debtor failed to list on her schedules.

Even if a Chapter 13 debtor cannot fully perform all requirements of the confirmed plan, the court may grant a discharge if it finds that the failure to make payments was due to circumstances for which the debtor should not be held accountable, that unsecured creditors have already received at least as much as they would have received in a Chapter 7 liquidation, and that a modification of the plan is not practical. This is called a hardship discharge.

After the discharge is granted, the case is closed.

Chapter 12 Family Farmer Reorganization

Chapter 12 provides the newest form of bankruptcy under the Code, relief for the family farmer. It blends the most favorable provisions of Chapters 11 and 13, giving family farmers even greater protections than other debtors. Like both Chapters 11 and 13, the debtor is a debtor in possession (DIP).

Chapter 12 relief is preferable to Chapter 11, first of all, because the court costs are substantially less expensive. In addition, payments to Chapter 12 creditors during administration may be much less than those to Chapter 11 creditors. For example, a secured creditor under Chapter 11 is entitled to adequate protection to maintain the value of his collateral, which can result in sizable payments by the DIP. Under Chapter 12, a secured creditor is entitled only to the rental value of the collateral. Where the price of farm land is low, its rental value will be quite low.

Unlike Chapter 11, where secured property cannot be sold unless the creditor consents or will be paid in full from sale proceeds, a Chapter 12 DIP can sell mortgaged farmland and secured equipment without the creditor's consent, even if the sale does not bring enough money to pay the creditor in full. Court approval is needed, however.

A trustee is appointed in all Chapter 12 cases, who may investigate the debtor's activities and farming operations in much the same way as a Chapter 11 trustee but who monitors payments under the plan in much the same way as a Chapter 13 trustee.

The Chapter 12 reorganization plan must be filed within 90 days after the date of the petition but can be filed only by the debtor. The plan must provide that at least a portion of future earnings will be paid to the trustee to fund the plan. It must classify claims and must provide for payments over three years, which can be extended to five years with court approval. Unlike Chapter 13, the residential mortgage of a Chapter 12 debtor can be modified in the same way that other secured debts can be modified.

A confirmation hearing must be concluded within 45 days after the proposed plan is filed. Similar to Chapter 13, creditors do not vote on approving the plan; it is approved by the court, using the same general criteria that is used to approve a Chapter 13 plan.

Once the provisions of the plan are fully performed, the Chapter 12 debtor receives a discharge; but the discharge is more like the discharge under Chapter 7 than under Chapter 13. For instance, the nondischargeable debts that apply to a Chapter 7 debtor under § 523 of the Code are also nondischargeable under Chapter 12. The discharge resembles one granted under Chapter 13 only in the fact that a Chapter 12 debtor may be considered for a hardship discharge (payments not completely paid under the plan through circumstances that were not the fault of the debtor). Upon discharge, the case is closed.

The material in this chapter, together with the self-test and the provisions of the Bankruptcy Code itself, should provide the applicant with thorough review of the substance of the Bankruptcy Law subsection of the CLA® examination. *See the Bibliography for additional study references.*

Bankruptcy Law Self-Test

Allow an uninterrupted thirty-minute period to answer all questions. At the end of thirty minutes, check your answers against those in the Answer Key Section of this Manual. Deduct two points for each incorrect answer (100 total possible points). Unanswered questions are counted as incorrect answers. Follow directions carefully and observe the time limit precisely to provide an accurate self-assessment.

Choose the most correct answer to each of the following questions unless a specific question instructs you to do otherwise.

1. True or False.   As is true of all federal courts, bankruptcy courts must demonstrate minimum contacts before they may exercise personal jurisdiction over persons not within their geographic boundaries.

2. True or False.   Under 11 U.S.C. § 704, a Chapter 11 Trustee is required to make § 521 filings (list of creditors, assets and liabilities, statement of debtor's financial affairs, and so forth) if they have not been filed by the debtor.

3. In addition to the other filings required, a debtor must file a statement of intentions concerning secured property:

   a. in all cases filed under Chapters 7 and 11.
   b. in all cases filed under Chapters 7 and 12.
   c. in all cases filed under Chapters 7 and 13.
   d. in all cases filed under Chapters 11 and 12.

4. True or False. Assuming that all other requirements are met, creditors may file an involuntary petition for relief when (1) they hold claims of totaling at least $20,000; and (2) they can show that the debtor generally is not paying debts as they become due.

5. True or False. In a Chapter 7 case, assumption or rejection of executory contracts must be made within 120 days of the order for relief.

6. An examiner may be appointed:

   a. in a Chapter 7 case.
   b. in a Chapter 11 case.
   c. in a Chapter 12 case.
   d. in a Chapter 13 case.

7. Nine weeks before filing for bankruptcy relief, Joe transfers his home valued at $55,000.00 to his Uncle Jim in consideration for the cancellation of an unsecured promissory note for $50,000.00. Within the bankruptcy proceeding, which of the following statements is most accurate?

   a. The transfer is void because Uncle Jim is an insider.
   b. The transfer is voidable as a preference.
   c. The transfer is voidable as a fraudulent transfer.
   d. Joe cannot receive a discharge because of this transfer.

8. True or False. Once a creditor raises the issue of lack of adequate protection in seeking relief from the automatic stay, the burden of proof shifts to the debtor to show that the creditor's interests in the property are protected.

9. True or False. A family farmer under Chapter 12 may sell his corn crop and use the money to purchase equipment for next year's farming without court approval or creditors' consent; for all other purposes, however, the sale proceeds are cash collateral and require court approval or consent of creditors before they can be used by the debtor in his farming operation.

10.   True or False.   Assuming that a debtor has filed under Chapter 7, he or she may convert to Chapter 11, 12, or 13 at any time, as a matter of right.

11.   True or False.   A debtor who originally filed under Chapter 11 and then converted to Chapter 7 may convert back to Chapter 11 as a matter of right.

12.   True or False.   Once a case has been filed under Chapter 7, creditors can request an order, requiring its conversion to Chapter 13 if that chapter will be more beneficial to unsecured creditors.

13.   True or False.   Other than Chapter 11 creditors, all creditors are required to file proofs of claim within 90 days after the date set for the § 341 meeting.

14.   True or False.   In prioritizing the payment of claims, a creditor which grants post-petition credit to the trustee with court approval will be paid before post-petition taxes are paid.

15.   True or False.   An individual debtor who cannot obtain a discharge under Chapter 7 because of fraud committed by her nevertheless may be entitled to discharge under Chapter 13.

16.   True or False.   Professionals employed to perform services for the estate (accountants, attorneys, and so forth) will not be paid for their services unless prior court approval has been obtained to hire such professionals.

17.   True or False.   Social security benefits or welfare benefits are included in the definition of "regular income" for purposes of qualifying as a Chapter 13 debtor.

18.   True or False.   A stockbroker who owns her own business as a sole proprietor may qualify for relief under Chapter 13.

19.   Exclusions from the Chapter 7 estate include:

    a.   Post-petition wages.
    b.   Property acquired by extortion.
    c.   Money paid into an employer-held pension plan.
    d.   Two of the above.
    e.   All of the above.
    f.   None of the above.

20. True or False.   A purchase money mortgage may be reduced to that amount that a debtor can pay under Chapter 13 over the term of the debtor's plan.

21. True or False.   Under the Bankruptcy Code, if a state's laws give more rights to a creditor whose execution has been returned unsatisfied than to a judicial lienholder who has not attempted to execute on the lien, the trustee may exercise the rights of a hypothetical creditor whose execution has been returned unsatisfied.

22. True or False.   A preferential transfer occurs when Ben's mother pays money to one of Ben's secured creditors on Ben's behalf within 90 days preceding the filing of Ben's petition for relief.

23. True or False.   Proceeds from the sale of personal property are included in the definition of "regular income" for purposes of qualifying as a Chapter 13 debtor.

24. True or False.   All interests and property of the debtor, whether in her possession or not, comprise property of the estate and remain property of the estate until disposed of by the trustee.

25. True or False.   A debtor may discharge a consumer loan on exempt property by paying the value of the property, regardless of the amount of the loan.

26. Which of the following groups of chapters apply to all bankruptcy proceedings?

    a.   Chapters 7, 11, and 13
    b.   Chapters 7, 11, and 12
    c.   Chapters 1, 3, and 5
    d.   Chapters 1, 5, and 7
    e.   None of the above

27. Under the federal exemptions, a debtor who owns no residential real estate may claim how much as a general exemption in addition to her other, specific exemptions?

    a. $750
    b. $7500
    c. $10,000

(see next page)

       d. $15,000

       e.   None is correct.

28.   After an order for relief is entered in a liquidation case, the court then:

       a.   appoints a receiver.

       b.   appoints a custodian.

       c.   appoints an examiner.

       d.   appoints an interim trustee.

29.   A reaffirmation agreement between a holder of a claim and a debtor, which is based on a dischargeable debt, is enforceable only if:

       a.   such agreement was made before the petition for relief was filed.

       b.   such agreement was made on or before the § 341 meeting.

       c.   such agreement was made before the discharge was granted.

       d.   such agreement was made at the discharge hearing.

30.   For purposes of the Bankruptcy Code, a family farmer is one engaged in farming operations with:

       a. $1,500,000 in total debt, 80% of which is from farming operations.

       b. $750,000 in total debt, 80% of which is from farming operations.

       c. $750,000 in total debt, 50% of which is from farming operations.

       d. $350,000 in total debt, 50% of which is from farming operations.

31.   True or False.   Adversary proceedings are governed by the Federal Rules of Civil Procedure.

32.   True or False.   A debtor must be either insolvent or generally not paying his debts as they become due before he can seek bankruptcy relief.

33.   True or False.   A corporate debtor is not eligible to receive a discharge.

34.   True or False.   Bankruptcy judges are appointed for life, subject to good behavior.

35.   True or False.   Claims related to personal injury or wrongful death are not included among those non-core proceedings that may be heard by the bankruptcy court.

36. True or False   Proper venue for a bankruptcy proceeding is that federal district in which the debtor has maintained her domicile, residence, or place of business for at least 180 days before filing for bankruptcy relief.

37. Which of the following acts is a trustee not authorized to do?

   a. Operate the debtor's business.
   b. Employ professional persons without prior court approval.
   c. File proofs of claim for creditors who have not timely filed claims.
   d. Sell or lease property of the estate.

38. When a corporate debtor has twenty creditors, how many of them are required to file an involuntary petition for bankruptcy relief?

   a. One
   b. Three
   c. Ten
   d. Twelve
   e. None of the above

39. Which of the following debtors is (are) ineligible to file for bankruptcy relief under Chapter 13?

   a. Stockbrokers
   b. Corporations
   c. Partnerships
   d. Sole proprietors
   e. Two of the above
   f. Three of the above

40. Using the federal exemptions, which of the following most accurately describes the maximum motor vehicle exemption for a married couple?

   a. Maximum of $1200 for one motor vehicle
   b. Maximum of $1500 for one motor vehicle
   c. Maximum of $1400 for each of two motor vehicles
   d. Maximum of $4800 for each of two motor vehicles

41. Cash collateral may include all of the following except:

   a. Proceeds from the sale of a secured vehicle.
   b. Cash from the sale of secured crops.

(see next page)

    c.   Rents from an apartment building held as security.

    d.   Cash from the sale of secured inventory.

    e.   All are cash collateral.

    f.   None are cash collateral.

42.   True or False.   Post-petition wages are excluded from the bankruptcy estate in Chapter 11 cases.

43.   True or False.   Property which is subject to a purchase money security interest may be claimed as exempt by a debtor in bankruptcy.

44.   True or False.   A bankruptcy trustee can avoid a federal tax lien which has not yet been filed of record.

45.   True or False.   A bankruptcy trustee can avoid a real estate transfer to a bona fide purchaser without notice of the bankruptcy proceedings if the transfer is made within 90 days before the bankruptcy petition is filed.

46.   True or False.   In a proceeding which seeks relief from the automatic stay, the creditor bears the burden of proving that the creditor's secured value in the property is not adequately protected in the hands of the debtor.

47.   True or False.   Pre-petition tax claims have lower priority for payment than do administrative expenses in a Chapter 7 liquidation.

48.   True or False.   Post-petition taxes are paid before court-approved, post-petition creditors are paid in a Chapter 11 case.

49.   True or False.   Post-petition taxes are paid before secured creditors are paid in a Chapter 7 case.

50.   True or False.   If a debt is found to be nondischargeable because of fraud in a Chapter 7 case, the debtor may receive a discharge for the debt by waiting six years and then filing another petition for relief under Chapter 7.

Chapter 10
BUSINESS ORGANIZATIONS

Go as far as you can see; and when you get there, you will be able to see farther.

—Anonymous

The law of business organizations covers the creation, operation, merger, and liquidation of various business enterprises. It includes sole proprietorships, general partnerships, limited partnerships, joint ventures, joint stock companies, and corporations. Of these, the sole proprietorship, the partnership, and the corporation are the three most common forms of business organization used in the United States. The legal assistant who works with the commercial clients of a law firm must have a thorough understanding of the concepts, rules, and procedures that govern the existence and activities of commercial entities.

In addition to the summary of general principles provided in this *Review Manual* and an up-to-date textbook or treatise covering business organizations, the applicant may find it helpful to review the complete texts of the Uniform Partnership Act (UPA), the Revised Uniform Limited Partnership Act (RULPA), and the Revised Model Business Corporation Act (RMBCA) in preparation for the CLA® examination. The materials in this chapter are based upon selected sections of these Acts, as well as upon general principles of jurisdiction, agency law, and contract law.

Sole Proprietorship

The most common form of business organization is the sole proprietorship. A sole proprietorship exists when one person owns a business operation and its assets and carries on the business enterprise as the sole owner. Unlike a corporation, the sole proprietorship requires no charter from the state to exist.

Advantages The greatest advantage of the sole proprietorship is its flexibility. As the only owner, a sole proprietor operates the business as he or she chooses within the bounds of the law. The owner may hire employees to assist with the business operation, but the owner retains ultimate responsibility for all decisions concerning the business.

If the business will sell goods, the owner must obtain a sales tax license (services are also taxed in some states); and if the business will have employees, state and federal tax identification numbers must be obtained. Certain types of businesses require special licensing (taxi service, physician services, child care); these licenses must be obtained where necessary. Otherwise, there are no special formalities required to begin a sole proprietorship.

The sole proprietorship is treated as an extension of its owner for income tax purposes, which allows the owner to apply business losses against other personal income in computing tax liability. Moreover, individual tax rates generally are less than corporate tax rates.

Disadvantages The disadvantages of the sole proprietorship stem from its complete identity with its owner. As a practical matter, the business and the owner are one. Capitalization of the business comes from the owner, either through direct contributions or through financing which generally is dependent—at least in part—upon the credit worthiness of the individual owner.

Likewise, liabilities of the sole proprietorship are the unlimited personal liabilities of its owner, which means that trade creditors look to the owner's personal assets to satisfy trade debts when business assets are insufficient. Unlimited personal liability exists for business contracts and business torts of the sole proprietorship, making it possible for the owner to lose all personal assets as well as all business assets if an unfavorable judgment is entered against the business. This is very different from the corporate business structure, in which an owner's personal liability typically is much more limited *(see below)*. A sole proprietor may negotiate to limit her contract liability to business assets only;

however, her tort liability for business activities generally cannot be limited by agreement.

The duration of a sole proprietorship is limited by the life of its owner. In the usual situation, this means that the sole proprietorship is liquidated upon the owner's death. The liquidation process can be difficult unless proper authority has been given to a trustee or to the personal representative of the owner's estate to operate the business, to sell its assets, and to distribute the sale proceeds. If the business is inherited or is purchased by another person, a new sole proprietorship is created in the new owner.

General Partnership

General partnerships are governed by the Uniform Partnership Act (UPA), which has been adopted in whole or in part in all states except Louisiana. A general partnership is an "association of two or more persons to carry on as co-owners a business for profit." U.P.A. § 6(1). The traditional law firm, for example, is organized as a general partnership.

By definition, a partnership requires at least two persons who intend to affiliate for the purpose of operating a business. The term *person* can include an individual, a partnership, a corporation, or other entity. The intent to associate as partners may be based upon a formal, written partnership agreement (always the preferred method); upon an oral agreement; or upon conduct of the partners. The concept of co-ownership implies that contributions, ownership of assets, rights to profits, obligations for losses, and management of the partnership are shared equally by the partners. Although a different arrangement is permissible, it must be stated specifically and clearly in a written partnership agreement to avoid application of the general rule.

Standing alone, however, mere co-ownership of property does not indicate that a partnership exists, even if the property produces income which is divided among the property owners.

Finally, the definition of a partnership excludes charitable, fraternal, religious, trade association, or labor union purposes, for example, because it requires the partnership to carry on a business "for profit." This means that the partnership must be operated with the intent to generate a profit, whether or not a profit actually is generated. Like other business organizations, partnerships can and do experience financial losses.

A partnership is a "pass-through" entity for taxation purposes, which means that each partner is taxed on his, her, or its proportionate share of deductions, credits, profits, and losses at the personal income tax rate applicable to that partner. The partnership is not taxed separately.

Formation and Existence   The requirements to form a partnership are similar to the requirements to establish a sole proprietorship (sales tax license and other licenses, if applicable; state and federal tax identification numbers if there will be employees). The prudent business person will insist upon a written partnership agreement, sometimes called articles of partnership, to govern the partners' rights and obligations; however, where there is no agreement or where the agreement fails to address a specific issue, terms will be supplied by the Uniform Partnership Act (UPA).

A partnership may exist for any length of time to which the partners agree. If the partnership is intended to exist for one year or more, there must be a written agreement to comply with the Statute of Frauds. If no term is stated, it will be presumed that the partnership is one "at will," which may be terminated by any partner upon notice to the other partners.

If the names of all partners are part of the partnership name, registration of the partnership's business name generally is not required. If less than all of the partners names are used or if an entirely different name is used, most states require registration of the business name. Sanctions for noncompliance vary from state to state, but typically deny the partnership the right to use that state's court systems until the partnership complies with the assumed business name statute by registering the partnership name.

A frequent question in partnership law is whether the partnership is an aggregate of its partners or whether it is a separate legal entity. Under common law rules, a partnership was viewed as an aggregate. This meant, for example, that all partners had to be named as defendants if a partnership were sued. If an entity theory were used, the partnership could be named as the defendant without the need to name each of the partners.

The UPA incorporates both theories in its provisions, treating the partnership as an aggregate for some purposes and as a separate entity for other purposes. For example, all partners are personally liable for partnership debts (aggregate theory). However, the partnership may acquire, hold, and convey property; and partnership assets, liabilities, and transactions are separate from those of individual partners (entity theory).

Many statutes follow the same hybrid approach, treating the partnership as an aggregate for some purposes and as an entity for others. Both the Uniform Commercial Code and federal bankruptcy law, for instance, define the term *person* to include a partnership. Most states allow a partnership to sue and to be sued in the partnership name. Tax laws, however, treat the partnership as an aggregate by attributing income and expenses to individual partners *(see above)*.

A. Partnership Property

Each partner generally contributes to the partnership's capital account when the partnership is formed. A partner's capital contribution may be in the form of real property (land and/or buildings), personal property (typically vehicles, machinery, or equipment), cash, or personal services. Although there is no legal requirement to do so, it is important to state the value of each partner's capital contribution if contributions vary from partner to partner. If no amount is stated, it will be presumed that each partner's capital contribution is equal to the capital contributions of all other partners. Each subsequent advance by any partner should be recorded, along with its value, for the same reason.

Property of the partnership may be held in the partnership's name or may be held in the name of any partner as an agent of the partnership. Property purchased with partnership funds is presumed to be partnership property, owned by all partners as tenants in common. No partner may sell partnership property without the consent of all other partners; neither can a partner, for instance, sell her fractional interest in specific partnership property. A partner's personal creditors cannot reach partnership property to satisfy the partner's individual debt. If a partner dies, partnership property belongs to the surviving partners and not to the heirs of the deceased partner.

Financial Structure

Initial capitalization of the partnership comes from contributions made by its partners. Contributions may or may not be equal in value. If no value is stated, it will be presumed that contributions were equal; and profits will be divided equally. Even if capital contributions are unequal, profits will be divided equally among all partners unless the partnership agreement provides for a different ratio of distribution.

> Anderson, Baker, and Cunningham form a partnership to operate a catering business. Anderson contributes a delivery van valued at $20,000; Baker contributes $40,000 in cash; and Cunningham will operate the business on a daily basis without salary for the first year, valued at $20,000. The business operates at a loss of $15,000 during the first year and generates a profit of $60,000 during the second year.

Absent a contrary provision in the partnership agreement, both the first year's loss and the second year's profit will be allocated equally among Anderson, Baker, and Cunningham.

At the beginning of the partnership described in the example, Anderson's partnership interest is $20,000; Baker's, $40,000; and Cunningham's, $0. At the end of the first year of operation, Anderson's partnership interest is $15,000 (the $20,000 van minus $5,000 loss); Baker's is $35,000 ($40,000 cash minus $5,000 loss); and Cunningham's is $15,000 ($20,000 salary minus $5,000 loss).

Although no partner may sell or assign specific partnership property to a third party without consent of the other partners, she may sell or assign her partnership interest. Her partnership interest (but not specific partnership property) also may be reached by her individual creditors or may be inherited by her heirs. The new owner of the partnership interest is entitled to payment of its value as well as to payment of profits to which his assignor would have been entitled, but the new owner does not become a partner and has no management authority *(see below)*. Partnerships often purchase insurance policies on the lives of individual partners to provide a method of paying the value of a deceased partner's partnership interest to his or her heirs.

The value of a partnership interest typically is calculated by a formula that includes the partner's initial contribution and subsequent advances, increased by surplus profits, and decreased by undistributed losses and withdrawals from the partnership. The precise valuation formula should be stated in the partnership agreement.

If a partner uses individual assets to pay undisputed debts to firm creditors, that partner is entitled to proportionate reimbursement from the other partners.

Management   The law presumes that all partners will devote their full time and attention to operating the partnership business without compensation and that each partner will have equal management authority concerning the business. If the partners desire a different management structure, they must provide for it in the partnership agreement.

In the example given above, for instance, Anderson, Baker, and Cunningham agreed that Cunningham should be compensated for his daily services to the business (implying that Anderson and Baker would not be involved in daily operations); and what would have been paid to him as salary should be applied, instead, as his capital contribution during the first year. Unless Cunningham is named as the managing partner, however, all three partners have an equal voice in management decisions. Without regard to the variance in their capital contributions, they each have one vote; and the partnership is authorized to engage in various activities by majority vote of its partners. The partnership agreement may alter this structure in any way which is satisfactory to the partners.

A *silent partner* is one who assumes all benefits and burdens of her partner status except in the area of management decisions.

Complete books and records must be maintained, and any partner is entitled to inspect the books or to receive an accounting at any time.

Liability of Partners

Like sole proprietors, members of a general partnership have unlimited personal liability to partnership creditors if the assets of the partnership are insufficient to satisfy partnership debts.

If any partner incurs liability or expenses in the ordinary course of the partnership business, she is entitled to reimbursement from the partnership or from the remaining partners. A partner who leaves the firm remains personally liable for debts incurred while she was a partner in the firm unless an indemnification provision is included in the original partnership agreement. New partners are personally liable for firm debts existing when they join the firm only if they agree to such liability. If a new partner does not assume existing debts, she is personally liable for only those obligations incurred after she becomes a partner.

Dissolution and Termination

When any partner is no longer associated with the partnership business, for whatever reason, the partnership is dissolved. However, the remaining partners (assuming there are two or more remaining) may elect to continue the business. Under strict interpretation of partnership law, a new partnership is created by the remaining partners and continues to operate under the terms of the original partnership agreement. In other situations, the dissolution may require termination of the partnership and "winding up" of the business operation.

Since a partnership is formed by agreement of the parties, it may be terminated by agreement of the parties. The original partnership agreement may provide for termination upon the occurrence of a specific event, such as the death or disability of a partner or a stated period of consecutive operating losses. Dissolution may be necessary if the partnership business becomes unlawful (statute adopted to outlaw all movie theaters after January 1 of next year) or when partners simply cannot agree about important matters related to the business. Whenever possible, a written dissolution agreement should be put into effect; the better practice is to include dissolution provisions in the original partnership agreement.

If the remaining partners cannot or do not wish to continue the business, dissolution requires that the partnership be terminated and "wound up." Notice of dissolution must be provided to all persons who may have a claim against the partnership. All partnership assets are gathered and liquidated, paying creditors (other than partners) first. All valid debts must be paid in full before anything can be distributed to partners.

Limited Partnership

A limited partnership is a partnership of two or more persons formed in compliance with a state's limited partnership statute with one or more general partners and one or more limited partners as members of the firm. General partners have unlimited personal liability for partnership debts, while limited partners have no liability for debts or losses beyond their investment in the partnership. If a person is both a general partner and a limited partner in the same partnership, she has the liabilities of a general partner in relation to creditors. It is also possible for a corporation to be a general partner in most states, which may diminish the concept of unlimited personal liability of the general partner in some circumstances.

The National Conference of Commissioners on Uniform State Laws adopted the Uniform Limited Partnership Act (ULPA) in 1916, which was adopted by all states except Louisiana. ULPA was updated and revised in 1976, with further amendments in 1985, by the Revised Uniform Limited Partnership Act (RULPA). RULPA and its amendments have been adopted by a substantial majority of states, although some states still operate under the former ULPA. (Louisiana has adopted neither version of the Act.)

Limited partnerships differ from general partnerships in two important ways:

1.   A limited partnership can be formed only by complying with specific statutory requirements, which include filing a certificate to provide notice to creditors that some partners have limited liability for partnership debts. A general partnership can be formed by private agreement without any formal filing requirements.

2.   Limited partners, unlike general partners, may not participate in the management or control of the business.

Formation and Existence   RULPA requires members of a limited partnership to sign and file a certificate with the secretary of state showing the name and address of the limited partnership, the name and address of each partner, and identification of an agent for service of process. Amendments to the certificate must be filed to show important changes in the limited partnership structure or capitalization. In addition to the certificate, members of a limited partnership typically execute a private limited partnership agreement to govern the affairs of the business.

The term limited partnership must be included as part of the firm name. In addition, the surname of a limited partner cannot be used as part of the firm name unless it is also the name of a general partner or unless the firm had used the name before admitting the limited partner. If this rule is violated, the limited partner may be liable to creditors to the same extent as a general partner.

RULPA requires a limited partnership to maintain an office in the state, which need not be its place of business, where the following records must be maintained for inspection:

> ● a current list of names and addresses of all partners;

> ● a copy of the certificate of limited partnership and all amendments;

> ● a copy of all financial statements and tax returns for three years; and

> ● a copy of any written partnership agreement that exists.

In addition, the limited partnership must maintain an agent for service of process within the state.

Financial Structure　　　　A limited partner's contribution may take the form of cash, property, or a promise to contribute future cash or property. RULPA permits contribution of services; the former ULPA does not. A limited partner must make the contribution represented in the certificate of limited partnership; and if she fails to do so, the contribution may be enforced against her or against her estate.

The profits, losses, and distributions are allocated among partners according to the limited partnership agreement. ULPA does not provide a basis for making these distributions if the partnership agreement fails to do so. RULPA, however, provides that if the limited partnership agreement is silent on the topic, profits, losses, and distributions are allocated on the basis of the value of contributions made by each partner as shown in the limited partnership records retained by the partnership. This is different from the rule applied to general partnerships by UPA, which provides that partners share profits and losses equally if the subject is not covered by the partnership agreement.

A limited partner may lend money to the partnership; however, ULPA restricts loans made by limited partners if the loans are secured by firm assets. RULPA contains no specific prohibition but, rather, defers to each state's fraudulent conveyance statute.

Management The general partners manage the business of the limited partnership and incur personal liability to creditors if partnership assets are insufficient. Limited partners are investors only and generally have no voice in management. They may be granted voting rights by the limited partnership agreement; without such a provision, however, RULPA provides no voting rights other than the unanimous consent required to admit a new general partner.

If a limited partner participates actively in the management of the partnership business, she loses her limited liability insulation and is treated as a general partner. ULPA reaches this result in all cases; RULPA, however, grants unlimited liability only as to those persons who transact business with the partnership with knowledge of the limited partner's participation—unless the limited partner exercises powers similar to those reserved for general partners.

RULPA attempts to clarify types of conduct by a limited partner which do not result in the loss of her limited liability status. Permissible conduct includes:

- serving as a contractor, agent, or employee of the limited partnership or of a general partner;

- consulting or advising a general partner concerning the limited partnership's business;

- acting as surety for the limited partnership;

- attending a meeting of partners or requesting such a meeting; and

- voting on vital partnership matters such as dissolution, changing the nature of the business, or the admission or removal of a general partner.

Liability   The liabilities of the general partners in a limited partnership are similar to those in a general partnership. Limited partners are liable only to the extent of their investments in the limited partnership unless:

> ■the limited partner's name appears in the name of the limited partnership;
>
> ■the limited partner participates in the management of the partnership business in an unlawful way; or
>
> ■false statements are made in the certificate of limited partnership, and the limited partner takes no action to correct the defect.

If any of these prohibitions occur, the limited partner involved loses the insulation of limited liability and is treated as a general partner.

Dissolution and Termination   Limited partnerships, like general partnerships, may be dissolved by agreement of the partners. The partnership is dissolved upon the withdrawal of a general partner unless the right to continue the business is stated in the limited partnership agreement or unless all partners consent to the continuation. Withdrawal of a general partner occurs upon the retirement or other voluntary withdrawal of a general partner, upon the death of a general partner, upon the dissolution of a corporate general partner, upon the removal of a general partner according to the terms of the limited partnership agreement, or upon the bankruptcy of a general partner.

Unless the business is continued, firm assets are collected and distributed according to statute. Outside creditors are paid first. After creditors are paid, ULPA gives preference to certain distributions to limited partners over general partners; RULPA, however, does not. Under the RULPA distribution scheme, limited and general partners are treated substantially the same.

Joint Venture

A joint venture involves the combining of efforts by two or more persons for one transaction or for one event only. It resembles a partnership in many respects and may be evidenced by a written agreement. A joint venture is different from a partnership, however, since it does not contemplate a continuing relationship between or among the parties. Once the transaction or event occurs, the joint venture is concluded.

A joint venture may exist between an entertainer and a promoter, for example, for a specific concert or show.

Joint Stock Company

The term *joint stock company* or *joint stock association* derives its name from the fact that its members pool their capital into a common fund (joint stock) rather than each member owning his or her own stock separately. This business form is not prevalent today; when it exists, it typically is an unincorporated business enterprise with ownership interests evidenced by shares of stock. It may have articles of association and may be subject to regulation by a particular state's statutes; however, it is not regarded or treated the same as a corporation.

Shareholders are personally liable for association obligations; and the association's affairs generally are managed by a board of directors and by officers who serve as agents or employees of the shareholders.

Corporation

A corporation is an artificial person created by or under authority of state statute to carry on a business or activity separately from its creators, owners, or investors. A corporation has unlimited liability for corporate obligations; however, its owners' liability is limited to the amount of their investment. A corporation may have perpetual existence, which means that it is unaffected by changes in ownership. Like a natural person, a corporation may own property, may sue and be sued, may enter into contracts, and may be subject to criminal liability. As artificial persons, corporations are entitled to many of the protections of natural persons under the federal and state constitutions.

For purposes of establishing personal jurisdiction, a corporation is a citizen of the state where it is incorporated, as well as of any state where it does business which is sufficient to establish minimum contacts with that state. A California corporation that sells insurance policies to Kansas residents from its office in California, for instance, is a citizen of California and a citizen of Kansas for purposes of personal jurisdiction and federal venue statutes.

Corporations are classified by type and may fit more than one classification. A ***public corporation*** is created by a government entity to administer government purposes. A local government may create a municipal corporation, for example, to administer the affairs of a city. The federal government has created public corporations, such as the Federal Home Mortgage Association, to administer special federal programs. A *private corporation* is created by private persons for private (as opposed to public) purposes. Private corporations generally are either nonprofit corporations or for-profit corporations.

A *nonprofit corporation*, sometimes called an eleemosynary corporation, is one organized typically for educational, religious, or charitable purposes. The income earned by a nonprofit corporation is devoted to its nonprofit purpose (such as providing educational programs or scholarships) and may not be used to enrich those who operate or manage it. By contract, a for-profit corporation, more typically called a *business corporation*, is one organized to operate a business enterprise, with profits from the business being distributed to its owners. The balance of this chapter is devoted almost exclusively to the business corporation.

A *publicly held corporation* is one owned by many shareholders and whose stock is publicly traded (bought and sold on the open market). Large corporations, such as General Foods or General Motors, are publicly held corporations. A *closely held corporation*, sometimes called a close corporation, is one owned by one shareholder or by a small, closely connected group of shareholders. Unlike shareholders of publicly held corporations, shareholders of close corporations often serve as directors and officers of the corporation as well.

The *professional corporation* is a type of close corporation formed by a small group of professionals (lawyers, accountants, doctors) to carry on the practice for which they are licensed. Unlike shareholders of other types of corporations, shareholders of a professional corporation remain personally liable for their professional activities affecting third parties. Professionals traditionally incorporated to take advantage of retirement plans and tax benefits available to corporate employees that were not available to self-employed persons. (Federal tax laws now have been changed to provide similar retirement benefits to self-employed persons as well as to corporate employees.)

A *domestic corporation* is one which operates in the same state in which is was organized or created. A *foreign corporation* is one operating in a state that is different from the one in which the corporation was organized or created. For example, a corporation organized in Tennessee and operating in Texas is a domestic corporation in Tennessee—but is a foreign corporation in Texas.

A *subsidiary corporation* is one whose stock is owned entirely or in substantial part by another corporation. The corporation owning the majority of shares in a subsidiary corporation is called a *parent corporation*.

A *Chapter S corporation* is a small business corporation which, under certain situations, may elect to have its undistributed taxable income taxed to its shareholders under federal tax laws as if it were a partnership. The ChapterS status generally avoids corporate income tax on profits, and corporate losses may be claimed by shareholders (*see below*).

A *limited liability company* is a corporate form authorized by a growing number of states, intended as a hybrid of the most attractive characteristics of the partnership and corporate forms of organization. Until more states enact statutes authorizing existence of the limited liability corporation, typical provisions and characteristics cannot be stated with reasonable accuracy.

The Decision to Incorporate   Distinctive attributes of the corporation, including centralization of management, free transferability of ownership interests, perpetual existence, and limited liability of owners (shareholders) make the corporate form advantageous for large businesses. For small businesses, however, the advantages often are illusory. Centralized management, transferability of ownership interest, and continuity of existence can be provided by specific provisions in a partnership agreement. The limited liability of the corporation loses much of its value when creditors require shareholders to guarantee corporate obligations personally, which happens fairly often in small, closely held corporations.

Creating and operating a corporation involves expense, complexity, and formalities not present in a partnership. For these reasons, the corporation is not always the most desirable form for a small business. Incorporation is most commonly indicated if limited liability is an important consideration and if federal income tax treatment is favorable.

Preincorporation   If the corporate form is desirable to operate a particular business, someone must take charge of bringing the corporation into existence. It is possible to create the corporation and then to organize it; however, the organization often is done before the statutory requirements to incorporate are met. The person or persons who plan and organize the business affairs of the intended corporation are called ***promoters***. A promoter's activities typically include discovery and development of the idea for the business, arranging for needed capital, securing property and personnel to operate the business, and ultimately complying with the statutory formalities to create the corporation.

A promoter who contracts on behalf of a proposed corporation is liable on the contract unless she discloses that the corporation has not yet been formed. If a preincorporation disclosure is made, the promoter may characterize the transaction as an offer to the corporation, to be accepted or rejected after its formation. The preincorporation agreement between the promoter and the third party may provide that the promoter is liable but will be released if the corporation is formed subsequently and assumes liability on the contract.

Once the corporation is formed, it may accept the preincorporation offer or may adopt or assume the preincorporation contract. Corporate liability for the promoter's actions requires some affirmative act by the corporation after its formation to shows its consent to the preincorporation transaction. After a corporation is formed, the promoter has a fiduciary duty to the board of directors and to the shareholders to act in good faith, to deal fairly, and to make full disclosure. A promoter may not take secret profits in violation of her fiduciary obligations.

Incorporation   Incorporation is governed by state statute. At one time, the corporation laws of Delaware were the least restrictive in the country; and, as a result, many corporations were incorporated there. The American Bar Association adopted a Model Business Corporation Act (MBCA) and, later, the Revised Model Business Corporation Act (RMBCA), which has been enacted in whole or in part by many states. As a result of this and other, more liberal laws affecting corporations, more states have become strong competitors of Delaware in attracting corporate citizens.

Specific incorporation procedures vary from state to state; however, they follow the same general pattern. In the usual situation, one or more persons, called *incorporators*, draft and execute a document called *articles of incorporation*. (Since a corporation is a person, a corporation may be the incorporator for another corporation.) The articles of incorporation and the required fee are filed typically with the secretary of state, who issues a *certificate of incorporation* if the articles meet all statutory requirements. Corporate existence generally begins when the certificate of incorporation is issued. Some states have additional requirements, such as recording the articles of incorporation in a local office (for example, the county clerk) or publishing a notice of incorporation in a newspaper of general circulation.

Required contents of the articles of incorporation vary according to the laws of the incorporating state; however, these requirements generally include:

- the name of the corporation;

- its duration (whether perpetual or for a specific, limited time);

- the purpose(s) for which the corporation is organized (many statutes allow a very broad statement of purposes, such as "to transact any and all lawful business for which corporations may be incorporated in this state");

■a statement of the authorized classes of stock, the authorized number of shares, the par value of shares, and the rights and preferences of shares or shareholders;

■the address of the corporation's registered office and the name and address of the registered agent (for service of process and notices);

■the names and addresses of the original directors comprising the board of directors; and

■the name and address of each incorporator.

Other information may be included as the incorporators believe appropriate. The articles of incorporation is the controlling document of the corporation. Amendment of the articles must follow specific statutory rules, which usually include a requirement that all amendments be filed with the secretary of state.

After the certificate of incorporation is issued, the organizational meeting is held by the directors named in the articles of incorporation. If no directors are required to be named in the articles, the organizational meeting is held by the incorporator(s). The overseer of this meeting generally is the attorney retained to complete the incorporation process. At the organizational meeting, subscriptions received from potential shareholders for the purchase of stock may be accepted or rejected; the form of stock certificate is adopted; the form of corporate seal is adopted (if a corporate seal is required by state law); preincorporation contracts may be accepted or rejected; a corporate bank account is authorized, together with a designation of those persons who will be authorized to sign checks and to borrow money on behalf of the corporation; and bylaws are adopted. If a particular state's statutes require it, first meetings of shareholders and directors may follow the organizational meeting to accept or reject the actions taken at the organizational meeting.

Bylaws are the written rules which supplement the articles of incorporation in governing the corporation's internal affairs. Bylaws may contain any terms or provisions desired by corporate shareholders which are consistent with the laws of the state and also are consistent with the controlling articles of incorporation. Bylaws usually are adopted during the corporation's organizational meetings of shareholders and directors and may be amended by the corporation's board of directors, although amendment can be reserved to shareholders only. A set of bylaws may cover things such as procedures required to sell and to value shares (in closely held corporations); the method of filling vacancies for directors or officers which occur between elections; the duties and authority of the board of directors and of officers of the corporation; and so on. Bylaws need not be filed with the secretary of state; rather, they are maintained with the corporation's permanent books and records.

A single corporation may be domesticated (incorporated) in more than one state at the same time or may incorporate in one state and operate in other states as a foreign corporation. The decision of whether to operate as a domestic corporation or as a foreign corporation depends upon many factors, including state tax laws and any differences in treatment of domestic and foreign corporations within a particular state. If it were advantageous to do so, a single corporation could be domesticated simultaneously in all fifty states.

Recognition or Disregard of Corporate Entity

A primary purpose for incorporating is to provide limited personal liability to shareholders for corporate obligations. By using the doctrines of "*de facto* incorporation" and "corporation by estoppel," corporation law sometimes permits limited liability to those who do business as a corporation which has not complied with statutory requirements. Conversely, a court may "pierce the corporate veil" in some situations to impose personal liability upon shareholders of a properly formed corporation.

Defective Incorporation   A *de jure corporation* is one which has complied with all statutory requirements governing its organization and existence.

A *de facto corporation* is not a corporation at all, having failed to comply with statutory requirements for organization and existence. Rather, a *de facto* corporation is a legal fiction created to identify an entity that has made a good faith effort to comply with statutory requirements, has failed to comply for some technical reason, and has conducted itself as a corporation. If these elements are present, third parties (such as creditors) may not assert lack of corporate status as a basis to impose personal liability on the owners.

Another doctrine used to insulate owners of a defectively formed corporation is *corporation by estoppel*. When a third party deals with a corporation, unaware of its defective organization and relying solely upon the corporation's credit, later discovers the defective incorporation, and attempts to hold either the promoters or the owners personally liable as general partners, the third party is estopped (prevented) from holding owners personally liable. Corporation by estoppel most likely will be applied when the defect is not caused by a willful failure to comply with incorporation statutes.

The RMBCA and many state statutes provide that a corporation is legally formed (*de jure* corporation) when the certificate of incorporation is issued by the secretary of state despite any technical defects that may exist. Where this type of statute exists, the *de facto* corporation and corporation by estoppel doctrines are unnecessary.

Piercing the Corporate Veil

Because a primary purpose of operating in the corporate form is limited liability, courts generally recognize the separate legal existence of the corporation from its shareholders. If a corporation incurs debts in excess of its assets, creditors' claims may be satisfied only with corporate assets, no matter how limited those assets are. However, if it would be unfair or unjust to allow shareholders to hide behind the corporate shield, a court may disregard the corporation's existence and may impose personal liability for corporate debts upon its shareholders. In such a case, the court is said to "pierce the corporate veil."

Cases which pierce the corporate veil (impose shareholder liability for corporate obligations) involve some or all of the following characteristics:

1. Insufficient capital invested, considering the nature and risks of the business.

2. Failure to observe corporate formalities, such as issuing shares of stock and holding meetings.

3. Failure to treat the corporation as a separate entity by mixing affairs of the corporation with affairs of the shareholders, such as failure to maintain separate corporate records, commingling corporate assets with shareholder assets, paying corporate debts with shareholder assets, or paying shareholder debts with corporate assets.

4. Excessive fragmentation of a single business into separate corporations.

5. Affirmative wrongdoing, such as creating the corporation to avoid an existing obligation or siphoning off corporate assets by a dominant shareholder.

Cases which seek to pierce the corporate veil typically arise in a one-shareholder, family, or other closely held corporation where the shareholder may use the corporate entity as a facade for personal dealings. They also arise in situations involving parent and subsidiary corporations where a parent corporation uses an undercapitalized subsidiary to undertake an especially risky venture.

Personal liability of shareholders may be sought in either contract or tort cases. A person who is injured in an automobile accident in which an employee of the corporation was the negligent driver may seek damages from the corporation under a theory of *respondeat superior*, for instance.

Courts are more reluctant to pierce the corporate veil in contract cases than in tort cases. A contract claimant deals with the corporation voluntarily and generally has the opportunity to secure the personal guaranty of one or more shareholders if she wishes to do so. If corporate credit is unacceptable and if the shareholders refuse to incur personal liability, the third party can refuse to enter into the contract. Tort claimants, on the other hand, are involuntary creditors. Their claims easily may be frustrated by undercapitalized, underinsured corporations; and courts are more willing to impose liability in these situations.

Corporate Financial Structure

A corporation must have a source of funds with which to acquire assets and to operate. Most funds of ongoing corporations are generated by reinvesting earnings back into the business. An additional method, and usually the initial method, of raising corporate funds is the issuance of corporate securities in exchange for cash, property, or services transferred to the corporation.

A *security* is a share or other interest in the property of the corporation (an equity security) or an obligation of the issuer (a debt security). Equity securities, such as stock shares, are those which create an ownership interest in the business. The owners of equity securities are called shareholders or stockholders. In contrast, debt securities are obligations of the corporation which must be repaid. A debt security creates a debtor-creditor relationship between the corporation and the holder of the debt security. Typical debt securities include notes, debentures, and bonds.

Corporations often use both equity securities and debt securities to finance the business. The combination of debt securities and equity securities of a particular corporation is known as the corporation's *capital structure*.

Equity Securities   The equity securities of a corporation (shares of stock) are the units into which the ownership of the corporation is divided. They represent the underlying ownership interests and confer three basic rights upon the shareholders:

1.   The right to share in distributions of corporate profits (dividends) when declared by the board of directors;

2.   The right to vote on important corporate matters and thereby to participate in control; and

3.   The right to a proportionate share of net assets upon liquidation of the corporation.

Not all ownership interests (shares of stock) are created equal. The articles of incorporation may divide shares into classes. If classes are created, the articles of incorporation must describe the designations, preferences, limitations, and rights of each class in relation to other classes. The voting rights of any class of shares may be limited or denied entirely, or special voting rights may be provided. In addition, a corporation may issue stock in preferred or special classes that have preference over other classes (1) in the payment of dividends or (2) in the distribution of assets of the corporation upon liquidation. Classes of shares which have these types of preferential rights are called *preferred shares*. Preferred shares generally are nonvoting shares.

By contrast, *common shares* are the residual ownership interest in the corporation. Common shares are entitled to payment of dividends only after shares with a dividend preference are paid. They are entitled to distribution of assets upon liquidation only after creditors (including holders of debt securities) and preferred shareholders receive distributions. If a corporation has only one class of shares, it is, in effect, common stock regardless of what it may be called.

Most states permit a corporation to have more than one class of common stock, each possessing different rights and privileges.

The articles of incorporation may make certain classes of stock subject to reacquisition (redemption) by the corporation at a fixed price. These are *redeemable shares*. Although redemption or "call" provisions typically apply only to preferred shares, some states permit redeemable common shares as long as there is at least one class of voting common shares which is not subject to redemption. Redemption of a class of shares may be mandatory or optional and may be total or partial, as determined by the articles of incorporation.

The articles of incorporation also may provide that shares of a given class can be converted into shares of another class on some predetermined ratio. These are *convertible shares*. The ratio generally takes stock dividends and stock splits into account to protect the conversion privilege against dilution. The MBCA and some state statutes prohibit conversion of one class of stock into a class (1) having prior or superior rights to dividends or (2) having prior or superior rights to corporate assets upon liquidation. Under these types of provisions, for example, preferred stock may be converted to common stock; however, common stock may not be converted to preferred stock.

A given class of shares often possesses both redemption and conversion privileges. If so, after the call for redemption, the shareholder generally has a limited time within which to exercise the conversion right. Redemption and conversion privileges often are found in debt securities as well (*see below*).

A corporation may create and issue ***stock options*** which entitle the option holders to purchase a stated number of shares of a given class from the corporation at a specific price and usually within a limited period of time. Options may be purchased either in connection with or independently of the corporation's issuance of other securities. They may be issued as incentives to corporate directors, officers, or employees.

Stock options generally are evidenced by certificates called ***stock warrants***, which characteristically are long term. By contrast, short-term share options are called ***stock rights*** and often are issued in connection with the issuance of debt securities or preferred stock. Both warrants and rights of publicly held corporations are freely transferable and are publicly traded. Their value depends on the difference between the stock's market price and the option price.

A shareholder has ***preemptive rights*** when she has the right to purchase a proportionate share of a new issue of common stock (or of securities which are convertible to common stock) before it is offered for sale to others. Whether preemptive rights are granted by the articles of incorporation or by statute, they provide a method of protecting a shareholder's proportionate interest in the corporation. Preemptive rights are more common in closely held corporations than in publicly held corporations (*see below*).

A. Issuance of Stock

A corporation has the power to create and to issue the number of shares stated or authorized in its articles of incorporation. The law generally places no limit on the number of shares of various classes that can be authorized; neither does it require that all authorized shares be issued. Some states, however, impose a tax according to the number of authorized shares, which creates a practical ceiling on the shares which are authorized.

Shares of issued stock are represented by stock certificates. The ***stock certificate*** merely is evidence of the holder's undivided ownership interest; it is not the stock itself. Because the ownership interest is undivided (cannot be separated from the corporate assets), a stock certificate is the method used to show the owner's stock interest.

Some or all of the authorized shares are issued to shareholders for consideration; these are known as **outstanding shares**. Shares are outstanding until they are later reacquired by the corporation through redemption, conversion, or repurchase. Shares reacquired by the corporation are known as treasury shares or **treasury stock**.

Shares may be issued with a par value or may be "no par" shares. **Par value** is the dollar amount stated as the value of the share in the articles of incorporation. Historically, par value was the selling price of the shares. Today, however, par value often has little connection with the selling price of the stock. Both par and no par shares are issued for the amount which is determined by the board of directors (unless the right to determine value is reserved to shareholders).

Stock may not be sold for less than par value. Consequently, par stock often shows a nominal par value (such as $1.00). Absent fraud, the judgment of the board of directors concerning consideration to be paid for stock is conclusive. Treasury stock may be sold for any price set by the board of directors without regard to the par value stated on the stock.

B.   Payment for Stock   Before a corporation is formed, stock subscriptions are one method to acquire investment capital or the assurance of investment capital. A preincorporation **stock subscription** is an offer by a would-be shareholder to purchase a specified number of previously unissued shares of the corporation. Stock subscriptions can be made either before or after the corporation is formed. When stock subscriptions are made after the corporation is formed, they constitute bilateral contracts between the subscriber and the corporation. When stock subscriptions are made before the corporation is formed, they constitute irrevocable offers under both MBCA and RMBCA provisions.

Payment terms for stock subscriptions generally are set by the board of directors; payment must be uniform for all shares of the same class. In general, the stock certificate is not issued until the subscription price is paid in full. If a subscriber defaults in the agreed payments, the board of directors may collect the debt in the same way as all other debts of the corporation are collected.

Securities registration requirements generally prevent the use of stock subscriptions for equity securities issued by publicly held corporations.

C. **Watered Stock** As consideration for issuance of stock, shareholders and subscribers must pay the value of the stock as determined by the board of directors. Although consideration usually is expressed in dollars, money is not the only consideration permitted. Some states permit the consideration to be paid in property or in services as well as in cash. Using this approach, a promissory note cannot constitute payment for the stock. However, the RMBCA permits stock to be issued either in exchange for a promissory note or in exchange for a contract for future services to the corporation.

Stock issued and paid for at the full value established by the board of directors are *fully paid and nonassessable* shares. Stock issued for something less than the full value established by the board of directors is **watered stock**. Issuance of watered stock can occur when a shareholder pays nothing for the shares (*bonus stock*) or when a shareholder pays less than full value for the shares (*discount stock*).

Watered stock dilutes the value of stock held by all other shareholders, because it dilutes their equity interests in corporate assets. When this occurs, the remedy is cancellation of the offending shares. Watered stock also inflates the corporation's capitalization, which may mislead creditors (securities regulations prevent many of the previous abuses in relation to creditors of publicly traded corporations). If creditors are involved, the offending shareholder(s) can be required to pay the additional amount necessary to reach the value of the stock set by the board of directors.

A subsequent good faith purchaser of the stock incurs no liability to the corporation or to its creditors for consideration that was not paid by the original shareholder. Likewise, a creditor to whom the stock is transferred as collateral is not liable. In both situations, the transferor (the original shareholder) remains liable for the watered amount of the stock: actual value less value paid.

Debt Securities Debt securities are issued in exchange for loans made to the corporation. As is true of any other loan, debt securities typically require periodic interest payments and ultimate repayment of principal. The holder of a debt security is a creditor of the corporation and, as a creditor, has a claim on corporate assets which is prior to the claims of any shareholders.

Publicly held corporations frequently issue debt securities in the form of either bonds or debentures. A **bond** is an obligation secured by a lien or a mortgage on specific corporate property; the holder of a bond is a secured creditor of the corporation. By contrast, a **debenture** is an unsecured corporate obligation; a holder of a corporate debenture is an unsecured creditor of the corporation.

Corporate bonds and debentures generally are long-term obligations, issued in fixed denominations (perhaps $1,000) with a fixed interest rate, which is called the coupon rate. Bonds and debentures most often are handled by a financial institution which serves as the trustee under a trust agreement—sometimes called a *trust indenture*—between the corporation and the trustee for the benefit of the security holders.

In addition to bonds and debentures, corporations frequently obtain either short-term or long-term loans from commercial banks and similar lenders in exchange for promissory *notes* from the corporation, either secured or unsecured. Suppliers of goods or services (trade creditors) also may extend credit or corporations on a secured or unsecured basis.

If money can be borrowed from outside creditors, one possible advantage of debt financing is *leverage*, sometimes called *trading on equity*. Leverage occurs when the total investment in the business (debt + equity) yields a higher rate of return than the cost of borrowing money (interest rate).

> Ajax Corporation has a total investment of $1,000,000 and generates $150,000 a year in earnings, which yields a 15% rate of return. As long as the interest rate stays below 15%, Ajax should borrow as much of the $1,000,000 investment as possible. The difference between the rate of return and the interest rate is additional profit. If, however, earnings are so poor that they fall below the interest rate, the difference is an additional loss.

Shareholders frequently lend a portion of their investment to the corporation, rather than use all of it to purchase stock. Since interest payments on the debt are deductible and dividend payments on the stock are not, shareholder debt often reduces the problem of "double taxation" associated with corporations (corporation is taxed on its profit, declares dividends, and shareholder is taxed on dividend income).

Because of the tax advantages of corporate debt which is payable to shareholders, the Internal Revenue Service has been able to reclassify some corporate debt as shareholder stock interest, particularly in those corporations with excessive debt capitalization. A corporation with a high debt-to-equity ratio (four to one or higher) commonly is known as a *thin corporation* and may be subject to debt reclassification under IRS regulations.

Dividends and Redemption

When a corporation transfers corporate money or property to its shareholders, the transfer is a *distribution*. When the distribution comes from the corporation's current or past earnings, it is a **dividend**. A dividend may or may not be proportionate to share ownership. Preferred shares, for example, may have preferential rights to dividends over other shares. In addition, a corporation's redemption or repurchase of its shares may produce a disproportionate distribution.

Any distribution (whether by dividend or by corporate liquidation) may affect the rights of creditors and of various classes of shareholders. As a result, limitations are placed upon the distributions that a corporation lawfully can make.

Dividends   Dividends typically take the form of cash, property (such as shares of stock of a subsidiary), or stock. A stock dividend means stock of the corporation declaring the dividend. (Stock of a subsidiary corporation is property—it is not stock—of the corporation declaring the dividend.) A corporation pays dividends only by declaration of its board of directors. Once declared, a dividend is a legally enforceable obligation of the corporation and cannot be repealed or retracted by the board of directors. Whether or not to declare dividends is influenced by such factors as corporate earnings, future capital needs of the business, and shareholder expectations. Federal income tax consequences to major shareholders can affect dividend and retention policies in closely held corporations.

Shareholders usually participate in dividends in proportion to their ownership interests, as determined by the classes of shares identified in the articles of incorporation. Preferred stock, for example, typically receives dividends before common stock receives dividends.

The articles of incorporation may provide that preferred stock be cumulative, cumulative-to-the-extent-earned, or noncumulative. **Cumulative preferred** stock receives a prescribed dividend for the current year as well as for all prior years in which a preferred dividend was not paid by the corporation—before any dividend may be paid for common stock. **Cumulative-to-the-extent-earned preferred** stock carries forward and accumulates any unpaid dividends to the extent that the corporation had earnings to pay the dividend but did not pay it.

> Ajax Corporation had earnings in 1991, no earnings in 1992, and substantial earnings in 1993. If the preferred stock is cumulative-to-the-extent-earned and if dividends are to be paid in 1994, the dividends for 1991, 1993, and 1994 must be paid for the preferred stock before any dividend is paid for common stock.

Noncumulative preferred stock receives only the prescribed dividend for the current year (prior years need not be paid) before dividends are paid for common stock.

Regardless of the cumulative or noncumulative status of preferred stock, the articles of incorporation may provide that preferred stock be either participating or nonparticipating. ***Participating preferred*** stock receives the preferred dividend fixed by the articles and also participates in dividends paid to other classes of stock. ***Nonparticipating preferred*** stock receives only the preferred dividend stated in the articles of incorporation; it does not participate in any other dividend payments made to other classes of stock.

A.   Stock Dividends   Unlike cash or property dividends (*see above*), stock dividends do not distribute corporate assets to the shareholder. Instead, a stock dividend distributes additional shares of stock (or fractional shares) for each share owned. A stock dividend increases the number of shares comprising the corporation's equity and, at the same time, proportionately reduces the percentage of ownership of each share. The additional shares generally—but not always—are of the same class as the original shares.

The MBCA permits—but does not require—a corporation to issue either (1) *fractional shares* of stock or (2) *scrip* in lieu of fractional shares. A particular state may follow the MBCA or may authorize corporations to issue only fractional shares or only scrip.

> Ajax Corporation declares a 1% stock dividend entitling shareholders to receive one additional share of stock for every 100 shares owned. John owns 150 shares of Ajax stock.

If the corporation issues fractional shares, John will receive 1.5 shares of stock as his dividend. The holder of a ***fractional share*** is entitled to a fractional voting right, a fractional dividend, and a fractional distribution if the corporation is liquidated. By contrast, ***scrip*** is a certificate representing a percentage of a full share. When the holder accumulates enough scrip certificates (scrip may be bought and sold), she may surrender them for one full share of stock. Unless the board of directors provides otherwise, scrip certificates do not entitle the holder to the same voting, dividend, or liquidation rights as fractional shares. In addition, the board of directors may provide that scrip becomes void if it is not exchanged for full shares within a certain time period.

B.   Stock Split   A stock split is similar to a stock dividend, since each increases the total number of outstanding shares without distributing corporate assets. They are different, however, in the way they affect corporate capital accounts. When a stock dividend is declared, the value of the stock is capitalized (transferred from the earnings surplus account to the capital account—either as additional stated capital or as additional capital surplus). There is no transfer of earnings to capital in a stock split.

A stock split simply creates more shares of stock (two-for-one, three-for-one), with each share valued at a proportionately lesser amount. In a two-for-one split, for example, shares valued at $100.00 each would be valued at $50.00 each after the split. Stock splits sometimes are used to reduce the per-share value of stock, making it more attractive to a larger group of investors. Stock splits typically require approval of the board of directors and may require amendment of the articles of incorporation to authorize the issuance of additional shares of stock or to change the par value of authorized stock.

Stock splits typically do not create tax consequences.

Funds Available to Pay Dividends

To protect corporate creditors and, to a lesser degree, to protect preferred shareholders, state law limits the distribution of corporate assets to shareholders. Although there is some variation, all states essentially follow the *insolvency test* found in both the MBCA and the RMBCA. Under the insolvency test, dividend payments are prohibited if the corporation is insolvent or would be rendered insolvent by the distribution. Insolvency may be either equity insolvency or bankruptcy insolvency.

Equity insolvency is the inability to pay debts as they become due in the ordinary course of business.

Bankruptcy insolvency is the excess of total liabilities over total assets.

If a corporation is insolvent under *either* insolvency test, the Model Acts prohibit payment of a dividend to shareholders.

When a corporation is solvent, all states permit dividends to be paid to the extent of the corporation's unrestricted and unreserved earned surplus. Earned surplus means retained earnings and typically includes all accumulated profits of the corporation since its formation, reduced primarily by prior dividend distributions.

When a corporation is solvent, some states permit dividends to be paid from either surplus capital or earned surplus. These states typically permit dividends to be paid unless the dividend would cause an impairment of the stated capital (total par value); however, dividends from surplus capital may be limited if there is no earned surplus.

Only a handful of states permit what are known as *nimble* dividends, where dividends can be paid from current profits even if a deficit exists in the earned surplus accounts from losses in prior years.

State statutes generally impose liability upon directors for unlawful dividends or for other unlawful distributions. Under both Model Acts, a director is liable to the corporation for the amount by which the declared distribution exceeds the legally permissible amount if she votes for or assents to the declaration of a dividend or other distribution in violation of statutory limits or in violation of the articles of incorporation. Such a director may have a defense to liability if she exercised *due care* in declaring the dividend by relying upon financial statements or upon the opinions provided by corporate officers, accountants, attorneys, or employees.

Repurchase and Redemption   Under both the MBCA and the RMBCA, a corporation has the power to acquire its own shares of stock through repurchase. It also has the power to issue stock (usually preferred stock), which can be redeemed by the corporation at a later time. These types of shares are called treasury stock after they are repurchased or redeemed, and are the functional equivalent of authorized but unissued shares. After the repurchase or redemption, each outstanding remaining share represents a proportionately larger interest in a smaller group of corporate assets.

A repurchase or a redemption is similar to a cash or property dividend, because the corporation distributes corporate assets to shareholders without consideration. Unlike a dividend, however, a repurchase or redemption involves an element of exchange: shares of stock in exchange for corporate assets. When the repurchase or redemption is partial, it causes a disproportionate distribution of corporate assets to the selling shareholders; dividends, on the other hand, generally are paid to all shareholders in proportion to their ownership interests.

A corporation may repurchase its own shares for one of several reasons. In a closely held corporation, the repurchase may be necessary to buy out one or more shareholders. In a publicly held corporation, the repurchased shares may be used to fund employee compensation plans or to acquire other corporations. Moreover, significant repurchases may drive up the price of the remaining shares as a defensive measure against a hostile takeover bid.

Repurchases and redemptions are classified as corporate distributions and are subject to the same legal restrictions as dividends, including the insolvency test (*see above*).

Corporate Taxation

Like individuals (and consistent with its identity as a separate legal entity), a corporation is subject to taxes levied by federal, state, and local governments based on the amount of income earned each year.

Double taxation occurs when corporate profits are taxed at the corporate rate, the after-tax balance is distributed to shareholders as dividends, and the dividend income is taxed again (to the shareholder) at the individual income tax rate. With parent-subsidiary corporations, this can become triple taxation. For example, when the subsidiary pays its tax and distributes remaining profits to its parent corporation (the sole shareholder) as dividends, those dividends become part of the parent's income; and the parent pays tax on it before distributing the balance to the individual shareholders as dividends, which are included in the shareholder's individual income tax.

Large corporations simply accept this disadvantage, because the corporate form offers many advantages that are critical to operating a large business. Small corporations, however, may have options available to minimize the double taxation effect. For example, when shareholders also are officers or employees of the corporation, as is frequently the case, they may be paid salaries by the corporation, which are deductible as a corporate expense and therefore not included in the net taxable income of the corporation. Another option is to use a portion of the shareholder's investment to lend money to the corporation rather than to buy shares of stock. In this way, the interest on the loan is an expense to the corporation. This works well, as long as the corporation's debt-to-equity ratio is not excessive (*see above*). In addition, shareholders may purchase equipment and lease it to the corporation (rather than buying stock); the shareholder then receives rental payments on the equipment, which is an expense to the corporation.

Another approach is to leave profits in the corporation as retained earnings; since no dividends are distributed, only the corporate tax is paid. This option has only limited advantages, because retained earnings increase the value of the remaining, outstanding stock, which means a capital gains tax for the shareholder if the stock is sold. Even more limiting is the fact that a separate accumulated earnings tax is levied against the corporation when it retains excessive earnings.

Chapter S Election   A small business corporation may elect not to be taxed at the corporate rate. Instead, its income (whether distributed as dividends or retained by the corporation) is passed through in proportion to shareholders' ownership interests and is taxed at each shareholder's respective individual income tax rate.   The corporation thus receives the same tax treatment as a sole proprietorship or partnership. This provides two advantages over corporate tax treatment: (1) profits are not subject to double taxation and (2) if the shareholder actively participates in the business, corporate losses may be taken as ordinary losses against the shareholder's personal income which, in turn, reduces the shareholder's personal income tax liability. The qualifications for a Chapter S election are:

- No more than 75 shareholders (spouses are treated as a single shareholder, no matter how the stock is held by them);

- Shareholders must be natural persons (no corporations or partnerships);

- There can be only one class of stock (different classes are permitted if their only difference is voting rights); and

- No nonresident aliens as shareholders.

Making the election to be taxed as a Chapter S corporation for a given fiscal year must be done within certain time limits (any time during the preceding fiscal year or no later than three months into the current fiscal year). Once made, the election continues until it is terminated by a majority of the shareholders; until the corporation receives more than 25% of its income from passive sources (rents, dividends, interest) for three consecutive years; or until the corporation acquires its 36th shareholder.

Chapter S status may be desirable during the first few years of operation, when the corporation is most likely to incur losses.

Section 1244 Stock   Section 1244 of the Internal Revenue Code provides a separate method for shareholders of small business corporations to receive favorable tax treatment if they sell Section 1244 stock or if the stock becomes worthless. Rather than take a capital loss, which is what ordinarily would occur with losses on stocks, the shareholder can treat the loss as ordinary loss—which means she can credit it against ordinary income to reduce her personal income tax liability.

The definition of a small business corporation is different for Section 1244 stock than it is for a Chapter S election. To qualify as Section 1244 stock, the amount of money to be raised by selling Section 1244 stock plus the corporation's equity capital cannot exceed $1 million total.

Another major difference is that a Chapter S election applies to all income and all shareholders of the corporation. By contrast, Section 1244 applies only to a specific group of stock shares to which Section 1244 benefits will attach when they are offered for sale to prospective shareholders. The number of persons to whom the stock is offered is quite limited and usually involves existing shareholders. A single shareholder, then, may own some shares which are from the Section 1244 group and some shares which are not. If losses are incurred, the Section 1244 shares receive a different, more favorable tax treatment (ordinary loss) than the regular shares (capital loss).

Other Tax Advantages Corporations traditionally have been allowed to deduct certain types of expenses incurred in providing fringe benefits to employees to encourage their long and faithful performance. In addition, there are some tax advantages to employees under qualified incentive plans without regard to whether the employee is also a shareholder or not. These include stock options; qualified pension and profit-sharing plans; medical and dental reimbursement plans; and life, health, and accident insurance programs.

For example, a qualified profit-sharing plan allows the corporation to deduct profits accumulated for employees under the plan. At the same time, the employee is not taxed on those amounts until payment is made, which often is not until the employee reaches retirement age and a much more favorable income tax bracket. Premiums for health and life insurance plans are expenses to the corporation but are not treated as taxable income to the employee.

Favorable tax treatment of these types of fringe benefit packages once was unique to the corporation. In recent years, however, many of the same tax incentives are available to self-employed persons.

Corporate Management

Once a corporation is formed, it is managed by individuals whose functions, rights, authority, and duties are governed by statutes, case law, administrative regulations, and internal sources such as the corporation's articles of incorporation, bylaws, resolutions, and private contracts. Corporate management responsibilities are divided among shareholders, the board of directors, and corporate officers. As owners of the corporation, shareholders elect a board of directors, which has ultimate responsibility to manage the corporation. The directors, in turn, elect or appoint corporate officers and give them authority to operate the corporation consistent with the management policy set by the board of directors. The officers frequently appoint executive officers, who hire employees to undertake the day-to-day activities of the business. Collectively, the officers and directors comprise the management of the corporation.

In a small, closely held corporation, the same individuals frequently are shareholders, directors, and officers simultaneously.

Shareholders   Shareholders (stockholders) are the owners of the corporation; however, their management involvement generally is limited to election of directors and extraordinary corporate matters such as amendments to the articles of incorporation, sale of corporate assets other than in the ordinary course of business, merger or consolidation, and dissolution. The power to adopt, amend, or repeal bylaws frequently is reserved to the shareholders by the articles of incorporation.

A.   Shareholder Meetings   Shareholder voting generally is done at either annual or special meetings. Corporations typically hold an annual shareholders' meeting at a time specified in the corporation's bylaws. The primary purpose of the annual meeting is to elect a board of directors; however, other business also may be conducted at the annual meeting. In addition, annual management reports may be given; bylaws may be amended or repealed; and management resolutions may be considered and adopted (or rejected) by vote of the shareholders.

In addition to the annual meeting, special meetings may be called by the board of directors, by the holders of a specified number of shares, or by other persons named in the bylaws or in the articles of incorporation. Special meetings are called to consider important matters that cannot wait until the next annual meeting.

Advance, written notice of the date, time, and place of both annual and special meetings must be given to each shareholder who is entitled to vote. In addition, notice of special meetings must include the purpose for the meeting, and only business related to that purpose may be conducted at the meeting.

Shareholders may cast their votes in person at either annual or special meetings or may authorize others to vote their shares by proxy. A quorum of shareholders must be present to conduct business, either in person or by proxy. A majority of the shares entitled to vote generally constitutes a quorum. Although the articles of incorporation may specify a different percentage, most state statutes provide that a quorum may not be less than one-third of those shares entitled to vote. Unless stated otherwise in the bylaws or articles of incorporation, a majority vote of the quorum is needed to deal with any matter brought before the meeting.

The MBCA and many state statutes allow shareholders to take action without a meeting if written **consent** to the action is signed by all shareholders entitled to vote on the issue. The consent-in-lieu-of-meeting avoids unnecessary formal meetings and can be especially useful in closely held corporations, where many decisions are unanimous.

To determine which shareholders are entitled to notice of a meeting, to demand a special meeting, to vote at meetings, or to take other shareholder action, the bylaws or the board of directors may set a **record date**. Persons listed in the corporate records as registered owners of voting shares on the record date are entitled to vote. Statutes generally require the record date to be set within a specified period before the meeting, such as "not more than seventy days before the meeting." Once the record date is established, the officer or agent in charge of the stock transfer books prepares a complete voter list or **voting record** of shareholders entitled to vote. The list must be made available to shareholders for inspection and copying at the time of the meeting and, in some states, in advance of the meeting.

B.   Shareholder Voting   Unless a different provision is made in the articles of incorporation, each outstanding share (regardless of its class) is entitled to one vote on each item presented at the meeting. The articles may permit more than one vote to any class of stock, but all shares within the class must have the same rights.

Treasury stock and stock held by other corporations which are controlled by the issuing corporation (subsidiaries) are not entitled to vote and are not counted in fixing the number of outstanding shares. Redeemable shares are entitled to vote—unless a notice of redemption has been mailed and there is sufficient money on deposit with a financial institution to redeem the shares.

The voting rights of any class of stock may be limited or denied by the articles of incorporation. However, if an amendment to the articles of incorporation that would alter the rights of the shares of that class (changing the number of authorized shares, preemptive rights, and so forth), shareholders are entitled to vote as a class, even though they have no voting rights otherwise. In addition, a non-voting class of shares is entitled to vote when the question relates to merger or voluntary dissolution of the corporation.

C.   Election of Directors   Shareholders may elect directors either by straight voting or by cumulative voting. ***Straight voting*** is the method by which each share is entitled to one vote on each matter, including one vote for each director position to be filled. Since directors generally are elected by a plurality of votes, the shareholder with the largest number of shares effectively elects all of the directors. State laws concerning shareholder voting generally follow this method; however, shareholders always may select a different method through bylaws or by shareholder agreement (*see below*).

To ensure representation of minority shareholders on the board of directors, many states require ***cumulative voting***, which applies to election of directors only. Under a cumulative voting method, each shareholder is allowed to aggregate her votes by multiplying the number of her total shares x the number of director vacancies to be filled. Her aggregate votes then may be cast in favor of one director or may be allocated in any way desired by the shareholder.

> Casey owns 800 shares of Ajax Corporation. At the annual meeting of shareholders, 9 directors will be elected to the board. Casey has 7200 votes, which he may cast for one director or may allocate among director vacancies as he sees fit. If he casts all votes for a single director, he cannot vote in the election of any other directors.

As the number of directors on the board increases, the number of minority shares needed to elect a single director increases; thus, the impact of cumulative voting of decreases.

D.   Proxy Voting   A ***proxy*** is the grant of authority to another to vote a stockholder's shares. Many states require the proxy to be in writing and signed by the shareholder. The proxy holder need not be a shareholder but must be competent to serve as an agent. A general proxy allows the proxy holder to vote on all issues presented at the meeting. Unless the proxy itself provides otherwise, both the MBCA and the RMBCA provide that a proxy is valid for eleven months.

Like other agency relationships, appointment of a proxy is revocable by the shareholder at any time; revocation also may occur upon the death or incapacity of the shareholder (the proxy holder must have notice under the RMBCA before the proxy is revoked). A proxy may be irrevocable if it is "coupled with an interest" or is "given as security." For example, when a shareholder pledges her shares as collateral for a loan, the lender may require her to provide an irrevocable proxy to vote the shares as well. When the debt is fully paid, however, the irrevocable proxy is extinguished.

E.   Voting Trusts and Agreements   A person who accumulates enough shareholder proxies can obtain control of a corporation or, at least, can ensure representation on the board of directors. Voting trusts and voting agreements can accomplish a similar result by controlling large blocks of stock. A *voting trust* is created when a group of stockholders transfers legal title to their shares to a trustee in exchange for voting trust certificates. The trustee has the power to vote the shares, subject to any limitations in the trust agreement. Corporate dividends and other distributions generally are passed through the trust to the equitable owners of the shares (the owners of the trust certificates).

Early cases refused to enforce voting trusts on the basis that separating the right to vote from other rights of ownership was against public policy; however, modern corporation statutes uniformly authorize voting trusts, subject to certain restrictions. For instance, the RMBCA requires a voting trust to be in writing and signed by all participating shareholders. In addition, it is valid only for ten years unless the parties extend it.

The voting trust may concentrate control of a large block of shares in one individual or in a small group of individuals, who can elect directors and thus control the corporation. Voting trusts frequently are used in corporate reorganizations to give control to former creditors whose debts are reclassified as stock as part of the reorganization plan.

A shareholder *voting agreement*, sometimes called a *pooling agreement*, is a less formal method of control. Unlike the voting trust, which transfers legal title of the shares to a third party, a voting agreement is a contract between two or more shareholders concerning the way in which their shares will be voted on certain issues, including election of directors. Shareholder voting agreements are enforceable under general contract principles and usually are authorized by statute. Shareholder agreements typically are used to allocate and to maintain control in closely held corporations.

F.   Shareholder Right to Information   The law requires every corporation to keep appropriate accounting books and records, minutes of its shareholders' and board of directors meetings, and detailed records of its shareholders. Shareholders have the common law and statutory right to be kept informed of corporate affairs and, therefore, have the right to inspect corporate records for "proper purposes." The articles of incorporation may grant an absolute right of inspection for some types of records, such as the articles of incorporation, bylaws, and so forth.

The statutory right of inspection generally is limited to those who own a minimum number of shares or who have been shareholders for a minimum time or both. For example, a state statute may provide inspection rights only to those shareholders who own at least 5% of the outstanding stock of the corporation or who have been shareholders for at least six months. The shareholder exercises the right by a written demand upon the corporation, which states the purpose of the demand.

A "proper purpose" is one gauged to protect the shareholder's interest in the corporation, such as determining the corporation's financial condition, the value of shares, the propriety of dividend payments, discovering the existence of dishonesty or mismanagement by corporate officers or directors, or communicating with other shareholders to solicit proxies or to publicize mismanagement. Improper purposes include harassment or extortion, acquiring trade secrets for personal benefit or for the benefit of a competitor, and obtaining the stockholder list to sell for profit.

G. **Preemptive Rights** An existing corporation may issue additional shares of stock to finance corporate operations or expansion. Existing shareholders may have a preemptive right in new shares of stock issued by an existing corporation. A *preemptive right* allows an existing shareholder to purchase a new issue of shares in proportion to her present interest in the corporation before any shares are sold to others. A preemptive right is more valuable in a closely held corporation than it is in a publicly held corporation. If it is exercised, a preemptive right prevents dilution of a shareholder's financial or voting interest in the corporation. Preemptive rights generally are governed by statutes which allow them to be limited or denied by appropriate provisions in the articles of incorporation.

Even when preemptive rights exist, they can be exercised only for new issues of stock—not for shares previously authorized but unissued. In addition, preemptive rights generally *do not apply* to:

- shares issued for property or services rather than for cash;

- shares issued in connection with merger, consolidation, or reorganization;

- shares issued to satisfy conversion or option rights;

- treasury shares; or

- shares issued to directors, officers, or employees under compensation or incentive plans.

Directors   All corporate power is exercised by or under the authority of the board of directors, which manages the business and affairs of the corporation. As part of its basic management function, the board of directors:

> ■*makes basic policy decisions (products, services, prices, labor relations, and so forth);*
>
> ■*appoints, supervises, and removes corporate officers and other executive personnel and delegates authority to them to act on behalf of the corporation;*
>
> ■*determines executive compensation, including pension and retirement plans;*
>
> ■*determines if, when, in what form, and in what amount dividends will be paid;*
>
> ■*determines financing and capital structure;*
>
> ■*adopts, amends, and repeals bylaws (unless that power is reserved to the shareholders in the articles of incorporation);*
>
> ■*participates with shareholders in major changes such as merger, consolidation, or dissolution; and*
>
> ■*supervises the overall operation of the business.*

Directors may be ***insiders***—individuals who are also officers or employees of the corporation or its affiliates. They also may be outside directors—individuals who are not affiliated with management. Boards of large publicly held corporations include a mixture of both inside and outside directors.

A.   Board of Directors   Older corporate statutes required a board of directors to consist of at least three persons; however, modern statutes typically permit one- or two-person boards of directors. The number and qualification of directors are specified in the articles of incorporation or in the bylaws.

The initial board of directors, named in the articles of incorporation or appointed by the incorporators, serves until the first meeting of shareholders. This meeting generally is held shortly after incorporation. Permanent directors are elected by the shareholders at that meeting and at each annual meeting thereafter.

Both the MBCA and the RMBCA provide that if a corporation has nine or more directors, the articles of incorporation may provide for two or three classes of directors. If two classes are authorized, each class serves a two-year term and is elected every other year, which results in staggered terms. If classes of directors are not specified in the articles, all directors are elected annually.

After incorporation, the number of directors may be increased or decreased by amendment of the articles of incorporation or bylaws. A reduction in the number of directors does not shorten any incumbent director's term. A director whose term has expired continues to serve until a successor is elected and qualified. Because directors continue in office until their successors are elected and qualified, the corporation's power to transact business is unaffected by delay or failure to hold an annual meeting of shareholders.

Vacancies on the board are filled according to statutory provisions or according to the bylaws. Typical statutes provide that remaining board members elect or appoint director vacancies caused by death or resignation. Vacancies caused by an increase in the number of directors may be filled by the directors as well, although some states require shareholder action. A director elected to fill a vacancy generally serves until the next meeting of shareholders at which directors are elected.

During her term of office, a director may be removed by the shareholders for cause (fraud, breach of duty, and so forth), usually by a majority vote. Both the MBCA and RMBCA allow a shareholder vote to remove a director without cause unless the articles of incorporation provide otherwise.

B.   Actions of Board of Directors   Management authority is vested in the board of directors as a group—not in its individual members. As a result, directors generally must act in properly called meetings which provide an opportunity to discuss, deliberate, and reach a collective judgment. The timing and details of board meetings typically are governed by detailed bylaw provisions. They may be either regular or special meetings and may be held either within or outside the state of incorporation. All types of business may be conducted at both regular and special meetings; however, directors are entitled to advance written notice of special meetings.

In general, a majority of the number of directors fixed by the articles or bylaws constitutes a quorum for the transaction of business. The articles or bylaws may require a greater number to reach a quorum, and some states allow less than a majority (one-third, for example) of the members to constitute a quorum. Many states also permit board meetings to take place by telephone. If a quorum is present, a majority vote of those directors present constitutes the act of the board unless the articles or bylaws require a greater number. Each director is entitled to one vote and generally cannot vote by proxy. Both Model Acts permit directors to act without a meeting if a written *consent* stating the action taken is signed by all directors. A consent-in-lieu-of-meeting has the effect of a unanimous vote.

A director who objects to an action authorized by a majority of the board must either request that her dissent be recorded in the minutes of the meeting or must give written notice of *dissent* within a short time after the meeting. Either action eliminates the dissenting director's potential personal liability for the action taken.

C.   Committee Action   The board of directors of a large corporation often delegates much of its management authority to corporate officers, to executive committees, or to other committees appointed by the board. If permitted by the articles of incorporation or bylaws, the board of directors may establish one or more committees and may appoint one or more members of the board to serve on them. A committee exercises the board's authority to the extent specified by the board or provided in the articles or bylaws. The most common is the executive committee, which performs board functions between meetings of the full board. Other committees might include an audit, a nomination, a compensation, and a finance committee. To prevent excessive delegation of board authority, committee powers are limited by statute. The Model Acts state that a *committee may not*:

- authorize distributions;
- approve a merger (even when shareholder vote is not required);
- fill vacancies on the board of directors;
- adopt, amend, or repeal bylaws; or
- authorize or approve reacquisition or sale of shares.

These important matters must be undertaken by a vote of the full board of directors.

Officers   Corporate officers conduct the day-to-day affairs of the business and are appointed (or removed) by the board of directors. Officers are agents of the corporation to whom the board delegates authority to administer policy decisions of the board of directors. Corporate officers typically include a president, one or more vice presidents, a secretary, and a treasurer. In addition, various junior officers may be appointed (assistant treasurer, assistant secretary, assistant vice president, comptroller). The duties of the corporate officers are outlined in the bylaws.

Officers generally serve at the pleasure of the board of directors and are subject to removal at any time. However, if a valid employment contract exists between the officer and the corporation, premature termination may constitute a breach of that contract.

A.   Authority of Officers   Unlike directors, officers are agents of the corporation; and their conduct is governed by general principles of agency law. Like all other agents, a corporate officer's authority to act for the corporation (the principal of the agent) derives from:

(1)   Actual authority, whether express or implied;
(2)   Apparent authority; or
(3)   Corporate ratification of a previously unauthorized act.

An officer's express authority derives from one of four sources: (1) state corporation statutes; (2) the articles of incorporation; (3) the bylaws; or (4) resolutions of the board of directors. The most typical and most reliable of these is a resolution of the board of directors which authorizes the transaction in question.

Like other agents, a corporate officer may possess a degree of implied authority to act which flows from her express authority. Although some courts have upheld an implied authority of a corporate president to bind the corporation in certain situations, prudent third parties always will require a resolution of the board of directors to ensure corporate liability on important transactions negotiated by officers.

Even if the officer possesses no actual authority (express or implied), the corporation may be bound by the officer's apparent authority or may be bound on the grounds of ratification. *Apparent authority* arises when a person (here, the corporation) leads third parties to believe that another (here, the corporate officer) has authority to act on that person's behalf. Third parties who reasonably rely on the officer's apparent authority may be able to bind the corporation despite the officer's lack of actual authority.

Notwithstanding actual or apparent authority, the corporation may be bound by an officer's conduct if it ratifies the previously unauthorized act of the officer.

Duties of Management   Corporate management (directors, officers, and sometimes controlling shareholders) has legal duties to the corporation and, in some situations, to its shareholders and creditors. The most important legal duties are based upon common law rules, which have been codified by statute in most states:

■*the duty to exercise reasonable care in managing the corporation;* and
■*the fiduciary duty of loyalty to the corporation.*

In addition to the duties of care and loyalty, state statutes typically impose liability upon officers and directors for commencing business before the required minimum capital has been contributed; for improper dividends or repurchase of corporate stock; for improper distribution of assets upon liquidation; and for unlawful loans to corporate directors, officers, or shareholders.

A.   Duty of Care   The MBCA and RMBCA require directors and officers to discharge their duties in good faith, in a manner which they reasonably believe to be in the best interests of the corporation, and *with the care that an ordinarily prudent person in a like position would exercise under similar circumstances.* Simply stated, officers and directors are liable to the corporation for negligence in the performance of their responsibilities. The duty of care does not, however, make management liable for mistakes or errors in judgment. Under the ***business judgment rule***, officers and directors are not liable for honest, unbiased transactions undertaken with reasonable care, even if it later turns out that the act was ill-advised or was mistaken.

Negligent mismanagement may involve negligent selection or supervision of employees, inadequate consideration or research of major decisions, or authorizing unnecessarily risky or unusual transactions. Directors and officers also are required to keep themselves reasonably informed of corporate affairs. Most state statutes allow officers and directors who act in good faith to rely upon information prepared by other corporate officers or employees, attorneys, public accountants, or a committee of the board of directors.

The business judgment rule insulates most management decisions from attack; however, recent court decisions have eroded its protection when, in the court's view, an officer or director fails to "act in an informed and deliberate manner" in reaching management decisions. In the wake of these decisions and faced with rising liability insurance costs, many outside directors resigned from the boards of publicly held corporations; declined to sit for re-election; or refused nominations. In response, most states have enacted statutes to limit the personal liability of corporate directors when money damages are involved. They fall into two categories: (1) ***charter option*** statutes, which permit the articles of incorporation to limit or eliminate a director's liability for damages or (2) ***self-executing*** statutes, which automatically limit a director's liability, subject to stated exceptions. The RMBCA uses a charter option provision, which permits the articles of incorporation to limit a director's liability for *money damages* (not for equitable relief) *to the corporation or to shareholders* (not to third parties) for any act or omission except:

●the amount of any financial benefit received by the director to which she is not entitled (such as money received as a result of breach of her duty of loyalty);

●intentional infliction of harm on the corporation or its shareholders;

●improper corporate distributions (dividends or repurchase of shares); or

●intentional violation of criminal law.

B.   Duty of Loyalty   Like other fiduciaries, corporate directors and officers have a strict duty to act honestly, in good faith, and solely in the interest of the corporation regarding matters which are within the scope of the fiduciary relationship.

The duty of loyalty may be breached when a director or officer has a ***conflict of interest*** (whether actual or potential) with the interest of the corporation (1) which she *fails to disclose* and (2) which *results in unfairness* to the corporation. In this context, fairness is judged by whether an independent corporate fiduciary dealing at arm's length would have entered into the transaction. The officer or director asserting the validity of the transaction has the burden of proving fairness.

Conflicts of interest may arise in transactions between the fiduciary (officer or director) and the corporation involving sale of corporate property to a director, purchase of property from a director, or contracts between a director and the corporation. Conflicts can arise in transactions (1) between the corporation and the fiduciary personally or (2) between the corporation and another entity in which the fiduciary is an officer, director, partner, or otherwise is financially interested.

In addition to the prohibition against conflict of interest, officers and directors cannot compete with the corporation in business transactions. This means that a fiduciary cannot use corporate assets or personnel to conduct personal business; cannot use customer lists or trade secrets for personal benefit or use them for sale to others; cannot solicit corporate customers for personal ventures; and cannot receive secret profits, kickbacks, or commissions on corporate transactions.

Many wrongful competition cases involve the ***corporate opportunity doctrine***, which prevents corporate officers and directors from diverting business opportunities in which the corporation may have some expectancy, property interest or right, or that in fairness should belong to the corporation. Corporate opportunity issues are tied closely to business ethics and are decided on a case-by-case basis. It is possible that a fiduciary may be permitted to divert opportunities which the corporation is unwilling or unable to pursue; however, recognizing that corporate inability is a defense to diversion may reduce management's incentive to use its best efforts to resolve the corporations inability to pursue the opportunity. The more prudent approach for fiduciaries is to steer clear of these types of opportunities without regard to whether the corporation can undertake them or not.

C. Duties to Minority Stockholders

Directors are under a statutory duty to manage in the best interests of the corporation as a whole. They have fiduciary responsibilities when they take actions involving issuance or redemption of shares and similar activities, which prevent them from attempting to favor one shareholder group at the expense of another. For example, directors who authorize issuance of additional shares in an attempt to dilute the voting power of minority shareholders unfairly (freeze them out) violate their fiduciary duties.

The typical shareholder has no fiduciary duty to the corporation and is entitled to vote her shares for directors or on other corporate matters in any way she chooses. However, a shareholder with controlling interest in a block of stock may have fiduciary duties to minority shareholders. For example, controlling shareholders may not use their ability to elect directors or to approve extraordinary corporate matters in order to take actions that unfairly affect the rights of minority shareholders.

Extraordinary Matters

Matters which are outside the scope of ordinary management transactions typically require participation by both the board of directors and shareholders. The most notable of these transactions include amendment of the articles of incorporation, merger, sale of substantially all corporate assets, and voluntary dissolution. *Dissolution is discussed at the end of this chapter.*

Extraordinary changes usually require notice and vote of the shareholders as well as filing with the secretary of state of the incorporating state. To protect minority shareholders who dissent from major corporate changes, statutes generally provide an ***appraisal remedy*** which allows dissenting shareholders to be paid in cash for their shares.

A. Amendment of Articles of Incorporation

A corporation may amend its articles of incorporation to include any provision permitted by law at the time the amendment is filed. Amendments typically involve changes in capital structure. If the change adversely affects the rights of one or more classes of shareholders, specific approval of the adversely affected class (usually be a majority or two-thirds vote) may be required in addition to the approval of the directors and shareholders. Dissenting members of the class generally are bound by the vote but may be able to assert statutory appraisal remedies (*see below*).

If the amendment is approved, documents reflecting the change are filed with the secretary of state.

B.   Merger and Consolidation   Any two or more corporations may be merged into one of them (called the surviving corporation) or may consolidate to form a new corporation. In a merger, one corporation survives and the other corporation dissolves. By contrast, in a consolidation, both corporations dissolve upon the creation of the new corporation. The corporation remaining after the merger or consolidation succeeds to the rights and liabilities of the prior corporation(s). Thus, creditors' rights are not affected by merger or consolidation.

To accomplish the combination, a plan of merger or a plan of consolidation is approved by resolution of the respective boards of directors and is submitted for approval by the stockholders of both corporations. An appraisal remedy is available to dissenting stockholders of either corporation.

A short-form merger is available for parent-subsidiary combinations, which allows the boards of directors to adopt a resolution to effect the merger (no shareholder vote by either corporation) when the subsidiary corporation is wholly owned or substantially wholly owned (90% or more) by the parent corporation. Short-form merger statutes create no appraisal rights in the minority stockholders of the parent corporation; however, dissenting stockholders of the subsidiary generally are provided with appraisal rights.

C.   Asset or Stock Purchase   When one corporation purchases all, or substantially all, of the assets of another, the corporate existence of both corporations is unaffected. Instead, the form of corporate assets changes. The selling corporation, for example, sells inventory, equipment, and real estate in exchange for cash or securities of equal value. After the sale is concluded, the selling corporation may liquidate and distribute the assets to shareholders or may remain in existence as a holding company or as an investment company.

The sale or lease of all or substantially all corporate assets outside the ordinary course of business is an extraordinary transaction and requires both board resolution and shareholder approval by the selling corporation. Dissenting shareholders are entitled to appraisal remedies. In addition, an asset sale may invoke the bulk sale provisions of a particular state's version of the Uniform Commercial Code.

Shareholder vote of the corporation purchasing the assets is not required (board resolution is required, however), and shareholders of that corporation who object are not entitled to appraisal remedies.

A similar result is achieved when one corporation purchases all, or a controlling block, of another corporation's stock. The stock purchase can be accomplished by a negotiated sale with one or more major stockholders, by purchase on the open market, or by **_tender offer_** to existing shareholders. Overall shareholder approval is not required; instead, individual shareholders of the target company decide whether or not to sell their shares. This is the method used to accomplish a hostile takeover. If the buyer accumulates enough shares to control the corporation, it may be operated as a subsidiary (if the buyer also is a corporation); it may be merged into the corporation that makes the purchase; or it may be liquidated. Because the sale involves no action by the acquired company's board and requires no shareholder approval, appraisal remedies are not available. Securities regulations may affect a tender offer (*see below*).

D.   Appraisal Remedy   State statutes afford shareholders a right to dissent from certain extraordinary corporate transactions and to obtain "fair value" payment for their shares. Fair value is the value of the shares immediately before the action was taken to which the dissenter objects. Fair value is determined by judicial proceeding only if the dissenting shareholder and the corporation cannot agree on a fair price for the shares.

The appraisal remedy typically is available to shareholders who dissent from major corporate action that requires shareholder approval (*see above*). Where the appraisal remedy is available, the statutory procedure must be followed strictly or the remedy may be lost. Generally speaking, if the action is one that creates dissenter rights, the notice of the meeting at which the vote will be taken must inform the shareholders of their right to dissent. Before the vote, an objecting shareholder must file a written notice of intent to demand fair compensation for her shares and must refrain from voting her shares in approval of the action. If the corporation and the shareholder do not agree on the fair value of the shares, a judicial proceeding is filed to appraise the shares. The corporation, then, is required to pay the fair value determined through the judicial appraisal.

Because dissenting shareholders must be paid in cash, a number of dissents may block the corporation's proposed action.

Special Problems of Closely Held Corporations

State corporation statutes apply to all corporations but are designed with publicly held corporations in mind, having freely transferable stock and a tri-level management structure. Most corporations, however, do not fit this model. Most are closely held corporations, with few stockholders (who generally play significant roles in all levels of management) and no public market for the stock. In fact, the stock of closely held corporations frequently is subject to transfer restrictions which limit the purchasers. As a practical matter, this often means that only other shareholders may purchase stock.

Because shareholders often serve as directors and officers as well, management is conducted on a much more informal basis than in a publicly held corporation. The business may operate by unanimous or majority shareholder consent, much like a partnership. As a result, it is easy to ignore or to forget corporate formalities; and management functions can become blurred. Disregard of corporate formalities may allow outsiders to pierce the corporate veil and to impose personal liability on the shareholders.

Shareholder agreements are extremely common in closely held corporations; and their effect sometimes extends to agreements concerning director functions, such as paying dividends or employing a particular shareholder as an officer. The trend in the RMBCA and in a growing number of states is to permit agreements of this type. Some states allow closely held corporations to dispense with the board of directors entirely. RMBCA § 7.32(a)(1).

Whether or not shareholder agreements are used, operating a closely held business as a corporation often leads to disputes. If any person or group within the corporation controls the power to elect a majority of the directors, this faction can out-vote the minority on a consistent basis and can effectively exclude them from management functions. In addition, the faction can "freeze out" the minority by refusing to pay dividends, while simultaneously draining corporate earnings in the form of salaries, bonuses, or rental payments to majority shareholders. Because there is no outside market for the stock, a disenchanted minority shareholder may be locked into the corporation.

If they are negotiated during the incorporation stage, various methods may be available to alleviate some of the problems. One method is to provide for greater than majority voting requirements, usually unanimous. This gives the minority a veto power over unfair management actions. Another method is to create separate classes of stock for majority and minority shareholders, with greater dividend rights to the majority but with both classes entitled to elect an equal number of directors.

Still another is a mandatory agreement requiring the majority shareholders or the corporation to buy out the minority at a price fixed by a predetermined formula.

The drawback to most of these methods is deadlock, which may be overcome by a provision requiring the parties to submit disputes to an arbitrator for a binding decision when they cannot agree. In addition, a provision can be included to require one faction to buy out the other. If all else fails, the shareholders (usually the minority) may petition the court for involuntary dissolution, which is available in both deadlock and oppression cases. The RMBCA allows the corporation or any shareholder to avoid dissolution by electing to purchase the shares owned by the complaining shareholder at fair market value.

Special Problems of Publicly Held Corporations

Publicly held corporations face entirely different sets of problems than those faced by closely held corporations. Their stock is freely transferable, usually on the open market through stock brokerage houses; but it is subject to strict and highly complex securities regulation. In addition, their larger size frequently subjects them to more rigorous scrutiny by various administrative agencies in the areas of antitrust, environmental protection, equal employment opportunity, and labor law.

Securities Regulation   The inherent characteristic of a publicly held corporation is publicly traded securities (stocks and bonds). Industrial growth at the turn of the century was aided by the sale of corporate securities to the general public to provide money for expansion. Most of the sales were legitimate, but many were not. To prevent citizens from being swindled by worthless stock schemes, many states adopted legislation in the early 1900s to regulate the distribution and sale of securities. The purpose of the statutes was to prevent fraud upon unsuspecting investors by selling them securities that were worth no more than "so many feet of blue sky." To this day, state securities statutes are known as *blue sky laws*.

State blue sky laws generally require registration of the securities brokers and dealers as well as registration of all securities offered or traded in the state. They also require disclosure of pertinent information concerning the security and its issuer. The state securities commissioner evaluates the merits of the investment before securities can be offered for sale in that state.

After the stock market crash in 1929, it became obvious that state blue sky laws were inadequate to police securities fraud. Congress used its (interstate) commerce clause powers to enact federal legislation for the purpose, beginning with the Securities Act of 1933 and the Securities Exchange Act of 1934, which created the ***Securities and Exchange Commission*** (SEC). The SEC continues as the primary securities regulator in the nation.

Securities laws and regulations strive for full disclosure of accurate information to investors concerning securities traded on the open market. They also prohibit insider trading. Certain types of small offerings (limited dollar value and limited number of investors) are exempt from SEC regulations, as are intrastate offerings; securities exchanged in corporate reorganizations and bankruptcy proceedings; offerings by banks and other regulated entities; insurance policies; and short-term commercial paper.

Securities regulation is a law practice specialty area of its own, and detailed discussions concerning it are beyond the scope of this *Review Manual*.

Antitrust Regulation   Also as a result of turn-of-the-century abuses, Congress used its interstate commerce power to enact the Sherman Antitrust Act, the Clayton Act, and the Federal Trade Commission Act to curtail the establishment of monopolies and the price fixing problems that came with them. During that time period, stockholders of large corporations had formed stock trusts which controlled virtually all commercial activity in specific areas (railroads, oil, sugar, cotton, whiskey). Federal legislation, together with administrative regulations and enforcement from the Federal Trade Commission (FTC), focused on "busting" the trusts and continue to police interstate commerce activities that resemble the older business trusts.

Today, the reach of the FTC extends not only to interstate monopoly activity (corporate consolidations and mergers) but also to price fixing, restraint of free competition, and unfair trade practices addressed by consumer protection laws. The break-up of AT&T in recent times was based on antitrust laws, for example; and today's franchises and chain stores must comply with antitrust laws.

Antitrust laws have resulted in the prohibition against corporate directors sitting on the boards of competing corporations, so that it is not permissible for a person to be a corporate director for both Standard Oil and Mobil Oil, for example. Antitrust laws also prevent tying one product to another in such a way as to require purchasers to pay a higher price than they otherwise would have paid. For example, a corporation cannot offer seminars requiring participants to purchase study tapes at a higher price than the study tapes cost when purchased alone.

Other Government Regulation   Small corporations are not immune to government regulation; however, their small size exempts them from some regulatory requirements. Large corporations tend to operate across interstate lines more frequently, tend to have more employees, and tend to become involved in more complex transactions. As a result, government regulation is more pervasive in relation to large corporations. Only a few of those areas are mentioned here.

The *Environmental Protection Agency* (EPA) controls toxic waste emitted by businesses into the environment. This includes land pollution, water pollution, and air pollution. A business can be fined for violating EPA regulations in addition to being required to pay the cost of rectifying the pollution problems. The EPA regulations extend not only to businesses who create waste but also to their lenders in some situations. Businesses are required to perform environmental impact studies for many of their business activities and to report to the EPA.

The *Equal Employment Opportunity Commission* (EEOC) controls discriminatory practices of businesses in the areas of hiring, promotion, and firing of employees who fall within the protected classes of race, color, gender, religion, and national origin. The EEOC enforces Title VII of the Civil Rights Act of 1964 and related statutes. Companies with more than five full-time employees are subject to its regulation; larger companies are expected to adopt affirmative action plans and to keep detailed records of all employees hired, promoted, and fired. (Age discrimination is covered by separate statute.)

The *Occupational Safety and Health Administration* (OSHA) controls safety of the workplace. Businesses must provide safety devices for workers (masks, safety glasses) in certain types of industrial fields and, in general, strive to avoid a dangerous working environment.

In addition, businesses that employ workers who are members of a collective bargaining unit (labor union) must negotiate satisfactory contracts with the union and must follow certain procedures established by the Wagner Act. A business that violates any of those provisions may be subjected to administrative processes before the *National Labor Relations Board* (NLRB).

The agencies mentioned here represent only a few of the regulatory bodies which control the activities of large corporations. A corporation's cost of compliance with the various regulations of so many governmental agencies is extremely high, but the cost of non-compliance is even higher.

Corporate Litigation

A corporation is an artificial person created by state statute. It has the capacity to sue and be sued in civil actions and can be prosecuted for violation of a criminal statute, such as the federal Racketeer Influenced Corrupt Organizations Act (RICO). Upon dissolution, the corporation's capacity to sue and be sued generally continues for a limited time.

Corporate litigation can involve claims by or against the corporation. Some claims can be asserted either by the corporation or by someone standing in its shoes, such as a trustee in bankruptcy or a shareholder in a derivative action.

Before any suit involving a corporation can be initiated, however, litigants must meet the threshold procedural requirements involving subject matter jurisdiction, personal jurisdiction, and venue. A state's subject matter jurisdiction and personal jurisdiction over domestic corporations is extremely broad, as is its *in rem* and *quasi in rem* jurisdiction over corporate property located within its boundaries. Many states require a foreign corporation operating within its borders to name an agent for service of process before the foreign corporation lawfully can conduct business in the state.

State and federal courts may exercise concurrent personal jurisdiction over corporations in diversity of citizenship actions, including shareholder derivative actions. *(See the General Law chapter for a more detailed discussion of jurisdiction and venue.)*

Shareholder Derivative Actions   When a corporation is injured by the negligence or wrongdoing of its officers or directors, it is unlikely that the wrongdoers will initiate a suit in the name of the corporation which names themselves as defendants. In this situation, one or more shareholders may bring a derivative suit in the name of the corporation against the insider-wrongdoer. The shareholder does not sue in her individual capacity but, rather, as a representative of the corporation. Any judgment resulting from the suit is paid to the corporation, not to the shareholders. The shareholder receives an indirect benefit, however, in the protection of her investment in the corporation. A successful plaintiff-shareholder is entitled to reimbursement from the corporation for her reasonable expenses, including attorney fees.

Most shareholder derivative actions are filed in federal court under federal securities laws or on diversity of citizenship grounds. To ensure that shareholders do not abuse the derivative action by filing ***strike suits*** (suits filed merely to secure a favorable private settlement rather than to redress a corporate wrong), derivative actions are subject to a number of restrictions.

A.   Exhaustion of Corporate Remedies   Before filing a derivative action, the shareholder must either (1) make demand upon the board of directors to enforce the claim or (2) prove that such a demand would be futile, such as where the wrongdoers control the corporation. Typically, the suit cannot be filed until 90 days after the demand unless the 90-day waiting period would cause irreparable injury to the corporation.

B. Contemporaneous Share Ownership   The plaintiff-shareholder in a derivative action must have been a shareholder at the time the alleged wrong took place. Persons acquiring shares after that time by operation of law (for example, by inheritance) also are eligible plaintiffs. In addition, the plaintiff must own shares both when the action is filed and continuing to the entry of final judgment. This requirement ensures that the plaintiff has a financial stake in the suit throughout the pendency of the action; prevents an outsider from "buying into a lawsuit" to harass corporate management; and, in federal cases, prevents collusion in establishing jurisdiction for diversity of citizenship.

C. Security for Costs   A few states require plaintiffs owning less than a stated percentage of the outstanding shares of the corporation to provide security (usually by posting a bond) to cover the reasonable costs of litigation, including attorney fees, that may be incurred by the corporation or others in defending the suit. Courts often permit the plaintiff to bring additional shareholders into the suit to satisfy the minimum percentage, which eliminates the need to provide security.

D. Settlement and Dismissal   To discourage strike suits and unfair settlements, the Federal Rules of Civil Procedure (Rule 23[1]) and the RMBCA require court approval for dismissal or compromise of derivative suits, as well as notice to other shareholders of the terms of the compromise. The RMBCA and a number of state statutes specifically require the dismissal of a derivative suit if an independent group of directors determines in good faith and after reasonable inquiry that maintaining the derivative action is not in the best interests of the corporation. To protect the corporation, however, the court must assess the good faith and independence of the directors and the reasonableness of their inquiry.

Indemnification for Litigation Expenses

When directors, officers, and other corporate personnel must defend lawsuits filed against them based upon execution of their corporate responsibilities, the statutes of all states allow some type of indemnification by the corporation. The MBCA permits indemnification if the defendant acted in good faith and in a manner reasonably believed to be in the best interests of the corporation in carrying out his or her duties. If the suit relates to criminal conduct, the defendant also must have had no reasonable cause to believe that the conduct was unlawful.

Statutory provisions concerning indemnification generally are not exclusive. Therefore, many corporations include detailed provisions concerning indemnification in their articles of incorporation or in their bylaws.

Corporate Dissolution

Unless its existence is limited in the articles of incorporation, a corporation's existence or duration is perpetual. Once created, therefore, some formal action must be taken by the corporation or by others to terminate the corporation's existence. Termination of a corporation's existence is done by dissolution, either voluntary or involuntary.

Voluntary Dissolution   The procedure for voluntary dissolution is similar to the procedure for other major corporate changes. The board of directors adopts a resolution which must be approved by the shareholders. As an alternative, the MBCA permits dissolution without board action by unanimous written consent of all shareholders. The document reflecting the decision to dissolve (articles of dissolution, for example) then is filed with the secretary of state. Upon dissolution, corporate assets are liquidated, creditors are paid, and any remaining proceeds are distributed to shareholders according to their respective ownership preferences and interests.

To protect creditors in the dissolution process, notice of dissolution is given to creditors directly and by publication (usually in a newspaper of general circulation in the place where the corporation's principal office is located).

The corporate existence continues for a stated time (for example, two years) after dissolution to "wind up" the corporation's affairs. During this time, the corporation may continue to sue and be sued on predissolution claims.

Involuntary Dissolution   State corporation statutes also provide for involuntary dissolution of a corporation, sometimes by judicial proceedings and decree. Proceedings may be initiated by the state attorney general, the secretary of state, shareholders, or creditors. The MBCA permits dissolution of a corporation in an action filed by the state attorney general if the corporation has (1) failed to file its annual report or to pay its franchise tax timely; (2) procured its articles of incorporation through fraud; (3) exceeded or abused its legal authority; or (4) failed to maintain or to appoint a registered agent or failed to notify the state of a change in registered agent.

In an action by shareholders, the court may order liquidation of the corporation if it is proved that:

●The directors are deadlocked over management of the corporation, the shareholders are unable to break the deadlock, and irreparable injury to the corporation is imminent;

●The acts of directors or those controlling the corporation are illegal, oppressive, or fraudulent;

●Corporate assets are being misapplied or wasted; or

●The shareholders are deadlocked in voting power and have failed for at least two consecutive annual meetings to elect successor directors for terms that have expired (or would have expired if new directors had been elected).

A creditor may obtain judicial dissolution by proving (1) that it obtained a judgment against the corporation, the judgment is unsatisfied, and the corporation is insolvent or (2) that the corporation has admitted in writing that the creditor's claim is due and owing and that the corporation is insolvent.

In addition, a corporation's assets may be liquidated in bankruptcy proceedings and the proceeds used to pay creditors. The bankruptcy court does not dissolve the corporation, *per se*; however, the effect is virtually the same. When all of a corporation's assets are liquidated, the corporation is nothing more than an empty shell.

The formation, operation, and dissolution of business organizations is a complex area of legal practice. The material in this chapter and the self-test provide a summary of its principles that a corporate legal assistant should know. Further references and study aids are listed in the Bibliography.

Business Organizations Self-Test

Allow an uninterrupted thirty-minute period to answer all questions. At the end of thirty minutes, check your answers against those in the Answer Key Section of this Manual. Deduct two points for each incorrect answer (100 total possible points). Unanswered questions are counted as incorrect answers. Follow directions carefully and observe the time limit precisely to provide an accurate self-assessment.

Choose the most correct answer to each of the following questions unless a specific question instructs you to do otherwise.

1. Each of the partners in a general partnership:

    a. has joint liability for all partnership debt.
    b. has joint and several liability for all partnership debt.
    c. is liable for partnership debt in proportion to his or her capital contribution.
    d. none of the above.

2. Each of the partners in a general partnership:

    a. has no personal tax liability for partnership income; it is the liability of the partnership.
    b. bears equal personal liability for tax on partnership income.
    c. bears personal tax liability in proportion to the partnership income received by him or her.
    d. none of the above.

3. If a limited partner were to participate in the operation of the partnership in any way,

    a. the limited partnership would be treated as a general partnership except for taxing purposes.
    b. the limited partner would become jointly and severally liable, along with the general partner, for all partnership debt.
    c. the partnership would be dissolved.
    d. none of the above.

4. Amy and Brenda form a partnership. Amy contributes $75,000 to the partnership, and Brenda contributes $25,000. At the end of the first year, the business realizes a profit of $10,000. Since no agreement concerning distribution of profits was made, how much will each receive?

    a. Amy will receive $7500; Brenda, $2500.
    b. Each will receive $5000.
    c. Amy will receive $3,750; Brenda, $1750.
    d. None is correct.

5. An advantage of incorporation is:

    a. perpetual existence.
    b. limited liability.
    c. corporations are separate taxing entities.
    d. all of the above.
    e. none of the above.

6. True or False. Corporations cannot be found guilty of criminal acts, because corporations cannot be sentenced to prison terms.

7. True or False. Corporate directors and officers generally owe no direct duty to individual shareholders of the corporation.

8. True or False. A close corporation may restrict the rights of shareholders to transfer stock by means of shareholder agreements.

9. True or False. A partnership may be a shareholder in an "S" corporation.

10. A foreign corporation:

    a. is chartered in a foreign country, such as Canada.
    b. is a synonym for the term "alien corporation."
    c. may require a certificate of authority to do business in states where it is not chartered.
    d. may transact business only in foreign states.

11. The "business judgment rule":

    a. applies to actions of the directors.
    b. protects directors from all liability.
    c. makes directors liable for errors in business judgment.
    d. makes officers liable for errors in business judgment.

12. For which of the following acts is a director most likely to be found personally liable?

    a. Investment of corporate funds in a venture that loses money.
    b. Failure to supervise the president's actions.
    c. Creation of a new product line that is unsuccessful.
    d. Breach of warranty for a faulty product made by the corporation.

13. Which of the following is *not* among the duties of a director?

    a. Declare dividends.
    b. Elect officers.
    c. Issue stock.
    d. Sign contracts on behalf of the corporation.

14. True or False.   A director is always an agent of the corporation.

15. True or False.   A share of stock with a stated par value of $10, which is sold and issued initially for $8, is an example of watered stock.

16. Ben owns 100 shares of ABC Corporation. The corporation makes a new issue of 10,000 shares. According to his share certificate, Ben is entitled to purchase an additional 100 shares at the time of the new issue. This is an example of:

    a. right of first refusal.
    b. shareholder restrictions on transfer and ownership.
    c. preemptive rights.
    d. participation rights.

17. Shareholders can be held liable for:

    a. illegal acts of the corporation.
    b. ultra vires acts of the corporation.
    c. full payment for watered stock received.
    d. fraud committed by the board of directors.

18. Angela, a Certified Public Accountant, sits on the board of directors of three corporations. Angela:

    a. has violated her duty of loyalty to each of the corporations.
    b. has violated the Sherman Act.
    c. has not violated her duty of loyalty if she refrains from voting on issues which concern more than one of the corporations.
    d. has not violated her duty of loyalty if the corporations do not compete directly with each other.

19. Which of the following classes of stock is *never* granted voting rights?

   a. Common stock
   b. Preferred stock
   c. Treasury stock
   d. Watered stock

20. Stock warrants are used to implement:

   a. cumulative voting.
   b. the preemptive right.
   c. access to corporate stock records.
   d. dissolution of the corporation.

21. Which of the following actions by shareholders requires more than a majority vote?

   a. Election of directors
   b. Election of directors by cumulative voting
   c. Resolution to merge with another corporation
   d. Resolution to amend the date of the annual meeting

22. The right of a shareholder to force the corporation to buy his or her stock following a merger is called:

   a. repurchase rights.
   b. appraisal rights.
   c. preemptive rights.
   d. preferred rights.

23. A four-lawyer firm incorporated. They did not elect to be a Chapter S corporation. At the end of the first year, they show a taxable income of $64,000. They have decided that they each will remove $5,000 from the corporation. They should:

   a. declare bonuses of $5,000 each.
   b. declare dividends of $5,000 each.
   c. receive loans of $5,000 each.
   d. none of the options is better than any other.

24.   A corporation is created:

      a.   by agreement of the parties.
      b.   by franchise.
      c.   by expanding business interests.
      d.   by statutory authorization.

25.   Piercing the corporate veil is:

      a.   obtaining the advantages of conducting business in corporate form.
      b.   obtaining a corporate charter.
      c.   disregarding the corporate entity.
      d.   suing a foreign corporation.

26.   The duration of a corporation may be:

      a.   dissolved by death of the parties.
      b.   perpetual.
      c.   subject to liability.
      d.   terminated by a lawsuit.

27.   A domestic corporation is:

      a.   a corporation whose officers reside in the state where the corporation transacts business.
      b.   a corporation whose principal place of business is in the forum state.
      c.   a corporation whose principal activities relate to family services.
      d.   a corporation chartered in the forum state.

28.   True or False.   A corporation sometimes is treated as a person within the meaning of the federal Constitution.

29.   True or False.   For purposes of federal litigation, a corporation is deemed to be a citizen of the state where it has its principal place of business as well as of the state where it is incorporated.

30.   True or False.   A corporation may be incorporated in more than one state.

31.   True or False.   A corporation must transact all or most of its business in a state where it is incorporated.

32.   True or False.   A corporation may be subjected to criminal charges.

33. True or False.   A partnership generally is treated as an aggregate for purposes of taxation and as a separate entity for purposes of litigation.

34. True or False.   Angela and Margaret form a partnership. If Angela sells her partnership interest to Priscilla, Priscilla will receive all of the benefits and burdens of partnership status when the sale is consummated.

35. True or False.   A corporation cannot be a domestic corporation and a foreign corporation at the same time.

36. Tom, Sam, and Mary form a partnership to operate a movie theater franchise. The partnership realizes a profit in the first year of operation. Under general partnership rules and assuming that all profit is distributed to the partners, what amount will each partner receive?

    a.   An amount equal to his or her percentage of the total capital contribution.

    b.   An amount equal to his or her percentage of the total capital contribution after taxes.

    c.   The same amount as all other partners.

    d.   The same amount as all other partners minus his or her capital contribution.

37. The Uniform Partnership Act and the Revised Uniform Partnership Act were formulated by the:

    a.   American Law Institute.

    b.   National Conference of Commissioners on Uniform State Laws.

    c.   National Association of Partnerships.

    d.   American Bar Association.

38. If the members of a limited partnership fail to provide a basis for making distributions of profit to partners, the Revised Uniform Limited Partnership Act:

    a.   provides for equal distributions to partners.

    b.   provides for distributions to limited partners only.

    c.   provides for distributions according to each partner's capital contribution.

    d.   makes no provision for distributions.

39. Under the Revised Uniform Limited Partnership Act, a limited partner may not:

    a.   vote on partnership matters such as dissolution.
    b.   serve as an employee of the limited partnership.
    c.   act as a surety for the limited partnership.
    d.   supervise employees of the limited partnership.

40. Which of the following business entities typically provides the most flexibility in terms of management policy?

    a.   sole proprietorship
    b.   partnership
    c.   limited partnership
    d.   corporation

41. True or False.   Stock splits and stock dividends achieve the same result in relation to the transfer of earnings to capital.

42. True or False.   Partnerships must be formed by written agreement and in strict compliance with the partnership statutes of a particular state.

43. True or False.   Each partner in a general partnership is an agent of the partnership for purposes of conducting partnership business.

44. True or False.   A debenture is a corporate obligation secured by a lien or by a mortgage on specific corporate property.

45. True or False.   Holders of fractional shares of stock and holders of scrip certificates generally enjoy the same voting rights within the corporate structure.

46. A public corporation is:

    a.   one whose stock is traded publicly.
    b.   one created by government to administer government purposes.
    c.   one whose activities are subject to public scrutiny.
    d.   one which has one or more subsidiary entities.

47. A de facto corporation is one which:

    a.   has complied with statutory rules and exists in fact.

    b.   is used by its shareholders as a conduit for personal activities.

    c.   has not complied with statutory rules but operates as a corporation.

    d.   is used by its shareholders to defraud creditors.

48. If the organizers of a small corporation anticipate losses during the first two to three years of operation, which of the following options will provide the best tax treatment for shareholders in the usual situation?

    a.   Chapter S election

    b.   Section 1244 stock

    c.   Nonprofit status

    d.   Leverage financing

49. Cumulative voting is a term that applies in which of the following situations?

    a.   Voluntary dissolution of a corporation

    b.   Election of shareholders

    c.   Election of directors

    d.   Election of officers

50. A shareholder derivative action may be initiated in response to:

    a.   negligence by management which injures a shareholder.

    b.   management's election to dissolve the corporation.

    c.   a strike suit filed by management.

    d.   negligence by management which injures the corporation.

Chapter 11
CONTRACT LAW

A verbal contract isn't worth the paper it's written on.

—Samuel Goldwyn

A contract is a single promise or a set of mutual promises, the performance of which is recognized as a legal duty and the breach of which will result in a remedy granted to the nonbreaching party. A contract may be categorized by its type (whether unilateral or bilateral), by its method of formation (whether express, implied, or quasi), by its validity (whether void, voidable, or unenforceable), and by its status (whether executory or executed).

Unilateral or Bilateral

The *traditional* **unilateral contract** consists of a single promise made by the offeror to the offeree, which seeks performance from the offeree rather than a promise of performance.

> Max promises to pay Sam $100 if Sam paints Max's house. If (and only if) Sam paints the house, Max will be obligated to pay him $100.

The *traditional **bilateral contract*** consists of a promise given in exchange for a promise (mutual promises). Under both the Uniform Commercial Code (U.C.C.) and the Restatement (Second) of Contracts, however, a bilateral contract may be created either by mutual promises *or* by the start of performance.

> Max promises to pay Arnold $100 if Arnold will promise to paint Max's house, and Arnold promises to paint Max's house for $100. *(bilateral contract)*
>
> Max promises to pay Arnold $100 if he will promise to paint Max's house, and Arnold begins painting the house. *(bilateral contract)*

Under the modern view, most contracts are classified as bilateral, with traditional unilateral contracts occurring only in two situations:

1. Where the offeror clearly indicates that performance is the only manner of acceptance, in which case no contract is formed until the act is done; and

2. Where there is an offer to the public that clearly contemplates acceptance only by performance, such as an offer of a reward for the return of a lost item.

Express, Implied, or Quasi-Contract

The classifications express, implied, and quasi-contract refer only to the way in which the contract was formed; they have no bearing on the enforceability of a contract.

An ***express contract*** is one formed *by specific words*, either *oral or written*.

An ***implied contract*** is one formed by an indication of assent other than specific words, such as *by conduct*. This is sometimes called a contract "implied in fact." Turning on the bathroom light and running the water every morning indicates acceptance of utility service and brings the concomitant obligation to pay for the utilities used.

A ***quasi-contract*** is not a contract in any technical sense. It is a legal fiction created by courts *to prevent unjust enrichment* of a defendant by allowing the plaintiff to seek restitution of a benefit conferred upon the defendant. This is sometimes called a contract "implied in law." For instance, a physician who treats an unconscious accident victim found in the middle of a street may be able to recover under quasi-contract, even though her services were not requested by the victim or by anyone else.

Void, Voidable, or Unenforceable

The term *void contract*, although a misnomer, is used to refer to a purported contract—an agreement that had *no legal effect* and was invalid from the start, such as an agreement to commit murder. It would be more precise to say that such an agreement is simply not a contract at all. No contract ever was created because of a defect in its formation (illegality of purpose). Nevertheless, the term "void contract" continues in popular use.

A *voidable contract* is one that one or both parties may *choose to avoid* or may ratify. Most contracts of minors are avoidable, for instance, at the option of the minor upon reaching the age of majority. An exception to this general rule is a contract made for the necessities of life, such as board and room, medical treatment, and the like.

An *unenforceable contract* is one that cannot be enforced because of *defenses to the contract*, none of which relate to its formation. Examples of such defenses include Statute of Frauds, statute of limitations, unconscionability, and so forth.

Executory or Executed

An *executory contract* is one in which *some obligation or duty remains to be done* by one or more of the parties.

An *executed contract* is one in which all parties have *fully performed* their obligations and duties under the contract terms.

Formation of a Valid, Enforceable Contract

Regardless of how they are presented, all issues concerning contract formation boil down to these three: (1) existence of **mutual assent**, (2) existence of **consideration**, and (3) absence of **defenses** that would prevent enforcement of the contract terms.

Mutual Assent

Mutual assent is often called the **meeting of the minds** or intent to contract. Whether a meeting of the minds has occurred is determined objectively, based upon the words and conduct of the parties. Each party is bound by the apparent intention manifested (shown or demonstrated) to the other. Mutual assent requires both *offer and acceptance*.

The Offer To create a power of acceptance in the offeree, the offer must be an objective expression of a *promise, undertaking, or commitment* to enter into a contract; the terms of the offer must be **definite and certain**; and the offer must be **communicated** to the offeree.

Distinguish between a promise or an undertaking that can form the basis of an offer and other types of communication or conduct:

Statements obviously made *in jest or in anger* are not offers and cannot create a contract, even if they are purportedly "accepted."

Generally, an **advertisement** is viewed as an *invitation to make an offer*, not as an offer to sell. The classic exception is where a defendant store, for instance, lists a specific item (rather than a group) for a specific price on a "first come, first served" basis.

An **auction** is considered a *solicitation for offers* (bids). The exception is where the auction is conducted without reserve, in which case the auctioneer cannot withdraw the goods once the bidding starts.

An **invitation to bid** is *not an offer* unless it contains language to indicate otherwise, such as, "I will sell my law library for the highest cash bid received by me within the next thirty days." This is an offer. Each bid received within the thirty-day period is an acceptance, which will be effective unless a higher bid is received. The situation would be different, however, if this statement were made: "I will consider selling my law library for the highest cash bid received by me within the next thirty days." This is not an offer but is merely an invitation to bid or a statement of preliminary negotiations.

The **terms of the offer must be definite and certain**. This means that there must be enough of the essential terms stated so that a contract based upon those terms could be enforced. Generally, essential terms include *identity of the offeree* and *subject matter*; the *price* to be paid; the *time* of payment, delivery, or performance; the *quantity* involved; and the **nature** of the work or performance required.

A.   Identity of Offeree   There must be some statement that identifies the offeree or the class to which the offeree belongs in order to substantiate that the offeror intended to create a power of acceptance.

> Alice offers a $100.00 reward to the person who finds and returns her lost cat. Here, the offeree cannot be identified specifically when the offer is made. Performance by returning the lost cat constitutes both an identification of the offeree and an acceptance of the offer.

B.   Definite Subject Matter   The subject matter of the offer must be certain. A court cannot enforce a promise if it cannot tell what the promise is. It is not necessary that every material term be spelled out, as long as there is some objective standard by which to supply missing terms.

In real estate transactions, for example, the offer must identify the land and the price. Courts will not imply terms to identify the property, the price to be paid, or the terms by which the price is to be paid (mortgage terms, for instance).

In sale of goods, the quantity offered must be definite or must be capable of being determined. If a seller offers to sell all of her outputs or if a buyer offers to buy all of his requirements, the quantity can be determined by extrinsic, objective facts (the history of outputs or the history of requirements). If there is no history of outputs or of requirements, which may be true of new businesses, the quantity cannot be implied.

The duration of an employment contract must be stated; otherwise, the offer will be construed as one contemplating a contract that can be terminated at will by either party. If the contract states a rate of pay, such as $2,000.00 a month, some courts will infer that the offer is for the minimum period stated (one month in the example).

Unless the parties have shown that they do not want a contract until they agree on price, a reasonable price will be implied for goods under U.C.C. § 2-305. Likewise, unless the parties have specified that time is of the essence, U.C.C. § 2-309 provides for performance within a reasonable time.

When terms are missing, the U.C.C. and modern cases presume that the parties' intent is to include reasonable terms. This presumption cannot be made, however, if the parties have included a term that is too vague to be enforceable.

An agreement to divide profits "fairly" is too vague.

An agreement to purchase a ring for "100.00 or less" is too vague.

If the uncertainty stems from the offeror having given a choice of acceptances to the offeree, the offer becomes definite when the offeree makes her selection.

> Bill offers to sell Jean any ring in the display case for $100.00.
> Once Jean selects a ring, the offer will have become definite.

If an offer specifically states that the price, quantity, or other material term will be agreed upon at a future date, the offer is too uncertain. This situation is different from having omitted a material term. Instead, the offeror has specifically reserved the right to name the term; there is no basis for a court to imply a reasonable term.

C. Communication to Offeree The offer must be communicated to the offeree before the power of acceptance can be created.

> Bill finds Jean's wallet containing her driver's license and all of her credit cards. He returns it to her, unaware that she had advertised a $50.00 reward. Because Bill did not know about the offer, there can be no mutual assent and, without mutual assent, no contract.

Termination of Offer When the power of acceptance created by a valid offer is terminated before acceptance, acceptance can no longer be made. Termination of the offer can occur in a number of different ways.

A. Revocation The offeror may terminate an offer by communicating revocation to the offeree before acceptance has occurred. The revocation may be communicated directly to the offeree by the offeror or may be communicated indirectly, where acts of the offeror, made known to the offeree by a reliable source, would indicate to a reasonable person that the offer has been revoked.

> Mrs. O'Leary offers to buy home-grown, white potatoes for her restaurant from Bill, a potato wholesaler, if he can find any for her. In his travels, Bill is told by one of his best customers that Mrs. O'Leary just signed a contract with the customer's neighbor to buy all of the white potatoes that he can produce. This information should indicate to Bill that Mrs. O'Leary's offer to him has been revoked.

Offers made by publication may be revoked by comparable means.

An offer published in the Portland Post may be revoked by publication of the revocation in the Portland Post but not by publication in People Magazine or in the Wall Street Journal.

A revocation becomes effective when it is received by the offeree. If the revocation is made by publication, however, it becomes effective when it is published.

B. **Limitations on Revocation Powers** In general, an offeror may revoke an offer at any time. This power may be limited in the circumstances shown below.

1. **Option** An option is an independent contract in which the offeror receives separate consideration from the offeree to keep an offer open for a stated period of time, such as an option to buy real estate. The consideration paid for the option is separate from any consideration that will be paid if the option is exercised. If the offeree does not exercise the option by purchasing the real estate, there is generally no refund to the offeree of the consideration paid for the option.

2. **U.C.C. Firm Offer** A firm offer by a merchant to buy or to sell goods, represented by a signed writing that promises to hold the offer open for a stated time, cannot be revoked for lack of consideration during that time. If no time is stated, a reasonable time is inferred, not to exceed three months. U.C.C. § 2-205.

3. **Detrimental Reliance** Detrimental reliance prevents revocation of an offer for a reasonable time when the offeror should expect that the offeree would rely on the offer to his or her detriment. At the very least, the offeree would be entitled to damages measured by the extent of detrimental reliance. Restatement 2d § 90.

4. **Part Performance of a Unilateral Contract** Unilateral contracts generally contemplate acceptance by full performance, rather than by a promise to perform. Where performance has been started but is not complete, it would be unfair to allow the offeror to revoke the offer.

The Uniform Commercial Code, as well as the First and Second Restatements, provide that such an offer becomes irrevocable once performance has begun; and the offeree is given a reasonable time within which to complete the performance.

The majority view is contained in § 45 of the First Restatement, which reasons that a contract is formed at the moment when performance begins, with the offeror's duty to perform conditioned upon completion of the act within a reasonable time or within the time stated in the offer. Under the Second Restatement, an option contract is formed upon the start of performance by the offeree, making the offer irrevocable for a reasonable time. It is as if the offeree's part performance is consideration to keep the offer open for a reasonable time.

C.   Rejection   The offer may be terminated by a simple rejection from the offeree, which is effective at the time the rejection is received by the offeror. It also may be terminated by a counteroffer from the offeree. Use care to differentiate between a counteroffer (which constitutes a rejection) and a mere inquiry (which does not terminate the offer when the inquiry is consistent with the offeree's continued consideration of the original offer).

> Adam offers to sell his farm to Bill for $100,000. Bill replies, "I am not willing to pay that much." When he sees that Adam is unwilling to lower the price, Bill says, "All right, I will pay $100,000." Because Bill's rejection terminated his power of acceptance, there is no contract.

> Adam offers to sell his farm to Bill for $100,000. Bill replies, "Let me think about it; but if you want to close the deal right now, I will give you $80,000." Adam does not respond, and Bill accepts the $100,000 price the next day. There is a contract.

D.   Lapse of Time   Lapse of time may terminate an offer, whether the lapse of the time specified for acceptance by the offeror or the lapse of a reasonable time when no time is specified. When the offeror's terms are unclear as to time, such as "by return mail," a reasonable time for return mail is implied.

E.   Termination by Operation of Law   If either party dies or is adjudged insane or incompetent prior to acceptance, the offer is terminated without the need to communicate the death, insanity, or incompetence to the other party. Restatement 2d § 48. The offer will not terminate, however, if any of the rules limiting the offeror's power to terminate apply (such as an option contract, where the offer is irrevocable because of the consideration given to keep it open).

If the subject matter of the proposed contract becomes illegal, the offer will terminate by operation of law.

The Gilded Lily Partnership offered to lease a building from Benny Bigtime to operate a bingo parlor. Before Benny accepted the offer, the city council outlawed bingo games within city limits. The offer automatically is terminated by operation of the new law.

The Acceptance   Acceptance is a manifestation of assent to the terms of an offer, given in the manner prescribed or permitted by the offer. By manifesting assent, the offeree exercises the power given by the offeror to create a contract.

Generally, only the person to whom an offer is addressed has the power of acceptance. One may also have a power of acceptance if he or she is a member of a class to which an offer has been directed. If the offer is made to the general public, anyone may qualify as an offeree. Performance by anyone knowing of the offer will cut off the power of every other person to accept, provided that the offeror desires only one performance (reward for return of lost property).

Unlike rights under an existing contract, the offeree's power of acceptance cannot be assigned. An exception exists for option contracts, since the power to accept is itself a contract right in a contract of this type.

A.   Common Law Rule   Under common law rules, different or additional terms in the acceptance make the response a rejection and a counteroffer, unless it is clear that the original offer is still being considered (*see above*). Distinguish the following situations:

> 1.   Statements by the offeree that make implicit terms explicit do not prevent acceptance, such as, "I accept provided that you can provide marketable title." This is a valid acceptance because the obligation to convey marketable title is implicit in the offer to sell.

> 2.   A grumbling acceptance is nonetheless valid, as long as it stops short of dissent, such as, "This is highway robbery, but I must have this briefcase. Wrap it up."

> 3.   A request for clarification does not necessarily indicate a rejection and counteroffer. For instance, "Would you be willing to come down another $10.00 on the price?" seeks clarification or further negotiation; it is not a rejection.

B.   U.C.C. (Battle of the Forms)   When the offer is for the purchase or sale of goods between merchants, the common law rules for acceptance have been altered substantially by U.C.C. § 2-207. Unlike common law rules, the proposal of additional terms by the offeree does not constitute a rejection and counteroffer if the acceptance is otherwise definite and timely. Under the U.C.C., a contract is formed nevertheless, subject to the limitations shown below. The only question is whether the additional terms will be included or excluded.

1. Consistent Terms The additional terms proposed in the offeree's acceptance become terms of the resulting contract if they are consistent with (do not materially alter) the allocation of economic risks and benefits or impair a remedy that would be available otherwise, and the offeror does not exclude them by objecting specifically to their inclusion within a reasonable time.

2. Inconsistent Terms If the additional terms proposed are inconsistent (materially alter the contract), a contract is formed; but its terms include only those contained in the offer. The inconsistent, additional terms become part of the contract only if the offeror expressly assents to their inclusion.

3. Either Party Can Avoid Effects of § 2-207 If an offeror wishes to avoid the addition of consistent terms proposed by an offeree under § 2-207, he may do so by expressly limiting acceptance to the terms of the offer. Similarly, an offeree who does not wish to form a contract unless the offeror consents to additional terms can respond with a clear rejection and a counteroffer.

C. Acceptance Must Be Communicated Subject to a few exceptions, the general rule is that the acceptance must be communicated to the offeror. Like the offer, the acceptance is judged by an objective standard. The offeree's subjective state of mind is irrelevant.

1. Common Law Whether an acceptance became effective upon dispatch or upon receipt depended upon whether the offeree used an authorized method of communication under common law rules. Unless a specific method of communication was required by the offeror, the method used by the offeror to transmit the offer was impliedly authorized for transmittal of the acceptance.

2. U.C.C. and Second Restatement Most courts today ignore the technical common law rules concerning acceptance. Under the U.C.C., an offer may be accepted by any "medium reasonable in the circumstances." U.C.C. § 2-206. The offeror still may limit acceptance to a particular method but must do so clearly, since any ambiguity will be construed to allow the offeree to use any reasonable means.

3.   The Mailbox Rule   Acceptance by mail or by a similar medium creates a contract at the moment of posting, properly addressed and stamped, unless:

(a)   The offer stipulates that acceptance is not effective until received; or

(b)   An option contract is involved (acceptance under an option contract is effective only upon receipt). Restatement 2d § 63.

In most states, a revocation is effective only upon receipt (*see prior discussion*). Under the mailbox rule, a contract is formed if the acceptance is sent before the revocation is received. This is true even though the acceptance is sent (by offeree) after the revocation is sent and is received after the revocation is received.

> Kathy made an offer to Dale on July 23 to purchase his 1955 classic Cadillac auto, specifying that acceptance must be made by United States mail. Dale received the offer on July 25 and mailed his acceptance on July 26. In the meantime, Kathy located a better vehicle and sent her revocation of the offer to Dale on July 25, which he did not receive until July 27. Kathy received Dale's acceptance on July 28. A contract is formed, and Kathy is obligated either to purchase Dale's auto or to pay damages.

4.   Acceptance by Unauthorized Method   If an acceptance is sent by an unauthorized method (or improperly sent by an authorized method), it still may be effective if it is actually received by the offeror while the offer remains open.

> Betty made an offer to Joe, specifying that acceptance should be by facsimile; but Joe's fax machine is broken, so he mails the acceptance. The acceptance will not be effective until it is received by Betty, assuming that the offer is still open at that time.

> Same as above, except that Betty specified that acceptance should be by letter. Joe incorrectly addressed the envelope when he sent the acceptance. His acceptance will not be effective until Betty receives it, assuming that the offer is still open.

5.   Crossing Offers   If offers containing exactly the same terms cross in the mail, they do not create a contract despite the apparent mutual assent. An offer cannot be accepted until there is knowledge that it has been made.

C. Acceptance Without Communication

An executory bilateral contract may be formed without communication of acceptance in limited situations:

1. Express Waiver An offer, by its terms, may waive any communication of acceptance. For instance, an application for insurance may state: "Your application is an offer only, pending acceptance by our home office." This is similar to the concept of solicitation of offers discussed previously.

2. Silence as Acceptance An offeree who silently receives the benefits of services (not goods) will be held to have accepted a contract for them if the offeree (1) had a reasonable opportunity to reject them and (2) knew or should have known that the offeror expected to be compensated. Restatement 2d § 72(1)(a).

> Alice, a local golf pro, gave a free golf lesson to Ben. She told him that a series of ten lessons would cost $100.00. Ben did not ask for the lessons and remained silent when he learned of the cost. Ben finally stopped the lessons after five had been given. By his silence, Ben accepted Alice's offer of a ten-lesson course and must pay the contract price, not just the value of the five lessons given.

When the offeree receives goods, he or she may be held to have accepted a contract for the goods, even though the offeror did not intend to do so. The unintentional acceptance may be made by exercising dominion over the goods in a way that is consistent with ownership of the goods. Restatement 2d § 72(2), U.C.C. § 2-606(1). If this occurs, the offeror has a choice among a contract action, a tort action for conversion, and a quasi-contract action for the fair value of the goods.

> Ann receives a mailer from Discriminating Book Club, soliciting her membership and asking her to complete a card and send it back to the Book Club. Although Ann did not complete or mail the card, the Discriminating Book Club began sending books to her. Ann gave the books away as gifts. Since giving the books away is inconsistent with the Book Club's ownership of them, Ann will be held to have accepted the Book Club's offer, even though she did not intend this result. (This contract will be effective, however, only if Discriminating Book Club elects to sue "on the contract," rather than in tort or in quasi-contract.) Had Ann simply kept the books and waited for the Book Club to ask for them back, there

would be no contract since Ann would not have exercised dominion
over them. Restatement 2d § 72, Illustr. 7, 8, and 9.

Note: Many states have adopted statutes that change this result
when unsolicited goods are sent by mail. They allow the recipient to
treat the goods as "unconditional gifts." These are sometimes referred
to as "Book of the Month Club" statutes.

Consideration

Most legally enforceable contracts contain a bargained-for exchange (change in
position) between the parties, which is called consideration. Although substitute
doctrines may permit enforcement of an agreement without consideration
(discussed *infra*), look for consideration first. It is only when consideration is not
present that substitutes for consideration should be considered.

There are two requirements for consideration: (1) there must be a
bargained-for exchange between the parties and (2) the bargained-for exchange
must provide some benefit to the promisor or must provide some detriment to the
promisee (legal value).

Mary promises to sell her used car to John for $100 in exchange for
John's promise to pay $100 to Mary.

Both requirements of consideration are present. The promise of Mary induced a
detriment in the promisee, John. John's detriment induced Mary to make the
promise. Therefore, Mary's promise was bargained for. Secondly, both parties
suffered a detriment: the detriment to Mary was the transfer of her ownership of
the car to John, and the detriment to John was the payment of $100 to Mary.

Although this definition may sound complicated, the gist of it is that a
promise is supported by consideration if:

1.   The promisee gives up something of value or restricts his
liberty in some way (suffers a legal detriment); and

2.   The promisor makes the promise as part of a bargaining
process, that is, he makes the promise in exchange for the promisee's
giving of value or restriction of liberty (the promisee's legal
detriment).

These two components of consideration generate two very different groups
of cases in which consideration problems arise. The "bargain" element appears

most often in cases that do not involve business dealings, such as a promise to make a gift. The "legal value" or "legal detriment" element appears most often in business-related contracts where it is unclear whether one of the parties has given up anything.

Bargained-For Exchange   For a promise to be supported by consideration, the promisee's "detriment" must have been bargained for by the promisor. One of the primary reasons to require a bargained-for exchange is to prevent the enforcement of a promise that is intended as a promise to make a gift.

A.   Gift   In the usual promise to make a gift, the promise is not enforceable in a court of law because it lacks consideration. Such a promise is not a bargained-for exchange; neither is legal detriment suffered by the promisee.

> George says to Henry, "I promise to give you $5,000 when I die."

George's promise is not supported by consideration and is unenforceable for two reasons. First, George did not make the promise as part of a bargain, that is, he was not trying to obtain anything from Henry. Second, Henry suffered no legal detriment; he didn't do anything, spend anything, or give up anything to obtain the promise from George.

A promise may be present even though the promisor does not receive economic benefit from agreement.

> Uncle Ed promises his niece, Karen, $10,000 if she does not marry before the age of 25. Karen waits until she is 25 to marry.

This promise is enforceable. Even though Uncle Ed received no economic benefit from Karen's restraint, he did obtain something that he wanted (his niece's forbearance); and he bargained for it. In addition, Karen sustained a legal detriment by not marrying until she reached age 25, which she had a legal right to do from the age of majority. The mere fact that the promisee incurs a legal detriment, however, does not always mean that the promisor obtains a corresponding benefit.

> "Come over to our house, and I will give you our old refrigerator."

> "If you take care of me in my old age, I will leave my entire estate to you."

The promise in the first example is unenforceable. Although the promisee incurs a detriment by going to the promisor's house (which she is not otherwise required to do), the promisor receives no benefit. Rather, coming to the house is the condition to receive the gift. If the promisee comes to the house to find that the promisor has changed her mind about giving away the refrigerator, the promisee has no cause of action. In the second example, however, the promisor receives a benefit that she has bargained for specifically: care in her old age. At the same time, the promisee incurs a detriment in caring for the promisor. Consideration is present and the promise is enforceable.

B. **Past Consideration or Moral Obligation**   If the detriment had already been given or performed before the promise was made, most courts would reason that it was not given or done in exchange for the promise and, therefore, does not satisfy the "bargained-for" requirement.

> After working for fifty years at Bilkum & Billum, Lee retired. At her retirement party, Henry Billum promised Lee a pension of $500.00 a month for life because of her many years of loyal service to the firm.

This promise is unenforceable under the general rule, because there is no "bargained-for" exchange for the promise of a pension. Note the exceptions below, however.

1. **Technical Defense**   If the past obligation would be enforceable except that a technical defense stands in the way—such as a *statute of limitations*, *discharge in bankruptcy*, and so forth—many courts will enforce the new promise if it is *in writing* or if it has been *partially performed*.

2. **Promise to Pay for Past Requested Act**   Under the modern trend, if acts previously performed were *requested* by the promisor, the new promise is enforceable (*see pension example above*). Many of states have extended this rule to cover *unrequested* acts as well if they were rendered during an emergency.

Legal Value   As a general rule, courts of law will not inquire into the adequacy of consideration. In other words, they will not intervene if one party contracts to sell an item of high market value for a low price. However, a court of equity may inquire into the relative values exchanged by the parties and may deny an equitable remedy where it finds a contract price to be unconscionable.

Where the consideration is *token* only (entirely without value), the consideration generally will be held insufficient. Courts reason that this indicates a gift rather than bargained-for consideration.

Parties to written agreements sometimes recite that the consideration is $1.00 or some other *nominal* sum. Frequently, the recited amount has not been paid; and it was never intended that it be paid. Most courts hold that evidence may be introduced to show that no consideration was paid. Do not confuse this situation, however, with the recitation of "$1.00 and other valuable consideration" that is often shown on deeds. The phrase "other valuable consideration" is used merely to avoid showing the precise purchase price in the deed records.

A.   Preexisting Legal Duty   The traditional rule has been that the promise to perform (or the performance of) a preexisting legal duty is not sufficient consideration to create a contract.

> Andrew offered a $100 reward for the return of his Rolex watch, which had been stolen while he was lunching at Benny's Burger Barn. Tom, one of the police detectives assigned to the case, recovered the watch. Tom's performance of his official police duty is not sufficient consideration to enforce payment of the reward.

Because the traditional rule is disfavored by so many courts, a number of exceptions have evolved.

1.   New or Different Consideration   If the promisee gives something new in return for the promise she now seeks to enforce or agrees to vary her preexisting duty in some way, there is consideration. It generally is immaterial how slight the change is, since courts are anxious to avoid the results of the preexisting legal duty rule.

2.   Honest Dispute as to Duty   If the scope of the legal duty owed is the subject of honest dispute, then a modifying agreement relating to it ordinarily will be given effect.

3.   U.C.C. Exception   Under U.C.C. § 2-209(1), an agreement modifying an existing contract that is subject to the Uniform Commercial Code is binding without consideration, as long as the parties act in good faith.

B.   Existing Debts   Existing debts present a recurring problem, which is only a variation of the preexisting legal duty rule. For instance, partial payment of a debt is not sufficient consideration to support a promise by the creditor to discharge the entire debt. However, courts generally will attempt to avoid this result by applying one of the exceptions.

C.   Forbearance to Sue   The promise not to sue or not to file a claim constitutes consideration if the claim is valid or if the claimant reasonably and in good faith believes the claim is valid. Forbearance of the right to have a claim decided by a court is a detriment recognized as consideration.

Mutuality of Consideration   Consideration must exist on both sides of the contract, that is, the promises must create mutual obligations.

> John promises to buy "all of the widgets that we may order" from Worldwide Widget Co.

John's promise is illusory, since he is still free to buy widgets anywhere else that he chooses or to buy no widgets at all.

    A. **Requirements and Output Contracts**   Requirements contracts (a promise to buy all that I require) and output contracts (a promise to sell all that I produce) are enforceable. Consideration is present, because the promisor suffers a legal detriment when she gives up the right to purchase the goods that she may need from (or the right to sell the goods that she produces to) another source. U.C.C. § 2-306.

    Requirements and output contracts may not be unreasonably disproportionate to a stated estimate. Absent a stated estimate, they may not be unreasonably disproportionate to any normal or otherwise comparable prior requirements or output. In this way, the promisee is protected if the promisor attempts to alter quantities in an unforeseeable way. This is so, even though the attempted alteration is made in good faith.

    The fact that one of the parties to a requirements or output contract may go out of business does not make the promises illusory. Some courts have refused to enforce such agreements where the promisor did not have an established business history, because there was no basis for estimating quantity. The Uniform Commercial Code avoids this problem by reading "good faith" into the agreement. That is, the promisor must operate the plant (or conduct the business) in good faith and according to commercial standards of fair dealing in the trade so that the output or the requirements will approximate a reasonably foreseeable amount.

    B. **Conditional Promises**   Conditional promises are enforceable (no matter how remote the contingency may be) unless the "condition" is entirely within the promisor's control.

> Kathleen promises to send her niece, Olivia, to law school if Olivia has stopped seeing her current boyfriend by the time she graduates from college.

> Kathleen promises to send her niece to law school if it snows on
> August 15.
>
> Kathleen promises to send her niece to law school if Kathleen loses
> ten pounds by the end of June.

The first two promises are enforceable; the third is not. Whether Kathleen loses ten pounds or not is entirely within her control—the arguments of lifelong dieters notwithstanding.

A promise to buy if satisfied with the goods is not illusory since one cannot reject the goods unless dissatisfied. The courts have assumed that the party will exercise his or her right to reject in good faith. The Uniform Commercial Code is in accord. U.C.C. § 1-203.

C. **Right to Cancel or Withdraw** Although reservation of an unqualified right to cancel or withdraw may be an illusory promise, the consideration is valid if this right is restricted in any way, for example, the right to cancel upon thirty days' notice.

D. **Best Efforts Implied** The promise furnishing mutuality may be implied by a court in appropriate circumstances. Courts have increasingly tended to supply such promises in order to sustain agreements that might otherwise appear to be illusory.

> Acme Corporation is granted the right to sell Worldwide Widgets
> exclusively in return for one-third of the profits. The agreement is
> silent about the obligations of Acme Corporation. Courts will
> imply a promise by Acme to use its best efforts to sell the widgets.

E. **Voidable Promises** Voidable promises are not objectionable on mutuality grounds. Restatement 2d § 80.

> Frank entered into a contract with 17-year-old William. William's
> power to disaffirm his contractual obligations will not prevent his
> promise from serving as consideration.

F. **Unilateral or Option Contracts** Unilateral contracts (enforceable once performance has started) or option contracts (enforceable because one has purchased the time to decide whether to accept the offer or not) are not objectionable on mutuality grounds.

G. **Choice of Alternative Courses** A promise to choose one of several alternative means of performance is illusory unless each alternative involves some legal detriment to the promisor. However, if the power to choose rests with some third party not under the control of the promisor, this is itself a legal detriment and supplies valuable consideration even if one or more of the other alternatives carries no legal detriment.

> Smith, who is Jack's English professor, tells Jack that in return for Jack's promise to pay $250, Smith will (1) give Jack swimming lessons, (2) paint Jack's portrait, or (3) teach Jack's English class on a regular basis during the balance of the term, with the choice of performances to be Smith's. Since alternative (3) represents a preexisting duty owed by Smith to the university, it involves no legal detriment; and Smith's promise does not constitute legal detriment for Jack's promise to pay $250.

> Same as above, except that Smith allows Jack to select the performance. Legal detriment is present, even if Jack chooses alternative (3).

> Same as first example, except that Smith selects either alternative (1) or (2). Either selection cures the problem of legal detriment.

Substitutes for Consideration

Although consideration is necessary to make an executory bilateral agreement enforceable, certain substitutes for consideration can make an agreement at least partially enforceable.

A. Promises Under Seal

Common law recognized the seal (a wax impression or notary's mark) as a substitute for consideration. A sealed promise was enforceable without anything more. However, the statutes in many states have abolished all distinctions between sealed and unsealed documents. In still other states, the seal raises only a rebuttable presumption of consideration. The Uniform Commercial Code has eliminated the seal entirely as consideration for sales contracts.

B. Promises in Writing

A promise in writing may be enforced despite the absence of consideration in a few states simply because it is in writing. Except to the extent that it has been adopted by the Uniform Commercial Code for transactions between merchants, most states do not follow this rule.

Under the Uniform Commercial Code, any claim arising out of an alleged breach of a sales contract can be discharged in whole or in part by a written document signed by the claimant. U.C.C. § 1-107. Neither is consideration required to modify a written contract in good faith. Likewise, oral modifications are valid, unless the contract specifically prohibits such modification. Modifications of contracts covered by the Statute of Frauds (goods valued at $500 or more) must be in writing.

Merchants may bind themselves to keep an offer open for a period of no longer than three months if the offer so states and if it is a signed writing. If the offer form is supplied by the offeree, the clause promising to make the offer irrevocable must be separately signed by the offeror. U.C.C. § 2-205.

C.   Promises to Pay Obligations Barred by Law   A promise to pay a legal obligation barred by law is enforceable if the promise is in writing or if there has been partial performance, such as a partial payment. The new promise will be enforceable according to its terms, not according to the terms of the original obligation.

> Bill owes Mary $1,500, the collection of which is barred by the statute of limitations. Bill promises in writing to pay Mary $1,000 of the original debt. Mary can enforce the new promise without further consideration on her part but only to the extent of $1,000.

Similarly, a contract made by a person who lacks capacity is not enforceable. However, if that person affirms the contract upon attaining or regaining capacity, the new promise is binding against him or her.

D.   Promissory Estoppel   Consideration is not necessary where the facts indicate that the promisee relied to his or her detriment upon the promise of the promisor. In that instance, the promisor will be estopped to deny liability to the promisee to prevent injustice, although the liability may be limited by the losses incurred by the promisee. To enforce a claim of promissory estoppel, the promisee must be able to show: (1) The promisor reasonably should have expected to induce action or forbearance on the part of the promisee; (2) of definite and substantial character; and (3) the action or forbearance occurs.

> Ann orally promises to sell her chicken farm to Betty. Betty, in reliance upon Ann's promise, buys 500 chickens for the farm. If Ann refuses to go through with the deal, Betty cannot enforce the sale because of the Statute of Frauds; however, she may be able to recover her losses related to purchase of the chickens because of promissory estoppel (her detrimental reliance).

Contract Defenses

To be enforceable, a contract must be free of legally recognized defenses. A contract defense is a defect that prevents enforcement of a promise or agreement of the parties. The defect may be based upon lack of capacity of one of the parties to the contract or it may be based upon certain types of errors, misrepresentations, or public policy concerning the subject matter or terms of the contract.

Lack of Capacity   Contract defenses based upon lack of capacity generally involve one of three types of incapacity: minority, mental incapacity, and intoxication. Contracts made with persons who lack the capacity to contract are voidable, at the election of the incapacitated person.

A minor, sometimes called an infant, is a person who has not yet reached the statutory age of adulthood (majority). Many states, however, have adopted legislation that terminates minority if the minor marries, enters military service, or is otherwise fully emancipated from his or her parents. Since the contract of a minor is voidable, the minor may ratify the contract upon reaching the age of majority. The minor may ratify the contract by expressly affirming it or by failing to disaffirm it within a reasonable time after reaching majority. Even though minors are not generally bound by contracts made during legal minority, adults who contract with minors are bound.

> Joe Adult entered into an installment sale contract with Gary Teen for a car when Gary was 17 years old, requiring payments to be made once a month for three years. The age of majority in Gary's state of residence is eighteen. Joe then changed his mind and wanted out of the deal.

> Hot Hits Recording Co. entered into a contract with Gary while he was 17 years old, the terms of which required Gary to purchase one musical selection a month for the next ten years.

In the first example, Joe Adult may not avoid the contract with Gary. Gary, however, may avoid the contract within a reasonable time after reaching his eighteenth birthday. In that event, Gary will be required to return the car and may be required to pay for its rental value while it was possessed and used by him.

In the second example, Gary may disaffirm the contract within a reasonable time after reaching his eighteenth birthday. If he continues to purchase musical selections every month until he is nineteen, however, his right to disaffirm may have been lost through the passage of time.

There are certain situations where the minor may not avoid contracts made during minority. If the minor misrepresents his or her age or if the contract provides the minor with necessities of life, the minor usually cannot avoid the contract. Necessities of life generally include such things as food, shelter, and so forth; what constitutes a necessity depends on the particular minor's station in life. The statute that carves out the necessity of life exception generally encompasses such things as student loans, insurance contracts, and the like.

A person whose mental capacity is so deficient that he or she is incapable of understanding the nature and significance of a contract may disaffirm it, either personally (in a lucid moment) or through his or her legal representative. One who has been adjudged insane or mentally incompetent by a court of law lacks the capacity to contract. As with minors, mental incompetents are liable for necessities of life furnished to them, not under the contract but, rather, under a quasi-contract theory.

A person who is so intoxicated as not to understand the nature and significance of a particular contract may either avoid or affirm the contract when he or she is sober. Again, there may be quasi-contractual liability for necessities furnished during the period of intoxication.

Lack of Consent   Even when a person has the legal capacity to contract, offensive pressure exerted by one party against the other may make any consent to the bargain ineffective. Lack of genuine consent may fall into one of four general categories: duress, undue influence, misrepresentation, and fraud.

A finding of **duress** requires a ***coercive threat*** of sufficient gravity that it induces the other party to manifest assent to an agreement to which he or she would not have assented otherwise. Advice, suggestion, or persuasion is not coercive standing alone. Likewise, fear of embarrassment or annoyance does not generally constitute duress. For coercion to exist, there must be threatened injury; and the victim must give assent while under the influence of this threat.

The coercion may be a gun held to the head of the victim or threatened harm to a family member or to property of the victim. Threat of criminal prosecution constitutes duress when fear of the prosecution overcomes judgment and deprives the victim of the exercise of free will. Threat of civil prosecution, however, is not duress. In extreme situations, economic distress or business compulsion may be grounds for duress (*see also unconscionability, infra*).

> ABC Parts Co. contracted with Weisenheimer Industries to supply super-widgets for Weisenheimer's federal contract. The super-widgets were specially manufactured according to unique specifications. After supplying a portion of the super-widgets, ABC found that it was losing money and submitted a price increase for Weisenheimer's approval. Because there was no other source for the super-widgets on such short notice, Weisenheimer had no choice but to pay the higher price. Weisenheimer then sued to have the price increase refunded and won based upon the business compulsion (duress) defense.

Undue influence results when the will of the dominant person is substituted for the will of the victim. Undue influence exists when a ***confidential relationship*** is used to create an ***unfair bargain*** for the victim. Family relationships, such as husband-wife or parent-child, often give rise to confidential relationships. Likewise, fiduciary relationships fit into this category, such as attorney-client, guardian-ward, or trustee-beneficiary.

A contract is not voidable simply because a confidential relationship exists. It is voidable because the dominant party uses the relationship to his or her own advantage in obtaining the assent of the weaker party. A legitimate suggestion or persuasion may influence the weaker party; but when methods go beyond persuasion and prevent the victim from acting freely, undue influence is present. Whether independent advice was provided to the weaker party is an important factor in determining fairness of the contractual arrangement.

Misrepresentation is the ***innocent or negligent misstatement*** of a material fact made by one party and relied upon by the other party as a basis for entering into an agreement to his or her damage. Distinguish actionable misrepresentation from the puffing that sometimes occurs when a salesperson touts his or her product as "the best on the market." Puffing is not misrepresentation. Likewise, giving an opinion is not misrepresentation.

Fraud is defined in the same way as misrepresentation, with the additional element of ***scienter*** required. If a defendant knows that what she says is false or if she recklessly disregards the truth or falsity of what she says, scienter is present. The burden then shifts to the plaintiff (victim) to show that he relied upon the intentional misstatement and that his reliance was reasonable or justifiable.

> Slick Sam says to a prospective buyer, "You won't find a better buy than this little beauty." *(Puffing)*

> Slick Sam says to a prospective buyer, "You won't find a better buy than this little beauty. It was driven only to church on Sundays." *(Unless it is true, the latter statement may be the basis for fraud.)*

> Slick Sam says to a prospective buyer, "I bought the Brooklyn Bridge last month and am prepared to let you have it for a reasonable price." *(No fraud—reliance on this statement is not justified.)*

> Slick Sam, repeating what he was told by the former owner, says to a prospective buyer, "Mary Todd Lincoln stayed in this house when she visited New York." *(Unless it is true, the statement is a misrepresentation; because scienter is absent, however, it cannot form the basis for fraud.)*

<u>Mistake</u> A mistake is an assumption that is different from the facts. Although textbooks often classify mistakes as either unilateral or mutual, these classifications are practically useless in determining when a mistake will constitute a defense to contract formation and when it will not. At the heart of the mistake defense is the concept that mutual assent is lacking. In other words, there is no agreement because of some confusion by one (unilateral mistake) or both (mutual mistake) of the parties about a material fact. Either way, the contract is voidable, using the remedies of rescission and restitution.

There are some underlying philosophies that affect the mistake defense when it is raised:

1.	Although contract law usually looks at the objective intent of the parties (shown by words and actions), the parties' subjective understanding of the facts is the focus in determining whether a mistake exists.

2.	Mistake as a contract defense means mistake of past or present (but not future) material fact, not mistake of law. That a party is mistaken about the legal results of a particular fact or conduct is not included among the bases of the mistake defense. The law does not relieve parties who have merely made a bad bargain.

3.	Negligence in failing to read the terms of a contract before signing it is not the kind of mistake contemplated by the mistake defense.

**A.	Mutual Mistake**		A mutual mistake occurs when both parties are mistaken about a past or present material fact relating to the agreement. A mutual mistake goes to the heart of the bargain and prevents the formation of a contract. This kind of mistake is sometimes referred to as a latent ambiguity.

> Slick Sam contracts with Frank Farmer to sell Frank a prize cow. Unknown to either Sam or Frank, the prize cow died during the night. No contract is formed.

> Ann agrees to sell goods to Betty and to ship them from Bombay on a freighter known as the Peerless. Betty agrees to the terms. Neither knows that there are two freighters known as Peerless, one scheduled to depart in September and one scheduled to depart in December. Ann believes she has sold goods to be shipped on the Peerless leaving in December. Betty believes she has purchased goods to be shipped on the Peerless leaving in September. No contract is formed.

**B.	Unilateral Mistake**		A unilateral mistake is one made by only one of the parties to the agreement.

Burt agrees to buy an expensive ring from Ernie, believing Ernie to be a wealthy person with a similar name. Ernie is unaware of Burt's mistake concerning identity and has done nothing to cause the mistake to be made. Burt may not avoid the contract, even though Burt would not have agreed to buy the ring if he had known Ernie was not the wealthy person whom Burt supposed him to be.

George advertises a computer system for sale. Sally's employee inspects the equipment and offers $2,000 for it. Afterward, Sally discovers that the equipment will not handle a particular software program. Sally may not avoid the contract based upon mistake, because George did not know of the mistake nor should he have known of it.

Where ambiguity exists and is known to one party (but not to the other), a contract will be enforced according to the intention of that party who was unaware of the ambiguity.

Kathy agrees to purchase Dale's classic Cadillac auto. Unknown to Kathy, Dale has two classic Cadillac vehicles. Kathy intended to purchase one of them, and Dale intended to sell the other. The contract will be enforced so that Kathy will purchase the one that she intended to purchase, because Dale knew of the ambiguity. Kathy did not.

C.   Mistake in Transmission   When a mistake is made by an intermediary in the transmission of an offer or in the acceptance, the party who chose the intermediary generally bears the risk of the mistake. However, if the party receiving the message should have been aware of the mistake, no contract is formed.

ABC Company solicited bids for building a parking lot. Better Parking, Inc. sent its $10,500 bid by telegram. The telegraph company made a mistake, transmitting the bid at $1050. All of the other bids received by ABC were in the $10,000 range. ABC may not accept the $1050 bid, because it is apparent that a mistake has been made.

D.   Mistake in Value   When parties make assumptions concerning the value of the subject matter of the contract, those assumptions will be upheld by courts. This is particularly true when the subject matter is subject to fluctuations of value, such as publicly traded stock. However, when both parties are mistaken about the value, the rules concerning mutual mistake will prevail.

Arnold agrees to sell his prize cow to George for a minimal price, both parties believing that the cow is no longer fertile. After the purchase, George discovers that the cow is carrying a calf. This mutual mistake will support a rescission of the contract.

Illegality   If either the subject matter or the consideration of a contract is illegal at the time of the offer, there is no valid offer; and no contract is formed. Contracts may be illegal because they violate a constitution, a statute, or public policy as defined by courts. Illegality problems arise most often in these areas: agreements made in restraint of trade; gambling contracts; usurious contracts; agreements obstructing justice; and agreements concerning torts or crimes.

If the illegality occurs after the contract is formed, the supervening illegality discharges the contract because its performance has become impossible.

Unconscionability   Unconscionability is an equitable theory applied to contracts which are so unreasonable that they offend the conscience of all reasonable people. Under U.C.C. § 2-302, a court may refuse to enforce the entire contract, may refuse to enforce only the unconscionable portion, or may limit the unconscionable provision to avoid an unconscionable result. Unconscionability is used as a defense when the bargain is one-sided and one of the parties has substantially superior bargaining power over the other party.

Whether unconscionability exists is a question of law to be decided by a judge rather than by a jury. There is no precise definition for unconscionability, but courts use these criteria to determine its existence:

A.   Hidden, Risk-Shifting Provisions   Standard, preprinted forms sometimes contain provisions that seek to shift a risk normally borne by the stronger party to the weaker party. Typically, these provisions are in fine print, are inconspicuous, and are incomprehensible to the average person even when brought to his or her attention. They generally include: (1) "add-on" clauses that subject all property of the buyer to repossession if the buyer fails to pay for a newly-purchased item; (2) unreasonable liquidated damage provisions; (3) disclaimers of warranty provisions; and (4) confession of judgment clauses, which are illegal in most states on constitutional grounds.

B.   Adhesion Contracts   Adhesion contracts are those that contain unconscionable provisions concerning procurement of necessary goods, such as a refrigerator or an automobile, when the buyer is unable to purchase similar items from any seller without agreeing to a similar provision. In other words, the buyer has no choice. These contracts generally involve illiterate or non-English-speaking consumers, who unwittingly agree to pay three or four times the normal price of the item.

Statute of Frauds   The Statute of Frauds is a statute enacted in most states that requires certain types of contracts to be in writing to be enforceable, even though all other elements of contract may be present. Agreements included among Statute of Frauds provisions are:

A.   Executor or Administrator   An agreement by an executor, administrator, or personal representative to pay the debts of the estate out of his or her own funds must be in writing.

B.   Debts of Another   A promise to answer for the debt of another must be in writing, such as a guaranty for a loan. A promise to be primarily liable for the debt need not be in writing, even though the benefits of payment are conferred upon another.

C.   In Consideration of Marriage   A promise made in consideration of marriage, as an inducement to marry, must be in writing (other than a return promise to marry).

D.   Interest in Land   A promise creating an interest in land must be in writing. Interests in land include such things as the sale or purchase of real estate; a mortgage or other security interest or lien in real estate; a lease for more than one year; timber or minerals to be severed by the buyer; or an easement. There may be others. A contract to construct a building does not create an interest in land and does not need to be in writing for purposes of the Statute of Frauds.

Where part performance has occurred, equity may take the contract out of the Statute of Frauds. For instance, if a seller conveys real estate under an oral contract to sell and if the buyer then refuses to pay the purchase price, a court of equity may intervene. Similarly, where the purchaser under a land contract has paid all of the payments and the seller refuses to convey title, a court of equity may intervene to take the contract out of the Statute of Frauds and to require specific performance.

E.   Performance Within One Year   A contract which, by its terms, cannot be performed within one year must be in writing. The date of the agreement (not the date when performance is to begin) is used to calculate the one-year period. If it is possible to complete the contract within one year, the contract need not be in writing, even though its actual performance is concluded beyond the one-year period.

F.   Goods Priced at $500 or More   U.C.C. § 2-201(1) requires that contracts for the sale of goods of $500 or more be in writing. Under common law, this type of contract was taken out of the Statute of Frauds if a partial payment on the goods were made. The Uniform Commercial Code modifies this result by making such oral contracts enforceable only to the extent of the payments made and accepted or to the extent of goods received and accepted.

The Uniform Commercial Code permits enforcement of oral contracts for goods of $500 or more in some situations:

  1. If goods are being specially manufactured for a particular buyer and are not suitable for sale to others, an oral contract may be enforced.

  2. If the party against whom enforcement is sought admits in pleadings, discovery, or testimony that the contract was made, the oral contract may be enforced to the extent that its existence is admitted.

  3. A written confirmation between merchants is sufficient against the sender of the confirmation and is sufficient against the recipient unless he or she sends written objection within ten days of its receipt.

  G. **Satisfaction of the Writing Requirement** To satisfy the requirement of a writing, there must be a note or memorandum that contains the essential terms of the agreement, including (1) identity of the parties; (2) identity of the subject matter; (3) the essential terms; (4) recital of the consideration; and (5) signature of the party (or agent of the party) to be charged.

Under the Uniform Commercial Code, the following elements satisfy the requirement of a writing: (1) quantity; (2) signature of the party to be charged; and (3) a writing "sufficient to indicate" that a contract was formed. U.C.C. § 2-201.

  H. **Effect of Noncompliance** Noncompliance with the Statute of Frauds may render the contract unenforceable. In almost all cases of noncompliance, however, the noncomplying party still can recover the reasonable value of his or her performance or restitution of a benefit conferred under a quasi-contract theory.

Rights and Duties of Nonparties

Once it is determined that a valid, enforceable contract has been formed, the next question is whether any nonparty to the contract has rights or duties in connection with it.

The general rule is that a contract confers benefits and imposes duties only on the parties to the contract. Two important exceptions to this general rule include third-party beneficiaries and those to whom contractual rights or duties are transferred. The rights and duties conferred upon third-party beneficiaries stem from the original contract. In the latter situation, the rights and duties do not stem from the original contract but, rather, are transferred subsequently when one of the original parties transfers rights (assignment) or duties (delegation) to a third party.

Third-Party Beneficiary Contracts   A third-party beneficiary is one who is intended to receive the benefits of a contract created by someone else. The first distinction to be made is whether the third party is an intended beneficiary (who can recover) or is an incidental beneficiary (who cannot recover).

> Bill lends money to Jack in exchange for Jack's promise to buy Bill's mother a Cadillac when Jack graduates from law school. Bill's mother is an intended beneficiary. The local Cadillac dealership is an incidental beneficiary and cannot sue to enforce Jack's promise.

Under traditional common law rules, there are two categories of intended beneficiaries: creditor beneficiaries and donee beneficiaries. A creditor beneficiary is one to whom the promisee owes a debt (or to whom a debt is claimed). A donee beneficiary is one to whom the promisee intends to make a gift of the benefit being conferred. Bill's mother is a donee beneficiary in the example shown above. The Second Restatement has dispensed with these distinctions; it uses only the term "intended" beneficiary, without any distinction between creditor beneficiaries and donee beneficiaries.

A.   Third-Party Beneficiary v. Promisor   The third-party beneficiary (Bill's mother in the above example) may sue the promisor (Jack in the above example) on the contract. The promisor may assert any defense arising from the formation of the contract. Defenses arising after the contract is formed (supervening illegality, impossibility, failure of a condition, and the like) may defeat a suit brought by the beneficiary.

B.   Third-Party Beneficiary v. Promisee   A third-party creditor beneficiary may sue the promisee on the existing obligation between them. Any contract between the promisor and the promisee does not discharge the promisee's obligation to the third party. The rights of the third party beneficiary are cumulative. She need not elect between the third-party promisor and her own debtor (the promisee). She may sue both but can obtain only one satisfaction.

A third-party donee beneficiary (Bill's mother) may not sue the promisee (Bill) because the promisee's act is gratuitous. This is true even when the third-party beneficiary has relied on the contract to her detriment (perhaps by building a garage for the Cadillac).

C.   Promisee v. Promisor   When the contract involves a creditor beneficiary and a promisee has been required to pay the beneficiary on the original debt, the promisee then may recover against the promisor. If the debt has not yet been paid to the third-party beneficiary by the promisee, the promisee can compel the promisor to pay as agreed by filing suit for specific performance.

Where a donee beneficiary is involved, the majority rule now is that the promisee has a cause of action against the promisor. Since the promisee rarely ever suffers any actual damage, however, the promisee usually will receive only nominal damages. For this reason, many courts have resolved the problem by allowing specific performance in this situation as well.

Assignment of Rights   When a contract already has been created and when one of the parties subsequently seeks to transfer rights under the original contract to a third party, this transfer is accomplished by assignment.

> Oscar agrees to provide cleaning service to the Super Shopper Store for a fee of $1500 a month. After the contract is underway, Oscar agrees to transfer his right of payment to the Second National Bank, with the payment to be applied to Oscar's equipment loan at the bank. The transfer is an assignment.

In the above example, Oscar is the assignor; Second National Bank is the assignee; and Super Shopper Store is the obligor.

Although nearly all contractual rights may be assigned, there are some exceptions:

A.   Obligor's Duty Changed   If assignment of rights would alter the obligor's duty substantially, assignment will be prohibited. One example is a personal service contract where the obligor would have to perform a service substantially different for the assignee than would have been performed for the assignor. Another example might be a requirements and output contract, where the requirements of the assignee may be substantially different than the requirements of the assignor.

B.   Obligor's Risk Changed   When the assignment would alter the obligor's risk substantially, assignment will be prohibited without the obligor's consent.

Bill's auto is insured by Best Insurance Co. Bill sells the auto to Susan, who intends to use it as a taxi. Bill cannot assign his rights under the insurance contract to Susan without Best's consent, since the assignment would alter Best's risk substantially.

C. **Assignment Prohibited by Law** A right cannot be assigned if the assignment is prohibited by law. For instance, many states have statutes that prohibit, or at least limit, wage assignments.

D. **Assignment Prohibited by Contractual Provision** The power to assign cannot be limited by contract; however, the right to assign can be. Where parties seek to bar assignment by contract provision, the provision must be clear and unequivocal that any purported assignment is void. A contractual provision barring assignment is ineffective against assignments by operation of law (bankruptcy, death, and so forth).

Assignment Requirements Assignments are not required to be in writing as a general rule; however, some assignments must be in writing to be effective:

1. Assignments of wages;
2. Assignments of interests in land;
3. Assignments relating to sale of goods of $500 or more; and
4. Assignments of security interests under U.C.C.'s Article 9.

A. **Partial Assignments** Contract rights may be transferred to one assignee or they may be divided and transferred to more than one assignee. Likewise, the assignee may transfer some of the rights under a contract and retain others.

B. **Revocability** If an assignment is given in exchange for consideration, it is irrevocable. An assignment given gratuitously (no consideration exchanged) is revocable unless the obligor has already performed or unless the assignee has changed his or her position in reliance upon the assignment (detrimental reliance). In the latter situation, the assignor is estopped from revoking the assignment.

C. **Effect of Assignment** The effect of assignment is to establish privity of contract between the obligor and the assignee. The assignee replaces the assignor as the real party in interest; and the assignee is entitled to performance under the contract, subject to any defenses that the obligor may have against the assignor.

D.   Successive Assignments   When the first assignment is revocable (gratuitous), a subsequent assignment will revoke the first one. Generally, when the first assignment is irrevocable, the first assignee has priority over any subsequent assignees.

The Uniform Commercial Code has resolved this problem by imposing filing requirements. U.C.C. § 9-302. If the filing provisions apply to a particular transaction, the assignee who is the first to file will prevail.

Delegation of Duties   Duties or obligations under a contract are not assigned. Rather, they are delegated when a party to the original contract wishes to have another person perform his or her duties under the contract.

> Oscar agrees to provide cleaning service to the Super Shopper Store for a fee of $1500 a month. After the contract is created, Oscar authorizes Mostly Maids, Inc. to perform the cleaning service for him at a fee of $1000 a month. This authorization is a delegation.

In this example, Super Shopper Store is the obligee; Oscar is the delegator; and Mostly Maids, Inc. is the delegate (sometimes called the "delegatee").

A.   Duties Subject to Delegation   In general, all duties are capable of delegation to third parties except duties requiring personal judgment or skill (artistic performance); duties involving a trust relationship (attorney-client); duties which, if delegated, would change the expectancy of the obligee (output contract); and duties which are covered by a contract provision that restricts or prohibits their delegation.

B.   Requirements for Delegation   No special rules or formalities are required to delegate duties under a contract. The delegation may be either oral or written. There is no requirement that the word "delegate" be used; the delegator need only manifest a present intention to transfer or to delegate the duty.

C.   Rights and Liabilities of Parties   The rights and liabilities of parties in relation to delegated duties are shown below.

1.   Obligee   Other than those duties that cannot be delegated (*see above*), the obligee must accept performance from the delegate.

2.   Delegator   The delegator remains liable on the contract even if the delegate expressly assumes the contract duties.

If the obligee expressly consents to the delegation, however, this situation may create a novation (see subsequent discussion under Discharge).

3. Delegate When the delegate promises to perform the contractual duties and when that promise is supported by consideration, a third-party beneficiary contract is created by the delegator and delegate, with the obligee as the third-party beneficiary. In that event, either the obligee or the delegator can compel performance or can bring suit for nonperformance.

Construction and Interpretation of Contracts

Courts use specific rules of construction when they interpret contracts. In general, contracts are construed as a whole, with specific clauses subordinated to the contract's overall intent. Words are construed according to their ordinary meaning, unless it is clear that they are intended to be used in a technical sense (term of art). When parties intend words to be used in a technical sense, it is prudent to provide the technical definition as part of the contract document.

When provisions appear to be inconsistent with each other, courts look to see whether some of the provisions are printed (a form contract), while others are written or typed. If both are present, written or typed provisions will be given more weight than printed provisions.

Courts look at the custom and usage of a particular business or industry in construing contract terms. Where possible, courts prefer to validate contracts rather than to invalidate them. Because of this inclination, courts try to construe provisions to make them operative unless this practice clearly would contradict the overall intention of the parties.

Parol Evidence

When parties express their contract in writing with the intent that it embody the full and complete expression of their agreement, any other expressions—whether oral or written—made prior to or contemporaneous with the writing are inadmissible to vary the terms of the writing. This is known as the parol evidence rule. In other words, the written terms expressed in the contract may not be changed by parol evidence of what the parties actually intended.

Notwithstanding its name, the parol evidence rule is regarded as a rule of substantive contract law rather than as a rule of evidence. It is designed to put the apparent intention of the parties (expressed by the writing) into effect and to assist in judicial interpretation by having a single source of proof (the writing) concerning the terms of the contract.

When the parol evidence rule is raised concerning a particular contract, the judge—not the jury—must decide (1) whether the written document was intended as a final expression of the parties' agreement and (2) whether the written document is a complete integration or is only a partial integration of the parties' agreement.

The more complete that a document appears on its face, the more likely that it was intended as a final expression. Where the document contains a merger clause, reciting that it is complete on its face, this clause strengthens the presumption that all negotiations were merged into the written document. If the judge determines that the written document is the final integration of the parties' agreement, no extrinsic evidence will be admitted to vary any of the terms contained in the document.

There are a number of situations where the parol evidence rule does not apply to exclude evidence. These are discussed below.

Attack on Validity   Any party to a written contract may attack the contract's validity. In this circumstance, the party concedes that the written document reflects the agreement but asserts that the agreement never came into existence because of formation defects (duress, mistake, illegality, misrepresentation, and so forth) or because a condition precedent never occurred.

> Jill signs a real estate contract, agreeing to sell her house to Jack,
> but Jill and Jack agree orally that the contract will not become
> effective until Jill finds another house to buy for herself.

The parol evidence rule does not come into play until a fully binding contract exists; therefore, Jill ordinarily will be allowed to introduce evidence that the stipulated event (the condition precedent) has not yet occurred.

To Clarify Ambiguity   If there is ambiguity concerning the terms of a written agreement or if there is a dispute concerning the meaning of those terms, parol evidence can assist the fact-finder in correctly interpreting the agreement. If the meaning of the agreement and its terms are plain, parol evidence is inadmissible.

To Refute Consideration   The parol evidence rule will not exclude extrinsic evidence to show the consideration actually paid. For instance, if a written contract recites that $100 has been given, parol evidence may be admitted from the defendant to show that $100 was never paid.

Subsequent Modification   Since the parol evidence rule applies only to prior or contemporaneous negotiations related to the agreement, parol evidence can be admitted to show subsequent modification of the written contract. In other words, parties may show that the written contract was changed in some way after it was originally made.

U.C.C. Rule   Under the Uniform Commercial Code, a party may not contradict the written document but may add consistent, additional terms unless (1) there is a merger clause or (2) the court finds that the writing was intended as a complete and exclusive statement of the terms of the agreement. U.C.C. § 2-202. Under this Code section, the terms of a written contract may be explained or supplemented by showing custom and usage in the trade or by showing the course of performance to date.

Enforcement of Contracts

The area of contract enforcement deals with discharge of contract duties, breach of contract, and remedies for breach. Before any of these things can be considered, however, there must be an initial determination that a party has a present duty to perform and has not done so. To make this determination, one must be able to distinguish between a promise to perform and a condition, sometimes called a condition precedent.

Promise v. Condition   A promise is a commitment to do or to refrain from doing an act. A promise in a contract may be unconditional or conditional. An unconditional promise is absolute; a conditional promise may become absolute by the occurrence of the condition. When the promise is unconditional, the failure to perform will constitute a breach of the contract.

A condition is an event, other than the passage of time, the occurrence of which will create an absolute duty to perform and the nonoccurrence of which will extinguish any duty to perform. There can be no breach if the condition has failed to occur. Instead, failure of the condition discharges the liability of the promisor, whose obligations never mature.

> Frank Farmer agrees to sell his prize cow to Jane for $500, with possession of the cow to be given on October 31. On October 15, the cow dies.

In the above example, is delivery of a specific cow a condition? If so, the death of the cow will discharge Jane's duty to pay; however, Jane will have no cause of action against Frank if the condition does not occur. Or, has Frank promised to sell his prize cow (whether the cow that died or another prize cow), giving Jane the right to sue for breach of contract?

As the example shows, it is important to know whether a provision will be interpreted as a promise or as a condition. The basic test is the "intent of the parties." In making this determination, courts look at the specific words used and the context of the entire agreement; the prior practices of the parties; and the customs within that business or industry. Recall that in doubtful situations, courts prefer to validate the contract rather than to invalidate it. However, if occurrence of the stipulation goes to the heart of the contract's consideration, it is probably a condition rather than a promise. In the above example, it is likely that a court would find that delivery was a condition to Jane's duty to pay. Alternately, the court may find that there was a mutual mistake, in that the subject matter of the contract (the prize cow) was destroyed.

Both Condition and Promise   A particular contract term may be a promise for one party and a condition for the other. These are often called constructive conditions.

> Ben promises to repair Adam's car by December 1 if Adam will promise to pay Ben $200 for the repairs on that date. Adam agrees.

In this example, Ben's promise to repair the car by December 1 is an absolute promise, and his performance is a condition of Adam's duty to pay $200.00 on December 1.

A contract term may be both a promise and a condition for the same party.

> Alice agrees to buy Jim's house if she can secure the necessary financing. Alice attempts to secure financing but is unable to do so.

Alice is subject to both a promise and a condition. The condition is that she be able to secure financing; the promise is that she will make reasonable attempts to secure it. If Alice makes reasonable attempts but is unsuccessful, the failure discharges any further duty on the part of either party.

Excuse of Condition   As a general rule, if a party's duty to perform is conditional, there is no duty to perform until the condition occurs. However, situations may exist that require performance even though the condition has not occurred. In these situations, the condition is excused.

A. Hindrance If a party's duty is conditioned on the occurrence of an event and that same party wrongfully prevents the event from occurring, the occurrence of the event (condition) may be excused; and the party must perform despite the non-occurrence. In determining whether a party has contributed to the non-occurrence of a condition to his or her own duty, the test is one of good faith. If the party acts in bad faith, the condition will almost always be excused; and that party will be required to perform.

> Alice agrees to buy Jim's house if she can secure the necessary financing. Alice later decides that she does not want the house and does not attempt to secure financing.

B. Breach A material breach of the contract when performance is due will excuse the non-breaching party's duty to perform. A minor breach, on the other hand, may suspend the non-breaching party's duty to perform but will not excuse it.

C. Anticipatory Repudiation Anticipatory repudiation occurs when a party, prior to the time required for performance, indicates unequivocally that he or she will not perform when performance is due. Under common law rules and under the Uniform Commercial Code, anticipatory repudiation occurs only when there is an executory bilateral contract (duties remaining on both sides).

When the nonrepudiating party has no duty remaining to be performed by him or her, the doctrine of anticipatory repudiation does not apply. The nonrepudiator must wait until the time originally agreed for performance before a cause of action arises. Until then, the repudiator may withdraw the repudiation and perform as required by the original contract.

> Bill agrees to pay $50 on December 1 for Frank's used aquarium, with the aquarium to be delivered on November 15. On November 1, Bill unequivocally informs Frank that he no longer wishes to buy the aquarium and will not pay $50 for it. (*Anticipatory repudiation applies.*)

> Bill agrees to pay $50 on December 1 for Frank's used aquarium, with the aquarium to be delivered on November 15. The aquarium is delivered as agreed; and on November 25, Bill announces that he will not pay $50 for it. (*Anticipatory repudiation does not apply, since Frank's performance is complete. Frank must wait until December 1 passes to initiate suit.*)

When anticipatory repudiation occurs, the nonrepudiating party may select one of four options:

1.   Treat the anticipatory repudiation as total repudiation and sue immediately;

2.   Suspend performance and wait until the performance date to sue;

3.   Treat the anticipatory repudiation as an offer to rescind, resulting in discharge of the contract; or

4.   Ignore the anticipatory repudiation and urge the promisor to perform as originally agreed.

D.   Substantial Performance   The   condition   of   full performance often may be excused if a party gives substantial performance. In other words, if a party has committed a minor (insubstantial) breach but has performed in all other respects, she has substantially performed. In this situation, the other party's duty of performance becomes absolute. The rule of substantial performance does not apply to an express condition, however, if it would contradict the stated intent of the parties.

> Dick agrees to build a new house for Jane, using plans that, among other things, call for Newton locks on all doors and windows. Dick uses Newton locks on the doors but cannot obtain Newton window locks for another eight weeks. He uses Benning window locks instead, which are of similar quality.

Although Dick breached the contract by not using Newton window locks, the deviation is minor. Accordingly, Dick has substantially performed; and Jane now has a duty to perform her duty by paying for the house. Because of the doctrine of substantial performance, Dick is able to enforce the contract rather than sue in quasi-contract. Jane will be able to deduct or to sue for damages (if any) that she suffers as a result of Dick's incomplete performance.

The substantial performance doctrine was developed primarily to prevent forfeiture for minor defects in construction contracts. When the sale of goods is involved, U.C.C. § 2-601 gives the buyer the right to reject goods (perfect tender rule) subject to six exceptions:

1.   The parties may agree otherwise;

2.   Rejection of goods under an installment contract is permitted only if the installment is nonconforming and if the nonconformity substantially impairs the value of the installment;

3.   The seller's failure to provide for reasonable shipment or promptly to notify the buyer of shipment gives the buyer the right to reject only if material delay or loss occurs;

4.   If the buyer has accepted the goods, she no longer has the right to reject;

5.   Bad faith rejection by the buyer for an immaterial defect may preclude her right of rejection; and

6.   Although the buyer has the right to reject for any defect in general, the seller has the right to cure if there is any time remaining for performance under the contract.

E.   Divisible Contracts   Like the doctrine of substantial performance, divisibility of a contract into units prevents the harsh result of forfeiture. Where a party performs one of the units of a divisible contract, she is entitled to the agreed equivalent for that unit, even if she fails to perform the other units. The other party, however, may have a cause of action for the remaining units and, at the same time, may withhold his counter-performance for those units.

The divisibility rule can be applied only when the contract can be divided into units in a reasonable way. The test is one of fairness. When contract terms expressly state that the contract is *entire* or is otherwise indivisible, courts will honor the parties' intent.

Under the Uniform Commercial Code, goods covered by a single contract must be tendered in a single delivery unless it is clear that the parties intended otherwise. When a contract for sale of goods authorizes or requires deliveries in separate lots, it is an installment contract. U.C.C. § 2-612 covers installment contracts:

1.   If the price may be apportioned, it may be demanded for each lot unless a contrary intent is shown.

2.   The buyer may reject an installment if the defect materially impairs the value of that installment and cannot be cured. If adequate assurance is provided by the seller, the buyer must accept the installment.

3.   The buyer may declare a total breach only if the defects materially impair the value of the entire contract. Even a material breach can be waived and the duties reinstated if the buyer demands further performance or if the buyer sues only for past installments.

F.   Waiver or Estoppel   One who is to receive the benefit of a condition may manifest words or conduct to waive the condition. If the condition is waived and if the other party changes her position in reliance upon the waiver, the waiver will be binding (estoppel). The waiver may be retracted, however, at any time before the other party has changed her position to her detriment in reliance upon the waiver.

> Frank agrees to buy a computer "in perfect working order" from
> Richard. When delivered, the computer has minor defects; but
> Frank elects to take delivery anyway.

By taking delivery, Frank waives the "perfect working order" condition. However, he may nonetheless be entitled to damages for the defects in the computer. Waiver relates only to waiver of the right to treat the failure of condition as a total breach for purposes of excusing counter-performance.

Discharge of Contract Duties

Duties under a particular contract may be discharged (released or extinguished) in a number of different ways. When a contract duty is discharged, that duty is no longer enforceable.

Performance   One way to discharge contract duties is by performance, and the vast majority of contracts are discharged in this way. A good faith *tender of performance*, made according to contract terms, likewise will discharge a party's duty to perform when the tendering party has the present ability to perform and when the other party refuses to accept performance.

> Joe pays $20 to Fred for a tennis lesson to be given on the following
> Tuesday. When Tuesday arrives, Joe fails to appear for the lesson,
> although Fred is present and ready to provide it.

Illegality   If the subject matter of the contract becomes illegal after the contract is formed, this supervening illegality will discharge the contract.

Impossibility   Contractual duties are discharged when it becomes impossible to perform them. The impossibility must be objective (could not be performed by anyone) and must occur after the contract is formed. If the impossibility exists when the contract is formed, the issue is one of formation—not one of discharge.

When a contract is discharged because of impossibility, each party is excused from duties yet to be performed under the contract. Either party may receive restitution under a quasi-contract theory for performance given before the impossibility occurred. If the performance to be given becomes impossible in part, the duty is discharged only to that extent. The remainder of the performance may be required, even if the remainder may involve additional expense or difficulty.

Temporary impossibility suspends contract duties but does not discharge them. When performance becomes possible, the duty of performance springs back into existence unless the burden on either party is substantially more than or is substantially different from the burden originally contemplated.

Death or physical incapacity of a party necessary to perform contract duties (personal services contract) discharges the contract. If the subject matter of the contract is destroyed through no fault of the promisor after the contract is formed, the contract is discharged unless the risk of loss has already passed to the buyer (such as certain sales of goods under the Uniform Commercial Code).

Impracticability   A number of courts will discharge contractual duties when performance becomes impracticable. To qualify for discharge by impracticability, the party required to perform must encounter extreme and unreasonable difficulty or expense that could not have been reasonably anticipated. It is not enough that performance has become more difficult or more expensive than anticipated; it must be extreme and unreasonable. Typical examples of commercial impracticability under the Uniform Commercial Code include war, labor strikes, or similar, unforeseen events that dramatically affect performance.

Frustration   If the purpose of the contract has become frustrated (without value or virtually without value) by a supervening event that could not have been foreseen reasonably when the contract was formed, performance may be discharged.

> Beth agrees to rent Mary's summer home at Myrtle Beach for her family's vacation during the last two weeks in August. On August 10, a hurricane causes extensive damage to the entire South Carolina coastline. Although the vacation home receives only minor damage, Myrtle Beach is declared part of a disaster area. The purpose of the contract is frustrated, since no one would want to vacation in a disaster area.

Rescission   A contract may be rescinded by agreement between the parties (mutual rescission). The agreement to rescind is itself a binding contract supported by the consideration of each party's giving up the right to performance by the other.

To be effectively discharged by rescission, there must be executory duties on both sides. The U.C.C. provides that the rescission of a contract for the sale of goods must be in writing when the original contract so requires. For contracts not governed by the U.C.C., many courts will permit oral rescission even though the original contract requires a rescission to be in writing.

When one party wants to rescind and the other party does not (unilateral rescission), the party seeking rescission must have adequate legal grounds to force the rescission. Adequate legal grounds may include mistake, misrepresentation, duress, undue influence, or failure of consideration.

Modification   If a contract is modified, the modification discharges those terms of the original contract that are the subject of the modification. The modification does not discharge the entire contract, however.

Ordinarily, the modification must be by mutual agreement. Under the doctrine of reformation, however, either party may bring an equity action to have written terms modified when the writing, through mistake or misrepresentation, does not state accurately the terms upon which the parties agreed.

No consideration is necessary when the effect of the modification is to correct an error in the original contract. Contracts for the sale of goods may be modified without new consideration. U.C.C. § 2-209(1).

Substituted Contract   A contract may be discharged by substituting a new contract in its place. The new contract may expressly revoke the original contract; but if the terms of the new contract are inconsistent with the terms of the original contract, the original contract is impliedly revoked and discharged.

Novation   Novation occurs when a new contract substitutes a different (new) party to receive benefits and to assume duties under the terms of the original contract. Novation requires agreement among all parties, including the new party; and when that agreement is reached, the contractual duties of original parties are extinguished (discharged).

Release   A release or an agreement not to sue will discharge contractual duties when the release is in writing and is supported by new consideration. When a contract for the sale of goods is involved, the release or agreement not to sue must be in writing but need not be supported by new consideration. U.C.C. § 1-107.

Accord and Satisfaction

An accord is an executory promise by one party to give a substituted performance and by the other party to accept the substituted performance as discharge of an existing duty.

> Eve owes Adam $1,000 under an existing contract. Eve offers Adam a new widget worth $750 in lieu of the existing debt. Adam accepts. The new consideration is sufficient to support a valid accord.

Where a genuine dispute exists concerning the amount due under an existing obligation, an agreement to pay a portion of the amount claimed will be treated as a valid accord by most courts.

Standing alone, an accord does not discharge the prior contract. Rather, it suspends the right to enforce the original contract in deference to the terms of the executory accord agreement. When performance under the accord agreement is complete, satisfaction occurs; and the combined accord and satisfaction will discharge the original contract.

Account Stated

An account stated is an agreement between parties concerning a final balance due from one party and payable to the other. The final balance covers a number of transactions and merges the transactions by discharging claims related to the individual transactions. To qualify as an account stated, there must have been more than one prior transaction between the parties.

An account stated need not be in writing unless one or more of the original transactions was subject to the Statute of Frauds. An account stated need not be express; it may be implied.

> After a number of individual sales between Betty and Ruth, Betty presents Ruth with a bill for $500 covering all previous transactions. Unless Ruth objects within a reasonable time, the bill will become an account stated. Betty then may sue for the account stated rather than for the combination of previous transactions.

Lapse

When the duty of each party is a condition to the duty of the other party, contractual obligations may lapse if neither party performs when his or her performance is due.

> Wally contracts with Sam to sell Sam 500 shoe horns on January 20 for $750. On January 20, Wally fails to tender the shoe horns

and Sam fails to tender $750. Six months later, Wally tenders the shoe horns but Sam refuses to accept them. The contractual obligations of both parties have been discharged by lapse.

Operation of Law   When a party to a contract obtains judgment against the other for breach of contract, the contractual duty of performance is merged in the judgment, which discharges the contract. Instead, the judgment debtor is obligated for whatever performance is required by the judgment, usually the payment of damages. An arbitration award works essentially the same way.

A discharge in bankruptcy likewise bars any right of action on the contract.

Breach of Contract

A breach of contract occurs when (1) a promisor is under an absolute duty to perform and when (2) the duty of performance has not been discharged. Implicit in the determination of whether the duty of performance has been discharged is an assessment of whether the nonperformance (breach) is material or minor.

Material Breach   A breach is material if the promisee does not receive the substantial benefit of her bargain as a result of the promisor's failure to perform or as a result of the promisor's defective performance. If the breach is material, the nonbreaching party may treat the contract as terminated, in which event her duty of counter-performance is discharged. In addition, she will have a right to one or more remedies for breach of the contract.

Minor Breach   A breach is minor if the promisee receives the substantial benefit of her bargain despite the promisor's defective performance. A minor breach may include small delays in completing the performance when time is not critical or small deficiencies in the quality of performance when precision is not critical. The effect of a minor breach is to provide a remedy to the nonbreaching party for the breach, but it does not relieve the nonbreaching party of the duty to perform under the contract.

When a minor breach is accompanied by anticipatory repudiation, however, the nonbreaching party may treat it as a material breach. In this situation, she is relieved of any further duty to perform under the contract; and she is permitted to sue immediately for damages.

Timely Performance   When the defaulting party has a duty to perform immediately, her failure to perform is a breach. Unless the nature of the contract makes performance at a specific time essential or unless the contract's terms provide that time is of the essence, the failure to perform on time ordinarily is a minor breach. Where merchant contracts are concerned, however, timely performance as agreed is important; and an unjustified delay is a material breach.

The nonbreaching party who sues for breach of contract must show both the ability and the willingness to perform but for the breaching party's failure to perform.

Contract Remedies

Once a plaintiff shows both (1) material breach by the defendant and (2) no material breach by the plaintiff, a remedy is available to redress the breach. Depending upon the facts of the case and the legal issues that they raise, there may be more than one remedy available to the plaintiff. In that event, the plaintiff must select the most advantageous remedy among them.

The purpose of a contract remedy is to put the plaintiff where he or she would have been if the contract had not been breached. In other words, a contract remedy attempts to give the plaintiff the benefit of his or her bargain. This is sometimes referred to as the plaintiff's expectation interest or expectancy and can take the form of damages or specific performance.

If a plaintiff wants to rescind the contract (does not want to buy the house if the defendant misrepresented that Mary Todd Lincoln slept there), she cannot obtain contract damages. Instead, the court will restore the plaintiff to her original position (before the contract was formed) by restoring to her any benefits that the defendant may have received, perhaps an earnest deposit or a down payment.

Similarly, when one party has conferred benefits on the other under an agreement that cannot be enforced, equity may intervene to disgorge the benefits from the defendant under a quasi-contract (restitution) theory.

Damages   The remedy awarded most often for breach of contract is contract damages. With some limited exceptions, damages must be proved to a reasonable degree of certainty; they cannot be speculative. Damages may be classified as compensatory (general), consequential (special), punitive, nominal, or liquidated.

A.   Compensatory (General) Damages   Compensatory damages are awarded to a plaintiff to put her where she would have been if the contract had been performed by the other party. Compensatory damages are designed to give the plaintiff the benefit of her bargain. This may be the contract price, the profits to have been realized from the contract, or the amount that she must pay to buy substitute performance.

> Andrew agrees to buy Ben's farm for $70,000. On the scheduled date of closing, the farm is valued at $73,000. If Ben refuses to sell, Andrew's general damages loss as a result of Ben's breach will be $3,000.

B. **Consequential (Special) Damages** In addition to compensatory damages, a plaintiff may be able to recover other losses incurred as a consequence of the breach, provided that they were reasonably foreseeable at the time the contract was made; that there is a causal ("but for") relationship between the damages and the breach; and that they can be proved with a reasonable degree of certainty.

> In the above example, Ben knows that Andrew intends to operate a chicken farm on the land. After signing the purchase agreement, Andrew contracts with ABC Poultry to purchase 900 chickens and makes a deposit of $500. Since Ben knew of Andrew's intention, it was reasonably foreseeable that Andrew would contract for chickens. If Andrew must forfeit the $500 deposit as a result of the breach, Ben may be liable for that amount as consequential damages.

C. **Punitive Damages** Punitive damages are designed to punish or to penalize the defendant for bad conduct above and beyond a simple breach of contract. In states where punitive damages are permitted, for instance, an employer who refuses to pay wages to an employee may be liable for punitive damages over and above the amount of the wages.

Punitive damages ordinarily are not allowed in commercial contract cases and are awarded in other contract cases only in very limited circumstances.

D. **Nominal Damages** Nominal damages may be awarded when the defendant has breached the contract but no monetary loss is proved. Nominal damages are awarded more frequently in tort cases than in contract cases, simply because breach of a contract usually results in a measurable monetary loss.

E. **Liquidated Damages** Liquidated damages are those damages agreed upon by the parties at the time the contract is formed. Liquidated damage provisions are used most often where the parties recognize that damages will be difficult to prove in the event of breach (such as lost profits of a new business, violation of a literary license agreement, and so forth). As long as a liquidated damages provision is reasonable (does not amount to a penalty), a court will enforce it without requiring that it be substantiated.

Measure of Damages Damages may be measured (calculated) in a number of different ways, depending upon the type of contract involved and the facts surrounding its breach. Implicit in all measures is the concept that a plaintiff is required to mitigate (minimize) his or her losses.

A. Sale of Goods When a contract involves the sale of goods, the Uniform Commercial Code prescribes the remedies available to both the seller and the buyer. U.C.C. § 2-703 describes the remedies of a seller when the buyer breaches, and U.C.C. § 2-711 describes the remedies of a buyer when the seller breaches.

Seller's Remedies When the buyer wrongfully rejects goods, wrongfully revokes acceptance of goods, or fails to make a payment, the seller may:

1. Withhold delivery of the goods;

2. Stop delivery of the goods in the hands of a carrier;

3. Resell the goods and recover the difference from the defaulting buyer, measured as the difference between the resale price and the contract price;

4. Cancel the contract;

5. Recover the contract price from the defaulting buyer if (a) the goods have been accepted or, if conforming goods have been lost or damaged, within a reasonable time after the risk of loss passes to the buyer; or (b) the goods have been identified to the contract and the seller is unable to find another buyer; or

6. Recover ordinary contract damages for nonacceptance, measured as the difference between the market price at the time and place for tender and the contract price, together with any consequential damages.

Buyer's Remedies   When the seller fails to deliver goods or when the buyer properly rejects goods or properly revokes acceptance of goods, the buyer may:

1.   Cancel;

2.   "Cover" by purchasing substitute goods on the open market and recover from seller the difference between the price of the substituted goods and the contract price;

3.   Recover specific goods identified to the contract if the buyer has paid all or a portion of the purchase price;

4.   Recover damages for nondelivery, measured as the difference between the market price at the time when buyer learned of the breach and the contract price, together with any consequential damages; or

5.   Obtain specific performance in limited circumstances (see U.C.C. § 2-716).

B.   Contracts for Sale of Land   The standard measure of damages for breach of contracts for the sale of land is the difference between the contract price and the fair market value of the land at the time when the land was to have been conveyed.

C.   Construction Contracts   The measure of damages in construction contracts depends upon the identity of the breaching party (whether the contractor or the owner) and the point at which the breach occurs.

Owner Breaches:

Before Construction Begins: Builder receives the profit she would have made on the contract.

During Construction: Builder receives the profit she would have made on the contract plus any costs that she has incurred to date.

After Construction Completed: Builder receives the full contract price plus interest.

Contractor Breaches:

Before Construction Begins: Owner receives the cost of completion (the amount over the contract price that it will cost to complete the construction).

During Construction: Owner receives the cost of completion unless completion would entail economic waste. In that event, owner receives the difference in the value of the land at the time of breach and the value of the land as it should have been if the contract had been performed.

If the contractor's breach is unintentional (negligent), she may be able to recover the reasonable value of her services and costs under a quasi-contract theory. She cannot recover under the contract, of course, if she is the breaching party. If the contractor's breach is intentional, she may be denied recovery of any kind—even in quasi-contract.

By Late Completion: Owner receives damages for loss of use (rental value) until construction is completed. If loss of use cannot be calculated readily or was not foreseeable at the time the contract was made, the owner may be limited to the interest on the value of the building as a capital asset.

Specific Performance
Specific performance is an equitable remedy by which a party is ordered by a court to fulfill his or her contractual obligations. Because it is an equitable remedy, the plaintiff must demonstrate to the court that there is no adequate remedy at law before specific performance can be granted. In other words, if the plaintiff can be compensated with money, she cannot obtain an order of specific performance.

As a general rule, specific performance in contract cases is limited to those situations where the subject matter of the contract is unique, because money will compensate for most contract losses. Notice the examples below, however.

> Mark agrees to sell an original painting to Ellen. Before delivery is to occur, however, Mark receives a higher offer for the painting. He informs Ellen that he will not honor their contract. Ellen may

be able to obtain an order of specific performance because the painting is an original and is therefore unique.

Alice agrees in writing to sell her house to Betty for $85,000. This is Betty's dream house. It is located one block from the school and six blocks from her place of employment. It is perfect in every way, right down to the red and green ceramic tiles in the kitchen. Alice subsequently changes her mind about selling the house. Because the house is unique (no other house is exactly like this one), Betty may be granted the remedy of specific performance.

Same situation, except that Betty (rather than Alice) changes her mind about buying the house. Specific performance is not appropriate on these facts, because Alice does not care whether she sells to Betty or to some other buyer, as long as she receives the $85,000 purchase price. If Alice is forced to sell the house for $82,000, she can obtain damages from Betty of $3,000; but she cannot force Betty to buy the house.

Rescission and Restitution   When a breach occurs, the nonbreaching party may elect to rescind the contract (treat it as if it had never existed). In that event, each party would be required to return any benefit or partial performance to the party by whom it was given. This is done either by returning tangible property or by returning the dollar value of the benefit or of the service. The purpose is to restore each party to the same position as before the contract was made.

Restitution damages focus on the gains of the defendant; compensatory damages focus on the losses of the plaintiff.

Reformation   Reformation is used in equity to correct errors in the document which contains the written terms of the parties' agreement. When an error is made in a written contract provision, the error can be "reformed" to reflect the correct provision. For example, if parties agree to sponsor an auto show on May 16 and if the written contract indicates a May 26 date, reformation is available to reflect the agreed date.

Reformation cannot be used to change the terms to which the parties agreed, however. When parties want to change an agreed term, a modification of the contract is used (*see above*). Modification discharges the old contract provision in favor of the new provision.

Quasi-Contract   Quasi-contract is not a contract at all. Rather, it is a legal fiction created by equity courts to prevent unjust enrichment of a defendant at the expense of a plaintiff. Quasi-contract is used as a remedy to obtain the reasonable value of services or other performance when no contract exists. It is also used by a breaching party to recover the reasonable value of her performance or services prior to the breach, such as the breaching contractor who builds part of the house but does not finish it (*see prior discussion*).

> Jack is hired by the Springfield Chamber of Commerce for $7,000 to organize a summer arts festival, payable upon conclusion of the festival. Two weeks before the festival, Jack becomes involved in a dispute with the Chamber's executive director and quits. As a general rule, Jack cannot bring an action on the contract if he is the breaching party. However, he can recover the value of his services under a quasi-contract theory, even if the value of his services proves to be more than the contract price.

Tort Actions   Courts have become increasingly receptive to imposition of a tort duty, as well as a contract duty, when there is a reasonably foreseeable risk of harm in connection with the performance of the contract duty. Therefore, improper performance of a contract may result in tort liability to the injured party as well. A few examples of this include the areas of products liability, professional liability, and infliction of emotional distress. The injured party may elect to waive the contract and sue in tort in this type of situation. In any event, she must choose one or the other; she cannot receive both contract damages and tort damages.

> Bill contracted with Morbid Mortuary to provide funeral services for his deceased wife. Everything proceeded routinely until the funeral procession was on its way to the cemetery. During the trip, the back door of the hearse flew open and the casket dropped onto the street; it was struck by the mortuary's limousine in which Bill was a passenger; and it broke apart, hurling the corpse into the oncoming lane of traffic.

On these facts, Bill may elect to bring a tort action against the mortuary for emotional distress, assuming the tort damages would be greater than the contract damages that he could recover.

The material in this chapter and the following Self-Test provide a basic review of the major issues and principles involved in contract law. The applicant who is unfamiliar with any of the issues or principles covered or who wants a more thorough review than can be provided in a text of this type should consult the Bibliography for additional study references.

Contract Law Self-Test

Allow an uninterrupted thirty-minute period to answer all questions. At the end of thirty minutes, check your answers against those in the Answer Key Section of this Manual. Deduct two points for each incorrect answer (100 total possible points). Unanswered questions are counted as incorrect answers. Follow directions carefully and observe the time limit precisely to provide an accurate self-assessment.

Choose the most correct answer to each of the following questions unless a specific question instructs you to do otherwise.

1.   True or False.   An offer made to B can be accepted by C.

2.   True or False.   An assignment generally cannot be made without the express consent of all parties.

3.   True or False.   Arnold rents a car to Ben for $50 a day. The car has a broken headlight, which Ben repairs. When the car is returned three days later, Arnold says, "In consideration of your repair of the headlight, I will not charge you for renting the car." Arnold cannot change his mind later and enforce the original rental agreement.

4.   The primary difference between fraud and misrepresentation is:

   a.   scienter
   b.   the amount of damages that can be obtained
   c.   the type of damages that can be obtained
   d.   two of the above
   e.   none of the above

5.   True or False.   A contract with an emancipated minor is voidable because the minor lacks capacity.

6.   True or False.   A woman, who is going to Europe for two years, contracts for the care of her car while she is gone. She agrees in writing to pay a man $500 to wax the car once every four months during her absence. This is a binding contract.

7. True or False.   A court is unlikely to set aside the exchange of an airplane for a car for lack of consideration.

8. Contractual intent generally is present:

   a.   in an agreement to meet for lunch made between two friends.
   b.   when a person signs a pledge for a charitable donation.
   c.   when an actor agrees to give an agent 15% of her earnings.
   d.   in two of the above selections.
   e.   in none of the above selections.

9. True or False.   The difference between a bilateral contract and a unilateral contract is the number of promises involved.

10. Duress probably exists when:

   a.   a man sells his house to pay for his wife's funeral.
   b.   a school withholds a student's diploma until his tuition is paid.
   c.   a gas station requires payment before putting gas in customers' cars.
   d.   an employee is told by a supervisor to buy company stock or be fired.
   e.   all of the above.

11. Dick and Jane enter an agreement whereby Dick agrees to purchase Jane's home subject to the sale of Dick's current residence. This is an example of a:

   a.   promise.
   b.   condition precedent.
   c.   condition concurrent.
   d.   condition subsequent.
   e.   none of the above.

12. Bert and Ernie contract for the construction of Bert's new home by Ernie for $225,000. After the home is approximately 75% completed, Bert and Ernie disagree about installation of the entry way doors. Bert becomes obnoxious, and Ernie leaves the job site in complete frustration. Ernie later calls Bert and tells him that he can't work on the house any longer and wants his money for the work already completed. Bert refuses, saying that unless Ernie completes the house, he will be paid nothing. Which of the following statements is true?

a. Ernie can receive contract damages of $225,000 because the house is substantially completed.

b. Ernie can receive contract damages equal to 75% of the contract price because the house is 75% completed.

c. Ernie can receive contract damages equal to 75% of the contract price because Ernie's conduct amounts to frustration of the contract's purpose.

d. Ernie cannot receive contract damages but can receive quasi-contract damages.

e. None of the above is true.

13. The difference between compensatory damages and restitution damages is:

a. Compensatory damages seek to compensate; restitution damages seek to restore.

b. Compensatory damages focus on what the defendant gained from the plaintiff; restitution damages focus on what the plaintiff lost.

c. Compensatory damages focus on what the plaintiff lost; restitution damages focus on what the defendant gained from the plaintiff.

d. None of the above statements is accurate.

14. True or False.   Acme Corporation is granted the right to sell Worldwide Widgets exclusively in return for one-third of the profits. The agreement is silent about the good faith obligations of Acme Corporation; consequently, courts will not enforce this contract.

15. Ann orally agrees to sell a building to Betty for use as a gymnasium. In reliance upon Ann's promise, Betty contracts for 100 pieces of exercise equipment. If Ann refuses to go through with the deal, Betty may be entitled to receive:

a. contract damages
b. collateral estoppel damages
c. promissory estoppel damages
d. restitution damages

16. True or False.   To prevail in an action based upon undue influence, the victim must prove, among other things, that he was subjected to an unfair bargain in which he lost money.

17.   True or False.   Under U.C.C. § 2-201, the requirements of a writing are satisfied if there is some memorandum that shows the quantity of goods ordered; no signature of the buyer or seller is needed.

18.   True or False.   Under the parol evidence rule, agreements made subsequent to the agreement in dispute are inadmissible to show the intended terms of the original agreement.

19.   When anticipatory repudiation occurs, the nonrepudiating party may:

   a.   Treat the anticipatory repudiation as a total repudiation and sue immediately.
   b.   Suspend performance and wait until the performance date to sue.
   c.   Treat the anticipatory repudiation as an offer to rescind, resulting in discharge of the contract.
   d.   Any one of the above.
   e.   None of the above.

20.   True or False.   Bill agrees to pay $100 on June 1 for Frank's used lawn mower, with the lawn mower to be delivered on May 15. The mower is delivered as agreed; and on May 25, Bill announces that he will not pay the $100. Anticipatory repudiation does not apply on these facts, since Frank's performance is complete. Frank must wait until June 1 to file suit.

21.   True or False.   An offer to purchase real estate is a contract.

22.   True or False.   An option contract must be supported by consideration.

23.   True or False.   Conditional contracts for the sale of land cannot be assigned.

24.   Legal grounds to rescind a contract may include:

   a.   mistake.
   b.   misrepresentation.
   c.   duress.
   d.   undue influence.
   e.   all of the above.
   f.   none of the above.

25.   An assumption of mortgage clause in an agreement for the sale of land is
       most advantageous to the:

       a.   seller.
       b.   buyer.
       c.   mortgagee.
       d.   broker.

26.   An option cannot be sold or assigned legally if the original consideration for
       the option was:

       a.   cash.
       b.   a promissory note.
       c.   love and affection.
       d.   a personal check.

27.   The law which requires contracts for the sale of real estate to be in writing
       is known as the:

       a.   Statute of Frauds.
       b.   statute of limitations.
       c.   adverse possession law.
       d.   parol evidence rule.

28.   Builder contracts with Owner to construct a garage on Owner's property for
       a price of $10,000. Assume that Owner commits a total breach of the
       contract at a point when Builder already has incurred costs of part
       performance of $3,000, and Builder would have to spend another $6,000 to
       finish the job. Builder is entitled to a recovery of:

       a. $1,000.
       b. $3,000.
       c. $4,000.
       d. $5,000.

Questions 29-32 are based on the following facts: Rusty's Typewriter Service
advertises used ICM typewriters for sale at $100 each at its store. Bertha Butte,
who lives 250 miles away, mails Rusty a check for $500, with a note stating, "Send
me five of the used ICM typewriters that you have advertised."

Rusty checks his inventory and finds that he has only two of the used ICM
typewriters left, but he has plenty of Ogilvie typewriters. He sends Bertha two

ICMs and three Ogilvies by common carrier. En route, the two ICMs are stolen. The carrier delivers only the three Ogilvie units.

Bertha is short of equipment, so she uses the machines that were delivered. One week later, however, the secretaries complain about the Ogilvie typewriters. Bertha then writes to Rusty, "I reject the three machines you sent me. Return my $500." Rusty refuses to do so.

29. Concerning the theft of the two ICM typewriters during shipment:

    a.   Rusty must bear the loss because he selected the carrier and made the arrangements for shipment.

    b.   Rusty bears the loss because he is a merchant and, in the absence of a contrary agreement, bears the risk of loss until the goods are delivered to the buyer.

    c.   Bertha bears the loss because the typewriters were advertised for sale at Rusty's store; therefore, the risk of loss passed there.

    d.   Bertha bears the loss because title to the goods passed to her upon shipment.

30. The legal effect of Bertha's retention and use of the Ogilvie typewriters for one week before notifying Rusty of her rejection was:

    a.   An acceptance of the three machines if Bertha knew they were not ICMs.

    b.   An acceptance only if Bertha's use was more than was reasonably necessary to determine whether the Ogilvies were acceptable substitutes.

    c.   Not an acceptance because the goods were nonconforming.

    d.   A waiver of any damage claim against Rusty based upon nondelivery of the ICM machines.

31. Assume that Bertha's retention and use of the typewriters did not constitute an acceptance. Which of the following remedies is available to her?

    a.   Damages measured by the difference between the contract price and the cover price.

    b.   Restitution of the $500 advance payment.

    c.   Resale of the Ogilvies, with Bertha retaining the profit from the sale proceeds.

    d.   Both "a" and "b" but not "c."

32. Assume that Bertha's retention and use of the typewriters did constitute an acceptance, which she subsequently and justifiably revoked. Which of the following remedies is available to her?

    a. Damages measured by the difference between the contract price and the cover price.
    b. Restitution of the $500 advance payment.
    c. Resale of the Ogilvies, with Bertha retaining the profit from the sale proceeds.
    d. Both "a" and "b" but not "c."

33. True or False. Mary promises to deliver goods to Frank "only if her son comes into the business." Valid consideration exists.

34. True or False. Benson offers a $10,000 reward for the return of his kidnapped child. Archie, the kidnapper, returns the child. Archie can collect the reward.

35. True or False. Benson offers a $10,000 reward for the return of his kidnapped child. Randolph, an FBI agent assigned to the case, recovers the child. Randolph can collect the reward.

36. True or False. An oral contract for the sale of goods valued at $2,000 may be voidable because of noncompliance with the Statute of Frauds.

37. True or False. Under the parol evidence rule, prior oral agreements are merged into the written agreement; however, prior written agreements are not.

38. True or False. John has an option until June 10 to buy Richard's automobile. John sends an acceptance by mail on June 9. It arrives on June 11. A valid contract exists.

39. True or False. A counteroffer serves as a rejection of the original offer.

40. True or False. Matthew and Angela enter into a written agreement which provides, "Angela will purchase a parcel of land for $8,000 or less from Matthew." The agreement is enforceable.

Questions 41-43 are based on the following facts: Jones purchased 100 bolts of standard blue wool, No. 1 quality from Martin. The sales contract provided that Jones would make payment prior to inspection. The bolts of fabric were shipped, and Jones paid the purchase price. Upon inspection, however, Jones discovered that the fabric was No. 2 quality. Jones tendered the fabric back to Martin and demanded return of the purchase price. Martin refused on the ground that there was no difference between No. 1 quality and No. 2 quality.

41. Which of the following statements regarding the contract provision for pre-inspection payment is most correct?

    a.   It constitutes an acceptance of the goods.
    b.   It constitutes a waiver of the buyer's right to reject nonconforming goods.
    c.   It does not impair the buyer's right of inspection or his remedies.
    d.   It is invalid.

42. What is Jones's remedy, assuming that the goods were nonconforming?

    a.   Specific performance.
    b.   Damages for the difference between the value of the goods delivered and the value of conforming goods.
    c.   Damages for the price paid plus the difference between the contract price and the cost of buying substitute goods.
    d.   None, since he waived his remedies by agreeing to pay prior to inspection.

43. Can Jones resell the wool fabric?

    a.   Yes, in a private sale.
    b.   Yes, in a private sale but only after giving Martin reasonable notice of his intention to resell.
    c.   Yes, but only at a public sale.
    d.   No.

44. Billings and Carson contract for 1000 pounds of lapoderm, an ingredient used by Billings to produce an expensive wax for wood, at $5.00 a pound. The lapoderm is to be delivered in four equal installments over a four-month period. After 250 pounds of lapoderm are delivered and paid for, Carson's lapoderm plant closes; and no further shipments are made. The market price of lapoderm at the time of the breach is $2.50 a pound. In a suit against Carson, what amount will Billings recover?

(see next page)

a. $7,500
b. $5,000
c. $1,875
d. $0

45.   Sam leaves his automobile, a 1951 Chevrolet, with the Ajax Garage for minor repairs. The car was a gift to Sam from his parents when he graduated from college. Sam has taken excellent care of the car, it has very low mileage, and it means a great deal to him now that both of his parents have died. The car is destroyed in an accidental fire at the Ajax Garage. In a suit against the Ajax Garage, what will Sam be able to recover?

a.   The market value of the car.
b.   The market value of the car plus mental anguish.
c.   The market value of the car plus punitive damages.
d.   Nothing, since a bailment contract existed between Sam and Ajax.

46.   True or False.   An offer creates a power of acceptance in the offeree and a corresponding liability on the part of the offeror.

47.   True or False.   Express contracts are formed by manifestations of assent other than oral or written language.

48.   True or False.   An unenforceable contract is one which one or both parties may elect either to avoid or to ratify.

49.   True or False.   Amy promises to buy goods only from Ben but reserves an option to cancel by giving written notice to Ben. Amy has given sufficient consideration to support a contract.

50.   True or False.   Ruth promises to buy certain goods from Sam "only if I (Ruth) take my son into the business." Valid consideration exists.

Chapter 12
CRIMINAL LAW

Injustice anywhere is a threat to justice everywhere.

—Martin Luther King Jr.

This chapter reviews the two central aspects of criminal law: (1) the types of conduct that constitute crimes (substantive criminal law) and (2) the rules that must be followed in redressing crimes (criminal procedure).

A crime is a ***wrong committed against society*** or against the community in general—as opposed to a wrong committed against one or more specific individuals or the property of one or more individuals (a civil wrong, also called a tort). *See the chapter on General Law to review the relationship between civil law and criminal law.*

Jurisdiction

The U.S. Constitution grants jurisdiction to the federal government to regulate in certain areas and reserves jurisdiction to the states in others. Jurisdiction is shared (concurrent) in still other situations.

> Ruth murders Mary outside a movie theater in Great Falls. Ruth surrenders immediately. *(state jurisdiction)*

If Mary were murdered in a post office (federal property), if Mary were a federal official, or if Ruth had fled across state lines, federal jurisdiction would have been activated. Concurrent jurisdiction would have existed, however, if Ruth had committed the murder while robbing a federal bank.

Federal Jurisdiction   The federal government has jurisdiction to define and to enforce crimes in these places and situations:

- the District of Columbia, U.S. territories, and federal property (such as military bases, national parks, federal buildings);

- Persons on American ships or in American aircraft in or over international territory;

- Conduct of American citizens located abroad; and

- Conduct or activities within individual states when the power to regulate the conduct or activity is expressly granted by the Constitution (such as taxation, federal officials, interstate commerce, and activities that cross state lines).

State Jurisdiction   In the United States, the majority of criminal offenses are prosecuted at the state level. Unlike the federal government, each state has inherent power to regulate its internal affairs to protect or to promote public health, safety, welfare, or morals (police power).

At common law, the state where the crime occurred had jurisdiction over it. For instance, if a libelous statement is written in one state but is published in another, the second state has jurisdiction. This is because publication—not writing—is the prohibited act.

Under modern principles, a person can be prosecuted by a state for an offense:

- Committed within the state, in whole or in part. The occurrence can be either conduct or a result that is an element of the offense. For homicide, for instance, the occurrence is either the physical contact causing death or the death itself.

●Conduct outside the state that constitutes an attempt to commit or conspiracy to commit an offense within the state.

●Conduct within the state that constitutes an attempt to commit or a conspiracy to commit an offense outside the state.

●Omission to perform a duty required by a state law is an offense in that state, regardless of where the offender is located at the time of the omission.

Sources of Criminal Law

Many sources are woven into the overall fabric of the American legal system, and criminal law is an important part of that system. The rules used to define criminal conduct are found in the common law, in the Constitution, in statutes, in administrative rules and regulations, and in the Model Penal Code where it has been adopted.

Common Law   The common law brought from England by the colonists defined common law crimes which were enforced by courts when specific statutes were unavailable. Although there is no federal common law of crimes (federal crimes are defined exclusively by statute), Congress recognizes common law crimes in the District of Columbia.

Some states still retain common law crimes either impliedly or by specific "retention statutes." The modern trend is to abolish common law crimes by an express statute of abolition or by adoption of comprehensive criminal codes to replace common law crimes. In these states, common law defenses may be retained; however, most defenses likewise are statutory.

Constitution   The United States Constitution gives Congress the power to legislate in certain areas, such as interstate commerce. Accordingly, Congress may define criminal conduct in these specific areas. All powers not given specifically to the federal government are reserved to the states for regulation.

Statute   Federal criminal law is governed exclusively by statutes adopted by Congress. The bulk of state criminal law is governed by statutes adopted by the state legislative body. Some states' statutes include comprehensive criminal codes, fashioned more or less after the Model Penal Code (*see below*).

Administrative   A legislature (either federal or state) may delegate the authority to administrative agencies to promulgate rules, the violation of which may be punishable as a crime. The legislature may not delegate the power to decide which regulations will carry criminal punishments; neither may it delegate the power of adjudication (determining guilt or innocence) concerning conduct that may result in criminal punishment. For instance, violation of anti-fraud rules adopted by the Securities and Exchange Commission (SEC) may result in criminal punishment; accordingly, persons charged with violation are tried in the federal court system and not by the SEC.

This is different from the quasi-judicial functions that can be delegated, such as issuance and revocation of certain kinds of licenses or fines imposed for violation of agency rules and regulations.

Model Penal Code   Though not a source of law in any technical sense, the Model Penal Code (M.P.C.) was a scholarly undertaking by the American Law Institute to compile a comprehensive body of criminal law as criminal experts believed it should be. Since its initial publication in 1962, the Model Penal Code has influenced the criminal laws adopted by various states and has been adopted, in whole or in part, by more than half of the states.

Theories of Punishment

Throughout history, a society's punishment of criminal conduct has been defended on various grounds. Restraint, deterrence, retribution, and rehabilitation are the primary theories advanced to justify criminal punishment, although there is considerable controversy about whether they serve their intended purpose.

Restraint   When a person is restrained or incapacitated by imprisonment, he or she has fewer opportunities to engage in conduct that is harmful to society in general.

Deterrence   Deterrence comes in two forms: individual deterrence and general deterrence. When a criminal is punished, he or she is deterred individually from committing future crimes. When a criminal is punished, others are deterred generally from committing similar crimes for fear of incurring the same punishment.

Retribution   As a theory of punishment, retribution serves the purpose of venting society's outrage at and its need for revenge for the offender's criminal conduct. In addition to society's need to get even with the criminal offender and to purge itself by removing the offender from its midst, proponents of retribution maintain that the availability of institutionalized retribution is essential to prevent forms of personal retribution (such as lynch mobs or personal retribution by a victim's family).

Rehabilitation   In theory, punishment (imprisonment) of criminal conduct provides the opportunity to reform or to rehabilitate the criminal into a person who will abide by society's rules at the end of the prison term. Whether criminals are rehabilitated by existing prison systems is the subject of much debate.

Classification of Crimes

Criminal conduct has always been classified according to its seriousness, with the most severe punishments reserved for the most serious crimes. At common law, all crimes were classified as treason, felonies, or misdemeanors. Murder, rape, manslaughter, robbery, sodomy, larceny, arson, mayhem, and burglary were classified as felonies under common law; all other crimes were misdemeanors. *Use the handy mnemonic "MR & MRS LAMB" to remember the common law felonies.* Statutory enactments have expanded the classifications of criminal conduct.

A crime *malum in se* is a crime that is wrong in itself or involves conduct that is inherently bad (murder, rape, or larceny). A crime *malum prohibitum* is one that involves conduct which is wrong because the legislature says it is wrong (fishing without a license, burning trash within city limits, or failure to post a required notice).

Treason is an attempt to overthrow the government or to betray the government in favor of a foreign power. A person can be convicted of treason only by the testimony of two witnesses or by confession in open court. Article III, Section 3, U.S. Constitution.

A *capital crime* is one for which the punishment may be death. Many jurisdictions do not have a separate classification for capital crimes; rather, they are included in the overall felony classification.

A *felony* is a crime for which the maximum punishment may be death or may be imprisonment for one year or more, although a person may be sentenced to a prison term of less than one year upon conviction of a felony. Recall that the key is the **maximum sentence** (punishment) **that *may* be imposed** upon conviction, not the sentence actually imposed.

A *misdemeanor* is a crime for which the maximum punishment may be imprisonment for less than one year. Also classified as misdemeanors are those statutory violations for which the maximum punishment may be only a fine.

Constitutional Limitations

The Due Process Clause of United States Constitution, found in the Fifth and Fourteenth Amendments, has been interpreted by the U.S. Supreme Court to require that no criminal penalty be imposed without fair notice that the conduct is prohibited. In addition, sections 9 and 10 of Article I of the Constitution place substantive restrictions on both federal and state legislatures in defining criminal conduct.

Void for Vagueness   Unless a criminal law gives citizens fair warning of the conduct that is prohibited by it, the law may be void for vagueness under the Constitution. A statute must give a person of ordinary intelligence fair notice of what conduct is forbidden. In addition, the statute must not encourage arbitrary arrests and convictions. In the latter situation, the statute may be attacked on overbreadth grounds, as well as on vagueness grounds.

These two considerations require special scrutiny of statutes that are capable of reaching conduct that is otherwise protected by the Constitution, such as freedom of speech, freedom to assemble and to petition the government, or freedom to move from one place to another. Statutes directed at vagrancy, restriction of parades, and the like are subject to particular scrutiny under these principles.

Ex Post Facto Laws   The U.S. Constitution specifically forbids adoption of *ex post facto* laws, which are laws that operate ***retroactively*** to:

A.   Make an act criminal, which was not criminal at the time it was performed;

B.   Aggravate a crime or increase the punishment for a crime, to make it more serious than when the criminal act was performed;

C.   Change the rules of evidence to the detriment of criminal defendants as a class, to make the rules more stringent for the defendant than when the criminal act was performed; or

D.   Change the rules of criminal procedure to deprive criminal defendants of a substantive right that the defendant would have had at the time the criminal act was performed.

Bill of Attainder   A bill of attainder is a legislative enactment that imposes a punishment or denies a privilege without a judicial trial. Although a bill of attainder may be an *ex post facto* law also, a distinction can be made in that an *ex post facto* law does not necessarily deprive the accused of a judicial trial. A bill of attainder always does. The Constitution specifically forbids adoption of bills of attainder.

Interpretation of Criminal Laws

Substantive criminal laws, whether created by statute or otherwise, are subject to accepted methods of interpretation.

Plain Meaning Rule   When the language of a statute is plain and its meaning is clear, a court must give it effect even if the court believes the statute is unwise or is undesirable. An exception exists if the court believes that application of the statute's plain meaning would result in injustice, oppression, or an absurd result.

Strict Construction   When the language of a criminal statute is ambiguous, the statute must be strictly construed in favor of the defendant. Ambiguity and vagueness are not the same. An ambiguous statute is one that is capable of two or more equally reasonable interpretations. A vague statute is one that is so unclear that a person of ordinary intelligence cannot tell what conduct is prohibited.

Effect of Repeal   Under common law rules and in the absence of a saving provision, the repeal of a criminal statute operates to bar prosecution for earlier violations, provided the prosecution has not yet commenced at the time of the repeal. Note that repeal of a criminal statute cannot be used to set free a person who has already been prosecuted and convicted under the repealed statute.

Many of the new, comprehensive criminal codes include a specific saving provision, so that crimes committed prior to the effective date of the new code are subject to prosecution and punishment under the law as it existed at the time when the offense was committed.

Merger

Under common law rules, if a person engaged in conduct that constituted both a felony and a misdemeanor, he or she could be convicted of only the felony. The misdemeanor was merged into the felony. If the same act or if a series of acts which were all part of the same transaction constituted several different felonies (or several different misdemeanors), there was no merger of any of the offenses of equal degree into any of the other offenses of equal degree.

The modern rule is that there is no merger in American criminal law, with the following limited exceptions:

Merger of Solicitation or Attempt into Completed Crime   If solicitation to commit a crime or attempt to commit a crime is itself a criminal act, one cannot be convicted of both the attempt (or the solicitation) and the completed crime. For instance, one cannot be convicted of both attempted homicide and homicide as to the same victim.

Merger of Lesser Offenses into Greater Offenses   Lesser offenses merge into greater offenses, in the sense that one who is placed in jeopardy for either offense may not be tried for the other at a later time. Neither can a person be convicted of both the greater offense and a lesser offense when the lesser offense is one that consists entirely of some, but not all, elements of the greater offense. This is often labeled a rule of merger but is also required by the constitutional prohibition against double jeopardy *(double jeopardy is discussed in more detail below)*.

No Double Jeopardy When Statute Provides Multiple Punishments for Single Act   Imposition of multiple punishments for two or more statutorily defined offenses, specifically intended by the legislature to carry separate punishments, even though they arise from the same transaction, does not violate the Double Jeopardy Clause, when the punishments are imposed cumulatively as a result of a single trial.

> Jill robs at store a gunpoint. She can be sentenced to cumulative punishments for armed robbery and for "armed criminal action" under a state's "use a gun, go to jail" statute.

Essential Elements of a Crime

Culpability under principles of Anglo-American criminal law rests upon certain requirements that are observed by legislatures and by courts when defining substantive criminal conduct. Consequently, the prosecution generally is required to prove the following elements of a criminal offense:

A.   ***Actus Reus*** (guilty act):   A physical act (or unlawful omission) by the defendant;

B.   **_Mens Rea_** (guilty mind): The state of mind (intent) of the defendant at the time of her act;

C.   **Causation**:   The defendant's act must be a proximate cause of the resulting harm; and

D.   **Harmful Result**: A harmful result caused (both factually and proximately) by the defendant's act.

The Physical Act _(Actus Reus)_   For criminal liability to exist, the defendant must have either performed a voluntary, physical act or must have failed to act when she had a legal duty to act. For this purpose, an act is defined as bodily movement. Bad thoughts alone cannot constitute a crime. Speech, however, may be an act that can create liability (such as perjury).

The act must be voluntary (a conscious exercise of will). Reflexive or convulsive acts, acts which are not the product of the defendant's determination, or acts performed while the defendant is unconscious or asleep are not voluntary.

> Adam pushes Betty, who stumbles into Carl's path, with the result that Carl slips and plunges to his death. With only these circumstances, Betty cannot be held criminally liable for Carl's death.

Some offenses treat possession as the wrongful act. For possession offenses, the possession may be actual, such as when a defendant is found with marijuana in her coat pocket, or the possession may be constructive, such as when marijuana is found in the automobile owned and driven by the defendant.

Although most crimes are committed by an affirmative act by the defendant, a defendant's _failure to act_ can result in criminal liability **_if_** _(1) the defendant had a legal duty to act and (2) it was reasonably possible for the defendant to perform the duty or to obtain the help of others to perform it._ The defendant can be subject to a legal duty to act:

●When a statute requires the action (such as filing an accident report);

●When the defendant contracts for the duty (such as a lifeguard);

●When the relationship creates the duty (parent's duty to prevent physical harm to his or her child);

●When the defendant voluntarily assumes the duty (good samaritan who does not satisfy reasonable standards of care); or

●When the peril was created by the defendant.

> Jill sees Adam, whom she despises, apparently drowning in a neighbor's swimming pool. Although Jill is an excellent swimmer, she does nothing to help. Jill has no criminal liability without some special relationship between herself and Adam that would create the duty to act.

> Mary tells her 12-year-old son, Bill, to stay out of the swimming pool for one hour after eating lunch. Bill is anxious to swim and jumps in anyway. He develops cramps and begins to drown. Mary is unable to swim and her screams for help produce no assistance. Although Mary has a special duty to her child, it was not reasonably possible for her to save her drowning child since she cannot swim. There is no criminal liability.

Intent *(Mens Rea)*

Intent is usually required to distinguish between inadvertent acts and acts performed with a "guilty mind" under common law rules, some of which have been incorporated into statutes. Acts performed with a guilty mind are more blameworthy. Intent may be specific or general. However, in some cases, *mens rea* is not required at all (such as strict liability crimes).

A.   Specific Intent   Some crimes are defined in such a way that a specific intent must accompany the wrongful act. A statute may define first degree murder to require premeditation, for instance. If so, the prosecutor must prove not only that the victim was killed by the defendant, but also that the defendant planned the killing ahead of time. Specific intent cannot be presumed simply from the doing of the act. Some defenses, such as intoxication, apply only to specific intent crimes.

Specific intent crimes may also include assault (intent to commit a battery); attempt (intent to complete a crime); larceny (intent to permanently deprive another of her personal property); and so forth.

B.   General Intent   All crimes (other than specific intent crimes or strict liability crimes) are general intent crimes. General intent requires merely that the accused is aware that the prohibited act is being committed and that the prohibited result is likely to occur. Since people are presumed generally to know the probable consequences of their acts, general intent can be inferred from the doing of the act.

C.   Transferred Intent   The concept of transferred intent is one borrowed from general tort rules, in which the defendant's intent is "transferred" to fit the result. Cases of transferred intent are sometimes called "bad aim" cases. For example, if A intends to shoot B but misses, shooting C instead, the concept of transferred intent allows A to be found guilty of C's murder even though A's intent was directed at B.

D. Strict Liability A strict liability crime is one in which the commission of the prohibited act renders the defendant guilty, without regard to her intent. Intent is conclusively presumed by the use of a legal fiction. Strict liability crimes often involve violation of a regulation and customarily result in a minor punishment, such as a fine. The failure to register firearms sold under federal law is an example of a strict liability crime.

E. Model Penal Code The Model Penal Code (M.P.C.) rejects the sometimes esoteric distinction between general and specific intent. Instead, the M.P.C. proposes four separate states of mind for which criminal liability may be imposed: purposeful, knowing, reckless, and negligent.

- A defendant acts ***purposely*** when she consciously desires or seeks her conduct to cause a particular result.

- A defendant acts ***knowingly*** when she is aware that her conduct is almost certain to cause a particular result.

- A defendant acts ***recklessly*** when she is aware that there is a risk that her conduct might cause a particular result.

- A defendant acts ***negligently*** when she should be aware that there is a risk that her conduct might cause a particular result.

The risk involved in the definitions of reckless and negligent under the M.P.C. must be substantial and unjustifiable. In addition, and unlike the common law rules, the M.P.C. assigns a particular state of mind to each element of the crime. For example, the crime of rape requires that the act of sexual intercourse with the victim be purposeful; however, the element of the victim's non-consent may require only negligence.

Concurrence of *Actus Reus* and *Mens Rea* The defendant must have the intent necessary for the crime at the time she commits the act constituting the crime. Moreover, the better view is that concurrence alone is insufficient; the intent must have placed the act in motion.

> Joan decided to kill her husband, Bill. On her way home from purchasing the rat poison that she intended to use for the murder, Joan negligently struck Bill with her car as she pulled into the driveway of the family home. Bill died from his injuries.

On these facts, for example, Joan cannot be found guilty of premeditated murder. She did intend to murder Bill, but her intent did not place that act into motion which caused his death. Although she is not guilty of premeditated murder, she may be found guilty of an offense based upon her negligent driving.

Liability for the Acts of Others

A crime may have many participants. The common law recognized four types of participants to a felony: principals in the first degree, principals in the second degree, accessories before the fact, and accessories after the fact. The distinctions were not used for treason or for misdemeanors, in which all parties were treated as principals. Today principals in the second degree and accessories before the fact are called accomplices, and the following classifications generally are made:

- A *principal or actor* is one who, with the required mental state, engages in the act or omission that causes the criminal result.

- An *aider and abettor* is one who aids, counsels, helps, procures, commands, or encourages another in the commission of the crime.

- A *co-conspirator* is liable for all crimes committed during and in furtherance of the conspiracy.

- An *accessory after the fact* is one whose involvement does not begin until after the crime has been completed.

Two other types of assistance after the crime can lead to criminal liability: misprision of felony and compounding a felony. *Misprision of felony* is simply the failure to report a known felony. Not all states make this act a crime, and there are few reported prosecutions of this crime in the United States. *Compounding a felony* is the acceptance of money or other consideration in exchange for not prosecuting (as to a victim) or in exchange for not reporting (as to a witness) a felony.

Inchoate Offenses

The three inchoate offenses are solicitation, attempt, and conspiracy. They are often classified as felonies. An inchoate offense is committed prior to and in preparation for what may be a more serious offense. It is a complete offense in itself, even though the act to be done may not have been completed. Under the doctrine of merger in common law, inchoate offenses were misdemeanors but rose to the level of felonies when the principal offense was carried out. The merger doctrine has been abandoned in many jurisdictions for conspiracy, and an accused can be convicted of both conspiracy and the principal offense. However, an accused cannot be convicted of either solicitation or attempt in addition to the principal offense.

Solicitation   It was a common law misdemeanor to solicit another to commit a felony or an act that would breach the peace or would obstruct justice. Solicitation consisted of inciting, counseling, advising, inducing, urging, or commanding another to commit a felony with the specific intent that the person solicited would commit the crime. The crime of solicitation was complete when the solicitation was made; it was not necessary that the person solicited agree to commit the crime or do anything else in response to the solicitation.

If the person solicited committed the crime, the solicitor would be liable for the crime as a principal or party; if the person solicited proceeded far enough to be liable for attempt, the solicitor would be a party to that attempt.

Modern criminal statutes often retain the crime of solicitation, but sometimes restrict it to the solicitation of serious felonies only.

A.   Defenses   Impossibility is not a defense (the crime could not have been successful), such as when the person solicited is an undercover agent. The solicitor's culpability is measured by the circumstances as she believes them to be. Withdrawal or renunciation (changing her mind) by the solicitor is not a defense once the solicitation has been made.

Conspiracy   Under common law rules, a conspiracy was a combination or agreement between two or more persons to accomplish a criminal or an unlawful purpose or to accomplish a lawful purpose by unlawful means. Modern state codes require that the object of the conspiracy be specifically prohibited by statute. The four elements of conspiracy are:

- An agreement between two or more persons;
- An intent to enter into an agreement;
- An intent to achieve the object of the agreement; and
- An overt act in furtherance of the conspiracy by at least one party.

Under the traditional definition, the agreement itself is the culpable act *(actus reus)*. Unlike attempt, an "overt act" or other conduct in furtherance of the conspiracy is required. Although half of the states now require an act in furtherance of the conspiracy, preparation usually will suffice.

> Betty, Barney, and Ken agree on a plan to rob a grocery store. Without the knowledge of Betty and Barney, Ken rents a car for the getaway. If an overt act is required, renting the car is sufficient.

A conspirator may, by his participation in the scheme, meet the requirements for aiding and abetting crimes committed by other participants. In addition, a separate doctrine provides that each conspirator is liable for the crimes of all other conspirators when the following requirements are met:

- The crimes were committed in furtherance of the objectives of the conspiracy; and

- The crimes were a natural and probable consequence of the conspiracy (foreseeable).

This doctrine applies only if the conspirator has not made a legally effective withdrawal from the conspiracy by the time the crime is committed by the co-conspirator(s).

Under common law, if the conspirators completed the crime, the crime of conspiracy "merged" into the completed crime; and the accused could be convicted only of the completed crime. Under modern statutes, successful conspirators can be convicted of both criminal conspiracy and of the crime they successfully completed.

A.   The Wharton Rule   When two or more people are necessary for the commission of the crime (adultery, gambling, drag racing on public streets, and so forth), the Wharton Rule states that there is no crime of conspiracy unless more parties participate in the agreement than are necessary for the crime.

> Alice and Betty agree to meet at midnight to drag race on a suburban highway. They are caught before the racing begins, however. Drag racing is a crime in the jurisdiction, and Alice is charged with conspiracy to drag race. Wharton's Rule prevents liability for conspiracy to drag race, because drag racing requires at least two parties. If Jane is also part of the conspiracy, however, Alice can be convicted of conspiracy to drag race.

B.   Agreement with Person in Protected Class   If parties agree to commit a crime designed to protect persons in a protected class, persons within that class cannot be guilty of the crime itself. Neither can they be guilty of conspiracy to commit the crime.

> Betty and Carl agree that Carl will drive Betty to the next state for the purpose of engaging in prostitution in violation of the Mann Act. The purpose of the Mann Act is to protect women, so Betty cannot be guilty of violating the Act and cannot be guilty of conspiracy to violate the Act. Moreover, Carl cannot be guilty of criminal conspiracy because there must be two guilty parties to the agreement.

C. **Effect of Co-Conspirator's Acquittal** Since conspiracy requires two guilty parties, acquittal of all parties with whom a defendant is alleged to have conspired prevents the remaining defendant from being convicted. Note that a prosecutor's decision to *nolle prosequi* (not prosecute) is not the same as an acquittal. In those states where an overt act is required in addition to the agreement, if the person who allegedly committed the overt act is acquitted, no other alleged co-conspirators can be convicted.

D. **Mental State** Conspiracy is a specific intent crime. Two different intents are necessary: the intent to agree and the intent to achieve the objective of the conspiracy. For examination purposes, remember that the intent to agree can be inferred from conduct. The intent to achieve the objective of the conspiracy must be proved as to each defendant. At least two persons must intend the same purpose. In other words, there must be a "meeting of guilty minds."

> Sam, Tom, and Ulysses agree to steal William's car, but only Sam and Tom intend to keep it permanently. Ulysses intends to keep it overnight and to return it in the morning. Only Sam and Tom are guilty of conspiracy to commit larceny because they are the only ones who intended to deprive William of the car permanently. If only Sam intended to deprive William of the car permanently, Sam could not be guilty of conspiracy to commit larceny. The crime of conspiracy requires at least two people.

Because conspiracy is a specific intent crime, conspiracy to commit a "strict liability" crime (for which intent is not required) nevertheless requires intent.

> Russell and Barney agree on a plan to persuade Rose, a 15-year-old girl, to have intercourse with them. They believe Rose is 21, but this is not a defense to the crime of statutory rape. It is a defense to a charge of conspiracy to commit statutory rape, however, because knowledge of the victim's age would be required.

E.   Defenses   Impossibility is not a defense to conspiracy. However, withdrawal from (renunciation) or termination of the conspiracy may serve as a defense or may limit the defendant's liability.

1.   *Withdrawal*   Withdrawal (renunciation) ordinarily is not a defense to conspiracy; however, a person may limit her liability for the subsequent acts of other conspirators if she withdraws or renounces.   To withdraw, she must perform an affirmative act that notifies all members of the conspiracy, and the notice must be given in time for them to have an opportunity to abandon their plan.

2.   *Termination of Conspiracy*   Because the acts or declarations of co-conspirators are admissible against each other only if they are made in furtherance of the conspiracy, it is important to determine when the conspiracy ended.   When the conspiracy ended is also important in calculating the statute of limitations.   Acts of concealment after the crime is committed generally are not viewed as part of the conspiracy unless the concealment was part of the specific, original plan.

F.   Punishment   Unlike the common law rule, conspiracy and the completed crime are now considered distinct offenses.   Therefore, a defendant may be convicted of both conspiracy to commit the crime and commission of the crime.   It is even possible that the punishment for conspiracy may be more severe than the punishment for the completed crime.

RICO   A federal statute directed specifically toward conspiracy and fraud is the ***Racketeer Influenced and Corrupt Organizations Act***, commonly known as RICO, which was enacted by Congress in the 1970s to curb organized crime in the business arena. Since then, the statute has been interpreted to include all businesses—not just those traditionally involved with organized crime.

A conviction under RICO requires the United States to prove that:

●The defendant received money or income
●From a pattern of racketeering activity
●And invested it in an enterprise (business)
●Which is in interstate commerce or affects interstate commerce.

Racketeering activity includes state and federal crimes that are associated with racketeering: murder, kidnapping, extortion, drug sales, drug transportation, mail fraud, wire fraud, white slave traffic, securities fraud, and bribery. A pattern may be proved by two or more acts.

Victims of RICO may file civil suit against the defendant for treble damages, costs, and attorney fees. RICO also provides for forfeiture of property as part of the criminal proceedings. A forfeiture is aimed specifically at obtaining all property or money connected to the crime upon which the conviction is based.

Attempt   A criminal attempt is an act which is done with the intent to commit a crime but which falls short of completing the crime for one reason or another. Attempt consists of two elements: intent and an overt act.

     A.   **Intent**   For intent to exist, the defendant must have the intent to perform an act for the purpose of obtaining a result which, if accomplished, would constitute a crime. Specific intent crimes require specific intent. For example, attempt to commit a burglary requires the specific intent to commit a felony inside a dwelling.

Although a strict liability crime does not require specific intent, an attempt to commit a strict liability crime does require an intent to bring about the prohibited result. For example, to convict a defendant of attempt to pollute a waterway, she must have intended to dump a waste product into the water and must have taken some overt act to dump the waste. She need not know that her act, if completed, would be illegal.

When a crime is defined as the negligent production of a result, there can be no attempt. If there were an intent to cause the result, the proper charge would be attempt to commit the crime, not attempt to negligently cause the harm.

     B.   **Overt Act**   The defendant must commit an act beyond mere preparation for the attempt offense to exist. To determine whether the overt act requirement has been satisfied, four tests have been developed:

     1.   *Final Step Test*   Although it has been abandoned in most jurisdictions, the final step test states that the defendant is not guilty of attempt until all steps necessary to bring about the intended result have been completed.

     2.   *Proximity Test*   Under this test, attempt requires an act that comes dangerously close to success.

3. ***Equivocality Test*** Under this test, sometimes called the *res ipsa loquitur* test, the act by itself must demonstrate that the defendant had an unequivocal intent to commit the crime.

4. ***Model Penal Code Test*** The M.P.C. requires that the act or omission constitute a "substantial step in a course of conduct planned to culminate in the commission of the crime." An act will not qualify as a substantial step unless it is a strong corroboration of the actor's criminal purpose.

C. **Defenses to Attempt** Traditionally, the law distinguished between inherent, factual, and legal impossibility. The modern view, reflected in the M.P.C., is that impossibility never should be a defense when the defendant's intent was to do an act or to bring about a result prohibited by law. For examination purposes, it will be important to notice whether the question relies upon the common law distinctions or not.

If the defendant has a change of heart and does not complete the crime, abandonment may be a defense. The abandonment must be voluntary. However, the defendant usually cannot claim abandonment as a defense if she has, with the required intent, gone beyond preparation.

D. **Prosecution for Attempt** A defendant charged with attempt may not be found guilty of the completed crime.

Criminal Capacity

To be guilty of most crimes, a defendant must have the capacity to form a criminal intent. Where that capacity is lacking, guilt cannot be established. The three mental states of a defendant where criminal capacity comes into question and may exempt a defendant from criminal culpability are insanity, intoxication, and infancy.

Insanity Insanity is a legal term, not a medical or psychiatric term. It is a generic term than can comprise many different mental abnormalities that may absolve the defendant of criminal liability. The insanity defense exempts a defendant because of an abnormal mental condition existing at the time of the crime. The various theories of insanity differ substantially as to what effect a mental illness must have to absolve the defendant. *M'Naghten* and the Model Penal Code are the two most common standards.

A. *M'Naghten* (Right or Wrong) Test

The traditional M'Naghten provides that a defendant is entitled to acquittal if the proof establishes:

- a disease of the mind,
- which caused a defect of reason
- such that the defendant lacked the ability at the time of her actions to either:
  - (1) know the wrongfulness of her actions; or
  - (2) understand the nature and quality of her actions.

If the defendant suffered from delusions (false beliefs), one must determine whether, if the facts had been as she believed them to be, her actions would have been criminal.

> Due to mental illness, Lenora believed that Charlie wanted to kill her so she shot him. Under the *M'Naghten* Test, Lenora would not be absolved on insanity grounds. Even if her belief were true, she would not have been entitled to kill Charlie just because he wanted to kill her.

A defendant is not entitled to acquittal under the *M'Naghten* Test if he believes his acts are morally right, unless he has lost the capacity to recognize that those acts are regarded by society as wrong. Likewise, if the defendant knew that his acts were wrong, but was unable to control himself to prevent the acts, *M'Naghten* would not acquit him on insanity grounds.

B. Irresistible Impulse Test

Under the irresistible impulse test, the defendant may be acquitted if the proof establishes that because of mental illness, she was unable to control her actions to conform to the law. Contrary to what the name implies, the inability to control her actions need not come upon the defendant suddenly.

Many jurisdictions use both *M'Naghten* and the irresistible impulse tests, so that a defendant is entitled to acquittal if she meets either test.

C. Model Penal Code Test

Under this test, the defendant is entitled to acquittal if the proof shows that:

- He suffered from a mental disease or defect; and

- As a result, lacked substantial capacity to either:

    (1) Appreciate the criminality (wrongfulness) of his conduct; or

    (2) Conform his conduct to the requirements of law.

Issues Related to Insanity Defense   Many theories of the insanity defense (including the M.P.C. test) specifically exclude the psychopathic criminal—the person who repeatedly commits crime without experiencing guilt. The terms "sociopathic" and "psychopathic" are synonymous for this purpose.

  From a procedural standpoint, a defendant is ***presumed sane*** until she shows that she was likely insane under the appropriate test. Depending on the jurisdiction, this may be shown by a mere shred (scintilla) of evidence or by evidence sufficient to raise a reasonable doubt as to sanity. Once the issue has been raised, some jurisdictions require the prosecution to prove the defendant sane beyond a reasonable doubt. In others, the defendant must prove her insanity—generally by a preponderance of the evidence.

  The defendant may raise the insanity defense at arraignment (when the plea is taken), but she usually is not required to do so. In most states, a simple "not guilty" plea does not waive the defendant's right to raise the defense at a future, reasonable time before trial.

  Some jurisdictions recognize the defense of ***diminished capacity*** by which the defendant may assert that as a result of a mental defect (neurosis, severe retardation, and so forth) short of insanity, she did not have the mental state required for the crime charged. This defense may be limited by some states to specific intent crimes only.

  Some states (such as California) use a two-stage (bifurcated) trial process when the insanity defense is raised. The first stage is used to determine guilt; the second stage is used to determine insanity. A new jury may be used for the second stage, at the judge's discretion. If both issues are determined affirmatively, the defendant is said to be "guilty but insane."

  Acquittal by reason of insanity generally means the defendant will be confined in a mental institution until cured; some jurisdictions require proof that the defendant is mentally ill and dangerous at the time of confinement. In others, the commitment is automatic. Confinement continues until the defendant regains her sanity or is no longer dangerous, even though this may be longer than the maximum imprisonment provided for the offense.

Intoxication   Intoxication is a state that can be caused by ingesting any substance, although alcohol, drugs, and medicine are the most common. The intoxication defense may be raised when the intoxication negates any element of a crime. The law usually distinguishes between voluntary and involuntary intoxication.

   A.   Voluntary Intoxication   Intoxication is voluntary (self-induced) if it is the result of intentional taking of a substance known to be intoxicating. The defendant need not have intended to become intoxicated. Voluntary intoxication is a defense to a crime that requires purpose (intent) or knowledge if it prevents the defendant from formulating the purpose or from obtaining the knowledge. Voluntary intoxication is not a defense, however, to crimes involving negligence, recklessness, or strict liability. The defense is not available if the defendant becomes intoxicated to establish the defense.

> After drinking heavily, Karen broke into a neighbor's house (believing it was her own). When she was surprised by the owner, Karen began beating the owner with her fists. While driving home, Karen was cited for speeding. Because of the intoxication, Karen is not guilty of burglary because she did not know the house belonged to someone else. However, intoxication is not a defense to battery (which may result from recklessness) or to speeding (a strict liability crime).

   B.   Involuntary Intoxication   Intoxication is involuntary only if it results from taking an intoxicating substance without knowledge of its nature, under duress by another, or under medical advice. Involuntary intoxication may be treated the same as mental illness, in which case a defendant is entitled to acquittal if, because of the intoxication, she meets whatever test the jurisdiction has adopted for insanity.

Infancy   Under common law rules, the defense of infancy raises three presumptions concerning the perpetrator's physical age (not mental age) at the time of the crime (not at the time of trial).

   A.   Under the age of seven, a child cannot be criminally liable. There is a conclusive presumption that a child who is six years old or younger is incapable of knowing the wrongfulness of his or her acts.

   B.   Between the ages of seven and fourteen, children are presumed to be incapable of knowing the wrongfulness of their acts. This presumption can be rebutted by clear proof in a specific case that the child appreciated the nature of his act (such as by conduct undertaken to conceal the crime). Children under the age of fourteen are conclusively presumed incapable of committing rape, however.

C.   Children fourteen and older may be treated as adults or may be treated as juveniles, depending upon the jurisdiction and its requirements.

A number of modern statutes provide that no child can be convicted of a crime until a stated age, generally thirteen or fourteen. Others retain the common law rule. A few others use a case-by-case approach, which—in theory— would allow prosecution of a child of any age for any crime.

Exculpation

Sometimes the commission of an otherwise prohibited act is justified, making it inappropriate to punish the perpetrator. This often involves the use of force.

Justifiable Use of Force   The defendant generally must raise the defense of justifiable use of force by introducing some evidence (more than a scintilla) tending to show justification as an affirmative defense. Once the defendant has done this, the state must prove beyond a reasonable doubt that the use of force was not justified.

    A.   Self-Defense   As a general rule, a person who is without fault may use such nondeadly force as reasonably appears necessary to protect herself from the imminent use of unlawful force upon her. There is no duty to retreat before using nondeadly force, even if retreat would result in no further harm to either party.

A person may use deadly force if she is without fault, is confronted with "unlawful force", and is threatened with imminent death or with great bodily harm. There is no duty to retreat before using deadly force.

Generally, one who begins a fight (the aggressor) has no right to use force in her own defense during that fight. But she can regain her right to use self-defense in two ways:

    1.   If the aggressor, in good faith, effectively withdraws (removes herself) from the fight or communicates to the victim her desire to remove herself, the aggressor regains the right to self-defense when the "victim" continues the fight; or

    2.   If the victim suddenly escalates a minor fight into one using deadly force, without giving the original aggressor the chance to withdraw, the original aggressor may use force in her own defense.

B.   Defense of Others   A defendant has the right to use force in defense of any other person, if the other requirements of the defense are met. A defendant's right to use force in defense of others is buttressed if the person defended is a member of the defendant's family, is the defendant's employee, or is the defendant's employer.

C.   Defense of Property   A person is justified in using nondeadly force in defense of his dwelling if he reasonably believes it necessary to prevent or to terminate another's unlawful entry into or attack upon the dwelling. He generally is justified in using *deadly force* in defense of his dwelling in only two situations:

1.   When the entry is made or attempted in a riotous or violent manner *and* the person reasonably believes that the use of force is necessary to protect himself or another in the dwelling; or

2.   When the person reasonably believes that force is necessary to prevent the entry into the dwelling by one who intends to commit a *felony* in the dwelling.

Concerning property other than a dwelling, *nondeadly force* may be used to defend one's property in one's possession from unlawful interference. In the case of (non-dwelling) real estate, unlawful interference means entry or trespass. In the case of personal property, unlawful interference means removal or damage. The need for force must appear to be imminent; force may not be used if a request to stop would suffice. In addition, the right to use force is limited to property in one's personal possession. Force cannot be used to regain property wrongfully taken except in "hot pursuit" of the taker.

D.   Crime Prevention   A person is privileged to use nondeadly force to the extent that it reasonably appears necessary to prevent a felony, riot, or other serious breach of the peace. However, some states (such as California) have extended the privilege to the prevention of any crime.

Generally deadly force may be used only if the crime is a "dangerous felony" involving risk to human life. This would include robbery, arson, burglary of a dwelling, and so forth. Once again, however, some states allow the use of deadly force to prevent the commission of any felony.

E.   Resisting Arrest   At common law, one could use force to resist an unlawful arrest. In most states today, however, one may not use force to resist even an unlawful arrest if the person making the arrest is known to be a police officer.

Necessity   Sometimes called the "lesser of two evils" defense, necessity may justify conduct that otherwise would be criminal if, as a result of pressure from natural forces, the defendant reasonably believes the conduct necessary to avoid harm to society exceeds the harm caused by the conduct. The test used to determine necessity is an objective one. Causing the death of another person to protect property is never justified. Likewise, the defense of necessity is not available if the defendant is at fault in creating the situation that requires her to choose between two evils.

> Discarding cargo at sea during a violent storm, if necessary to save the lives of people on board, would constitute the defense of necessity if the defendant were charged with criminal destruction of property. Throwing people overboard to save the cargo, however, would not be justified.

Duress   Duress involves a human threat, as opposed to pressure from physical or natural forces. A person is not guilty of a crime, other than homicide, if he performs an otherwise unlawful act under the threat of imminent death or great bodily harm to himself or to a member of his immediate family. The excuse of duress may extend to those who are not members of the immediate family as well. Acts committed under duress are excusable rather than justifiable. The reason for the distinction is that acts performed under duress are condoned by society rather than encouraged.

> If Sam points a gun at George and threatens to kill George if he does not break into Milton's house and steal food and if George complies, George may raise the defense of duress. On the other hand, if George is a starving victim of a plane crash in a desolate area and if he breaks into Milton's house to steal food, he may raise the defense of necessity.

Mistake   A mistake of fact affects criminal liability only if it shows that the defendant did not have the state of mind required for the crime.

If general intent is required for the crime, the mistake must be the type of mistake that a reasonable person would have made under the circumstances. If specific intent is required for the crime, any mistake of fact, reasonable or unreasonable, is a defense.

> Arnold takes an umbrella from a restaurant's coat room, believing it to be his. In fact, it belongs to Ronald. Arnold is not guilty of larceny because he believed the umbrella to be his own. Since his mistake negates a specific intent required for larceny, it does not matter whether the mistake was reasonable or not.

Since intent is not an element of strict liability crimes, mistake of fact is not a defense.

Rarely does a mistake of law, albeit a reasonable mistake, constitute a defense to a criminal act. Recall the adage: "Ignorance of the law is no excuse."

Consent   Consent of the victim generally is not a defense. If it negates some element of the crime, however, it is a complete defense. For example, proof that the victim consented to intercourse is a complete defense to a charge of forcible rape. However, proof that the victim of statutory rape consented is not a defense.

Entrapment   Entrapment arises when the intent to commit a crime originates through the creative activities of a law enforcement officer rather than with the defendant. In this situation it is presumed that the legislative intent is not to classify the conduct as criminal. The defense of entrapment requires proof of two elements:

1.   The criminal design must have originated with the law enforcement officer(s); and

2.   The defendant must not have been predisposed in any way to commit the crime.

It is not entrapment if the law enforcement officer provides the opportunity for the commission of a crime by one who is otherwise ready and willing to commit it. For example, if a narcotics officer poses as a drug addict who wants to buy drugs and if the defendant sells drugs to the officer, there is no entrapment. By posing as an addict, the officer merely provided an opportunity for the defendant to make an unlawful sale.

A defendant cannot be entrapped by a private citizen. In addition, if the defendant denies his participation in the offense, he has, in effect, elected not to pursue the entrapment defense and cannot raise the issue, even if the facts would otherwise permit him to do so.

Offenses Against the Person

Specific offenses against the person vary widely from state to state. The following are general, common law crimes, which may be altered substantially by the statutes of a particular state.

Assault   An assault is either:

1.   An attempt to commit a battery; or

2.   The intentional creation (other than by mere words) of a reasonable fear in the mind of the victim of imminent bodily harm.

Simple assault is a misdemeanor. Aggravated assaults (with a dangerous weapon, with a deadly weapon, or with intent to maim, rape, or murder) are treated more severely and generally are felonies.

If there has been an actual touching of the victim, the crime is a battery. If there has been no touching, the act may or may not be an assault, depending upon the situation.

Battery   Battery is an unlawful application of force to the person of another which results in bodily injury or results in an offensive touching. Simple battery is a misdemeanor. Aggravated battery generally is a felony.

A battery need not be intentional; it is enough if the defendant causes the application of force with criminal negligence. Moreover, the force need not be applied directly. If it is applied by means of another force or by a substance placed into action by the defendant, it is sufficient (such as causing a dog to attack a victim or causing a victim to ingest poison).

Mayhem   Under common law rules, the felony crime of mayhem required dismemberment, disablement of a bodily part, or disfigurement. Modern statutes typically retain mayhem in some form, although the trend is to abolish mayhem as a separate offense and to treat it as a form of aggravated battery, extending its scope to include permanent disfigurement.

Homicide   At common law, criminal homicides were divided into three different offenses: murder, voluntary manslaughter, and involuntary manslaughter.

Murder was the unlawful killing of a human being with malice aforethought. Malice aforethought could be express or implied. In the absence of facts excusing the homicide or reducing it to manslaughter, malice aforethought existed if the accused had any of these states of mind:

- Intent to kill (express malice);
- Intent to inflict great bodily harm (implied malice);
- Awareness of an unjustifiably high risk to human life (implied malice); or

●Intent to commit a felony (implied malice).

Intentional use of a deadly weapon created an inference of intent to kill. The deadly weapon rule encompassed situations in which a person drove a car through a crowded park; a person fired a bullet into a room full of people; or a professional boxer beat and killed an uncooperative gas station attendant.

Voluntary manslaughter was an intentional killing for which adequate provocation existed. This was sometimes known as "passion killing." For example, provocation was adequate when the defendant was exposed to an imminent threat of deadly force or when the defendant discovered his spouse in bed with another. Mere words were never adequate provocation.

Involuntary manslaughter was an unintentional killing, such as the type that occurred as a result of criminal negligence or the type that occurred while committing a misdemeanor crime.

A.   "Year and a Day" Rule   The death of the victim must occur within one year and one day from the infliction of the injury or wound. If death occurs after this time, there can be no prosecution for homicide even if it can be proved that "but for" the defendant's actions, the victim would not have died when he did.

B.   Modern Statutes   Modern statutes often divide murder into degrees. Under such statutes, *first degree murder* occurs in these situations:

●Deliberate and *premeditated* killing (intentional and planned); or

●A killing that occurs while committing certain felonies (usually arson, robbery, burglary, rape, mayhem, or kidnapping). This is the *felony murder* rule; the state generally does not need to show that the killing was deliberate and premeditated. A few states have backed away from the felony murder rule on the ground that intent to commit first degree murder requires premeditation, and planning to rob a bank is not the same as planning to kill.

Depending upon the law of a particular jurisdiction, *second degree murder* may be a "passion killing" or a killing that occurs while committing a felony other than those listed above.

Voluntary and involuntary manslaughter continue to exist (*see above*). Many states have added motor vehicular homicide as a type of involuntary manslaughter.

C. **Felony Murder** The malice aforethought required for murder is implied from the intent to commit a felony. When combined with conspiracy law, the scope of liability becomes very broad. It applies to all co-conspirators if a death is caused in furtherance of the conspiracy and was a foreseeable consequence of the conspiracy.

The defendant must be found guilty of the underlying felony before the felony murder rule can be applied. In addition, the death must have been a foreseeable result of committing the felony, although most courts have been willing to find most deaths foreseeable. The death must be *caused during the commission* of the felony. The death of a co-felon that results from resistance of the victim or of the police cannot be charged against the defendant, based upon the case of *Commonwealth v. Redline*, 391 Pa. 496, 137 A.2d 472 (1958).

> Arnie and Barney rob a liquor store, during which Arnie shot and killed the owner when he tried to resist. As they were fleeing the scene, a police officer tried to stop them; and in the process, shot and killed Barney. Arnie got away and hid in the basement of his sister's home. Six hours later, Arnie heard someone trying to get in the front door and, believing it was the police, shot through the door, killing his sister.

In this example, Arnie is guilty of felony murder of the liquor store owner but not of his co-felon, Barney, who was killed by a police officer. He is also guilty of killing his sister but not under the felony murder rule, since it did not occur during the felony or while fleeing from the scene of the felony.

The M.P.C. recommends rejection of the felony murder rule except as a rebuttable presumption of malice for killings that occur while committing a felony. However, most states have not yet adopted this recommendation.

False Imprisonment The common law misdemeanor of false imprisonment is the unlawful confinement of a person without her consent.

Confinement requires either that the victim be forced to go where she does not want to go or that the victim be compelled to stay where she does not want to stay. The confinement may be accomplished by force, by a show of force, or by threats. Blocking a person's path is not confinement, as long as alternative routes are available to her.

Confinement is unlawful unless it is specifically authorized by law or by the consent of the person. However, the consent must be freely given by one who has the capacity to consent. Consent is invalidated by coercion, threats, deception, or incapacity resulting from youth, retardation, or mental illness.

Kidnapping   Kidnapping is the confinement of a person which involves either:

- Some movement (asportation) of the victim; *or*
- Concealment of the victim in a "secret" place.

Modern statutes often define aggravated kidnapping as a separate offense. Aggravated kidnapping occurs when a person is kidnapped for a ransom; for the purpose of committing another offense, such as robbery; with the intent of harming the person or with the intent of committing some sexual crime with the victim; or when child stealing is involved.

As with false imprisonment, free consent by one who has the capacity to consent is a defense to a kidnapping charge.

Sex Offenses   The term *sex offenses* encompasses a wide array of sexually motivated conduct: rape (included as a form of sexual assault under some statutory schemes), incest and other sex offenses against children, sodomy, obscenity, prostitution, and so forth. The common law crimes of adultery and fornication either have been abolished or are no longer enforced in most jurisdictions.

Some sex offenses are universally prohibited, while others vary from state to state. For instance, rape (first degree sexual assault or first degree sexual battery) is a crime in all states; prostitution is not (in Nevada, for instance).

    A.   **Rape**   The common law crime of rape required:

    (1)   Sexual intercourse with
    (2)   A woman, not the man's wife
    (3)   Committed without the woman's consent, by use
    of force.

Nearly all states have altered the common law requirements. For instance, many states have eliminated gender reference, making it possible to convict women and minors of the crime as well. (The M.P.C. is gender-neutral concerning all sex offenses except rape.) The spousal exception has been eliminated by most states. Further, a victim need not risk his or her life or risk serious bodily injury to prove resistance.

The M.P.C. punishes rape as a felony in the second degree, unless serious bodily injury occurred or unless the victim was not a social companion of the rapist, in which case the rape is a felony of the first degree.

The crime of **statutory rape** involves one who is under the age of consent (the age of sixteen, for example). Even if the minor consents, the defendant is guilty of statutory rape, since minors under a certain age are incapable of giving legal consent.

Statutory rape is a strict liability crime, so that even a reasonable mistake about the victim's age generally will not absolve the defendant.

B.   Incest   Incest is a statutory offense, usually a felony, which consists of either marriage or a sexual act (intercourse or deviate sexual conduct) between persons who are closely related. There is no uniformity among states as to the degree of relationship required. The majority restricts the crime to blood relatives, but a significant number of states includes some non-blood relatives.

C.   Obscenity   Obscenity crimes usually relate to the sale, display, or publication of material that appeals to a prurient sexual interest; involves patently offensive sexual conduct; and lacks serious literary, artistic, political, or scientific value.

Offenses Against Property

This section deals with a number of property offenses. Since there seems to be consistent difficulty in distinguishing among three of them—larceny, embezzlement, and false pretenses—the following table is provided. The major differences relate to the type of misappropriation of property.

	Conduct	**Method**	**Intent**
Larceny	Taking and asportation of property from possession of another person	Without consent or with consent obtained by fraud	With intent to steal
Embezzlement	Conversion of property held on behalf of another	Use of property in a way inconsistent with the ownership of another	With intent to defraud
False Pretenses	Obtaining title to property	By consent gained through fraudulent misrepresentation	With intent to defraud

Larceny   Larceny is:

- A taking
- And carrying away (asportation)
- Of personal property
- Of another
- By trespass
- With intent to deprive permanently (or for an unreasonable time) the person entitled to its possession.

Property that is severed from real estate and is taken before it comes into possession of the landowner cannot be the subject of larceny. If the landowner gains possession of the severed material, a later taking of the material is larceny. Gas and electricity are considered tangible goods; they can be the subject of larceny.

Under common law rules, documents and instruments were regarded as merged with the item which they represented (such as a deed for real estate or a bill of sale for dairy cows). Unless they had monetary value themselves, they could not be the subject of larceny. Modern statutes have expanded larceny to include written documents that embody intangible rights.

Real estate and its fixtures cannot be the subject of larceny. Neither can services or intangibles be the subject of larceny.

Larceny is a crime against possession. All that is required is that the property be taken from someone who has a possessory interest superior to the defendant's. The property must be taken from one with possession by the defendant who does not have possession. If the defendant has possession of the property when she takes it, the resulting crime is not larceny (although it may be embezzlement). If, however, the defendant has custody and not possession, her crime is larceny.

> While shopping, Joe asks the store owner if he may take a suit home on approval. The owner consents. Joe then asks to see some ties. After a few minutes, Joe absconds with the suit and with two ties. Joe is guilty of larceny as to the ties (he asked only to look at them) but not as to the misappropriated suit because of the control over the suit given to Joe by the owner.
>
> Alice takes her car to Dean's Garage for repairs. Gary makes the repairs and has a mechanic's lien on the car as a result. Alice takes the car without paying Gary. Alice has committed larceny because

> Gary has a possessory interest and the car was in his possession.
> It is immaterial that Alice holds the title to the car.

Employees usually have custody and not possession of their employer's property. They may have possession, however, if the employer has given them broad power over the property. Abandoned property has no owner, and larceny cannot be committed by taking it. Lost or mislaid property, on the other hand, is in the constructive possession of the owner; if it is found and taken, larceny may be committed if these circumstances exist:

■ The finder must know or have reason to believe that she can find out the identity of the owner; and

■ The finder must, at the moment she takes possession of the property, have the intent necessary for larceny.

For larceny to exist, there must be a "taking" of such character that the defendant obtains actual control over the property.

> Willie knocked an expensive piece of crystal from Ronald's hand, causing it to fall and to break. Willie is not guilty of larceny. Even though Ronald lost possession of the crystal, Willie never obtained control.

In addition, larceny requires asportation. In other words, all parts of the property must be moved; and this movement, which may only be slight, must be part of the carrying away process.

> Joyce entered Anne's yard where two tricycles were overturned. Joyce turned them both right side up and moved one of them about six inches toward the street. Turning the tricycles over is not part of the carrying away movement and is not asportation. Moving one of the tricycles, however, is asportation for the purpose of a larceny charge.

Embezzlement   Embezzlement is defined differently from state to state but generally requires:

- Fraudulent
- Conversion
- Of property
- Of another
- By a person in lawful possession of the property.

Embezzlement differs from larceny in that a defendant who embezzles has lawful possession of someone else's property when the embezzlement occurs. Larceny requires a taking (asportation) with the intent to permanently deprive, while embezzlement requires intentional conversion with the intent to defraud. The conversion required for embezzlement generally requires only that the defendant deal with the property in a way that is inconsistent with the agreement under which he holds it. It is not necessary that the defendant receive any direct personal gain from the embezzlement.

> Pete, a pawn broker, acquires a unique emerald ring from Judy as security for a 15-day loan. After five days, Pete gives the ring to his mother for her birthday. This is embezzlement, even though Pete received no direct personal gain from his act.

False Pretenses The offense of false pretenses is part of the common law of crimes and consists of these elements:

- Obtaining title
- To property of another
- By an intentional (or knowing) false statement of past or present fact
- With intent to defraud the other.

False pretenses differs from larceny by trick. If only possession is obtained by a defendant, the crime is larceny by trick. If title is obtained, the crime is false pretenses.

> James wanted to buy Ruth's car and offered a demand note signed by Ben Bigbucks in payment. In fact, James had forged Bigbucks' signature on the note. Ruth agreed to sell the car but told James the sale would not be final until she had collected the note from Bigbucks. Ruth then allowed James to use the car until she had located Bigbucks. James has committed larceny by trick, not false pretenses, because Ruth did not intend to transfer title to the car. She intended to transfer only possession, pending collection of the note.

For false pretenses to exist, the victim must be deceived by, or act in reliance upon, the misrepresentation. This must be a major factor (or the sole cause) of the victim's passing title to the defendant. In addition, the defendant either must have intended that the victim rely upon the misrepresentation or must have known the statement to be false. Subjecting the victim to a risk of loss will suffice.

> Lenora obtained money from Rutherford by representing that she would secure the loan with a first mortgage on property located in another state. Lenora intended to pay back the loan but knew that

> the property was already mortgaged and that she could give only a second mortgage to Rutherford. Lenora is guilty of false pretenses because Rutherford was subjected to a greater risk of loss than he agreed to. This is sufficient basis to find intent to defraud by Lenora.

Many states have enacted specific laws to cover conduct that resembles false pretenses but is different and requires separate treatment. Most states have **bad check** laws that prohibit the giving of an insufficient funds check or a no-account check with the intent to defraud. Many states also have laws that prohibit the knowing use of a **fraudulent credit card** (one that has been stolen, forged, cancelled, revoked, or is otherwise unauthorized) to obtain property.

Another crime related to false pretenses is **mail fraud**. Using the United States mail with the *intent* to defraud another of money or of property is mail fraud. This is exclusively a federal offense. The intended victim need not be defrauded; the intent to defraud is sufficient for mail fraud. Computer larceny or **computer fraud** also falls into the category of false pretenses.

Forgery   Forgery is the

- Making of a false document or
- Altering an existing document to make it false and
- Passing the document to another (uttering a forged document)
- With intent to defraud.

Common law divided forgery and uttering (passing) a forged document into two separate crimes. The purpose of prohibiting forgery is to preserve the commercial system and the documents that are transferred within it.

> Carla painted a picture and signed it "Whistler's Mother." She sold it to Xavier, representing it as an original work of Whistler's Mother. Carla is not guilty of a forgery, although she probably is guilty of false pretenses in connection with the sale.

Robbery   Robbery is a felony in all jurisdictions. It consists of:

- A taking
- Of personal property of another
- From the other's person or presence
- By force or intimidation
- With the intent to permanently deprive the other person of it.

Robbery is basically an aggravated form of larceny in which the taking is achieved by force or threats of force.

If threats are used, they must be threats of immediate death or serious physical injury against the victim, a member of the victim's family, or a person in the victim's presence at the time the threats are made. A threat to damage property is not enough unless it is a threat to destroy the victim's dwelling. The force or threats must be used to gain possession of the property or to retain possession immediately after the unlawful possession has been achieved.

> Ralph grabs Mrs. Evans' handbag as he passes her on the street. Mrs. Evans turns around and grabs Ralph as he tried to run away. Ralph pushed her to the ground and fled. Ralph has committed a robbery, since the force used to prevent the victim from regaining her property is sufficiently related to the taking.

Statutes often create a form of aggravated robbery, generally defined as robbery accomplished with a deadly weapon.

Extortion   The common law misdemeanor of extortion consisted of the corrupt collection of an unlawful fee by an officer under color of his office.

Modern statutes define extortion *(blackmail)* as obtaining property from another by means of oral or written threats. In some states, extortion occurs when the threats are made with the intent to obtain money or something of value; the threat is the heart of the defense. In others, the money or property must be obtained as a result of the threat (the threat alone is not enough).

Extortion may be achieved by threats that are not sufficient for robbery. For extortion, the threats need not be to do physical harm; nor do they have to be threats of immediate harm.

Receiving Stolen Property   The common law crime of receiving stolen property requires the receiving of possession or control of personal property known to have been obtained in an unlawful manner, with the intent to deprive the owner of his property permanently. Although physical possession constitutes "receiving", it is also receiving if the thief puts the stolen property in a place designated by the defendant or if the defendant arranges for the thief to sell the stolen property to a third party for profit.

Modern Changes   Some states and the M.P.C. have consolidated many of the separate offenses involving deprivation of another's property into one crime, most commonly called *theft*. The specific consolidation varies from state to state but often combines all forms of larceny, embezzlement, false pretenses, bad checks, receiving stolen property, and extortion. Robbery and forgery generally are treated as separate and more serious offenses.

Because substantial losses occur each year as a result of destruction of property, many states have adopted statutes that prohibit **criminal mischief**, sometimes called *malicious mischief*. It generally is a specific intent crime and includes all types of destruction that affects the value or the dignity of the property. For example, painting swastikas on the doors of a Jewish synagogue would fall under the category of criminal mischief.

Offenses Against a Dwelling

Burglary   At common law, burglary was defined as the trespassory breaking and entering of the dwelling house of another in the night with the intent to commit a felony therein. The term "breaking" requires the removal of anything blocking entry. Opening a closed but unlocked door was always sufficient, while further opening a partially open door was not always sufficient. A constructive breaking could occur if false pretenses were used to gain entry, such as claiming to be an employee of the gas company, checking for leaks.

There must be an intent to commit a felony within the dwelling. A person who breaks and enters, intending only to obtain shelter on a rainy night, is not guilty of burglary even though she changes her mind once inside and ultimately steals a valuable stereo system.

Modern statutes have altered common law burglary rules significantly, with the result that it is possible under some statutes to break without entering —or to enter without breaking—and still be guilty of burglary. Burglaries committed during the day frequently are punished less severely than those committed at night. The protection of the dwelling has been extended to all occupied buildings and even to automobiles in some states. Sometimes the results are inconsistent. For instance, it may be a more serious offense if a defendant breaks into a vehicle and steals a tape player than if the defendant steals the entire vehicle.

The M.P.C. suggests that a defendant is guilty of burglary "*if he enters a building or occupied structure, or separately secured or occupied portion thereof, with the purpose to commit a crime therein, unless the premises are at the time open to the public or the actor is licensed or privileged to enter.*" The crime is upgraded to a more serious felony if it is "*perpetrated in the dwelling of another at night*" or if the defendant "*purposely, knowingly, or recklessly*" injures or attempts to injure another or "*is armed with explosives or a deadly weapon.*"

Arson   At common law, arson was defined as the malicious burning of the dwelling house of another. As with murder, the malice requirement did not mean ill will but, rather, an intentional or reckless burning of another's house was sufficient. Based upon the common law rules, scorching was not arson; however, a slight charring of wood was arson, even if no flames ever appeared. Using explosives to destroy a house was not arson unless the house caught on fire. Even then, if the exploded fragments of what was once the house caught on fire, it was not arson; fragments of a house were not the same as a house intact. Burning one's own house was not arson under the common law.

As with burglary, modern statutes have changed the common law rules significantly. Buildings other than dwelling houses are frequently protected by current statutes. Under the M.P.C., a defendant is guilty of arson if she starts a fire or causes an explosion for the purpose of destroying the building or occupied structure of another. In addition, anyone who burns her own building or structure is guilty of arson unless she can prove that she did not endanger other people or other property.

Crimes Involving Judicial Procedure

Perjury   Perjury was a criminal offense at common law and is prohibited by specific statute in each state and by federal statute. Perjury involves making of a false statement, with knowledge that the statement is false, while under oath. The most difficult element to prove is the defendant's "knowledge that the statement is false"; however, the finder of fact is permitted to infer the defendant's knowledge from the surrounding facts.

A statement made under oath includes more than testimony given in court. It also includes affidavits, testimony in a deposition, testimony before a grand jury, a certification, or any other statement that requires it to be given in front of a person authorized to administer oaths. If a person's religious beliefs prevent her from giving an oath, she will be permitted to give an affirmation. For purposes of perjury statutes, affirmations are treated the same as oaths.

Some states require that the statement be "material" to the outcome of the case. If a statement is not material, a defendant cannot be convicted of perjury if it is false in a state with the materiality requirement.

Truth is a complete defense to a charge of perjury.

Subornation of Perjury   Subornation of perjury occurs when a defendant convinces someone else to commit perjury. The defendant who commits subornation of perjury is treated the same as the perjurer for purposes of sentencing.

Bribery   Although it originated in common law, bribery is prohibited by statute in every state, as well as by federal statute. Bribery is defined as the solicitation or acceptance of anything of value with the purpose of violating a duty or trust. Bribery generally is classified either as bribery of a public official or as commercial bribery.

> Joe Bigbucks, President of ABC Corporation, offers $10,000 to Pete Politician, who is the mayor of the city, in exchange for awarding a contract for cable services to ABC Corporation. Pete Politician accepts.

Both Bigbucks and Politician are guilty of bribery, since one solicited the bribe and the other accepted it. If Politician had refused the bribe, Bigbucks still would be guilty of bribery. Even if the mayor had no influence concerning the contract award, bribery exists if Politician believed the mayor could influence the decision. Finally, bribery would exist even if the cable contract were awarded to a company other than ABC corporation.

Commercial bribery exists when a person who is engaged in business breaches a duty or trust owed to someone (including a business organization) in exchange for something of value.

The M.P.C. classifies commercial bribery as a misdemeanor and applies to people in specific positions: attorneys, accountants, trustees, and officers of corporations. Anyone who makes an offer to a person in any one of these positions to violate the trust or duty created by the position is guilty of bribery. Anyone who accepts such an offer also is guilty of bribery.

Criminal Procedure

Criminal procedure is the term used to describe the methods used to enforce substantive criminal law. Every jurisdiction (state and federal) has its own procedural rules. Because the focus of the CLA® examination is national, this section of the *Review Manual* emphasizes federal rules as they apply to federal and state criminal proceedings.

At the federal level, procedural rules in criminal cases derive from the United States Constitution, statutes found in the United States Code, and the Federal Rules of Criminal Procedure (F. R. Crim. P.).

Constitutional Restraints

The restraints on governmental action in relation to citizens' rights are found in the Bill of Rights. Until the Fourteenth Amendment was adopted in 1868, the Bill of Rights applied only to the federal government. This amendment is aimed specifically at state action and provides in pertinent part:

> *No State shall make or enforce any law which shall abridge the **privileges or immunities** of citizens of the United States; nor shall any State deprive any person of life, liberty, or property, without **due process** of law; nor deny to any person within its jurisdiction the **equal protection** of the laws.* (Emphasis added.)

Using the Fourteenth Amendment as the conduit, the U.S. Supreme Court (using its *selective incorporation doctrine*) has declared through judicial decision that certain other amendments within the Bill of Rights apply to states in the same way that they apply to the federal government.

Requirements Binding on States   By judicial decision in various cases, the following rights are binding on states under the due process provisions of the Fourteenth Amendment.

Fourth Amendment	unreasonable searches and seizures exclusionary rule (see below)
Fifth Amendment	privilege against forced self-incrimination double jeopardy
Sixth Amendment	right to speedy trial right to public trial right to trial by jury right to subpoena witnesses right to confront witnesses right to assistance of counsel
Eighth Amendment	excessive bail prohibited cruel and unusual punishment prohibited

Requirements Not Binding on States   By judicial decision, the U.S. Supreme Court has held that the right to indictment by grand jury for capital crimes is not binding on states.

The Supreme Court has not yet defined applicability of the Eighth Amendment's prohibition against excessive bail as it relates to states. However, most state constitutions create a right to bail and also prohibit excessive bail.

Exclusionary Rule

The exclusionary rule is one of the remedies for violations of a defendant's Fourth, Fifth, and Sixth Amendment rights. Other remedies include civil suit, injunction, and administrative and criminal sanctions against the offending officer. The exclusionary rule was first announced in 1914 but was not incorporated into the Fourteenth Amendment (applicable to states) until the 1961 case of *Mapp v. Ohio*.

The gist of the exclusionary rule is to exclude evidence obtained in an unconstitutional way (such as an illegal search); it also excludes all evidence derived from that evidence (***fruit of the poisonous tree***). Both the primary evidence and the derivative evidence becomes tainted.

> Police officers threaten and beat Arnie until he confesses to robbing the liquor store. Arnie also tells them where he hid the remaining, stolen cash (he spent some of it). The officers retrieve the cash as evidence.

Because Arnie's confession was obtained illegally, it cannot be used against him at trial. Neither can the cash be used as evidence, since it would not have been located but for the illegal confession.

Illegally obtained evidence cannot be used in forfeiture proceedings.

Exceptions   Evidence that is tainted can be made admissible in one of three ways:

1. If the state can show that it was obtained from *a source independent* of the original illegality (such as an eyewitness).

2. If an *intervening act of free will* of the defendant breaks the chain between the evidence and the original illegality (defendant returns to police station the next day and confesses voluntarily).

3. If the state can show that the evidence *inevitably would have been discovered* anyway (if, for example, a proper search warrant would have led to discovery of the cash in the trunk of defendant's car).

Limitations   The exclusionary rule does not apply in grand jury investigations unless the federal wiretap statute has been violated. It does not apply in civil proceedings. For instance, if the IRS were to bring a civil action concerning the cash that Arnie spent in the above example, it could use the illegally obtained evidence, even though the government could not use it in the criminal case.

The exclusionary rule does not apply if the police acted in good faith on a facially valid statute (even though the statute is later declared unconstitutional) or acted in good faith on a facially valid search warrant.

Although inadmissible in the state's case in chief, illegally obtained evidence may be used to impeach the defendant's credibility if she testifies at trial or in a forfeiture proceeding. Tainted evidence also may be used at sentencing.

Enforcement   The exclusionary rule is enforced by a motion to suppress at the pretrial stage and by objection at the trial stage. The state must establish admissibility by a preponderance of the evidence.

If a motion to suppress is filed, the defendant has the right to testify at the suppression hearing without her testimony being admitted against her on the issue of guilt at the time of trial.

Harmless Error   When the admissibility of evidence is appealed by the defendant on the basis of the exclusionary rule, the state must show beyond a reasonable doubt that admission of the evidence was harmless error (made no difference in the outcome). One method is to show that there was other, overwhelming evidence of guilt.

Some errors, such as denial of the right to counsel, are never harmless.

The Fourth Amendment

The Fourth Amendment prohibits unreasonable search and seizure. This prohibition applies both to search of a defendant (including her dwelling and—in some situations—her car) and to arrest of a defendant.

Arrest   Because an arrest is the seizure of a person, it must meet Fourth Amendment requirements. The remedy for unlawful arrest is a civil suit for false arrest. If the person is still in custody on an unlawful arrest, a writ for *habeas corpus* may be available.

A police officer can arrest a person without a warrant when there is **probable cause** to believe that a *felony* has been committed and that this person is the one who committed it. An officer can arrest without a warrant when a misdemeanor is committed in her presence. A misdemeanor is committed *in the officer's presence* if she is aware of it through any of her senses.

In contrast to search cases, the police do not need an arrest warrant to arrest (seize) a person in a public place, but they must have an arrest warrant to make a non-emergency arrest of a person in his own home. (Domestic violence cases may be an exception.) All warrantless searches of homes (for the person to be arrested) are presumed unreasonable. If the police believe the person to be in the home of a third party, they must have a separate search warrant for the third party's home.

A criminal statute requiring persons who wander or loiter on public streets to provide "credible and reliable" identification when stopped by police is unconstitutionally vague for failure to clarify what will satisfy the identification requirement. Likewise, police may not randomly stop an automobile unless they have probable cause to believe that the driver has violated a traffic law. (Boats *can* be randomly stopped.) The police can, however, stop vehicles at a checkpoint to check license and registration, for example, as long as they have a neutral method for stopping the cars—such as stopping all cars or stopping every sixth car or the like.

No warrant is required to command a person to appear before a grand jury (a subpoena is used).

Search and Seizure

Search and seizure problems generally follow an analysis similar to this:

1.   Does the defendant have a Fourth Amendment right?
    (i).   Was there government conduct?
    (ii).   Did the defendant have a reasonable expectation of privacy?

2.   If so, did the police have a valid warrant?

3.   If not, did they make a valid warrantless search and seizure?

A.   Government Conduct   The Fourth Amendment protects only against governmental conduct, not against searches by private persons. Government agents include police personnel and citizens acting at their direction or request, as well as public school officials. Private security guards are not government agents unless they are deputized by the official police.

B.   Reasonable Expectation of Privacy   A person is presumed to have an expectation of privacy in her home and on her person unless her conduct indicates otherwise (such as an uncovered patio door or an open briefcase). However, officers are entitled to see what is left in *plain view*—the use of binoculars, though enhanced viewing, may still come within the "plain view" rule. Prisoners, on the other hand, have no expectation of privacy in their cells or in any personal property located in their cells.

A person has no expectation of privacy in things held out to the public, such as one's handwriting, paint on the outside of a car, account records held by a bank, a vehicle's movement on a public street, or arrival and departure at a private residence. Police do not need a warrant to attach an electronic beeper to a vehicle, but must obtain a warrant to place a beeper in a residence. There is no expectation of privacy outside the curtilage (dwelling and outbuildings). These areas are subject to search under the *open fields doctrine*. Police may search these areas on foot or by airplane and can even take aerial photographs. The use of trained dogs to sniff luggage for narcotics is not a search.

C.   Warrant Requirement   All searches without a warrant are prohibited unless found among the six exceptions discussed below.

A warrant must be based upon a showing of probable cause. Probable cause is demonstrated by affidavit(s) stating sufficient underlying circumstances to allow the magistrate to make a common sense determination of probable cause, independent of the officer's conclusions. The reliability and credibility of the informant, together with her basis of knowledge, are considered for this purpose.

The search warrant must describe precisely the place to be searched. Premises belonging to third parties not suspected of a crime may be searched if there is probable cause to believe that evidence of the defendant's guilt can be found there.

The police must knock and announce their purpose except in cases of genuine emergency. Once inside, they may seize any contraband, fruits, or instrumentalities of crime that they find within the scope of a proper search warrant, whether specified in the warrant or not. A search warrant does not authorize the police to search persons found on the premises who are not named in the warrant. If the police have probable cause to arrest a person discovered on the premises, however, that person may be searched incident to the arrest. A warrant to search for contraband on a premises implicitly carries a limited authority to detain the occupants while a proper search is conducted.

Exceptions   There are **six exceptions** to the warrant requirement. A valid warrantless search must meet all of the requirements of any one exception.

- Search incident to a lawful arrest
- Exigent circumstances plus probable cause
- Inventory searches
- Consent
- Stop and frisk
- Hot pursuit, disappearing evidence, and other emergencies

A.   Search Incident to a Lawful Arrest   The police may conduct a search incident to an arrest when a full, custodial arrest is authorized. If the arrest is unlawful, the search is unlawful also. Incident to a lawful arrest, police may search a suspect and those areas into which she might reach to obtain weapons or to destroy evidence (her wingspan). This includes the entire passenger compartment of an automobile, including its contents, after arresting the occupants. A search incident to an arrest must be contemporaneous in time and place with the arrest.

B.   Exigent Circumstances Plus Probable Cause   Exigent circumstances may be found in an emergency situation. The police may enter a place without a warrant if they have probable cause to believe that a person is inside who is in distress or if they have probable cause to believe that evidence inside is about to be destroyed or removed.

This exception also applies to automobiles, aircraft, and other "fleeting targets." Automobiles have less Fourth Amendment protection than homes have. Not all automobile searches qualify under this exception, however. To qualify, there must be probable cause to believe that the automobile contains evidence of crime and that the vehicle likely will be unavailable by the time a warrant is obtained.

If, on the other hand, the police have full probable cause before beginning the search, they can search the entire vehicle (interior compartment and trunk) including any package, luggage, or other container that may reasonably hold the item for which they had probable cause to search originally. In this situation, the police may have the vehicle towed for a later search. It need not be searched when and where the vehicle is stopped.

C.   Inventory Searches   If a vehicle has been taken lawfully into police custody (an abandoned vehicle, a vehicle towed from an accident scene or after the driver was arrested, and so forth), police may make a routine inventory of the vehicle's contents without probable cause, including any containers found within it, provided that inventories are performed routinely on *all* vehicles taken into custody. The rationale is that police have a duty to preserve and protect the property in the vehicle, since they would be held accountable for its loss. In addition, police must ensure that the vehicle does not contain items that may create danger to officers and impound lot personnel, such as explosives, toxins, weapons, and the like. *(See discussion of the plain view rule below.)*

D. Consent A warrantless search can be conducted if the police have consent to do so, voluntarily and intelligently made. Knowledge of the right to withhold consent is not required for the consent to be voluntary and intelligent. The scope of the search may be limited by the scope of the consent; and if the consent is revoked, the search must stop.

Any person with equal right to use or occupy the property can give consent, and any evidence found can be used against the other owners or occupants.

E. Stop and Frisk An officer can conduct a protective frisk if she reasonably believes that the person may be armed and dangerous. Generally, the scope of the frisk is limited to a patdown of the person's outer clothing for concealed instruments of assault, unless the officer has specific information that a weapon may be hidden in a particular area of the person's clothing.

If the occupant of a vehicle is believed to be dangerous, the passenger compartment of the vehicle can be searched without a warrant. Once a vehicle has been stopped properly for a traffic violation, for instance, the officer may order the driver out of the vehicle even without suspicion of illegal activity.

Admissibility of evidence obtained during a stop and frisk depends upon whether the officer reasonably could have believed it to be a potential instrument of assault. (A gun found during a stop and frisk will be admissible, but a plastic bag containing narcotics will not.)

F. Hot Pursuit Police in hot pursuit of a fleeing felon can make a warrantless search and seizure and can pursue the suspect into private dwellings. To qualify as "hot," the search must be continuous.

Administrative Inspections Inspectors generally must have a warrant to search private residences and commercial buildings. A showing of a general, neutral enforcement plan will justify issuance of a warrant.

Administrative inspection of highly regulated industries and situations involving contaminated foods are excused from the general warrant requirement.

Similarly, courts routinely uphold searches of airline passengers prior to boarding.

Schools and Government Offices   Schools and government offices that previously have notified students and workers the premises are public property, without any expectation of privacy, may search lockers and work spaces without a warrant. Only "reasonable grounds" are necessary.

Border Searches   Neither citizens nor non-citizens have any Fourth Amendment rights at the United States border. Border officials may stop a vehicle at fixed checkpoints inside the U.S. border to question occupants concerning the presence of illegal aliens, but they must have probable cause or consent to search the vehicle. Roving patrols inside U.S. borders may stop an auto for the same purpose and under the same conditions.

Permissible border searches include opening international mail when postal authorities have reasonable cause to suspect that the mail contains contraband. Regulations prohibit authorities from reading any correspondence contained inside, however. Once customs agents lawfully open a container into which illegal contents have been placed, its subsequent reopening after it has been resealed and delivered to the defendant is not a search under the Fourth Amendment. Additionally, officials who "reasonably suspect" that a traveler is smuggling contraband in her stomach may detain her for a reasonable time.

I.N.S. officials may conduct a "factory survey" of an entire work force in a particular factory to determine citizenship of each employee without raising Fourth Amendment issues. Even if evidence is obtained illegally (preventing its use in a criminal prosecution), it may be used in a civil deportation hearing.

Plain View Rule   Not every seizure involves a search. Police may make a warrantless seizure when they (1) are legitimately on the premises; (2) inadvertently discover fruits or instrumentalities or crime; *and* (3) see the evidence in plain view.

This rule covers unspecified property that may be seen while executing a warrant, as well as warrantless seizure of property found during a *routine inventory* of an impounded vehicle (*see above*). Likewise, the Fourth Amendment does not extend to an established, routine inventory of the shoulder bag of an arrestee.

Wiretaps   Wiretaps and other forms of electronic surveillance that violate a reasonable expectation of privacy constitute a search under the Fourth Amendment. *Katz v. United States* (1967). In 1968 Congress passed Title III of the

Omnibus Crime Control and Safe Streets Act, which showed a legislative intent to require more protections than the constitutional minimum in this extremely sensitive area.

A magistrate may issue a warrant authorizing a wiretap if these criteria are shown: (1) a showing of **probable cause** to believe that a specific crime has been or is being committed; (2) the persons suspected, whose conversations are to be intercepted, must be **named**; (3) the warrant must **specifically describe** the conversations that can be intercepted: (4) the wiretap must be **limited in time**—extensions can be given upon an adequate showing; (5) provision must be made to **terminate** the wiretap once the necessary information has been obtained; and (6) a **return** must be made to the court, showing what conversations have been intercepted. Once a valid warrant has been issued, officers do not need authorization for a covert entry to install electronic surveillance equipment.

A person always assumes the risk that the party with whom she is talking may be an informer and has no Fourth Amendment claim if no attempt is made to keep the conversation private.

A pen register is used to record only the telephone numbers dialed from a particular phone. They do not require prior judicial approval under the Fourth Amendment. In fact, officers may obtain a court order requiring the telephone company to provide the technical assistance necessary to use a pen register.

Unconscionable Methods   Evidence is inadmissible if it is obtained by methods that shock the conscience or that offend the sense of justice inherent in due process, even if the methods do not violate any specific prohibition.

Since a person's strongest expectation of privacy is in his or her own body, Fourth Amendment requirements apply to any intrusion of the human body. Courts use a "reasonableness" standard, weighing society's need for the evidence against the magnitude of intrusion to the individual, including the threat to health, safety, and dignitary interests. Taking a blood sample (such as from suspected drunk drivers) by common medical procedures involves little risk and, therefore, is a reasonable intrusion. However, a surgical procedure that involves a general anesthetic involves significant risks to health and is a significant intrusion on privacy.

If a crime is induced by official action that itself shocks the conscience, any conviction resulting from the action offends due process.

Pat is subpoenaed to appear before a legislative commission and is told that she may invoke the privilege against self-incrimination, although the fact is that she could be convicted for failure to answer questions. If Pat is then convicted for refusing to answer questions, the conviction could be reversed because her crime was induced by methods that shock the conscience. *Raley v. Ohio* (1959).

Confessions   Under the early law of confessions, due process required that a confession be voluntary considering the totality of the circumstances, including age, education, mental and physical condition, as well as the setting and duration of the interrogation. In *Massiah v. United States* (1964), the Supreme Court shifted its focus to the Sixth Amendment, holding that the use of incriminating statements made by an indicted person in the absence of his attorney, violates his right to counsel. *Massiah* still applies to noncustodial, post-indictment interrogations. In *Miranda v. Arizona* (1966), the Fifth Amendment privilege against self-incrimination became the basis for ruling upon the admissibility of a confession. Since *Miranda*, the Burger and Rehnquist Courts have launched a steady move back toward a concern for totality of the circumstances and reliability of the confession.

A.   **Fifth Amendment Privilege:** *Miranda* **Warnings**   After the *Miranda* case, a person in custody must be informed before interrogation:

1.   He has the right to remain silent;
2.   Anything he says can be used against him in court;
3.   He has the right to have an attorney present; and
4.   If he cannot afford an attorney, one will be appointed if he desires.

The warnings need not be given literally, although ***substantial compliance*** is required; and the warnings must be understood. Depending on the circumstances, for example, failure to advise a suspect of his right to appointed counsel may be harmless error.

Anyone in police custody and accused of a crime must be given the *Miranda* warnings prior to interrogation. Interrogation refers to express questioning, as well as to any words or actions by the police that the police should know are reasonably likely to elicit an incriminating response from the suspect. An interrogation is custodial if the suspect is not free to leave (a routine traffic stop is not custodial, however).

Miranda does not apply to spontaneous statements which are not made in response to interrogation, although officers must give the *Miranda* warnings before any follow-up questions are asked.

If a suspect indicates in any way, at any time before or during questioning, that he wants to remain silent, the interrogation must cease. Also, if a suspect requests counsel, interrogation must cease until the suspect is provided with an attorney or until the suspect himself initiates further communication with officers.

B. *Miranda* **Limitations** *Miranda* applies only to interrogations by publicly paid officers or by private persons acting at the direction of publicly paid officers.

A suspect may waive her *Miranda* rights, but the prosecutor must prove that the waiver was knowingly, voluntarily, and intelligently made. Waiver cannot be presumed from the suspect's silence or from the fact that a confession eventually is obtained. Neither is a suspect's refusal to sign a written waiver conclusive as to the absence of waiver. The request for an attorney must be specific; a suspect's request to see her probation officer is not the same as a request for an attorney, so that it is possible that waiver of the right to counsel still may be found.

A confession obtained in violation of a defendant's *Miranda* rights (but otherwise voluntary) may be used to impeach the defendant's testimony if she takes the stand at trial, even though it is inadmissible in the state's case as evidence of guilt. A genuinely involuntary confession is inadmissible for any purpose. A defendant's silence after receiving *Miranda* warnings is not evidence of her guilt; neither can it be used to counter her insanity defense. Evidence based upon a psychiatric interview of the defendant is inadmissible if the defendant was not warned of her right to remain silent.

The *Miranda* requirements do not apply to a witness testifying before a grand jury, even if the witness testifies under compulsion of a subpoena. A witness who has not been charged or indicted does not have the right to have counsel present during questioning but may consult with an attorney outside the grand jury room. Even without the *Miranda* warnings, a witness who gives false testimony to a grand jury may be convicted of perjury.

Pretrial Identification

Although pretrial identification can include fingerprints, blood tests, and deoxyribonucleic acid (DNA [genetic]) tests, this section deals primarily with lineups. A *lineup* occurs when officers exhibit a group of people, including the suspect, to a witness or to a victim for identification of the perpetrator.

The purpose behind all rules concerning pretrial identification by witnesses or victims is to ensure that when the witness identifies the suspect at trial, she identifies the person who committed the crime—not merely the person whom she saw at the police station. If the lineup was faulty, the subsequent in-court identification will be faulty also. Showing mugshots to a witness or victim for identification is permissible, as is requiring the suspect to supply handwriting samples or to submit to voice testing.

To ensure that physical evidence, such as a blood test, remains unchanged and is not confused with evidence from other investigations, the police must maintain the ***chain of custody*** for each piece of evidence from the time it is obtained until the time of trial. All contacts with the evidence, whether by forensic officers or others, must be recorded precisely.

A suspect can be compelled to appear in a lineup without violating the fifth amendment privilege against self-incrimination. Likewise, a suspect can be required to shave, wear a hat or a wig, or engage in a physical act (walking, gesturing, and so forth). None of these things rises to the level of testimony that is protected by the fifth amendment.

A defendant can attack a lineup or showup identification on due process grounds if the identification is unnecessarily suggestive ***and*** if there is a substantial likelihood of misidentification. Both requirements must be met. There is no right to counsel at a pre-indictment lineup; however, the suspect is entitled to counsel at any post-indictment lineup. The suspect is not entitled to any particular type of identification procedure; neither may the suspect demand a lineup

A witness can make an in-court identification despite an unconstitutional pretrial identification if the in-court identification has an independent source. The factors used to determine an independent source include the opportunity to observe the defendant at the time of the crime, the ease with which the witness can identify the defendant, and the existence or absence of any prior misidentification. *U. S. v. Wade* (1967).

Pretrial Procedures

The Criminal Procedure Timeline on the following page may be helpful for those who have not worked actively with criminal procedure for a time. Minor variations are possible from jurisdiction to jurisdiction.

Criminal Procedure Timeline

Police Investigation	Grand Jury Investigation
↓	↓
Complaint	↓
↓	↓
Arrest	↓
↓	↓
Initial Appearance (Bail)	↓
↓	↓
Preliminary Hearing	↓
↓	↓
Information	Indictment

	Arraignment (Enter Plea)	

Guilty or Nolo Plea	Not Guilty Plea	
↓	↓	
↓	Trial	Acquittal (Not Guilty)
↓	↓	
↓	Guilty Verdict	
↓	↓	
→ → → →	Presentence Investigation	
	↓	
	Sentencing	→ → → Punishment
	↓	↑
	Appeal	→ → → → ↑

Assuming there is sufficient evidence, a prosecutor may file a formal complaint (F. R. Crim. P. 3), and an arrest warrant is issued at an *ex parte* hearing based upon the complaint. Following arrest, the defendant is taken before a federal magistrate (usually within 24 hours) for an initial appearance; bail is set; and a preliminary hearing is scheduled. The prosecutor may request that a summons be issued instead of an arrest warrant. After the preliminary hearing, the prosecutor files an information. The ***information*** replaces the complaint as the formal, charging document. This procedure is used predominantly by state systems west of the Mississippi River; it is also used by the federal system but in a more limited way than are grand juries.

State systems east of the Mississippi, as well as the federal system, use a ***grand jury*** to investigate crimes and to bring an ***indictment*** if there is probable cause to believe that the defendant committed a crime. The U.S. Constitution mandates that a grand jury must be used in all federal capital cases, as well as in federal cases dealing with infamous crimes. Federal grand juries consist of 16 to 23 jurors and are secret (closed to all but the prosecutor and the jurors). Witnesses generally are subpoenaed to testify, which may or may not include the defendant. No witness has the right to have an attorney present during the testimony. Neither the defendant nor her attorney has a right to be present or to produce evidence. When all evidence has been presented, the grand jury decides by secret ballot whether to bring an indictment or not against a particular defendant.

The indictment of a grand jury is the functional equivalent of the information filed by a prosecutor. For state traffic offenses and some misdemeanors, the complaint acts as both a summons to appear in court and as the charging document. The ticket is used in place of an information or indictment, and the defendant usually appears in court only once.

Pretrial Detention   The U.S. Supreme Court has yet to decide whether the Eighth Amendment requires pretrial release (bail). Most state constitutions or statutes create a right to be released on bail but may limit the right in capital cases. Where bail is permitted, it can be set no higher than necessary to assure the defendant's appearance at trial. Clearly, the Eighth Amendment does prohibit excessive bail.

Many jurisdictions have preset schedules for bail based upon the nature of the crime. Defendants who can pay 10% of the bail amount are released. Some crimes do not require bail, in which case the defendant may be ***released on her own recognizance*** (ROR).

Issues related to bail can be appealed immediately.

Preliminary Hearing   A later preliminary hearing may be held to determine whether there is probable cause to prosecute. The accused has a right to counsel at this hearing. Either side may use this hearing to preserve the testimony of a witness who may be unavailable at trial, provided there was an opportunity to cross-examine the witness during the hearing. The accused may waive the preliminary hearing.

There is no preliminary hearing in grand jury proceedings.

Speedy Trial   The Sixth Amendment provides the right to a speedy trial. Whether this right has been violated concerning a particular defendant will be determined by a totality of the circumstances. Factors considered are length of delay, reason for delay, whether the defendant asserted her right, and prejudice to the defendant.

The right to speedy trial does not attach until the defendant has been arrested and charged. A prosecutor cannot suspend charges indefinitely, permitting reinstatement of the charges at any time. This is a violation of the defendant's Sixth Amendment right.

Prosecutor's Duty to Disclose   The prosecutor has a specific duty to see that justice is done. As a result, she must disclose any exculpatory information. However, nondisclosure is not grounds for reversal unless there is a reasonable probability that the nondisclosed evidence would have affected the outcome of the trial.

In the absence of a specific defense request, the prosecutor still must disclose information that, considered in light of other information available, creates a reasonable doubt that would not exist otherwise as to guilt.

A defendant must be given reciprocal discovery rights before she can be compelled to give the prosecutor notice of an intent to present either an alibi or an insanity defense at trial. The prosecutor may not comment at trial on the defendant's failure to produce a witness named as supporting the alibi or on the failure to present the alibi itself.

Competence to Stand Trial   Competence to stand trial relates to a defendant's mental condition at the time of trial. Insanity, by comparison, relates to the defendant's mental condition at the time of the crime. Incompetency is not a defense but, rather, is a bar to trial. If a defendant later regains competency, she then can be tried and convicted.

The defendant's mental condition is also an issue for purposes of trial and of execution (for capital crimes). ***The Due Process Clause of the U.S. Constitution prevents a defendant from being tried, convicted, or sentenced if, as a result of mental disease or defect, she is unable:***

•*To understand the nature of the proceedings; or*

•*To assist her lawyer in the preparation of her defense.*

A defendant is incompetent to stand trial if she either (1) lacks a rational, as well as a factual, understanding of the charges and proceedings or (2) lacks the ability to consult with her lawyer with a reasonable degree of understanding.

If no one else raises the issue of competency, the trial judge has a duty to raise it if it appears that the defendant is not competent. A defendant found to be incompetent to stand trial may be detained in a mental institution for a reasonable period of time for evaluation and treatment but cannot be hospitalized indefinitely. If warranted, however, a separate, civil proceeding may be initiated for commitment of the defendant to a mental institution.

Pretrial Publicity   Excessive pretrial publicity that is prejudicial to the defendant may require a ***change of venue*** or may require retrial. The theory is that when most, if not all, jurors have seen, heard, or read news accounts concerning the crime or the defendant, they may base their decision on the publicity, at least in part.

Trial

A defendant is entitled to a fair trial, which includes a guarantee of the Sixth and Fourteenth Amendments of the right to a public trial. This applies to nearly every stage of the criminal process except a pretrial hearing if one is held; this hearing may be closed by agreement of the prosecution and the defense. Both the press and the public have a First Amendment right to attend the trial itself. In addition, criminal proceedings may be televised without violating constitutional protections, even if the defendant objects to their being televised.

Due process is violated if the trial is conducted in a manner or in an atmosphere making it unlikely that the jury will give the evidence reasonable consideration, such as excessive disruption, excessive interruption, and the like. The defendant cannot be forced to stand trial in prison clothing. Jurors cannot be exposed to influence that is favorable to the prosecution, such as deputy sheriffs who eat lunch with and run errands for the jurors.

Right to Trial by Jury   The constitutional right to trial by jury applies only to serious offenses. An offense is serious if it carries a possible punishment of more than six months' imprisonment. There is no right to jury trial for civil contempt proceedings. For criminal contempt proceedings, however, cumulative penalties totaling more than six months' imprisonment cannot be imposed without affording the defendant a right to jury trial.

A judge can impose punishment summarily for contempt during trial; and, as long as no single contempt is punished by imprisonment for more than six months, additional contempts may aggregate more than six months without a jury trial. In addition, a judge can place a contemnor on probation for up to five years without giving her the right to a jury trial, as long as revocation of probation would not result in imprisonment for more than six months.

There is no constitutional right to a jury of twelve persons, but there must be at least six jurors to satisfy the right to jury trial. The Supreme Court has upheld less-than-unanimous convictions when the vote was 9-3. However, a six-person jury must be unanimous in its vote to convict. Unlike federal criminal trials, some states require a unanimous vote to convict, regardless of the number of jurors.

The defendant is entitled to a jury selected from a representative cross-section of the community. A particular defendant needs to show only the under-representation of a district and a numerically significant group to show that her jury trial right was violated. She is not entitled to proportional representation of all groups on her jury. The Equal Protection Clause forbids either the prosecutor or the defense counsel from using peremptory challenges to exclude potential jurors solely because of race. A defendant is entitled to *voir dire* questioning that is specifically directed to racial prejudice when race is relevant.

The prosecutor cannot challenge for cause all those who express a doubt or a reservation about the death penalty in capital cases. Before a particular juror can be excluded, it must be determined whether the juror's views would prevent or would substantially impair the performance of her duties.

Right to Counsel   A defendant has the right to be represented by counsel at each of these stages of the criminal process: (1) custodial police interrogation; (2) post-indictment interrogation, whether custodial or not; (3) preliminary hearing to determine probable cause to prosecute; (4) arraignment; (5) post-charge lineup; (6) guilty plea and sentencing; (7) a felony trial; (8) a misdemeanor trial when imprisonment is imposed; and (9) appeals as a matter of right.

There is no right to be represented by counsel at any of these stages: (1) blood sampling; (2) taking of handwriting samples; (3) precharge or investigative lineups; (4) photo identifications; (5) initial hearings to determine probable cause to detain; (6) discretionary appeals; (7) parole and probation revocation proceedings; and (8) post-conviction proceedings.

The Sixth Amendment right to counsel includes the right to *effective assistance of counsel*, which extends through the first appeal. Effective assistance of counsel is a rebuttable presumption. A defendant claiming ineffective assistance of counsel must show (a) deficient performance by counsel; and (b) but for the deficiency, the result of the proceeding would have been different. The claim cannot be based only upon inexperience, lack of time to prepare, gravity of charges, complexity of defenses, or accessibility of witnesses to counsel. Circumstances that *do not* give rise to ineffective assistance include trial tactics, failure to argue non-pivotal issues, or rejection of a defendant's request for continuance.

A defendant is entitled to automatic reversal, even without a showing of prejudice, when one attorney represents clients with conflicting interests.

When a defendant has made a preliminary showing of need to the court, the state must provide expert witnesses (physician, firearms expert, and the like) for preparation of the defense.

Right to Confront Witnesses   The Sixth Amendment guarantees the defendant's right to confront adverse witnesses. The right is not absolute, however. A judge can remove a disruptive defendant or the defendant may leave the courtroom during trial (trial will continue in her absence).

If two defendants are tried together and if one has given a confession that implicates the other, the right to confront witnesses prohibits the use of that confession. This type of confession may be admitted, however, if:

1.   All portions referring to the other defendant can be eliminated;

2.   The confessing defendant takes the stand and subjects himself to cross-examination concerning the truth or falsity of what the confession alleges; *or*

3.   The confession of co-defendant #1 is used to rebut co-defendant #2's testimony that his (co-defendant #2's) confession was coerced.

Hearsay evidence, if admitted, denies a defendant the right to confront that person unless (a) the prosecution has made a good faith but unsuccessful effort to obtain the person's in-court testimony **and** (b) the defendant has had an opportunity to cross-examine the person concerning the hearsay testimony or otherwise has had an opportunity to test its accuracy.

Burden of Proof   Due process requires that the prosecutor be able to prove guilt beyond a reasonable doubt in all criminal cases. However, a state may place the burden of proof upon the defendant concerning an affirmative defense, such as insanity.

The presumption of innocence is a basic component of a fair trial. Any rule that shifts this presumption or that shifts the burden to the defendant violates the defendant's constitutional rights under the Fourteenth Amendment.

Plea Bargaining   Sometimes at the arraignment and sometimes before or during the trial, the prosecution and the defense may negotiate for and agree to the dismissal of one charge in exchange for the defendant's guilty plea to another or to a reduction to a less serious charge. This is called *plea bargaining*, and it accounts for the disposition of approximately 90% of all felony cases.

A plea bargain is enforceable against a prosecutor but not against the judge, who is not required to accept the plea. A plea is voluntary even if it is entered in reaction to the prosecution's threat to charge the defendant with a more serious crime if she does not plead guilty. Moreover, there is no improper misconduct on the part of the prosecutor if she charges a more serious offense when the defendant demands a jury trial.

A.   The Guilty Plea   A guilty plea is a waiver of a defendant's Sixth Amendment right to a jury trial, to confront witnesses, and so forth. Because of the importance of these rights and their waiver, the judge must assure herself (1) that the guilty plea is entered knowingly and voluntarily and (2) that there is a factual basis to support the guilty plea.

A record must be made when the guilty plea is entered, and the judge must advise the defendant personally: (a) of the nature of the charge to which the plea is offered; (b) of the maximum penalty that is possible and of any mandatory minimum; (c) that the defendant has a right not to plead guilty; and (d) that by pleading guilty, the defendant waives the right to a trial.

The remedy for failure to meet the standards required for taking a guilty plea is withdrawal of the plea and pleading anew.

B. **The *Nolo Contendere* Plea**   A plea of *nolo contendere* (no contest) neither admits nor denies that the defendant committed the crime charged. For purposes of sentencing, it is treated the same as a guilty plea.

The advantage of entering a *nolo contendere* plea is that it cannot be used in a subsequent civil proceeding against the defendant; a guilty plea can be used.

C. **Collateral Attack**   A guilty plea that is shown to be an intelligent choice made from the defendant's alternatives is immune from collateral attack. *(Note: collateral attack means after the case is concluded.)*

The bases for collateral attack of a guilty plea include: (a) ineffective assistance of counsel; (b) failure to honor a plea bargain; (c) lack of jurisdiction; (d) prosecution was barred by double jeopardy; (e) failure to meet constitutional standards for taking the guilty plea.

Sentencing

Legislatures ordinarily set a range of punishments that can be meted out for a specific crime. Once a defendant has been found guilty of that crime, the sentencing process is used to decide which punishment within the prescribed range will be used. Generally, a presentence investigation is conducted for felony crimes and for some misdemeanors; it includes a background check, interview with the defendant, and so forth. If a presentence report is prepared in the federal system, the defendant has the right to review it before sentencing occurs and may attempt to disprove any factual statements at the time of the sentencing hearing.

Federal Sentencing Guidelines   The Federal Sentencing Guidelines were adopted in 1987 to remove the wide disparity that often occurred in sentencing for federal crimes, as well as the arbitrary and inconsistent way in which parole was granted. With the Federal Sentencing Guidelines, Congress eliminated parole and provided a specific time that must be served, reduced by 54 days of good time that may be earned each year (after the first year).

In addition, the judge's discretion in imposing sentence is reduced dramatically. A numbering system is provided to rate the defendant's criminal history and her offense level, with a formula for making the rating computation. The end result is a very small range of sentences which a judge can impose. The guidelines continue to be the subject of much controversy. The primary complaint is their rigidity, which sometimes leads to absurd results. For instance, a young honor student with no prior record, who was involved in one drug transaction, was sentenced to ten years in prison.

Procedural Rights   The usual state sentencing may include hearsay, as well as aggravating or mitigating circumstances. When a magnified sentence is based upon a statute (such as one permitting an indeterminate sentence) requiring that new findings of fact be made (such as recidivism), the defendant must be given the constitutional rights of confrontation and cross-examination of witnesses. Defendants convicted of capital crimes must be given more opportunity for confrontation than is given to defendants convicted of lesser crimes.

Substantive Rights   The Eighth Amendment forbids cruel and unusual punishment. A punishment which is grossly disproportionate to the seriousness of the offense is cruel and unusual. Twenty years at hard labor is a cruel and unusual punishment for forging an official document. The death penalty is a cruel and unusual punishment for sexual assault of an adult female.

The death penalty is not cruel and unusual *per se*. However, the death penalty can be imposed only under a statutory scheme that gives a judge or a jury reasonable ***discretion***, full ***information*** concerning the defendant, and ***guidance*** in making the decision. A trial judge can impose a death sentence even though an advisory jury has recommended a life sentence.

Status crimes, such as being a drug addict, violate the Eighth Amendment, but it is permissible to punish those who sell or who possess narcotics.

A mandatory life sentence imposed under a recidivist statute is not cruel and unusual punishment, even when the three felonies that form the basis for the sentence are nonviolent, property-related offenses.

A punishment of greater length or severity cannot be reserved for those who assert their rights to plead not guilty and to demand a jury trial. For instance, if the death penalty could be imposed for federal kidnapping defendants who insist on a jury trial but not for federal kidnapping defendants who plead guilty. *United States v. Jackson* (1968).

Appeal

The U.S. Constitution grants no right to appeal any criminal conviction. If an avenue of appeal is provided, any condition that makes that avenue less accessible to the poor than it is to the rich violates the equal protection guarantee of the Constitution.

Indigents must be provided with counsel at state expense during a first appeal that is granted to all defendants as a matter of right. In a jurisdiction that uses a two-tier system of appellate courts, with discretionary review by the highest court, the state need not provide an indigent defendant with counsel during the second, discretionary appeal.

When a defendant's conviction is reversed on appeal, due process prohibits retrying that defendant for any offense more serious than the one for which she was convicted at the first trial. For example, suppose that a defendant is charged with murder but is convicted of manslaughter and that the manslaughter conviction is reversed on appeal. The defendant can be charged with nothing more serious than manslaughter if a second trial is held.

Habeas Corpus **Proceedings**

If appeal is no longer available (or if appeal was unsuccessful), a defendant still may be able to attack her conviction collaterally with a new and separate civil action that involves an application for a ***writ of habeas corpus***. The action focuses on the legality of the detention and names the person having custody as the respondent.

There is no right to counsel in a *habeas corpus* proceeding, even if the petitioner is indigent. The petitioner has the burden of proof (by a preponderance) to show that the detention is unlawful.

Federal *Habeas Corpus* Proceedings   Federal defendants may file an application only in federal court; state defendants may file in both state and federal court, provided that the following requirements are met: (a) the state defendant must be "in custody"; (b) the state defendant must have exhausted all available state remedies; (c) with limited exceptions, findings of fact by the state court must be respected; and (d) the state defendant must prove that he is in custody in violation of his federal rights (such as a constitutional right violated during trial). Federal *habeas corpus* statutes are found at 28 U.S.C. §§ 2241-2255.

If the defendant fails to comply with procedural rules, he must show cause for the noncompliance and actual prejudice before he can obtain federal *habeas corpus* relief.

Punishment

A convicted defendant is entitled to assistance of counsel in all situations in which she is entitled to counsel at trial (such as revocation of probation which involves imposition of a new sentence). If the case relates to parole revocation, however, the right to counsel is much more limited.

Prisoner Rights   Deliberate indifference to serious medical needs of prisoners constitutes cruel and unusual punishment, but the negligent failure to provide care does not violate the Eighth Amendment.

Prisoners have no reasonable expectation of privacy in their cells or in the personal property in their cells. Although prison inmates cannot be subjected to broad, overall censorship of mail, censorship is permissible if it is shown to further an important governmental interest related to suppression of expression; if it is no more stringent than required to accomplish the governmental purpose; and if inmates have an opportunity to protest the censorship of their mail.

An inmate can be deprived of "good time" earned or can be placed in solitary confinement only if the disciplinary proceeding meets certain requirements, including (a) advance, written notice of the charges; (b) a hearing; (c) the inmate is allowed to call witnesses and to produce evidence; (d) the decision must be supported by "some evidence"; and (e) reasons for the disciplinary action are in writing.

Prison inmates must be given reasonable access to courts; no unreasonable limitation can be placed upon their ability to develop and to present arguments. Indigent inmates have no Sixth Amendment right to counsel prior to the initiation of adversarial judicial proceedings, however.

Due process places no procedural requirements upon the transfer of an inmate to another institution, including a prison in another state. However, a prison inmate cannot be transferred to a mental institution without a hearing.

There is no right to federal parole, and a right to parole may or may not exist in a particular state. The effects of conviction may continue even after the prison term has been completed (such as loss of voting rights).

Double Jeopardy

The Fifth Amendment of the U.S. Constitution prohibits double jeopardy: (1) a defendant cannot be tried twice for the same offense; and (2) a defendant cannot be punished twice for the same offense. Jeopardy does not attach in civil proceedings but does attach in criminal proceedings:

1.   When a guilty plea is entered and accepted by a court;

2.   In a jury trial, when the jury is empaneled and sworn;

3.   In a bench trial, when the first witness is sworn; and

4.   At the commencement of a juvenile proceeding which bars subsequent criminal trial for the same offense.

Same Offense   Two crimes do not constitute the same offense if each crime requires proof of an additional fact that the other crime does not require, even though some of the same facts may be necessary to prove each crime. Cumulative punishment for two or more statutory offenses, specifically intended by the legislature to carry separate punishments though based on the same conduct, does not violate the double jeopardy rule when multiple punishments are imposed following a single trial.

Attachment of jeopardy for a greater offense bars retrial for lesser-included offenses. Attachment for a lesser-included offense bars retrial for the greater offense, except that retrial for murder is permitted if the victim dies after attachment of jeopardy for battery. A state may continue to prosecute a charged offense despite the defendant's guilty plea to a lesser-included or to an allied offense that stems from the same incident.

Exceptions Permitting Retrial   Even if jeopardy has attached, a defendant can be retried if the first trial ends in a hung jury or if the first trial is aborted or terminated on behalf of the defendant for any reason that does not amount to an acquittal. The state may retry a defendant who has successfully appealed a conviction unless the ground for reversal was insufficient evidence to support a guilty verdict. Retrial is permitted when reversal is based on the weight (rather than the sufficiency) of the evidence.

Separate Sovereigns   The prohibition against double jeopardy does not apply to trials by separate sovereigns. A defendant can be tried for the same conduct by both the state and the federal government or can be tried by two different states, but she cannot be tried for the same offense by a state and any of its municipalities.

Forfeiture Actions

State and federal statutes may provide for the forfeiture of property (such as automobiles or real estate) used in the commission of a crime. Actions for forfeiture are brought against the property itself and are regarded as quasi-criminal. A forfeiture action is a ***civil proceeding***, and its outcome is not dependent upon the success or failure of any criminal prosecution.

Neither the property owner nor others who may have interests in the property is entitled to notice and hearing under the Constitution before property is seized initially. However, a hearing is required before final forfeiture of the property.

Although a person with an interest in the property may be able to avoid forfeiture by showing that she took all reasonable steps to avoid having the property used for illegal purposes, simply establishing lack of knowledge about or lack of participation in the illegal activity will not avoid forfeiture.

Juvenile Court Proceedings

Some of the rights developed for defendants in criminal prosecutions apply to juveniles who are subject to delinquency proceedings in a juvenile court. They include: (a) written ***notice*** of the charges, with sufficient time to prepare a defense; (b) assistance of ***counsel***; (c) the opportunity to confront and to ***cross-examine witnesses***; (d) the privilege against ***self-incrimination***; and (e) the right to have delinquency established ***beyond a reasonable doubt***. *In re Gault* (1967); *In re Winship* (1970).

Other rights accorded to defendants in criminal proceedings are not required in juvenile proceedings. Among these is the right to trial by jury, although some states do provide jury trials in juvenile courts when the juvenile is accused of conduct that would be a crime in adult court. In addition, a juvenile can be detained before trial if she is determined to be a "serious risk" to society. The goal of the juvenile court is also different; it is geared toward protective rehabilitation—not punishment.

A prosecutor may attempt to have a serious criminal charge involving a juvenile defendant filed and tried in criminal court. Similarly, a juvenile court may, after inquiry, determine that a particular child is not an appropriate candidate for juvenile court proceedings and may transfer the case to adult court for trial on criminal charges. If a 17-year-old minor intentionally shoots and kills another, for example, the range of possible dispositions (sentences) available in juvenile court typically are less severe than those available in criminal court. Moreover, the jurisdiction of a juvenile court ends when the juvenile reaches the age of majority, which means the juvenile must be released when he reaches adulthood. This factor may weigh heavily in favor of charging older juveniles as adults for serious offenses.

If the juvenile court adjudicates the child as a delinquent, however, jeopardy attaches; and the constitutional prohibition against double jeopardy prevents him from being tried as an adult for the same conduct.

The review of criminal law and procedure contained in this chapter, together with the following Self-Test, provide a summary of the type of material tested in this subsection of the CLA® examination. Additional study references are contained in the Bibliography section of this *Review Manual*.

Criminal Law Self-Test

Allow an uninterrupted thirty-minute period to answer all questions. At the end of thirty minutes, check your answers against those in the Answer Key Section of this Manual. Deduct two points for each incorrect answer (100 total possible points). Unanswered questions are counted as incorrect answers. Follow directions carefully and observe the time limit precisely to provide an accurate self-assessment.

Choose the most correct answer to each of the following questions unless a specific question instructs you to do otherwise.

1. True or False. A crime is a civil wrong against the state.

2. True or False. Embezzlement involves the asportation of personal property from the possession of its true owner.

3. True or False. One who wrongfully gains possession of real estate may be charged with the crime of larceny.

4. True or False. If a criminal defendant intends to plead insanity, she generally may do so at the time of arraignment.

5. True or False. Joe Anitopo shot and killed a married couple after burglarizing their home. If Joe receives two life sentences as punishment for this crime, he will be able to show double jeopardy.

6. True or False.   A defendant charged with a completed crime may be found guilty of both the completed crime and attempt to commit the crime; however, a defendant charged with attempt to commit a crime may not be found guilty of the completed crime.

7. True or False.   Ben Williams, who tricked his elderly uncle into signing a deed to convey title of the uncle's farm to Ben, may be found guilty of embezzlement.

8. True or False. Defendants are generally permitted to make their opening statements first in criminal cases.

9. Acquittal is most accurately defined as:

   a. exoneration of a criminal charge.
   b. non-liability in a civil action.
   c. dismissal of an appeal.
   d. none of the above.

10. A RICO charge may be filed against:

   a. businesses infiltrated by organized crime.
   b. businesses engaging in interstate mail fraud.
   c. businesses engaging in interstate wire fraud.
   d. all of the above.
   e. none of the above.

11. Double jeopardy is prohibited by:

   a. the Fifth Amendment.
   b. the Sixth Amendment.
   c. the Eighth Amendment.
   d. the Fourteenth Amendment.

12. The doctrine that prohibits evidence from being introduced against a defendant when it is the "fruit of the poisonous tree" derives from:

   a. the Fourth Amendment.
   b. the Fifth Amendment.
   c. the Sixth Amendment.
   d. all of the above.
   e. none of the above.

13. True or False.   A suspect can be required to produce voice and blood samples even though she has not been charged with a specific crime.

14. True or False.   A person who is the subject of a grand jury investigation is entitled to be present and to produce evidence for consideration by the grand jury in making its ultimate decision.

15. True or False.   Once a grand jury has filed its indictment, the next step is the preliminary hearing.

16. True or False.   Under Federal Sentencing Guidelines, a first-time offender is entitled to parole unless the prosecution can show that the crime committed is so grave that parole should be denied.

17. True or False.   A defendant is not entitled to assistance of counsel in a proceeding for parole violation.

18. True or False.   Generally speaking, a defendant is entitled to parole upon conviction of a criminal offense.

19. True or False.   A felony is a criminal act for which the maximum possible sentence is imprisonment of one year or more.

20. True or False.   Double jeopardy forbids prosecution by both the state and federal governments for the same conduct.

21. True or False.   *Nolle prosequi* means that the prosecutor is unable to prosecute on due process grounds.

22. True or False.   Under common law rules, a married man could not be convicted of raping his wife.

23. True or False.   Under common law rules, one could not be convicted of arson for bombing another's home and causing it to explode into a million pieces.

24. True or False.   Illegally obtained evidence cannot be used against a defendant in the case in chief; but if the defendant takes the stand, such evidence can be used to impeach her.

25. When a defendant suffers from a psychopathic disorder which renders her unable to feel remorse for her acts, which of the following statements most accurately applies to her criminal culpability?

a. She is not culpable for her acts but may be found insane.
b. She is not culpable for her acts under the irresistible impulse test.
c. She is not culpable for her acts under the Model Penal Code test.
d. She is culpable for her acts.

Questions 26 - 28 are based on the following facts: Arnold, Betty, and Charlotte agree to hold up a hot dog stand. Arnold waits in the car around the corner while Betty and Charlotte approach the stand, their guns drawn. The attendant gives them all of the money in his possession, which is $10.79. As Betty and Charlotte turn to run away, the attendant grabs his own gun and fires several times. He intends only to wound Betty and Charlotte but kills Charlotte instead. Meanwhile, Arnold hears the gunfire, becomes frightened, and flees the scene before Betty gets back to the car.

26. The attendant cannot be prosecuted for murder because:

a. He intended only to wound Charlotte.
b. The robbery constituted a provocation.
c. He was trying to get his money back.
d. He was attempting to apprehend a fleeing wrongdoer.

27. If Betty is accused of felony murder, her most promising defense will be:

a. She had no desire to see her partner harmed.
b. The fatal act was performed by the attendant.
c. The killing occurred after the robbery was over.
d. The robbery was not a felony, since only $10.79 was involved.

28. Betty plans to plead insanity. In a state which uses the M'Naghten test, what will be the best way for her to frame her defense?

a. She is mentally retarded, and her partners convinced her the robbery was only a game.
b. She gets sudden, uncontrollable urges to steal.
c. The robbery was caused by severe schizophrenia.
d. She was stoned out of her mind on drugs at the time.

29. Arnold is charged with robbery and conspiracy to commit robbery. His best partial defense is:

      a.   He cannot be tried for both offenses; the prosecutor must choose between them.

      b.   He cannot be convicted of conspiracy if Betty was insane and if Charlotte was an undercover police officer.

      c.   He cannot be convicted of conspiring with Charlotte because Charlotte is dead and cannot be convicted with him.

      d.   He abandoned the conspiracy before the commission of the robbery.

30.   True or False.   Alex refused to permit Ben to enter a building, even though Ben had a right to enter it. Alex is guilty of false imprisonment.

31.   True or False.   Joe and Sam meet at a bar. Joe threatens to kill Sam's child (who is at home) if Sam does not help Joe rob the liquor store next door. If he is captured and tried, Sam will have no valid defense.

32.   True or False.   Arthur called Bob a name reflecting on Bob's mother and her moral character. Bob became so incensed that he grabbed Arthur by the throat and choked him to death. The facts indicate that Bob committed a passion killing.

33.   True or False.   In an effort to kill Kathy, Joe obtained a rifle, smashed the window of Kathy's residence with it, and pushed the barrel of the rifle into the house to shoot Kathy. However, Joe was apprehended before any shots were fired. Joe is guilty of burglary.

34.   True or False.   A statute makes it a misdemeanor to provide intoxicating beverages to a minor. In a prosecution under this statute, the state is required to prove that the defendant knew the substance provided to the minor was an intoxicating beverage.

35.   True or False.   Ruby holds a gun on spectators to keep them from interrupting Laura as Laura sets fire to Rachel's residence. Ruby is guilty of the crime of arson as a principal.

36.   True or False.   Steven is tried for the murder of Bill and is acquitted. Steven then is charged with aggravated battery based on the same facts. Double jeopardy precludes a trial on the battery charge.

37.   A defendant's right to the effective assistance of counsel is guaranteed by the:

      a.   Fifth Amendment.

      b.   Sixth Amendment.

(see next page)

    c.   Seventh Amendment.

    d.   Eighth Amendment.

38.   A defendant is entitled to legal representation during:

    a.   a habeas corpus proceeding.

    b.   probation revocation proceedings.

    c.   a post-charge lineup.

    d.   parole revocation proceedings.

39.   An information is:

    a.   the charging document of a grand jury.

    b.   filed after the complaint.

    c.   filed before the complaint.

    d.   the predecessor for an arrest warrant.

40.   Chris entered Barbara's residence late at night and took an antique clock. When apprehended, Chris asserted that she believed she was entitled to the clock because Barbara owed her an amount of money equal to the clock's value. Chris is guilty of:

    a.   larceny.

    b.   embezzlement.

    c.   false pretenses.

    d.   nothing.

41.   In which of the following situations is the defendant most likely to be found guilty of the crime charged?

    a.   Without the permission of Owner, Defendant takes Owner's car with the intention of driving it ten miles to the grocery store and back. Defendant is charged with larceny.

    b.   Defendant obtains permission to borrow Owner's car for the evening by falsely promising to return it, although he does not intend to do so. Two days later, he changes his mind and returns the car. Defendant is charged with larceny by trick.

(see next page)

      c.   Defendant obtains permission to borrow Owner's car for the evening by misrepresenting his identity and by falsely claiming that he has a driver's license. He returns the car the next day. Defendant is charged with obtaining property by false pretenses.

      d.   With permission and promising to return it by 9:00 p.m., Defendant borrows Owner's car. Later that evening, Defendant decides to keep the car until the next morning and does so. Defendant is charged with embezzlement.

42.   True or False.   Helen persuades Clarence to meet her at a bus station, intending to defraud him of a large amount of money when he arrives. This is a felony. While waiting for Helen, Clarence is struck by a negligently driven bus and is killed. Helen is guilty of felony murder.

43.   True or False.   John is employed as a driver for a dry cleaning company. While delivering dry cleaning to customers, John stops at his apartment. He removes several items of clothing from the van, intending to keep them. John is guilty of larceny.

44.   True or False.   Martin removed numerous stock certificates from Edward's office, intending to keep them. Martin is guilty of larceny under common law rules.

45.   True or False.   The F.D.A. typically must obtain a search warrant to inspect a meat packing plant.

46.   True or False.   Robert comes upon the scene as Arnold is pummeling John to the ground. Robert pulls Arnold off John and pushes Arnold away. Arnold hits his head on the side of a building and is injured. It later evolves that John was the initial aggressor in the fight between Arnold and John. Even if self-defense is not available to Arnold, defense of others is available to Robert on these facts.

47.   True or False.   Ken threatens to destroy Bill's business unless Bill gives Ken everything that Bill has in his pockets. Bill does so. Ken is guilty of robbery.

48.   True or False.   Ann is suffering from a terminal illness and asks Joe to give her a lethal injection. After thinking about it for a few days, Joe decides it is the humane thing to do. Joe gives the injection to Ann, and Ann dies. Joe is guilty of premeditated murder.

49.   True or False.   Susan leaves a rake where she knows that Jim will trip on it. Jim trips on the rake and breaks his ankle when he falls. Susan is guilty of battery.

50.   True or False.   A wiretap can be issued for "as long as it takes to ascertain probable cause" against a bookie.

Chapter 13
ESTATE PLANNING AND PROBATE

There are no traffic jams when you go the extra mile.

—Anonymous

Estate Planning

An estate is an interest in property (an asset). An individual's estate consists of the total real and personal property interests owned by her, whether during life or at her death.

Estate planning is the process of preserving an individual's assets with two ultimate goals in mind: (1) meeting the financial needs of the individual during his or her life and (2) maximizing the individual's assets transferred at death to heirs and beneficiaries by minimizing estate and death taxes.

The collective assets owned by an individual determine the value of the gross estate, without regard to whether those assets are classified as probate or non-probate property. Ownership is the key factor in determining whether an asset is part of an individual's gross estate. In other words, if an individual may exercise control over an asset, the asset is part of his or her gross estate. Estate planners must be familiar with the range of devices used to facilitate an individual's estate planning needs and objectives. The most common of these devices include title

699

options for property ownership, gifts of property during life, life insurance, retirement plans, trusts, and wills. Estate and gift tax laws are major factors in any estate plan.

Tax Legislation Overview

To understand present estate and gift tax laws, it may be helpful to know something about their evolution. The past decade or so has produced many changes and reversals by Congress in estate and gift tax legislation, necessitating both agility and patience in estate planners.

The most comprehensive modifications came with the passage of the Tax Reform Act of 1976 (TRA-76). The changes included a larger marital deduction, a new unified credit system combining estate and gift tax *(see below)*, an orphan's deduction, special valuation guidelines for farmland and closely held business realty, replacement of the stepped-up income basis at death with a carryover basis, and liberalization of extensions for payment of tax.

The Windfall Profits Tax Act of 1980 repealed carryover basis retroactively.

Among other things, the Economic Recovery Tax Act of 1981 (ERTA) included an unlimited marital deduction (changing the 1976 Act), the introduction of "qualified terminable interest property" (QTIP), an increase to $10,000 for the annual gift tax exclusion, an increase in the unified credit, a reduction in the upper rate brackets, and the repeal of the orphan's deduction (established in the 1976 Act).

The estate tax exclusion for qualified plan benefits (such as Keogh plan benefits, IRA plan benefits, and certain annuities) was reduced to $100,000 under the Tax Equity and Fiscal Responsibility Act of 1982 (TEFRA).

Under the Tax Reform Act of 1984 (also known as the Deficit Reduction Act of 1984 [DEFRA]), the alternate valuation of assets reported on the estate tax return was restricted, the $100,000 estate tax exclusion for retirement plans was eliminated, I.R.C. § 6166 (installment payments of estate tax) was slightly liberalized, and procedures for reforming charitable trusts were established.

The previous generation-skipping transfer tax was repealed and was replaced by a new tax structure under the Tax Reform Act of 1986. Estate tax on excess accumulation of retirement benefits was added, and tax was imposed on unearned income of youngsters under the age of 14 at the parent's tax rate.

The Omnibus Budget Reconciliation Act of 1987 (OBRA) imposed a five per cent surtax on taxable estates in excess of ten million dollars and added I.R.C. § 2036(c) to eliminate estate "freeze" techniques. This surtax was imposed on decedents' estates coming into existence after 1987.

Under the Unemployment Compensation Amendments of 1992, significant changes in treatment of lump-sum distributions from qualified retirement plans were adopted. The new law imposed a mandatory 20-percent withholding tax on distributions not directly transferred to another qualified retirement plan and eliminated previous distinctions between partial and total distributions.

Unified Credit   Before the Tax Reform Act of 1976 (TRA-76), there were separate tax tables for gift taxes and for estate taxes. Gifts were not considered when computing estate taxes unless the gifts were made in contemplation of death. With TRA-76, however, a new unified system was established that combined the gift tax tables and the estate tax tables. The Act also made gifts subject to the tax under the unified rate, replacing specific lifetime gift exemptions with the unified credit. Thus, gifts made after December 31, 1976 are included when computing tentative estate tax, and credit is allowed for tax paid on gifts that were made during the decedent's lifetime under the new tax rate schedule.

The amount of the unified credit gradually increased until 1987. Since 1987, the unified credit has remained $192,800, which means that taxable estates valued at $600,000 or less are not subject to estate tax.

Property Ownership

Property ownership is one of many devices used by estate planners to maximize the benefits of an individual's estate during life and to maximize assets transferrable at death to his or her heirs and beneficiaries. Property is classified either as probate property or as non-probate property based upon the legal characteristics attached to its ownership (whether solely owned, jointly owned, commonly owned, and so forth).

Probate Property   Property owned solely by the deceased at death is probate property. These assets are subject to the jurisdiction of the probate court and are distributed according to the laws of intestacy or according to the terms of the decedent's will. Probate proceedings are necessary to transfer ownership of probate assets to the decedent's heirs or beneficiaries.

The key element in determining whether an asset is probate property is the title of ownership. If the deceased owns real estate, stocks, bonds, bank or savings accounts, leases, mortgages, promissory notes, real estate, automobiles, and other property in her name alone, it is probate property. If the deceased owns life insurance and designates her estate as the beneficiary, the policy proceeds are probate property and are distributed under the deceased's will or under intestacy statutes.

If an individual owns property with one or more other persons or entities (without right of survivorship), the ownership interest is a *tenancy in common*. As a tenant in common, each owner holds an undivided interest in the property, which can be sold, transferred, or devised separately from the interests of the other owners without destroying the tenancy of the property. Each individual's undivided fractional share is classified as probate property. The value of a deceased owner's fractional share is included in the probate inventory.

> Ann, Betty, and Carl own a farm as tenants in common, each owning an undivided one-third interest in the property. Ann sells her interest to Donna, who becomes a tenant in common with Betty and Carl. When Donna dies, her undivided one-third interest will be probate property.

Mandated by law in some states, *community property* means that all property acquired during a marriage automatically is marital property and is owned equally (50-50) by each spouse. Each spouse has an undivided right to one-half the property acquired by the other spouse during the marriage. Each spouse has complete control over his or her half. From this standpoint, community property is similar to a tenancy in common and is classified as probate property.

Non-probate Property   Property owned by the deceased is non-probate property if its disposition (transfer) is made automatically or by operation of law at death. Non-probate property is valued as of the date of death and is included in the decedent's gross estate.

The most typical type of non-probate property is an asset owned in *joint tenancy* with others. Two or more individuals may own a single asset jointly and may contribute to the total value. During the lifetime of all owners, the law assumes the jointly owned asset belongs to the parties equally, regardless of the contribution made by each. At the death of one of the owners, the decedent's share vests by operation of law to the surviving joint tenants in equal shares.

> P. Bailey, A. Hill, and V. Chappin are joint owners of a savings account. P. Bailey originally contributed 50% to the total sum on deposit, and A. Hill and V. Chappin contributed 25% each. P. Bailey dies in a racing car accident, leaving a total balance of $50,000 in the joint account at her death. By operation of law, the

ownership interest of A. Hill and V. Chappin, the surviving joint
owners, is $25,000 each.

Another common type of non-probate account is a ***P.O.D. account***,
sometimes called a Totten Trust. The abbreviation means **payment on death**.
The individual who establishes a P.O.D. account is called the original payee. He
retains ownership and receives income during his lifetime, but he is able to
designate specific individuals to receive proceeds of the account at his death.

> Vicki established a P.O.D. account naming her two children as the
> P.O.D. beneficiaries at her death. When Vicki died, the balance of
> the account was $20,000; each of her children received $10,000.

Two or more original payees may establish a P.O.D. account; however, no proceeds
are paid to the P.O.D. beneficiaries until death of the survivor of the original
payees.

> Vicki and Dick established a P.O.D. account naming their two
> children as the P.O.D. beneficiaries. When Vicki died, Dick
> assumed total ownership of the P.O.D. account. The children did
> not receive any proceeds until Dick's death.

The right of survivorship under express contract terms (whether a joint
account, a beneficiary designation, or a P.O.D. payee designation) cannot be altered
by a will. As useful as it can be in some situations, joint tenancy ownership is no
substitute for a will.

Tenancy by the entirety is similar to a joint tenancy ownership, except that
it can exist only between people who are married to each other. Accordingly, it is
terminated upon divorce. Couples may terminate a tenancy by the entirety by
transferring the property or by mutual agreement. Since this is a variation of joint
tenancy ownership which automatically vests in the surviving joint owner, these
types of assets are non-probate property.

From an estate-planning view, joint tenancies (including P.O.D. accounts
and tenancies by the entirety) can create a variety of problems, particularly for
large estates. Joint ownership precludes any type of post-mortem control by the
estate of the deceased joint tenant; the survivor, by operation of law, has complete
control of the joint property. If the survivor does not possess the management
skills necessary to preserve the asset, it likely will disappear or will diminish in
value. Should the survivor remarry and then die, the property could pass to the
new spouse and then to the heirs of the new spouse.

Life Insurance   A life insurance policy payable to a beneficiary other than the deceased's estate is a non-probate asset and is included in the decedent's gross estate—provided the decedent was the policyowner at his or her death.

> Harry purchased a $50,000 of life insurance policy from Grand Central Life Insurance Company. Harry was the owner and insured under the policy. The primary beneficiary was Sally, Harry's spouse. When Harry died five years later, Sally received $50,000 from the insurance company. On Harry's federal estate tax return, the policy was reported on Schedule D as an asset owned by Harry. However, the insurance proceeds were not included in Harry's probate proceeding, because the insurance policy named a beneficiary other than Harry's estate.

If the insured is *not* the owner of the life insurance policy, the insurance proceeds are *not* included in the deceased's gross estate. For example, a husband may own life insurance policies insuring his wife, and vice versa. In this event, the husband controls the policy insuring his wife and designates the beneficiary, which likely will be himself or a trust created by him. If the wife dies first, the insurance proceeds are paid directly to the owner/husband or to his trust. Because the wife does not own the policy at her death, the proceeds are not included in her gross estate.

> Randy and Jenny purchased two life insurance policies from Kent Life Insurance Company. The policy insuring Randy's life was for $300,000 and the one on Jenny's life was for $200,000. Jenny was the policyowner insuring Randy, and Randy was the policyowner insuring Jenny. Randy designated his *inter vivos* trust as the beneficiary of the policy insuring Jenny's life, and Jenny designated herself as the beneficiary of the policy insuring Randy's life. When Jenny died seven years later, the insurance company paid the $200,000 death benefits directly to Randy's trust. The insurance proceeds are not included in Jenny's gross estate because she had no incidents of ownership.

If the policyowner dies before the insured dies, the cash value of the policy is included in the policyowner's gross estate. The cash value is considerably less than the face value of the policy.

> Continuing with the above example: At Jenny's death, she was the owner of a policy insuring the life of her husband. The cash value of the policy is an asset in Jenny's estate and is reported on the federal estate tax return.

Under I.R.C. § 2035, however, the insurance proceeds (rather than the cash value) are included in the insured's gross estate if ownership of a policy is created or assigned within three years of death. Although I.R.C. § 2035 generally does not include gifts made within three years of death as part of the gross estate, life insurance transfers are an exception.

> John assigns ownership of his $250,000 life policy to Mary, his wife. Eighteen months after the completed assignment, John dies. Because three years have not yet elapsed since the assignment, the insurance proceeds are included in John's gross estate.

To keep insurance proceeds out of an insured's estate, the insured must surrender all "incidents of ownership" in the policy and must live three years after purchase or transfer of the policy. "Incidents of ownership" under estate tax regulations (Reg. § 20.2042-1[c]) include the power to change the beneficiary, to assign, to revoke an assignment, to pledge the policy for loans, to cancel the policy, or to borrow against the cash value. Other regulations address powers over the payout options as incidents of ownership.

Indirect incidents of ownership over a life insurance policy will cause the proceeds to be included in the decedent's gross estate. If incidents of ownership are held by a corporation controlled by the decedent, proceeds of an insurance policy insuring the decedent's life are included in the decedent's gross estate. Ownership control is defined as 50 percent or more of the total voting power of the corporation at the time of the decedent's death. Voting power includes stock owned by the decedent, by any agent for the decedent, or by a trustee of a voting trust owned by the decedent.

The U.S. Tax Court has ruled that incidents of ownership by a partnership over a life insurance policy on a decedent are not included in the gross estate, even though the decedent was a 50 percent general partner. The rationale was that the proceeds of the policy were received by the partnership, which increased its net worth. Thus, the proceeds effectively were included in his gross estate by virtue of the increased value of the decedent's partnership interest.

As a part of an estate plan, a married couple may want to consider a *survivor life insurance policy*, sometimes called a second-to-die policy. This is a single policy insuring a married couple simultaneously. It costs less than two separate whole life policies, because it pays only upon the second death. With the unlimited marital deduction, often no estate tax is due at the death of the first spouse. As a consequence, when the surviving spouse dies, his or her estate stands the full burden of the estate tax and related expenses. A survivor life insurance policy provides the liquidity to meet these expenses.

Retirement Plans   A qualified retirement plan may be a pension plan, a profit-sharing plan, or an annuity plan. Other retirement programs may include

401(k) plans, a Keogh plan, an employee stock ownership plan (ESOP), and an individual retirement account (IRA). The following material is not an in-depth discussion of retirement plans but, rather, provides definitions of the various plans for review purposes. If there are benefits remaining to be paid at death, the value of the retirement plan is included in the decedent's gross estate for estate tax purposes. Income tax treatment of retirement plans must be scrutinized closely for proper reporting.

A qualified *pension plan* must be established and maintained by the employer, the benefits of which are definitely determinable and systematically paid to a retired employee for a specific period of years (usually for life). Benefits are determined by the employee's rate of compensation and by her length of service with the company.

A *profit-sharing plan* is a defined contribution plan to which the employer may make discretionary contributions. Under most plans, employees may make discretionary contributions also. If a profit-sharing plan uses a trust, the trustee requirements must be met. The IRS requires a profit-sharing plan to be a written instrument to be recognized for tax purposes.

A qualified *annuity plan* can use contributions to buy retirement annuity contracts from insurance companies. For the annuity to be effective, a contract must be signed by the annuitant and issued by the insurance company. Most annuity plans provide a menu of payout options from which the annuitant may select. Again, the key to determine if any annuity benefits are included in an estate is whether any benefits remain to be paid at death.

Under *401(k) plans*, an individual contributes pre-tax dollars up to a specific limit, which are tax free at the time of contribution. When benefits eventually are paid, the recipient pays income tax in the year the benefits are received. Upon death, beneficiary designations determine who is to receive any remaining benefits, all of which remaining benefits are included in the gross estate.

A *Keogh plan* is a self-employment retirement plan, which is a written program created for the benefit of employees. These self-employment plans can be created only by an employer, who typically is the employee as well. Partnerships or proprietorships are eligible for self-employment plans. If a self-employed individual has more than one trade or business that earns income in any tax year, each business is considered separately for purposes of contributing to a plan. The value of the plan at decedent's death is included in the gross estate for federal estate tax purposes.

An *employee stock ownership plan* is a defined contribution plan which invests primarily in the company's (employer's) securities. These plans are available only to employees of a company offering such a plan. Purchase of securities usually is done through a stock bonus plan or through a money purchase plan created by the employer. To determine the stock's value for federal estate tax purposes, the corporation's accountant typically will be involved.

Individuals may contribute up to $2,000 each year until age 70½ to an *individual retirement account*. Contributions are deductible except by active participants in qualified retirement plans with adjusted gross income above certain levels. Additional contributions may be made to a spousal IRA for a spouse who does not work outside the home.

Under the Unemployment Act Amendments of 1992, new penalties apply to lump sum distributions made from retirement plans to individuals who retire or who leave their current employers. This Act imposes a 20 percent withholding tax on lump-sum distributions unless the recipient elects to have the distribution transferred directly into an IRA, a 403(a) or (b) annuity, or a new employer's qualified plan. The employee also has the option of leaving the funds in the former employer's plan if that option is available. If the recipient personally receives any portion of the plan benefits outright, the 20 percent withholding tax is imposed on the total proceeds of the plan. To avoid imposition of income tax on a distribution or on a rollover, the account should be transferred or rolled over by the company (not by the employee) directly into a qualified retirement plan.

> Jack, age 64, works at Second National Bank and decides to retire. He requests his employer to transfer his lump-sum distribution of $300,000 from the employer's qualified plan to a new IRA. No amount is withheld from the $300,000 and the entire sum begins to accrue tax-free earnings.
>
> Same facts as above except that Jack requests a check for the entire lump-sum distribution. The employer is required to withhold 20 percent, or $60,000, giving Jack the remainder, or $240,000.
>
> Same facts as above except that Jack requests only a partial lump-sum distribution of $100,000. The employer still is required to withhold 20 percent of the entire plan proceeds, or $60,000, giving Jack the remainder of his requested distribution, or $40,000.

Under the 1992 Act, plan administrators must give a written explanation of distribution options before making a distribution.

Trusts

A trust is an estate planning device which permits one person to hold legal title to an asset or to a group of assets, while the equitable title rests with the beneficiaries of the trust. Equitable title may be granted in different proportions to the trust beneficiaries. Trusts are major tools in family estate planning because of tax considerations and because of their management benefits. Trusts originally were used to minimize death taxes and probate expenses on assets transferred from generation to generation. Although this is still a consideration, it is not the sole motivation to create a trust.

An individual may create a trust to ensure that safety devices are in place to protect beneficiaries. For example, if a parent dies with minor children surviving her, a trustee provides not only the management skills necessary to maintain the principal of the trust, but also is responsible for making distributions for the care, education, and general welfare of the beneficiaries. If a parent dies owning a small business, minor beneficiaries will not have the ability, experience, or training necessary to continue the business operation.

An individual may establish a trust for his own benefit. It is common for individuals to establish trusts while they are capable of managing their own affairs so that if they become incompetent, trust administration can continue without the assistance of the creator.

Other non-tax reasons to create a trust are:

(1)   Lack of confidence in a beneficiary's ability to manage property;
(2)   Preservation of property for a spendthrift beneficiary during life;
(3)   Assurance of family income;
(4)   Protection of a disabled family member;
(5)   Desire to "rule from the grave"; and
(6)   Avoidance of publicity and probate.

A trust can have a long duration but only to the extent that it does not violate the Rule Against Perpetuities. The common law Rule Against Perpetuities in effect in most states requires that an interest must vest no later than a life (or lives) in being at the creation of the trust plus 21 years. The purpose of this rule was to prevent persons from ruling from the grave by holding assets in trust forever. *Refer to the chapter on Real Estate Law for further discussion.*

The Uniform Statutory Rule Against Perpetuities (USRAP) was adopted by the National Conference of Commissioners on Uniform State Laws in 1986 and changed the common law rule. The USRAP requires property to vest within 90 years. Few states have adopted the USRAP rule.

A trust may be *revocable* or *irrevocable*. The right to revoke, modify, or amend the trust may be reserved by the creator in a revocable trust. An irrevocable trust cannot be revoked and should not be amended in any way. The assets of a revocable trust are included in the deceased's estate. The assets of an irrevocable trust are not included in the deceased's estate unless life insurance for the deceased was purchased or transferred within three years before death. If death occurs within that three-year period, the life insurance proceeds are included in the deceased's gross estate.

The legal requirements for all trusts are: (1) intent to create a trust; (2) a trustee; (3) trust property; (4) at least one beneficiary; and (5) trust purposes.

Trustor, Grantor, Settlor   A person who creates a trust is a trustor, grantor, or settlor. One who creates a trust by a will typically is called a *settlor*; one who creates a living trust typically is called a *grantor*.

Trustee   The operation of a trust requires a trustee to hold legal title to the trust property. If a trustee dies, becomes incapacitated, resigns, or is removed after the trust is established, a successor trustee is appointed. If the trust document fails to appoint a successor, a new trustee will be appointed by an appropriate court upon application by an interested party. The court normally will consider the wishes of the beneficiaries and the intent of the grantor to provide sound administration. Generally, however, the trust agreement provides the selection process of a successor trustee; appointment may be made by the grantor (if living), by the spouse, by adult beneficiaries, or by a person designated in the trust agreement.

The trustee can be any person or institution in which the grantor has faith and trust. Institutions serving as trustee are granted special trust powers by state law and/or by federal regulatory agencies. Many times the grantor serves as her own trustee until she dies or becomes unable to serve.

A trustee is entitled to reasonable compensation for administering trust property. Compensation may be provided by the terms of the trust agreement, which generally will control even though the compensation is not within the norm established by statute or by the local marketplace. If extraordinary events take place during the course of administration, the court may allow additional compensation.

A.   Powers of the Trustee   To administer a trust effectively, the fiduciary (trustee) must have the power to act. A trustee has powers that are specifically conferred by the terms of the trust agreement as well as powers that are necessary or appropriate for carrying out the purposes of the trust and that are not forbidden by the trust agreement.

An *express* trust power is one which is granted specifically by the trust instrument (agreement) or by statute. A power not granted by instrument or by statute may be *implied* to administer the purposes of the trust properly. The exercise of a power is *mandatory* when a trust provision directs the trustee to perform a specific function. The trustee is given *discretionary* power when she is given the option to perform a specific function. A court will not interfere with the discretionary authority of the trustee so long as the trustee acts reasonably.

An example of an express trust power is one directing the trustee to pay all trust income to a certain beneficiary; a mandatory, express trust power may direct the trustee to pay the trust income to a certain beneficiary at least quarterly. Requiring the trustee to pay all income to a beneficiary grants an implied power to invest the trust assets so that a reasonable income can be generated to pay the beneficiary. If, on the other hand, the trust instrument provides that the trustee *may* pay income or principal to a beneficiary for support, the trustee has discretionary power to make the payment. In other words, if the trustee has authority to withhold either income or principal in her complete, uncontrolled discretion, the trustee has discretionary power.

B.   Prudent Person Rule   A trustee is required to exercise the same reasonable care and skill that a person of ordinary prudence would exercise in administering her own property. If, however, a particular trustee possesses greater skills than an ordinary person, that trustee will be held to a higher standard. For example, if a trust company serves as a trustee and holds itself out as having special investment facilities and knowledgeable employees, the trust company and its employees are held to a higher standard of performance than is an ordinary person who serves as a trustee.

Testamentary Trusts   A testamentary trust is created by a will and is a part of the will. If the will is revoked, the testamentary trust is also revoked. Funding this type of trust does not take place until after the testator's or testatrix's death. Individuals who use testamentary trusts frequently are unwilling to relinquish control of assets during their lifetimes. A testamentary trust is revocable, because the will that creates it is revocable.

Depending upon the purpose and language of the trust, trust property can be protected from successive estate tax liability as it is distributed from beneficiary to beneficiary. If the trust is funded by property with a low tax basis but with a strong potential for appreciation, the tax savings to the family can be enormous.

The estate tax savings and income tax savings of a testamentary trust are not realized until the will takes effect at death. The flexibility of the trust permits the testatrix to tailor the dispositive provisions to the intended beneficiaries. The interests of the beneficiaries can be limited or adjusted to meet unique circumstances. The trust may provide for management of property for beneficiaries who are minors, elderly, or inexperienced in business matters to preserve estate assets.

A will may create a variety of trusts (a marital trust, a credit shelter trust, and a generation-skipping transfer trust, to name a few) to maximize the tax benefits and to accomplish specific trust purposes. One disadvantage of testamentary trusts, however, is that the disposition of the decedent's property is subject to public surveillance. A will becomes part of the probate court's public records, and this loss of privacy is a concern to some.

Inter Vivos Trusts   An _inter vivos_ trust, also called a **_living trust_**, may be either revocable or irrevocable. The goals of the grantor determine whether to use a revocable trust or an irrevocable trust.

If the grantor is primarily tax motivated, an irrevocable trust can be used to shift income tax burdens and to reduce the grantor's taxable estate at death. Transferring assets into an irrevocable trust means that the grantor relinquishes control of the assets and of the right to receive income from those assets. Assets of more than $10,000 are subject to gift taxes at the time of transfer. Because the grantor retains no incidents of ownership at death, however, irrevocable trust assets are not included in the gross estate. The exception is the purchase or transfer of insurance on the life of the decedent within three years of death.

On the other hand, if the grantor chooses not to relinquish ownership or if she wants to receive the income generated from the assets but wants to avoid probate, transferring assets to a revocable trust allows the grantor full control during her lifetime. After the grantor's death, the revocable trust may dispose of property privately (without estate administration) if all of the grantor's property is in the trust. A living trust lends itself to continuity of management for trust assets and to maintenance of an income flow to beneficiaries during the life of the trust.

The grantor of a revocable trust may serve as her own trustee for as long as she is able. When the grantor is no longer able to serve as the trustee, the successor trustee designated in the trust instrument automatically becomes the trustee.

At the grantor's death, the revocable trust becomes irrevocable. The trust estate is allocated among any specific trusts established by the trust instrument.

The assets usually are divided between a marital trust and a credit shelter trust and are administered according to the terms of each separate trust.

Credit Shelter Trust   The nonmarital trust commonly is called the *credit trust*, the *family trust*, or the *residue trust*. Assets having a value equal to the federal estate tax exemption equivalent normally are allocated to the credit shelter trust and are exempt from federal estate tax. Funding a family trust with assets equal to the exemption equivalent (the unified credit) and allocating the balance of the estate to the marital deduction trust allows the decedent's estate to maximize the unified credit and to minimize the marital deduction. The result is no federal estate tax liability at the first death between spouses. Upon the death of the surviving spouse, the credit shelter trust does not become a part of the surviving spouse's estate and is not taxed a second time.

Benefits which may be provided to the surviving spouse under a family trust and which are not taxable to the spouse's estate at his or her subsequent death include:

(1)   All of the income during his or her lifetime;

(2)   Amounts of principal necessary for support, maintenance, welfare, and care;

(3)   Withdrawals of principal by the spouse equal to the greater of 5% or $5,000 on a noncumulative, annual basis; and

(4)   A special power of appointment allowing the spouse to leave the trust property to anyone *except* the spouse, the spouse's estate, the spouse's creditors, or the creditors of the spouse's estate. The decedent normally wants assurance that the family trust ultimately will be distributed to her children or to specific charities. With the special power of appointment, the decedent can designate what class of beneficiaries are eligible for consideration by the surviving spouse if the special power of appointment is exercised.

After the death of the surviving spouse, the remaining principal and any accumulated income are distributed to designated beneficiaries chosen by the decedent, which usually are her children. Depending upon the terms of the family trust, children may receive their shares in one lump sum or in installments as predetermined by the decedent.

Marital and QTIP Trusts   The decedent may give his entire estate to the surviving spouse, which would pass free of federal estate tax under the unlimited marital deduction. Depending upon the size of the estate, however, this could create an unnecessary tax burden on the surviving spouse's estate. To minimize the tax burden between the two estates, the credit trust or family trust should be funded with the exemption equivalent when the first spouse dies.

All assets allocated to the marital and/or QTIP trusts must qualify as marital deduction property. Property owned jointly between a decedent and his spouse qualifies for the marital deduction, as do assets owned solely by the decedent. However, assets owned jointly among the decedent, the decedent's spouse, and a third party do not qualify as marital deduction property. Life insurance proceeds paid to an individual other than the spouse or the decedent's trust likewise do not qualify as marital deduction property.

The marital trust must grant all of the net income to the surviving spouse at least annually, as well as grant the right to control and dispose of the trust property either during life or by will through a power of appointment. If the spouse does not use all of the trust property during life and does not dispose of it by will through the power of appointment, the remaining trust property is distributed according to the grantor-decedent's directions. (Generally, the balance is administered under the terms of the decedent's family trust or credit trust.) At the death of the surviving spouse, the value of the remaining assets in the marital trust are included in the spouse's estate and are subject to federal estate taxes.

By contrast, the *qualified terminable interest property (QTIP) trust* does not give the surviving spouse control or a power of appointment over the trust assets. In fact, the major difference between a marital trust and a QTIP trust is that the grantor of a QTIP trust controls the final disposition of the trust property after the death of the surviving spouse.

QTIP trusts are useful planning tools for a second marriage when the grantor has children from a prior marriage who are the ultimate beneficiaries. The grantor is able to safeguard the children's interests, while preserving the marital deduction and allowing the spouse to receive the income during life. At least annually, all income must be paid to the surviving spouse; and at the spouse's death, any accrued income must be paid to the spouse's estate. Because qualified terminable interest property (QTIP) qualifies for the marital deduction, the value of the assets are included in the estate of the surviving spouse even though the spouse has no control over the assets of the trust.

For trust assets to be regarded as QTIP assets, the personal representative makes the election on the federal estate tax return. The personal representative may select a percentage of the marital deduction property as QTIP assets and may allocate the remaining assets to a regular marital trust and/or a family trust. In some instances, the personal representative may elect to have all marital deduction property treated as QTIP assets. Once the QTIP election is made and the federal estate tax return is filed with the Internal Revenue Service, the election is irrevocable.

Sprinkle Trust   A *sprinkle trust*, also called a *spray trust*, is a discretionary trust. Its purpose is to provide the trustee with uncontrolled discretion to distribute as much income or principal to a beneficiary for care and education as the trustee thinks best. The trustee becomes the parent substitute for children who are beneficiaries. If there is a surviving parent, the trustee typically will rely upon the parent's suggestions for distributing funds among the beneficiaries. However, when there is no surviving parent, the trustee is extremely cautious about making uneven (sprinkling) distributions to beneficiaries. Among the advantages of a sprinkling trust are:

1.   It provides spendthrift protection, since the beneficiaries do not have any right to income until it is allocated to them.

2.   Estate tax savings are achieved when the spouse is also a beneficiary and receives only needed income rather than unnecessary increases in the value of the spouse's estate.

3.   Savings on family income tax are achieved when income is distributed to a low-bracket beneficiary.

4.   Funds are allocated among beneficiaries according to need.

The disadvantage of a sprinkling trust is that it places complete control in the trustee.

Spendthrift Trust   A spendthrift provision in a trust allows a grantor to transfer assets for the benefit of a beneficiary and to protect those assets from creditors. The beneficiary cannot transfer his right to any future distributions, and his creditors cannot attach a claim to any future distribution. Protection against creditors depends upon the amount of discretion granted to the trustee. If the beneficiary receives income or principal at the complete discretion of the trustee, the trust is more creditor-proof. Spendthrift provisions are placed in trusts not only to address the problem of minors receiving sums of money but also to assist adults who lack the capacity to manage money and assets prudently.

The protection offered by a spendthrift trust is not ironclad. Not all states limit creditors' reach on the assets to the same extent. There have been cases where the trustee has been forced to make discretionary distributions to a beneficiary. In addition, spendthrift provisions are never effective against a federal tax lien.

Generation Skipping Transfer (GST) Trusts   To understand the application of generation skipping transfer (GST) trusts, knowledge of their terminology is essential. The most common terms used in GST trusts are defined below.

A *skip person* is one who is two or more generations below the grantor's generation. A trust can be regarded a skip person if all beneficiaries with an interest in the trust are skip persons. A skip person may be a grandchild, a great-grandchild, or a trust in which all beneficiaries are skip persons.

A *non-skip person* is a member of the generation "jumped over" to get to the next descending generation. A non-skip person may be a child of the grantor or one who stands in the shoes of a child of the grantor.

The *transferor* is the deceased or the grantor whose property is subject to estate tax. The transferor also may be a donor who makes a gift of property which is subject to gift taxes. An individual who exercises a general power of appointment granted by will or by trust instrument is the transferor of that property.

Generation skipping transfer *interests* apply only to present interests and not to future interests in property. A *present interest* is a right to receive income or principal now. For example, a parent may provide that a child is to receive income for life and as much principal as needed under the trust agreement. By contrast, a *future interest* is a right to receive income or principal upon the occurrence of an event or a condition. For example, a parent may provide that after the death of the child, the grandchild will receive the remaining principal and any accumulated income. The grandchild's right is a future interest.

A *direct skip* is a transfer made directly to (or in trust for) a grandchild while the parent of the grandchild is living. If a grandmother gives a grandchild $2,000,000, this is a direct skip if the grandchild's parent is living. If the grandchild's parent is not living, the grandchild (and all succeeding lineal descendants of the grandchild) moves up one generation. Thus, no GST tax is imposed on that grandchild's share.

A *taxable termination* occurs in property when the present interest of a non-skip person ends (no more distributions can be made to him or her), and the present interest in the property is held by a skip person as a result.

> A sprinkle trust established by the grantor provides that the income is to be paid to the child for life, with the remainder to be paid to grandchildren and great-grandchildren. When the child dies, no more distributions can be made to him; and the present interest in the trust automatically is transferred to the grandchildren and great-grandchildren. In this situation, GST tax may be levied upon the trust. If, however, the child has a general power of appointment under the sprinkle trust which is exercised at death, the child's interest is included in his estate for estate tax purposes; and a taxable termination does not occur. Thus, no GST tax is imposed.

A ***taxable distribution*** is a distribution of principal or income to a skip person. A taxable distribution occurs when payments are made to a grandchild under a sprinkle trust while the child is living.

The generation skipping transfer tax is a surcharge (an extra tax) at the maximum estate tax rate (currently 50%) on assets transferred to skip persons. Every individual has a $1 million generation-skipping-transfer exemption. With proper planning, a married couple has a combined $2,000,000 GST exemption. One way for married couples to utilize the GST exemption is to create a three-trust plan by using a credit trust, a GST tax-exempt QTIP trust, and a nonexempt QTIP trust as follows:

1. The credit trust is funded with the exemption equivalent. The total value of assets allocated to this trust is exempt from the generation skipping transfer tax if *no* life estate is provided for the surviving spouse and if the assets are distributed outright to the decedent's beneficiaries.

2. The GST tax-exempt QTIP trust is designed to absorb the $1 million GST tax exemption after allocation to the credit shelter trust. If no life estate is granted to the surviving spouse in the credit shelter trust ($600,000), $1 million may be transferred to the GST tax-exempt QTIP trust. However, if $600,000 is allocated to the credit shelter trust (which provides a life estate for the surviving spouse and the remainder to the children and their descendants), the personal representative will elect specifically that the balance of the GST exemption ($400,000) be allocated to the GST tax-exempt QTIP trust, which will bring the GST allocation to the full $1 million. This is called a *reverse election* under I.R.C. § 2652(a)(3). The reverse election treats the deceased grantor as the transferor of the assets for

GST tax purposes. This allocation avoids paying GST tax on property distributed to grandchildren if their beneficiary parent dies after the grantor but before the surviving spouse.

The GST-exempt trust typically does not permit principal to be distributed for the benefit of the surviving spouse unless there are no other funds available to the spouse. The income of this trust, however, is paid at least annually to the surviving spouse. The purpose of this trust is to preserve the assets for the skip generation.

Because it is a QTIP trust (which receives only assets that qualify for the marital deduction), the principal is subject to estate tax at the death of the surviving spouse. Most estate planners attempt to shift the burden of paying the estate tax to the nonexempt trust.

3.   The nonexempt QTIP trust receives the balance of the deceased grantor's estate, which qualifies for the marital deduction. Upon the death of the surviving spouse, this trust will be subject to estate tax. The surviving spouse's estate is considered the transferor of the trust property from this nonexempt QTIP trust for GST purposes.

There are many aspects and variations of GST trusts to consider when planning for clients. This discussion is limited and does not encompass all of the many variables that can affect planning for a particular client.

Trusts for Disabled Children   Trusts intended to protect a disabled child must be drafted with extreme care to preserve the child's entitlement from public assistance programs. Some states allow the use of spendthrift trusts to prevent local and state agencies from seeking reimbursement from the trust.

Trusts created to avoid reimbursement to welfare agencies of public assistance must indicate clearly the intent of the grantor or testator. The trust should not provide for payments of income or principal for the care, maintenance, support, welfare, or education of the beneficiary if the grantor intends that public assistance be available to the disabled beneficiary. If payment is allowed for these needs, the disabled beneficiary may be disqualified from receiving public assistance. The use of an independent trustee or someone other than a family member provides additional protection.

As a cautionary measure, the trust may provide that the principal must be paid to a contingent beneficiary if the trust is determined to be against public policy; and upon payment to the contingent beneficiary, the trust terminates.

Standby Trusts   Standby trusts, sometimes called ***conduit trusts***, originally were used by individuals who traveled abroad extensively or who were suffering from a disability. Management of trust assets frequently is controlled by someone other than the grantor. Upon the grantor's death, the trust assets are distributed to another trust for distribution.

Charitable Remainder Annuity Trusts and Unitrusts   The grantor of a charitable remainder annuity trust retains an income interest in the trust property for a stated period, either for herself or for specified trust beneficiaries. The period typically does not exceed 20 years. Alternately, the period can be contingent upon the life of a trust beneficiary. The remainder interest of the trust is distributed to a qualified charity upon termination of the term or of the life interest. Termination of the income interest can be contingent as well. The Internal Revenue Code requires that a charitable remainder trust be either an annuity trust or a unitrust.

An annuity trust requires an annual, fixed payment from the trust which is equal to at least five percent of the original contribution to the trust. The beneficiaries receive no more than this annual fixed dollar amount regardless of their needs and inflation. Any excess earned by the trust and not distributed to the beneficiaries ultimately will be distributed to the charity. If the income from the trust is not adequate to meet the annual payment, principal may be invaded.

A unitrust does not require annual, fixed payments to noncharitable beneficiaries. The beneficiaries must receive a fixed percentage of the value of the trust annually, but the payment is never less than five percent of value of the trust. If value of the trust increases, the beneficiaries receive larger payments. Conversely, if the value of the trust declines, the payments will be smaller. If the investments of the unitrust are managed well, it provides some protection against inflation. The unitrust is preferable to an annuity trust in inflationary times.

Wills

A person dies **testate** when he or she dies with a valid will that disposes of his or her property.   The term *testate* derives from the creator of a will: a male who executes a will is the ***testator***; a female, the ***testatrix***. Each state has its own version of the Statute of Wills. The purposes of this statute are to permit individuals to dispose of their assets at death in a clear, orderly manner and to eliminate fraud and undue influence by others in arranging for that disposition. The legislation also ensures implementation of the decedent's testamentary intent.

The Uniform Probate Code defines a **will** as any testamentary instrument, including a codicil, which appoints a personal representative, revokes or revises another will, nominates a guardian, or expressly excludes or limits the right of an individual or class to succeed to property of the decedent passing by intestate succession.

For historical reasons, disposition of real estate by will is a **devise**; and a conveyance of personal property is a **bequest**. Because it sometimes is difficult to distinguish between real and personal property or because the characteristics of a group of assets may change over time, many estate planners advocate the use of both terms for all testamentary dispositions.

Requiring written terms forces the testator to leave evidence of his desires for disposing of his estate. Genuineness of the will is evidenced by the signature of the testator and by the attestation. The attestation ceremony is a protective formality. It requires individuals to witness the fact that the testator signed the will voluntarily. When the formalities for execution of a will are followed, many will contests are eliminated; and probate costs are reduced.

Codicil   To amend or modify an existing will, a **codicil** is executed in the same manner as the original will. A codicil normally refers to the date of the original will and ratifies those provisions of the original will which are not specifically revoked, amended, or modified by the codicil. A properly executed codicil becomes a supplement to the original will and is incorporated with the will in the probate process.

A will is **ambulatory** (changeable), which means that it disposes of property owned at the date of death without regard to what property was owned when the will was signed. For purposes of interpretation, however, the meaning of the testator's words is determined by the conditions existing when the will was signed. When codicils are executed to update the will, conditions existing when the codicil was signed likewise are taken into account in determining testamentary intent.

Holographic Wills   Nearly half of the states authorize a holographic will—one which is in the handwriting of and signed by the testator. All holographic wills must be signed, but only a few states require the testator's signature at the end of the document. Nearly any act performed with the intent that it be a signature is sufficient, even though it may not be legible or may not be the formal name of the testator. Where holographic wills are valid, there is no requirement that they be witnessed.

Many states also require that a holographic will be dated by the testator. The date must be complete (month, day, and year) and may be expressed in numbers.

Some state statutes impose very stringent conditions, such as requiring that the will be entirely in the handwriting of the testator. As a result, some courts have declined to admit documents offered as holographic wills because they were typed or because they contained printed text or printed captions.

Nuncupative Wills   A nuncupative will is an oral will, which a majority of states will admit for probate. This type of will permits a person to dispose of limited amounts of personal property (usually up to $1,000), and it must be made during the testator's last illness. Witnesses must be present and at least one must be willing to testify in court if requested to do so. Many states require that the testator's wishes be reduced to writing and that the writing be admitted to probate within a specified time.

Validity of Wills

An estate planner must know the formal requirements for executing a will in all states. With today's mobile society, a will may be offered for probate in a different state than the state where it was executed. The general rule is that the validity of a will is determined (1) by the law of the *situs* for immovable assets and (2) by the law of the decedent's domicile at death for movable assets. To establish the validity of wills, courts require substantial compliance with statutory formalities.

Age   UPC § 2-501 provides that any person who is 18 or more years of age and who is of sound mind may make a will.

Statutory Formalities   The formalities required to execute a will are relatively simple. Wills must be in writing; they may be in any language and may be written in any form which has some permanency. The writing materials used for wills have been as varied as the imaginations of the writers. Many wills have been handwritten in pencil, some have been written on brown wrapping paper, and a few even have been carved on hard surfaces.

Testator's Signature   The requirement that a formal will must have the signature of the testator is accompanied in nearly all jurisdictions with the provision that another individual may sign on behalf of the testator (in the testator's presence and with his express permission). Any completed act of the testator is a sufficient signature so long as the testator intends the act to be his signature. Consequently, a testator can sign his will with a mark, with initials, or with a nickname.

The UPC does not require that the testator publish his will. (Publication typically is a simple declaration that a particular instrument is his will.) Neither does the UPC require that the signature of the testator be subscribed or that the signature be at the end of the will. If the testator chooses to sign his name in the body of the will or in the margin and if he intends it to be his signature, it will satisfy the UPC standard.

Witnesses   Two or more witnesses typically are required for the execution of formal wills. The qualifications to be a witness to a will are the same as the qualifications of witnesses generally. The witness should be able to observe, to understand, and to relate what happened when the will was signed. No minimum age is required to be a witness to a will.

Under the UPC, at least two individuals must sign the will, each of whom witnessed at least one of the following: the signing of the will; the testator's acknowledgment of the signature; or the testator's acknowledgment of the will. The signing of a will by an interested witness (one who is a beneficiary under the will) does not invalidate the will or any of its provisions under the UPC; however, some jurisdictions require that at least one witness be disinterested.

Many statutes require the witness to be competent; others require the witness to be credible. Regardless of the statutory language, the standards are the same as those used to determine competency of the testator or of the testatrix at the time the will is executed. If a witness becomes incompetent or dies after the will is executed, the validity of the will is not affected.

Self-Proving Clause   A will may be simultaneously executed, attested, and self-proved by an acknowledgment of the testator and affidavits of the witnesses, each made before a notary public. A self-proved will normally is admitted to probate without the testimony of any subscribing witnesses; otherwise, the will is treated no differently than a will which is not self-proved. Thus, a self-proved will may be contested (except regarding signature requirements), revoked, or amended by a codicil in exactly the same manner as a will which is not self-proved.

Testamentary Capacity

Individual intellectual capacity and mental power vary to such a degree that only general guidelines can be established to determine whether mental capacity exists to make a will. The legal standard merely outlines some elements of the mental comprehension necessary for testamentary capacity: (1) the testator must know the nature and extent of his estate; (2) the testator must be able to identify the persons who are the objects of his bounty and his relationship to them; and (3) the testator must understand the nature of his act in disposing of his property. He must have sufficient mind and memory to understand all of these elements and how each relates to the other.

Capacity to make a will must exist at the time the will is executed (signed). If a testator had capacity at the time the will was signed but later loses his capacity, the validity of the will is not affected. On the other hand, if a testator does not have capacity when the will is made but subsequently acquires capacity, his will would not be considered valid. Re-executing another will after acquiring capacity does, however, establish a valid will.

Witnesses may be required to testify about the testator's capacity to make the will, including the testator's age, sanity, and freedom from undue influence. This point may be overlooked by the witnesses, who often think they are attesting only to the legal formalities of signing the will.

The standard of testamentary capacity does not mean the testator must comprehend each of the technical legal terms used by the estate planning lawyer who drafts the documents. However, the testator should understand the legal effect and intent of the instrument which disposes of his property.

Nature and Extent of Estate   To establish testamentary capacity, the testator generally must know what his property is. Understanding the relative value of properties comprising a large estate requires more knowledge than does remembering the balance of a single savings account. However, the fact that an individual cannot remember details concerning all of his assets does not mean his capacity is insufficient.

Objects of Bounty   The testator should be able to identify the claims against his property and the names of those who are the natural objects of his bounty (property). Relatives generally are the natural objects of a testator's bounty. An understanding of the condition of his property and the persons related to him (the objects of his bounty) are important in establishing testamentary capacity. Not only should the testator know who his relatives are, but he also should have the ability to recollect their treatment of him.

A testator must be able to identify the recipients of his property and to identify those relatives to whom no disposition will be made. A testator may choose to give his property to some unrelated person or may choose specifically to omit heirs by stating those desires in his will and by identifying those who otherwise might have a claim against his estate.

Nature of Disposition   A testator has testamentary capacity if he understands his plan of disposition, whether he possesses an intelligent perception of the disposition or whether he merely has a reasonable comprehension of the basic facts. The ability to grasp essential facts with minimal assistance or prompting carries considerable weight in some jurisdictions. Capacity to understand the consequences of disposing of property generally is sufficient.

Grounds for Invalidity   One who disputes a will must initiate a court proceeding to contest the will. The contestant may assert several grounds for contest. The most common grounds for invalidating a will are incapacity, fraud, duress, and undue influence. Because every state has its own unique statutes to define each of these grounds, all matters connected with drafting and execution of the will must be analyzed closely. If acts which may invalidate the will are alleged, those acts must be scrutinized carefully in relation to the specific statutory language.

A.   Incapacity   Litigation regarding incapacity often centers on mental capacity, which may be one of two types: (1) mental deficiency or (2) mental derangement. The test applied in *mental deficiency* cases is the same as the test applied for testamentary capacity (*see above*). *Mental derangement* usually relates to insane hallucinations or delusions. Simply stated, if a testator imagines facts to exist against all evidence to the contrary, he may be mentally deranged. However, simply having irrational beliefs does not make his will invalid on grounds of mental derangement if those beliefs do not affect the will.

B.   Fraud   Fraud occurs when false statements are knowingly made by an heir or a beneficiary with the intent to deceive the testator, causing the testator to change his will in reliance upon the statements. Fraud generally is one of two types: (1) fraud in the execution, also called fraud in the *factum* or (2) fraud in the inducement.

Fraud in the execution of a will occurs when a will is executed by a testator who believes it to be something other than a will or when the contents of the will are withheld. If a testator is deceived about the contents of his will, the fact that he had an opportunity to read the will does not make the will valid if, in fact, he did not read it. Death-bed wills sometimes result from fraud in the execution, usually because the testator no longer has the physical or mental strength to comprehend the contents of the will. If unusual dispositions are made to persons with influence over the testator at the time of his last illness, fraud in the execution of the will may have occurred.

Fraud in the inducement, however, occurs when the testator or the testatrix has a genuine intent to create a will, but the intent is induced by false statements of a beneficiary under the will. When the inducement or deceit unjustly enriches that beneficiary, the will may be invalidated. Knowledge by the beneficiary of the falsity of the statement, coupled with the intent to deceive the testator, are essential to prove fraud. For example, if false statements are made to a testatrix by one of her daughters that another of her daughters is immoral and if the testatrix makes a new will disinheriting the allegedly immoral daughter, the will may be invalid (1) if the testatrix was induced to make the will because she believed the statements and (2) if the person making the statements benefited from the new will.

If a provision of a will has been induced by fraud and if that provision can be separated from the remaining provisions, the remaining provisions may remain in effect.

C.   Duress   The exercise of force over the testator which destroys his free will and which causes him to create a will that he would not have made otherwise falls into the category of duress and invalidates the will. The use of threats or violence toward the testator or toward his family to induce him to create a will is duress. Duress often exists in conjunction with undue influence.

D.   Undue Influence   Undue influence exists when the testator is induced to execute a will which appears to be his but which contains the wishes and dispositive plan of someone else. Thus, it is not the will of the testator at all. Although the will is executed by the testator, it is the product of a captive mind. When undue influence is proved, it may invalidate all or part of the will. The legal elements of undue influence are: (1) susceptibility of the testator to undue influence, (2) opportunity to exert undue influence, (3) disposition to exert undue influence, and (4) the result of undue influence.

When considering susceptibility to undue influence, courts weigh the testator's physical and mental health, age, personality, and ability to administer business affairs. Although forgetfulness does not prevent one from creating a valid will, mental impairment may provide an avenue for others to influence the testator unduly. It is not the nature or extent of the influence but, rather, the effect upon the testator's mind which determines whether undue influence exists.

Opportunities to exert undue influence over a testator are limited only by the imagination. Threats of abandoning a sick testator, appeals to the affection and emotions of the testator, flattery combined with deceit and solicitation of the testator, and misrepresentations to the testator are only a few examples of the methods used to overpower the mind.

The disposition to influence unduly means that a person is willing to act in a manner which is wrong or which is patently unfair to obtain a share of the estate.

The result of undue influence relates to the naturalness of the bequest. However, omitting heirs from a will does not prove undue influence if a supportable reason is given for their omission.

Revocation of Wills   An essential characteristic of a will is its revocability. A will conveys no present interest in the property devised or bequeathed. The ownership of property remains with the maker of the will until she dies. The will may be revoked in whole or in part by the testatrix at any time by creating another will that specifically revokes all prior wills, by writing the word "revoked" across the original will and initialing it, or by destroying the original will.

A will may be burned, torn, cancelled, mutilated, obliterated, or destroyed with the intent to revoke it by the testator (or by another person in his presence and by his direction). Some statutes expressly provide that the revocation of a will also revokes codicils related to it. Litigation arises when the testator's intent is unclear because, for example, the will is only singed (burned only along the edges) or because only the first page of the will is cross-marked. These types of situations have led to inconsistent results in different jurisdictions.

A will may be revoked by a subsequent will or codicil. Generally, a revocation signed under the same formalities as the original will is sufficient to declare the previous will revoked. If a will is revoked in part, a codicil may be used (*discussed previously*).

A court may declare a will revoked by operation of law under special circumstances. UPC § 2-508 revokes will provisions for a spouse if there is a later divorce or annulment. The estate is distributed as if the former spouse predeceased the testator.

Revocation occurs in many states when a will has been executed before marriage and the subsequent birth of children. However, marriage alone generally does not revoke a will, because a spouse has other protections (*see below*).

Limitations of Wills   Generally speaking, a testatrix may dispose of her property at death in any way she chooses by executing a valid will. She may disinherit everyone, including her children; but she cannot totally disinherit her spouse. The Uniform Probate Code gives a surviving spouse the option to elect against the will (take a statutory share) when the testatrix intentionally omits the surviving spouse from the will or leaves only a small part of the estate to the surviving spouse. (*See the section on Elective Share discussed later in this chapter.*)

Intestacy

An individual who dies without a valid will is **intestate**, and her estate is distributed to her heirs according to the laws of intestate succession. Different intestacy statutes may apply to the same estate if the decedent owns real estate in more than one state. To transfer real property located in other states to the deceased's heirs, a separate court proceeding is required (an **ancillary administration**) to appoint a personal representative to execute the deeds of distribution. Personal property generally is distributed according to the laws of the state where the deceased was domiciled. Occasionally, however, a court may assert jurisdiction over personal property which was kept in that state's jurisdiction, even though the deceased was domiciled elsewhere.

Intestacy statutes, similar to the Canons of Descent under the English common law, provide for progressive distribution until there is a taker. The term "descent and distribution" comes from the Canons of Descent. The term **descent** originally pertained only to realty; the term **distribution** pertained only to personalty. Over time, the distinction between realty and personalty has become blurred or has been eliminated.

Although intestacy statutes vary, many contain provisions similar to the following:

    (1)   The surviving spouse may take a specific cash amount plus either one-third or one-half of the estate (depending upon whether the children are issue of that marriage);

    (2)   Surviving descendants of the deceased share the remaining estate equally;

    (3)   If there is no surviving descendant of the deceased, the surviving spouse takes the entire intestate estate;

    (4)   If there is no surviving spouse or descendant, the surviving parents of the deceased take the intestate estate;

(5)   If there is no surviving spouse, descendant, or parent of the deceased, the descendants of the deceased's parents shall take the estate; or

(6)   If there is no surviving spouse, descendant, parent, or descendant of a parent, but the deceased is survived by one or more grandparents or descendants of grandparents, then half of the estate passes to the decedent's paternal relatives and half to the decedent's maternal relatives.

A **descendant** is an offspring of the deceased, one who has descended from the body of the ancestor (such as a child, grandchild, great-grandchild, and so on, to the most remote degree). Descendants sometimes are classified as *lineal descendants* (those in a direct line of descent from the deceased) and *collateral descendants* (those who are neither direct ascendants or direct descendants of the deceased, but who share a common ancestor). An **ascendant** is one to whom the deceased is related as a direct descendant (such as a father, grandfather, great-grandfather, and so on).

Heirs   An **heir** is a person entitled to receive the deceased's property as determined by the statutes of intestate succession. The Uniform Probate Code intestacy provisions require that an heir survive the decedent by 120 hours to be eligible for inheritance. An individual may be named as an heir in an estate without receiving any property at all if, for example, the decedent died without a will but provided for transfer of her assets through joint tenancy, gifts, trusts, or insurance designations.

Pretermitted heirs are those born or acquired after the execution of a will. If a will fails to provide for the descendant born after signing the will and fails to show an intention to exclude that descendant, pretermission occurs. Pretermitted heir statutes are designed to protect heirs who are omitted from a will unintentionally. The descendant often is a child of the deceased, and the statutes operate on the assumption that the testator would have wanted to provide for such a child. Courts have interpreted pretermitted heir statutes to protect issue of a deceased child and his or her spouse as well. A person who marries after a will is executed also is protected under the doctrine of pretermitted heirs unless the will provides to the contrary.

Adopted Persons   The right of an adopted person to inherit as an heir is created by statute. Many statutes treat the adopted person as if he had been born into the adoptive family, allowing him to inherit through—as well as from—his adoptive parents. State statutes vary concerning whether inheritance is permitted *from* as well as *by* an adopted person and concerning the adoptee's status with respect to both his natural relatives and his adoptive relatives.

Persons Born Out of Wedlock   State statutes differ concerning the inheritance rights of persons born out of wedlock. A child born out of wedlock clearly inherits as an heir from the mother in all states. However, unless there is a subsequent marriage between the mother and the father or unless the father acknowledges paternity, most jurisdictions do not permit the child to inherit from the father.

Distribution of Intestate Estate

There are different statutory approaches to distributing the assets of an estate: *per stirpes* and *per capita*. Under a ***per stirpes*** approach, sometimes called taking by right of representation, the decedent's estate is divided into as many shares as there are (1) living children plus (2) deceased children leaving issue (children). The living children of the deceased take their shares directly; the issue of deceased children stand in the shoes of their parent, taking his or her share by representation and dividing it among themselves equally.

> Adam is a widower who dies leaving three children: Cain, Abel and Janice. Cain has three children, Abel has one child, and Janice has two children. Since all three children survive Adam, each child receives one-third of Adam's estate.

> Same facts as above, except that Cain predeceases his father, Adam. The estate is divided into three equal shares: Abel and Janice receive one-third each; Cain's three children divide Cain's share equally, each receiving one-ninth of Adam's estate.

> Same facts as above, except that when Adam dies, all of his children have predeceased him. Adam's estate is divided into three equal shares, representing his three deceased children. The issue of Adam's children each will receive a different percentage of the estate. Cain's three children each will receive one-ninth of the total estate, Abel's only child will receive one-third of the total estate, and Janice's two children each will receive one-sixth of the total estate.

> Same facts as above, except that when Adam dies, all three of his children and one grandchild, who is the issue of Janice, have predeceased him. The deceased grandchild has two children. Adam's estate is divided into three equal shares and distributed as follows: Cain's three children each will receive one-ninth, Abel's only child will receive one-third, and Janice's surviving child will receive one-sixth. The remaining one-sixth will divided between the two children of Janice's deceased child, giving each one-half of the parent's one-sixth share, or one-twelfth of the total estate.

Under a ***per capita*** approach and the 1990 amendments to the Uniform Probate Code (UPC), the estate is divided into as many shares as there are (1) surviving heirs in the nearest degree of kinship and (2) deceased heirs of the same class with surviving issue. The estate is distributed equally to individuals of the same generation, even though part of the estate may be given to a different generation. This is referred to as the *per-capita*-at-each-generation approach. To illustrate the UPC *per capita* distribution, consider the following examples, which use the same family facts as the preceding examples.

> Adam dies, leaving no surviving children. Each of his six grandchildren will share his estate equally.

> Adam dies, leaving one surviving child (Janice) and issue of predeceased children. Under the 1990 UPC, Janice receives one-third of the entire estate; the remaining estate is treated as a single share and is divided equally among the four surviving issue of Adam's deceased children.

Escheat   If a person dies both intestate and without surviving heirs, the entire estate will ***escheat*** (pass) to the state. If a person dies testate and if all of his beneficiaries and heirs are deceased, his estate also will escheat to the state. Most statutes provide that the state must hold the assets for a period of time and that a diligent search must be conducted to locate heirs. If no heirs are found within the statutory time, the estate becomes the property of the state.

Probate

Whether testate or intestate, the decedent's estate (property owned by her at death) must go through a liquidation and distribution process to convey legal title to the decedent's heirs or beneficiaries. The ***purposes of probate*** proceedings are to determine validity of the will (to determine legal heirs if there is no will), to collect and preserve the assets of the decedent, to pay from the estate all expenses and outstanding debts of the deceased, and to distribute the remaining assets to those who are entitled to receive them.

Formal probate proceedings to administer an estate (collect assets, pay debts, and distribute to heirs and devisees) under the continuing supervision of the court are ***in rem proceedings***. Actions which may affect administration of an estate but which are not part of the administration itself are ***in personam proceedings***. Typical *in personam* proceedings include: (1) actions concerning the elective share of the surviving spouse; (2) actions by the personal representative against a debtor of the estate; and (3) actions against the estate by a creditor of the estate.

If a will exists, it must be located as quickly as possible to prevent its loss or destruction. If the will is in the possession of someone who is unwilling to relinquish it, legal proceedings may be initiated to compel production of the will. Once the will is located, it is filed with the probate court (admitted for probate); a personal representative is appointed; and the decedent's estate is probated (administered according to the testator's intent).

Jurisdiction and Venue

Jurisdiction relates to the power of a particular court to hear a particular case. Venue relates to the geographical location within a jurisdiction where the case should be filed and tried. (*Refer to the chapter on General Law for more detailed discussions of jurisdiction and venue.*)

Every state court system includes jurisdiction of probate matters within that state and establishes a probate court to hear those types of cases. Probate courts generally are located in many different places throughout the geographic boundaries of the state. The most typical pattern is to establish a branch of the probate court within each county of the state.

When a person dies with assets that require probate, two questions must be answered:

1. Which (state) probate court has jurisdiction? and

2. Which (county) probate court within that state has venue?

The answers to both questions are easy for a decedent who lived in the same city (Omaha, Nebraska) for most or all of her life and who owned property only in that state. Nebraska has jurisdiction, and the county court in Omaha has venue. If a decedent owned a home or owned other property in several different states at her death, each of those states may be able to assert jurisdiction over at least a portion of her estate.

Primary Jurisdiction   The primary jurisdiction to administer an estate, sometimes called *domiciliary administration*, is in the state and county where the deceased had established his or her domicile (permanent home) at the time of death. A person may have several residences but can have only one domicile. If there is confusion about the deceased's domicile, the court may investigate the location where the deceased last voted. Establishing primary jurisdiction is particularly important when more than one state may have jurisdiction and when the estate and inheritance tax laws are more liberal in one state than in another.

All probate assets of the deceased located in the state with primary jurisdiction (the deceased's domicile) are subject to the jurisdiction of the probate court. In addition, personal property located in other states generally—but not always—is subject to the authority of the probate court with primary jurisdiction.

Ancillary Jurisdiction   Jurisdiction over real property owned by the deceased in states other than where his or her domicile is established is subject to ancillary jurisdiction. A separate probate proceeding in each state where the deceased owned real property is necessary to properly convey the real estate to the heirs or beneficiaries. In some states, an ancillary administration may be necessary even to distribute certain personal property.

Venue   Venue refers to the geographic location of the court within a jurisdiction (state) where the probate proceedings should be conducted. Generally, the county where the deceased was domiciled is the preferred venue. If the location of domicile is questionable, the next-preferred venue is the county where the majority of assets are located. Under the Uniform Probate Code, if a proceeding can be maintained in more than one court in the same state, the court where the proceeding is commenced first has the exclusive right to proceed.

Admitting Will to Probate/Appointment of Personal Representative

The first stage of a probate proceeding involves admitting the will for probate (if there is a will) and appointing a personal representative. The proceeding is initiated by an application filed by any interested person. In the usual situation, the person nominated in the will as personal representative is the person who files the application. If there is no will or if the named personal representative does not initiate the proceeding, a relative or a creditor may file the application. Probate proceedings may be initiated formally or informally in either testacy or intestacy situations. State statutes describe in detail the contents of the petition, the notice requirements, and the time and method of hearing the application.

Testate or Intestate   Testate and intestate applications contain essentially the same information: background information about the decedent, identification and relationship of heirs, and a request for appointment of a personal representative. A testate application requests admission of the decedent's will for probate and determination of heirs; an intestate application requests a determination of heirs.

Formal or Informal Proceedings   Probate proceedings may be initiated formally or informally without regard to whether the decedent died testate or intestate. In a testate situation, the application for an *informal proceeding* includes the information stated above, information concerning the will, and a request for informal appointment of a personal representative. The will accompanies the application if it is in the possession of the applicant. By verifying an application for informal probate or informal appointment, the applicant submits personally to the jurisdiction of the court in any proceeding for relief from fraud relating to the application. Letters appointing the personal representative are issued soon after the application is filed.

A petition to probate the will by *formal proceeding* recites all of the same information and requests an order of testacy regarding the will and determination of heirs. Again, the will accompanies the petition if it is in the petitioner's possession. Notice must be given to decedent's heirs, devisees, and the personal representative named in the will of the pending petition for appointment of a personal representative. At the hearing, the named personal representative is appointed if there are no objections. After the hearing, letters of appointment are issued by the court; and notice is given to all creditors, notifying them of the deadline to file their claims with the court. The procedure is the same in an intestate situation, except there is no will to be filed and no order of testacy; however, there is a determination of heirs by the court.

Notice to Creditors and Interested Parties   The UPC requires that notice be given to all interested parties, including creditors, when formal or informal probate proceedings are commenced. Under the UPC, if the address or the identity of any person is unknown, notice is published in a newspaper having general circulation in the county where the hearing will be held. As a practical matter, most jurisdictions require a published notice even though all creditors, beneficiaries, and heirs are known.

The notice to creditors states the deadline for creditors to file their claims with the probate court. The personal representative examines each claim filed to determine its legitimacy. If the personal representative determines the claim should not be paid, a notice of disallowance is filed with the probate court and a copy is mailed to the creditor. If the creditor wishes to dispute the disallowance, he files a petition to allow the claim; and the judge ultimately will make the decision concerning whether or not to allow the disputed claim.

Proof of Will   All wills admitted to probate must be proved by one of the following methods: (1) by a self-proving clause, which simply states that the will was executed properly, or (2) by an affidavit (or testimony) of a witness to the will, reciting what occurred at the time of its execution.

Appointment of Personal Representative

With the Uniform Probate Code came the term *personal representative*, which replaced the term *executor* (used in testate proceedings) and *administrator* (used in intestate proceedings). Some jurisdictions still use the term administrator to identify a personal representative in some situations. For example, *administrator de bonis non* means a successor personal representative, and *administrator with will annexed* means that the personal representative nominated in decedent's will was unable to serve.

The term *executor* or *administrator* identifies a male fiduciary; the term *executrix* or *administratrix* identifies a female fiduciary.

The person nominated in the decedent's will as the personal representative is preferred for appointment unless he is incompetent or is otherwise disqualified. If none of the named individuals can serve, local statute determines those who have priority. If there is no will (intestate), local statute determines who has priority to serve as the personal representative. This statute typically ranks priority according to degree of interest in the estate and degree of relationship to the decedent. The order of priority of appointment under the UPC is:

1. The person nominated in the decedent's will;
2. The surviving spouse of the decedent who is a devisee;
3. Other devisees of the decedent;
4. The surviving spouse of the decedent;
5. Other heirs of the decedent;
6. 45 days after the death of the decedent, any creditor.

Some states require that the personal representative be a resident of the state; others do not require residency. Still others permit a nonresident personal representative to serve if a local process agent is designated.

Before letters of appointment are issued by the court, the personal representative must file an acceptance of appointment with the court. The letters reflect the date of appointment, whether the probate is formal or informal, and whether the decedent was domiciled in that state. Some jurisdictions may issue letters testamentary for a testacy estate and letters of administration for an intestacy estate.

If a personal representative exercises her fiduciary duties improperly, she can be removed for cause; and her letters of appointment can be revoked. Local statutes provide for appointing a successor personal representative.

Bond Requirements   The personal representative may be required to post a bond before letters of appointment are issued. Any person or creditor with an interest in the estate may make a written demand to the court that a personal representative give a bond. If the court determines that a bond is desirable, an order will be issued. The amount of the bond is based upon an estimated value of the estate and of the expected annual income.

No bond is required if the will waives the bond, if the beneficiaries (testate) or the heirs (intestate) file a waiver of bond with the court, or if the court determines a bond is not necessary.

Renunciation by Personal Representative   An individual with priority or nominated by the decedent's will to serve as the personal representative may not wish to take on those responsibilities. Before any letters of appointment are issued, a person may renounce the appointment and may nominate a qualified person to act. The UPC defines a qualified person as one who is at least 21 years of age or who is otherwise suitable to the court.

If an individual is appointed as the personal representative and subsequently becomes unable to serve, each jurisdiction follows its own statutes for appointment of a successor personal representative.

Estate Administration

Estate administration is a liquidation process used for winding up the property and business affairs of the deceased. Once a personal representative is appointed, he or she has the responsibility to initiate the administrative procedures necessary to conclude the decedent's affairs.

1. *Assemble and inventory estate assets.* This includes storing or protecting personal effects and furnishings; transferring bank accounts; collecting income and insurance proceeds; inspecting real estate, leases, and other business ventures; establishing asset values; obtaining appraisals; preparing an inventory of estate assets; and determining if any ancillary proceeding is necessary. If the deceased owned trust assets, those assets must be valued for tax purposes but are not probate assets.

2. *Pay claims, debts, and taxes.* The personal representative must analyze and determine whether to allow or to disallow claims filed with the court and must arrange for payment in the order of priority if the estate is insolvent or is short of funds. Obtaining information to file tax returns is also part of the administration process. Tax returns which may be required are the

decedent's final individual income tax return, federal and state estate tax returns, gift tax return, and the estate's fiduciary income tax return. Arrangements for paying these taxes are necessary to obtain releases from the IRS. If an audit is initiated, the estate usually remains open until an estate tax closing letter is issued by the Internal Revenue Service.

3. *Manage estate assets.* Management of estate assets begins when the probate proceeding is commenced and ends when all assets are distributed. Analysis of liquidity requirements; safeguarding and managing investments, real estate, and business interests; and arranging for cash needs are included among the personal representative's responsibilities.

4. *Account for and distribute assets.* Preparation and filing of interim and final accountings may be required by the court. Timing of certain expenses, such as professional fees and other major expenses, can maximize their income tax benefit to the estate and to the beneficiaries. Once a determination is made concerning entitlements of the beneficiaries, final distribution may be made according to the will or intestate succession statutes.

Forms of Administration   If 120 hours have elapsed since the decedent's death, ***informal administration*** can be requested by application, with appointment of the personal representative made by the registrar of the court. As provided under the UPC, notice is published to announce the personal representative's appointment and to notify creditors to present claims within four months from the date of the first publication of notice.

Informal administration is used when there is no likelihood of disagreements or contests among the beneficiaries or heirs over the administration of the estate or distribution of assets. Court involvement is minimal.

Under ***formal administration***, the court closely supervises management of the estate. A formal administration generally is used when heirs are difficult to determine, devisees are difficult to locate, or controversy is imminent. In these instances, the court determines who the heirs are and may provide special arrangements to hold assets for individuals who are difficult to locate.

If disagreements are likely, if the validity of the will is questioned, or if a controversial issue arises, formal administration is appropriate. If an estate is opened informally and if subsequent problems arise, the estate can be converted to a formal proceeding.

Small estates may be processed through a ***summary administration*** procedure. If it appears from the inventory that the value of the entire estate (less liens and encumbrances) does not exceed the homestead allowance, exempt property, family allowance, costs and expenses of administration, funeral expenses, and medical expenses of last illness, the personal representative may (without notice to creditors) disburse assets immediately to those entitled to receive them. A closing statement is filed with the court, and administration is concluded.

The initial administration typically is opened in the state where the decedent was domiciled. The personal representative appointed in the domicile state is the primary or the *domiciliary personal representative*.

If the decedent owned real property in other states, an *ancillary personal representative* must be appointed in each of those states to convey the real property within that jurisdiction to the heirs or beneficiaries. The ancillary personal representative is responsible for paying any creditors and death taxes due in the ancillary proceeding.

Sometimes the domiciliary personal representative is permitted to serve as the ancillary personal representative also, provided that appropriate documentation is filed in the ancillary state.

Identifying Assets (Probate and Non-Probate)   Probate assets are those which were owned solely by the decedent. Non-probate assets include those owned by the decedent in joint tenancy, life insurance contracts, annuity trusts, revocable trust assets, retirement benefit interests designating specific beneficiaries, and other assets which do not pass under the decedent's will.

Locating the assets and verifying the title are necessary to determine whether the property is a probate or a non-probate item. Careful review is also necessary to determine if an estate tax return must be filed. In some instances, it may be necessary to file an estate tax return but not a probate proceeding. If the deceased transfers all of his or her assets to a revocable trust during life, this eliminates the need for probate but may not eliminate the need to file an estate tax return if the value of the estate exceeds the exemption equivalent.

Estate property is valued as of the date of death even though no probate proceeding or estate tax return is required. At the decedent's death, all estate assets receive a stepped-up basis, which passes to the heirs or to the beneficiaries.

> When the decedent purchased 100 shares of AT&T stock, her basis was $10 a share. When the decedent died, the value was $50 a share. The new, stepped-up basis of $50 passes to the beneficiaries of the decedent's estate.

Stepped-up basis is the value of the asset as of the date of death of the decedent. When the beneficiary receives an asset from the estate, she acquires the new basis (the date of death value). Stepped-up basis is important if the asset is later sold by the beneficiary. The gain or loss of the asset is determined by subtracting the basis of the asset from the sale price. If the sale price exceeds the basis, there is a gain; if the sale price is less than the basis, there is a loss.

> Shannon received 100 shares of AT&T shares from her father's estate. The stepped-up basis on each share was $50. Shannon later sold 50 shares for $70 each. The gain to be reported on her income tax return is $20 a share, or $1,000.

Once probate assets have been segregated from non-probate assets, the probate assets are further classified as either real or personal property. Real estate situated in the domicile state is conveyed to the beneficiaries by the domiciliary personal representative, and real estate located outside the state of domicile is conveyed to the beneficiaries by the ancillary personal representative. Personal property, whether tangible or intangible, generally is conveyed by the domiciliary personal representative.

Inventory and Appraisal of Assets   By statute, the personal representative is required to prepare and file an inventory within a specific time, listing each asset owned by the decedent at death. Each item of property on the list shows its fair market value as of the decedent's death and identifies the type and amount of any encumbrance against the asset.

The personal representative may employ a qualified and disinterested appraiser to ascertain the date-of-death value of any asset. Appraisers are most often employed to value real estate, patents, copyrights, coins, antiques, art objects, silver, jewelry, and any other collections of personal property. If a closely-held business (whether sole proprietorship, partnership, or corporation) is among the assets of the estate, an expert valuation of the business is desirable. Of course, different experts are employed to appraise different kinds of assets.

The UPC requires that appraisals be filed with the inventory, stating the name and address of the appraiser. It is also prudent to include the qualifications of the appraiser, any comparable sales analysis, and the basis upon which the appraisal is made.

Stocks and bonds owned by the decedent are valued according to the securities market. Stockbrokers can provide the date-of-death high and low market value for inventory purposes. The personal representative calculates the average of the high and low values to determine the date-of-death value. Any stock dividends declared but not yet paid at death, as well as any accrued interest on bonds, are listed separately from the security (the stock or the bond) on the inventory. To determine if the declared dividend is included in the gross estate, it is necessary to know the stockholder-of-record date declared by the corporation. (*See the chapter on Business Organizations.*)

> Bertha owned U.S.A., Inc. stock. A $1.50 dividend was declared on September 1, payable September 30 to stockholders of record as of September 15. Bertha died on September 20. Thus, the dividend is listed separately as part of her gross estate. However, had Bertha died on September 10, before the stockholder-of-record date, the dividend would not be listed as a part of the estate.

Cash accounts (checking accounts, money market accounts, certificates of deposits, savings accounts, and similar accounts) are reported on the inventory, with any accrued interest on each account listed separately.

To document asset valuations, letters should be obtained from the stock brokerage firm and the banks showing the value of each asset. This information is retained in the event any valuation is contested by a beneficiary or by the Internal Revenue Service.

The domiciliary personal representative includes all the real estate located in the domicile state and (usually) all personal property of the estate, regardless of where the personal property is located, in the inventory. Real estate located in other states is reported on an inventory filed by the ancillary personal representative for the ancillary jurisdiction.

For federal estate tax purposes, all assets are listed on the estate tax return without regard for the location of the asset.

Management of Assets   The personal representative is a fiduciary of the estate and has a duty to administer the property for the benefit of the creditors and the beneficiaries. The fiduciary is obligated to refrain from all actions of self-dealing, to avoid placing her own interests before those of the estate beneficiaries. The personal representative is charged with making all the administrative decisions. There is also a duty to keep estate assets separate from the assets of the personal representative and others to avoid confusion of title. Another obligation of the personal representative is to make the estate assets productive during the administrative process and to avoid unnecessary loss to the beneficiaries. Throughout the administration, the personal representative is required to use reasonable care and skill and to deal impartially with the beneficiaries. If the exercise of power concerning the estate is improper, the personal representative is liable to interested persons for damage or loss resulting from breach of fiduciary duty.

In a testate estate, the will may provide certain limitations upon the personal representative's powers and duties. In an intestate estate, statutes govern the administrative functions of the personal representative.

Unless otherwise provided in decedent's will, the personal representative has a right to take possession or control of the estate property, except real property or tangible personal property which may be left with or surrendered to the person entitled to it by decedent's will or by operation of law. If necessary the personal representative may initiate an action to recover possession of property if it is not voluntarily delivered.

In some states, the personal representative must obtain a court order to carry on the business of a decedent unless this power is authorized by will. The personal representative who continues the decedent's business without authority may incur personal obligation to those with whom he deals. He may be liable for all losses and must account to the estate for all profits.

A.   Personal Property   Once it is determined that there are adequate funds available to pay taxes, allowances, administration expenses, and creditors, the specific bequests may be paid to the named beneficiaries. As soon as practical to do so, the personal representative may begin making partial distributions of assets to the beneficiaries or heirs. It is prudent to distribute or to sell certain *depreciable assets* such as motor vehicles (including boats and planes) early in the administrative process to minimize liability. Before distributions are made to the residuary beneficiaries, however, the income tax ramifications should be considered both for the estate and for the beneficiaries.

If the estate has insufficient funds to meet its obligations, the personal representative may need to sell property that otherwise would be used to satisfy a bequest. However, personal property specifically bequeathed is sold last.

In the absence of a will, the power of the personal representative to sell personal property is governed by local statute. Particularly where securities are held as an investment, prior authority or subsequent approval by a court is required to sell them.

In many states, the personal representative has an obligation to prepare a distribution proposal to persons entitled to estate assets. The distributee has a right to object to the proposed distribution on the basis of the kind of asset he is to receive or to object to the value of the asset. To evidence the assignment, transfer, or release of assets distributed in kind to heirs or beneficiaries, the personal representative executes appropriate instruments of distribution.

B.   Real Property   If there are adequate funds in the estate to meet its obligations, the real estate may be distributed to those entitled to it at any time during the administration process. Unlike personal property, the heirs (intestate) or the beneficiaries (testate) have an automatic, vested interest in the real property upon the decedent's death. To convey real estate, a personal representative's deed or a *deed of distribution* is filed with the proper county recording office.

If real estate is to be sold, the personal representative must be given specific power under the will to do so. If there is no will or if the will does not grant authority to sell real estate, a petition for sale is filed with the court. After notice is given to all interested persons, the court issues an order authorizing the sale of the real estate if it determines that a sale is appropriate. Before conveyance can be finalized to the new purchaser, IRS tax liens must be released if the estate is subject to estate tax and if no closing letter has been issued by the IRS.

Creditors' Claims   When the personal representative is appointed, notice to creditors is published. This begins the period within which creditors must file their claims or be barred by statute. Under the UPC, the period is four months; but this varies from state to state. When a claim is filed with the court, proof of decedent's indebtedness should be included.   The personal representative determines which claims are valid and objects to disputed (disallowed) claims within the statutory period. Claimants' disallowed claims may be litigated, either in the probate court or in a court of general jurisdiction within the state. If the disputed claim is compromised, the probate court can grant authority for settlement.

After expiration of the time to file creditor claims, the personal representative pays allowed claims. UPC § 3-805 outlines the priority for payment of claims against insolvent estates. Allowances for homestead, exempt property, and family maintenance take priority over all other claims, after which administration expenses, funeral expenses, debts and taxes preferred under federal law, last illness expenses, and debts and taxes preferred under state law are permitted in that order. Some states require insolvent estates to pay claims pro rata.

Settlement of the Estate

Settlement of the estate involves distribution of the remaining assets to heirs (intestate) or to beneficiaries under the will (testate), the personal representative's accounting, and discharge. Filing appropriate tax returns is part of the settlement process; however, this topic is discussed separately at the end of this chapter.

Intestate Distributions Once heirs are determined in an intestate proceeding, the state's intestate succession statutes control distribution. When a decedent gives property to one of her children before her death, this irrevocable gift is called an advancement. The recipient has no obligation to declare the gift; however, states have equalized its potential for unequal treatment among surviving children through the ***doctrine of advancements***. If the recipient of an advancement wants to participate in additional distributions from the intestate estate, he must acknowledge the advancement and must agree that it will be deducted from his share of the estate. If the advancement exceeds his share of the estate, however, he may retain it without sharing in the estate.

Testate Distributions Vague will provisions concerning distribution of assets can create problems for the personal representative and for the court. Different problems may be presented, depending upon whether the testamentary disposition is specific, demonstrative, general, or residuary.

Specific bequests and specific devises A particular item of personal property is a specific bequest; a particular parcel of real estate is a specific devise.

> Stacy's will provided the following specific bequest of stock: "I give 200 shares of Berkshire Hathaway common stock to my mother." Her will further provided a specific devise of real estate: "I give and devise the following described property to my brother Kenneth: Lot 23, Block 66, Park Place Addition, Erie County, Pennsylvania."

Demonstrative bequests If a testamentary disposition is to be made from a specific source, with any deficit to be paid from general funds or residue of the estate if the specific source is insufficient, the bequest is demonstrative.

> Jenny's will has the following demonstrative provision: "I give the sum of $5,000 to John Simon, payable from my savings account at ABC National Bank, but if this is insufficient then from my other property."

General bequests Payment from the general estate rather than from a particular asset indicates a general bequest.

> Pamela's will provided the following general bequest: "I give the sum of $25,000 to Richard Deck."

Residuary Dispositions After all debts and specific bequests and devises have been paid, any gift of the remaining estate (residuary estate) is a residuary disposition.

> Ron's will contains this residuary disposition: "I give the remainder of my estate, wherever located, to my spouse."

A.   Ademption   The rule of ademption applies only in **testate** estates for specific bequests and specific devises. If the property specifically bequeathed or specifically devised no longer exists at the decedent's death, the legatee takes nothing. This is called *ademption by extinction*.

Ademption by satisfaction in testate estates is similar to the doctrine of advancements in intestate estates. If, after signing his will, the testator distributes general or residual property to the beneficiary, the bequest (or devise) may be treated as satisfied.

B.   Abatement   If, after payment of claims and expenses, the testator's remaining property is insufficient to satisfy all bequests and devises, a reduction (abatement) of some or all of the beneficiaries' shares must occur. If the testator's will addresses the method of abatement to be used, that method will apply. More often, however, testator's intent is not known; and the state statute is applied.

Generally, the order of abatement is first from the residuary beneficiaries, then general bequests, then specific and demonstrative bequests. Within a given class of beneficiaries with equal priority, the gifts normally are abated ratably. Decisions in some states have given relatives priority over strangers.

Elective Share   The surviving spouse may (1) accept the dispositive provisions of the decedent spouse's will or (2) elect against the will and take a statutory share of the decedent's augmented estate. Under § 2-201 of the Uniform Probate Code, the surviving spouse of a testator has a right to take an elective share equal to a specific percentage of the augmented estate. The percentage of the augmented estate typically increases with the longevity of the marriage. The UPC provides that the surviving spouse may receive as little as $50,000 or as much as 50% of the augmented estate, depending upon the size of the estate. However, state statutes provide many variations for determining the elective share and for making its election.

Most states provide the surviving spouse with a homestead allowance, exempt property, and family allowance in addition to the elective share. Gifts, insurance proceeds, annuity contracts, probate assets, trust assets, and any other assets in which the decedent may have had an interest are included in computing the augmented estate and eventually the elective share of the spouse. The personal representative and beneficiaries are notified of the surviving spouse's intention to elect against the will and are entitled to receive copies of the computations determining the elective share.

The UPC provides that the surviving spouse must petition the court for the elective share within nine months after the decedent's death or within six months after the probate of the decedent's will, whichever is later. Once the court makes a final determination concerning the elective share, the election becomes irrevocable. If the surviving spouse's right to election is granted, disposition of the decedent's estate is amended; and the remainder of the estate is distributed as provided by the will or by intestate succession.

Renunciation/Disclaimer   The 1990 amendment to the Uniform Probate Code liberalized renunciation provisions. It provides that a person or her representative who is entitled to receive property by will or by intestate succession may disclaim the property within nine months of the decedent's death.

A written disclaimer is filed in the probate court where the administration proceedings are commenced. It must describe the property clearly, must declare the extent of the disclaimer (whether whole or in part), and must be signed by the disclaimant. If an interest in real property is disclaimed under the UPC, a copy of the disclaimer is recorded in the office of the recorder of deeds of the county where the real estate is located.

A person who disclaims is regarded as having predeceased the decedent, and the disclaimer relates back to the date of death of the decedent for all purposes. Thus, the disclaimed interest is distributed to the descendants of the disclaimant unless the decedent's will or trust provides otherwise.

If a federal estate tax return is filed, a copy of the timely filed disclaimer should accompany the return.

Accounting   As part of the administrative process, the personal representative must maintain an accounting of receipts and disbursements and of the assets and liabilities of the estate. In a complex estate or one which extends over a long period of time, the personal representative may file interim accountings with the probate court, with copies to the beneficiaries or heirs.

If an estate is closed informally, the UPC provides that a full written accounting be furnished to the distributees of the estate. Under the formal closing procedures, however, the personal representative files a full accounting with the probate court so that the court may approve the distribution and settlement, with copies provided to distributees. The distributees may execute waivers of the final accounting to prevent details of the accounting from becoming part of the public records. Even with the waivers of the accounting, the court may require the personal representative to furnish the court with a full accounting.

Final Distribution and Discharge   To close an estate informally under the UPC, the personal representative files a verified statement no earlier than six months from her original appointment. (Some state statutes permit the verified statement to be filed earlier). The verified statement reports to the court that a published notice to creditors occurred, the estate has been fully administered and assets distributed, and the distributees received a full accounting. The personal representative is discharged one year from the date the verified statement is filed. Closing informally is inexpensive and efficient.

Under the UPC, a formal closing requires a petition for an order of complete settlement of the estate, which may be filed after one year from the appointment date of the original personal representative. Before an order is entered approving distribution of the estate, a notice to all interested parties and hearing by the Court are required. Once an order is entered, then an order of discharge of the personal representative is issued. This process may take as long as six to eight weeks, depending upon the court's calendar.

The formal closing process is preferred in estates where the parties have not been congenial or cooperative during the administration. Providing copies of the accounting and proposed distribution to the distributees prior to a hearing gives the parties an opportunity to object to any questionable transaction at the scheduled court hearing. The court's review and approval of the accounting and distribution provides protection to the personal representative. The court's findings are conclusive upon all parties. After receipts are filed, an order of discharge is issued to the personal representative, which is used to release any bond and surety.

Estate Taxes

An estate tax, imposed at death by the federal government, is a type of excise tax levied on the privilege of transferring assets. An inheritance tax, imposed by most states, is levied on the privilege of receiving property from a deceased. Federal estate tax liability is determined by the size of the decedent's estate. Inheritance tax is determined by a rate structure and exemptions which vary, depending upon the relationship to the decedent.

When a person dies, the personal representative is responsible for filing not only an estate tax return, if one is required, but also the final 1040 for the decedent and the fiduciary (1041) income tax returns. Careful analysis determines which deductions are reported on which returns to provide full benefit of tax laws to the estate and to beneficiaries. Thus, cautious planning and coordination are required among fiduciaries, accountants, and attorneys.

Decedent's Final Income Tax Return - Form 1040   If the decedent had been filing joint returns with the spouse, then a joint return also may be filed for decedent's final return. Income and deductions pertaining to decedent's assets are included on the final return from the first day of the taxable year through the date of death. If filing jointly, the full year's income and deductions on jointly owned assets are included. Since the personal representative is responsible for filing the final return, he signs on behalf of the decedent, attaching evidence of his appointment.

The due date for the final 1040 remains unchanged: the 15th day of the fourth calendar month following the close of the taxable year. If the decedent's taxable year ended December 31, his final return is due April 15.

It is prudent for the personal representative to investigate whether the decedent filed 1040s for the last three years and to request the Internal Revenue Service to provide a written release of liability on decedent's last three years of 1040s. This request must be made early in the administration process to give the IRS time to review the returns and to provide the release by the time the estate is closed. If the request is made, the estate should not be closed until the release is issued by the IRS. The release does not need to be filed with the court, but it should be retained permanently.

Fiduciary Income Tax Return - Form 1041   The personal representative is responsible for filing the estate's fiduciary income tax return, Form 1041, which is due on the 15th day in the fourth month following the end of the taxable year. Unlike the tax year for the deceased taxpayer's income tax return, the estate's initial fiduciary income tax return may be either a short tax year or a full 12 months, at the election of the personal representative. This election establishes the remaining reporting periods for the estate. If a short tax year is elected for the first year, the estate fiduciary income tax return must be timely filed or the option is lost. Subsequent returns will cover a full 12-month period except the final return. If a 12-month reporting period is elected for the first estate income tax return, the fiscal year ends on the last day of the month preceding the anniversary of the deceased's death. The IRS does not allow the reporting period to extend over 12 months or allow a fiscal year to end in the middle of a month.

If an estate has income of less than $600 annually, a fiduciary return is not required if there are no nonresident, alien beneficiaries. Because the final 1040 income tax return for the decedent reports income received through the date of death, the estate begins reporting income received and deductions incurred as of the day after death. Since the Tax Reform Act of 1986, estates are required to make estimated income tax payments if the estate is open for two or more years after decedent's death.

If trusts were established by the decedent, a separate fiduciary income tax return is filed annually for each trust. Trust income tax returns must be filed on or before the 15th day of the fourth month following the end of the tax year. Trusts are required to make estimated income tax payments.

A. Distributable Net Income - DNI Distributable net income (DNI) was established by the 1954 Internal Revenue Code, and it has a number of functions. DNI is taxable income received by an estate or by a trust. It establishes a ceiling on the fiduciary's distribution deduction, a maximum amount taxable to the beneficiaries, and the character of income distributed to the beneficiaries.

Categories of gross income are reported by the fiduciary of an estate in the same manner as the decedent reported the income: dividends, interest, royalties, rents, capital gains, and other income from assets under the control of the estate fiduciary. The estate income is generated from assets which belong to the estate. Once an estate asset is distributed, then any income earned after the date of distribution must be reported by the distributee.

In the case of specific bequests, any income received by the estate on assets specifically bequeathed is reported according to state law. If applicable state law provides the estate with the right to all income from estate assets, the income is reported on the estate tax return. Once the asset is distributed, the distributee is responsible for reporting income. Some states, however, take the position that the specific legatee has an immediate right to the asset upon the decedent's death and is responsible for reporting any income.

The fiduciary of an estate who prepares the entity's income tax return must furnish each beneficiary with a Schedule K-1, which reports the beneficiary's share of income, deductions, credits, and items of tax preference from the estate or trust. For beneficiaries receiving a *specific bequest* under a will, DNI does not apply; thus, no Schedule K-1 is issued to specific legatees.

B. Income in Respect of Decedent - IRD Income in respect of a decedent (IRD) may include many types of income to which a decedent is entitled at the time of death but has not received. This accrued income is included in the decedent's gross estate and is reported on the federal estate tax return. Examples of income in respect of a decedent are: (1) postmortem bonus or wages; (2) crop shares; (3) dividends declared prior to death but paid after; (4) accrued interest; (5) investment income earned prior to death but unpaid at death; and (6) sales consummated by decedent prior to death but paid after death.

Income in respect of a decedent which is declared on the federal estate tax return is also subject to income tax. However, any federal estate tax assessed as a result of the IRD may be a deduction on the income tax return.

C. Decedent's Funeral and Final Medical Expenses   Funeral expenses include not only the expense of preparing the body for burial, the casket, and funeral service but also a reasonable sum paid for a headstone or monument and a burial plot. Transporting the deceased's body to the place of burial is included as funeral expense. If the deceased made a bequest to a cemetery association for perpetual care of his or her gravesite, this may be deducted as a funeral expense. Funeral expenses must be reduced by the amount of any death benefit received from the Department of Veterans Affairs and the Social Security Administration.

Some community property states provide that funeral and last illness expenses are chargeable in full to the deceased's estate (the same as non-community property states), while others provide that only half of the expenses may be used as deductions. The remaining half is regarded as an obligation of the survivor's share, which is not a part of the deceased's estate. Often a special formula is used to arrive at the estate's share of the funeral expenses when there is both community property and separate property of the deceased.

Schedule J of the federal estate tax return is used to record deductible funeral expenses.

Medical expenses paid before decedent's death are deducted only on the decedent's final 1040. Medical expenses paid within one year of decedent's death may be deducted either (1) on the decedent's final income tax return (Form 1040) or (2) on the estate tax return (Form 706). Medical expenses are reduced by any reimbursements received from insurance or other sources.

Careful analysis is required to obtain the maximum tax advantage for the medical expense deduction. The deduction is wasted on the estate tax return if no estate tax is due; thus, it is more advantageous to deduct the expense on the decedent's final income tax return. On the other hand, if estate tax is due, the medical expense is more valuable as an estate tax deduction than it is as an income tax deduction. The income tax deduction is subject to the adjusted-gross-income floor; the estate tax deduction is not. Another consideration is that the estate tax rate is higher than the income tax rate.

D. Administration Expenses   Deductions for administration expenses must meet two basic requirements: (a) local law must allow the expense and (b) the deduction must fit under one of the following categories: (1) funeral expenses; (2) administration expenses; (3) claims against the estate; or (4) unpaid indebtedness on property included in the decedent's estate.

Administration expenses may include personal representative fees, attorney fees, accountant fees, appraiser fees, surrogate fees, court costs, filing fees, and miscellaneous administration expenses. Miscellaneous administrative expenses may include preservation costs for estate assets, maintenance costs, selling costs relating to estate property, payments for discovering and collecting estate assets, investment advice costs, auctioneer's commissions, and farm management fees. This is not an exhaustive list but is representative of allowable expenses in larger estates.

The above administration expenses may be taken as deductions either on the estate tax return or on the estate's income tax return. It is also possible to split the expenses, claiming part as an fiduciary income tax deduction and part as an estate tax deduction, provided there is no duplication.

Deductions for administrative expenses on a timely filed estate tax return do not require a declared election. However, to allow administrative expenses on the income tax return, the fiduciary files a waiver of the right to include those items on the estate tax return and a statement that no deduction has been taken on the estate tax return for those items. The waiver and statement are filed with the income tax return claiming the deduction. The waiver operates as an irrevocable relinquishment of the estate tax deduction.

Federal Estate Tax Return - Form 706

At death, federal estate tax is imposed upon the transfer of a decedent's property. The tax is imposed upon the taxable estate, which is the value of the total property transferred reduced by allowable deductions. The unified rate schedule (applicable to both gift taxes and estate taxes) is used to calculate the tax liability.

The federal estate tax return must be filed no later than nine months after death unless an extension for time to file has been granted by the Internal Revenue Service. An estate tax return must be filed if the gross estate's value at the date of death exceeds the exemption equivalent—even though no tax is due. The personal representative is responsible for filing the estate tax return and for paying the tax. If no personal representative is appointed, the tax liability falls upon the individuals in possession of the property.

A.   Gross Estate   The gross estate includes full or partial ownership of property owned by decedent at death regardless of its location. In addition to the previously discussed properties included in a decedent's estate, if the deceased held a general power of appointment over specific property, its value is included in the gross estate. A ***general power of appointment*** is exercised in favor of an individual who may direct property to be paid to him personally, to his estate, to his creditors, or to the creditors of his estate.

B.   Alternate Valuation   For purposes of the federal estate tax return, the assets of the estate may be valued either on the date of death or on the alternate valuation date, which is six months after death. Alternate valuation may be used only if it results in reductions of the gross estate, the estate tax, and any generation skipping transfer tax. Once the election is made, it is irrevocable; and all property must be valued in the same manner. If certain assets are sold, distributed, or otherwise disposed of before the end of the six-month period and if the alternate valuation date is elected, the value at the date of the sale or distribution is used.

If there is no numerical date which corresponds to the date of death in the sixth month following the date of death, the alternate valuation date is the last day of the sixth month following the deceased's death.

> Joyce dies on March 31. The alternate valuation date is September 30 because that is the last day of the sixth month.

C.   Special Use Valuation   Provided certain conditions exist, a personal representative may elect to value qualified farm or other closely held business real estate on the basis of actual use, rather than its fair market value. The fair market value is based on the highest and best use to which the property can be utilized. This means that if the real estate has a greater value for residential or commercial development than it does for its actual use, the property is valued at the higher and better use for estate tax purposes. Electing to value the property on the basis of its actual use in farming or other trade or business provides a lower basis for estate tax purposes. This special use election also may be used for standing timber on qualified woodlands. Once made, the election for special use valuation is irrevocable.

If the qualified property later is distributed or sold to someone other than a family member or if it ceases to be used for the same purpose within ten years of the decedent's death, recapture of the estate tax savings may apply. The IRS attaches a special lien on qualified real estate, which continues until the liability for recapturing the estate tax is satisfied or unenforceable. The special use value becomes the income tax basis for real property.

Special use valuation property (included in the decedent's gross estate and allocated to the surviving spouse) is valued at its special use value for purposes of computing the marital deduction. If the decedent solely owned property valued at special use, the full mortgage may be deducted for the special use property.

D.   Taxable Estate   The taxable estate is the gross estate less allowable deductions. Allowable deductions include: (1) funeral and administration expenses, claims against the estate, and unpaid mortgages and debts against estate assets; (2) losses from casualty or theft during estate administration; (3) charitable transfers; and (4) the marital deduction. This is a general classification because in some instances certain taxes are deductible, while in others they are not. Recall that some deductions may be taken both for estate tax and income tax purposes; others may be taken only for one or the other.

Tentative estate tax is computed on the taxable estate. The unified credit and the state death tax credit (if applicable) are applied against the tentative tax to arrive at the estate tax liability. State death tax credit is given for estate, inheritance, or succession taxes paid to a state or to the District of Columbia. The benefits of the unified credit are phased out for taxable estates exceeding $10,000,000. If the unified credit exceeds the estate tax, the unused unified credit cannot be claimed as a refund.

State death tax credit may need to be allocated among those states where estate property is located. The IRS requires proof of payment of the state death taxes because the maximum credit is allowed on the federal estate tax.

Once the tax liability has been determined, estate taxes may be paid in full on the due date of the return (which is nine months after death) or in installments over ten years if the estate qualifies for the installment method.

E.   Marital Deduction   On Schedule M of the federal estate tax return, a marital deduction is allowed for property included in the decedent's gross estate that passes to the surviving spouse. To qualify for the marital deduction, these requirements must be met: (1) The decedent is survived by a spouse; (2) The surviving spouse is a U.S. citizen; (3) Property must pass from decedent to the surviving spouse; *and* (4) The property must be a deductible interest. Property may pass to the surviving spouse by bequest or devise, inheritance, joint property between the decedent and the surviving spouse, power of appointment, or beneficiary designation of insurance on the decedent's life.

Under present law, there is no cap on the value of property passing tax free to the spouse. This applies to gifts between spouses during lifetime and to property distributed to the surviving spouse by decedent's estate. This is known as the unlimited marital deduction which was passed by Congress under the Economic Recovery Tax Act (ERTA) of 1981. The Act permits spouses to distribute assets between each other without tax penalty. More significant, ERTA allows the postponement of estate tax until the death of the second spouse. A surviving spouse is able to enjoy full benefit of assets accumulated during marriage.

F.   Qualified Domestic Trust   A marital deduction may be allowed, even though the surviving spouse is a noncitizen if one of the following exceptions are met: (1) Property passes to the surviving spouse in a qualified domestic trust (QDT); (2) Before the decedent's estate tax return is filed, the spouse becomes a U.S. citizen and meets certain U.S. residency requirements; *or* (3) If the decedent died before December 19, 1992 and was a resident of a foreign country, the denial of the deduction would be inconsistent with treaty provisions.

A qualified domestic trust is a trust which requires at least one trustee to be a U.S. citizen or a domestic corporation, permits no distribution unless the U.S. trustee has the authority to withhold estate tax from the distribution, meets tax regulations for collection of estate tax, and allows the executor to elect the trust to be treated as a QDT. Property passing under the QDT to a noncitizen spouse must meet requirements generally applicable to the marital deduction.

G.   Joint Property   Part I of Schedule E of the federal estate tax return lists property owned only between decedent and the surviving spouse. Although the total value of jointly owned assets is reported, only one-half is included in the decedent's estate and on Schedule M. Thus, the surviving spouse receives a stepped-up basis on only one-half of the jointly owned assets; the remaining half retains the original basis. The same rule applies to any mortgage or lien on joint property between decedent and spouse. One-half of the mortgage or lien is applied against the joint property listed on Schedule M to arrive at the net marital deduction.

Part II of Schedule E of the federal estate tax return reports joint ownership of assets between the decedent and other individuals. If the decedent owned an asset jointly with her spouse and a child, for instance, this asset does not qualify as a marital deduction asset and is reported in Part II of Schedule E. All joint owners are identified, and each shares equally in the decedent's ownership of the asset. (*See prior discussion of joint tenancies.*)

H.   Deductible Items   With the exception of deductions relating to income in respect of a decedent and payment of certain support and maintenance obligations, the estate cannot take double deductions on its estate and income tax returns. Administration expenses and losses during administration may be taken either as a deduction on the estate income tax return *or* as a deduction on the estate tax return. However, if the expense is used as an income tax deduction, the fiduciary must file a formal election waiving the expense as an estate tax deduction.

Funeral, burial, and related expenses are deductible only on the estate tax return. Debts and expenses outstanding as of death not deducted on decedent's final 1040 are deductible on the estate tax return.

Deductions for business and non-business expenses, interest, taxes, and other items accrued at the decedent's death are allowed as deductions for estate tax purposes and as after-death deductions for estate income tax purposes. These deductions are attributable to income in respect of a decedent.

Tax law changes frequently affect the estate planning and probate areas. A skilled legal assistant is one who has mastered the intricate technicalities of the Internal Revenue Code and related statutes. Armed with this invaluable knowledge, the attorney-legal assistant team is better able to assist clients to effect the most efficient means to preserve and to distribute estates.

The review of estate planning and probate contained in this chapter, together with the following Self-Test, provide a summary of the type of material tested in this subsection of the CLA® examination. Additional study references are contained in the Bibliography section of this *Review Manual.*

Estate Planning and Probate Self-Test

Allow an uninterrupted thirty-minute period to answer all questions. At the end of thirty minutes, check your answers against those in the Answer Key Section of this Manual. Deduct two points for each incorrect answer (100 total possible points). Unanswered questions are counted as incorrect answers. Follow directions carefully and observe the time limit precisely to provide an accurate self-assessment.

Choose the most correct answer to each of the following questions unless a specific question instructs you to do otherwise.

1.   True or False.   Elective share means that beneficiaries may choose those assets which they want to have distributed to themselves.

2.   True or False.   The purpose of estate administration is to collect the decedent's assets, pay claims against the estate, and distribute whatever remains.

3.   True or False.   All wills admitted to probate must be "proven" either by witnesses who recognize the decedent's signature or by a special seal of the court.

4.   True or False.   A testate estate means that the decedent has died with a valid will that disposes of his or her property.

5.   True or False.   An ancillary proceeding is required if the decedent owed creditors in a different state.

6.   True or False.   A testamentary trust is one which takes effect if the grantor becomes incapacitated.

7.   True or False.   Bequeath means to give real property by will.

8.   True or False.   A Totten trust is distinguished as one created by a person who deposits money in his name as trustee for another, which is made in contemplation of death.

9.   True or False.   A nuncupative will is one written in the testatrix's own handwriting.

10.   True or False.   Gift tax exclusions apply to annual gifts from one person to another which are valued at $3,000 or less.

11.   True or False   A generation-skipping transfer tax applies to direct skips only, such as from grandmother to a grandchild.

12.   True or False.   Pretermitted children are those who were adopted by the decedent.

13.   A sprinkle trust:

   a.   allows the trustee to decide which beneficiaries will receive distributions.
   b.   permits the trustee to control the amount of distributions.
   c.   permits the trustee to use her own judgment in distributing income.
   d.   all of the above.
   e.   none of the above.

14. Abatement occurs when assets of an estate are insufficient to pay:

    a.   creditors.
    b.   administration costs.
    c.   funeral expenses.
    d.   devisees.
    e.   all of the above.
    f.   none of the above.

15. True or False. By definition, *inter vivos* trusts are those trusts which are created and become effective during the lifetime of the trust beneficiary.

16. True or False To obtain payment from the estate, secured claims must be filed directly with the court; and a copy must be sent to the personal representative.

17. True or False Property in escheat goes to the state because there remains no living person who is a legitimate heir of the decedent.

18. True or False. A trustee may exercise only those powers specifically given to her by the trust document.

19. True or False. *Per stirpes* means taking by the roots or stocks of lineage from the decedent.

20. True or False. A gift list is a formally executed change in the terms of a will.

21. A personal representative of an estate is comparable to:

    a.   an executor.
    b.   an administrator.
    c.   a fiduciary.
    d.   all of the above.

22. A trust or an estate recognizes gain or loss when property is:

    a.   distributed under intestate succession.
    b.   distributed as part of the residuary estate.
    c.   sold to satisfy a specific monetary gift.
    d.   sold during administration.

23. A legacy is:

a.   any personal property given under a will.
b.   any realty given under a will.
c.   any property held in trust.
d.   any inheritance.

24.   One element necessary for every estate proceeding is:

a.   fiduciary income tax return.
b.   formal administration.
c.   federal estate tax return.
d.   none of the above.

25.   The formal document issued by the court appointing the personal representative of an estate is called:

a.   registrar's statement.
b.   letters of personal representative.
c.   order of appointment.
d.   statement of personal representative.

26.   True or False.   A fiduciary is a representative of a trust or of an estate.

27.   True or False.   If the grantor of a trust reserves the power to take back title to the trust property for himself, the trust is a taxable asset upon his death for estate tax purposes.

28.   True or False.   A codicil is an oral will.

29.   True or False.   An intestacy proceeding will result from a disclaimer of a surviving spouse who was the beneficiary under the last will and testament of her husband.

30.   True or False.   Decedent dies, leaving his gold mine and 100 shares of Ajax Corporation stock in trust to his son, "to pay income to Bertha for life, remainder to my son Richard." Six months later, Ajax declares a quarterly dividend. The dividend should be allocated proportionately between Bertha and the Richard.

31.   Daniel Dapper is a widower with two living, adult children (Ruth and Carl) and two deceased children (Susan and Karen). Ruth has no children. Carl has two children. Susan is survived by three children, all of whom are adults. Karen is survived by one adult child. Dan dies intestate. Based on

these facts, which of the following statements is most accurate under the UPC?

a. Ruth and Carl each receives one-half of Daniel's estate.
b. Ruth, Carl, and Karen's child each receives one-fourth of Daniel's estate; Susan's children each receive one-twelfth..
c. Ruth and Carl each receives one-fourth of Daniel's estate; the children of Susan and Karen each receives one-eighth.
d. Ruth and Carl each receives one-fourth of Daniel's estate; the children of Susan and Karen each receives one-sixteenth.

32. Inter vivos trusts are:

a. irrevocable trusts only.
b. testamentary trusts.
c. trusts created and effective during the grantor's lifetime.
d. trusts created during the grantor's life but not effective until his death.

33. A spendthrift trust is:

a. one created for a spouse who spends money too freely.
b. one created for a beneficiary who is either physically or mentally disabled.
c. one created for a beneficiary who receives public assistance.
d. one created for a beneficiary who is unable to manage money.

34. Under the statutes of most states, a testatrix may:

a. disinherit any heir, regardless of his or her relationship.
b. disinherit any heir except his or her spouse.
c. disinherit any heir except his or her children.
d. disinherit any heir except pretermitted children.

35. Which of the following is a proper general bequest:

a. 25 shares of AT&T stock
b. all AT&T stock owned by me at my death
c. all real estate owned by me at my death
d. the $500 certificate of deposit in my safety deposit box

36. True or False.   Harold leaves "all of the rest and residue of my personal property, wherever situated," to Luther. This is a valid residuary gift.

37. True or False.   Thatcher, a college professor, signs a will in which he leaves certain property to "my college." Thatcher graduated from Rutherford College and teaches at Baines College. Since a latent ambiguity exists concerning which college should receive the property, a court may consider evidence outside the will to determine which college Thatcher intended to receive the property.

38. True or False.   When construing the provisions of a will, courts use a "reasonable person" standard to determine how the testator intended to dispose of his property.

39. True or False.   Joe Bartlett executed a will in 1989, leaving the bulk of his estate to his surviving children. Joe and his wife had three adult children at the time. Unknown to Joe, he also had an older daughter from a college relationship many years ago. At Joe's death, this daughter will be included in the category of Joe's "surviving children" as a pretermitted heir.

40. True or False.   Bill executes a will which leaves his summer cabin to Margie. Bill borrows $5,000 one year later and gives a security interest in the cabin as collateral for the loan. If Bill dies without repaying the loan, the UPC requires Margie to take the property subject to the security interest unless some different provision is made in the will.

41. True or False.   Descent and distribution in a particular state is governed by statute and by common law.

42. True or False.   The informal probate procedures of the UPC contain more safeguards against possible abuse by the personal representative, but they are not much easier to use than the formal probate procedures are.

43. True or False.   Joe executes a will which provides, "All of my property shall go to my son and daughter-in-law, Dick and Jane. If Dick predeceases Jane, then all of my property shall go to my close friend, Isaac." Dick and Jane die simultaneously. Several years later, Joe dies. On these facts, Isaac should inherit Joe's estate.

44. True or False.   QTIP property is that property which qualifies for a marital deduction in which the spouse has a life income interest.

45. True or False.   Aliens cannot make a will that is intended to be probated in the United States.

46.   True or False.   Because a partnership is a pass-through entity for tax purposes, the proceeds of life insurance on a deceased partner's life pass through the partnership and are included in the deceased partner's gross estate if she owned 50% or more of the partnership.

47.   Which of the following statements is least correct?

    a.   The grantor controls disposition of a QTIP trust.
    b.   The grantor controls disposition of a marital trust.
    c.   The grantee controls disposition of a family trust.
    d.   The trustee controls disposition of a sprinkle trust.

48.   Sam and Sue are married to each other and own their home in joint tenancy. Sam dies. The family home now:

    a.   is Sue's sole property.
    b.   may be included among the bequests made in Sue's will.
    c.   is non-probate property.
    d.   "a" and "c" are correct.

49.   A beneficiary who wishes to renounce a bequest may do so by:

    a.   presenting himself to the court and orally renouncing the bequest.
    b.   refusing to accept the assets or to negotiate any checks received.
    c.   filing a written disclaimer with the court within the required time.
    d.   notifying the personal representative in writing not to distribute assets from the estate to him as a beneficiary.

50.   Fred is both the owner and the beneficiary on a policy insuring the life of Wilma, his wife. The policy was issued in 1992. In 1993 Wilma died. Three months later, Fred died. Which of the following statements is most correct concerning estate tax treatment of the insurance policy?

    a.   The cash value of the policy is included in Wilma's gross estate.
    b.   The face value of the policy is included in Wilma's gross estate.
    c.   The cash value of the policy is included in Fred's gross estate.
    d.   The face value of the policy is included in Fred's gross estate.

Chapter 14
FAMILY LAW

Most folks are about as happy as they make up their minds to be.

— Abraham Lincoln

Family law or domestic relations law covers many topics related to the status of the family and its members. Among them are adoption, marriage, divorce (called dissolution of marriage in some jurisdictions), conservatorships, guardianships, and the like. The family law practitioner wears many hats in serving the various needs of his or her family practice clients. Both lawyers and legal assistants who work in the area of family law frequently find themselves embroiled in a complex legal and psychological quagmire with people who are in the worst personal crisis they may ever face. Professionals in this field of law may be likened to ringmasters and trapeze artists in a perpetual circus of human emotion.

Although much of a family law practice is based on the laws of a particular state, there are general principles that exist in the majority of states as well as minority positions that should be familiar to all applicants for this section of the CLA® exam. For example, common law marriages cannot be created in most states; however, the examinee must be familiar with the requirements for a common law marriage in those states that allow them. In addition, certain uniform laws, federal statutes, and federal constitutional provisions relate to various aspects of family law.

References are made to major family law cases for resource and reference purposes throughout this chapter. Examination applicants are not expected to cite specific cases as part of the examination process.

Historical Background

The family unit can be found at the center of nearly every society since Biblical times. We can trace the laws and traditions of the typical American family back to Anglo-Saxon England, through their evolution under Norman rule, and continuing into their transplant to America.

In feudal England, the custom of *betrothal* developed, by which the bride's family agreed to transfer custody of the bride to the groom. In turn, the groom agreed to protect, care for, and make a settlement for the bride. This financial settlement, which was paid by the bride's family, came to be known as *dower*. The Church and ecclesiastical courts established procedures for a marriage, including publication of notice (called *banns*) of the intended marriage; performance of the marriage ceremony in the Church; and gift of a ring by the groom to the bride. The bride frequently gave a ring to the groom as well. Ecclesiastical courts, which came to be known as courts of chancery and then as equity courts, also had the power to annul or terminate a marriage on established grounds. This may account, at least in part, for the continued role of equity courts in today's divorce proceedings.

Women had few, if any, legal rights under early English matrimonial law. They could not inherit or own property and were themselves considered property, first of their fathers and then of their husbands. In addition to caring for and protecting his wife, a dutiful husband was expected to beat his wife with a stick no thicker than his thumb when she was disobedient. The legal disabilities of women were shed, one by one over hundreds of years, and were replaced with legal rights that ultimately placed women in America on an equal legal footing with men.

Children likewise were the property of their fathers until they were either betrothed (females) or emancipated (males). Their labor was for the benefit of their father. This fact, coupled with a high incidence of childhood illness and death, may account for the many large families in England and in early America. In the extremely rare event of divorce, the husband always retained custody of the unemancipated children. It was not until child labor laws were passed in early twentieth-century America that courts began — coincidentally and increasingly — to award young children, who had become financial liabilities rather than assets, to their mothers.

Autonomy of the early family was sacrosanct, and its governance was determined solely by the husband/father as the family head. The government declined to interfere except in cases of extreme maltreatment of a family member. Against this historical backdrop, family law in America has evolved and developed over time to meet the needs and standards of an ever-changing society.

Marriage

Although family law comprises many facets, substantially all of them are related directly or indirectly to the marital relationship. *Marriage* is the legal union of one man and one woman, traditionally for the purpose of creating a family.

The traditional marriage always has been fostered by the government as the basic social, economic, and religious unit of American society. Until the last few decades, several assumptions generally were accepted concerning marriage: (1) marriage was designed to last until the death of one of the spouses and would be ended during their joint lives only on very serious grounds; (2) the marital union was to be emphasized over the personality of either spouse; (3) the primary purpose of marriage was to have and to rear children; and (4) within the family, the husband-father was the predominant decision maker and provided for the family's material needs, while the wife-mother tended the house and the children.

The right to marry is a basic freedom that is protected by the U. S. Constitution, provided that parties meet the legal qualifications for marriage under state law. When a state statute has restricted the right to marry on unconstitutional grounds, however, the Supreme Court has not hesitated to strike it down. Examples of those statutes declared unconstitutional include one that prohibited prison inmates from marrying and one that prevented those with child support arrearages from marrying. Most significant were the miscegenation statutes that existed in many states. A *miscegenation* statute prevents persons from marrying across racial lines. The Supreme Court held that a state's restriction against marriage was unconstitutional when it was based solely on racial classifications. *Loving v. Virginia*, 338 U.S. 1 (1967).

Legal Requirements

As basic as the right to marry is, that right is subject to certain valid restrictions. Every state has established legal requirements to enter into a valid marriage. These generally involve competence to marry (no legal disabilities exist), gender, and a good faith agreement to create a genuine marital relationship. Among the types of legal disability contemplated by most marriage statutes are consanguinity, being under the minimum age of consent, health, mental incapacity, and a preexisting marriage by one or both parties.

Consanguinity   *Consanguinity* refers to the blood relationship between persons who intend to marry. All states and the District of Columbia forbid marriage between parent and child, brother and sister, and uncle and niece. Marriage between first cousins also is forbidden in thirty states. Nearly all courts have held that the prohibition applies similarly to relatives by half-blood, and most courts extend the prohibition to step-relatives. A purported marriage between relatives in this group is void. Moreover, the criminal charge of *incest* may result from having sexual relations with any person within the prohibited group of relatives, whether marriage occurs or not.

> Harry marries Wilma. Wilma has a daughter, Dora, by a prior
> marriage. Harry and Wilma divorce. Harry now is free to marry
> Dora, since her relationship as a step-daughter ended with Harry
> and Wilma's divorce.

Surprisingly, many — but not all — courts allow marriage by persons who are related only by adoption.

Minimum Age   All states have established a minimum age (typically 18 or 19) that must be reached before a person legally may consent to marry. One who is too young to consent to marriage under state law must obtain the consent of a parent or guardian before the marriage can take place.

Health Standards   Most states require parties to meet certain health standards before they can marry, that is, they must be free of venereal disease. Many states now have included AIDS in the health standard requirement.

Mental Capacity To be competent to marry, parties must have the mental capacity to understand the nature, effect, and consequences of marriage *at the time of the marriage*. The level of capacity is different for marriage than it is for entering into other types of contracts. To annul a marriage on this ground, the petitioning spouse must prove lack of capacity by clear and convincing evidence.

> Harry married Wilma. Two years later, Harry was committed to
> a mental institution. Wilma sought an annulment based on lack of
> mental capacity.

> Harry married Wilma sometime during a week-long drinking
> binge. One week later, Harry sought an annulment based on lack
> of mental capacity.

In the first example, Wilma likely will lose unless she can show that Harry was mentally incapable of understanding the concept of marriage or consenting to it at the time the marriage took place. In the second example, Harry likely will win based on his intoxication at the time of the marriage.

Preexisting Marriage   Neither party can be married to someone else at the time the marriage. This situation not only prevents the offending party from entering into the second marriage lawfully, but also subjects her to criminal prosecution for *bigamy* (being married to two different people at the same time).

Mutual Consent   Both parties must consent to the marriage, including all of its rights and responsibilities, voluntarily and in good faith. Consent given under duress (genuine threat of imminent physical harm) can provide a basis for annulment. Similarly, a marriage entered into for a limited purpose (to gain legal alien status to remain in the United States, for example) may be declared a sham marriage and invalidated on that basis.

Gender   Statutes in all states require individuals who apply for a marriage license to be of opposite gender. Court challenges to this statutory requirement have been largely unsuccessful, even on equal protection grounds.

Because the equal rights amendment to Hawaii's state constitution is more expansive than the federal Equal Rights Amendment, Hawaii's Supreme Court has held that banning same-gender couples from marrying may violate the state constitutional provision unless the ban is narrowly drawn and serves a compelling state interest. Anticipating that homosexual couples would rush to Hawaii to marry and then return to their home states, many states already have declared that regardless of how Hawaii resolves the question, no homosexual marriage will be recognized in their jurisdictions.

A homosexual relationship between consenting adults remains a crime in some states. The U. S. Supreme Court has upheld such statutes against challenges based on privacy. *Bowers v. Hardwick*, 478 U.S. 186 (1986).

Formalities   All states have enacted some process to formalize marriages. Whether the formalities are mandatory or discretionary varies from state to state. If a formality is mandatory, the marriage is void unless the formality takes place. If it is discretionary, absence of the formality does not invalidate the marriage, although the offending parties may be subject to criminal penalties or to civil liabilities.

Typical among the formalities required by states are blood tests, grant of a marriage license, a waiting period before the marriage ceremony, some type of solemnization (ceremony) by an authorized official (an ordained minister or a judge, for example), and registration of the marriage (for example, with a county clerk or in the state office of vital statistics). Not every state requires all of these formalities, but all states require some portion of them.

Types of Marriage

Generally, a marriage validly created in one state is valid in all other states, even though it could not have been created in those states. One possible exception is Hawaii's allowance for the possibility of homosexual marriage, *supra*. Marital status can be accomplished in a number of ways.

Ceremonial Marriage   The traditional marriage in the United States is a *ceremonial marriage*. All states have enacted statutes to allow ceremonial marriage according to formalities that also are set by statute (discussed *supra*).

Common Law Marriage   A *common law marriage* is an agreement between a man and a woman to enter into a marital relationship, to cohabit, and to hold themselves out as husband and wife without complying with the formalities of a ceremonial marriage. Common law marriages can be created only in thirteen states (Alabama, Colorado, Georgia, Idaho, Iowa, Kansas, Montana, Ohio, Oklahoma, Pennsylvania, Rhode Island, South Carolina, and Texas) as well as in the District of Columbia. These states have declared either by statute or by judicial interpretation that since marriage is a civil contract, no specific ceremony is required.

Common law marriages arose at a time in history when it often was difficult to find a minister or appropriate official to solemnize the marriage. Therefore, all that was required were words of present intent to live together as a married couple, spoken by each party to the other. Once the words were spoken, the couple was married. This is different from a promise to marry at a future time, which is an engagement or betrothal. Rather than words, today's courts largely look to the actions of the parties. They must have the legal capacity to marry; they must have agreed to become husband and wife (some states require express words, others will infer agreement based on conduct); they must cohabit openly and hold themselves out as husband and wife in the community. Whether all of these requirements are met usually is not determined until a much later time, when the case comes before a court for some reason.

If a valid common law marriage is created, it is recognized as valid by most other states.   Thus, if the couple separates either in the state where they contracted the marriage or in a state that recognizes the marriage, they must obtain a divorce to terminate their legal relationship. Legal problems arise when the couple moves from state to state, especially when they move to a state that neither sanctions nor recognizes common law marriage. States in this category include Connecticut, Illinois, Indiana, Minnesota, Mississippi, Missouri, Rhode Island, South Dakota, Vermont, and Wisconsin.

> Harry and Wilma formed a valid common law marriage in Iowa and moved to Illinois several years later, where they continued the relationship for 25 more years. Harry became ill and died without a will. Wilma's claim against Harry's estate will fail because Illinois does not recognize common law marriage, regardless of where it was created.

> Hunaan and Wanda agreed to live together as if married and held themselves out as husband and wife in Nebraska, where common law marriages cannot be created. They occasionally traveled to Iowa, which allows common law marriage, for a week or so at a time to visit Wanda's parents over the following 20 years. During these visits, they continued to hold themselves out as husband and wife. If Hunaan dies and if Wanda applies for Social Security survivor benefits, a Nebraska court likely will recognize the common law marriage (created in Iowa) even though the couple always was domiciled in Nebraska.

The result in the second example is even more probable because a governmental benefit is involved.

Putative Marriage   A *putative marriage* is one in which at least one of the parties contracted to marry in good faith and without knowledge that some legal impediment existed to prevent a valid marriage. For example, the intended bride may represent that she is old enough to marry or that she has not been married previously. In a putative marriage, the innocent spouse makes a good faith commitment and goes through the ceremonial requirements for marriage.

A few states have acknowledged the putative spouse doctrine by statute to provide some degree of protection for the innocent spouse.

Successive Marriages   Within the American legal system, monogamy is the rule. No state permits a person to be married to more than one person at one time. When this situation occurs, successive marriages exist; and the offending spouse may be subject to criminal charges (bigamy for being "married" to two persons at once; polygamy, for more than two). The results for the putative spouse will vary depending on the statutes in his or her state.

When there is evidence of more than one marriage, the law presumes the most recent one to be valid. This presumption may be rebutted, however, by proof from the first spouse that the marriage never was terminated legally.

> Hans and Winona entered into a common law marriage in South Carolina. Hans later deserted Winona and moved to California, where he entered into a ceremonial marriage with Melanie without telling her of his first marriage. One year later, Hans died. Both wives filed claims against his estate.

In this example, a court will presume that Melanie's marriage to be valid, because it is the more recent of the two. However, if Winona can prove that she and Hans never were divorced, the legal presumption is rebutted; and Winona's marriage will be recognized as the valid one. Where does that leave Melanie? Since Melanie and Hans lived in California, which is one of the states with a putative spouse statute, she will be permitted to pursue her claim against Hans's estate on an equal footing with Winona, the lawful wife.

If Hans and Melanie had lived in a state without a putative spouse statute but where common law marriages from other states are recognized (Colorado, for example), Melanie would not be allowed to proceed with her claim. She is not the lawful spouse, and no putative spouse statute protects her. On the other hand, if Hans and Melanie had lived in a state where common law marriages from other states are not recognized (Indiana, for example), Winona could not be recognized as a lawful spouse at all; and Melanie would prevail.

Proxy Marriage A *proxy marriage* is contracted or solemnized by one or more agents of the parties rather than by the parties themselves. Proxy marriages become slightly more prevalent during times of war. In peace time, they are rare. If a particular state requires the personal presence of parties to a marriage, a proxy marriage is invalid. However, if state statutes are silent on the point, they may be interpreted to allow proxy marriages.

By federal statute, a marriage by proxy may not be used to circumvent federal immigration laws. For instance, a foreign national who lives outside the United States cannot use marriage by proxy to become married to a United States citizen and thus gain entry to the United States.

Breach of Promise to Marry

If Harry and Wilma agree to marry and if Harry later changes his mind, approximately fifty percent of all states will allow Wilma to sue for breach of promise under a contract theory. This type of suit also is known as a *heart balm action*, because it serves as a balm to the plaintiff's broken heart. Most breach-of-promise-actions are brought by women but may be filed by either party in substantially all of the states that recognize this type of suit.

In states where heart balm actions are allowed, most courts are willing to award consequential (special) damages for the expenses incurred in reliance on the promise of an upcoming wedding. Many courts, however, are more reluctant to award damages for the improved financial position that the plaintiff has lost because of the breach. Specific performance never is granted.

Gifts   When couples become engaged, the man frequently gives the woman an engagement ring to celebrate the event. If the engagement is broken, most state courts will require the ring to be returned. This is especially true if the ring is extremely expensive or if it is a family heirloom.

Gifts given to each other before the couple's engagement typically remain the property of the person to whom they were given. Gifts given after the engagement, particularly very expensive gifts, typically follow the general rule for engagement rings and must be returned. If a friend or a family member gives a gift in contemplation of the marriage, that person can enforce return of the gift if the engagement is broken.

Contracts Related to Marriage

Individuals may make some types of agreements before marriage. These agreements may restrict the right to marry until a certain event or condition has occurred, or they may restrict the right to remarry. By far, the most common is the type of agreement made in relation to a planned marriage.

A contract that forever restricts the right to marry probably is not enforceable, even if it is supported by consideration. Contracts supported by consideration (or conditional gifts made) which restrict marriage until a specified, reasonable event occurs (completion of college education or reaching the age of 25, for instance) are much more likely to be enforced by a court. Courts also will enforce contracts restricting the right to remarry if the restriction serves some beneficial purpose, such as rearing children.

> As part of a divorce settlement, Harry and Wilma agree that if either of them remarries before their youngest child reaches age 20, that party will forfeit $10,000 of his or her property to the other party. This agreement was upheld by an Iowa court.

A married couple also may create contracts to govern their legal separation, which are submitted to a court for approval in a legal separation proceeding and sometimes, but not always, are merged into a divorce decree at a later time.

Antenuptial Agreement   Sometimes called a prenuptial agreement or a premarital agreement, an ***antenuptial agreement*** is created prior to marriage and sets out the terms that will govern the parties' financial matters in relation to property and support in the event of death or divorce. An antenuptial agreement is particularly useful in second marriages where one or both parties have been married previously and have acquired both children and property from the previous marriage.

Section 3 of the ***Uniform Prenuptial Agreement Act*** (UPAA) allows parties to contract concerning:

1.   Rights and duties of each party in any property of the other or both of them, whenever and wherever located;
2.   The right to buy, sell, use, transfer, exchange, abandon, lease, consume, expend, assign, create a security interest in, mortgage, encumber, dispose of, or otherwise manage and control property;
3.   Disposition of property upon separation, marital dissolution, death, or the occurrence or nonoccurrence of any other event;
4.   Modification or elimination of spousal support;
5.   Making of a will, trust, or other arrangement to carry out the provisions of the agreement;
6.   Ownership rights in and disposition of the death benefit from a life insurance policy;
7.   Choice of law governing construction of the contract;
8.   Any other matter, including personal rights and obligations, not in violation of public policy or a statute imposing a criminal penalty.

Section 3(b) of the UPAA further provides that the right of a child to support cannot be affected by a premarital agreement.

In many states, the consideration to support enforceability of an antenuptial agreement is the marriage itself. The UPAA, however, provides that the agreement is enforceable without consideration.

In most states, an antenuptial agreement will be enforced if it:

1.   Is in writing;

2. Is made after full disclosure by each party of his or her assets; and
3. Demonstrates that each spouse has sufficient support (is fair and reasonable).

To determine whether a particular agreement is fair and reasonable, a court will consider the overall circumstances, including the situation of the parties in relation to each other; their respective ages, health, and experience; their respective property; their family ties and connections; the needs of each party; and factors tending to prove (or to disprove) that the agreement was made with understanding.

Cohabitation Agreements   The term cohabit refers to a couple living together, whether married or not. A ***cohabitation agreement***, however, is a contract between two individuals who intend to live together for the foreseeable future without becoming married. Their contract typically covers property and support matters during the period of cohabitation as well as upon separation.

Under the traditional view — and still the majority view, at least for now — courts will not enforce this type of contract between unmarried partners, holding that a contract to cohabit is nothing more than a contract for prostitution. As such, it violates public policy. The dramatic rise in cohabiting couples since the 1960s, however, has prompted courts to take another look at the issue. Many (but certainly not all) courts have taken a somewhat softened view by showing a willingness to ignore the sexual aspect of the relationship and to deal only with the pooling of property, resources, and energy. They have used various legal theories to do this: express contract, implied contract, *quantum meruit*, partnership, and joint venture, for example.

The landmark case in this area law is *Marvin v. Marvin*, 557 P.2d 106 (Cal. 1977), which involved the actor Lee Marvin and his female companion of seven years, who had gone so far as to change her last name to his even though they were not married. The case was heard and appealed three times, ultimately resulting in payment to the female companion of a mere $104,000. The case received significant coverage in the national press; and from it, the term ***palimony*** was coined to denote support paid to an ex-pal as opposed to an ex-spouse.

Even in those state courts where cohabitation agreements have won some degree of acceptance, judges continue to require that no part of the agreement can be conditioned upon sexual activity between the couple. Otherwise, a cohabitation agreement performs much the same function as an antenuptial agreement. Unlike antenuptial agreements, however, courts generally do not require cohabitation agreements to be in writing despite the fact that many of them are.

Although a number of family law scholars and judges have taken strong, opposing positions on this topic, it remains unresolved.

Separation Agreements   A *legal separation* (called separation from bed and board in older cases) is a declaration by a court that the parties may live apart; yet, they remain married. There is no law that requires married parties to live together, of course; but unless the couple obtains either a decree of divorce or a decree of legal separation, nearly all of their marital rights and duties continue whether they live together or not.

Legal separation is useful for the couple that wants a divorce but does not yet qualify under a particular state's residency requirement, for example. By seeking a legal separation, they can obtain a court decree that divides property, grants custody of children, and awards support. When the residency requirement is met, the parties can use a summary proceeding to merge the decree of separation into a divorce decree.

In other situations, parties may seek a legal separation without any intention to divorce. Religious beliefs or the social stigma of divorce, for example, makes legal separation a viable, permanent solution for some parties.

Similar to a property settlement agreement in a divorce proceeding, parties may prefer to reach a voluntary agreement concerning property division and the like instead of leaving these decisions entirely to the court. They may wish to include recommendations concerning child custody and support, although matters related to children are not binding on the court.

If the couple reconciles (resumes their marital relationship) after a separation agreement is signed, the separation agreement is terminated. However, if property was transferred to one party or the other as a result of the agreement, the conveyance is not affected. If the conveyance was made to waive inheritance rights, the waiver also may survive.

Family Relationships

This section considers the legal status of intact families and the legal relationships of family members. The traditional family consists of a husband, a wife, and one or more children. The law always has recognized that family members have certain obligations to each other and are entitled to certain benefits. The nature of those legal obligations and legal benefits has changed dramatically over time and continues to change at an even faster rate today. Courts are challenged to balance the rights of individual family members against the privacy rights generally associated with the family unit.

Spousal Rights and Duties

Within an intact family, the husband historically was the undisputed head of the basic family unit. Husbands and wives were treated as one person under the law, with the husband as the legal spokesperson for the marital union. He controlled all property and made all decisions concerning members of the family, including his wife. Over the last 150 years, this situation gradually has evolved to a point where husbands and wives are more or less equal partners in a marriage, at least as far as the law is concerned.

Obligations of Support   The husband had a legal obligation to provide food, clothing, shelter, and medical care (the necessities of life) to his wife under traditional common law rules. This became known as the *necessaries doctrine*. The wife had no similar obligation for her husband's basic needs. Older cases reflect that as long as the necessaries were being provided by a husband, judges were reluctant to interfere with their quality or the manner in which they were provided. The statutes of most states now apply the necessaries doctrine equally to both husband and wife, and most states consider legal fees part of the group of necessary expenses for which a spouse is liable if they are incurred to defend a criminal charge.

> Wilma became so angry one day that she left her husband, Harry. Over the next two years, Wilma fell on hard times and ultimately began receiving public assistance. The state agency filed suit against Harry for support, seeking reimbursement of the money that it had paid on Wilma's behalf.

Even though Wilma in the example abandoned her husband, he nevertheless is responsible to provide support for her, at least for as long as the marriage continues.

Until recently, if a spouse became seriously ill, nearly all of a couple's assets had to be depleted before one of the spouses could qualify for government subsidy (of nursing home care, for example). This often forced the healthy spouse to sell the family home and to apply all but a small portion of the proceeds toward the ill spouse's care. Under current law, the healthy spouse is allowed to exempt the primary residence from the depletion requirement, up to a maximum of $125,000.

When a spouse incurs debt for things other than necessities, the other spouse generally is not liable.

> Harry and Wilma are married. Harry has a credit card in his own name (Wilma did not sign the credit agreement and is not a signer on the account). Harry used the card to purchase a Rolex watch and then failed to pay the credit card issuer. Wilma is not liable for this debt. A Rolex watch is not a necessity, and she did not sign anything that requires her to pay charges on the account.

If Wilma were signed on the credit card account, she could be forced to pay the debt without regard to whether the watch was a necessity.

Property of Women   In early England, women generally could not own property other than their own clothing and jewelry. Even property inherited from a wife's family became the property of her husband. This common law tradition continued into the American colonies and persisted until the mid-1800s, when women's property acts first were passed by state legislatures. Regardless of their marital status, women today may inherit or purchase property on an equal footing with men.

Procreation and Birth Control   The primary, traditional purpose of marriage has been to **procreate** (to reproduce). Not until *Griswold v. Connecticut*, 381 U.S. 479 (1965), however, did the Supreme Court announce that penumbras of privacy found within the Constitution prevented states from interfering with a married couple's right not to procreate. The case involved an agency that counseled married couples on the use of contraceptives in violation of Connecticut's statute forbidding their use. The statute was struck down, but the more important outcome of this case was the Court's recognition of a right of privacy. That recognition was the springboard for much of the privacy litigation leading to *Roe* and beyond (*see discussion below*).

Griswold's holding was extended in other cases to include contraceptive use by unmarried persons and then to minors in a more limited way. Despite these rulings, however, the Court never has recognized a general right of privacy in sexual matters. Thus, state statutes regulating homosexuality, sodomy, fornication, sexual activity by minors, adultery, and so forth are not affected by these decisions.

Abortion   *Abortion* is the intentional termination of pregnancy and was illegal except in cases of rape, incest, or to save the mother's life in every state until 1973. Nontherapeutic abortions always had occurred, however. Women who sought an abortion typically did so in back alleys and dingy offices, frequently at the hands persons with little or no medical training. Many of these women died.

The landmark case of *Roe v. Wade*, 410 U.S. 113 (1973) held that a pregnant woman has a fundamental right to choose whether or not to have an abortion, leaving the decision almost exclusively to her and to her physician during the first trimester of pregnancy. An avalanche of cases followed *Roe*, each of them reflecting the turmoil among Americans who had aligned themselves on opposite sides of this emotional issue. That turmoil remains and likely will continue for the foreseeable future, no matter what judicial decisions are made.

Although Roe was not overturned, its precepts were limited in *Planned Parenthood v. Casey*, 505 U.S. 833 (1992), which upheld Pennsylvania's laws requiring: 1) except in a medical emergency, a physician must give a woman information on the nature of as well as alternatives to abortion, which information must be given at least 24 hours before the abortion occurs; and 2) except in a medical emergency, an unemancipated minor must obtain informed parental consent to the abortion (the statute allowed a court to consent if the minor had given informed consent and if the abortion would be in her best interest). However, the Court struck down that portion of the statute which required a woman to inform her husband of the intended abortion, holding that this provision placed an undue burden on a woman's right to choose. Many states since have enacted ***informed consent statutes*** along the lines of the *Casey* decision.

States cannot be required to fund abortions, which largely affects women on state aid (welfare mothers). In addition, a state can prohibit a public hospital from performing abortions and can require that all second-trimester abortions be performed in a hospital (rather than in an abortion clinic or some other place).

Domestic Violence   Domestic violence has existed throughout history, frequently with the explicit or tacit approval of church rulers, courts, and society (*see above*). A wife was considered a type of personal property of her husband. He could not be convicted of rape, assault, or battery of his own wife. Laws eventually were passed to prohibit wife beating, but the practice continued.

In recent years, states began to take wife beating more seriously. Most states have enacted a procedure to issue a ***protective order***, which is a type of injunction that prevents one person from threatening or inflicting physical harm on another. Many of these statutes do not require involvement of a lawyer and can be issued in an ongoing marriage as well as in nonmarital relationships of various types. As an alternative, the abusive partner can be arrested; and many police departments prefer this approach.

In 1994 Congress enacted the ***Violence Against Women Act***, which created a federal civil rights action for victims of violence motivated by gender. The violence can include wife beating, stalking, rape, and other types of sexual assaults. The Act allows a victim to file suit in federal court to obtain damages, injunctive relief, and attorney fees.

Despite state and federal legislation, domestic violence continues. Occasionally, an abused wife kills her husband. If the killing occurs while she is in imminent danger of physical harm, she may be able to claim self-defense. When she kills him at a later time, however, self-defense does not apply. In recent cases, a new argument has been raised to fit this type of siutation. It is the *battered wife syndrome*, which claims essentially that the self-defense time frame should be extended for women who have been abused over a long period of time. The argument is that after years of terror and abuse, a woman can suffer a type of "flashback" in which she genuinely believes that she is in imminent danger and acts upon that belief to defend herself. This defense has not been accepted widely, but a few courts have been willing to allow testimony along these lines.

Most states today, however, still prohibit prosecution of a husband for *spousal rape* that occurs while the couple continues to live together. If married but living apart, however, a husband can be prosecuted for rape of his wife in eleven states. Approximately nine states have eliminated the marital rape exemption completely, allowing a rape charge to be prosecuted in relation to a cohabiting couple.

Parental Rights and Duties

At one time, parental rights and duties resembled spousal duties, at least in relation to the husband/father. A father legally was responsible to provide the necessities of life to his children (food, clothing, shelter, and medical care). As women's rights have evolved, mothers now bear equal responsibility to provide necessities for their children. What constitutes a necessity for a particular child depends on the unique needs of the child as well as his or her station in life. Often in conjunction with the Married Women's Property Acts, states enacted *family expense statutes* that allow third parties to execute against the property of a parent or spouse to enforce necessary family expenses.

In addition to civil remedies, a parent who refuses to support a minor child can be charged with criminal nonsupport if he or she is capable of providing support. Implicit in the duty of parents to support their minor children is the children's duty to obey reasonable regulation of the parents.

> Harry and Wilma have one daughter, Rayette, now 16 years old. Against her parents' wishes, Rayette became involved with a teenage boy and frequently came home drunk. She often skipped school and became unmanageable. Ultimately, she became pregnant and moved in with the boy (who is unemployed) and his

family. Harry and Wilma ordered her to come home and to return
to school. Rayette refused to do either.

On these facts, a slight majority of courts would allow Harry and Wilma to stop supporting Rayette based upon Rayette's ongoing conduct in rejecting parental regulations and discipline. If Rayette receives welfare benefits, this rule also prevents the state agency from pursuing her parents for reimbursement. Unless a child is emancipated, parents typically are obligated to continue support for the child even if the child does not live at home (a child placed in foster care, for example).

In addition to parents, states have an interest in ensuring that children receive proper care, including medical care and a basic education. If a parent refuses to allow a child to receive life-saving medical treatment, even on religious grounds, most states can intervene to provide the treatment and/or can prosecute the parents for manslaughter, child endangerment, or a similar charge.

Education   All states have some type of mandatory education requirement. A typical statute requires children to attend school until age 16, until emancipation, or until graduation from high school, whichever happens first. If a child does not attend school, he or she is ***truant***; and sanctions can be imposed against both the child and the parents. This rule is not absolute, however. The Amish community, for instance, allows children to attend school only through completion of the eighth grade because of religious beliefs. Authorities in one state convicted Amish parents of violating truancy statutes. The Supreme Court, however, reversed the conviction on the basis that the parents had observed the spirit of the statute and, in their unique situation, were not required to send their children to school until the age of 16. *Wisconsin v. Yoder*, 406 U.S. 205 (1972).

States are divided on whether parents in an intact family must pay for a child's college education. A few recent cases have held that parents are required to pay this cost if they can afford to do so; however, this is still far from the majority view. As long as the family is intact, the majority of courts remain reluctant to interfere with its values and budgetary processes. When a divorce or separation occurs, courts are more willing to issue orders related to college education.

Filial Responsibility   Under common law rules, an adult child has no legal duty to provide for the needs of an indigent parent. However, a majority of states have enacted filial responsibility statutes, sometimes called relative responsibility statutes, that alter the common law rule.

Filial responsibility statutes usually require an adult child to support a needy parent if the adult child has the resources to do so after providing for his or her immediate family (spouse and minor children). Enforcement of this type of statute most generally arises when an agency has provided some type of support for a needy parent and then looks to the adult child or children for reimbursement. A number of legal scholars question the rationale of filial responsibility statutes, particularly in situations where the now elderly parent either had abandoned or had abused the defendant during the defendant's childhood.

Legal Disabilities of Minors   In most states, a person less than 18 years of age is a minor under the law (sometimes called an infant). Lacking judgment and maturity, a minor is subject to certain legal disabilities designed to protect him. For example, a minor cannot marry without a parent's or guardian's consent; and a minor cannot make a will or other testamentary instrument. Contracts of minors generally are voidable *(see Contracts chapter in this text)*. A minor must sue or be sued through a "next friend," parent, or guardian *ad litem* in civil actions.

In dealing with minors, older cases rested on an irrebuttable presumption that a child under the age of seven could not be held accountable when she committed a tort or a crime. That presumption has been discarded by nearly all courts. When a minor commits a tort, she is held to a subjective test to determine her capacity to understand the consequences of her act (and, therefore, whether she should be held responsible), taking into account her age, intelligence, and experience. Many states have enacted statutes that hold parents liable for the torts of their minor children up to a stated amount ($500, for example). In some states, the statutory amount varies, depending on whether the minor causes property damage or personal injury.

When minors engage in activities normally reserved only for adults, such as flying an airplane, they generally are held to the same standards as adults. Likewise, when a minor commits a crime involving malice or involving a gun, courts increasingly are willing to grant prosecutors' motions to try them as adults (which subjects them to adult punishment if found guilty) rather than referring them to the state's juvenile court system.

A minor may hold title to property, both real and personal, in his own name. In this situation, the creditors of other family members (parents, for example) cannot seize the minor's property. Although it is almost never pursued by today's parents, a parent is entitled to the earnings of his or her child. This is one carryover from the common law that has not been changed.

Abuse and Neglect   As the *parens patriae* of children, states have an interest in protecting children from the abuse and/or neglect of their parents. The abuse may be physical or psychological. As a general rule, courts attempt to rehabilitate parents (through family court or juvenile court) when neglect or mild abuse is at issue. When a pattern of abuse or neglect develops (or when a single abuse is very serious) that makes continued parenthood detrimental to a child, a court may terminate parental rights. When a parent's rights are terminated, his or her support obligations end.

Usually, this type of action is initiated by a state agency or by a state attorney. In recent years, however, a few cases have been initiated by children who filed suit through a guardian or next friend to terminate the parental rights of their own parents. Although these cases received wide media attention, with news accounts of children "divorcing their parents," they certainly do not indicate a trend.

Intra-Family Immunities

In tort law, an immunity is a defense to tort liability that is based on a potential defendant's status or relationship to the plaintiff. With an immunity, the tort is not eliminated; but the liability for it is avoided. At common law, familial immunities existed between husband and wife as well as between parent and child. No immunity ever has existed between siblings. However, immunity is not the rule in every case.

Because husbands and wives were viewed as a one person under common law, it would have been illogical to allow one to file a tort suit against the other. When Married Women's Property Acts were passed, courts began to allow suits related to property interests between spouses. The same is true when a parent damages a child's property. There is no longer a family immunity for property suits.

An overwhelming majority of states have abolished the spousal immunity, even in personal injury suits, either by statute or by judicial decision. Some states, however, do not allow one spouse to sue the other; neither can a child sue a parent in these states. Even where immunity is the rule, there are exceptions. For example, some states grant immunity for negligent injury only, allowing suits between family members for intentional injury to the person.

Like the spousal immunity, the parent-child immunity has been abolished in a substantial majority of states. Even in states where the immunity still exists, certain exceptions apply, including suits by emancipated children; suits based on intentional torts; and suits based on the wrongful death of the other parent.

Torts Involving Third Parties   Where third parties (persons outside the family unit) are concerned, the two primary types of claims involving family relationships are loss of consortium and loss of services.

For example, when a wife is injured by the negligence of a third party, her husband may have a claim for *loss of consortium* against that party based on his injury from the loss of her companionship, affection, and sexual relationship. Similarly, parents may have a claim for *loss of services* based on a parent's right to the services of his or her unemancipated children.

If a physician makes a mistake that results in the birth of a deformed child when the parents had tried to avoid the birth either by sterilization or by abortion, the parents can bring a wrongful birth action. If the child is healthy, the parents may be able to sue for wrongful pregnancy, but their damages generally would be limited to the losses incurred from the pregnancy itself (they could not recover the costs of rearing the child). In either situation (deformed child or healthy child), courts usually will not hear a child's claim based on *wrongful life*.

Vicarious liability exists when one person is liable for the torts of another. As a general rule, vicarious liability does not exist among family members. There are two major exceptions to the general rule, however. 1) Many states' statutes impose limited vicarious liability on parents for the torts of their children (*see above*); and 2) Under the *family purpose doctrine*, the owner of an automobile can be liable for a tort committed by a family member while driving the automobile for a "family purpose."

Evidentiary Privilege   The Federal Rules of Evidence and the rules of evidence in most states grant a special privilege that permits one spouse to refuse to testify against the other in a civil or criminal trial. The theory behind the privilege is to preserve the confidential relationship that marital partners share.

Legal scholars continue to debate whether this privilege belongs to the spouse who is asked to testify or to the spouse against whom the testimony is sought. Several things seem clear, however. This evidentiary privilege exists only in an ongoing marriage. If a married couple is living apart, for example, some courts will not recognize the privilege. Moreover, if the litigated matter involves claims of one spouse against the other (such as a divorce or a charge of spousal abuse), the privilege does not apply.

The privilege applies only to spouses. There is no evidentiary privilege that allows a child to refuse to testify against his or her parent (or visa versa), even if the information was provided to the child in confidence by the parent.

Annulment

An ***annulment*** is the legal method by which a marriage is invalidated retroactively to the date of its creation. In other words, the marriage is canceled, as if it never happened. Unlike other areas of matrimonial law, which can trace their beginnings back to English common law, annulment is primarily a creature of legislative action. Generally, but not always, an annulment occurs within a short time after the marriage.

Annulment may be granted in relation to a ***voidable marriage*** or a ***void marriage***. A marriage is voidable if it is created in the manner prescribed by law but lacks an element considered essential to the marital union (an undisclosed inability to have children, for example). A marriage is void if it cannot be created legally (for instance, marrying someone while legally married to someone else). A void marriage simply can be ignored, since it never had a legal existence. However, annulment for a void marriage may avoid complications and confusion in the future.

Jurisdiction to grant an annulment exists in the courts of the state where one or both of the parties are domiciled. Once jurisdiction is established, the court will apply the law of the state where the marriage was created to determine whether an annulment should be granted.

Grounds for Annulment

Most states provide for annulment if fraud, duress, impotency, or mental incapacity existed at the time the marriage was created. Generally speaking, an annulment action may be filed only by the aggrieved spouse. For example, a spouse who uses fraud to induce the marriage cannot later seek annulment based upon his or her own fraud. The doctrine of ***marriage by estoppel*** prevents the offending spouse from using his or her own offense to have the marriage annulled.

In jurisdictions where divorce typically is based on specific types of fault, an annulment may have broader grounds that make it more viable in the proper case. In no-fault divorce states, however, parties may find it easier to obtain a divorce than to obtain an annulment.

Fraud   Fraud is a knowing misrepresentation, made with the intention that the other party will rely on it to his or her detriment. As it relates to annulment, the fraud must relate to some element that is essential to the concept of marriage.

> After knowing her a few weeks, Harry married Wilma, who
> represented through the courtship that she had not had sexual
> relations with any other man. In fact, Wilma was pregnant with
> another man's child at the time of the marriage.

Many courts would grant Harry an annulment in this situation. Likewise, if Wilma had told Harry that she was pregnant with his child when the child belonged to another man, most courts would grant the annulment. However, if Wilma had told Harry that she was pregnant with his child when she was not pregnant at all, most courts would *not* grant the annulment.

Misrepresenting either a willingness or the ability to have children is grounds for annulment. Likewise, misrepresenting a condition related to health sometimes can provide grounds for annulment (having AIDS at the time of the marriage). Some courts permit misrepresentation of character to form the basis for annulment.

> Harry represented to Wilma that he is a devout Catholic, knowing
> that she would not marry him otherwise. After the marriage,
> Wilma discovered that Harry is not Catholic at all; and he refused
> to embrace Catholicism. Wilma is granted an annulment.

For Wilma, shared religious beliefs were essential to her ability to carry out her duties as a wife and mother. Where the misrepresentation concerns social position or income, however, courts are less likely to annul the marriage.

Standing alone, misrepresentation of love and affection is not enough to annul a marriage. However, it can be coupled with other facts to provide grounds for annulment based on fraud (for example, marriage solely to obtain an immigration visa or marriage solely to gain access to property, followed by desertion).

Duress   Depending on the particular pressure brought against a spouse, duress may be grounds for annulment. Certainly, the use of force or threat of imminent harm is duress and provides grounds for annulment. Threat of legal action for fornication, seduction, or the like generally does not constitute duress, however.

> Haywood seduced Martha, a minor, who also was the daughter of
> the local judge. Upon learning of the seduction, Martha's father
> threatened Haywood with charges of fornication and contributing
> to the delinquency of a minor. He further threatened to impose the
> maximum sentence upon conviction. The alternative was to marry
> Martha, in which case her father would not pursue the charges.
> Haywood married Martha and then sought an annulment based on
> duress.

In this situation, a court is unlikely to find that duress existed. Haywood did have a choice, although it was not an attractive one.

Impotence   Implicit in the concept of marriage are procreation and consortium, both of which are essential elements of marriage. When a man is impotent (unable to engage in sexual relations) at the time of the marriage, this fact can support annulment of the marriage. Likewise, if a woman is impotent at the time of the marriage, her husband can seek an annulment. In most jurisdictions, it makes no difference whether the reason for the impotence is physical or psychological.

Mental Incapacity   A marriage may be annulled for mental incapacity which existed at the time of the marriage. The mental capacity to marry is judged on a lesser scale than is the mental capacity to enter into most other contracts (*see previous discussion*).

> Horace, diagnosed a schizophrenic, had been committed for many years to Ivy Halls, a high-security mental institution. While on a group outing, he escaped. During this time, he met and married Wilhelmina, telling her that he was a retired colonel from the Canadian Air Force. Shortly after the marriage, Wilhelmina noticed something was wrong. Horace behaved erratically and frequently did not know who she was.

> Hank, a elderly man of some wealth, met and married Wolanda, who had cared for him after a surgery for cancer that had left him partially paralyzed. Hank's daughter from his first marriage petitioned to have the marriage annulled, claiming that Hank was insane at the time of the marriage and was incapable of consent. His appearance and health had declined, he had become slovenly, and he sometimes did not recognize the daughter or her family.

The marriage in the first example probably can be annulled based on mental incapacity at the time of the marriage. The marriage in the second example is unlikely to be annulled, however, unless the daughter can prove such a lack of understanding at the time of the marriage that Hank was rendered incapable of giving his consent. On the facts stated, this seems improbable.

Defenses   An action for annulment usually can be defended or resisted on the following grounds: 1)knowledge, when the complaining spouse knew of the impediment before the marriage took place; 2) ratification, when the couple continues to live together after the impediment is known; 3) *res judicata,* when the issues previously have been litigated and decided; 4) statute of limitations imposed by many states in relation to an annulment; and if there is no statute of limitations, 5) laches, when the complaining spouse simply has waited too long.

> After a short marriage, Hiram and Whitley filed for divorce. The
> final divorce decree was entered; and during the waiting period,
> they jointly asked the court to vacate the decree. They had been
> reconciled for only a few months when Hiram saw that he never
> would convince Whitley to have sexual relations with him. He filed
> for annulment of his marriage to Whitley.

Because the court had found the marriage to be valid in the previous divorce action,
the doctrine of *res judicata* applies; and Hiram's annulment action will be
dismissed on that basis.

Effects of Annulment

Once a marriage is annulled, the marital bonds are canceled as if they never
existed. However, the parties cannot always go back to square one concerning
every aspect of the relationship. Certainly, they cannot cancel children who may
have been born before the annulment; and something must be done with property
that may have been acquired. Even thornier questions are raised concerning
alimony, both past and future.

Children   Regardless of whether the marriage is void or voidable, nearly all
states have enacted statutes declaring children born of the union to be legitimate.
This is a dramatic change from the old common law rule, which turned such
children into bastards following annulment of their parents' marriage based on the
"relation back" doctrine.

Annulment does not alter a child's right to support from his or her parents.
This aspect of the annulment process is very similar to support awarded following
a divorce.

Property and Alimony   Upon annulment, the majority of states hold that
permanent alimony and marital property rights cannot be granted unless a specific
state statute provides otherwise. Without this type of statute, a needy party in a
traditional jurisdiction has very limited contractual or equitable remedies (an
implied partnership theory, express or implied contract, or unjust enrichment, for
instance).

A growing number of states have recognized the plight of the needy party
when annulment occurs and have enacted legislation that allows permanent
spousal support and marital property division in an annulment proceeding. This
type of statute is similar to divorce legislation. A state statute that allows
permanent alimony to be awarded likely includes a provision for temporary alimony
as well. In those states without such a statute, courts typically will award

temporary alimony if the needy spouse is the one trying to defend the validity of the marriage, but will not award temporary alimony if the needy spouse is the one seeking annulment.

The following example presents a more difficult situation:

> Hazelton and Winnifred divorced, and the divorce decree required Hazelton to pay alimony (spousal support) to Winnifred until either of them died or until Winnifred remarried. Winnifred did remarry, but the second marriage later was annulled.

States are divided into three distinct postures concerning the effect of annulment on Hazelton's support obligation. One group of courts takes the view that the original support obligation is not terminated. Using the relation back doctrine, the second marriage never existed; therefore, Hazelton's support obligation continues. A second group takes the view that Hazelton's support obligation is terminated if the second marriage is voidable and is annulled, but his support obligation is not terminated if the second marriage is void (for example, if the second husband already was married when he married Winnifred). A third group takes the view that Hazelton's support obligation terminates, regardless of whether the second marriage is voidable or is void.

Divorce

A **divorce** (called dissolution of marriage in some states) is the legal termination of a valid marriage. Depending on the state, this process may include common law marriages (*see above*) as well as ceremonial marriages. Divorce actions affect not only the parties' legal status, but also the rights and obligations related to property division, support of dependent family members, and custody of children. Divorce and legal separation procedures in the United States are a strange mixture of English common law, equity law as it has developed in America, and statutory law.

Jurisdiction

The authority to grant a divorce and to resolve its related issues rests with individual states under the domestic relations exception to federal subject matter jurisdiction. This is true even though diversity of citizenship exists. A federal court may be able to hear cases related to issues touching on family law because of specific federal statutes (violence against women, for instance), but it has no jurisdiction to grant a divorce or to determine property division and support issues attendant to granting a divorce. Within each state, the authority to grant a divorce is vested in a court with equity jurisdiction.

Jurisdiction to grant a divorce rests in that state where at least one of the parties has established a domicile. A ***domicile*** generally is defined as the place where a person physically is present, with the intention to make that place his or her permanent home. Although some states use the term "residency requirement" in their statutes, courts universally interpret this term to mean domicile. The Uniform Marriage and Divorce Act (UMDA) and most states make an exception for military personnel stationed in a state for a specified period of time. In addition to being domiciled there, most states do require some minimum time of residence (one year in many states).

In a state like Nevada, where the minimum residency requirement is very short (six weeks), many migratory divorces are granted. A ***migratory divorce*** results when a party travels from his home state to another state, establishes domicile and residence, and obtains a divorce there. Frequently, the party returns to his or her home state at a later time. This type of "quickie divorce" may be pursued because it can be achieved quickly, but factors such as local publicity in the home state and more lenient substantive law also affect parties' decision to migrate.

To grant a divorce, a state must have personal jurisdiction over one or both of the parties. When a state has personal jurisdiction of one party only, it may grant an ***ex parte divorce*** in which the marriage is dissolved. Unless it has personal jurisdiction of both parties, however, the court cannot divide property, award support, or decide custody issues.

A ***foreign divorce*** is one obtained in a foreign country. Since a state is not required to acknowledge a divorce obtained in a foreign country, the Full Faith and Credit Clause of the U. S. Constitution does not apply. A state may ignore a foreign divorce in favor of following its own policies.

Grounds for Divorce

Before the twentieth century, divorce was rare and was a remedy available only to husbands in most cases. Divorce petitions originally were heard by the state legislature, not by courts. The first divorce laws allowed adultery as the only type of fault that could warrant the grant of a divorce. The fault statutes later were amended to add desertion, cruelty (physical and mental), or gross neglect as permissible grounds in nearly all states. One exception was the State of New York, which retained adultery as the only grounds for divorce until 1966.

Because of the rigidity of such limited grounds for divorce, parties sometimes simply agreed to manufacture or to simulate situations that could qualify as permissible grounds. This was known as ***collusion***; and if it was discovered, the divorce was not granted. Nevertheless, parties who no longer wanted to be married continued to contrive the requisite fault with increasing frequency in order to obtain a divorce.

California passed the first no-fault divorce statute in the 1960s, which soon was followed by the Uniform Marriage and Divorce Act (UMDA). Proposed by the National Conference of Commissioners on Uniform State Laws, the no-fault concept of the Act has been adopted in whole or in part by every state. A **no-fault divorce** is exactly what it seems it would be: neither spouse is required to show fault of the other spouse in order to obtain a divorce. States variously use terms such as irremediable differences, irreconcilable differences, or irremediable breakdown of the marital bonds; but the meaning essentially is the same.

Some states provide no-fault as the only type of divorce that can be granted. Others have added it to the existing list of grounds based on fault; parties in those states may choose which option to use. Even in those states where all divorces are of the no-fault variety, evidence of fault continues to be important in issues related to alimony and child custody.

> Hueston and Winnie are married; they have two children. Hueston did not finish his education and has never held anything but unskilled, entry-level jobs. His wife, Winnie, however, managed to put herself through school during the marriage and to secure a well-paid position in a large company. Through the years, Hueston became increasingly abusive to Winnie and the children, drank heavily at times, and seldom held a job for more than two or three months. After Hueston injured her severely enough to require hospitalization, Winnie filed for divorce.

In a state where no-fault divorce is one of several options, Winnie is more likely to pursue a fault option (probably based on extreme cruelty), where Hueston's conduct will be admitted as direct evidence in granting the divorce and in determining issues of child custody and alimony. In a state where no-fault divorce is the only option, Hueston's conduct may not be admissible in determining whether to grant the divorce, but it will be admissible in determining child custody and alimony questions.

Divorce Procedure

The exact procedure to file, prosecute, and obtain a divorce differs from state to state. Within a particular state, procedures also may vary according to whether the divorce is contested or not. However, there are recurrent themes in every state's divorce procedure.

Once jurisdiction is established (both domicile and residence), one of the parties initiates the process by filing a complaint or petition for divorce. Some states label the parties as plaintiff/defendant; others, as petitioner/respondent. Most state statutes allow a court to enter temporary orders (sometimes called interim orders) during the pendency of the action. These typically relate to temporary child support and visitation, support for a dependent spouse if appropriate, prohibition on disposing of property, occupancy of the family home, and so forth.

In many jurisdictions, parties are allowed to negotiate a separation document that reflects their agreement concerning property division and their proposals concerning the type and amount of support that should be paid as well as child custody. If the court finds the agreement reasonable, it can make the terms binding in granting the final divorce.

In some jurisdictions, all divorce issues are tried at the same time; in others, each major aspect of the divorce is tried separately, called a ***bifurcated*** trial. Most states provide some type of waiting period between the time the petition is filed and the time that a decree can be entered, even in uncontested cases. The purpose of the waiting period (sometimes termed a "cooling off" period), is to allow parties to reflect on the serious step they have initiated and, hopefully, to reconsider it. Many couples do reconcile, but many more do not.

At the end of the waiting period, a trial is scheduled and held according to the procedural rules of that particular court. The judge may accept the parties' agreement and recommendation (*see above*), approving its terms as part of the divorce decree. A ***decree*** in an equity case is analogous to a judgment in other types of civil cases. If the parties have not reached such an agreement, the judge makes all decisions concerning property, child custody, and support.

Nearly all states impose a waiting period between the time of the decree is entered and the time it becomes final (six months, for example). During this time, the decree is ***interlocutory*** (not final); and the parties remain married. An interlocutory divorce decree generally can be vacated (canceled) upon the joint motion of the parties, which means that it has no further legal effect; and the parties remain married. If either spouse dies during the interlocutory waiting period, the survivor becomes widowed rather than divorced and generally inherits as a surviving spouse (whether under a will or under the statutory marital share).

Once the waiting period expires, the interlocutory decree becomes a final decree; and the parties' marital status is terminated. The parties are free to remarry. In addition, many states have enacted statutes that automatically remove ex-spouses from each other's will (if a will exists), as if he or she had predeceased.

In states where no such statute exists, parties are well advised to make the necessary changes to their estate plans as soon as possible.

Property Division

Under common law, the person who held title to property was the person who owned it; and generally this was the husband. Not until passage of Married Women's Property Acts did American courts begin to view marriage as having characteristics of an economic partnership. When this occurred, distribution statutes began to change, albeit slowly.

When a couple seeks a divorce today, they need to unravel their financial affairs so that each may function independently following the divorce. In addition to alimony and child support allocations, the parties' assets and liabilities must be divided. Married people often own property together, including a home, vehicles, bank accounts, and so forth. The longer the marriage, the more complicated the property issues that are likely to arise. How marital property division is accomplished in a particular state depends on whether the state follows principles of 1) equitable distribution or 2) community property.

Equitable Distribution   Most states follow the equitable distribution approach to divide property upon divorce. Today's equitable distribution statutes are the direct descendants of earlier distribution statutes that recognized, to some degree, the nature of marriage as an economic partnership.

Although not all states adopting equitable distribution statutes have classified the property, many have. Where those statutory classifications exist, they identify property as either separate property or marital property. *Separate property* is that property which was owned by each party before marriage. It also includes property received by a spouse as a gift or inheritance during the marriage. Separate property is not subject to equitable distribution when property division occurs. However, if a spouse commingles separate property with marital property, most courts take the view that the entire commingled portion becomes marital property.

Marital property is all other property (nonseparate property) acquired by the parties during the marriage. All marital property is subject to equitable distribution when parties divorce. Property that the parties own together is marital property. Many states treat vested pensions (those in which ownership rights have matured) as marital property. If one spouse helps to put the other spouse through school to acquires a professional license, many courts likewise will treat the value of the license as a type of marital property.

In an equitable distribution state, the court must identify, classify, and value the assets of each spouse; the marital assets; and the debts that exist. Without other factors, such as children and/or alimony, the court must make a fair distribution of the marital assets and liabilities. To distribute the marital assets fairly, the court may award specific items of property to each spouse; may order property to be sold, with the proceeds divided between the spouses; or may order some combination of these two approaches.

> Hank and Wilma were married. Before the marriage, Wilma's parents gave her a home, titled in her name only. During the marriage, Hank and Wilma were employed, worked hard, and became comfortable financially. They continued to live in the home and, over the years, remodeled various parts of it. Hank did all of the remodeling work himself as well as general maintenance for the home. When her parents died, Wilma received a large inheritance from their estates. Hank also inherited from his parents, although it was a small amount. With her inheritance, Wilma purchased a substantial annuity for herself as well as a new car that was titled in both names. She deposited the rest into a joint checking account. Hank used his inheritance to fund a Caribbean cruise for himself and Wilma. From his employment, Hank had amassed a sizeable pension fund for his retirement. Only a few years before retirement, the parties filed for divorce.

In reviewing Hank and Wilma's assets strictly from the standpoint of property distribution, the home was Wilma's separate property at the beginning of the marriage. One reasonably may infer the parties had been married for some time when they filed for divorce, with substantial remodeling work and routine maintenance of the home performed by Hank. Because of this, many courts would treat the home as marital property, regardless of how it is titled.

The facts do not state how large Wilma's inheritance was; but since she purchased an annuity for herself with part of it and since Hank's name is not on the annuity contract, this asset likely will be treated as Wilma's separate asset. She titled the car in both names (making it a marital asset), and she deposited money into a joint check account (commingling it with marital assets, which causes the entire account to become a marital asset).

Hank's inheritance does not enter into the formula because he spent it. His pension fund, however, will be classified as a marital asset by most courts. This assumes, of course, that no part of the pension fund was accumulated prior to his marriage to Wilma.

Structuring the distribution of marital property is left entirely to the court unless the parties have entered into a separation agreement. Without such an agreement and assuming the assets have similar values, a court might award the home to Wilma and the pension fund to Hank. Alternately, it could order the home to be sold (with proceeds divided equally) and then award one-half of Hank's pension fund to Wilma. Other alternatives may come to mind. Of the two given here, the first alternative requires the least monitoring; and for that reason alone, many judges will prefer it purely on grounds of efficiency.

Community Property   Eight states have enacted statutes that use a community property approach to assets owned by married people. These states are Arizona, California, Idaho, Louisiana, Texas, Nevada, New Mexico, Washington, and Wisconsin. In a *community property* state, there is a legal presumption that all property acquired during the marriage that is not separate property belongs to both spouses equally. This presumption exists regardless of how the property is titled or who purchased it. Both spouses are entitled to make management decisions in relation to community property, including whether it is invested, leased, sold, or the like. Upon death or divorce, each spouse owns one-half of the community property of the marriage, although a few community property states have modified the presumption slightly by moving to equitable distribution principles upon divorce.

The more significant difference of community ownership is that if one spouse dies, the survivor is entitled to one-half of the community property. Because of this, community property states do not have a statutory elective share for the spouse as part of their probate codes. They do not need such a provision.

The community property presumption can be rebutted by evidence showing that all or part (if it was commingled) of a particular asset is the separate property of one spouse. When the presumption is rebutted properly, that portion which is separate property is subtracted from the community property grouping.

Alimony

In appropriate circumstances, nearly all states grant authority to a court to require an economically strong spouse to provide financial support to an economically dependent spouse. This financial support is called *alimony* in most states, although many call it *spousal support*. Alimony traditionally was awarded to the wife, because she nearly always was the more dependent spouse in the marital relationship. The changing roles and economic positions of men and women have resulted in larger numbers of alimony awards being made to the husband.

Alimony awards are discretionary with the court, and some states allow a court to deny or to limit alimony to any spouse who is guilty of marital fault (for instance, if a spouse commits adultery). On this issue, then, marital fault would be admissible evidence in such a state, although it may not be admissible in a no-fault divorce state for any purpose other than determining whether alimony should be awarded. There is no requirement that alimony must be awarded. In fact, if the parties are in relatively equal economic positions, a court may decide not to award alimony at all.

Types of Alimony   If alimony is awarded by a court, it may be either permanent or rehabilitative. If **_permanent alimony_** is awarded, it typically is paid as periodic payments of a set amount that continue until either spouse dies or until the recipient remarries. Permanent alimony also may be awarded as a fixed amount, which can be paid either as a lump sum or in installment payments. This type of permanent alimony sometimes is referred to as **_alimony in gross_**. If installment payments for alimony in gross are ordered and if the payor spouse dies before all installments are made, the unpaid portion is a claim against the estate of the payor spouse. Permanent alimony generally is awarded to a wife who was married in an earlier social time frame, when women were expected to devote their lives exclusively to caring for their homes and families and when men were expected to support their wives for life.   As society has changed, awards of permanent alimony have declined.

With more women working outside the home, a court may order **_rehabilitative alimony_**, which is intended to provide support while the recipient obtains training or education to strengthen his or her employment opportunities. Rehabilitative alimony generally is awarded for a specified number of years (five, for example) to give the recipient time to complete an educational program and to become established in an employment or in a profession.

In awarding any type of alimony, courts consider many factors, including the length of the marriage and the era in which the parties were married; the existence or nonexistence of marital fault; each party's earning capacity, future earning prospects, and health; and the likelihood that the recipient spouse will take advantage of training and/or educational opportunities.

Termination or Modification   Generally speaking, once alimony is fixed by the court in a final decree of divorce, the obligation to pay it continues for the time stated in the decree. There are exceptions, however. If either spouse dies, alimony generally terminates as of the date of death. In addition, nearly all states provide for termination of alimony upon the remarriage of the recipient spouse. Parties may alter these general rules by specific provisions contained in a property settlement agreement.

The amount of alimony to be paid can be changed if the requesting party can prove a "substantial change in circumstances" since entry of the divorce decree to justify the change. The UMDA arguably imposes a greater burden on the requesting party, since it requires "a showing of changed circumstances so substantial and continuing as to make the [existing] terms unconscionable . . . ." The substantial change may warrant either an increase or a decrease in the amount of alimony originally awarded. If no alimony was awarded in the original decree, however, alimony never can be awarded as part of a modification proceeding.

When a modification of alimony is granted, all but a few states provide that the change applies only to prospective payments. If the modification order is entered today, it applies to all future alimony payments to become due; but it does not apply to any prior payments that were due, regardless of whether or not the payments were made. As to the few states that allow alimony modification to take effect retroactively, courts in other states have held that the alimony award need not be honored under the Full Faith and Credit Clause because it is not a final order.

Child Custody and Support

Over time, American legislatures and courts have adopted many new rules that are used in granting divorces. One of the things that has changed very little with the passage of time is the court's concern about the interests of minor children of the marriage, who are innocent casualties of the divorce process.

Child Custody In an ongoing family, each parent is entitled to joint legal custody and joint legal possession of the children born to them. This status continues until a valid custody order is entered by a court. For this reason, many courts award temporary custody during the pendency of the litigation and permanent custody as part of the final decree. Child custody cases typically involve a dispute between parents over custody; however, they also can involve a parent and a grandparent or a parent and a third party. This can occur when a parent leaves a child with someone else and returns years later to reclaim the child. In an action between a parent and a third party, the general rule is that the parent is entitled to custody of his or her child unless shown by clear evidence to be unfit.

When the issue of child custody arises within a divorce proceeding, courts traditionally have used criteria designed to determine the "best interests of the child." Even though both parents were morally and financially fit to have custody, the court usually was required to determine which parent was the more fit to serve the child's best interests. This standard continues today, with only slight differences in the way it is applied.

State statutes often list the factors that a court must consider to evaluate each parent in relation to the best interests of the child. These typically include the age of the child; the physical and mental health of the child; each parent's fitness to care for the child, including emotional stability and/or patterns of moral misconduct; the financial situation of the parents; and the desires of the child if the child is of an age or maturity level to state his or her desires. Many states allow a child of a certain age (typically 12 or 14) to elect his or her preference; however, courts always will consider a stated preference made by a younger child.

In the past, courts used a legal presumption that the custody of a "child of tender years" should be awarded to the mother unless she was unfit or was unavailable. Most states have abolished this "tender years" presumption. Either by statute or by judicial decision, a parent's gender is disregarded today in determining child custody. Instead, many courts consider factors geared at demonstrating which parent is the ***primary caretaker*** for the child. All else being equal, awarding custody to the child's primary caretaker generally serves the best interests of the child. In today's society, it may well the father who is the primary caretaker of the children, sometimes going so far as being the parent who stays at home while the mother attends to the demands of her career and provides the major portion of income for the family.

Courts are divided over the extent to which custody should be affected by a parent's adulterous activities. However, there is no question that courts generally are more tolerant about this issue than they ever were in the past. Especially when the activity is heterosexual, most courts give it much less weight in their decision making than they did even ten years ago, reasoning that adultery in itself does not make a parent unfit. When it has a negative impact on the child, however, most courts consider it a factor in determining custody. Where custody is concerned, a court is even less likely to consider extramarital sexual activity in a modification proceeding than in the original divorce action.

When the adulterous activity of the parent is homosexual, courts are more strongly divided on its proper weight in determining custody issues. Many courts view a parent's homosexuality heavily against that parent where original custody is concerned. Other courts view it much less heavily against the parent unless it is shown that the homosexual activity will affect the child adversely (potential teasing by other children is not enough).

Custody issues cannot be decided on the basis of race, religion, or a parent's disability that affects only that parents's ability to engage in physical activities.

Types of Custody   Courts traditionally awarded custody of children either to one parent or to the other, called the custodial parent, with visitation rights awarded to the noncustodial parent. Many courts continue to award custody under the traditional model. However, a growing number of courts provide for joint custody. In fact, some states have enacted a statutory presumption in favor of joint custody. Of those states without a presumption in favor of joint custody, most allow a court to award joint custody if both parents agree.

The term *joint custody* may apply at least to two different custodial arrangements. In a joint legal custody situation, both parents have an equal voice in important matters related to rearing the child, such as where the child attends school and so forth, with possession granted to one parent and visitation rights granted to the other. In a joint physical custody situation (sometimes called *split custody*), the parents share the day-to-day living arrangements. For example, the child might spend four days at the mother's home and three days at the father's home each week. Because of the much larger commitment to cooperate and effort required by joint physical custody, courts are more inclined to award joint legal custody.

Modification   When a parent seeks to modify an existing custody decree, a different and more difficult standard applies than it applied in granting custody originally.   The petitioning parent must show a "substantial change in circumstances" from the time the original decree was entered. Courts have interpreted this standard to require a showing that the welfare of the child has been altered so greatly that there is a strong possibility that the child will be harmed if she continues under the present arrangement.

> Horace and Wanda divorce, and Wanda is awarded custody of the couple's child. Wanda then marries a man of a different color and race, and Horace petitions for custody based on a substantial change of circumstances. The evidence shows that Wanda and her new husband are devoted to the child, have adequate housing, and the new husband is a respectable man.

Horace's petition for change in custody will be denied. The Fourteenth Amendment does not permit custody to be denied solely on the basis of a racially mixed household. Except for the fact that Wanda married a man of a different race, her fitness to have custody apparently has not changed since custody originally was awarded to her.

Custody Jurisdiction   When both parents and all of their children reside in the same state, that state clearly has jurisdiction to decide custody matters if there are no prior custody orders on record and if no other custody proceedings are pending. The question of jurisdiction is not so clear when one state has issued a custody decree and when one or both parents move to another state (with or without the child) or when a court is asked to modify the custody decree of another state.

Two important statutes exist to help unravel the complexities of custody jurisdiction. One is the ***Uniform Child Custody Jurisdiction Act*** (UCCJA), which has been adopted in all 50 states as well as in the District of Colombia. The UCCJA sets the ground rules in each state for deciding whether that state (the forum state) has jurisdiction to issue a custody decree if custody proceedings are not pending in any other state and if no other state already has issued a custody decree. Under the UCCJA, the forum state has jurisdiction only if at least one of these four criteria is met:

> 1.   If the forum state was the "home state" of the child at either of two dates: a) the date the proceedings were commenced; or b) any date within six months before the proceedings were commenced, but only if the child is now absent from the forum state because of his removal or retention by a person claiming custody . . . and a parent or person acting as parent continues to live in the forum state;

> 2.   It is in the best interest of the child that the forum state assumes jurisdiction because: a) the child and his parents, or the child and at least one contestant, have a significant connection with the forum state; and 2) there is available in the forum state substantial evidence concerning the child's past or future care, protection, training, and personal relationships . . . ;

> 3.   If the child is physically present in the forum state and either has been abandoned or there is an emergency requiring protection of the child against mistreatment, abuse, or neglect; or

> 4.   If no other state has (or is willing to exercise) jurisdiction), and it is in the child's best interest that the forum state hear the matter.

Under the UCCJA, then, the presence of the child in the state is not enough to confer jurisdiction on a particular state. This rule is intended to avoid giving a parent the incentive to abduct a child. Conversely, the presence of the child in the forum state is not a prerequisite to jurisdiction, so long as the proceeding is started within the first six months after the child's removal.

The UCCJA does not specifically require that the forum state obtain personal jurisdiction over the absent parent for the court to exercise jurisdiction over the custody dispute. If a parent does not have minimum contacts with a state, that state cannot order him or her to pay child support; however, most courts hold that deciding the status of custody does not require personal jurisdiction.

The second major law relating to child custody is the **Parental Kidnaping Protection Act** (PKPA), a federal statute that deals with parental kidnaping, as its name implies; but it also deals with all cases where one state is asked either to enforce or to modify another state's custody decree. Both the UCCJA and the PKPA contain rules to govern these two situations; however, the PKPA takes priority because of the Supremacy Clause of the Constitution. Taken together, the UCCJA and PKPA require a state to enforce a custody decree of a sister state without modification except when the court that issued the original decree no longer meets certain jurisdictional requirements and when the forum state does meet those requirements.

If a second court (State B) becomes involved in a custody battle either by beginning a case while a case is pending in another state (State A) or by modifying a prior custody order issued by another state (State A), State B first must determine whether State A had jurisdiction by analyzing State A's version of the UCCJA. If it did, State B cannot proceed. If State A did not have jurisdiction, State B may issue its own decree (actually an original decree rather than a modification). If State A did have jurisdiction when it issued the original decree, but State B now has jurisdiction (using the UCCJA tests), State B determines whether State A has continuing jurisdiction; and if it does, State B must enforce State A's decree. If State A did have jurisdiction originally but no longer has jurisdiction, State B may exercise its jurisdiction to reconsider the decree originally issued by State A.

Recall that federal courts do not have jurisdiction to grant a divorce, to award alimony, or to decide child custody. The PKPA lays out the procedure that states must follow but does not attempt to confer jurisdiction on federal courts. Moreover, federal courts do not have authority to decide which of two conflicting custody decrees is valid. Litigants must resolve the battle of the decrees in state court.

<u>Visitation</u> The noncustodial parent nearly always will be granted the right of reasonable visitation with his or her child unless the court is convinced that visitation would harm the child in a serious way.

Generally speaking, visitation rights and payment of child support are not interrelated. If a mother fails to pay child support, for instance, the father cannot withhold visitation until child support is paid. If a child refuses to visit and if the court determines it is the child's wish (particularly if the child is older) and not the orchestration of the custodial parent, most courts will not force the child to visit.

When a custodial parent repeatedly thwarts court-ordered visitation, several remedies are possible.

In the first instance, the noncustodial parent can initiate contempt proceedings that can result in jailing the custodial parent and suspending the sentence if he or she complies with the visitation order. In very serious situations, the court can change custody to the other parent.

Visitation rights may be granted to grandparents in nearly all states. Some states allow visitation by any person whom the court determines to be in the best interest of the child.

Child Support   Even though parents are divorced, each parent is obligated to contribute to the support of their children. Courts typically order the noncustodial parent to pay support to the custodial parent as part of the divorce proceedings. The custodial parent provides support in the form of food, housing, clothing, and the like. If custody is shared, the higher-income spouse generally pays support to the lower-income spouse.

Federal law requires every state to maintain *child support guidelines*, which provide a precise method for computing the amount of child support that a court should order. However, these are guidelines only. A court may adjust the amount up or down based on other circumstances in a particular case.

As a general rule, child support obligations continue until a child reaches the age of majority, dies, or is emancipated. However, a court may order support to continue beyond the age of majority if the child has special needs (spinal cord injury, for example). Even though most states do not require parents in an ongoing family to pay for college education, a divorce decree may require a noncustodial parent to contribute to the child's college education and/or to provide support while the child attends college.

Child support can be modified by showing a change in circumstances since the original support was awarded. If a noncustodial parent's income increases, most courts will find this to be a sufficient change to award increased support. This is different from a request to increase alimony, where increased income alone would not be sufficient to change the original award.

Enforcement of Child Support   For many custodial parents, obtaining a child support order is simple compared to enforcing it. Of all parents who are awarded child support, 24% have received nothing; and another 25% have received only partial payment. The traditional methods of enforcing civil judgments are largely ineffective when used to collect child support. Attorney fees are expensive, the noncustodial parent often moves out of the state (sometimes from state to state), and the judicial delays are a nightmare to a mother, for instance, who is trying to support her children alone.

The Uniform Reciprocal Enforcement of Support Act (URESA) and its revised version, **Revised Uniform Reciprocal Enforcement of Support Act** (RURESA), make this dilemma somewhat easier when the parents live in two different states. Some form of the URESA or RURESA is in force in every state, and the two uniform laws are virtually the same in their essential provisions. When RURESA is mentioned in in this text, it refers to URESA equally.

RURESA can be used to enforce alimony as well as to enforce child support. Each provides a procedure to collect an existing court order for support across state lines; it does not relate to any substantive issues in the support area (who should pay support or how much it should be, for example).

RURESA provides two types of action to enforce a support decree. The first type can be used only in those situations where a support decree already exists. Under this method, the support decree from State A is registered in State B where the obligor (person owing support) resides. State B then enforces the decree as if it originally had been entered by a court in State B.

The second type of RURESA enforcement is a two-state proceeding, which can be used regardless of whether State A (where the parent seeking enforcement lives) has entered a support decree. Using this method, the claimant files a petition in the courts of State A, called the **initiating state**. The State A court does not decide whether support is due. Instead, it decides whether there is probable cause to believe the defendant has a duty of support. No notice is given to the out-of-state defendant at this point of the proceeding, and no adversary hearing is held. If the initiating state finds there is probable cause to believe that the defendant will be found to owe a duty of support and probable cause to believe that the defendant can be found in State B, called the **responding state**, State A will transfer the case to State B. State B then locates the defendant and serves him with notice to obtain personal jurisdiction. Trial for support is held in State B, much like any other trial except that the plaintiff need not appear personally; affidavits can be submitted instead.

In addition to URESA and RURESA, which have been enacted as state statutes, Congress has enacted legislation to make child support collection easier. The primary statute is the **Child Support Enforcement Act of 1984**, as amended. It provides a number of tools that can be used either by a parent seeking enforcement or by a state making welfare payments in return for an assignment of support rights. They include the following:

A. Automatic Withholding   By paying a small fee, the person or agency seeking enforcement can have child support payments withheld from an obligor's wages (even if the obligor is current in his or her payments) in the same way that taxes are withheld. States have been required to enact this type of withholding law in order to receive various federal funds.

B. Tax Refund Intercept   If the obligor is in arrears, the parent or agency can have both state and federal income tax refunds intercepted and forwarded to the parent or agency rather than to the obligor.

C. Liens   Liens can be placed on the obligor's real and personal property for child support obligations.

D. Federal Parent Locator Service   This service is operated by the Department of Health and Human Services and is authorized to use all federal government records, including IRS and military service records, to locate a missing obligor.

E. Health Insurance   If the obligor has access to low-cost health insurance, a state court must enter an order requiring the obligor to make this insurance available as part of a child support order.

Although the federal statute uses the term "child support enforcement," its enforcement tools can be used to collect alimony as well, provided that alimony collection is sought in conjunction with child support collection.

Another device used to enforce child support payments is the revocation or denial of specific types of license (license to practice law or medicine or driver's license) to those who are delinquent in their child support payments. Some form of this enforcement tool already had been enacted by more than thirty states when the federal government intervened to require all states to consider such legislation if they wanted to continue receiving federal funding for their Aid to Dependent Children programs.

Tax Considerations

As parties and their attorneys strive to reach equitable solutions to division of property and allocation of support in divorce cases, they must take all tax consequences of those solutions into account. The full range of tax rules affecting divorce are outside the scope of this text (capital gains, gift taxes, recapture rules, and so forth). Legal assistants should be familiar with the most obvious tax consequences, however.

Child support payments are not income to the recipient for income tax purposes; nether are they deductible by the payor parent. Under IRS rules, children may be taken as dependent exemptions by the parent who had custody of them for the majority of the calendar year if the children received over half of their support from that parent. In cases of joint custody, the parent with whom the child resided for a majority of the calendar year may take the exemption. These rules can be changed by the parties, either as part of a settlement agreement contemplating divorce or from year to year on special forms provided by the IRS. Divorces granted before 1985 are subject to different dependent exemption rules, which are not covered here.

Provided that payments from one spouse to the other qualify as alimony (using IRS guidelines), alimony is income to the recipient spouse and is deductible by the payor spouse. The guidelines require:

1. The payments must be in cash, not in property.
2. The payments must be paid under a divorce decree or separation agreement.
3. The decree or separation agreement cannot expressly state that the payments are *not* to be treated as alimony for tax purposes.
4. The spouses cannot be members of the same household when the payments are made.
5. The payments must terminate on the death of the recipient, either by state statute or by order of a court.
6. The spouses cannot file a joint tax return.
7. The payments cannot represent child support.

Parentage Issues

The legal relationship of parent and child traditionally arises within a marriage when a wife gives birth to the biological child of her husband. This is not the only way to create a lawful parent-child relationship, however.

The two most common nontraditional methods to create a parent-child relationship are adoption and paternity proceedings. All states have enacted statutory procedures for adoption of a child by someone other than her biological parent, which legally substitutes one parent for another. In other situations, a paternity proceeding may be used to establish the legal relationship of a father to his biological child when the father is not married to the mother.

Changing social structures and technological advances have combined to bring new parentage issues to the courts related to artificial insemination, ownership of frozen embryos, surrogacy, and the like. The cases in these areas are very new and very few in number, making it impossible to draw from them any general legal theories or principles that are likely to be accepted by a majority of states.

Adoption

Adoption is the legal process by which the parental relationship legally is transferred to another. Adoption did not exist in common law; it is purely statutory. All states have enacted statutes that regulate adoptions. A few states permit adoption of adults in limited situations, but most adoptions involve children.

Adoptions traditionally occurred when both of a child's parents either had died or had abandoned the child, leaving her an orphan. With today's complex family relationships, adoptions occur in a myriad of situations. For instance, an unwed mother may give up her child voluntarily for adoption. Parental rights can be terminated for abuse or neglect, making the child available for adoption. A second husband may be able to adopt his stepchild in some situations.

Adoption Placement   Whether an adoption is privately arranged or is arranged by an adoption agency, state statutes dictate the procedures that must be followed and the criteria that must be considered. Unlike their European counterparts, which focus on the adoptive parent and lines of property succession, American adoption statutes focus on the welfare of the child. This has led a few states to ban private placements altogether. In those states, a private party other than the child's relative cannot act as an intermediary in arranging the adoption. This type of ban seeks to limit incidents of "baby brokering." All states allow agency placement.

An adoption agency must be licensed by the state. The agency is required to conduct a thorough investigation of all prospective parents to determine their suitability to meet a particular child's needs. Adoptive parents generally pay a fee, including the costs associated with the adoption process and the investigation. Agency placement typically is lengthy and rigorous, with only a limited number of children made available for adoption.

In states where private placement is permitted, the process usually does not take as long as agency placement because the parties arrange the adoption themselves, usually with an attorney acting as the intermediary to ensure privacy for both the natural and adoptive parent(s). Adoptive parents generally pay all costs of adoption, including attorney fees and medical expenses connected with the pregnancy and birth. Paying additional amounts to the mother, however, generally constitutes "baby buying" in many states and is not allowed.

Children with special needs (serious medical afflictions, for example) present another type of placement problem. Without regard to financial ability, finding suitable adoptive parents is more difficult when the child will require intensive and/or long-term care. If the expense of this type of care is added to the list of requirements, most otherwise suitable families would be excluded. To alleviate this situation, many states now provide for a **subsidized adoption** that allows the child to obtain all or part of his required medical care at the expense of the state. The subsidy may continue for an indefinite period or for a limited time, depending on the language of a particular state's statute.

Parental Consent   Before a child is made available for adoption, the parental rights of her biological parents must be waived voluntarily or must be terminated by a court. The U. S. Constitution, through its Due Process Clause and its Equal Protection Clause, requires adoption statutes to guarantee certain rights to biological parents, including the right to notice of hearings and the right to equal treatment under the law. A statute cannot favor the mother over the father, for example.

A biological parent may waive his or her rights by consent, which generally must be in writing, often must be witnessed or notarized, and must be approved by a court to be binding. Some states will not acknowledge a consent that is obtained before the birth of a child, and many states require a minimum waiting period following the child's birth (48 hours, for example) before a consent can be obtained. Once a mother gives her written consent, states often allow her a period of time (from two to ten days) within which to change her mind by revoking her consent.

With fewer children available for adoption than in the past, a biological mother often is able to secure the adoptive parents' agreement that the child may know who the biological mother is and/or that the biological mother will have visition rights with the child following adoption. This situation (or some variation of it) is called an **open adoption**.

Unless a biological father has abandoned his child, he must be given written notice of the adoption proceeding as well as the opportunity to appear to present his position concerning the proposed adoption. Moreover, if he has lived with the child, has supported the child, or has maintained contacts with the child, he generally is given the same right as the mother to veto the proposed adoption.

Alternately, a biological parent's rights can be terminated by the court in a separate proceeding on the basis of abuse or extreme neglect. Abandonment, nonsupport, or conviction of certain types of crimes also can form the basis to terminate parental rights. Once a parent is shown to be an unfit by clear and convincing evidence, his or her parentel rights can be terminated. When parental rights are terminated, that parent's consent to a proposed adoption no longer is required.

Adoption Requirements   Each state grants jurisdiction to hear adoption cases to a specific court. This court reviews the adoption petition according to factors that are provided by statute, designed to make that match which is in the best interests of the child.

Although state statutes vary, they generally list certain criteria by which a proposed adoptive parent's suitability is to be gauged by the court. These may include religion, age, health, economic status, home environment, and physical or character defects of the adoptive parents. By federal mandate, race no longer can be considered as a factor in determining the best interests of the child. Religion may be considered as a factor; however, a state cannot ban adoptions based on religious beliefs.

In the past, states required adoptive parents to be married. Single-parent adoptions are now fairly common. In addition, cases allowing adoption by homosexual parents have begun to appear in a number of states. These generally involve one homosexual partner adopting the biological child of the other homosexual partner. At least two states (Florida and New Hampshire) specifically forbid adoption by a homosexual, however.

Once the court has assured itself that all procedural requirements have been met, that the adoptive parents are suitable, and that the adoption is in the best interests of the child, it will enter an interlocutory decree of adoption. After a stated period of time, a final hearing will be held which is much less rigorous than the first; and the decree will become final if no problems have arisen.

Once the adoption proceeding is concluded, the adoption records are sealed. Other than upon a showing of good cause, most states provide that no one can gain access to the records to discover information about any of the parties involved. Good cause may be shown, for instance, if an adoptive child contracts a disease for which hereditary information is needed for treatment. If an adopted child grows up and seeks his or her natural parent(s), a few courts have granted limited access to the records. Some states now provide a registry system, which allows biological parents to register their desire to know the whereabouts of their children. Adopted children also may register to know the whereabouts of their biological parents; and if there is a "match," the state notifies each of the other's name and address.

Effects of Adoption   With certain exceptions discussed above, a biological parent's rights and duties toward his or her child cease when the adoption proceeding is concluded. Those rights and duties are assumed by the adoptive parent(s), including the duty to support the child.

When the word "child" or "issue" appears in a will or in a trust document, most states interpret the word to include both biological and adopted children. In addition, nearly all states would allow an adopted child to inherit solely from and through her adoptive parents. There are exceptions, however.

> Carol is the daughter of Hagaar and Wilma, who were divorced in 1990. Neither had any other children. Wilma then married Horace, and Horace adopted Carol. Calvin was born to Wilma and Horace after their marriage. Several years later, Horace and Wilma died in an auto accident. Neither had a will. Hagaar's father drafted a will in 1994 that left his estate to "Hagaar, but if Hagaar predeceases me, then to any child or children of Horace's body who shall be living at my death, in equal shares." Hagaar died without a will in 1996. He had not remarried and had no other children. Hagaar's father died in 1997.

In this example, both Carol and Calvin inherit equally from the estates of Wilma and Horace. Because Carol was adopted by Horace, she is entitled to the same inheritance rights as Calvin, Horace's biological child. Notwithstanding the adoption, Carol continues to have inheritance rights in her mother's estate as the biological child of Wilma (Wilma's parental status was not affected by the adoption).

Carol cannot inherit from Hagaar under the intestate succession statutes of most states, since she was no longer his legal child at the time of his death. However, she probably will be able to take under the will of her biological grandfather in nearly all states. Hagaar's father drafted the will in 1994, after the adoption had taken place. Presumably, he knew of the adoption when the will was drafted. Certainly, he knew by the time of Hagaar's death in 1996 that Hagaar would have no children except Carol; yet, he did not change his will. No statute prevents a person from voluntarily transferring property to anyone he or she chooses. If Carol's grandfather had died without a will, however, intestate succession statutes would have required a different result.

When an adopted child dies, the vast majority of states give inheritance rights to the child's adoptive family rather than to the child's biological family.

Paternity Proceedings

When a married woman gives birth, the law presumes her husband to be the child's father, making him legally responsible for the child's support and care. This legal presumption may be rebutted in an action to determine **paternity** (fatherhood), either as a separate proceeding or in connection with a divorce case. It is the husband who generally would raise the paternity issue (usually as part of a divorce action). If the mother raises the issue of paternity by claiming that someone other than her husband is the father of her child, most states require her husband's consent before a paternity action can be commenced.

When an unmarried woman gives birth, the child is **illegitimate** (termed *born out of wedlock* in more recent cases and in some state statutes). This is the situation in which paternity proceedings most commonly are filed. By establishing the child's paternity, the mother establishes the child's right to support as well as to inheritance from the father's estate. If the state provides welfare benefits to the child, a state agency frequently is the party who initiates the paternity proceeding to obtain support from the child's father.

A paternity proceeding is a civil action. Evidence in these cases historically centered around the putative father's cohabitation with the mother, his acknowledgement of the child as his own either before or after birth, or similar facts. The law of the domicile of the putative father of an illegitimate child generally determines whether he has legitimitized the child. The law of the child's domicile does not govern.

These types of facts still are probative in a parternity proceeding; however, the reliability of DNA blood tests makes this type of evidence much more probative than the traditional methods. If the putative father is indigent, he has a right to state-subsidized DNA evidence to attempt to disprove his paternity. *Little v. Streater*, 452 U.S. 1 (1981).

Nearly all states have established some type of statute of limitations for paternity proceedings. The exact time limit in a particular state may be moot, however. Any state that receives federal funding via an Aid to Dependent Children program (all states receive this type of funding) must allow paternity actions to be filed until the child is 18 years old in compliance with the federal Child Support Enforcement Act Amendments of 1984. Notwithstanding this federal mandate, only a handful of states allow a paternity action to be brought after the death of the putative father.

Effects of Paternity　　When a man is determined to be the lawful father of a particular child, that child is entitled to support and to inheritance rights on the same level as any other child or children of his. Without a parternity proceeding, however, the child's legal rights may be lost.

The general rule is that a state cannot abolish completely the inheritance rights of a child who was born out of wedlock. However, many states require the child to have been acknowledged in some way during the parent's life in order to be included under the intestacy statutes of that state at the father's death.

In matters other than inheritance, state law often is inconsistent. For instance, a state cannot exclude illegitimate children from sharing with other, lawful children in the award of worker compensation benefits. Likewise, a state cannot provide a cause of action to children for wrongful death of a parent and exclude illegitimate children from pursuing the same right. However, state welfare legislation can discriminate against illegitimate children by denying welfare benefits to households in which the adults are not married.

Reproduction Technology

Advances over the last few decades in medical technology have made it possible for individuals to become biological parents who otherwise would not be able to give birth to children of their own. While innovations in the areas of artificial insemination, surrogacy, egg donation, and frozen embryos have made childbirth possible for many, they also have presented the judicial system with novel and sometimes complex legal issues concerning parentage, custody, visitaiton, and support.

Artificial Insemination　　　Through artificial insemination, a woman may be impregnated with a donor's sperm by medical procedure rather than by sexual intercourse. If the couple is married and if the donor is the husband, the child's legal status is the same as any other child born of the marriage. Either by statute or by case law in most states, the same result is reached if the couple is married and if the donor is not the husband, provided the procedure was performed by or under the direction of a physician and provided the husband consented to the procedure. The husband, then, is responsible for child support even if the couple separates; and if the child is to be relinquished for adoption, the husband must consent.

When the mother is unmarried at the time she is artificially inseminated and remains unmarried at the time of birth, the results may vary from state to state. Some have resolved the matter by statute, which commonly provides that the donor is not the legal father when the procedure is performed by or under the direction of a physician. If no statute exists, it is possible that the donor can be treated as the legal father of the child. This is particularly true if he seeks paternity rights.

Surrogacy   Surrogacy originated when a married couple could not have children of their own, either because the wife was unable to conceive or was unable to carry a child to full term. The couple would agree with another woman to act as the surrogate mother. The woman would be impregnated artificially with the husband's sperm and would waive all parental rights to the child upon its birth. The wife, then, would adopt the child. The husband need not adopt, since he would be the biological father. Most surrogacy arrangements go as planned. It is only in the rare situation where the surrogate mother changes her mind that the courts become involved.

Very few states have enacted statutes to deal with surrogacy. Where no statute exists, most courts are opposed to the concept and tend to disregard any surrogacy contract that may exist, holding it void as against public policy. This is especially true when the surrogate mother is also the donor of the egg from which the child is born. When a custody battle ensues between the child's biological parents (the surrogate and the sperm donor), the wife of the child's father has no legal rights at all. The losing party in the custody litigation may be entitled to visitation rights as the child's lawful parent. This was the result in the most famous surrogacy case, *In Re Baby M*, 537 A.2d 1227 (1988), where the child's father was granted custody, with visitation rights awarded to the child's mother (the surrogate).

In at least three states (Arizona, Indiana, and North Dakota), surrogacy contracts are unenforceable. Other states may follow. Eleven states have enacted statutes that deal with surrogacy, largely making the practice very difficult to enforce. Virginia and New Hampshire have enacted statutes that attempt to regulate surrogacy contracts, but Virginia has the only statutory framework that would enforce a surrogacy contract against the wishes of the surrogate if the contract is approved by a judge under fairly rigorous criteria and before pregnancy occurs. Even then, the surrogate can change her mind until the end of the sixth month of pregnancy.

The Uniform Status of Children of Assisted Conception Act was proposed in 1988 to provide guidelines for approval of surrogacy contracts. No state has adopted this uniform law to date.

Another type of surrogacy results from the procedure known as in vitro fertilization. Here, conception occurs in a test tube, using the egg of the wife and the sperm of the husband. The resulting embryo is implanted into the surrogate, who carries it to term and then gives birth. Sometimes called gestational surrogacy, this procedure is different from conventional surrogacy in that the biological mother and the birth mother are not the same person. Only a handful of cases have been decided on this issue, because it is so new. The few cases that exist, however, have been decided in favor of the biological mother. This is consistent with the conventional surrogacy cases, in which genetics seem to be the predominant factor in determining who is the child's legal mother.

Embryos   Just as sperm may be donated for use in artificial insemination, medical technology now makes it possible for eggs to be donated for in vitro fertilization. The embryo is then implanted in the intended mother. Under the Uniform Status of Children of Assisted Conception Act, the third-party egg donor is viewed much like a third-party sperm donor. She never would be considered the legal mother under the Act. Case law on this specific issue is sparse to nonexistent, because the medical procedure is so new.

In other situations, litigation concerning embryos has occurred only slightly more often; but a few trends emerge.

> While Hiram and Wanda were married, Wanda contracted a serious illness that threatened her ability to have children. She and Hiram decided to undergo in vitro fertilization and to freeze the embryos in case they decided to have a family later. Wanda recovered from her illness, and a divorce followed. Wanda then decided to have one of the embryos implanted so that she could have a child. Hiram objected.

In this situation, Hiram's objection generally will be honored. Both parties own the embryos, and either party may veto a pregnancy based on their use. In a similar situation, the Social Security Administration has refused death benefits to a child born as a result of in vitro fertilization that took place after the death of the child's biological father.

Guardians and Conservators

The family law practitioner is certain to encounter situations in which a conservator or a guardian either has been or should be appointed to protect the interests of a person under legal disability. The person who needs protection is called a *ward*. The ward (sometimes called the "protected person") may be a minor, may be an elderly person, or may be an adult who is either mentally or physically so impaired as to be unable to handle his or her own affairs and/or finances.

Guardians

In some states, a guardian protects both the property and the person of the ward. As the term is used here, however, **guardian** refers to one who is appointed by a court to protect only the person of the ward. If both parents of a child die, for instance, a guardian may be appointed for the child until he is no longer a minor or until he is adopted. Similarly, if an adult becomes incapable of making basic decisions concerning her life, a guardian may be appointed for her.

> Marian is the adult daughter of Joseph and Elizabeth. As a result of a car accident, Marian was in a coma. No one could be certain when or if she would become conscious.

In this situation, Joseph and Elizabeth could apply to a court to become Marian's guardians. While Marian was a minor child, her parents were her natural guardians. Since this status ended when Marian became an adult, her parents must be appointed as guardians by a competent court if they wish to assume this role.

A guardian may be a relative of the person to be protected, but this is not always the case. One frequently sees situations in which a private attorney, an officer of a bank, or some other responsible person is appointed as guardian for the ward. State statutes generally state the specific requirements to be appointed as a guardian. Once appointed, the guardian makes all important decisions concerning the ward's living arrangements, care, education, and the like. If a guardian has been appointed, for example, the ward (whether a minor or an adult) cannot marry without the guardian's consent. A guardian has some limitations, however. For instance, he or she cannot create a will for the ward in most states.

Guardians typically are required to report periodically to the court concerning the ward's living arrangements and status throughout the time that the guardianship exists. To avoid the type of public scrutiny of their personal affairs that exists in a guardianship arrangement, adults often execute a power of attorney to name a specific person to act on their behalf in the event of their disability.

Conservators

In those states where guardians and conservators are separate, a **conservator** is appointed by a court of proper jurisdiction to manage the financial affairs of the ward. This text assumes the duties to be distinct from those of a guardian, since a family law legal assistant must know the difference between the two even if the laws of his or her own state do not provide separately for a conservator.

> Raymond is an elderly man for whom the court has appointed a conservator. Raymond lives in an assisted care facility; however, he does not require round-the-clock care. Raymond falls in love with Heloise, a widow who lives in the same retirement facility, and wants to marry her.

Since a conservator—not a guardian—has been appointed in the example, the state where Raymond lives apparently separates the duties of guardians and conservators. Raymond will not need the conservator's permission to marry. The conservator may block the marriage, however, by refusing to pay for the marriage license, blood tests, and so forth. The conservator also may require an antenuptial agreement to protect Raymond's financial interests in relation to the marriage.

A conservator may be a relative of the ward; but more often, a court will appoint a disinterested third party who has some business acumen to manage the ward's financial affairs. Depending on the provisions of a particular state's statutes, a conservator may be a bank, an attorney, or other qualified person or entity. A conservator may do all things on behalf of the ward related to financial matters except write a will.

Similar to a guardian, a conservator must report periodically to the court concerning the ward's financial affairs, usually in the form of an accounting that lists the ward's income, expenses, and assets. A conservatorship is a matter of public record; and for this reason, many people find that a power of attorney executed before the onset of disability or a trust arrangement is better suited for their own needs or for the needs of their family members.

In some states, a conservator must be appointed to receive a damage award on behalf of a minor when the award exceeds a stated amount ($5,000.00, for example). In this situation, the conservator typically is one or both parents of the child. As conservators, the parents then are required to report periodically to the court concerning disposition and status of the funds awarded on the child's behalf.

Family Law Self-Test

Allow an uninterrupted thirty-minute period to answer all questions. At the end of thirty minutes, check your answers against those in the Answer Key Section of this Manual. Deduct two points for each incorrect answer (100 total possible points). Unanswered questions are counted as incorrect answers. Follow directions carefully and observe the time limit precisely to provide an accurate self-assessment.

Choose the most correct answer to the following questions unless a specific question instructs you to do otherwise.

1.   True or False.   The first no-fault divorce statute in the United States was enacted in Nevada.

2.   True or False.   Under common law rules, a parent is entitled to any wages earned by his or her child.

3.   True or False.   By Supreme Court decision, a state may refuse to issue a marriage license to a person if he or she is delinquent in paying child support.

4.   True or False.   A state law that prohibits marriage between persons of the same gender is called a miscegenation statute.

5.   True or False.   In family law, consanguinity refers to the act of an adult woman and an adult man in living together as husband and wife without benefit of a ceremonial marriage.

6.   True or False.   A state lawfully may impose a restriction that prevents a person with AIDS from marrying.

7.   If a person has married three different people without ever obtaining a divorce from any one of them, he or she can be convicted of:

    a.   Bigamy.
    b.   Polygamy.
    c.   Trigamy.
    d.   All are correct.
    e.   None is correct.

8.   Which of the following factors will not be considered by a court in determining whether an antenuptial agreement is fair and reasonable?

    a.   The respective property of each spouse.

    b.   The financial needs of each spouse following termination of marriage.

    c.   The respective ages, health, and experience of each spouse.

    d.   The ability of each spouse to understand the agreement before signing.

    e.   All are factors that will be considered.

9.   Which of the following cannot be properly included in the terms of an antenuptial agreement?

    a.   Division of assets in the event of divorce.

    b.   Payment of alimony.

    c.   Payment of child support.

    d.   Inheritance rights of each spouse at the other's death.

10.   The equity defense used when a party attempts to assert a wrongful act by the other, all or part of which was of the asserting party's own making, is:

    a.   Laches

    b.   Fraud

    c.   Clean hands

    d.   Estoppel

11.   Property acquired by spouses during their marriage is called:

    a.   Joint property

    b.   Marital property

    c.   Equitable property

    d.   Common property

12.   Which of the following obligations ends when a marriage is terminated?

    a.   Property division

    b.   Child support and custody

    c.   Consortium

    d.   Alimony

13.   True or False.   The Latin phrase that means "in the place of the parent" is *parens patriae*.

14.   True or False.   Under existing federal tax laws, alimony is income to the recipient and is deductible for the payor.

15.   True or False.   When facts show successive marriages by the same person, the law presumes the first marriage to be the valid one.

16.   True or False.   Under Supreme Court rulings, states no longer can impose criminal sanctions against consenting adults who engage in homosexual conduct.

17.   True or False.   By Supreme Court decision, states no longer can prohibit marriage between persons of different race.

18.   True or False.   By Supreme Court decision, states no longer can prohibit marriage between persons of the different gender.

19.   In states where the following arrangements are recognized, which must be in writing to be enforceable by a court?

      a.   Antenuptial agreement.
      b.   Cohabitation agreement.
      c.   Separation agreement.
      d.   (a) and (c) but not (b).
      e.   All must be in writing.

20.   Which of the following can be modified only upon proof of fraud by one of the parties?

      a.   Child support.
      b.   Property division.
      c.   Alimony.
      d.   None can be modified.

21.   URESA is used primarily:

      a.   To collect support from an out-of-state obligor.
      b.   To collect support from the obligor, regardless of his or her location.
      c.   To intercept tax refunds due the obligor from the IRS.
      d.   To reimburse support provided by a IV-D agency.

22.   Once Dick and Jane were married, Jane discovered that Dick was impotent. Under the laws of most states, Jane would be successful if she filed suit for:

      a.   Annulment.
      b.   Divorce.

(see next page)

    c.   Legal separation.
    d.   Any one of the above.
    e.   Two of the above.

23.   True or False.   A parent who has been ordered to pay child support can be forced to have the payments withheld from wages, even though s/he never has been late with any of the payments as they became due.

24.   True or False.   Either the mother or the father of a child may inititate paternity proceedings concerning that child.

25.   True or False.   Because of the Uniform Marriage and Divorce Act, an abused spouse can file an action in federal court for damages and for future protection from the abuser.

26.   A child can become emancipated before the age of majority if the following event(s) occur(s):

    a.   The child joins the military.
    b.   The child's parents divorce.
    c.   The child enters into a contract for necessaries.
    d.   The child commits a crime and is tried as an adult.
    e.   a and d.

27.   The type of alimony awarded most frequently by today's courts is:

    a.   Permanent alimony.
    b.   Rehabilitative alimony.
    c.   Alimony in gross.
    d.   Compensatory alimony.

28.   The right of dower has been replaced in many states by:

    a.   Intestate distribution.
    b.   The elective share.
    c.   Curtesy.
    d.   Married women's property acts.

29.   Before a court can issue a child support order that is binding upon an individual parent:

a. The parent must appear before the court in person.

b. The court must have personal jurisdiction over the child.

c. The court must have personal jurisdiction over the parent.

d. b and c.

e. All are correct.

30. An order for support can be modified in relation to:

a. Arrearages only.

b. Future payments only.

c. Both arrearages and future payments.

d. Payments that become due after notice of the proceeding to modify is filed on the payor parent.

e. All of the above.

31. True or False. Palimony can be enforced by the courts of most states.

32. True or False. When a state enacts an informed consent statute, it cannot include a provision that requires a wife to inform her husband of her pending abortion or that requires him to consent.

33. True or False. Except in a medical emergency, a physicial must give a woman information concerning her pending abortion, as well as concerning alternatives to abortion, at least 48 hours before the abortion can occur.

34. True or False. Under the law of most states, a husband cannot be convicted of raping his wife while the couple continue to live together.

35. True or False. A filial responsibility statute is a state law that requires a parent to continue to support his or her adult child if that child is sufficiently disabled as to be unable to provide his or her own support.

36. Under the Federal Rules of Evidence:

a. One spouse cannot be required to testify against the other in an ongoing marriage where the parties continue to live together.

b. One spouse cannot be required to testify against the other in an ongoing marriage where the parties are separated.

c. One spouse cannot be required to testify against the other in a criminal case.

d. a and c.

37. The following proceedings originated in common law except:

a.   Adoption.
b.   Annulment of marriage.
c.   Legal separation.
d.   a and b.
e.   None is correct.

38.   While a divorce decree is interlocutory:

a.   It can be vacated by joint motion of the parties.
b.   If either party dies, the other is treated as a surviving spouse.
c.   Neither party can remarry.
d.   a and c but not b.
e.   a, b, and c are correct.

39.   In community property states:

a.   Elective share statutes are not necessary.
b.   Property division in divorce actions are based on equitable distribution principles.
c.   Neither spouse can lease the property without consent of the other.
d.   All are true.

40.   When deciding issues of child custody, which of the following factors is most probative to most courts?

a.   Extramarital affairs in which each parent may have engaged.
b.   The financial condition of each parent.
c.   Identification of the child's primary caretaker.
d.   The race of each parent in an interracial marriage.

41.   True or False.   The Uniform Child Custody Jurisdiction Act is a federal statute that applies in all 50 states as well as in the District of Columbia.

42.   True or False.   The Parental Kidnapping Protection Act is a federal statute that sets out procedural requirements to be met when one state is asked to enforce or to modify another state's custody decree.

43.   True or False.   A child custody arrangement in which the child lives with one parent for part of the time and with the other parent for part of the time is called joint custody.

44.   True or False.   Federal law requires every state to adopt child support guidelines for use by state courts in determining the amount of child support that should be paid.

45.   True or False.   If a noncustodial parent fails to pay child support when it becomes due, the custodial parent is not required to comply with visitation orders that may have been made.

46.   True or False.   The Child Support Enforcement Act of 1984 and its amendments can be used to collect both child support and alimony previosuly ordered.

47.   True or False.   A divorce is an equity action.

48.   True or False.   Common law marriage can be created in all but thirteen states.

49.   True or False.   If a common law marriage is created properly in a state that recognizes common law marriage, every other state must recognize the marriage under the Full Faith and Credit Clause of the Constitution.

50.   True or False.   A child born out of wedlock cannot inherit from his biological father in most states without a paternity proceeding or some other type of acknowledgement of the child by the biological father.

Chapter 15
LITIGATION

If you find a path with no obstacles, it probably doesn't lead anywhere.

—Anonymous

Litigation is the heart of the American legal system. Everything that lawyers do is gauged either to avoid litigation or to prepare for litigation. Therefore, every legal assistant, regardless of his or her practice area, must know litigation fundamentals. Litigation legal assistants must know substantially more than the fundamentals, however, to succeed on this portion of the CLA® certification exam.

Applicants who select Litigation as one of their substantive law subsections will be familiar with state laws and rules concerning litigation, of course. However, a national examination can test applicants' knowledge of state rules only in a very general way. Applicants will be well served by focusing on general litigation principles as well as by intensive study of the Federal Rules of Civil Procedure. Review the Federal Rules of Evidence, the Federal Rules of Appellate Procedure, and federal statutes related to jurisdiction and venue as well. *(Specific statutes are referred to throughout this chapter.)* In addition to these materials, refer to the General Law chapter of this *Review Manual* for summaries related to court systems, subject matter jurisdiction, personal jurisdiction, standing, and venue. The materials related to segregation of relevant facts, which are found in the Judgment chapter of this *Review Manual*, likewise will be helpful.

817

Unless stated otherwise, when the term *Rule* is used throughout this chapter, it refers to a rule of the Federal Rules of Civil Procedure.

One of the most effective ways to study any technical area is to create a timeline or a flow chart. Use this tool in addition to—not in place of—other study methods. A sample form for a flow chart for the Federal Rules of Civil Procedure is included on the following page.

The sample form is not complete. It represents an initial draft or outline of the flow chart, with only the most basic procedural elements of a federal litigation. Re-create and increase the flow chart's physical size by transferring it to several sheets of paper (continuous-feed computer paper works well). Imagine a hypothetical case and plot it from beginning to end on the flow chart, adding to and expanding each of the basic elements to show the significant features about each element (how, when, and why it is used), timing, requirements, and exceptions stated in the Rules or in related statutes.

Once the basic flow chart is completed, it can be expanded to include step-by-step procedures for various hypothetical contingencies (methods of serving summons on multiple defendants in varying situations, obtaining a deposition of an out-of-state witness, and so forth).

Working with a flow chart similar to this one helps to clarify the system that controls the litigation process. Flow charts are helpful to learn or to review any area of substantive or procedural law, because each area has its own system. Familiarity with the system makes it easier to recall details in a testing situation or on the job.

FEDERAL CIVIL LITIGATION FLOW CHART

PLEADINGS

Complaint
Rule 3
Rule 8(a)
Rule 9

Summons
Rule 4

Answer
Rule 8
Rule 12(a)

Reply to
Counterclaim
Rule 7(a)

Preliminary
Motions
Rule 12(b)

Motion for
Judgment on
the Pleadings
(after pleadings
closed)
Rule 12(c)

DISCOVERY

Interrogatories
Rule 33

Request to Produce
Rule 34

Request for
Physical or Mental
Examination
Rule 35

Depositions
Rules 30, 31

Requests for
Admission
Rule 36

Motion to Compel
Rule 37

Motion for Summary
Judgment
(during/after
discovery)
Rule 56

TRIAL

Pretrial
Conference
Rule 16

Pretrial Order
or Scheduling
Order
Rule 16

Voir Dire

Opening
Statements

Plaintiff's Case

Direct Testimony
& Exhibits
Cross-Examination
Rebuttal

Motion for Judgment
as a Matter of Law
(jury trials only)
Rule 50

Motion for Judgment
on Partial Findings
(nonjury trials only)
Rule 52(c)

Defendant's Case

Direct Testimony
& Exhibits
Cross-Examination
Rebuttal

Motion for Judgment
as a Matter of Law
(both jury and
nonjury trials)
Rule 50

Closing Arguments

Jury Instructions

Jury Deliberation

Verdict

Judgment

POST-TRIAL

Motion for Judgment
as a Matter of Law
Rule 50

Motion to Amend Judgment
Rule 59(e)

Motion for New Trial
Rule 59(a)

APPEAL

Notice of Appeal

Appellate Briefs Filed

Oral Arguments

Decision
(Affirm, Reverse,
or Remand)

Selecting the Proper Court

Selecting the proper court involves three separate and distinct issues, considered in this order: (1) subject matter jurisdiction, (2) personal jurisdiction, and (3) venue. *Subject matter jurisdiction* is the power or authority of a particular court to decide a specific type of case. *Personal jurisdiction* is the power or authority of a particular court over specific litigants. *Venue* refers to the geographical location(s) within a jurisdiction where the case should be tried. *(Refer to the General Law chapter for a discussion of other types of jurisdiction.)*

Subject Matter Jurisdiction The United States District Court (federal trial court) is a court of limited jurisdiction, which means that it does not have authority to decide all types of cases. Rather, its subject matter jurisdiction is conferred by statute. Of all of the areas for which subject matter jurisdiction is granted to the United States District Court, the three invoked most frequently are (1) cases in which the Unites States, its agencies, or its officers are parties; (2) cases involving federal questions; and (3) cases involving diversity of citizenship.

1. The United States, its agencies, or its officers are parties if named either as a plaintiff or as a defendant in the lawsuit. 28 U.S.C. §§ 1345, 1346.

2. A case involves a federal question if it is a "civil action arising under the Constitution, laws, or treaties of the United States." 28 U.S.C. § 1331.

3. A case involves diversity of citizenship if it is a civil action "where the matter in controversy exceeds the sum or value of $75,000, exclusive of interest and costs, and is between . . . citizens of different states." 28 U.S.C. § 1332. Special rules apply in determining whether both parts of diversity jurisdiction requirements are met.

The amount in controversy, exclusive of interest and costs, must exceed $75,000 in diversity cases, which means that it must be at least $75,000.*01*. A claim valued at $75,000 or less does not meet the jurisdictional requirement. If a suit involves a statute which awards attorney fees, the attorney fees may be included to reach the jurisdictional minimum. A plaintiff with more than one claim against a defendant may combine her claims to reach the required amount. If there are multiple plaintiffs, however, each plaintiff's claim(s) must exceed $75,000; the claims of different plaintiffs cannot be combined to reach the required amount. If multiple plaintiffs are common owners of property and if the property is the subject of the dispute, the total value of the property is used to determine whether the minimum amount is met—not the value of each plaintiff's undivided interest in the property.

The diversity of litigants in diversity cases must be complete diversity, based upon each litigant's state of citizenship (domicile). **Domicile** is the permanent home of the litigant. In determining domicile, a court may consider where the litigant is registered to vote, where automobiles are registered, or other factors that indicate a permanent home. For example, a retiree domiciled in New York may reside in Florida during the winter months, returning to New York in the spring. Even though the retiree maintains a residence in Florida, her domicile continues in New York.

A person may have several residences but can have only one domicile. By contrast, a corporation may be domiciled both in its state of incorporation and in the state where its principal place of business is located for purposes of federal diversity claims. If a corporation is incorporated separately in several different states, it may be domiciled in each of those states at the same time for purposes of determining diversity. If the corporation issues insurance policies, it is domiciled in the state of its incorporation, in the state where its principal offices are located, and in the state of the insured. 28 U.S.C. § 1332(c).

Complete diversity means that no plaintiff can be a citizen of the same state as any defendant. If there is a common state of domicile between any plaintiff and any defendant, diversity jurisdiction is destroyed even if the claims exceed $50,000. For purposes of establishing diversity, the District of Columbia is treated as a separate state.

> (1) Alice and Bob are citizens of Colorado. They want to join in a suit against the Charter Corporation, which is incorporated in Delaware and maintains its headquarters office in New Jersey.
> (2) Daniel is a citizen of New Jersey. Eugene is a citizen of New York. They want to join in a suit against the Charter Corporation, which is incorporated in Delaware and maintains its headquarters office in New Jersey.

(1) Assuming the jurisdictional minimum amount is met, complete diversity exists in the first example; and the case may be filed in the United States District Court. No plaintiff is a citizen of the same state as any defendant; it makes no difference that both plaintiffs are citizens of the same state. (2) In the second example, however, diversity is not complete. Daniel is a citizen of New Jersey, and the corporation's headquarters office also is in New Jersey. If Daniel were dropped as a plaintiff in the suit, complete diversity would exist for purposes of federal jurisdiction; and Eugene could proceed in the federal trial court. If Daniel and Eugene want to sue as joint plaintiffs, however, they must do so in state court.

Diversity of citizenship must exist (1) when the complaint is filed in federal court or (2) both when the action is filed in state court and when the action is removed to federal court (*discussed below*). Once established, diversity remains in effect for the duration of the lawsuit even if a litigant changes her domicile (permanently moves to a new state) during that time.

When a federal court sits in diversity, it applies state (not federal) substantive law, using conflicts of law principles. *(Conflicts of law are discussed in the chapter on General Law.)* Diversity jurisdiction cannot be exercised in probate or domestic relations cases.

Supplemental Jurisdiction   Supplemental jurisdiction is a new term for old concepts. First codified in 28 U.S.C. § 1367 in 1990, supplemental jurisdiction allows additional claims and additional parties to be added to an existing federal case without independently satisfying the requirements of federal subject matter jurisdiction. Before this statute was enacted, additional claims and additional parties were added through the judicially created doctrines of pendent jurisdiction and ancillary jurisdiction.

Under the ***pendent jurisdiction*** doctrine, a state-created claim between parties sometimes could be added to a *similar federal question claim* pending in federal court between the same parties, even though the federal court would not have had jurisdiction if the state-created claim were filed separately.

> Alice is a citizen of California and is employed by the Baker Corporation, which is incorporated and has its principal place of business in California. Alice is next in line for promotion to a supervisor's position, but the position is given to a younger male because he is the sole support of his family. Alice ultimately files suit in federal court based upon equal employment opportunity provisions of Title VII. Alice believes that her employer also has violated the California statute concerning equal employment opportunity.

There is no independent federal subject matter jurisdiction for Alice's state claim against her employer (no federal question and no diversity of citizenship). However, under the doctrine of pendent jurisdiction, Alice could have added the claim for violation of state law to her federal claim, since both would have been similar and would have arisen from a *common nucleus of operative fact*. She now may achieve the same result through the supplemental jurisdiction provisions of 28 U.S.C. § 1367. The same statute makes it clear that supplemental jurisdiction may be used to require additional parties to defend a state-created claim in federal court, even though they are not named as defendants in the federal question claim.

Before statutory supplemental jurisdiction was enacted, the ***ancillary jurisdiction*** doctrine was created by judges for use in cases where diversity existed for at least one claim between one plaintiff and one defendant and where additional claims or additional parties were sought to be added to that core claim. Ancillary jurisdiction generally was used to provide federal jurisdiction over claims made by parties other than the plaintiff when there was no independent federal subject matter jurisdiction for the claim (counterclaim, cross-claim, or third-party complaint).

> Bob, a citizen of Missouri, took his van to Charlie's Garage, also located in Missouri, for brake work. After the van was picked up, the brakes failed within three blocks of the garage, striking a car driven by Alice, a citizen of Illinois. Alice filed a diversity action against Bob in federal court, alleging negligence.

In this example, Bob likely will want to file a third-party complaint against Charlie's Garage because of the failed brakes. However, since Bob and Charlie's Garage are citizens of the same state, there is no diversity between them; and Bob's third-party complaint could not meet the federal requirement for subject matter jurisdiction if it were filed independently. Under the former judicial doctrine of ancillary jurisdiction (now statutory supplemental jurisdiction), this problem would be resolved in favor of allowing Bob to file the third-party complaint.

To avoid situations in which parties may contrive to circumvent the federal diversity jurisdiction statute, 28 U.S.C. § 1367 prevents supplemental jurisdiction from being invoked in some situations where the core claim is based upon diversity only. Supplemental jurisdiction in diversity cases does not apply to:

- Claims by a plaintiff against a third-party defendant.

- Claims by or against one who was made a party to the action under Rule 19's compulsory joinder provisions.

- Claims by a plaintiff against a defendant who was made a party to the action under Rule 20's permissive joinder provisions. (The exclusion does not apply to claims by a plaintiff against a co-plaintiff who was made a party to the action by permissive joinder.)

- Claims by a prospective plaintiff who attempts to intervene under Rule 24.

Although the federal court has authority to exercise supplemental jurisdiction in relation to compulsory counterclaims, cross-claims, or claims of third-party defendants, it may decline to exercise supplemental jurisdiction if the claim presents a novel or complex question of state law, if the claim predominates over those claims for which the court has original jurisdiction, or if the court has dismissed all claims for which it had original jurisdiction.

Supplemental jurisdiction is designed to facilitate subject matter jurisdiction only. It does not remove the requirements for exercise of personal jurisdiction or for service of process.

Removal Jurisdiction   Removal jurisdiction evolved in an era when defendants from other states were viewed with suspicion and may have been prejudiced in favor of local plaintiffs in state court actions. Allowing the out-of-state defendant to remove the case to federal court was designed to minimize the "home town" advantage enjoyed by the plaintiff. Although state boundary lines no longer present the barriers that they once did, removal jurisdiction continues as a way of means of permitting defendants to avoid favoritism for the plaintiff, whether real or perceived.

As a general rule, any case filed in a state court may be removed by the defendant to federal court if the federal court could have exercised original jurisdiction over the case. 28 U.S.C. § 1441. *A plaintiff never can seek removal.* In diversity cases, removal can occur only if no defendant is a citizen of the state in which the state court action was filed. Moreover, the defendant is subject to the additional requirement that complete diversity of citizenship must exist both at the time the original state action was filed and at the time when removal is sought.

A federal court may exercise removal jurisdiction only if the state court in which the action was pending originally had jurisdiction.

> Alice files suit against Bob in state court for relief on a patent held by Bob. The federal court has exclusive jurisdiction of patent matters. Realizing the error, Bob attempts to remove the case to federal court.

This example highlights what can be a ridiculous result: The federal court cannot exercise removal jurisdiction because the state court did not have jurisdiction to hear the case in the first place. Bob's best option is to raise the issue of lack of subject matter jurisdiction in the state court proceeding. If Alice's claim is dismissed by the state court on that basis (which it should be), Alice will be forced to file a new action in federal court.

Removal generally is determined from the facial allegations of the plaintiff's claim. Assume that a plaintiff has a federal claim that could be raised but elects not to raise it. With neither diversity jurisdiction nor a federal claim, the defendant has no basis for removal.

28 U.S.C. § 1441(c) provides that when a federal question claim is joined with a "separate and independent" claim that could not be removed if it were filed alone, the entire case may be removed to federal court; and the federal court may decide all issues or, in its discretion, may decide the federal question issue and remand all issues in which state law predominates. The same is not true of federal diversity claims. If a diversity claim is joined with a "separate and independent" claim that could not be removed if it were filed alone, no part of the case may be removed to federal court. This is a change in the law that became effective in 1990.

If a defendant has taken extensive action in the state court proceeding, she may not be able to remove the case at all. When removal is possible, notice of removal generally must be filed in the federal court within 30 days after the defendant receives service of the state court claim. All but nominal defendants must join in the notice of removal. The notice must contain those facts which entitle the defendant to remove the case to federal court. Once the notice has been filed, the state court may take no further action in the case unless the federal court determines that removal jurisdiction does not exist and remands the case to state court. 28 U.S.C. § 1446 *et seq.*

Personal Jurisdiction

Personal jurisdiction, also called *in personam* jurisdiction, is the court's authority to reach a decision affecting a particular person or entity. Personal jurisdiction involves the due process requirement that a party must be given notice and an opportunity to be heard. Intertwined with the due process requirement is a particular court's authority to give notice; its power to require a party to appear before it; and, if the party fails to appear, its power to impose sanctions.

Personal jurisdiction over plaintiffs is not a problem, because plaintiffs voluntarily subject themselves to the court's jurisdiction when they file their complaints. Therefore, personal jurisdiction issues generally relate to a court's authority over defendants.

Personal jurisdiction historically has been limited by state boundary lines. Although state lines continue as an important limitation for personal jurisdiction, enactment of long-arm statutes and conduct of the defendant make it much easier to acquire authority over out-of-state defendants than it once was. A ***long-arm statute*** typically allows courts to "reach out with a long arm" and pull defendants back to the forum state to defend themselves when they engage in conduct which causes injury in the forum state. Where a long-arm statute exists, both the state and the federal courts of that state may use it to acquire personal jurisdiction over out-of-state defendants.

Notwithstanding any other rules, jurisdiction over a defendant cannot be exercised unless the defendant has at least *minimum contacts* with the state in which the forum court sits. This means that the defendant must have engaged in some voluntary, affirmative act directed at the forum state (selling products, goods, or services in the state; telephone solicitations into the state; visiting the state; flying over the state; incorporating in the state). Once personal jurisdiction is established, it continues throughout the litigation.

In general, personal jurisdiction over an individual may be exercised when the individual:

- Is domiciled within the forum state;
- Is present within the forum state;
- Consents to suit within the forum state;
- Commits tortious acts which cause injury within the forum state; or
- Does business within the forum state.

A state may exercise personal jurisdiction over a domestic corporation (one incorporated in the forum state). A state also may exercise personal jurisdiction over a foreign corporation by requiring the corporation to appoint an agent to receive in-state process when it is registered or licensed as a foreign corporation in that state. In federal diversity cases, a corporation is a citizen both of the state where it is incorporated and the state where it has its principal place of business.

Service of Process   As a general rule, service of process in federal court cases can be made only within the territorial limits of the state in which the federal court sits. However, Congress has enacted laws to increase the territory of possible service in certain types of cases. For example, Rule 14 third-party defendants and Rule 19 indispensable parties may be served anywhere outside the state so long as it is within a 100-mile radius of the place (courthouse) where the case is filed. Nationwide service of process is permitted in interpleader cases *(discussed below)* and in cases filed against federal officials or federal agencies. In addition, services of process in federal cases can be made according to the forum state's long-arm statute. A defendant who is not within the forum state cannot be served with process if she cannot be served under one of these provisions, even if she more than meets the minimum contacts requirement.

Other than the summons, complaint, or a subpoena, all federal service must be made by the U.S. Marshal, a deputy U.S. Marshal, or a person specially appointed. A summons, complaint, or subpoena may be served by the Marshal if a party first obtains a court order. Absent a properly signed waiver of service of summons *(discussed below)* from the defendant, the summons and complaint may be served by anyone 18 or older who is not a party by delivering the summons and complaint to the party personally (personal service) or by leaving them at his dwelling with a person of suitable age and discretion who resides there (substitute service). A subpoena likewise may be served personally by anyone 18 or older who is not a party to the action. An attorney, for instance, can serve a summons, complaint, or subpoena.

Process can be served upon corporations by serving an officer or a general/resident agent of the corporation. In addition, service of process can be made in any way permitted by state law, including certified mail.

Venue   Venue refers to the place (the geographic location) within a jurisdiction where trial should occur. Venue does not become an issue until personal jurisdiction has been established. Venue in state court actions typically lies where the cause of action arose, where the defendant resides, or where the defendant has either a place of business or an agent. The venue statute of a particular state may provide for other places as well.

Under 28 U.S.C. § 1391 (1990), there are three basic methods to determine whether venue exists in a particular federal judicial district (some states have more than one federal judicial district):

1.   If any defendant resides in the district and all defendants reside in the state in which the district is located (applies both to federal question cases and to diversity cases);

2.   If a substantial part of the events or omissions giving rise to the claim occurred in the district or if a substantial part of the property that is the subject of the action is located in the district (applies both to federal question cases and to diversity cases); or

3.   If all defendants are subject to personal jurisdiction in the district (applies to diversity cases only) or if any defendant "may be found" in the district and there is no other district in which the action may be brought (applies to federal question cases only).

> Alice, a citizen of Minnesota, files suit in federal court against Bob, a resident of the Eastern District of Michigan, and against Charles, a resident of the Western District of Michigan.

> Allen, a citizen of Maine, files suit in federal court against Barbara, a resident of the Southern District of New York, and Charlotte, a resident of Massachusetts.

In the first example, venue is proper either in the Eastern District of Michigan or in the Western District of Michigan, because either district is the residence of at least one defendant; and each is located in a state in which all defendants reside. Since there is no state in which all defendants reside in the second example, venue must be based either upon the "place of events or property" or upon the catch-all provisions (see #3 above). Recall that personal jurisdiction must be satisfied before venue is considered.

The older "where the claim arose" language was replaced in 1990 with the language found in #2 above.

When a case is filed in a particular federal judicial district, the court may decline to hear the case if it determines that the district is a *forum non conveniens*. In other words, if more than one federal court meets jurisdictional and venue requirements and if trial of the case in the forum court would pose substantial inconvenience to the defendant and to witnesses, the court may decline to hear the case in favor of a court that would provide a more convenient forum. Although federal courts occasionally do apply the doctrine of forum *non conveniens* to move a case to another judicial district, the majority of cases indicate that if a defendant meets the requirements for personal jurisdiction, including minimum contacts, it generally is difficult for her to convince a judge that the forum is not convenient.

Parties

Within the context of litigation, a party is a principal in the lawsuit (either a plaintiff or a defendant). Rule 17(a) requires parties to be real parties in interest. A *real party in interest* is either one who was damaged or one who caused damage (directly or indirectly) in a specific transaction or occurrence. In other words, a manufacturer which produces a defective product may be a real party in interest. The manufacturer's lender, however, is not a real party in interest even though it has a definite interest in the outcome of the suit. An entertainer who loses her vision permanently from using the defective product is a real party in interest. Her spouse also may be a real party in interest if the spouse is denied love and affection of the entertainer as a result of the injury. The entertainer's manager, however, is not a real party in interest.

A real party in interest is one who has standing in the suit; she often is a necessary or indispensable party *(discussed below)*.

Rule 17(b) requires that a party must have the capacity to sue or to be sued. Minors or incompetent persons, for example, do not have this capacity. As a result, they must sue or be sued through a legal representative. If a guardian does not already exist (a parent may be a natural guardian of a minor child), a *guardian ad litem* may be appointed by a court for purposes of the litigation. A corporation has the capacity to sue or to be sued, since it is an artificial person created by the state of its incorporation.

Joinder of Parties More than one plaintiff or more than one defendant may be joined in a single suit (1) if their claims arise from the same transaction or occurrence (or same series of transactions or occurrences); and (2) if their claims present a common question of law or of fact that will apply to all of them. This is a *permissive joinder*. Rule 20. The common question must be a substantial one in relation to all claims. The existence of other questions that are not shared by all parties does not bar joinder, however. An airplane crash, for example, may produce multiple plaintiffs who qualify for permissive joinder. If any plaintiff does not want to join in the action of the other plaintiffs, she may file her own, separate action if she wishes to do so.

When multiple plaintiffs are joined in a diversity case under Rule 20, the claims of each plaintiff must meet the jurisdictional minimum amount. A single plaintiff is allowed to aggregate her claims to reach the jurisdictional amount. However, multiple plaintiffs are not allowed to combine their claims.

> Eugene has a claim against Bob of $60,000 based upon an auto accident. Alice has a claim against Bob of $20,000 for negligence based upon the same auto accident. She also has a claim against Bob of $30,000 for breach of contract. Connie and David have claims against Bob of $25,000 each for negligence arising out the same auto accident in which Eugene and Alice were involved.

Assuming that all other requirements of diversity are met in the above example, Eugene and Alice may join as plaintiffs in the same action against Bob under Rule 20. Eugene's claim meets the jurisdictional amount, and Alice's aggregate claims meet the jurisdictional amount. Neither Connie or David, however, may join in the action; neither meets the jurisdictional minimum, and they cannot combine their claims for that purpose.

When multiple defendants are joined under Rule 20, the requirements of personal jurisdiction, including minimum contacts, must be met for each defendant. Federal courts in diversity cases follow the long-arm statutes of the state in which they are located. Venue requirements also must be met. When codefendants reside in different states, it still may be possible to satisfy venue requirements in diversity and federal question cases by filing suit in that district where a substantial portion of the events occurred.

Rule 19 covers situations in which additional parties must be joined once the jurisdictional requirements are met. Joinder under Rule 19 is a ***compulsory joinder***. Two types of parties are addressed in Rule 19:

(1) **Necessary Parties** A ***necessary party*** is one who has an interest in the controversy and who should be joined if possible for the sake of justice; however, if the party's joinder is impossible because of jurisdiction or venue problems, the suit could continue without him. A junior lienholder in a foreclosure action might be a necessary party, for example.

(2) **Indispensable Parties** An ***indispensable party*** is one whose interest is so essential that litigation without him would be unjust. If an indispensable party cannot be joined because of jurisdiction or venue problems, the suit must be dismissed. For example, if only two of six endorsers of a promissory note can be joined, the remaining four endorsers likely will be indispensable parties. *Shields v. Barrow*, 58 U.S. 130 (1855).

Dismissal resulted in the *Shields* case because some of the defendants were residents of the same state as the plaintiff, which destroyed diversity. In this type of situation, dismissal by a federal court does not prevent the plaintiff from pursuing a remedy in state court. Today's long-arm statutes avoid many of the personal jurisdiction problems that the *Shields* plaintiff faced.

Intervention Rule 24 allows a person who was not an original party to the suit to enter the suit upon her own initiative. This process is called intervention, and the person who intervenes is the *intervenor*. The intervention may be either ***of right*** (Rule 24[a]) or ***permissive*** (Rule 24[b]).

A stranger to the lawsuit has an automatic right to intervene (permission is not required) if she has an interest in the property or transaction which is the subject of the lawsuit, if disposition of the suit may impair that interest, *and* if her interest is not adequately represented by the existing parties.

> The Small Business Administration (SBA) sues the principals of a leasing company for loan default and seeks, among other things, repossession of certain equipment. A lessee of the equipment sought to be repossessed may be able to intervene as a matter of right.

In addition to the intervention provided under the Federal Rules of Civil Procedure, federal statutes sometimes give outsiders the right to intervene. For example, the United States has a statutory right to intervene when the constitutionality of an act of Congress is in issue.

Even if the lessee in the above example cannot intervene as a matter of right, it is possible that permissive intervention may be allowed by the court under Rule 24(b) if there is a common question of law or fact. For example, if a restrictive easement on land leased by the federal government is in dispute and if Bill's land (also leased by the government) contains the same type of restrictive easement, for instance, Bill may be able to obtain permissive intervention even if he cannot intervene as a matter of right.

Interpleader   Interpleader is allowed in federal courts and in most state courts to protect a party from having to pay the same claim twice in situations where he is uncertain who the proper claimant is.

> Gibraltar Insurance Company issued an insurance policy on the life of Sam Finkel. The named beneficiary is "Susan Finkel, spouse of the insured." Sam was married to Susan when the policy was issued in 1960. They divorced last year, and Sam married Bunny two months before his death. Both Susan and Bunny claim the policy proceeds.

If Gibraltar pays the policy proceeds to Susan and if it evolves that the proceeds should have been paid to Bunny, Gibraltar will have to pay the proceeds again. Faced with this situation, Gibraltar can protect itself by filing an interpleader action in which both Susan and Bunny are named as defendants and can require the claimants to litigate the beneficiary issue. In this way, Gibraltar avoids exposure to double liability.

In federal practice, interpleader actions may arise under Rule 22 or under the statutory interpleader provisions of 28 U.S.C. § 1335. The differences between the two types of interpleader actions relate to subject matter and personal jurisdiction.

Without a federal question, a Rule 22 stakeholder (Gibraltar in the above example) cannot be a citizen of the same state as any claimant; and the amount in controversy must exceed $50,000. Service of process is made according to the general rules for federal civil suits. The stakeholder is not required to deposit the disputed property with the court, however.

Without a federal question, statutory interpleader requires only that some pair of claimants must be citizens of different states. What this means is that the stakeholder and one or more claimants can be from the same state, as long as there is diversity between at least two of the claimants. For example, if Gibraltar and

Susan were citizens of the same state in the example above, jurisdiction still would be possible so long as Susan and Bunny were from different states. The amount in controversy must be in excess of $500 under statutory interpleader, which is substantially less than in Rule 22 interpleader actions. Service of process may be made anywhere in the United States. However, unlike Rule 22 interpleader actions, the stakeholder must deposit the disputed property with the court.

Impleader   If a defendant claims that a third person is liable to the defendant for all or part of the plaintiff's claim (generally due to indemnity, subrogation, contribution, or breach of warranty), the defendant may ***implead*** that person by filing a third-party complaint. In the third-party complaint, the original defendant is identified as the *defendant and third-party plaintiff*; the third person is identified as the *third-party defendant*.

Both subject matter and personal jurisdiction requirements are relaxed somewhat for third-party claims. Third-party claims fall within the court's supplemental jurisdiction, and third-party complaints may be served anywhere within 100 miles of the federal courthouse—even if the place of service is outside the state and is beyond the scope of the state's long-arm statute (the ***100-mile bulge*** provision).

Class Actions   When there are large numbers of people with similar claims against the same party, which could lead to many lawsuits and potentially inconsistent results, Rule 23 allows a class action to be filed if certain requirements are met:

> •*The class must be so large that joinder of all of its members is not feasible;*
>
> •*There must be questions of law or fact which are common to the class;*
>
> •*The claims or defenses of the representatives of the class must be typical of class members; and*
>
> •*The representatives must represent the interests of the class fairly and adequately.*

A class action may be warranted, for example, when a national mortgage company appears to have overcharged the escrow accounts of many thousands of mortgagors located all over the country. Such a case likely would qualify as a class action under Rule 23(b)(3). Of the three types of class actions permitted, the most common type by far is the one provided by Rule 23(b)(3). Its requirements are (1) that the questions of law or fact which are common to the class predominate over any questions which affect individual members only; and (2) that a class action is superior to other, available methods to adjudicate the controversy fairly and efficiently. Members of a Rule 23(b)(3) class action may "opt out" of the class if they wish to do so, which is not true of other types of class actions.

Within 90 days after a complaint in a class action suit is filed, the plaintiff must file a motion with the court to determine whether the case can be maintained as a class action. Rule 23(c)(1). This is called "certifying the class."

Consolidation   Even though claims are made by filing separate complaints, a court nevertheless may order multiple suits to be consolidated for trial and judgment if the suits involve the same parties and contain common issues of law or fact. For example:

> A bankruptcy trustee for a national trucking company files 1000 separate lawsuits in the same court against 1000 separate freight customers to collect under-charges billed by the bankrupt trucking company over the preceding seven years. The court could order all cases consolidated for trial at the same time in this situation.

Pleading

Pleading in state and federal courts historically has taken three different forms: (1) *common law pleading* (different form required for each type of action, highly technical, significant for historical reference more than anything else); (2) *code pleading* (designed to disclose the facts upon which the claim is based); and *notice pleading* (designed only to give sufficient notice of the claim or defense).

Many states still follow the rules of code pleading, which emphasize the statement of facts—not conclusions of law—in the pleadings filed with the court. The federal courts use notice pleading exclusively, with facts to be determined through discovery procedures and with issues to be determined at the mandatory pre-trial conference.

Under the Federal Rules of Civil Procedure, only three pleadings are allowed: a complaint, an answer, and a reply to a counterclaim (if a counterclaim has been filed). Rule 7. Unlike the procedure in many states, a federal plaintiff need not respond to new issues raised by the answer; it is presumed that the new issues are denied under federal procedure. Counterclaims, cross-claims, and third-party complaints are the procedural equivalents of a complaint. The proper responsive pleading to a cross-claim or to a third-party complaint is an answer. The proper responsive pleading to a counterclaim is a reply to counterclaim *(see Rule 7)*.

The form of pleadings in federal court is governed by Rule 10 and may be supplemented by local court rules.

Complaint   All civil actions in federal court are commenced by filing a complaint. Rule 3. The federal complaint is equivalent to the petition used to initiate civil actions in many state courts.

As a general rule, the complaint should contain:

●the caption of the case, which identifies the court, the parties, and the name of the pleading (complaint, in this case);

●a jurisdictional allegation (statement of the statute or other basis for invoking the jurisdiction of the federal court);

●a short, concise statement of the claim(s) or defense(s) showing that the pleader is entitled to relief. Rule 8. This statement is the heart of the complaint and may be presented in several, separate paragraphs (refer to Form 9 of the Federal Rules for an example);

●a statement of the relief or remedy sought by the pleader (whether general and special damages, punitive damages, an injunction, or other relief);

●the demand for judgment (sometimes called the *ad damnum* clause, the prayer, or the "wherefore" clause) against the opposing party;

●signature of the pleader's attorney. Under Rule 11, the attorney's signature indicates that the attorney has made reasonable inquiry and believes the allegations are well grounded in fact. If it evolves that the pleading was made frivolously, the attorney may be subjected to personal sanctions by the court; and

●verification, if required. Very few types of claims require verification in federal court. The subscription of the attorney (*see above*) generally is sufficient. When verification is required, it takes the form of an affidavit of the party, swearing that she has read the pleading and that the statements contained in it are true to the best of her knowledge, information, and belief. The party signs the affidavit, typically before a notary public.

If the complaint refers to documents, such as a promissory note, a copy of that document should be attached to the complaint as an exhibit. Rule 10. Pleading special matters (such as fraud, conditions precedent, or special damage) must comply with Rule 9. The complaint is filed with the clerk of the U.S. District Court for the appropriate district, together with a Civil Cover Sheet; a request for jury trial (if a jury trial is desired and if the request is not stated in the complaint); a request *(praecipe)* for issuance of summons upon each of the named defendants; and the appropriate filing fee. Local court rules generally contain detailed procedures for filing a complaint within a particular federal judicial district.

The court clerk issues a summons for each named defendant. The court clerk issues a summons (sometimes called process) for each named defendant. The summons provides (1) notice of the suit and (2) an opportunity to be heard by filing a timely answer or other timely response. As a general rule, the plaintiff's attorney must send to each defendant a summons, a copy of the complaint, a form for waiver of service, and a notice of the consequences for failure to waive service. *See Official Forms 1A and 1B of the Federal Rules.* Rule 4(d) amended to 12-31-93. If the waiver of service is signed and returned to the plaintiff's attorney within 30 days after it was sent (60 days if the defendant is located in a foreign country), the defendant is given additional time in which to answer or to otherwise respond to the complaint. If any defendant fails to sign and return the waiver within the prescribed time, service may be made by anyone who is 18 years old or more and who is not a party in the case *(see additional discussion of service of process under personal jurisdiction, above)*; and that defendant will pay the costs of service, no matter who ultimately wins at trial. Either a signed waiver of service of summons (or service of the summons) must be obtained within 120 days after the complaint is filed; otherwise, the action is subject to dismissal without prejudice.

The signed waiver of service is filed with the court for each defendant. If particular defendant fails to sign and return the waiver timely, however, a proof of service of summons is filed with the court after the summons has been served.

After the action has been commenced, all pleadings, motions, notices, and so on are served upon all adverse parties or, if adverse parties are represented by counsel, upon their attorneys by U.S. mail. Rule 5.

Challenges to the Complaint   If any defendant wants to challenge the sufficiency of the complaint or matters connected with it, the proper procedure is to file a motion for that purpose within the statutory twenty-day period. If a motion is filed, the answer need not be filed until the motion matters have been resolved.

A motion is not a pleading; it is a request to the court for an order granting relief to the moving party. Motions may be made before, during, and after trial. However, this section deals specifically with preliminary motions—those which seek relief based upon some defect in the complaint, improper joinder of parties, improper court, or similar deficiency in filing the complaint.

Some types of defects, if not objected to at the beginning of the suit, are waived and cannot be raised at a later time. Lack of personal jurisdiction is one issue that must be raised immediately or it is waived. By contrast, lack of subject matter jurisdiction can be raised at any stage of the lawsuit, including the appeal.

The bases for preliminary challenges to a complaint in federal court are found substantially in Rule 12. Of these, the most common are:

> •*Lack of subject matter jurisdiction.* Rule 12(b)(1).

> •*Lack of personal jurisdiction.* Rule 12(b)(2). In state court, this may be called a *special appearance*.

> •*Improper venue.* Rule 12(b)(3).

> •*Insufficiency of process.* Rule 12(b)(4).

> •*Insufficiency of service of process.* Rule 12(b)(5).

> •*Failure to state a claim upon which relief can be granted.* Rule 12(b)(6). In state court, this may be called a *demurrer*.

> •*Failure to join a Rule 19 indispensable party.* Rule 12(b)(7).

•*Motion to make more definite and certain,* when the complaint is so lacking in facts or is so vague that it is difficult to tell whether a claim has been stated or not. Rule 12(e).

•*Motion to strike* "from any pleading any insufficient defense or any redundant, immaterial, impertinent, or scandalous matter." Rule 12(f).

The form of motions in federal court is governed by Rule 7(b). Unless it is made during trial or during a hearing, a motion must be in writing; must set forth the specific grounds for the motion; and must be signed by the attorney. Local court rules frequently require motions to be accompanied by a notice of hearing and a short memorandum of law which contains arguments and legal authorities in support of the requested relief. A copy of the motion and related documents must be served upon all adverse parties or their attorneys.

At least five days' notice must be given under Rule 6(d) for hearings in federal court. That time frame may be enlarged or reduced in state court.

The Answer   By signing a waiver of service, the defendant has 60 days after the waiver was sent to her (90 days if in a foreign country) to file an answer. Rule 12(a). Without a signed waiver, the answer is due 20 days after service of summons. Time is calculated by omitting the day of service and by including the last day of the period unless the last day is a Saturday, a Sunday, a holiday, or a day when the clerk's office is inaccessible. Rule 6. In that event, the last day for filing becomes the next day that the office is open.

If, instead, preliminary motions are filed to attack the complaint, the defendant has ten days in which to file her answer after the ruling on the motion is made. If a defendant has filed Rule 12(b) motions that were overruled, she may elect to restate them as part of her answer.

The answer in federal court must respond to each of the allegations stated in the complaint in one of the following ways:

- •Admit it;
- •Deny it;
- •Admit part of it and deny the rest of it; or
- •Neither admit nor deny based upon lack of personal knowledge.

Any allegation in the complaint which is not addressed in the answer is deemed admitted. Unlike federal courts, some state courts permit the filing of an answer in the form of a ***general denial***, in which the defendant "denies each and every allegation of the complaint except those allegations which are against the interests of the plaintiff." Even if an answer denies each allegation separately, it merely prevents default judgment from being entered and holds the plaintiff to strict proof of the allegations made. It does not raise affirmative defenses.

More typical—and more desirable—is an answer which responds to each of the allegations of the complaint and, continuing in the same numbered paragraph format, asserts any and all affirmative defenses that the defendant may have to those allegations. An ***affirmative defense*** is an assertion which—if it can be proved at trial—will negate the plaintiff's claim. Payment of a claimed debt, expiration of a statute of limitations, or noncompliance with the Statute of Frauds are three examples of affirmative defenses that might be pleaded in the defendant's answer. There are many others, the most common of which are listed in Rule 8(c).

In addition to (or instead of) affirmative defenses, the defendant's answer may claim a setoff against the plaintiff's claim. A ***setoff*** is an assertion which—if it can be proved—will reduce the plaintiff's claim but will not cancel it entirely.

Counterclaim and Cross-Claim

A counterclaim is the pleading used by a defendant to state a claim against a plaintiff, which typically is filed with the defendant's answer in a combined pleading labeled *Answer and Counterclaim*. A counterclaim is either compulsory or permissive. Rule 13.

A ***compulsory counterclaim*** arises from the same transaction or occurrence upon which the plaintiff's complaint is based. It is compulsory because the defendant is required to raise it in the same litigation; and if she fails to do so, it will be barred and never can be raised again. Because the defendant is required to raise all compulsory counterclaims, the Federal Rules waive the $50,000 jurisdictional requirement for compulsory counterclaims in diversity cases. The counterclaim's value does not matter in federal question cases *(discussed above)*.

A ***permissive counterclaim*** arises from a different transaction or occurrence than the one upon which the plaintiff's claim is based. The defendant is not required to raise a permissive counterclaim; therefore, a permissive counterclaim in a diversity case must meet the same jurisdictional requirements as the plaintiff's original complaint.

> Benjamin was a driver and tour guide with Jolly Trolley Co. His salary was $1200 a month. Benjamin took his friends on a tour during off-duty hours last July. During the tour, Benjamin lost control of the trolley, and it smashed into a building. The trolley was destroyed, and Benjamin was injured. Jolly Trolley fired him and then sued Benjamin for destruction of the trolley. Benjamin

> believes the trolley malfunctioned and wants to sue Jolly Trolley
> for his injuries as well as for his last four months' wages, which
> were not paid.

In the example, Benjamin's claim for injuries arises from the same transaction or occurrence as the destruction of the trolley; therefore, it is a compulsory counterclaim. If he does not raise it, he will have waived the right to do so. His claim for wages, however, arises from the employment relationship between Benjamin and Jolly Trolley and is a permissive counterclaim. He may raise it in the existing litigation or may file a separate suit. If the existing suit were filed in federal court, the wage claim would not meet the $50,000 requirement and could not be filed. It could, however, be filed separately in a state court.

A *cross-claim* is one filed against a co-party, either plaintiff v. plaintiff or defendant v. defendant (usually defendant v. defendant). It must involve the same subject matter (transaction, occurrence, or property) as the original complaint or a counterclaim. A cross-claim generally is filed at the same time as the answer to the complaint or at the same time as the reply to a counterclaim.

The proper responsive pleading is a *reply to counterclaim* (or **answer *to* cross-claim**), which must be filed within 20 days after service (60 days for the U.S.). The reply (or answer) addresses itself only to the allegations of the counterclaim (or cross-claim) and is the procedural equivalent of an answer to the complaint.

Amendment of Pleadings

If the pleading is one to which the opponent must respond (such as a complaint), Rule 15 allows the pleading to be amended without court permission at any time before the responsive pleading is served. If the pleading is one to which no response is required (such as an answer to a complaint that is not accompanied by a counterclaim or cross-claim), the pleading may be amended without court permission within 20 days after it is served.

> Plaintiff files her complaint in federal court and serves it upon the
> defendant. On the 9th day after service, the defendant files a Rule
> 12(b)(6) motion. Since the motion is not a pleading, the plaintiff
> may amend her complaint as of right during the remaining eleven
> days of the 20-day period unless the defendant files an answer
> before the amendment is filed.

If the responsive pleading already has been served or if more than 20 days have passed, the pleading may be amended by permission of the court or by consent of the opponent. The federal courts, like most state courts, are very liberal in granting leave to amend pleadings—even during trial if it can be done in such a way that the opponent is not subjected to unfair surprise.

Default Judgment   If no responsive pleading or motion is filed in connection with a complaint, counterclaim, cross-claim, or third-party complaint within the 20-day time limit (60 days for the U.S.), the non-responding party is in default; and judgment may be entered against her without a trial.

If the claim is for a *sum certain* (an amount not subject to reasonable dispute), the clerk of the federal court may enter default judgment upon submission of an affidavit concerning the amount due. Rule 55(a). If the claim is not for a sum certain, the request for default judgment is submitted to the court with affidavits. The court may require a hearing to prove damages before the default judgment is entered. Rule 55(b)(2). In either situation, the plaintiff is limited to the amount of damages claimed in the complaint.

If multiple defendants are involved and if only one defendant defaults, entry of a default judgment may preclude the plaintiff from proceeding against the remaining defendants. This rule varies from jurisdiction to jurisdiction.

Once a default judgment has been entered, it can be enforced in the same way as any other judgment.

Even though a default judgment is entered, the defendant can move to have it *set aside* Rule 55(c) *for good cause* under Rule 60(b). Good cause may include, among other things: mistake, inadvertence, surprise, excusable neglect, fraud, or misrepresentation by the opposing party.

Discovery

Subject to certain limitations, discovery is a formal, pretrial process designed to give all parties access to the same evidence that will be available to all other parties at the time of trial. If each party knows what all other parties know about the case, a more accurate assessment of the case is possible; and pretrial settlement is more probable. Discovery is available in both federal and state courts, and many state discovery rules mirror the federal rules very closely.

The purposes of discovery are to obtain evidence that might not be available at trial because of a witness' age, poor health, or absence from the jurisdiction; to narrow the issues for trial; to avoid unfair surprise during trial; and to encourage settlement before trial. When discovery procedures are used improperly (purely to harass, to delay, or to increase costs), the discovering attorney may be subject to court sanction. Rule 26(g). In addition to the Federal Rules, the Model Rules of Professional Conduct provide disciplinary sanctions against attorneys who make frivolous discovery requests.

Discovery is ***self-executing***, that is, the parties implement discovery procedures on their own, with little court intervention. In general, counsel for parties must meet to establish an overall discovery plan (Rule 26[f]) and, within ten days afterward, must make certain disclosures (Rule 26[a]) before any formal discovery occurs *(see below)*. Under Rule 29, for example, they may agree to increase the number or depositions or interrogatories or to extend the time to answer discovery requests under Rules 33, 34, and 36 if it does not conflict with other rules. Prior court approval is required for mental or physical examinations under Rule 35. Otherwise, the court becomes involved in the discovery process only when problems arise that the parties cannot resolve themselves.

The Federal Rules of Civil Procedure allow local courts to decide whether to require filing of all discovery requests or responses with the court in a particular jurisdiction. Most local jurisdictions allow requests and responses to be *served* upon the appropriate party or parties, with copies to all other parties and with only a notice of service *filed* with the court.

Discovery Devices   Several types of discovery devices are permitted by the Federal Rules, including interrogatories, requests to produce documents or things for inspection, requests for physical and mental examination of persons, requests for admission of facts, and depositions upon either oral or written questions. Discovery devices may be served upon *parties only* (except depositions, which may be taken of parties and nonparties alike). The permitted discovery devices can be used in any sequence desired and can be used in combination with other discovery devices once the Rule 26(f) meeting has occurred and once the required disclosures have been made.

Rule 26(a) requires the parties to disclose either at their discovery meeting or within ten days thereafter: (1) name, address, telephone number, and subject matter for anyone "likely to have discoverable information" about disputed facts; (2) description of all relevant documents, data compilations, and so forth; (3) computation of damages and supporting documents; and (4) liability policies, if any, related to the dispute. At least 90 days before trial, parties must disclose expert witnesses, including their opinions, data, exhibits, qualifications, amount received for testifying, and so forth. At least 30 days before trial, parties must disclose all witnesses that will or may be called at trial and must provide a list of exhibits that will or may be used. Disclosures are designed to avoid many of the routine topics of discovery in which parties historically engaged, although traditional discovery devices still play an important role.

A. **Interrogatories** Interrogatories are a series of written questions served by one party upon another party, which must be answered under oath. Rule 33. Interrogatories provide a very inexpensive method to obtain background material such as personal data, employment or medical history, or prior involvement in lawsuits. As a result, interrogatories often are among the initial discovery devices used.

No party may serve more than 25 interrogatories, including subparts, without (1) a stipulation to serve more or (2) permission of the court. State courts often limit the number of interrogatories as well. When multiple sets are used, many courts require that the interrogatories be *numbered sequentially* from one set to the next. For example, if the first set of interrogatories to a party ends with Interrogatory No. 7, a second set to the same party must begin with Interrogatory No. 8. Some courts require ***engrossment*** of interrogatories, which means that the propounding (discovering) party must provide enough space between interrogatories to insert answers. Even if engrossment is not required by court rule, the job of the litigation team is much simpler if interrogatory questions and answers—including any supplemental answers—are engrossed (combined) in one document.

The responding party must answer interrogatories in good faith and must supply the requested information unless a privilege or other basis for objection exists. However, the responding party is not required to provide information which is not in her custody or control or which is in the public domain. Neither is she required to compile reports or summaries, for example, that are not required by the Federal Rules and that do not exist already if the cost and degree of difficulty required to search the records will be about the same for either party. Instead, the responding party is allowed to specify in her answers to interrogatories those business records which contain the information so that the propounding party can examine the records himself to obtain the information he seeks.

Rule 33 requires the responding party to answer interrogatories within 30 days of their service. Answers to interrogatories are signed under oath by the party upon whom they were served, but objections to any particular question(s) are signed by the responding party's attorney. Objections are made to those interrogatories which are outside the scope of discovery (*discussed below*), too burdensome, too vague, too broad, or which request information that is privileged or that is classified as attorney work product.

When the attorney for the propounding party receives objections (or receives incomplete or unresponsive answers) to interrogatories, she may elect to compel answers under Rule 37 (*discussed below*), to redraft and resubmit the offending interrogatories, or to do nothing. ***Note:*** For a detailed review of helpful techniques in drafting interrogatories and answers to interrogatories, refer to the chapter on Litigation Skills found in the *NALA Manual for Legal Assistants*, Second Edition (West).

B.   Request for Production of Documents, Things, and Land for Inspection   Rule 34 provides that any party may request any other party to produce documents and things or to allow inspection of land which is under the control of the responding party. The request can be served any time after compliance with the Rule 26(f) meet-and-confer requirement, provided that the initial disclosures required by Rule 26(a) have been made *(see above)*.

The responding party must either comply with the request or file appropriate objections within 30 days of service. If the request is for production of documents and if the number of documents is small, the responding party may elect to forward copies of the documents to the propounding party's attorneys.

However, when large numbers of documents are involved, the responding party may find it easier to make them available for inspection by opposing counsel. In that event, the responding party must identify all documents which may be responsive to the request, often grouping them by categories named in the request. This means that a document control system must be devised and implemented. Legal assistants typically participate actively in this and most other discovery procedures. Opposing counsel, then, visits the document production site—often with one or more legal assistants—to inspect, select, and copy those documents which she believes are relevant. ***Note:*** A detailed discussion of document control systems and procedures is contained in the *NALA Manual for Legal Assistants*, Third Edition (West).

Nonparties cannot be subjected to a direct Rule 34 request to produce; however, the 1991 amendment to Rule 34(c) provides that nonparties can be required to produce documents and things under Rule 45 subpoena procedures. Under Rule 45, a nonparty can be served with a ***subpoena duces tecum***, which is an order "to appear and to bring with you" those items listed on the subpoena. This change creates the functional equivalent of a Rule 34 request to produce served on a party.

Unless the nonparty's attendance is required for deposition, hearing, or trial, he does not need to appear personally if the requested documents or items are produced for inspection. Objections to a subpoena *duces tecum* must be served on the party who initiated the subpoena within 14 days after the subpoena is served. If the time for compliance is less than 14 days, objections must be served before the time for compliance.

C. Request for Physical or Mental Examination Unlike other discovery devices, a Rule 35 examination is not self-executing. The requesting party must file a motion to request it. An order for examination will be entered if the requesting party can show existence of both of the following conditions:

1. *The physical or mental condition of a party (or a person in the custody or control of a party) is an issue in the case;* **and**

2. *Good cause.*

The constitutional right of privacy makes the scope of discovery under Rule 35 more narrow than it is under the other discovery rules. It is not enough that a party's physical or mental condition is relevant; it must be part of the actual controversy in the case. For example, one who claims permanent disability resulting from an accident may be subjected to a Rule 35 physical examination. However, mental examination of a plaintiff is not warranted simply because the defendants believe he filed suit as a result of mental delusions—not even if their belief is true.

D. Requests for Admission After the discovery meeting and initial disclosures, any party may serve upon any other party written requests for admission under Rule 36, seeking admission of the truth of:

- *statements of fact;*
- *opinions of fact;*
- *application of law to fact; or*
- *the genuineness of any document.*

The purpose of a request for admission is to narrow the facts and issues to be proved at trial—not to obtain information (Rule 33 interrogatories) and not to inspect documents (Rule 34 request to produce). Answers or objections to requests for admission are due in 30 days or the requests are deemed admitted.

A party cannot be compelled to answer requests for admission under Rule 37; however, if a party fails to admit the truth of any request and if the requesting party proves conclusively the subject matter of the request at trial, the court may require the non-answering party to pay reasonable expenses connected with proving the matter.

E. Deposition A deposition is a discovery device used to record the sworn testimony of a witness prior to trial. No witness may be deposed more than once, and depositions are limited to a maximum of ten per side except by stipulation or court order. Depositions may be oral (Rule 30) or upon written questions (Rule 31). They may be taken of any party or of any nonparty who is believed to have information related to the case. A Rule 30 deposition may be videotaped or may be taken by telephone if the parties agree or if the court orders it. If a deposition is taken either before the complaint is filed or before the Rule 26 discovery meeting, court permission must be obtained.

After the discovery meeting, depositions of parties may be taken simply by providing notice to the party-deponent and to all other parties; court permission is not required. If the party-deponent fails to appear, her attendance can be compelled under Rule 37. Because a nonparty witness is not subject to the sanctions of Rule 37, caution dictates that a subpoena be used to ensure attendance even though the Federal Rules do not require it. Failure to obey a subpoena subjects the nonparty to contempt of court.

A *subpoena* is a document typically issued by the court clerk (an attorney also can issue a subpoena as an officer of the court under the Federal Rules) commanding a person to appear personally at a specified time and place to give testimony. Rule 45. A *subpoena duces tecum* requires a person to appear to testify and to bring documents, books, records, papers, or other tangible things.

A subpoena must be served personally and may be served by anyone who is 18 or more years old. The server might be a deputy from the U.S. Marshal's office, a professional process server, or a legal assistant. A subpoena must be accompanied by the current witness fee and round-trip mileage (no witness fee or mileage accompanies a subpoena issued by a United States agency or official). Proof of service is filed with the court issuing the subpoena.

When a corporation is subpoenaed, the corporation—not the deposing party—selects the person who will testify on its behalf. Neither a nonparty nor an agent of a nonparty can be commanded to travel to a deposition which is more than 100 miles from her home, place of employment, or place where she regularly transacts business. If the subpoena contemplates testimony at a trial, however, a nonparty witness can be commanded to travel to the trial, without regard to distance, from anywhere in the same state where the action is pending.

> Ann lives in California. Her deposition testimony is sought in a federal court action pending in New York; Ann is not a party in the case. Attorneys for the parties may take Ann's deposition in California by traveling to California and having a subpoena issued by the appropriate California federal court to take Ann's deposition in California. Her attendance at the New York trial cannot be compelled, however, because she is outside the subpoena range of

the New York federal court and does not live, work, or regularly transact business in New York.

Before a deposition occurs, the deponent's attorney usually reviews the deposition procedure as well as questions likely to be asked with the deponent. Lawyers often provide a written checklist to the deponent, which contains suggestions such as (1) listen to the entire question before attempting to answer it; (2) if you don't understand a question, ask to have it repeated or explained; (3) if you do not know the answer to a question, say that you do not know; do not guess or make assumptions; and (4) tell the truth. Caution is exercised in allowing review of data before the deposition because once any portion of any document is used to refresh the deponent's recollection, the entire document must be made available to opposing counsel.

In the typical situation, the deposition is conducted in a lawyer's office, with the attorneys for the deponent and for each party present. The deponent is sworn by the court reporter or other person authorized to administer oaths, is questioned by the discovering party's attorney, and usually is cross-examined by one or more of the attorneys for the other parties. The deposition proceeds roughly in the same way as examination and cross-examination of witnesses at trial, except that attorneys often agree to reserve certain types of objections for trial (other than form of the question, form of the answer, or similar irregularity—which cannot be reserved until trial). Rule 32(d)(3)(B). Reserving as many objections as possible allows the deposition to flow more smoothly, which saves time and expense for all parties.

The deposition questions and responses are recorded, usually by a court reporter or stenographer, who then transcribes the deposition and presents it to the deponent for signature. The deponent reviews the deposition and signs it, noting transcription errors contained in the deposition, if any. A transcription error occurs when the court reporter transcribes something different from what the deponent actually said. An erroneous statement, which actually was made by the deponent, is not a transcription error.

Many attorneys prefer oral depositions for discovery, because they allow spontaneous exchanges between the attorney and the deponent. Response to a particular question may suggest additional questions that could not have been foreseen or asked if discovery were limited to interrogatories, for example. Equally important is the opportunity to see the witness in person and to evaluate his demeanor, style of presentation, and familiarity with the facts prior to trial.

A Rule 31 deposition upon written questions is similar to an oral deposition, except that the questions to be asked are provided by the discovering party's attorney in advance of the deposition. Written cross-examination questions likewise are provided in advance by attorneys for the other parties. The presiding officer asks the questions, which are answered by the deponent, followed by cross-examination questions. The questions and answers are recorded and transcribed. The lack of flexibility and the absence of spontaneity makes a deposition upon written questions much less attractive to most attorneys than is an oral deposition. As a result, Rule 31 depositions are used infrequently.

Whether the deposition is oral or is upon written questions, the deponent's attorney may object to a particular question if it is outside the scope of discovery and may instruct the deponent not to answer. The deposing attorney has several options in this situation:

1. Rephrase the question;

2. Announce a continuance of the deposition until a judicial ruling is obtained concerning the question and whether the deponent is required to answer it; or

3. Have the court reporter note both the question and the objection in the transcript and proceed with other questioning. Near the close of the deposition, announce a continuance of the deposition until a judicial ruling is obtained concerning this and any other questions to which objections have been made.

Scope of Discovery Rule 26 generally provides that parties may discover anything (not privileged) which is relevant to the subject matter of the action or which is reasonably calculated to lead to admissible evidence. Even before formal discovery begins, the Federal Rules require parties to disclose the identity of persons likely to have knowledge of any discoverable matter, to calculate their damages, to describe or to provide relevant documents, and to disclose the existence and content of any related liability insurance policies. Identity of expert witnesses and their opinions must be disclosed before trial. Privileged information, however, need not be disclosed and cannot be discovered.

A *privilege* is a protection against compulsory disclosure which is given to certain types of information, such as a trade secret or a communication between certain categories of people (attorney-client, physician-patient, clergy-parishioner, or husband-wife, for example). A person cannot be required to disclose privileged matters either at a deposition (Rule 26) or at trial (Federal Rule of Evidence 501 in federal question cases or state privilege rules in diversity cases).

In addition, a **work product immunity** applies to a lawyer's preparations for trial. This immunity may be absolute or qualified, depending on the circumstances. **Absolute immunity** is given to documents containing the subjective thoughts of a party's lawyer or other representative, including legal theories, conclusions, opinions, or mental impressions and is nearly impossible to overcome. (Although an opposing party cannot obtain documents of this type, her attorney can ask by interrogatory what a party's legal theories are as they apply to the facts in the case.) A **qualified immunity** is given to other documents prepared for trial, which can be overcome only with a strong showing that the opposing party has a substantial need for the materials and that their equivalent cannot be obtained by other means. If a lawyer or representative took notes during an interview with a potential witness who later died without giving any other statements or interviews, for example, the notes may be discoverable because of the qualified immunity.

Both parties and nonparties always can obtain copies of their own prior statements concerning the subject matter of the action.

A matter is **relevant** to the subject matter of the action if it makes the existence of a material fact more or less probable than it would be otherwise. However, a matter may be relevant without being admissible at trial. Even if information is not relevant, it still can be discovered if it is *reasonably calculated to lead to admissible evidence*.

> Bill is sued in federal court for negligence in connection with an automobile accident. He receives interrogatories which contain these questions: (1) "How fast were you driving at the time of the accident?" and (2) "How old is your wife?"

Bill's answer to the first question is both relevant and admissible in a negligence action. If he was speeding at the time of the accident, that fact may have substantial probative value in determining negligence. Bill's answer to the second question, no matter what it is, is not relevant to any of the issues in a negligence case; and it is not reasonably calculated to lead to admissible evidence. The question is objectionable, at the very least.

Resisting Discovery   Anyone (whether a party or a nonparty) from whom discovery is sought may resist the discovery attempt either (1) by obtaining a **protective order** or (2) by raising a timely **objection** to the question or request.

If the person wants to resist the time, place, or method of discovery or wants to resist an entire area or line of questioning, a Rule 26(c) protective order may provide the better solution. For example, a protective order can prevent discovery of a trade secret; can order a deposition sealed after it is taken (to be opened only by court order); or can order that discovery not be made in certain topic areas. A judge can fashion the scope of a protective order to fit the situation presented.

A protective order always can be issued by the court in which the main case is pending. If a deposition is involved, the protective order can be issued either (1) by the court in which the action is pending or (2) by the court in the district where the deposition is scheduled to be taken.

By contrast, if the person wants to resist a specific question or a few specific questions, making timely objection may be the better course of action. Objections are made to discovery requests in the same way that objections are made at trial. The most commonly raised objections are that the request is outside the scope of discovery under Rule 26 or that it seeks privileged information. In addition to these, objections to interrogatories may arise if the interrogatories are unnecessarily burdensome.

Compelling Discovery If a person makes a timely objection, fails to comply, or refuses to answer a discovery request or a deposition question, the burden falls upon the party making the request (or asking the deposition question) to seek a court order compelling discovery if he or she wishes to pursue the matter. An evasive or incomplete answer is treated as a failure to answer.

If a person then refuses to obey an order compelling discovery, the court may impose sanctions. Initial sanctions typically include requiring the person to pay the extra expenses (costs and attorney fees) incurred because of his noncompliance. If the person is a party and persists in disobeying the order, a court may prevent the disobedient party from making certain claims or from raising certain defenses. It can strike any portion of the pleadings, or it can go as far as dismissing a disobedient plaintiff's complaint or entering default judgment against a disobedient defendant. The court's contempt powers may be used in connection with either parties or nonparties except when the disobedience relates to a Rule 35 physical or mental examination.

Like protective orders, an order compelling discovery may be entered by the court where the action is pending or, in the case of a deposition, the order may be entered either by the court where the action is pending or by the court where the deposition is to be taken.

Orders compelling discovery generally are *interlocutory* (not final) orders and, therefore, are not subject to immediate appeal. There are exceptions:

1. *When a party is subject to criminal contempt for failing to comply with the order.* This is because criminal contempt carries

criminal sanctions, including imprisonment. Incarceration arising from civil contempt, however, is imposed for coercive reasons: when the person complies with the court order, incarceration ends.

2. *When the discovery order is directed to a nonparty, it may be appealed immediately.* This type of order is interlocutory for the main action and parties, but it is final for the nonparty witness. If the nonparty were to wait until the end of the case, she could not appeal because she would not be a party to the final decision.

3. *A discovery order may be appealed under the Interlocutory Appeals Act* if it presents a "controlling question of law" in the case, if immediate appeal will expedite the litigation, and if the appellate court agrees to accept the appeal. 29 U.S.C. § 1292. Parties seldom are able to meet all three of these criteria.

A party can appeal a discovery order once a final judgment is entered in the case, either alone or with other claimed errors; however, the discovery issue generally will have become moot by that time.

Use of Discovery at Trial Whether information obtained through discovery is admissible at trial depends on the discovery device and, in some situations, depends on the way in which a party seeks to use the discovery.

Rule 33 answers to interrogatories can be used by an adverse party for any purpose, including impeachment and as evidence of the truth of the answer. If the party who answered the interrogatory wishes to contradict the answer in her trial testimony, she may do so; and the trier of fact must weigh the credibility of the conflicting information.

Documents and records produced under Rule 34 are subject to the same admissibility rules as any other document and record offered in evidence. There are no additional requirements or limitations imposed because of the discovery device.

Rule 35 physical and mental examinations nearly always are admissible at trial, because this type of examination could not have been conducted in the first place unless a court previously had determined that the party's physical or mental condition was in controversy in the case. There may be a question of doctor-patient privilege, but that privilege is waived if the examined party requests and obtains a report of the examining physician. Rule 35(b)(2).

If a party has not exercised the limited right to rebut or to amend his answers, Rule 36 admissions conclusively prove the items admitted. Rule 36(b).

If a party has not exercised the limited right to rebut or to amend his answers, Rule 36 admissions conclusively prove the items admitted. Rule 36(b).

Rule 32 governs the use of depositions taken under Rule 30 or Rule 31. The first question to be answered is whether the deposition statement would be admissible if the deponent were testifying at trial. For instance, if a deponent makes a hearsay statement (one to which none of the hearsay exceptions apply) during a deposition, the statement remains hearsay for trial purposes; and it cannot be admitted as evidence at the trial. The issue of admissibility is raised by objection at trial, made at the time the statement is offered into evidence at trial. (Recall that certain objections, including admissibility, are reserved when depositions are taken.)

Even if the deposition statement would be admissible if it were made in person by the deponent at trial, it will be allowed in its deposition form only if it falls within one of these categories:

1.   Subject to its admissibility, the deposition statement of any trial witness may be used to impeach that witness' credibility. Rule 32(a)(1).

2.   Subject to its admissibility, the deposition statement of an adverse party—including depositions of officers or directors if the adverse party is a corporation—may be used for any purpose at trial. Rule 32(a)(2).

3.   Subject to its admissibility, the deposition statement of any party or nonparty may be used for any purpose if:

    a.   the witness is dead;

    b.   the witness is more than 100 miles from the place of trial;

    c.   the witness is too ill to testify;

    d.   the witness is outside the subpoena-range of the court; or

    e.   exceptional circumstances exist to justify use of the deposition rather than live testimony. Rule 32(a)(3).

If only part of a deposition is offered into evidence at trial, an opposing party may offer any other parts of that deposition which should be considered in fairness with the first part. Rule 32(a)(4). This prevents a statement from being taken out of context.

Termination Without Trial

Not every complaint results in a full trial on the merits. For example, if Rule 12(b) defects in the complaint are not or cannot be cured, the complaint is dismissed; and no trial occurs. A dismissal can be either with or without prejudice to future action. A *dismissal without prejudice* means that the claim may be filed again if the party elects to do so. A *dismissal with prejudice* means that the claim cannot be filed again, which invokes the *res judicata* doctrine (*discussed later in this chapter*).

This section reviews the ways in which a case may be ended without a full trial. Although termination generally is discussed in terms of the complaint, keep in mind that counterclaims, cross-claims, and third-party complaints are subject to termination on any of the same grounds as a complaint.

Voluntary Dismissal A plaintiff in federal court may dismiss her own complaint *once* without prejudice if she does so before the defendant serves his answer or moves for summary judgment. After the answer or motion for summary judgment is filed, the plaintiff must obtain court permission to dismiss her complaint.

The first dismissal is without prejudice; but if the plaintiff refiles the complaint and then voluntarily dismisses a second time, the second dismissal is with prejudice. Rule 41(a)(1). Many state court systems have adopted a similar rule.

Involuntary Dismissal A complaint in federal court can be dismissed involuntarily under Rule 12(b). In addition, it can be dismissed involuntarily under Rule 41(b) either for failure to prosecute the claim or for disobedience of a court order. If the involuntary dismissal results from lack of jurisdiction, insufficient service of process, improper venue, or failure to join an indispensable party, the dismissal generally is without prejudice.

After the pleadings are closed (both the claim and its responsive pleading are filed), a party may move for *judgment on the pleadings* under Rule 12(c). The moving party must show that she is entitled to judgment based solely upon the contents of the pleadings. If a complaint claims nonpayment of a promissory note and if the answer admits the note but claims the defendant did not pay because he was studying in Brazil, for example, a Rule 12(c) motion is appropriate.

A slightly different variation is the procedure to obtain a **summary judgment** available under Rule 56. To prevail on a motion for summary judgment, a party must show that there is *no genuine issue of material fact* and that she is *entitled to judgment as a matter of law.* Unlike Rule 12(c), however, Rule 56 permits the judge to go beyond the pleadings to the facts established by discovery or by sworn affidavits filed with the motion. Affidavits must include only those facts about which the affiant has personal knowledge and which would be admissible at trial.

The party opposing a motion for summary judgment must be given at least ten days' notice of the hearing and is permitted to file a resistance to the motion, together with opposing affidavits. In deciding whether to enter summary judgment, the judge must consider all of the facts in the light most favorable to the nonmoving party (resolving any doubt in favor of the non-moving party). Using that standard, if the evidence (affidavits and discovery results) establishes that there is no genuine dispute for a trier of fact to decide, the judge enters judgment according to the substantive legal rules which govern the issues in the case.

The judge may enter either a summary judgment or a partial summary judgment. A **partial summary judgment** is one which resolves one or more issues in the case but which leaves others for the trier of fact to decide. For example, affidavits and discovery results may show conclusively that liability of a party exists; but if there is a genuine factual dispute concerning damages, a partial summary judgment is entered on the issue of liability only.

If the case proceeds to trial and if the plaintiff fails to prove facts supporting her claim for relief, the judge can dismiss the complaint before the defendant begins his case. The procedure in a *nonjury* trial is for the defendant to make a motion for **judgment on partial findings** under Rule 52(c) when the plaintiff rests. In a *jury* trial, the defendant makes a motion for **judgment as a matter of law** under Rule 50 when the plaintiff rests, which is the functional equivalent of a directed verdict in state court actions. As a result of 1991 changes in the Federal Rules, a directed verdict no longer exists in federal courts. As was true of directed verdicts under prior federal rules, either party may move for judgment as a matter of law when the defendant rests. The judge grants judgment as a matter of law if there is *no legally sufficient evidentiary basis for a reasonable jury to have found for that party with respect to that issue.* Rule 50(a)(1).

When a Rule 50 motion for judgment as a matter of law is made by either party at the close of the defendant's case in a jury trial, the judge may reserve her decision until after the case has been submitted to the jury—even though she believes that judgment should be granted to the moving party as a matter of law. By waiting, she avoids a judicial catch-22. If the jury decides in favor of the moving party, the motion is moot. If the jury decides against the moving party, the judge still may enter judgment as a matter of law on the basis that no reasonable jury could have found against the moving party. This effectively overturns the jury verdict in much the same way as a judgment notwithstanding the verdict (judgment NOV) under prior federal rules. (Judgment NOV no longer exists after the 1991 amendments to Federal Rules; however, it continues in many state courts.)

Pretrial Conference

Rule 16 of the Federal Rules (and similar provisions in state court systems) give the judge authority to conduct a pretrial conference, which is used to identify uncontested issues, to define and simplify contested issues, to identify witnesses and exhibits for trial, and to set case progression deadlines for motions, discovery, and related matters. The theory of a pretrial conference is that if parties are required to define their legal and factual issues clearly, they will be more willing to settle the case.

Even if the judge in federal court does not conduct a pretrial conference, she must issue a scheduling order *within 120 days* after the complaint is filed. Rule 16(b). A *scheduling order* sets a time limit for joinder of additional parties, amendment of pleadings, filing motions, and completion of discovery.

If a party anticipates that an opposing party may attempt to introduce evidence at trial which is both irrelevant and unfairly prejudicial, it may be that a simple objection will be inadequate to remove the information from the jurors' minds. For example, if a party's counsel anticipates that her adversary may ask the question, "Isn't it true that you have been married 17 times?" during cross-examination of her client in a negligence case, an objection to the question most certainly would be sustained. However, just hearing the question likely will prejudice many of the jurors. In this type of situation, the attorney may file a *motion in limine* to preclude all lines of questioning concerning the client's prior marriages. This type of motion generally is considered at the pretrial conference, if there is one; if not, then it is considered at some point shortly before trial begins. If the order is granted to preclude the topic and if opposing counsel disregards the order during trial, his disregard could result in a mistrial.

If a pretrial conference is held, it is followed by a *pretrial order* issued by the judge, which summarizes the results of the pretrial conference in terms of contested and uncontested issues as well as identification of witnesses and exhibits. (Witnesses and exhibits to be used for impeachment purposes only need not be identified.) Case progression deadlines are included. A final pretrial order is binding on all parties and effectively replaces the pleadings in establishing the basic outline for the trial.

Any party (or the lawyer for any party) may be subject to sanctions if he or she fails to participate in the pretrial conference, participates in bad faith, or fails to comply with progression deadlines or with any other requirement established by the pretrial order. Rule 16(f).

Trial Procedure

As the time for trial draws near, the litigation team stays in touch with individuals on its witness list and organizes the evidence amassed during discovery for use at trial. Legal assistants have become increasingly important in this process. The trial notebook is prepared, which contains final pleadings, the outlines for the opening statement and closing argument, witness lists, exhibit lists, and short briefs on evidentiary issues which are expected to arise during the trial (called pocket briefs). When the trial date is set, witnesses are contacted once again, their testimony is reviewed with them, and subpoenas are issued for all nonparty witnesses. (*Issuance of Rule 45 subpoenas was discussed earlier in this chapter.*)

The purpose of trial is to present all admissible facts to an impartial factfinder, who then decides which party should win (reaches a verdict) based only upon (1) those facts which the factfinder believes are true and (2) the trial judge's instructions concerning the legal results of those facts. In the traditional trial setting, the jury decides the facts; and the judge decides the law.

The federal civil trial process is governed substantially by the Federal Rules of Civil Procedure and by the Federal Rules of Evidence. State courts are governed by similar rules. The material in this section reviews the basic procedural rules governing trials. Evidentiary rules are addressed only in a peripheral way.

Trial by Jury   The Seventh Amendment to the U.S. Constitution guarantees the right to a jury trial in all cases "at common law" in which the amount in controversy exceeds twenty dollars. This amendment applies to federal trials, but not to state trials.

The Seventh Amendment does not state how many individuals must serve on a jury. The twelve-person jury is a product of history and tradition. The Federal Rules require a jury of "not fewer than six members. . . ." Rule 48. If the jury shrinks to fewer than six members during the trial, a mistrial is declared unless the parties agree to continue. To avoid this situation (alternate jurors were eliminated in the 1991 amendments), the local court rules of many federal courts provide for more than six jurors to be selected. If one or more jurors must be excused for illness or for some other reason before the trial is finished, there still are "not fewer than six" to render the verdict.

Although trial by jury is the hallmark of the American judicial system, not every case is tried to a jury. Juries are not permitted in equity cases, for instance, or in tax court. Even if parties are entitled to a trial by jury, they may waive that right if they prefer to have the case tried to a judge. In these situations, the judge sits as both the factfinder and the trial judge; and her final judgment generally includes both findings of fact and conclusions of law. In federal court, parties who are entitled to a jury trial must request it specifically when their complaints are filed; otherwise, jury trial is waived.

When a trial by jury is permitted and is not waived, the jury's verdict in federal civil cases must be unanimous unless the parties in the case agree otherwise. Many states permit jury verdicts which are less than unanimous in civil cases.

Jury Selection   The pool of potential jurors must be drawn from a representative cross-section of the community. The jury pool may be taken from lists of persons holding a valid driver's license, from voter registration lists, or from other sources likely to produce the required cross-section.

Potential federal jurors (the precise number varies from district to district) are selected to serve as jurors through a process called *voir dire*. During ***voir dire***, potential jurors are examined first by the trial judge and then by the attorneys to determine whether they are able to reach a fair and impartial verdict. If a potential juror answers questions in a way which shows that she cannot reach an impartial verdict, she is ***challenged for cause*** by an attorney for one of the parties and is excused.

Cause exists if the potential juror knows any of the parties, their attorneys, or any prospective witnesses in the case or if the potential juror demonstrates bias or prejudice which would influence a verdict for or against either party. If a potential juror states that she might be influenced, for example, by pretrial publicity about the case, she may be challenged for cause. Because there is no limit to the number of challenges for cause that can be made, jury selection for cases involving controversial issues or controversial parties may extend over a period of days or weeks.

In addition to challenges for cause, each party in a federal civil trial receives three peremptory challenges. A ***peremptory challenge*** allows a party to dismiss a potential juror without demonstrating cause for dismissal. Peremptory challenges are useful when a potential juror provides information to indicate bias, but insists upon questioning that he is able to render a fair and impartial verdict. For example, a potential juror in an auto negligence case may be the husband of an insurance adjuster; yet, the juror may insist that he could be fair to both parties in reaching his verdict. Most plaintiffs claiming damages for injuries likely would use one of their peremptory challenges to dismiss this potential juror.

Opening Statements   Once the jury is selected, the trial begins with opening statements. Because production of witnesses and evidence at trial rarely follows the precise chronology of the transaction or occurrence being litigated, opening statements allow each party to explain to the jury how the evidence will be presented and what it will prove. Attorneys cannot argue the merits of the case or comment on the credibility of witnesses during opening statements; these are reserved for closing arguments. The plaintiff's attorney generally makes the first opening statement, followed by the defendant's attorney.

Opening statements generally are limited to ten or fifteen minutes for each party. Experienced trial attorneys agree, however, that these few minutes are critical to the rest of the trial. Although the attorney cannot argue her client's case during her opening statement, she certainly can capitalize on this opportunity to present her client's case in its best light without using argumentative language or demeanor. If she knows, for example, that her opponent intends to offer damaging evidence, she can talk about the evidence that minimizes its impact when the jurors hear it during trial. If her client is a large corporation, she can use the opening statement to provide it with human qualities through those officers or directors who will testify at trial. A well-organized, thoughtfully prepared opening statement can be a major factor in winning or losing a very close case.

Sequence of Trial   After opening statements are concluded, the plaintiff presents her case by offering evidence in the form of witness *testimony* (testimonial evidence offered through fact witnesses and expert witnesses); *exhibits* (documentary evidence or tangible evidence), and *audiovisual aids* (demonstrative evidence in the form of photographs, charts, diagrams, or models). The Federal Rules of Evidence govern the required foundation for and admissibility of specific evidence forms. Attorneys must object to the admissibility of evidence immediately as it is presented during trial, or the objection is waived. When an objection is made, all questions stop until the trial judge rules on the objection by sustaining it or by overruling it.

The plaintiff's goal is to prove facts to support each of the contested legal issues stated in the complaint (in the pretrial order, if one was entered). To achieve that goal, the plaintiff's case proceeds from witness to witness, with the plaintiff's attorney conducting a ***direct examination*** of each witness and with the defendant's attorney conducting a ***cross-examination*** of each witness if desired. If cross-examination produces facts which were not covered by direct examination, the plaintiff's attorney generally may conduct a ***redirect examination*** concerning those new facts only. She cannot re-hash facts disclosed during the direct examination. If redirect examination occurs, the defendant's attorney likely will be permitted to ***re-cross-examine*** the witness. In addition to testifying about the facts of the case (or offering opinions, if the witness is an expert), witnesses are used to lay foundation for the introduction of exhibits into evidence unless the parties' attorneys previously have stipulated to their foundation. When all evidence has been presented, the plaintiff rests.

At the close of the plaintiff's case, the defendant may make a motion for judgment on partial findings under Rule 52(c) or a motion for judgment as a matter of law under Rule 50(a) if the defendant believes that the plaintiff failed to prove (offer evidence on) any element which is necessary for an ultimate verdict in favor of the plaintiff. As a cautionary procedural measure, the defendant's attorney may make this motion without regard to his assessment of the outcome. By making the motion, even if he thinks that it may be overruled, he preserves his client's right to raise the issue on appeal. (*Both motions were discussed earlier in this chapter.*)

If the defendant's motion for judgment on partial findings is overruled, the defendant begins his case in chief. The defendant's goal is either or both (1) to refute the evidence produced by the plaintiff and (2) to prove the required elements of the affirmative defenses stated in his answer (or stated in the pretrial order, if there is one). The defendant's case proceeds from witness to witness in the same way as did the plaintiff's case. When all evidence has been presented, the defendant rests.

If new issues are raised by the defendant's case, the plaintiff may be permitted to present further evidence in ***rebuttal***. In that circumstance, she must confine her evidence to the new issues only; she cannot re-hash her case in chief.

At the close of all evidence, either or both the plaintiff and the defendant may make a motion for judgment as a matter of law under Rule 50(a), which replaces the motion for directed verdict under previous federal rules. The trial judge may rule on the motion(s) when they are made but is more likely to reserve the ruling until after the jury's verdict is returned. (*Judgment as a matter of law was discussed earlier in this chapter.*)

Closing Arguments   After each party rests (and if motions for judgment as a matter of law are either overruled or reserved for decision), closing arguments are made to the jury. The plaintiff's attorney is allowed to address the jury first, but she may choose to be last if she believes there is a tactical benefit in doing so.

Generally speaking, more time is allotted for closing arguments than for opening statements. This is the attorney's opportunity to persuade the jury to the justness of his or her client's position. The attorney may point out any gaps between what the opposing counsel said in his opening statement that he would prove and what he did prove; may comment on the credibility of witnesses, using care not to alienate the jury; and may argue the sufficiency or weight of evidence. Although there are some limitations on what can be said or done during closing argument, the attorney is given fairly wide latitude in attempting to persuade a jury.

Jury Instructions At the close of all evidence, any party may file written request(s) with the trial judge that a specific jury instruction be given to the jury. Rule 51. The requests typically include supporting legal authority for the judge to consider. (Many states have compiled a reference book of standard jury instructions, which are grouped according to subject matter.) The judge considers all such requests and, when appropriate, incorporates them with the full set of jury instructions that ultimately will be given.

After closing arguments are concluded, the trial judge instructs the jury concerning those rules of law which apply to the jury's findings of fact, generally by reading the jury instructions aloud to the jury and then by providing them in writing. They typically include instructions on the evidence, burden of proof (*discussed below*), pertinent law, and application of the law to the facts as the jury determines the facts to be. In federal courts, and in some state courts, the trial judge has the right to comment on the quality and weight of evidence if she chooses to do so.

Objections to jury instructions must be made before the jury retires for deliberation.

Burden of Proof The term *burden of proof* may have one of several meanings when it is used in connection with civil trials. Its most general meaning is the standard of proof which is assigned to a claimant as the ***burden of persuasion*** in the case. For example, the standard of proof assigned to the government in a criminal trial is "beyond a reasonable doubt." The standard of proof (burden of persuasion) assigned to a claimant in a civil trial is "by a preponderance of the evidence." A matter is proved by a ***preponderance*** if the jury believes it is *more likely than not* that the matter is true.

The preponderance standard frequently is explained to juries by using the example of tipped scales. In the example, the plaintiff and the defendant begin the case with evenly balanced scales. If the weight of the plaintiff's evidence tips the scales in her favor, however slightly, she wins by a preponderance of the evidence. If the combined weights of evidence on the plaintiff's side and the defendant's side tip the scales in favor of the defendant or if the combined weights tip the scales back and forth but end evenly weighted at the end of the case as to each party, the plaintiff (the claimant) cannot win by a preponderance of the evidence.

In addition, the jury's belief (sometimes called a finding) must be actual— not one based on statistics or on mathematical probabilities. For example, the statistical fact that more teenage males drive carelessly than do teenage females does not justify a jury's finding that an unidentified teenager, who was seen driving carelessly, was a male.

The Verdict   Once the jury has been charged (provided with jury instructions), members of the jury retire to a private jury room where they select a foreman and deliberate their verdict. If a unanimous verdict is required, a jury that cannot reach a unanimous decision is called a *hung jury*, which generally provides the basis to declare a mistrial. If a mistrial is declared for this or for any other reason, a new trial is conducted with a new jury.

The jury may return a general verdict, a general verdict with interrogatories, or a special verdict, depending on the jury instructions. A *general verdict* simply declares which party is the winner.

A *general verdict with interrogatories* declares which party is the winner and, in addition, requires the jury to answer answers to questions about specific findings of fact. Rule 49(b). If the findings of fact are consistent with the general verdict, the verdict is entered. If the findings of fact are inconsistent with the general verdict, the judge may either (1) enter judgment according to the findings of fact or (2) order a new trial. If the findings of fact are inconsistent with each other, the just must send the case back to the jury for further deliberation.

A *special verdict* requires a special, written finding for each fact in the case. Rule 49(a). Special verdicts have been frowned upon by several U.S. Supreme Court Justices on the basis that they allow a trial judge to exercise too much control in deciding the ultimate outcome of a case. Whether for that reason or for some other reason, special verdicts are used infrequently by federal courts.

Procedures and Motions after Verdict or Judgment   After the jury returns its verdict in the case, an order of judgment (sometimes simply called a judgment) is prepared and entered as part of the official court file. Absent an appeal, the entry of judgment generally is the final action taken in the trial process. This is how most cases end. However, if procedural matters are pending or are raised when the verdict is returned, those matters must be resolved before the judgment can be entered.

A.   Motion for Judgment as a Matter of Law   If any party moved for a judgment as a matter of law under Rule 50(a)(1) at the close of evidence and if a ruling on the motion was reserved by the trial judge (which often will be the case), the judge must rule on the motion before any judgment is entered. If the verdict is in favor of the moving party, the motion becomes moot. If the verdict is against the moving party, however, and if the judge determines there was no legally sufficient evidence upon which a reasonable jury could have found as it did, the judge may enter judgment as a matter of law in favor of the moving party. This effectively overturns the jury verdict in much the same way as did a judgment notwithstanding the verdict (judgment NOV) under prior federal rules. Judgments NOV and directed verdicts no longer exist after the 1991 amendments to the Federal Rules; instead, they are combined under Rule 50(a)(1) in the (new) judgment as a matter of law.

B.   Motion for New Trial   A motion for new trial must be filed *within ten days of the entry of judgment* (Rule 59) and may be accompanied by supporting affidavits, giving the adverse party ten days after the motion for new trial to file opposing affidavits. Filing a motion for new trial is a prerequisite for appeal in many state courts, but this is not true in federal court.

The goal of a motion for new trial is to allow the trial judge to correct prejudicial errors which occurred during the trial. A ***prejudicial error*** is one which both (1) affects a substantial right of the moving party in the trial process and (2) was objected to by the moving party at the time of its occurrence. By contrast, if a mistake was made which did not affect a substantial right of the moving party, it is a ***harmless error***. Prejudicial errors require a new trial to be conducted; harmless errors do not. If a motion for new trial is denied, the moving party either may accept the judgment as it stands or may appeal if the party believes that prejudicial errors occurred during trial.

Prejudicial error which justifies the grant of a new trial can include any one or more of the following:

1.   *Judicial error*, such as the improper admission or exclusion of evidence or an improper jury instruction.

2.   *Improper conduct of a party, witness, or attorney* during the trial if there is substantial risk that the conduct influenced the verdict.

3.   *Improper conduct of a juror*, such as allowing himself to be exposed to outside influence or concealing bias during *voir dire*.

4.   *A verdict which is against the weight of the evidence.* In federal courts, the verdict must be against the clear weight of the evidence, must be based upon evidence which is false, or must be one which will result in a miscarriage of justice. It is not enough that the judge disagrees with the verdict.

5.   *Newly discovered evidence* which is material and which was not, and could not have been, known at the time of trial.

6.   *The verdict is excessive or is inadequate.* When damages are fixed by law or are liquidated as part of a contract and when a verdict is returned in excess of that amount, the verdict may be set aside as a matter of law and a new trial ordered. Similarly, when damages are fixed by law or are liquidated as part of a contract and when a verdict is returned for less than that amount, the verdict may be set aside as a matter of law.   When the amount of damages is within the discretion of the jury, but the verdict clearly is out of line with the evidence, the verdict may be set aside.

When a trial judge determines that the excessiveness of a verdict is caused by the jury's miscalculation (mathematical error) of the damages, she may be able to correct the error through **remittitur**, under which the winning party agrees to reduce the damages to a specific amount. If the winning party does not agree, the judge may order a new trial. Conversely, when the damages awarded by a verdict are grossly inadequate because of jury miscalculation, the trial judge may correct the error by ordering a new trial unless the losing party agrees to increase the damages to a specific amount (**additur**). *Remittitur* is well-established both in federal and state courts. However, the U.S. Supreme Court has ruled that *additur* cannot be used in federal courts because it violates the Seventh Amendment. The Seventh Amendment does not apply to state courts, however, which continue to use *additur* to correct inadequate damage awards.

As an alternative to *remittitur* or *additur*, a trial judge may grant a partial new trial on the issue of damages only.

C.   Motion for Order *Nunc Pro Tunc*

A motion for an order *nunc pro tunc* generally seeks to correct clerical types of errors when there is no question about what the order of judgment should have contained. For example, if the order of judgment states that judgment is entered in favor of the "plaintiff, Joe Brown" when the plaintiff's name is Joe Bowen, an order *nunc pro tunc* is used to correct the error in the order of judgment. In federal court, the same result is accomplished by filing a ***motion to alter or amend judgment*** within *ten days* after the judgment is entered. Rule 59(e).

Appellate Review

The losing party in the trial court may have a higher court review the trial court proceedings for prejudicial error by filing an appeal. Similarly, the winning party may assume the procedural posture of a losing party for purposes of appeal if she does not win as much as she thinks she should have won. In general, the party who appeals to a higher court is the ***appellant***. The party who defends an appeal is the ***appellee***. In some state courts and under some federal statutes, the parties are identified as the petitioner and the respondent.

Appellate Procedure

Appeal of a federal trial court's decision is governed by the Federal Rules of Appellate Procedure (Fed. R. App. P.). An appeal of right (one which does not require permission from the appellate court) is initiated by filing a ***notice of appeal*** with the clerk of the federal trial court, which must be done either (1) within 30 days after entry of the final judgment or order in the case or (2) within 30 days after motions under Rules 50, 52, or 59 are denied (including denial of a motion for new trial under Rule 59). Fed. R. App. P. 4(a)(4). This period is enlarged to 60 days if the United States or any of its officials or agencies is a party. In addition, if a party can show excusable neglect, the period can be extended for an additional 30 days after the expiration date or for an additional ten days after the order of extension, whichever is later. Once a notice of appeal is filed, any other party also may file a notice of appeal (called a ***cross-appeal***) within 14 days after the first notice of appeal is filed or within any time period set by Fed. R. App. P. 4, whichever is later. If a notice of appeal is filed prematurely (before a final judgment is entered), it has no effect and must be refiled at the proper time to perfect the appeal.

Recall that certain federal appeals, such as an appeal under the Interlocutory Appeal Act (28 U.S.C. § 1292), require the permission of the appellate court before they can be filed. This type of appeal is not an appeal of right. Instead, a petition for permission to appeal is filed. The specific procedure is outlined in Fed. R. App. 5.

When the notice of appeal is filed, the appellant also must pay a ***docket fee*** under Fed. R. App. P. 3(e) and may be required to a ***bond for costs***, which is called an appeal bond. Fed. R. App. P. 7. A transcript of the record must be ordered by the appellant within ten days after filing the notice of appeal (Fed. R. App. P. 10), which must be prepared by the court reporter of the federal trial court and filed in the court of appeals court within 30 days after the transcript of the record is ordered. Fed. R. App. P. 11. The ***record*** consists of the pleadings, the transcript of testimony, the exhibits received in evidence in the trial court, and the docket entries of orders and other matters which are certified by the clerk of the trial court.

Appeals in state courts generally require a notice of appeal within a specified time, typically 30 days from the entry of the final judgment or from the order denying a new trial (when a motion for new trial is required before the appeal can be filed). Unlike federal court, however, there is no provision for enlargement or extension of the appeal time in many state courts.

Once the appeal is docketed in the appellate court (the court of appeals in the federal system), the appellate court assumes jurisdiction of the case. In both state and federal courts, the appellant and the appellee file ***appellate briefs***, which must conform to the rules of procedure and local court rules of the appropriate appellate court. Fed. R. App. P. 31 requires the appellant's brief to be filed and served within forty days after the date on which the record is filed in the court of appeals. The appellee then has thirty days to file her brief, running from the date of service of the appellant's brief. If the appellant files a reply brief to the appellee's brief, the reply brief must be filed and served within fourteen days after the appellee's brief.

After all briefs are filed, ***oral arguments*** are scheduled. In some situations, the appellate court may waive oral argument on its own motion. When oral argument occurs in a federal court of appeals, it generally is conducted before a three-judge panel and usually is limited to no more than 30 minutes for each side. Once oral arguments are concluded (or waived, if that is the situation), the appellate judges hold conferences to determine how they will rule. One judge usually is selected to write the opinion. The ***decision and opinion*** may take several months, depending on the court's case load and the complexity of the issues in the case.

If the losing party on appeal disagrees with the federal court of appeals decision, she may request a ***rehearing*** under Fed. R. App. P. 40; and, if she still loses, she may file ***petition for writ of certiorari*** with the United States Supreme Court. (*See chapter on General Law for further discussion.*)

Stay Pending Appeal   To prevent enforcement of the judgment entered by the trial court while the appeal is pending, the appellant (or the losing party) files a motion for an ***order of stay***. If the order is granted, the moving party typically must file a ***supersedeas bond*** in connection with the order. The purpose of the bond is to assure the winning party that the judgment will be paid if the appellant ultimately loses the appeal. If the motion for order of stay is denied for any reason, the trial court winner is free to enforce the judgment without waiting for the appeal process to be concluded.

Scope of Appellate Review   Appellate review in state court actions may be either *de novo*, *de novo* on the record, or on the record. An appeal *de novo* usually arises when an appeal is taken from a court or agency where no record is made, such as a small claims court or a property tax board, to a court of record. An ***appeal de novo*** means that the appellate court is allowed to try the case anew, as if no prior proceedings had occurred. Witnesses are allowed to testify, and evidence is received; the appellate court is not bound by the findings of fact or by the conclusions of law of the lower court or agency.

More typical in state court actions is an ***appeal de novo on the record***, which means that the appellate court's review is limited to the record made in the trial court. The appellate court generally does not re-evaluate the evidence or the findings of fact (whether by the judge or by a jury) unless they are clearly erroneous, but the appellate court is not bound by the conclusions of law reached by the trial court.

An ***appeal on the record*** is one in which the findings of fact reached by the trial court are given the greatest deference by the appellate court. However, the appellate court gives no greater deference to the trial court's conclusions of law for this type of review than for any other. Appeals from administrative agency decisions frequently are on the record.

The scope of appellate review generally operates in federal courts in much the same way as an appeal *de novo* on the record in state courts. Findings of fact are set aside only if they are "clearly erroneous." Rule 52(a). The federal Court of Appeals is not bound by the conclusions of law reached by the federal trial court, however (*see above*).

Disposition by Appellate Court   If a case is filed improperly (untimely notice of appeal, no record filed with the appellate court, or other material defect), the appellate court may dispose of the appeal by dismissing it without decision. Absent dismissal, the appellate court may dispose of the appeal by a decision which invokes one of the following actions:

1.   ***Affirm*** the lower court decision if, upon review of the record, the appellate court determines that findings of fact were not clearly erroneous and that no prejudicial errors were made. Most appellate cases are disposed of in this way.

2.   ***Reverse*** (change) the lower court decision (1) if, upon review of the record, the appellate court determines either that findings of fact were clearly erroneous or that prejudicial errors were made and (2) the facts in the record are sufficient for the appellate court to render a fully informed judgment on the merits.

3.   ***Reverse and remand*** with instructions for further proceedings (1) if, upon review of the record, the appellate court determines either that findings of fact were clearly erroneous or that prejudicial errors were made but (2) the facts in the record are *insufficient* for the appellate court to render a fully informed judgment on the merits. For example, if the appellate court reverses the trial court's summary judgment, the record will not contain sufficient facts to render a fully informed judgment on the merits. In that situation, the case will be remanded to the trial court for further proceedings (in this case, a trial).

Res Judicata

Res judicata literally means *the thing adjudged*. A basic premise of the American legal system is that every person is entitled to her day in court—but she is entitled only to one. She cannot relitigate the same case over and over again. The doctrine of *res judicata* limits a party's litigation right to one time only when the parties, issues, or claims are the same. If a final judgment on the merits is entered in a case, that judgment is *res judicata* as to all future suits involving the same parties and the same issues (claims). Recall that a dismissal with prejudice to future operates as a judgment on the merits and invokes the *res judicata* doctrine (*discussed above*).

Res judicata may be asserted either in a preliminary motion as a defect of a complaint or in an answer as an affirmative defense.

Although the term *res judicata* frequently is used in the generic sense defined above, it technically encompasses two subsidiary doctrines which are slightly different from each other: (1) merger and bar and (2) collateral estoppel.

Under the doctrine of *merger and bar* (sometimes called *claim preclusion*), the claims of the parties are merged into the judgment. The claims no longer exist, and any future action between the same parties on the same claims are barred because of the merger. Merger and bar applies to claims that actually were litigated as well as to claims that could have been litigated but were not.

> Adam sues Bill for a claim of negligence of $1000. Judgment ultimately is entered in favor of Adam for $500 on his claim. Adam's $1000 claim is merged into the $500 judgment. By operation of law (merger and bar), Adam cannot sue Bill for $1000 again. Neither can he sue Bill for the remaining $500 of his claim. The entire claim is merged into the judgment.

By contrast, the doctrine of *collateral estoppel* (sometimes called *issue preclusion*) prevents the same issues from being litigated by the same parties in different actions. Determination of the issue in the first case disposes of the same issue in the second case. Collateral estoppel applies only to those issues litigated; it does not apply to issues which could have been litigated but were not.

> Patty sues Elizabeth for negligence resulting in property damage to Patty's automobile. Judgment is entered in favor of Elizabeth. Then Patty files a second complaint, this time claiming personal injuries caused by Elizabeth's negligence in the same accident. Because the issue of Elizabeth's negligence was decided in the first case, that issue must be decided in the same way in the same case involving the same parties—even though the claims are different (property damage v. personal injury).

> Patty sues Elizabeth for an installment payment on a rental agreement and wins. Patty sues Elizabeth again for a different installment payment due on the same rental agreement; but this time, Elizabeth defends that the rental agreement never was signed. Collateral estoppel does not apply to the second suit if the validity of the rental agreement was not raised and actually litigated in the first suit.

Many intricacies exist in applying the rules for merger and bar and for collateral estoppel; however, they are beyond the intended scope of this *Review Manual*.

Parties Bound   If an issue or a claim is litigated in one action and appears again in a subsequent action, only certain parties in the subsequent action are bound by the first judgment on the merits. Clearly, the parties to the first litigation are bound by a final judgment on the issues and claims. In addition, persons *in privity* with those parties also are bound, including:

- successors in interest, such as a subsequent owner of property;

- •beneficiaries of a trust in which the trustee was a party to the action;
- •principal or agent of a party to the action; or
- •bailor or bailee in relation to a party to the action.

One who is a stranger to the first action (neither a party nor in privity with a party) is not bound either by the claims or by the issues litigated in the first action.

Enforcement of Judgments

In the usual situation, a judgment (unlike a decree) simply is an order or declaration by a law court that one party owes money to another party. The party who owes the money is the *judgment debtor*; the party to whom the money is owed is the *judgment creditor*.

A judgment does not include a requirement that the money owed must be paid by a certain time or that it must be paid at all. Unless a judgment debtor voluntarily pays the judgment, the judgment creditor must initiate proceedings to enforce (execute) the judgment. These proceedings are ancillary to the main litigation in which the judgment was entered.

Rule 64 provides that the procedure for execution of judgments is the same procedure used in the state where the federal district court is located. If a federal statute is involved, the federal statute governs to the extent that it applies; however, most federal judgment executions follow state rules.

Although procedures for judgment execution vary from state to state, the execution devices are similar. For example, nearly all states provide some type of *writ of execution*, which is used to *levy* against personal property assets of the judgment debtor which are in the possession of the judgment debtor (vehicle, boat, art collection). The property is seized, usually by a local law enforcement official, and is sold. After expenses of levy and sale (and satisfaction of any lienholders of the property), the proceeds are applied against the judgment. If the proceeds are insufficient to satisfy the entire judgment, additional personal property can be seized and sold. Any other enforcement remedy available can be used either in place of or in addition to execution and levy.

Garnishment is used to obtain personal property assets of the judgment debtor which are deposited with or are in the possession of a third person (someone other than the judgment debtor). The most common garnishees are banks holding deposits for the judgment debtor and employers holding earned wages for the judgment debtor. The specific amount of money subject to garnishment is the amount held by the garnishee at the moment when the garnishment notice is received. For example, if a checking account has a balance of $40.00 when the bank receives the garnishment notice, only $40.00 can be subjected to the garnishment proceeding—even if the judgment debtor deposits $10,000.00 into the account one hour later.

Some types of deposits cannot be garnished. For instance, Social Security benefits are not subject to garnishment. However, once the benefits are deposited into a recipient's bank account, they lose their character as Social Security benefits and are subject to general garnishment statutes.

Most states provide statutory exemptions of certain property amounts from levy or garnishment. For example, many states provide a wage exemption to a judgment debtor which is equal to the minimum hourly wage then in force. Garnishment of a debtor's wages, then, would be subject to the minimum wage limitation *if the debtor claims the exemption*. If the exemption is not claimed, it is not given. If the exemption is claimed, however, the judgment creditor can receive only that portion of the judgment debtor's earned wages which exceed the hourly minimum wage amount.

Most states allow a judgment to be enforced as a lien against real property owned by the judgment debtor through the process of judicial ***foreclosure and sale***. Foreclosure and sale of real property operates much the same as levy of personal property, but it generally involves a more detailed and time-consuming procedure to arrive at the point of sale. When real property ultimately is sold to satisfy the judgment lien, the judgment creditor receives the proceeds after expenses, prior lienholders' claims, and the interests of other owners of the property (such as a spouse) are paid. Unless the judgment debtor has a substantial equity interest in the real estate, foreclosure and sale may not be cost effective.

If the judgment creditor believes that the judgment debtor may have concealed assets or may have transferred assets for less than their fair market value (a fraudulent conveyance), Rule 69 allows the judgment creditor to conduct ***post-trial discovery*** (usually interrogatories or depositions) to obtain details concerning the judgment debtor's assets. State courts provide a similar device, sometimes called a debtor's examination.

A judgment debtor who has no assets, who owns assets with liens that equal or exceed the value of the assets, or whose assets consist entirely of exempt property is ***judgment proof***. Because this situation arises often, the wise plaintiff and her litigation team should check the prospective defendant's financial situation carefully and quietly before suit is commenced.

This chapter, together with the chapter on General Law found earlier in this *Review Manual* and with the self-tests provided for both chapters, should provide a basic review of the principles and procedures that may be encountered on the certifying examination. If the applicant is unfamiliar with any of the material covered, he or she is advised to consider close study of a relevant textbook or other study aid as well as the applicable Rules and statutes. *See the Bibliography for additional study references.*

Litigation Self-Test

Allow an uninterrupted thirty-minute period to answer all questions. At the end of thirty minutes, check your answers against those in the Answer Key Section of this Manual. Deduct two points for each incorrect answer (100 total possible points). Unanswered questions are counted as incorrect answers. Follow directions carefully and observe the time limit precisely to provide an accurate self-assessment.

Choose the most correct answer to each of the following questions unless a specific question instructs you to do otherwise.

1.   True or False.   The usual method of serving process on a corporation is to serve its board of directors.

2.   True or False.   Interpleader is initiated by one who already is a party to an existing lawsuit.

3.   True or False. Depositions cannot be conducted before a civil complaint is filed.

4.   True or False. Juries may decide issues related to both law and fact in simple cases.

5.   True or False. The basic pleadings in a federal civil case include the complaint, the answer, and the reply to counterclaim.

6.   True or False. A permissive counterclaim is one which requires the court's permission before it can be filed in a civil case.

7.   True or False. If a criminal charge is pending, the defendant may not be sued in a related civil case until the criminal case is concluded.

8. When a case is appealed, the appellate court will base its decision on:

    a. the credibility of the witnesses.
    b. the record of the lower court.
    c. re-evaluation of the facts presented to the jury.
    d. none of the above.

9. True or False. It is unethical for a lawyer to knowingly offer evidence during litigation which he or she knows is perjured.

10. True or False. Interrogatories under Rule 33 may be served on any person who may have personal knowledge of the facts involved in a particular litigation.

11. If a legal assistant is instructed to ensure that a particular witness personally appears and brings specific documents with him, which of the following should be issued?

    a. summons
    b. subpoena
    c. subpoena duces tecum
    d. subpoena capias

12. If a person fails to answer interrogatories within the time specified, which rule of the Federal Rules of Civil Procedure provides the remedy for this failure?

    a. Rule 33
    b. Rule 34
    c. Rule 36
    d. Rule 37

13. The purpose of a summons is to:

    a. notify the defendant to appear at the stated place and time.
    b. notify the defendant that suit has been filed and the time limit in which to respond.
    c. notify the defendant that depositions have been scheduled.
    d. notify the defendant that trial has been scheduled at a stated place and time.

14. True or False.   Since answers to interrogatories are given under oath, the answering party may use his or her own answers to prove the truth of their contents.

15. True or False.   A civil action is commenced in federal court when the complaint is filed.

16. True or False.   The answer day for interrogatories can be extended without court approval if all parties agree to the extension.

17. True or False.   Objections to interrogatories must be filed within ten days after the interrogatories are served.

18. When computing the deadline for response:

   a.   include the day of service.
   b.   count only ordinary working days.
   c.   exclude the day of service.
   d.   schedule it for Friday if the last day falls on Saturday.

19. If a plaintiff denies the allegations of a counterclaim, she must respond:
   a.   10 days from date of service.
   b.   20 days from date of service.
   c.   30 days from date of service.
   d.   none of the above.

20. General discovery provisions are contained in:

   a.   Rule 16.
   b.   Rule 26.
   c.   Rule 27.
   d.   Rule 28.

21. True or False.   If subject matter jurisdiction is defective, the parties may agree among themselves to waive this requirement.

22. True or False.   An interlocutory appeal is the method used to obtain appellate review of a discovery order prior to the time of trial.

23. True or False.   Summary judgment exists in most state court litigations but no longer exists in federal court litigations.

24. True or False.   Pretrial conferences are mandatory in federal civil litigation.

25. A local court rule is an example of:

    a.   substantive law.
    b.   procedural law.
    c.   adjective law.
    d.   a and c.
    e   b and c.

26. Eleanor (a citizen of Michigan) and Stanley (a citizen of Minnesota) want to sue Ken (a citizen of Iowa) and Wilma (a citizen of Minnesota) in connection with violation of a federal mail fraud statute. The fraud occurred in Iowa. Which of the following courts has subject matter jurisdiction of the case?

    a.   Michigan federal court
    b.   Minnesota federal court
    c.   Iowa federal court
    d.   All of the above
    e.   None of the above

27. The United States District Court is a court of _____ jurisdiction.

    a.   general
    b.   personal
    c.   limited
    d.   none of the above

28. Redirect examination of a witness during trial may occur:

    a.   only during the plaintiff's case in chief
    b.   only during the defendant's case in chief
    c.   only during the plaintiff's rebuttal
    d.   none are correct

29. All post-trial motions are calculated:

    a.   from the time the verdict is entered
    b.   from the time the parties rest
    c.   from the time the judgment is entered
    d.   from the time the jury is sequestered

30. When a nonparty witness is subpoenaed for a deposition in a particular case, which of the following sanctions may be imposed if she refuses to appear and to testify?

    a.   criminal contempt sanctions
    b.   civil contempt sanctions
    c.   entry of judgment against her
    d.   dismissal of her complaint

31. Proceedings to enforce a judgment are called:

    a.   execution proceedings
    b.   garnishment proceedings
    c.   ancillary proceedings
    d.   judgment proceedings

32. In a civil bench trial in federal court, which of the following motions properly may be filed by the defendant's attorney at the close of the plaintiff's case?

    a.   motion for judgment on partial findings
    b.   motion for judgment as a matter of law
    c.   motion for directed verdict
    d.   motion for dismissal

33. The proper method for objection to the issuance of a subpoena in a civil case is:

    a.   motion to suppress
    b.   motion to quash
    c.   motion in limine
    d.   motion to dismiss

34. In a civil trial in federal court, which of the following motions properly may be filed at the close of the defendant's case?

    a.   motion for judgment on partial findings
    b.   motion for judgment as a matter of law
    c.   motion for directed verdict
    d.   motion for dismissal

35. True or False.   Neither the court nor any of the parties every can waive personal jurisdiction.

36. True or False.   A state court of general jurisdiction may hear a case based upon a federal civil rights statute.

37. True or False.   The term "engrossment" is used to indicate that interrogatory questions and their answers related to a particular party are numbered sequentially from one set of interrogatories to the next.

38. True or False.   Answers to interrogatories must be verified by the party to whom they are addressed.

39. True or False.   All of the discovery methods provided in the Federal Rules of Civil Procedure are self-executing.

40. True or False.   The Federal Rules of Civil Procedure govern procedural matters such as the use of privileged communications in federal civil trials.

41. True or False.   The time limitation for responding to a counterclaim is 20 days after the date of its service.

42. True or False.   A plaintiff may aggregate her claims against a single defendant to reach the minimum dollar amount required to establish federal diversity jurisdiction.

43. True or False.   In a federal diversity action, the plaintiff may be able to invoke the federal court's supplemental jurisdiction to file a claim against a third-party defendant.

44. Joe (a citizen of Colorado) sues Andrew (a citizen of Wyoming) in Wyoming state court for an auto accident that occurred in California. Joe claims $100,000 in damages arising from Andrew's negligence related to the auto accident. If Andrew wants to remove the case to federal court under diversity of citizenship jurisdiction,

    a.   he cannot remove the case to any federal court.
    b.   he can remove the case to a Colorado federal court.
    c.   he can remove the case to a Wyoming federal court.
    d.   he can remove the case to a California federal court.

45. Mary holds a second mortgage on property which is the subject of a foreclosure action filed by the Small Business Administration (the first lienholder) in federal court. If Mary cannot be served with summons under any applicable statute or federal rule, which of the following statements is most accurate?

a. the suit must be dismissed because Mary is an indispensable party.
b. the suit must be dismissed because Mary has no minimum contacts with the forum state.
c. the suit must be dismissed because Mary is a necessary party.
d. the suit may continue because Mary is a necessary party.

46. Which of the following rules of pleading operate under the Federal Rules of Civil Procedure?

a. fact pleading
b. notice pleading
c. code pleading
d. claim pleading

47. Which of the following issues is waived if it is not raised immediately by the defendant in a federal civil action?

a. personal jurisdiction
b. subject matter jurisdiction
c. ancillary jurisdiction
d. removal jurisdiction

48. Ruth is sued in federal court for nonpayment of a promissory note in a diversity case. The complaint alleges that Ruth has made no payments on the note, but Ruth has cancelled checks showing that she has paid more than $2,000 to the lender. Which of the following terms most accurately states the way in which Ruth's payments should be characterized in her answer?

a. a denial of the plaintiff's claim
b. an affirmative defense to the plaintiff's claim
c. a setoff against the plaintiff's claim
d. a reduction of the plaintiff's claim

49. Sam Smith sues Bill Barnes and Mary Mitchell in federal court for negligent operation of an amusement park. Mary claims she should be indemnified by Bill for any negligence that may have occurred, since she is a limited partner in the business that operates the park. Mary should file:

a. a counterclaim
b. an answer and counterclaim
c. a cross-claim
d. an answer and cross-claim

50. Donald Defendant has been sued in federal court and timely filed his answer to the complaint. Shortly after the answer was filed, Donald wanted to add an additional defense. Which of the following statements is most correct?

    a.   Without the court's permission, Donald has ten days from filing to amend his answer.

    b.   Without the court's permission, Donald has 20 days from filing to amend his answer.

    c.   Without the court's permission, Donald has 30 days from filing to amend his answer.

    d.   Without the court's permission, Donald cannot amend his answer.

Chapter 16
REAL ESTATE LAW

The only difference between a rut and a grave is the depth.

—Gerald Burrill

Real estate law concerns the many ways in which real property is acquired, used, and transferred. It combines principles of contract law with principles of estates (interests) in land, many of which stem from feudal English law.

In feudal England, all land originally belonged to the king. Later, some of the lands were given by feoffment to certain lords for particularly faithful service to the king. Feoffment (delivery of the fee) gave a lord an ownership interest in the land. The lord could create tenancies (rights of possession and use) that could be held by a common man; but when a tenant died, the land reverted to the lord. Principles of real estate ownership and tenancy have changed substantially since feudal times; yet, some of the concepts and many of the terms continue today.

Freehold Possessory Estates

The concept of seisin (pronounced "season"), which was developed in feudal times, meant that a man owned both a freehold estate in land (free of the right of reversion either to the king or to a lord) plus the right of possession.
Possession could be exercised either by the freeholder himself or by a tenant of the freeholder.

When land was conveyed, it had to be conveyed in a certain way. The right words had to be used to create a proper estate in another: words of purchase and words of limitation. Both had to be present; if they were not, the conveyance was void.

To A = **words of purchase**, showing in whom the estate is created.

And his heirs = **words of limitation**, showing the type of estate created.

Fee Simple   The fee simple estate, sometimes called "fee simple absolute" was created by the words *To A and his heirs* (see above). It included all of the rights that possibly could go with the land, sometimes referred to as the "maximum bundle of rights." Today that bundle of rights includes the right to use it, to sell it or to give it away (alienate it), to give it by will (devise it), to pass it to heirs when no will exists (intestate succession), to waste it, to lease it, and so on.

The fee simple estate was, and remains today, the largest estate (interest) that could be created in land. Then and now, land may be conveyed in fee simple; or the bundle of rights connected to the fee simple estate may be split, (1) with only part of the bundle being conveyed or (2) with part being conveyed to one person and part being conveyed to others. When the bundle of rights are split, however, the resulting interests are something less than a fee simple estate.

Fee Tail   An estate in fee tail was created by the words *To A and the heirs of his body*. This estate could be inherited only by lineal descendants. In early real estate law and because of the doctrine of **primogeniture**, this type of conveyance meant that the estate could be inherited only by the first male heir born to the freeholder (owner). The rule was later relaxed to mean that any male heir born to the freeholder could inherit.

The more modern term for "heirs of the body" is **issue**. Land conveyed by will, for instance, can be devised to "my son Jack and his issue." This means that Jack will own the land at the testator's death; but if Jack is not living when the testator dies, the land will pass to his lineal descendants (children, grandchildren, great-grandchildren, and on down the line). Jack's wife cannot own the land, because she is not included in the definition of the term "issue." She is among Jack's heirs but cannot be among his issue.

Life Estate   A life estate is a freehold possessory estate conveyed for the life of the grantee or for the life of a person other than the grantee. If the life estate is conveyed for the life of a person other than the grantee, a life estate **pur autre vie** is created.

To A for life = A has the right to possess and to use the land until A's death.

To A for the life of B = A and his heirs have the right to possess and to use the estate until the death of B. If B dies next year, the life estate ends even though A is still living. If A dies next year instead of B, the life estate is inherited by A's heirs and continues until B's death. A is the life tenant *pur autre vie*; B is the **cestui que vie** (the measuring life).

In theory, a life estate can be sold. As a practical matter, however, few people may want to buy it because the only thing that can be purchased is a possessory estate that will terminate upon the death of the seller.

A life tenant has the right to use the estate during her life (grow crops and keep the profits, rent it to another and keep the rents, or some other use) but does not have the right to commit waste upon the land. **Voluntary waste** is committed by using the land in a way which results in an unreasonable reduction of the value that will be passed to those estates that follow the life estate. Strip mining is voluntary waste. **Permissive waste** is committed by permitting the land to fall into disrepair, resulting in its reduced value. The holder of a subsequent estate may bring an action for damages or for an injunction if waste is either committed or threatened.

Ameliorative waste results when improvements are made to the land which destroy the original condition of the land but which increase its value, such as tearing down a house to build an office complex.

Future Interest   A future interest is a freehold, *non*possessory, present interest in land that is capable of becoming possessory. The interest exists now but cannot become possessory until a future time. Future interests are classified as (1) those retained by the grantor and (2) those conveyed to third persons (someone who is neither the grantor nor the grantee of the possessory estate).

Future Interests Retained by Grantor   A future interest retained by a grantor may be classified as a reversion, a possibility of reverter, or a right of entry.

51. **Reversion** A reversion is a future interest retained by the grantor when land is conveyed by sale or by will. A reversion is created, for instance, when a life estate is conveyed without conveying the remainder interest. Upon the death of the life tenant, the land reverts automatically to the grantor.

a. **Possibility of Reverter** Also known as a *fee simple determinable*, the possibility of reverter exists when land is conveyed, for example, *to A as long as the land is used for religious purposes*. If the land is used to advance a religious purpose, A's ownership interest could last forever. If it is sold to build a brewery, however, the ownership interest reverts to the grantor automatically (to the grantor's heirs if the grantor is no longer living).

b. **Right of Entry** Also known as a *fee simple subject to condition subsequent*, the right of entry is similar to the fee simple determinable with one important difference. A fee simple determinable ends automatically upon the occurrence of the prohibited use or event; a fee simple subject to condition subsequent does not. Instead, the grantor or her successors must take some affirmative step to terminate the estate, such as entering the premises or commencing a lawsuit to enter the premises.

A fee simple subject to condition subsequent might be stated as *to A and his heirs as long as the land is used for religious purposes; and if the land is no longer used for religious purposes, Grantor or her heirs may enter and terminate the land conveyed*. This language creates a right of entry, which may or may not be used if the condition occurs. The future interest possessed by the grantor and her successors is a *right of entry for condition broken*, also called a power of termination.

Future Interests Conveyed to Third Persons A future interest conveyed to a third person (someone other than the grantor or the grantee of the possessory estate) is classified as either a remainder or an executory interest.

a. **Remainder** A remainder is a future interest that becomes possessory upon the natural termination of the preceding estate.

To Alice for life, then to Bob in fee simple conveys a life estate to Alice, with the remainder to Bob. Bob is a remainderman, and his remainder interest will become possessory when the preceding life estate terminates naturally at Alice's death. The grantor retains no interest in the estate. She has conveyed her entire "bundle of rights" to Alice and to Bob collectively.

In the preceding example, Bob holds a ***vested remainder***, meaning that it is certain to become possessory when Alice dies.

A ***contingent remainder*** exists when the identity of the remainderman is uncertain or when the remainderman's interest depends on the occurrence or nonoccurrence of an event. A conveyance *to Alice for life, remainder to Bob's first child* creates a contingent remainder if Bob has no children at the time of the conveyance. The remainder may not vest at all if, for example, Bob remains childless at the time of Alice's death. If that occurs, the contingent remainder becomes a reversion to the grantor.

On the other hand, if Bob has a child before Alice's death, the contingent remainder becomes vested. It is certain to take effect. The child's interest does not require that she outlive Alice, however. If the child predeceases Alice, the vested remainder becomes part of the child's estate to be inherited by the child's heirs (but not to become possessory until Alice's death).

b.   Executory Interest   An executory interest is similar to either a fee simple determinable or a fee simple subject to a condition subsequent, except that the interest is created in a third person rather than in the grantor or in the grantee of the possessory estate.

A conveyance to *Bob and his heirs; but if Bob dies without leaving children surviving him, then to Carol and her heirs* gives a fee simple determinable to Bob. In other words, Bob owns the property until such time as he may die without children surviving him. Carol owns an executory interest, which will cut off Bob's fee simple estate if Bob dies without children who survive him. The situation in the example describes a ***shifting executory interest***, meaning that it destroys the estate created in Bob and shifts that estate to someone other than the grantor, namely, Carol.

A ***springing executory interest***, sometimes called a springing use, is created by a conveyance to *Bob and his heirs, Bob's interest to commence upon his attaining the age of 25 years*. If Bob's interest vests at all, it will spring from the grantor; it will not shift from a third party.

The interest conveyed in the preceding example must not be confused with a continent remainder. Although the interest is contingent in the sense that it may never vest (Bob may die before reaching the age of 25), it cannot be a remainder. A remainder takes effect only upon the natural termination of the estate that precedes it, such as a life estate or an estate created for a specified term of years. In the example, the preceding estate is a fee simple held by the grantor; a fee simple estate does not end naturally. If the contingency occurs (if Bob reaches age 25),

Bob's interest will cut off or destroy the preceding fee simple estate. Because of this characteristic, Bob's interest is classified as an executory interest.

A remainder never cuts off the preceding estate before the time when it will end naturally. An executory interest almost always does.

Rule Against Restraints on Alienation

Since the Statute Quia Emptores (1290), which established the principle that land should be alienable, courts have fashioned a number of rules to advance the transfer of land. Among these is the rule against direct restraints on alienation. As a result, any attempt at *total restraint of alienability* of a fee simple estate *is void*. For example, a conveyance to *Alice and her heirs; but if Alice attempts to transfer the property, this conveyance shall be null and void* will not be given effect. Because courts will not recognize the attempted restraint, Alice may transfer the property as she chooses and without penalty.

A partial restraint is one that attempts to restrict transferability of land to specific persons only, by a specific method, or until a specific time. Partial restraints are attempts to control entry into a particular neighborhood or subdivision. They generally are treated the same as total restraints and are held void. There are a few exceptions, however:

> ### Cooperative Apartment Agreements
> A provision in a cooperative apartment agreement that restrains sale of stock ownership without the consent of the cooperative's board of directors may be upheld. Since tenants in a cooperative are liable for the entire mortgage on the building, they will be required to rectify any default by any individual tenant. This plus the need for tenants to live in very close proximity to one another creates a need to assure themselves of a new tenant's financial responsibility and desirability. A similar restriction on transferability of condominium units likewise may be valid.

> ### Right of First Refusal
> A right of first refusal if the owner decides to sell the property is less burdensome than requiring the consent, for instance, of a neighborhood association before sale can occur. If a cooperative housing association is given the first right to purchase the property at a fair market price, this preemptive right generally is valid.

> ### Cotenant Agreements
> An agreement not to seek partition of property, which is made by joint tenants or by tenants in common,

generally is valid if it is limited in time and if its purpose is reasonable.

A restraint on the *use of property* makes it less alienable by eliminating would-be purchasers who may want to use the property for the forbidden purpose. Nevertheless, restraints on the use of property almost always are upheld.

a.   Rule Against Perpetuities

The Rule Against Perpetuities is designed to prevent the hand of the dead from reaching out from the grave to control the living forever. The Rule states:

> *No interest is good unless it must vest, if at all, not later than twenty-one years after some life in being at the creation of the interest.*

Much of the confusion related to the Rule Against Perpetuities can be eliminated if the legal assistant keeps in mind that the Rule applies *only* to contingent remainders and to executory interests. If a problem relates to a reversionary interest or to a vested remainder, for example, the Rule simply does not apply.

When the Rule Against Perpetuities does apply (when a contingent remainder or an executory interest exists):

> ■Look for a life in being at the time of the original conveyance and use this person as the measuring life (a child in gestation can be the measuring life). If the interest *must* vest (or fail to vest) within 21 years after the end of the measuring life, the conveyance is valid.

> ■Use the "what might happen" test: If anything *might* happen that could prevent the interest from either vesting or failing to vest within the required time (the measuring life + 21 years), the conveyance is void from the beginning, whether or not "what might happen" ever happens or not. Consider these examples:

> In 1992 Mary conveys Blackacre *to the first child of Bill who marries*. Bill has two children, ages three and five, in 1992. The conveyance is void.

> In 1992 Joe conveys Greenacre *to the first child of Andrew who reaches the age of 21 years*. Andrew has no children in 1992. The conveyance is valid.

The conveyance in the first example is void, because it is possible that the first child of Bill to marry will be a child who was neither born nor in gestation when the conveyance was made in 1992. For instance, it is possible that both of Bill's children who were living in 1992 could die without having married. It is also possible that Bill could have a third child (let's name her Judy) born in 1994 and that Bill could die one month after her birth. If Judy were to marry at age 25 and were to claim Blackacre under the conveyance, she could not receive Blackacre—because more than 21 years would have elapsed after the death of Bill (the measuring life). Judy cannot be the measuring life, because she was not a "life in being" (born or in gestation) at the time the conveyance was made in 1992.

This hypothetical scenario represents only what *might* happen; but if it might happen, the conveyance is void from the beginning, regardless of whether any part of the hypothetical events ever happens or not. Even if one of Bill's children who was living in 1992 actually marries at age 18, the conveyance still is void—the Rule Against Perpetuities must be applied as of the time when the conveyance was made, using the "what might happen" test.

The conveyance in the second example is valid, because no hypothetical situation can be imagined in which the interest would not either vest—or fail to vest—within 21 years after Joe's death. The worst case scenario would be that Joe could die with no children living, in which case the interest absolutely would fail to vest not later than the prescribed 21 years after Joe's death.

Concurrent Ownership

Concurrent ownership of real property requires that more than one person holds a possessory ownership interest in the same property at the same time. These owners may be called co-owners or cotenants.

Unless clearly stated otherwise, co-owners are presumed to have equal, undivided interests in the property. This means that each co-owner has a simultaneous, proportionate share of the entire property, but no co-owner owns any specifically identifiable portion of the property. In other words, if three people own the same parcel of real estate, each owns an undivided one-third of the property. However, each owner has an equal right to possess and to enjoy any portion or all of the property subject to the rights of the other co-owners. This is the unity of possession that is characteristic of all forms of co-ownership.

Included among the rules that govern concurrent ownership of land are the *four unities* of property. A unity is a characteristic of property ownership that the owners have in common. The number of unities that exist in a particular co-ownership indicates the type of ownership held by them as well as the rights that attach to it. The four unities are:

1. Time (ownership created at the same time);
2. Title (ownership obtained from the same source);
3. Interest (each owner has an equal interest); and
4. Possession (each owner holds an undivided share).

The most common forms of concurrent ownership are tenancy in common, joint tenancy, and tenancy by the entirety. The primary difference among these forms of ownership is the right of survivorship that are inherent in joint tenancy and in tenancy by the entirety. No right of survivorship exists in a tenancy in common.

Tenancy in Common　　　　When real estate is purchased by more than one person whose interests are not stated specifically, the parties are presumed to own the property as ***tenants in common***. There is no right of survivorship.

The only unity that must be present in a tenancy in common is the unity of possession. Ownership interests can be created at different times and by different sources (by deed, by will, by intestate succession, and so forth). Interests of owners can be unequal (undivided 1/2 interest for one owner and undivided 1/4 interest for each of the other two owners, for instance). Because of the unity of possession, each cotenant can use the property as if he or she owned all of the property. However, no cotenant can use the property in a way that interferes with or that reduces the value of the rights of the other cotenants.

When tenants in common cannot agree about the use of the property or about any other rights associated with the property, any one or more of them may file an action for ***partition***. In a partition proceeding, the court divides the property into parcels according to the percentage owned by each cotenant. If the land cannot be divided reasonably (a small lot upon which a large house is located), the court may order the property sold so that the proceeds can be divided among the cotenants.

Joint Tenancy　　　　A joint tenancy ownership differs from a tenancy in common in several important ways:

1. Joint tenancy must be stated specifically in the document which conveys title (it will not be presumed); and

2. Joint tenancy includes all four of the unities of ownership: time, title, interest, and possession (*see above*).

3.   The right of survivorship is inherent in joint tenancy and will be inferred even though not specifically stated unless a statutory provision of a particular state provides otherwise.

Right of survivorship means that when one of the joint tenants dies, his or her interest vests automatically in the remaining joint tenant(s). The interest of the deceased joint tenant does not pass to his or her estate or descendants.

A joint tenancy continues only as long as the four unities continue. When one joint tenant conveys his or her interest to an outsider, only the original, remaining joint tenants continue as joint tenants. The new owner does not become a joint tenant but, rather, is a tenant in common. What this means is the new owner does not acquire a right of survivorship when one of the original joint tenants dies.

> Ann, Betty, and Connie own a parcel of land as joint tenants with right of survivorship (JTROS). While all three are living, Ann sells her interest in the parcel to Dick. Betty then dies and wills all of her property to Frank. Who are the owners of the property after Betty's death? What interest does each owner hold?

After Betty's death, the owners of the property are Connie and Dick. Ann sold her interest to Dick, destroying the joint tenancy in relation to herself and her buyer (Dick). At that point, Dick owned an undivided 1/3 interest in the parcel as a tenant in common; and Betty and Connie continued as joint tenants in relation to the remaining, undivided 2/3 interest.

The parcel was not included among the property willed to Frank. Because of the characteristics of joint tenancy ownership, Betty's joint tenancy interest passed to the surviving joint tenant (Connie) automatically upon Betty's death, making Connie the owner of the entire, undivided 2/3 interest.

Following Betty's death, then, Dick and Connie own the parcel as tenants in common. Connie was the only remaining joint tenant to survive. Since she now shares the four unities of ownership with no one, the joint tenancy no longer exists. Connie owns an undivided 2/3 interest, and Dick owns an undivided 1/3 interest.

Like tenants in common, joint tenants enjoy the unity of possession (all cotenants have equal right to use all of the property as long as that use does not interfere with the rights of the other cotenants). A joint tenancy can be terminated by partition, similar to a tenancy in common.

Tenancy by the Entirety   Tenancy by the entirety is a special form of joint tenancy. It has all of the characteristics of a joint tenancy but, in addition, requires that the joint tenants be married (husband and wife) to each other. If they continue to own the land following divorce, they automatically become tenants in common. Only a few states continue to recognize tenancy by the entirety as a form of ownership distinct from joint tenancy.

Duties and Rights of Cotenants

Each cotenant has certain duties to other cotenants in the use and maintenance of jointly owned real estate. They include:

- The cotenant cannot commit waste upon the property;

- The cotenant may need to account to cotenants for profits realized from the property; and

- When one cotenant advances money or services to maintain the property, that cotenant generally is entitled to contribution from the remaining cotenants.

<u>Marital Rights</u> When a married couple owns land, the rights of each spouse are derived from his or her ownership interest. When a married person owns land which is not also owned by his or her spouse, the spouse may have an interest in the land even though the spouse's name is not shown on the deed as an owner.

a.   Common Law Marital Rights Common law marital rights were found in the laws of dower and curtesy. These laws provided certain property rights for the surviving spouse in the marital relationship.

The law of ***curtesy*** was for the benefit of the surviving husband. It provided that he would inherit all of his wife's property at her death, without regard to surviving children. A wife's property often included lands inherited by her from her family.

The law of ***dower*** applied to the surviving wife. Unlike her male counterpart, a surviving wife *with children* generally received a life estate in 1/3 of the lands owned by her husband at his death, with the remaining 2/3 passing to the children. Upon the death of the surviving wife, her life estate passed to the children as well. Dower provided nothing for a surviving wife without children—not even a life estate.

b.   Statutory Marital Rights   Although modern statutes vary, they tend to be more equal in their treatment of surviving spouses without regard to gender. A person can disinherit a child completely but cannot disinherit a spouse. If a person does not provide adequately in his or her will for the surviving spouse, state statutes allow the survivor to claim a forced share, sometimes called a marital share, of the deceased's estate.

Under statutory provisions, the surviving spouse is entitled to a percentage of the deceased's estate. The spouse's statutory share is superior to all other claims of heirs and devisees, even though it may reduce or eliminate the devises and bequests made to them by the will.

There is no requirement that there be surviving children for the spousal share to be effective, and all real property received under the forced share statutes is in fee simple absolute rather than in a life estate. *(Refer to the chapter on Estate Planning and Probate for a more thorough discussion.)*

c.   Community Property Rights   Some states have adopted the concept of community property for married persons, which means that all property acquired during a marriage is marital property and is owned equally (50-50) by each spouse. The community property concept applies as a matter of law, without any action by either spouse.

Community property does not include:

• Property individually owned by a spouse prior to the marriage; or

• Property which comes to a spouse as an inheritance or gift after the marriage.

To the extent that separate property in either category is commingled with community property, making it difficult to tell which is which, it is treated as community property.

<u>**Trusts, Cooperatives, and Condominiums**</u>   Additional ways to divide ownership interests among multiple parties include trusts, cooperatives, and condominiums.

A trust may relate to land only or it may include land as well as other types of property. A *trust* is a fiduciary relationship concerning property in which one person, the *trustee*, holds legal title to the property (the *res*) and manages it for the benefit of one or more beneficiaries, who hold equitable title. In the usual situation, the trust has a life beneficiary and one or more remaindermen. (*See Estate Planning and Probate.*)

A *cooperative* is a form of real estate ownership in which residents in a multiple-unit building own shares in a corporation which, in turn, owns the building. Ownership of shares in the corporation entitles each owner to lease a unit in the building and to use common areas. As part of the shareholder agreement, each resident makes a monthly payment that represents a prorated share of the cost to repay the loan secured to pay for the building and a prorated share of the building maintenance costs. Generally, each resident is jointly and severally liable on the loan. Therefore, if any resident fails to make a monthly payment, the other residents must arrange to pay that tenant's share of the loan to avoid default.

Because of problems created by the joint and several liability characteristic of cooperatives, the condominium has evolved as a more popular form of ownership of multiple-dwelling buildings.

In a *condominium* system, each resident individually purchases (in fee simple) a unit in the building; and all residents own the common areas as tenants in common, such as hallways, basement storage, roads, and recreational facilities as tenants in common. Although a resident may obtain a loan to finance the purchase of his or her unit, the other residents do not assume liability for that loan.

Condominiums typically have some type of condominium association that is responsible for operation of the building; each resident is a member. Residents pay a monthly fee to the condominium association to cover the costs of maintaining common areas.

Most states regulate condominium ownership by statutes that require condominium developers to adopt a master deed and condominium association bylaws. These documents describe the specific interests held by each condominium owner and the methods of maintaining and paying the expenses of the common areas. A purchaser of a condominium unit is entitled to receive copies of these documents before ownership is transferred under most statutes.

Nonfreehold Estates

A nonfreehold estate in real property is one in which there are specific rights to possess and control land, to the exclusion of the true owner. These estates generally are created by agreement, are limited in time, and do not include any ownership interest. Nonfreehold estates created between the owner and possessor of real estate are called leaseholds.

Landlord and Tenant   The most typical nonfreehold estate is that created by the landlord/tenant relationship. This nonfreehold estate is called a leasehold. There are four types of leasehold estates that can be created:

- Tenancy for Years;
- Tenancy from Period to Period;
- Tenancy at Will; and
- Tenancy at Sufferance.

A.   Tenancy for Years   This is the most prevalent type of tenancy, characterized by a fixed beginning date and a fixed ending date. The duration of the term is unimportant; it can be as short as one day or as long as ninety-nine years (or longer). This tenancy expires automatically on the fixed date. Absent a contrary provision in the lease, no notice of termination is required by either party.

B.   Tenancy from Period to Period   A tenancy from period to period continues indefinitely for successive periods (week to week, month to month, or year to year) until notice of termination is given by either party. Periodic tenancies may be express (stated in words, either oral or written) or may be implied (parties fail to state a period but tenant pays rent periodically, such as by the week or by the month).

A periodic tenancy from year to year generally must be in writing to comply with the Statute of Frauds.

A periodic tenancy may arise by implication when a tenant "holds over" (continues in possession) following expiration of a tenancy for years. In that event, the landlord may elect (1) to treat the tenant as a trespasser and evict her or (2) to continue the tenancy from period to period by accepting further rental payments.

C.   Tenancy at Will   A tenancy at will is the lowest form of leasehold estate but is treated as an estate because it confers the right of exclusive possession upon the tenant. This characteristic distinguishes a tenant at will from a licensee or a lodger. No notice is required to terminate a tenancy at will under common law; however, many states have adopted statutes that require a minimum advance notice of termination, such as thirty days.

Tenancies at will ordinarily arise by implication. If a tenant takes possession without any specific agreement about rent, a tenancy at will is created. A tenant in possession under an invalid lease, such as one that fails to comply with the Statute of Frauds, is a tenant at will until periodic rental payments are made to create a periodic tenancy. A purchaser of property who takes possession prior to receiving legal title is a tenant at will.

D.   Tenancy at Sufferance   A tenancy at sufferance is not an estate in any real sense. The term is used to describe the situation when a hold-over tenant wrongfully remains in possession upon expiration of the lease term. The landlord may elect to treat the hold-over tenant either as a trespasser or as a tenant under a new periodic tenancy (*see above*). If the landlord elects to treat the tenant as a trespasser, the tenant's possessory interest is merely at the sufferance of the landlord, pending the landlord's action to evict.

The only difference between a tenant at sufferance and an ordinary trespasser is that the original possession of a tenant at sufferance was rightful.

Effect of Death of Either Party

Unless provided otherwise in the lease agreement, a tenancy for years or a periodic tenancy is not terminated by the death of either party. The interest passes as part of the decedent's estate by will or by intestate succession, and the rights and duties under the lease are enforceable by or against the decedent's estate. The lease continues until expiration of the term (in a tenancy for years) or until termination by proper notice (in a periodic tenancy).

A tenancy at will depends upon the continuing will of both the landlord and the tenant that the leasehold should continue. The death of either party extinguishes the will of that party and therefore terminates the tenancy on the date the survivor becomes aware of the death.

Landlord Rights

The landlord has the right to be paid the agreed rent for the duration of the lease term and has the right to return of the property in the same condition at the end of the lease term, less reasonable wear and tear.

A landlord generally has the right to enter the property to make repairs which are necessary to prevent waste of the property by the tenant (when tenant has failed to make the needed repairs).

Landlord Duties

Along with her rights, a landlord has certain duties that must be performed in relation to the tenant and the leased land.

•*Delivery of Possession*   The tenant has the right to possess the leasehold during the term of the lease.

●*Tenant's Quiet Enjoyment*   The tenant has the right of quiet enjoyment of the leasehold, which stems from the landlord's ownership right of quiet enjoyment. The landlord may not interfere with this right. Either actual or constructive eviction is a breach of this duty. The tenant must have vacated the premises for constructive eviction to have occurred. Upon actual eviction, the tenant's duty to pay rent ceases.

●*Habitable Premises*   The landlord must provide a habitable premises. This means there can be no latent defects. A latent defect is one which a tenant could not discover easily by inspection. In addition, habitability implies that the landlord must provide access to electricity, hot water, heat, and other basic services.

●*Mitigation*   If the tenant breaches the lease agreement by moving before the end of the lease term, the landlord must mitigate her damages (minimize her losses) by trying to find a replacement tenant.

The tort liability of a landlord varies substantially from state to state. As a result, only general principles are stated here. Under traditional common law rules, a landlord had no duty to make the leasehold premises safe. That rule has been altered by statute in many states.

Many state statutes require a landlord to disclose latent defects to the tenant at the beginning of the lease term; however, the landlord is relieved of liability once disclosure is made. When the premises will be used by the public (such as a physician's office), the landlord is liable for latent defects existing at the beginning of the lease term unless she makes reasonable efforts to remedy the defect.

The landlord generally is not liable for dangerous conditions which arise after the tenant takes possession of the premises unless a lease provision requires the landlord to make repairs. If a landlord voluntarily undertakes repairs, however, she must use reasonable care in doing so. If a landlord agrees to make repairs under the lease agreement, she is liable for injuries to tenants and to guests that result from her failure to repair.

When the landlord retains control of common areas, she is liable for defects and repairs and may be liable for the foreseeable, tortious acts of others as well (such as assault in an apartment hallway).

Tenant Rights   A tenant's rights correspond roughly with a landlord's duties (*see above*). In general terms, they include the right of quiet enjoyment, habitability, and cessation of rent upon actual eviction by the landlord. If the premises are condemned in eminent domain proceedings before the end of the lease term, the tenant may be entitled to a percentage of the condemnation award.

Tenant Duties   Along with his rights, a tenant has certain duties to the landlord in relation to the leased premises. Paramount among a tenant's duties is the duty to pay rent to the landlord. Under common law rules, the duty to pay rent continued even if the premises were destroyed. This rule has been modified by statute in most states, allowing a tenant to terminate the lease when the premises are destroyed. Short of actual eviction, the tenant's duty to pay rent is not affected by a landlord breach of the lease agreement. If the landlord agrees to install new carpeting, for example, the tenant cannot withhold rental payments until the landlord fulfills her agreement. Withholding payment in this situation may result in lawful eviction by the landlord.

Traditional common law rules require the tenant to make all repairs. This rule has been modified by statute in many states, some of which require the landlord to make repairs. This is especially true with apartment rentals. The traditional common law rule concerning repair can, of course, be changed by specific agreement of the parties.

The tenant is required to return the premises to the landlord in substantially the same condition as when the tenant originally took possession, except for normal wear and tear.

Remedies for Breach   The remedies available to a landlord or to a tenant concerning residential property are covered in the Uniform Residential Landlord and Tenant Act, which has been adopted (with modification) in fifteen states: Alaska, Arizona, Florida, Hawaii, Iowa, Kansas, Kentucky, Montana, Nebraska, New Mexico, Oregon, Rhode Island, South Carolina, Tennessee, and Virginia.

The Uniform Act does not cover the rights, duties, and remedies concerning commercial leases. In the lease of commercial property and in those states where the Uniform Act has *not* been adopted for residential property, typical provisions may include the following.

- Common law rules allowed a landlord to enter the premises and to seize goods of the tenant as security. This practice is questionable in most states today. Most states do provide a statutory lien on the tenant's property, which must be enforced by specific court order and peaceful seizure by a law enforcement officer.

●Security deposits or damage deposits may be obtained from tenants (such as the last month's rent) to assure the landlord of full payment of the rental amount. The deposit is returned to the tenant at the expiration of the lease term, minus any unpaid rent or any actual damage to the premises that was caused by the tenant. Some states require the landlord to pay interest on the deposit while it is held.

●An acceleration clause may be included in a lease agreement, allowing the landlord to leave the tenant in possession if the tenant defaults and to accelerate all rents due through the end of the term.

Lease provisions under which the tenant agrees to waive notice or to confess judgment in advance are invalid and unenforceable.

The most typical breach is where the tenant remains in the premises but fails to pay the rental amount when it becomes due. When this occurs, the landlord may evict the tenant by judicial proceeding which seeks restitution of the premises. The tenant typically must be given a notice to quit (usually three days) before the proceeding is filed. Some statutes allow the landlord to seek damages for accrued but unpaid rent as part of the restitution proceeding.

Assignment and Subletting   Unless the lease agreement provides differently, a tenant may assign his or her interest in the leasehold. The assignee comes into privity of estate with the landlord, and the landlord comes into privity of contract with the assignee. This simply means that both the assignee and the landlord may sue each other concerning the leasehold premises.

Alternatively, a tenant may sublet his or her leasehold interest unless the lease agreement provides otherwise. Under a sublease, however, the tenant assumes the position of landlord of the sublessee. There is no privity between the sublessee and the original landlord. If the sublessee fails to pay rent, for example, the original landlord must sue the original tenant; she cannot sue the sublessee directly.

Rights in the Land of Another

One may acquire specific, limited rights in the lands of others by easement, by license, or by covenant.

Easement   An easement is a nonpossessory interest in another's land that gives the holder of the easement the right either to use another person's land for a limited and special purpose (affirmative easement) or to prevent another from using the owner's land in a specified way.   Rights-of-way (the right to use driveways, roads, sidewalks) are the most common form of easements. Easements can be granted to public utility companies to run power lines, telephone lines, or sewer lines under or over a person's land.

The owner of the land which is burdened by the easement has complete right to possess and to use the property, subject only to the easement. An easement granted for one purpose does not entitle the grantee to use it for another purpose.

If the right to use another's property involves the right to remove part of the land or the products of the land (dirt, sand, minerals, timber) the right is called a *profit*. The right to remove things from the land distinguishes a profit from an easement.

An *easement appurtenant* involves two tracts of land: one benefited by the easement (*dominant tenement*) and one burdened by the easement (*servient tenement*). An easement appurtenant benefits land owned by the holder of the easement—the dominant tenement. Easements appurtenant usually involve adjacent tracts of land. The right to use a neighbor's driveway is an easement appurtenant.

An *easement in gross*, on the other hand, is not obtained for the benefit of any land owned by the easement holder. In other words, there is no dominant tenement. The most common example of an easement in gross is one granted to a utility company to erect poles or to lay underground cable.

a.   Creation of Easements   Easements can be created by express act of the parties (either express grant or express reservation); by implication (from existing use or from necessity); by prescription (adverse use); or by eminent domain.

1.   Express Easement   Because it is an interest in land, an easement generally is created by a deed describing the nature and extent of the easement conveyed. If there is no writing to satisfy the Statute of Frauds, a license is created (*see below*).   For example, if Ann grants an easement to Bob, allowing Bob to use Ann's driveway, Bob obtains the easement by express grant. If, on the other hand, Ann conveys part of her land to Bob, reserving to herself an easement to use the driveway, Ann retains an easement by express reservation.

2.   Easement by Implication   An easement can be created in either the grantor or the grantee by implication, based upon the presumed intention of the parties. Easements by implication arise most often when a grantor divides a tract of land and sells one or more of the parts to others.

An *easement implied from existing use* usually occurs when a landowner uses one part of her property to benefit another. For instance, if Ann owns property where the house is located on the eastern boundary line and if a highway is built along the western boundary line, she likely will build a road across the tract to provide access to the highway. If Ann then sells the eastern half of the tract (which includes the house) to Bob but fails to mention an easement from Bob's tract to the highway, an easement implied from existing use likely would be granted to Bob. Conversely, if Ann sells the western half of the tract to Bob, keeping the tract where the house is located for herself, an easement across Bob's tract may be implied (an implied reservation) in favor of Ann, the grantor.

An easement also may be implied because of necessity, without regard to prior use of the property. An *easement by necessity* arises when an owner of a single tract conveys part of it and, as a result of the conveyance, *landlocks* either the part conveyed or the part retained, leaving no way to enter or to exit the land without trespassing upon neighboring property. In that case, an easement by necessity is created in favor of the grantor if the landlocked land is retained (or in favor of the grantee if the landlocked land is conveyed). Unlike an easement implied from existing use, which continues indefinitely, an easement created by necessity continues for only so long as the need for the use continues.

3.   Easement by Prescription   Fee simple title, a possessory interest in property, may be acquired through a person's adverse possession of another's property for the required period stated in the Statute of Limitations. Likewise, an easement, which is nonpossessory, may be obtained through the adverse use of another's property for the required statutory period. This is a prescriptive easement. The requirements to create an easement by prescription are similar to those needed to acquire title by adverse possession. Thus, an easement by prescription may be created by the use of another's land if the use is hostile, is open and notorious, and is continuous and uninterrupted for the required period established by the Statute of Limitations.

4.   **Eminent Domain**   Unlike easements created by express grant or reservation, prescriptive easements are created involuntarily. An easement also may arise involuntarily through a sovereign's exercise of its eminent domain powers: the power of the sovereign to take private property for public use. Eminent domain easements generally are taken for highways, streets, utility lines, underground pipes or cables, or flight clearance near airports.

b.   **Transfer of Easements**   Easements may be transferred, without regard to how they were created. As a general rule, the easement follows the ownership or possession of the dominant tenement for easements appurtenant, and the grantee of the servient tenement takes subject to the easement. Both easements in gross and profits in gross generally are assignable, absent a contractual provision to the contrary.

C.   **Termination of Easements**   An easement is terminated (extinguished) when one person acquires title to both the servient and dominant tenements. The easement is not revived automatically by a later division of the combined tract into two or more parcels.

An easement can be terminated by the owner of the dominant tenement (the land benefitted by the easement) in writing, usually by quitclaim deed. The dominant owner may release the easement orally *if* the oral release is *accompanied by an act showing intent to abandon*. The mere failure to use an easement does not extinguish it. An easement by necessity is terminated when the necessity ends.

An easement can be terminated by the owner of the servient tenement (the land burdened by the easement) if he acts inconsistently with the easement, for instance, by building a fence across a right-of-way previously granted easement and by leaving it (the fence) there for the required period of the Statute of Limitations. In other words, the servient owner takes back the easement by prescription.

License   If the privilege to enter another's land or to perform acts on another's land lacks one or more of the requirements to create an easement, the privilege is called a license. The person in possession of the land who grants the right to its use is the licensor; the person granted permission to use the land is the licensee. A license simply gives the licensee the right to use another's land without incurring liability as a trespasser.

A license is revocable at the will of the property owner. A license ends upon the death of either party, upon a conveyance of the servient estate by the licensor to a third party, or upon the licensee's attempt to transfer the license. A license does not run with the land.

Covenants   A covenant is a contractual promise concerning land use. An *affirmative covenant* requires the promisor (the covenantor) to do something on her land, such as erecting or maintaining a party wall. A negative covenant, also called a *restrictive covenant*, limits the permissible uses of the land or the acts that can be performed upon it. Like a negative easement, a restrictive covenant limits the property owner in the use of her own land. Restrictive covenants comprise the vast majority of covenants affecting land use.

Restrictive covenants most commonly are used in residential subdivisions to achieve a coordinated, consistent pattern of land use within the area covered by the covenants. Common examples of restrictive covenants are those restricting the use of all lots of certain lots to residential purposes only, imposing a minimum cost for all buildings constructed, or requiring that any building constructed must be a minimum distance from streets or the rear lot line (setback restriction) or from adjoining lots (sidelot restriction). Most restrictions are upheld as beneficial tools of private land use control.

Restrictive covenants that attempt to limit those who may purchase property in a subdivision to one specific race, for example, are void and will not be enforced under any circumstance.

A.   Creation of Covenants   Covenants governing land use may be imposed with or without the conveyance of land, although restrictive covenants generally are created by the grantor when land is conveyed. A covenant created by the grantor seeks to limit the grantee's use of the land. A restrictive covenant may be included in the deed itself. If the property is located in a residential subdivision, however, the more likely method is to include the restrictive covenants with the plat.

When property is subdivided, a *plat* (map) of the subdivision is filed in the county recorder's office and provides the basis for the legal description of property located within the area covered by the plat. A declaration or list of the restrictions imposed by the person subdividing the property is filed for record in conjunction with the map. These restrictions, then, are incorporated by reference into the individual deeds used to convey lots within the subdivision, even though they are not stated fully within each deed. Therefore, the person performing a title search on property in a subdivision must read the plat restrictions to determine whether the property under examination complies with the limitations imposed upon its use.

To be enforceable, promises concerning land use (restrictive covenants, in this case) must be in writing under the Statute of Frauds. The Statute of Frauds ordinarily requires that the writing be signed by the person against whom enforcement is sought. Although covenants often are contained in or are incorporated into the deed and although modern deeds generally are signed only by the grantor, most courts hold that the grantee, by accepting the deed, is bound by the covenants that come with the deed, even without having signed it.

If a covenant is breached by one of the parties, the remedy is contract damages, enforceable in a court of law. *Compare equitable servitudes (discussed below), which are enforced by the grant of injunctive relief in equity courts.*

B.   Effect Upon Subsequent Transferees   Property subject to restrictive covenants is often transferred from one owner to another. Whether the covenants can be enforced by and against subsequent owners (assignors and assignees of the covenants) depends upon whether the burden or the benefit of the covenant runs with the land.

The burden runs with the land if:

- *the parties so intend;*
- *there is privity of estate (usually grantor-grantee relationship);*
- *the covenant "touches and concerns" the burdened land or*
- *the covenant "touches and concerns" the benefitted land; and*
- *the assignee has notice of the covenant before purchasing the land.*

Any one of the restrictive covenants mentioned previously (limitation to residential use only, minimum cost for buildings, setback and sidelot restrictions) touch and concern the land. In other words, the burden of the covenant touches and concerns the land if it decreases the use or value of the land in the hands of its owner (the covenantor-promisor). The benefit of a covenant touches and concerns the land if it increases use or value of the land in the hands of its owner (the covenantee-promisee). Any activity performed away from the location of the land does not "touch and concern" the land.

If all of these conditions exist, the covenant can be enforced against a subsequent transferee by filing an action for damages.

Equitable Servitudes   Because of the stringent requirements to enforce covenants at law and because enforcement can result in money damages only (rather than injunctive relief), the equitable servitude has become the primary tool for developing restricted areas (both residential and non-residential) and for enforcing beneficial covenants.

An equitable servitude is a covenant that can be enforced in equity against assignees of the burdened land who have notice of the covenant. An equitable servitude is an interest in land. Since an equitable servitude is an interest in land, most courts require a writing signed by the promisor unless a scheme (pattern) of restrictions exists for all or for a majority of the lots in the subdivision. In that event, a negative servitude may be implied as to all lots within that subdivision. Injunctive relief is the usual remedy.

Covenants and equitable servitudes are similar in that each must touch and concern the land, and neither is enforceable against a bona fide purchaser (BFP) without notice. An equitable servitude, however, differs from a covenant in several ways:

● An equitable servitude is enforced in equity by the grant of injunctive relief, while a covenant is enforced at law by the award of money damages.

● Many states will imply an equitable servitude from the overall scheme of restrictions in a subdivision, but a covenant must be in writing.

● Because an equitable servitude is an interest in land, privity of estate is not required to enforce it; privity is required to enforce a covenant.

Termination of Covenants and Servitudes   If the burdened land and the benefitted land become the property of one person, all covenants and servitudes merge into the resulting fee simple estate; the covenants and servitudes cease to exist. If the burdened land is taken by eminent domain, the covenant is condemned along with the burdened land; and the covenant ceases to exist. The owner of the benefitted land may be entitled to damages, however.

When an equitable servitude is claimed, equitable defenses to enforcement may include:

● Acquiescence in the breach.
● Estoppel.
● Hardship caused by the servitude greatly outweighs benefit.
● Change of conditions in the neighborhood.

Limitations Upon the Use of Land

A landowner has the right to possess, use, and enjoy his land. As is true of all rights, however, this right has limitations. The landowner's right is limited by the rights of neighboring landowners and others who may be affected by way in which a landowner seeks to exercise his rights. Legal rules restrict certain uses of land when those uses interfere unreasonably with the rights of others.

Nuisance   A nuisance is an activity conducted on land or a physical condition of land that is harmful or annoying to neighboring landowners or to members of the public in general.

Under some circumstances, the person responsible for creating or maintaining a nuisance on her property may be subject to criminal sanctions. In other situations, the person responsible for the nuisance may be liable in tort for injuries caused by the nuisance. The nature and extent of the liability depends on whether the nuisance is public or private.

A.   Public Nuisance   A public nuisance involves invasion of public rights: those rights common to all members of the public. This is a catch-all, minor criminal offense that encompasses a wide range of conduct which is offensive to public health, safety, morals, peace, and comfort. All states have statutes declaring certain specified conduct or conditions to be minor nuisances. Examples of public nuisances include maintenance of houses of prostitution or structures used in the commission of other criminal offenses (crack houses, for example), obstruction of public highways or streets, manufacture or storage of explosives within city limits, maintenance of excessive numbers of animals in a confined area, and the like.

B.   Private Nuisance   Unlike a public nuisance, a private nuisance results in a strictly private tort that is related to the tort of trespass. Prohibitions against private nuisances are designed to protect against invasions of the private use and enjoyment of land. Trespass, by contrast, involves an invasion of the right to possess land and requires a "breaking of the close"—a physical entry upon the land of another either by the trespasser or by an instrumentality of the trespasser.

Conduct or conditions that may constitute a private nuisance include vibration caused by blasting; destruction of trees or crops; pollution of water; excessive noise, smoke, fumes, or odors from a manufacturing process; excessive noise from barking dogs; or storing explosives or other dangerous materials. Most nuisances are intentional only in the sense that the defendant has created or has continued a condition that she knew or should have known would interfere with the rights of the owners and possessors of adjacent land.

Not all intentional interference with the private use and enjoyment of land is actionable. The rules related to nuisance attempt to balance the conflicting interests of landowners. On one hand, a person should be able to use her property as she sees fit; on the other, a person is required to use her property in such a way that it does not interfere unreasonably with the use and enjoyment of neighboring properties.

Right to Support A landowner cannot hold adjacent landowners accountable for natural changes in the terrain of her land caused by acts of nature (erosion, flooding, hurricanes). She can, however, hold adjacent landowners accountable if they alter the terrain of their own lands in such a way that natural support of her land is removed, causing her land to collapse.

For example, if Bob excavates part of his land to build a tennis court near his neighbor's lot line, he will be liable to the neighbor if the excavation causes the neighbor's land to collapse, to shift, or to erode. For this reason, Bob likely will include a retaining wall of some type to preserve the existing terrain of his neighbor's land.

Water Rights A landowner has the right to use the water that flows naturally across her land. This is her *riparian water right*. She cannot, however, use her riparian water rights in such a way that she obstructs the rights of other landowners who have the same rights in the same flowing water. She cannot, for instance, erect a dam to prevent the flow from reaching downstream (servient) land.

Some states permit an upstream landowner to use flowing water but require that the water be replaced into the stream or river in the same condition, without substantial change in the volume or velocity of the flow. Others permit a reasonable use of the flowing water. This means that the upstream landowner can use the water in any way she wishes as long as she does not interfere with the reasonable needs of downstream landowners.

Surface water is that water which collects on land, usually as the run-off from rains and melting snows. If a landowner wishes to erect dams on her property to capture all of the water that collects on her land, she is free to do so. In the ordinary circumstance, however, landowners want to expel surface water—not collect it.

One line of cases follows the *common enemy doctrine*, which treats surface water as the common enemy of all landowners and gives all landowners the right to fend it off in any way that they can. The more recent cases in this line have added a requirement of reasonableness to the landowners' right to expel waters. Another line of cases follows the *natural servitude doctrine*, which provides that lower lands are servient to the natural flow of surface waters. The owner cannot obstruct the flow in a way that injuries other landowners above or below her own land. Once again, the modern trend is to inject a reasonableness standard, which allows the owner to channel the drainage to some extent.

Airspace Rights   One of the early tenets of property law was that ownership of land included all of the land below it to the center of the earth and all of the land above it to the heavens. That principle remains true today, with some modification.

Aircraft have a navigational servitude (right to cross airspace) above surface land. The height at which the servitude begins is determined by the government. Owners of land which is located in an airport's flight path may have an action for ***inverse condemnation*** if the noise of low-flying aircraft interferes substantially with their use of the surface land. Inverse condemnation may be brought against a governmental body to recover the value of land that has been taken for governmental use without a formal eminent domain proceeding.

The owners of land whose airspace has not been invaded by aircraft but whose use and enjoyment of their land has been impaired substantially by aircraft noise may have an action for nuisance against the airline(s). Sovereign immunity generally prevents suing the government for nuisance; inverse condemnation is not available unless the landowner's airspace has been entered.

Public Land Use Controls

In addition to the restrictions placed on land use by private agreement, land use may be regulated by governmental action. A sovereign may impose restrictions on land use through zoning laws, for instance; and private property may be taken for public use without the consent of the owner under a sovereign's power of eminent domain.

Zoning   Zoning is the process by which a municipality (1) regulates the use that may be made of property and (2) regulates the physical configuration of land development within its jurisdiction. The power to zone is derived from the general police powers of a state. Although zoning usually is implemented by local governments, the power of local governments to zone comes either from the enabling statute adopted by the state legislature, which delegates zoning authority to local governments, or from a state constitutional provision that gives local governments specific zoning authority .

Under traditional zoning plans, the land affected is divided into zones or districts. Only certain uses or types of property are permitted within each zone. Zoning restrictions are of three general types:

1.   Limitations on use (residential, commercial, industrial, or special);
2.   Height, bulk, and area restrictions; and
3.   Architectural limitations on exterior building design.

All exercises of a state's police power, including zoning restrictions, are subject to Constitutional limitations requiring that the regulation must be reasonable by its terms and in its application. Zoning ordinances that impose an arbitrary, unreasonable, oppressive, or unreasonably discriminatory interference with the rights of property owners violate the Due Process and Equal Protection Clauses of the Fourteenth Amendment.

A zoning ordinance or any other exercise of a state's police power is given a strong presumption of validity. If there is any rational connection between the ordinance and public health, morality, safety, or welfare, the ordinance will be upheld. State courts examine the validity of zoning regulations as applied to particular parcels of land on a case-by-case basis. This approach allows the court to relieve landowners from excessively burdensome restrictions without striking down an entire ordinance.

A.   Objectives of Zoning   To avoid constitutional objection, all zoning regulation must be based upon a comprehensive plan. A comprehensive plan is an overall program for the future physical development of an area, including the provision of city services (streets, sewers, police and fire protection). Responsibility for the comprehensive plan generally rests with the city's zoning commission or planning commission. In addition to formulating the plan, zoning commissions study and determine the community's zoning needs along with any necessary changes; give notice and hold hearings; and make recommendations to the city's legislative body.

The comprehensive plan must be consistent with the objectives for which zoning ordinances may be enacted—the protection of public health, morals, safety, or welfare. Regulations that ensure adequate light and air or that limit the density of land use (such as building height and lot size restrictions) are designed to protect public health. Regulations aimed at reducing the risk of fire (by restricting the location or existence of gasoline stations or refineries) or street congestion (by regulating the existence of multifamily dwellings in single-family residential districts and the location of shopping centers, hospitals, and public facilities) are justified on grounds of public safety. Aesthetic zoning, or zoning to enhance community appearance, is justified as promoting the general welfare. Included under this heading are regulation of junk yards and mobile homes as well as zoning to preserve open spaces and historical districts and buildings. Ordinances regulating the location of adult bookstores and theaters by dispersing them throughout allowable districts or by concentrating them into one district are attempts to protect public morals and the property values of nearby residences and businesses.

B. Altering the Zoning Plan Zoning enabling statutes require that zoning regulations be uniform for each class or kind of building throughout each district. The uniform operation of zoning classifications may be modified by various devices, including nonconforming uses, amendments, variances, and special permits. Substantial use of these devices may defeat the basic purpose of comprehensive land use planning, however.

Nonconforming Uses When a zoning ordinance is enacted, it affects previously developed land as well as undeveloped land. Invariably, certain developed property is being used for purposes now prohibited by the new ordinance, such as a drugstore in a newly established residential zone. In this case, the affected property is known as a (grandfathered) nonconforming use, meaning that it does not conform to the current restrictions on the zoned area but lawfully existed when the ordinance went into effect and has continued in existence since that time.

Zoning ordinances usually permit nonconforming uses to continue, thereby reducing both political opposition to the passage of the ordinance and the likelihood that the ordinance will be declared unconstitutional as a deprivation of property without due process of law. The ordinance may permit the nonconforming use to continue indefinitely or may require it to be eliminated within a specified period of time. Eliminating nonconforming uses, however, has proven a difficult task.

Amendments The local legislative body which enacted the zoning ordinance may alter the plan by amendment. Amendments commonly take one of two forms: (1) reclassification of property to a different zone known as *rezoning* or (2) changes made in the uses allowed in a particular zone. Amendments must be enacted in accordance with the comprehensive plan. If not, they are subject to judicial attack as invalid spot zoning. **Spot zoning** occurs when a zoning amendment classifies a single property or group of properties within a district to a use that is inconsistent with the general zoning pattern of the surrounding area and is designed primarily for the economic benefit of the owner.

Variances   Zoning amendments involve a legislative change in the ordinance itself. In addition, zoning ordinances usually provide for administrative relief—for example, from a zoning board of appeals, zoning board of review, or zoning board of adjustment—by allowing an adversely affected landowner to apply for a variance or special permit under certain circumstances. Variances, which are designed to prevent rigidity, are commonly of two types: (1) *use variances*, which permit a different use than that authorized by the ordinance, and (2) *area variances*, which permit modification of area, yard, height, setback, or similar restrictions. An area variance is less disruptive of the zoning plan because it does not threaten neighboring property with an incompatible use and is therefore more commonly granted.

Special Use Permits   Unlike a variance, which involves a use prohibited by the ordinance, special use permits (also called special permits, special exceptions, or conditional exceptions) allow a landowner to use his or her land in a manner expressly permitted by the ordinance, provided that certain conditions and standards set forth in the zoning regulations are met. A basic function of the administrative zoning board is to hear and act on applications for special use permits. Special use permits commonly are used to control uses posing safety, traffic, or noise problems to neighboring property; uses that are necessary but incompatible within a specific zone; and facilities customarily located in residential zones that attract large numbers of people. Uses that might be allowed by special use permit include gas stations, parking lots, churches, schools, parks, utility substations, funeral homes, bowling alleys, or golf courses.

Eminent domain   Private property sometimes is required by a government (local, state, or federal) for a public purposes such as public housing, highways, airports, schools, public utilities, and the like). The power is inherent in a sovereign to take, or to authorize the taking of, private property for public use without the owner's consent upon payment of just compensation. This is known as eminent domain.

The power of eminent domain may be exercised by the federal or state legislature or may be delegated to a municipal corporation or other governmental subdivision or public corporation, or, in some cases, to a private corporation or individual, such as a railroad or a utility. Like all governmental action, the eminent domain power is subject to Constitutional restrictions. The federal Constitution contains a specific eminent domain limitation in the last clause of the Fifth Amendment:

> . . . Nor shall private property be taken for public use, without just compensation.

If the government or a governmental agency desires property for public use, such as an interstate highway, it will offer to buy the property from the owner for a stated price. If the owner refuses to sell at the price offered, the government initiates a ***condemnation proceeding*** to exercise its eminent domain power. The condemnation proceeding is necessary to satisfy due process requirements that the owner be afforded a notice and a hearing before the property can be taken. *(Note that inverse condemnation proceedings are initiated by the property owner.)*

The government's eminent domain power may be exercised to acquire a fee simple or some lesser interest in property, such as an easement. When a taking occurs, as opposed to the mere regulation of property under a state's police power, the owner must be justly compensated. This generally means that she must be paid the fair market value for property being taken on the date of the taking. When only a partial taking occurs, the owner receives the amount by which the remaining land is depreciated by the taking.

The owner is compensated for the land and not for the loss of its particular use. Under the general common law rule, the owner generally is not entitled to recover anything for the value of a business conducted on the property or for loss of goodwill. Some states have adopted statutes that specifically authorize recovery for the value of a business as a going concern in eminent domain cases.

If property is taken for a program or project of the federal government or for a state or local project funded with federal money, federal law provides relocation expenses for displaced persons. This assistance is provided in addition, not in place of, just compensation for the property taken.

Sale of Land

The sale (conveyancing) of land is a complex transaction. It blends concepts of real estate titles and conveyancing with contract law. In addition to the basic contract to convey the real estate, other contracts typically are involved: the contract to employ a real estate agent *(listing agreement)* to find a buyer and, if the sale is financed, a contract with the lending institution for a loan secured by the real estate. The legal assistant must be familiar with the creation of security interests, with customary lender requirements, and with applicable federal regulations. When commercial real estate is conveyed, still further federal regulations come into play, particularly in the environmental protection area.

In addition to these basic agreements, the parties should agree upon risk of loss; payment of taxes; rights on default; the required condition of the premises (plumbing, heating and cooling, and electrical systems); and the effect of termites or other problems that may indicate structural defects. These issues are best handled in a comprehensive, written contract which outlines the rights and duties of both parties.

Contract for Sale of Land   A contract for the sale of land contains the seller's promise to convey title to real estate to the buyer in exchange for the buyer's promise to pay the purchase price. The Statute of Frauds of most states requires that all contracts for the sale of land must be in writing to be enforceable. The contract must contain, at a minimum, the identity of the parties, a description of the property, and the purchase price.

Unless stated otherwise in the real estate sale contract (purchase agreement), it is implied that the seller will convey a fee simple absolute to the buyer and that the title will be merchantable (marketable). A *merchantable title* is one that is free of defects, such as unsatisfied liens against the property or indications that someone other than the seller may have a claim to ownership of the real estate. A seller's title does not have to be perfect; but defects, if any exist, are *clouds on the title* and must be resolved to make the title marketable. The new buyer cannot be forced to "buy a lawsuit" by accepting a defective title.

If either party fails to perform according to the sale contract, the other is entitled to an appropriate contract remedy, either money damages or specific performance. Note that specific performance ordinarily is limited to the buyer *(see the chapter on Contract Law)*.

Deed   The deed is the written instrument used to convey an interest in real property. The parties to the deed are the grantor (the person conveying the interest) and the grantee (the person to whom the interest is conveyed). A deed is used to convey any ownership interest in real property by sale or by gift, whether the interest is a fee simple estate or some lesser estate.

The formalities required to transfer a real estate interest effectively by deed ordinarily are set by state statute. Although the exact requirements vary from state to state, these statutes typically require that a deed must:

- Be in writing;
- Identify both the grantor and the grantee;
- State the type of state conveyed (fee simple, life estate, or other interest);
  Note that a fee simple absolute is presumed if no specific estate is described.
- Contain words of conveyance (transfer, sell, grant, or convey); and
- Contain a sufficient legal description of the property being transferred.

A deed merely transfers an interest in land and is not itself a contract. Therefore, no consideration must be stated or paid for the deed to be valid. Because a consideration clause was required in certain early common law deeds, modern deeds customarily contain a clause for reciting the consideration. This may be stated as "One Dollar and Other Valuable Consideration" but has no bearing on the amount paid by the grantee for the property.

A deed fails, however, if an insufficient legal description makes it possible for more than one tract of land to be identified by the language used. No particular method of description is required by law; however, the precise description used by the land recorder's office is advisable to protect marketability of the title. Deeds commonly describe the property by metes and bounds, by the rectangular survey system, or by reference to a subdivision plat or map.

Under a ***metes and bounds*** description, which is the oldest of the three, distances (metes) and directions (bounds) are used to trace the perimeter of the property by starting from a fixed point and moving either clockwise or counterclockwise—along straight lines and arc of curves—and ultimately returning to the starting point. This is the method used throughout most of the eastern portion of the United States.

The ***rectangular survey system***, which was adopted by the Continental Congress in 1785, is the dominant form of legal description. It is used in thirty states: Alabama, Florida, Mississippi, all states north of the Ohio River, and all states west of the Mississippi River (except Texas). This system is based upon a government survey conducted to aid in the development and settlement of areas west of the original thirteen colonies. Under this system, all of the land was divided into a grid formed by north-south lines (principal meridians) and east-west lines (principal base lines); and each square of the grid was further divided into squares (squares within squares). The basic unit of measurement and description is called a *township*, which is a square six miles long and six miles wide. East township is divided into further squares, called sections. There are thirty-six sections in each township; each *section* is one mile square and contains 640 acres of land. Smaller parcels of land (less than 640 acres) are described in *half sections* and *quarter sections*. For instance, the N½ of the SW¼ of Section 16 describes 80 acres of land.

Subdivided land in urban areas typically is described by reference to a ***subdivision plat*** or map prepared by a surveyor and filed in the land recorder's (register of deeds) office of the county where the land is located. Lots within the plat or map are either numbered or lettered; and the property subsequently is described by that number or letter, the subdivision name, and the book and page in the recorder's office where the plat or map is located. The plat itself frequently contains additional information about easements, covenants, setback and sidelot requirements, and lot measurements. These become part of the description and are incorporated into the deed by reference (without stating them specifically in the deed).

Execution of the Deed   In addition to the required contents, a deed must be executed properly to convey the intended interest to the grantee. The requirements of valid execution are summarized by the expression "signed, sealed, and delivered." Attestation or acknowledgement of the deed may be required as well.

Signature   The deed must be signed by each grantor. Although the grantee must be named in the deed, the grantee need not sign the deed. A deed signed only by the grantor is known as a ***deed poll***; nearly all deeds are of this type. If a deed is signed by both the grantor and the grantee, it is known as an ***indenture***.

Seal   The seal was used to authenticate an instrument in an era when few people could write. Although few states still require seals on deeds or on other instruments, seals are sometimes used as a matter of custom. At common law, the seal was a wax impression, but in modern deeds it may be evidenced by the word "Seal" or "L.S." printed on the deed form.

Delivery and Acceptance   The deed must be delivered to and accepted by the grantee to be effective. By accepting the deed, the grantee is bound by its terms, whether expressed or implied, which eliminates the need for her signature. The deed transfers title on the date it is delivered to the grantee.

<u>Attestation and Acknowledgement</u>   Approximately 20% of the states require that deeds be attested to transfer title effectively. ***Attestation*** is the act of witnessing the execution (signature) of a written instrument, at the request of the person making it (here, the grantor), and subscribing (signing) it as a witness. Other states require attestation as proof of authenticity before the deed can be recorded.

Acknowledgement is a more formal witnessing by a public official, such as a notary public, of the grantor's declaration that her execution of the deed was a free and voluntary act.

Types of Deeds   The ***warranty deed*** (also called a full warranty deed or a general warranty deed) is the most common type of deed used to convey title. It contains a number of promises, called ***covenants of title***, concerning the status of the grantor's title. Typical among them are the covenants of seisin and right to convey, the covenant against encumbrances, the covenant of quiet enjoyment, and the covenant of warranty and further assurances.

<u>Covenants of Seisin and Right to Convey</u>   These two covenants essentially mean that the grantor owns the estate which she purports to convey in the deed and that she has both the right and the power to transfer it.

<u>Covenant Against Encumbrances</u>   This covenant means that the property is transferred free of encumbrances except those specifically stated in the deed. An ***encumbrance*** is a right or interest in land which diminishes its value or diminishes its use but which does not prevent the transfer of a fee simple title. Encumbrances include:

- Liens against the property representing monetary obligations such as mortgages, taxes, special assessments, or judgments;

- Interests in the land which are less than a fee simple, such as leaseholds and life estates; and

- Restrictions on the use of the property, such as easements or restrictive covenants.

To avoid breaching this warranty, deeds often state that the property is free of all encumbrances "except those shown of record."

<u>Covenant of Quiet Enjoyment</u>   This covenant promises that the grantee will enjoy quiet and peaceable possession of the property (will not be ousted by a person holding a better title).

<u>Warranty and Further Assurances</u>   This covenant promises that the grantor will defend the grantee's title against any lawful claims existing at the time of transfer and that the grantor will perfect the grantee's title if necessary.

If a covenant of title is breached, the injured party generally is entitled to money damages. A buyer may be entitled to return of the full purchase price plus interest for a total failure of title or may be entitled to a proportionate reduction for a partial failure of title. If the grantor conveys a lesser title than stated in the deed (conveys a life estate instead of a fee simple), damages equal the price paid minus the value of the life estate received. If the breach involves an encumbrance, the amount paid to remove the encumbrance and to clear the title may be recovered, as long as it does not exceed the purchase price. If the easement or other encroachment cannot be removed, damages measured by the reduction in value of the burdened property may be appropriate.

The *limited warranty deed* or *special warranty deed* contains all of the same warranties as a general warranty deed but covers only defects that were created or came into existence while the grantor was the owner of the property.

The *quitclaim deed* makes no warranties or promises to the grantee concerning title. The grantor in a quitclaim deed says, in effect, "I convey to you whatever interest I may have in the property, and I may have none."

Merger   Under the doctrine of merger, the buyer's acceptance of the deed extinguishes her rights under the purchase contract as those rights relate to title. For instance, if title later proves defective, the buyer's recourse is for breach of the covenants contained in the deed, not for breach of the sale contract.

Generally, however, merger applies only to matters of title and not to collateral promises in the purchase contract, such as the seller's promise to make improvements or repairs. These promises survive the deed and can form the basis of an action by the buyer against the seller on the purchase contract.

Methods of Title Assurance

Although a seller may be obligated by a purchase contract or deed to transfer a fee simple title, a deed conveys only the interest that a seller lawfully has in the property. For this reason, the seller's representations concerning title are valuable to the buyer only if the seller (1) lawfully owns the represented interest or (2) is solvent and amenable to suit when a defect becomes known.

Because title assurance based upon the seller's representations provides such limited protections to the buyer, the buyer must independently determine whether the seller holds title to the interest that she purports to convey. This determination must be made before delivery of the deed. The task is accomplished by professional examination of the public record of land titles.

Recording Statutes   Each state has adopted a recording statute designed to provide reliable public information concerning the status of real estate titles. By examining the public records, a prospective buyer or a lender can determine whether the seller possesses the interest that she has contracted to convey (or that she proposes to use as security for a loan) and whether any liens or encumbrances exist against the property.

Generally speaking, any instrument related to the creation or the transfer of an interest in real property (deeds, contracts, mortgages, trust deeds, leases, assessments, tax liens, or mechanic's liens) are recordable. The instrument is recorded in a local office that may be called a recorder of deeds, registrar of deeds, or county recorder, usually in the county where the land is located. Instruments accepted for recording generally must meet statutory formalities to ensure authenticity, such as attestation or acknowledgement.

Recording is not necessary to make the instrument effective between the immediate parties to the transaction. A deed is effective to transfer interest from the grantor to the grantee upon delivery, even if it is never recorded. Conversely, recording does not validate an otherwise invalid instrument. Recording statutes are designed to protect the purchaser and the mortgagee against conflicting claims to the same property by third parties. They purchasers and mortgagees acting in good faith against prior, unrecorded ests in the property.

Recording provides *constructive* notice to third parties of the existence of prior, recorded interests in the property (even though they have no actual knowledge of the interests). Third parties will take subject to those interests. A purchaser or protected by the recording statute in two ways: and clear of prior, unrecorded interests

■S'

■When she records, the recording provides constructive notice to all third parties of her interest.

Recording simply provides constructive notice of the existence of an instrument; it has no bearing on the legal effectiveness of that instrument.

Recording statutes generally protect only those purchasers or lenders who act in good faith and who give value (consideration) for their interest in the property. To meet the good faith standard, the purchaser or lender must take without actual (subjective) knowledge of the prior interest. In addition, the purchaser or lender who has knowledge of facts that would prompt a reasonable person to investigate further is charged with the knowledge of facts that would be disclosed by a reasonable inquiry. For example, if someone other than the grantor occupies the property, further inquiry should be made.

Because a donee (recipient of a gift) or a devisee under a will or by intestate succession does not give value for the transfer of property, such a person generally is not protected by the recording statute and takes the property subject to prior, unrecorded interests.

The Title Search By recording each document affecting ownership of real property, a chronological public record of transactions concerning the property is created. Systematic examination of this record is known as a title search. Through a title search, a prospective purchaser or lender may determine whether the seller owns the interest she proposes to convey and what interest others, including creditors, may have in the property.

To facilitate the location of documents affecting the title under examination, all recording statutes require that documents accepted for recording be indexed. Instruments may be indexed under the names of both the grantor and the grantee (a grantor-grantee index). They may also be indexed according to the legal description of the real property involved (a tract index).

A prospective purchaser or lender has constructive notice of all instruments recorded within the chain of title to the specific tract in question. The *chain of title* refers to the succession of ownership of the property (and other deeds and other instruments by which the owner back to the original patent or grants in it) can be traced from the present first private owner. from a governmental authority to the

In some states, the title is searched back to the original grant from a sovereign. In others, search of a more limited period—30 to 100 years, for example—is sufficient. Several states have adopted *marketable title acts* that reduce the necessary period of title search by extinguishing all claims and title defects after a stated length of time, such as 30 to 40 years, unless they are preserved by filing statutory notice.

Even if a title search discloses an unbroken chain of ownership, the prospective purchaser is not assured of receiving a clear, unencumbered title due to events not disclosed by recording. Some of these include:

- Forgery of a grantor's signature;

- Minority or other incapacity of the grantor;

- Failure of delivery of a deed in the chain;

- Misrepresentation of marital status by a grantor, leaving a potential claim by the spouse or the spouse's heirs; or

- Failure of all persons holding an interest to join in a conveyance, leaving a potential claim by an omitted person or her heirs.

The county recorder's office is not the only source of public information concerning land titles. A thorough search requires examination of all relevant public records. Court records may show an outstanding judgment against the record owner that affects her title. Probate, tax, and assessment records also contain important information.

In addition to searching public records, the purchaser or lender always should inspect the premises in person to determine the rights of parties in possession and any other information that may not be disclosed by the public record. Physical inspection should include a precise determination of lot lines (boundary lines). Unless the property lines are evidenced by locating surveyor's stakes or from a prior survey, a survey may be required. The physical inspection and survey are important because neither a title opinion nor title insurance (discussed below) protects the buyer against defects that an inspection would reveal.

A.   Abstract of Title   In nearly all states, private abstract companies or title companies maintain a private duplicate set of real estate records. These records are updated on a daily basis with information obtained from the recorder's office. The information obtained over time is used to prepare an **abstract of title**, which is a chronological summary of the contents of all recorded instruments pertaining to a particular tract of land. The abstract is then rented or sold to persons who want to examine the title. Although a buyer, lender, or another could conduct an independent title search, the task usually is contracted to a professional abstracter.

B.   Title Opinion/Title Insurance   Once an abstract of title has been prepared (or updated), the status of the title may be evaluated either through a title opinion issued by an attorney or through title insurance. A *title opinion* involves an attorney's examination of the title as disclosed by the abstract and issuance of a formal, written opinion concerning its marketability. The opinion typically notes any areas of concern and lists any liens or encumbrances that burden the property. The attorney does not insure the title but, rather, is liable only for injury caused by negligent errors or omissions.

An alternative protection is title insurance. ***Title insurance*** is a contract between the insurer (a title insurance company) and an insured (usually a property owner or a lender). The insurer agrees to indemnify (reimburse) the insured against losses resulting from specified defects in the title of the property covered by the insurance policy. Title insurance provides slightly more protection than an attorney's title opinion, because the insured need not show negligence in order to recover and because the insurance company bears the expense of suit necessary to protect the title.

Note that the title is not insured in a title insurance contract; rather, the insured owner or insured lender is indemnified against loss resulting from failure of the title. In addition, a title insurance contract between a title insurance company and a lender does not indemnify the owner of the property; the owner must be named as an insured to obtain protection. The importance of this fact is shown by the following example.

> Ann buys Blackacre from Bob for $150,000; Bob relocates to Argentina. Ann pays $15,000 down and finances the balance with First Lender Bank. Bank obtains a title insurance policy, naming Bank as the insured. When Ann is $5,000 away from paying off the mortgage, a title defect is discovered, which causes a complete failure of Ann's title but which is covered by the title policy. Bank will receive $5,000 against its loss, but Ann will receive nothing. She is not a named insured on the policy.

Title Registration (Torrens System)

Under a recording statute, the buyer or lender must draw a conclusion concerning the status of a title from an ever-expanding body of information (deeds, mortgages, and so forth). This is an expensive, cumbersome process. It requires multiple searches and examinations of the same title as a tract is conveyed from owner to owner.

The **Torrens system** is an alternative involving registration of the title rather than recording evidence of the title. Under the Torrens system, the title is registered in a judicial proceeding in which all parties claiming an interest in the property are notified and are given the opportunity to present their claims. After a hearing, a certificate of title (similar to an automobile title) is issued to the person found to be the title owner. The certificate indicates the type of title owned (usually a fee simple) and any liens or encumbrances against the property. Once the title is registered in this way, the owner as well as subsequent buyers or lien holders take free of all claims or interests except those shown on the certificate.

To transfer the property, the owner simply executes a deed to the grantee. The deed and the owner's certificate are filed with the registrar of titles (the Torrens equivalent to the county recorder of deeds), who cancels the grantor's certificate and issues a new one to the grantee. Any liens or encumbrances surviving against the grantee are noted on the new certificate. Accordingly, once registration occurs, title can be transferred quickly and without a costly title search.

The Torrens system has not achieved wide acceptance, with fewer than one-fourth of the states providing for land title registration. Even where it is permitted, registration often is optional or may exist only in certain geographic areas.

Priority Among Successive Purchasers

A basic purpose of recording statutes is to protect purchasers or lenders by providing a public record that discloses the status of the title of the land to be purchased or to be taken as security. By its nature, however, the recording statute effectively allows a property owner to make successive conveyances of the same property, even though she may have no right to do so.

> Ann, the fee simple owner of a tract of land, transfers it by warranty deed to Bob, who pays fair market value. The next day, Ann transfers the same tract to Connie, who also pays fair market value for the property. Ann leaves for Tahiti. Between Bob and Connie, the innocent purchasers, who is entitled to the property?

In the absence of a recording statute, the common law rule is *"first in time, first in right."* Bob would prevail as the first purchaser in time under common law. After the conveyance to Bob, Ann had no remaining interest to transfer to Connie.

With a recording statute in place, however, priority is determined by the terms of the recording statute and not by the time of conveyance. This approach is designed to protect the integrity of the recording system and to enable a prospective buyer to rely upon the public record to indicate the status of title. Recording statutes generally are classified according to the manner in which the priority issue is resolved.

Pure Race Statute   A pure race statute is one under which the buyer who wins the "race" to the courthouse and records the deed first is the buyer who prevails.

Pure Notice Statute   Under a pure notice statute, a subsequent buyer (Connie, in the above example) who takes without actual knowledge of a prior, unrecorded conveyance prevails. This is so, even if Bob subsequently records before Connie records. If Bob had recorded before Ann's conveyance to Connie, Bob would have prevailed because Connie would have had constructive notice of Bob's interest in the property.

Race-Notice Statute   Race-notice statutes combine the first two types of recording statutes and have been adopted in approximately one-half of the states. Under a race-notice statute, the subsequent buyer (Connie, above) prevails if she *both*:

- takes without actual knowledge of the prior conveyance and

- records first.

Under a race-notice statute, then, Bob will prevail if he records first, even if Connie has no actual notice of Bob's interest. However, if Connie records first and has no actual knowledge of the conveyance to Bob, she will prevail.

In addition to purchasers and lenders with interests in the underlying real estate, recording statutes also may affect the rights of purchasers of goods which are closely associated with the land but which are sold apart from it (minerals, crops, timber, or fixtures). Section 2-107(3) of the Uniform Commercial Code provides that the buyer of such goods takes them subject to the rights of a prior purchaser or mortgagee of the underlying real estate who records her interest.

The buyer of such goods also may be jeopardized by subsequently created interests in the real estate. For example, a purchaser of real estate generally receives crops which are growing on the real estate. This raises the possibility of conflicting claims between a person who buys the crops and a later person who purchases the underlying real estate before the crops are harvested. U.C.C. § 2-107(3) provides that the crop sale agreement may be recorded in the real estate records, where it will provide constructive notice to third parties of the crop buyer's interest. Even if he fails to record the contract, some courts will protect the crop buyer in this situation by holding that the crops are personalty to which the recording act does not apply or that a "constructive severance" is effected at the time the crops are sold.

Land Financing

The typical real estate buyer rarely has the financial resources to pay cash for the property. In the usual situation, the buyer makes a down payment and borrows the balance of the purchase price. Lenders who finance real estate generally require security, usually in the form of a mortgage on the real estate. In some cases, an installment contract is used *(discussed below)*.

The Mortgage   A mortgage is an interest in specific real property that is created to secure performance of an obligation. The obligation normally involves repayment of a debt. The person creating the mortgage is the ***mortgagor***; this is the owner-debtor. The person receiving the benefit of the security given by the mortgage is the ***mortgagee***; this is the lender-creditor. If the obligation secured by the mortgage is not performed, the mortgagee has recourse against the real estate given as collateral.

The mortgage is not the debt. The debt is evidenced by a separate promissory note, generally calling for installment payments over an extended time. The note is evidence of the "underlying debt." Most notes given in connection with real estate financing are ***amortized*** over the term of the loan, which means that each equal installment is part principal and part interest. The principal amount due on the note gradually is reduced over the term of the loan, and interest is charged on the unpaid balance. The debtor builds increasing ***equity*** in the property as each payment is made. Equity refers to that portion of the real estate that is not subject to a lien.

A mortgage interest is created by a separate instrument (called a mortgage or a mortgage deed) which identifies the mortgagor and the mortgagee, describes the property, contains the typical language of conveyance, and is signed by the grantor of the mortgage interest (the mortgagor). In addition, the mortgage instrument describes the underlying loan secured by the mortgage and typically includes the mortgagor's promises to keep the property insured and in good repair and to pay taxes, assessments, and other liens against the property.

Approximately one-third of the states use a security device known as a ***deed of trust*** or ***trust deed***, which is the functional equivalent of a mortgage. Like other trusts, a trust deed uses three parties: the *grantor* (borrower) transfers the property to the *trustee*, who holds it in trust for the benefit of the *beneficiary* (lender) as security for payment of the debt. Most statutes do not allow the lender-beneficiary to serve as the trustee. The rights of the parties are determined by the trust instrument, including the borrower's right to reconveyance upon satisfaction of the obligation and the lender's rights upon default. Under a trust deed, the trustee typically may sell the property if a default occurs and pay the lender with the sale proceeds; any excess is paid the borrower-grantor. No judicial proceeding is required; therefore, the sale generally proceeds much more quickly than a mortgage foreclosure.

Two theories have developed to describe the property interest created by the mortgage (or trust deed). Under the traditional *title theory*, a mortgage is an outright conveyance of the property to the mortgagee, subject to reconveyance upon satisfaction of the secured obligation. Under the title theory, a mortgage is similar to a fee simple subject to a condition subsequent: the title to the property remains in the mortgagee until repayment of the underlying debt—the condition subsequent. Using this theory, if the mortgagor defaults, the mortgagee retains the property even if the value of the property exceeds the value of the underlying debt.

Because of the windfall to the mortgagor in a strict application of the title theory, the *lien theory* has gained widespread use in characterizing the mortgage interest. Under this approach, the mortgage creates only a security for a debt; and the mortgagee's interest is limited to the unpaid obligation. If the value of the property exceeds the unpaid debt at the time of a default, the sale proceeds are paid first to satisfy the debt; and the balance is paid to the mortgagor.

Ordinarily, the mortgagor is personally liable for payment of the debt secured by the mortgage because of the underlying promissory note. This liability becomes important in the event of a deficiency. A *deficiency* occurs when the mortgaged property is worth less than the underlying debt. Because the mortgage is given as security for the debt, not as a substitute for it, a mortgagor who also signs the promissory note is liable for the deficiency upon default. Conversely, a property owner may be liable on the mortgage but not on the underlying debt (husband and wife sign mortgage but only husband signs promissory note for business purpose loan). In that case, the mortgagor loses her interest in the property but has no liability for the deficiency on the underlying debt.

A mortgagor who satisfies the secured obligation is entitled to have the encumbrance evidenced by a mortgage removed from the public record. This is accomplished by a written *release of mortgage*, which is recorded to clear the mortgagor's title. A *deed of reconveyance* from the trustee to the grantor is used to extinguish a deed of trust.

A. Priority of Mortgages

A property owner may borrow money from two or more lenders and may give each lender a mortgage on the same property.   When the property is worth less than the combined value of the mortgages, priority of the various mortgagees then must be determined.

Priority among successive mortgagees, similar to priority among successive purchasers, is determined by the recording statute, without regard to which mortgage occurred first in time. Recording protects the mortgagee against a subsequent sale or a subsequent mortgage of the same property to another. If the mortgagee fails to record, subsequent buyers or mortgagees without actual notice take free of the unrecorded mortgage.

The first mortgagee to record is paid first (first mortgage), the second to record is paid second (second mortgage), and so on until the money generated from a sale of the property is exhausted. For this reason a first mortgage generally is termed the senior mortgage; all subsequent mortgages are junior mortgages.

Notwithstanding the rules established by the recording statute, a mortgagee may agree to relinquish a right to priority by a *subordination agreement*. A mortgagee bank may be willing to subordinate, for example, to a subsequent mortgage of the Small Business Administration (SBA) as part of a borrower's overall business plan for expansion. In this circumstance, the bank's underlying debt may be reduced by a lump sum payment from SBA loan proceeds to induce the bank to subordinate its mortgage lien.

Although no rule limits the number of mortgages that can burden a given tract of land, there are seldom more than two. Many lenders, by statute or as a matter of policy, will lend only upon first mortgage security. Additionally, second and subsequent mortgages commonly are available only for much shorter terms and at much higher interest rates than a first mortgage.

Sale of Mortgaged Property   As a general rule and in the absence of a contrary agreement, the mortgagor is free to sell the mortgaged property without consent of the mortgagee. The sale, however, has no effect on either the mortgage itself or the mortgagor's liability on the underlying debt. In other words, the mortgagee's rights against both the mortgagor personally and against the property are unaffected by the sale. The sale may take place with or without retiring the existing mortgage.

When property is sold without retiring the existing mortgage, the new buyer simply pays the seller for her equity in the property and continues to make payments on the mortgage. The new buyer takes either *subject to* the existing mortgage or agrees to *assume* the mortgage debt. A buyer who takes **subject to** the existing mortgage incurs no personal liability for payment of the underlying debt secured by the mortgage. In this case, if the new buyer fails to repay the debt, she will lose the property if the mortgagee forecloses but will not be liable if the amount realized from the sale is not enough to satisfy the outstanding debt. If the foreclosure sale generates more than the outstanding debt, the excess is paid to the new buyer because the seller has already been paid for her equity in the property.

Alternatively, the new buyer may agree to **assume** the underlying indebtedness. Although it frequently is said that the new buyer "assumes the mortgage," what the new buyer assumes is the underlying debt. The buyer's promise to assume the mortgage debt may be made either to the seller or to the lender. Either way, the promise is enforceable by the lender. If the promise is not made directly to the lender, the lender can enforce the promise as a third-party creditor beneficiary.

Under traditional contract principles, the seller remains liable for repayment of the debt despite the buyer's assumption. If the new buyer defaults, the seller can be compelled to satisfy the unpaid obligation. However, the seller may be relieved of liability if the mortgagee agrees to release her and to look only the new buyer for payment. In that case, a **novation** occurs in which one contracting party (the buyer) is substituted for another contracting party (the seller), whose liability is extinguished.

Acceleration Clause   An acceleration clause, sometimes called a *due-on-sale clause*, is a contractual provision in the promissory note or in the mortgage that permits the mortgagee, at its option, to declare the entire balance of the mortgage immediately due and payable if the secured property is sold or is otherwise transferred without the prior consent of the mortgagee. Acceleration clauses originally were designed to protect the mortgagee from impairment of its security or from increased risk of default by a new buyer who was less credit worthy than the original buyer. In recent years, however, acceleration clauses have been used primarily to retire old, unprofitable mortgages when the encumbered property is sold. This enables the lender to maintain its long-term loan portfolio at current interest rates.

Regulations of the Federal Home Loan Bank Board provide that if a mortgage contains an acceleration clause, the lender is not required to exercise it upon sale. Instead, the lender may waive it and allow the new buyer to assume the existing mortgage if the assumption agreement is in writing and is executed before the transfer is made. In this situation, the new buyer becomes contractually obligated on the original loan; and the lender is allowed to adjust the interest rate upward. After the assumption, however, the lender must release the original borrower from all obligations for the loan. This differs from the traditional contract approach, under which the original mortgagor remains liable after assumption.

Default and Foreclosure   Upon default of any of the underlying obligations, the mortgagee always has the option to proceed upon the underlying promissory note; obtain a judgment; and attempt to enforce the judgment against the debtor's general assets. Since these assets usually are insufficient or are subject to the claims of other creditors, however, the mortgagee generally will elect to enforce its interest in the secured real estate. Foreclosure is the method by which the mortgaged property (or the proceeds of its sale) is applied to satisfy the underlying debt.

Literally, *foreclosure* refers to barring or terminating the mortgagor's equity of redemption. The concept of *equity of redemption* was developed to allow the mortgagor to "redeem" her property by satisfying the debt plus interest within a reasonable time after default. Because the mortgagee could not sell or dispose of the property while a possibility of redemption remained, a method of fixing the duration of the mortgagor's equity of redemption was required. The method developed was the foreclosure action, which is filed as an equity proceeding.

Under early *strict foreclosure* actions, the mortgagee filed a petition with the court following default and obtained a decree ordering full payment within a fixed time, usually six months to one year. If the mortgagee failed to pay, her equity of redemption was extinguished; and title was vested in the mortgagee without any sale of the property. Only a few states continue to use the strict foreclosure action.

Foreclosure by sale is the predominant type of foreclosure action used today, either foreclosure by judicial sale or foreclosure by power of sale. Foreclosure by judicial sale is the more prevalent of the two. In a *foreclosure by judicial sale*, the mortgagee files a petition and, after hearing, obtains a decree of foreclosure that gives the mortgagor a specified time to pay the outstanding obligation, after which the property is sold at public auction. A majority of states also give the mortgagor an additional "statutory redemption period," allowing the mortgagor to redeem the property for a limited period of time, even after its sale. Ultimately, the proceeds of the sale are used to pay the senior mortgagee's debt and then to pay junior mortgage holders in the order of their priority. Any surplus remaining after all secured parties are paid is returned to the mortgagor.

Far less time-consuming and less expensive is the *foreclosure by power of sale*, which is used by more than one-third of the states. Under this method, a foreclosure sale may be held without judicial proceedings if the mortgage instrument (or trust deed) gives the power to sell the property in the case of default. Conduct of the sale by public auction is regulated by statute to protect the mortgagor.

Installment Sale Contract In mortgage financing, the buyer typically makes a down payment, borrows the balance from a third-party lender, and receives a deed from the seller. The contract of sale remains executory (yet to be performed) for a brief period of time from the inception of the contract until delivery of the deed. If mortgage financing is unavailable for any reason, the parties may enter into an installment sale contract, also called a *contract for deed, agreement for deed,* or *land contract.*

In an installment sale contract, the seller finances the buyer, who generally takes possession of the property at the beginning of the contract; makes periodic installment payments against the price; and ordinarily assumes responsibility for payment of taxes, assessments, insurance, and repairs on the property during the contract period. The seller retains title as security for performance of the contract and delivers the deed to the buyer only after the purchase price is paid in full. Unlike the ordinary real estate contract, the installment contract remains executory for an extended period of time. Because the buyer has no deed to evidence her interest, the installment contract usually is recorded to give third parties constructive notice of the buyer's interest in the property. Recording protects the buyer against a subsequent sale or mortgage of the property by the seller.

Escrow Agreement An escrow is a convenient and flexible device for closing many types of real estate transactions, including installment sale contracts. In an ***escrow agreement***, parties to the contract deposit a deed, other instrument, or money with a third party, called an ***escrow agent***, who holds the deposited items until the performance of a condition or until the occurrence of an event outlined in the escrow agreement.

Escrow agreements are common in installment sale contracts. Because the seller retains title until the buyer performs, the buyer runs the risk that the seller will be unwilling or unable to convey the property at the time when the contract calls for him to do so. For instance, the seller may be dead, incompetent, or absent from the jurisdiction when the duty to convey arises under the contract. To prevent this result, installment contracts generally require the seller to deposit a deed with the escrow agent to be delivered to the buyer upon payment of the purchase price.

An escrow agreement creates an agency relationship between the parties and the escrow agent. As an agent of both the buyer and the seller, the agent stands in a fiduciary capacity to both parties. Once created, the escrow agent's authority is not terminated by death or incapacity of either party prior to performance of the conditions of the installment sale contract.

This type of escrow arrangement is different from an escrow account. Typically, an escrow account is a bank account maintained in the names of a mortgagor and a mortgagee into which the mortgagor makes periodic payments to satisfy recurring charges while the mortgage is in effect, such as property taxes or insurance premiums.

Real Estate Closing

The sale contract (purchase agreement) generally fixes a date for performance, commonly three to eight weeks after the contract is made. Unless otherwise agreed, real estate contracts require simultaneous performance by the parties. On the agreed date, then, the seller will convey the property by delivering her deed to the buyer; and the buyer will pay the purchase price. This performance is known as the *settlement*, *title closing*, or *closing*. In addition to the basic duties of conveyance and payment of the purchase price, other expenses incident to the sale (costs of financing, cost of establishing a merchantable title, commissions of the real estate agent, attorney fees, and filing fees) generally are paid at the time of closing. Proration of prepaid real estate taxes and other, miscellaneous matters connected with the sale and transfer may be handled at this time as well.

For residential property, the *Real Estate Settlement Procedures Act (RESPA)*, a federal statute, requires an advance, itemized disclosure of closing costs to the buyer. For commercial property, lenders increasingly require an environmental impact study before closing concerning any property to be used as collateral to assure themselves that no toxic waste or disposal exists on the property (such as underground gas and oil tanks). Failure to perform this study can result in liability of both the buyer and the lender under existing environmental protection regulations.

For both residential and commercial property, a *closing statement* or settlement statement is prepared for the buyer and for the seller. The seller's closing statement typically lists the sale price and any expenses of sale attributable to the seller, together with credits to the seller, and shows a net purchase price payable to the seller. The buyer's closing statement likewise lists the purchase price to be paid, together with those expenses for which the buyer is responsible and any credits to which the buyer is entitled (including buyer's down payment), and shows a net purchase price payable by the seller.

Closing statement forms for the buyer and for the seller, respectively, are shown on the following pages. It may be helpful to work through one or more hypothetical real estate sale transactions by inserting the appropriate information where it belongs on each form.

REAL ESTATE CLOSING STATEMENT
BUYER'S SETTLEMENT SHEET

Date_____

Name of Buyer_____
Address_____
Property_____

	Debit	Credit
Purchase Price	$_____	$
Earnest Money Paid		_____
Additional Payments Prior to Closing		_____
Old Mortgage Assumed		_____
New Mortgage		_____
Contract with Seller		_____
Loan Closing Costs	_____	
Pro-rated Insurance or New Insurance Premium	_____	
Pro-rated real estate taxes (general)		_____
Pro-rated real estate taxes (special)		_____
Pro-rated rent		_____
New/Replacement escrow fund deposited with mortgage holder	_____	
Interest Adjustment	_____	_____
Tax Adjustment	_____	
Abstracting Cost	_____	
Appraisal Fee	_____	
Attorney Fee	_____	
Credit Report	_____	
_____	_____	_____
_____	_____	_____
Credit Balance, Seller		_____
TOTALS	$	$

RECEIVED, READ, AND APPROVED:

_____, Buyer

_____, Buyer

REAL ESTATE CLOSING STATEMENT
SELLER'S SETTLEMENT SHEET

Date_____

Name of Seller_____
Address_____
Property_____

	Debit	Credit
Sale Price	$	$ _____
Earnest Money Paid	_____	
Additional Payments Received Prior to Closing	_____	
Contract Carried Back by Seller	_____	
Existing Mortgage	_____	
Rebate of escrow fund		_____
Pro-rated insurance (unearned premium)		_____
Pro-rated real estate taxes (general)	_____	
Pro-rated real estate taxes (special)	_____	
Pro-rated rent	_____	
Interest Adjustment	_____	_____
Recording Fees—Release of Mortgage	_____	
Affidavit	_____	
Revenue Stamps	_____	
Abstracting Cost	_____	
Land Survey	_____	
Appraisal Fee	_____	
Attorney Fee	_____	
Sales Commission	_____	
_____	_____	_____
_____	_____	_____
Debit Balance, Buyer	_____	
TOTALS	$	$

RECEIVED, READ, AND APPROVED:

_____ , Seller

_____ , Seller

Adverse Possession

Adverse possession is a method of acquiring property through the statute of limitations that applies to actions by owners of real estate against persons who wrongfully possess it. The statute of limitations for this type of action varies from state to state; it can be as little as five years or as long as thirty years. If the owner fails to file suit for recovery of possession from the adverse possessor within the statutory period, two legal results follow: (1) the owner's claim against the possessor is extinguished; and (2) the adverse possessor acquires title to the property.

> Ann and Bob own adjacent tracts of real estate. Ann builds a privacy fence along the boundary line, ten feet beyond her tract and onto the tract owned by Bob, resulting in wrongful possession. If Ann's possession of Bob's land continues for the statutory period, she will acquire title to it by adverse possession.

The adverse possessor's title is an original title, rather than a derivative title. A ***derivative title*** is one derived from the original owner by sale, gift, will, or intestate succession. In adverse possession, an ***original title*** destroys the owner's title and vests automatically by operation of law when the legal requirements are met. A person may have acquired title by adverse possession, even though the public record discloses record title in another. The adverse possessor need not announce the interest publicly by recording it to be protected against subsequent buyers from the original owner. For this reason, a prospective buyer of real estate always should conduct a physical inspection or survey of the property to determine precisely where the boundary lines are. In this way, adverse possession claims not disclosed by an ordinary title examination procedures may be discovered.

Title to property owned by the federal or a state government generally may not be acquired by adverse possession. This result is dictated by statute in many states. Similarly, no title may be acquired by adverse possession against land registered under the Torrens system.

To be effective, adverse possession must be:

- *Open and notorious possession;*

- *Hostile, exclusive, and adverse to the original owner's interest, under a claim of right by the adverse possessor; and*

- *Continuous, uninterrupted possession for the statutory period.*

Open and Notorious Possession   To establish title by adverse possession, the occupation of the property must be sufficiently obvious to put the owner on notice of the possession. The owner need not have actual knowledge; he is deemed to know facts that would be disclosed by reasonable inspection of the property. Accordingly, an absentee owner may be especially susceptible to losing her title by adverse possession.

Hostile, Exclusive, and Adverse Possession Under Claim of Right
Hostile possession does not refer to antagonistic conduct by the possessor. It simply means that the possession is without the owner's permission, either express or implied. The possession must be under a "claim of right," meaning that the adverse possessor must indicate an intent to possess the land as against the whole world, including the true owner.

There is some question about whether the adverse possessor must intend to possess the land of another or whether a mistaken or innocent possession is sufficient. Most courts hold that subjective intent of the possessor is irrelevant. Physical possession beyond the property line is sufficient to make the possession hostile and adverse under a claim of right, whether the claim of right is intentional or mistaken. The intent that is required is the intent to possess.

The adverse possessor must prove that possession was exclusive over the statutory period. Shared or common possession with the record owner generally defeats an adverse possession claim. Likewise, exclusive possession of land by a cotenant (either a joint tenant or a tenant in common) usually is not considered hostile to the interests of other cotenants. If an ouster occurs, however, the statute of limitations begins to run against the ousted cotenant. An *ouster* is conduct by the cotenant in possession which excludes other cotenants and indicates that the cotenant in possession holds adversely to their interests.

Some but not all states require that the adverse possessor pay property taxes during the period of adverse possession.

Continuous and Uninterrupted Possession for the Statutory Period
When hostile and adverse, open and notorious possession occurs, the statute of limitations begins to run. From that point forward, it must be continuous and uninterrupted for the duration of the statutory period.

Continuous possession requires only the type of possession that an average owner ordinarily would take over the property. For instance, adverse possession of a summer home would require physical possession only during the summer months, with an intent (state of mind) to possess it again the next summer. If the adverse possessor abandons the property or if the true owner re-enters it, an interruption occurs; and any subsequent adverse possession causes the statute of limitations to begin anew.

Tacking is a doctrine which allows an adverse possessor to "tack" (add) adverse possessions of others on her own, provided the predecessors were in privity with her (shared a common interest through contract or by blood). This would allow a buyer of Ann's tract of land in the above example to tack Ann's adverse possession onto the buyer's. It also would allow Ann's heirs to do the same thing if Ann were to die.

Under Color of Title

Although adverse possession generally occurs without any hint of actual title in the adverse possessor, it sometimes occurs under *color of title*. In this situation, the adverse possessor claims the land under an instrument purporting to pass title but which is ineffective to operate as a conveyance. This can occur if the grantor's signature is forged or if a deed is executed by a grantor with defective or nonexistent title. Some states require that the instrument constituting color of title be recorded.

The effect of possession under color of title differs from possession under a claim of right. In many states, the statutory period is shortened if possession is under color of title, provided that the possessor pays the annual property taxes against the property. The extent of the property acquired also differs when property is possessed under color of title. Ordinarily, the adverse possessor may claim only that portion of the land actually possessed and occupied during the required statutory period. A person possessing under color of title, however, may acquire title to the entire tract if it is adequately described in the instrument, even though actual possession is limited to only a portion of the tract.

The review of real estate law and procedure contained in this chapter, together with the following Self-Test, provide a summary of the type of material tested in this subsection of the CLA® examination. Additional study references are contained in the Bibliography section of this *Review Manual*.

Real Estate Law Self-Test

Allow an uninterrupted thirty-minute period to answer all questions. At the end of thirty minutes, check your answers against those in the Answer Key Section of this Manual. Deduct two points for each incorrect answer (100 total possible points). Unanswered questions are counted as incorrect answers. Follow directions carefully and observe the time limit precisely to provide an accurate self-assessment.

Choose the most correct answer to each of the following questions unless a specific question instructs you to do otherwise.

1. True or False.   Concurrent ownership of real property involves the three unities of time, title, and possession.

2. True or False.   Joint owners of real property hold undivided shares.

3. True or False.   A tenancy at will provides more rights to the tenant than other types of tenancies.

4. True or False.   If a parcel of real estate is landlocked, this means that it is surrounded by land on all contiguous sides.

5. True or False.   Riparian rights refer to the rights of a landowner to any crops growing on the land.

6. The language "to A and his heirs" indicates:

   a.   a fee simple estate.
   b.   a fee tail estate.
   c.   a defeasible fee estate.
   d.   a joint tenancy estate.

7. An easement differs from a license in that:

   a.   a license confers a personal privilege to do an act.
   b.   an easement is a possessory interest in land.
   c.   an easement is created through eminent domain.
   d.   all of the above.
   e.   none of the above.

8. Which of the following is an example of a fixture?

    a. a helicopter pad
    b. a built-in dishwasher
    c. a bird bath
    d. none of the above

9. The conveyance of real property by will is referred to as a(n):

    a. inheritance.
    b. devise.
    c. bequest.
    d. gift.
    e. none of the above.

10. Adam conveys property to Ben for the life of Carol, then to Jane. At Ben's death, the property owner is:

    a. Carol.
    b. Jane.
    c. Ben's heirs.
    d. Adam.
    e. none of the above.

11. Ann, Barbara, and Casey own property as joint tenants with right of survivorship. While all three are living, Ann sells her interest in the property to Dafney. Barbara then dies and wills her property to Frances. Who are the owners of the property after Barbara's death?

    a. Dafney and Casey
    b. Dafney, Frances, and Casey
    c. Ann, Frances, and Casey
    d. Casey
    e. None of the above

12. True or False.   When owners of real property are tenants by the entirety, the death of one spouse will result in the surviving spouse owning the property as a whole.

13. True or False.   Property acquired as a gift from his parents by a married man living in a community property state is community property.

14. True or False.   Land upon which an easement is located is known as the burdened tenement.

15. True or False.   Foreclosure of a first mortgage generally will terminate a second mortgage lien on the secured real estate.

16. True or False.   A "due on sale" provision in a mortgage means that if the mortgage is sold, the debt secured by the mortgage will become due and payable; these clauses generally are not enforceable.

17. True or False.   A *lis pendens* is used to provide notice of a federal tax lien against real property.

18. True or False.   Absent a specific provision preventing it, a lease generally may be assigned.

19. True or False.   When one tenant sublets to another tenant, the first tenant becomes, in effect, the sub-landlord because no privity of contract is created between the original landlord and the second tenant.

20. True or False.   An easement by prescription is one created when the owner allows a license to lapse but fails to remove the licensee.

21. True or False.   Generally speaking, covenants are easier to enforce than equitable servitudes are.

22. True or False.   Title to real estate may pass without the consent of the owner.

23. True or False.   In a tenancy in common, one person may own a 1/5 interest and another person may own a 4/5 interest.

24. True or False.   A deed cannot be recorded unless it is signed by the grantee.

25. Deeds are attested:

    a.   to make them binding on the grantee.
    b.   to enable them to be recorded.
    c.   because of ancient custom.
    d.   to establish legal capacity.

26. Chain of title means:

 a. listing of all recorded instruments affecting the title.
 b. a measurement used by a surveyor.
 c. certificate of title.
 d. burdens of ownership.

27. Title to real estate passes to the buyer at the time the deed is:

 a. written.
 b. notarized.
 c. signed.
 d. delivered.

28. Emma needs more space in her garden to grow tomatoes. Her neighbor, Nigel, has plenty of space but refuses to lease to Emma the small strip of land next to Emma's garden. Frustrated, Emma plants tomatoes there anyway and continues to do so for a number of years. Based only on these facts, Emma most likely has established a(n):

 a. easement by reclamation.
 b. easement by prescription.
 c. easement by necessity.
 d. easement by implication.

29. Roy conveys land to Jack by deed. Unknown to the parties, there was a cloud on Roy's title at the time of the conveyance. Which of the following deeds puts Roy in the worst legal position if Jack demands that Roy defend the title?

 a. guaranteed deed
 b. special warranty deed
 c. warranty deed
 d. quitclaim deed

30. True or False. An acknowledgement on a deed is unnecessary to make it effective.

31. True or False. When a zoning plan is put into effect by a legislative body, any nonconforming use must be allowed to continue until legal title to the nonconforming property passes to a new owner.

32. True or False.   Joe and Willie agree in writing that Joe will purchase Willie's farm for $350,000, with closing to occur in 60 days. Joe makes an earnest deposit of $20,000. Joe's financing does not come through until 2½ months later, at which time Willie informs Joe that the farm has been sold to Tom. On these facts, Joe has no cause of action against Willie to enforce the purchase agreement.

33. True or False.   Assume that Joe elects not to pursue legal action seeking to enforce the sale in the preceding question. In that event, Joe nevertheless is entitled to a return of his earnest deposit.

34. True or False.   Snob Hill Owners' Association adopts a series of covenants for its new subdivision, one of which requires that property owners hold at least a master's degree in their chosen professions. Maurice Chivalrous wants to sell his property to a sanitation engineer who holds only a bachelor's degree. On these facts, the covenant likely can be enforced to prevent the sale.

35. True or False.   A group of Texans obtain licenses from Bertha to hunt on her Colorado land. Two years later, Bertha sells the Colorado land and moves to San Diego. If the Texans want to continue hunting on the land, they must obtain new licenses from the new owner.

36. In return for $8,000, Sarah gives George a 30-day option to purchase a rental property that Sarah owns for $117,000. Sarah dies one week later, leaving a will which gives all of her real property to Samson and all of her remaining property to Delilah. If George decides to exercise the option before it expires, who is entitled to the purchase price?

   a. Samson
   b. Delilah
   c. George
   d. Sarah's heirs

37. John and Karen Smith rent a house in Faircity from Jack Nimble. The lease agreement does not indicate who is to make repairs to the house. Two weeks after they move in, the furnace stops working. The cost to repair it is $750. Which of the following statements is most correct?

   a. Common law rules require the landlord to pay for repairs.
   b. Common law rules require the tenants to pay for repairs.

(see next page)

    c.   Statutes require the landlord to make repairs of rental houses.

    d.   Statutes require the tenants to make repairs of rental houses.

38.   Herbert Highpockets prepares a deed for his house to Donna Dreeme and records the deed in the appropriate registrar's office. Herbert places the recorded deed in his safe and does not tell Donna about it. Which of the following statements is most correct?

    a.   Herbert owns the property because there was no consideration for the deed.

    b.   Herbert owns the property because he did not deliver the deed to Donna.

    c.   Donna owns the property because it is recorded in her name.

    d.   Donna owns the property because she has the equitable title.

39.   Ruth dies, leaving a life interest in all of her real property to her husband, Seth, and the remainder of her property to her adult children. One year later, Seth marries Ruby. Three months after their marriage, Seth dies. Which of the following statements is most accurate concerning the real estate?

    a.   Seth's heirs will take legal title to the remainder interest.

    b.   Ruby will take legal title to the remainder interest.

    c.   Ruth's adult children will take the reversion interest.

    d.   Ruth's adult children will take the remainder interest.

40.   Jordan leases her roadside property to Erin for a three-day craft fair. Erin is a:

    a.   tenant at sufferance.

    b.   tenant at will.

    c.   tenant from period to period.

    d.   tenant for years.

For the next group of questions, match each term in the first column with the phrase in the second column which defines or relates to it best (no phrase is used twice).

41.   _____ habendum clause   a.   deed signed by both grantor and grantee

42. _____ fee simple determinable   b.   cuts off prior estate

43. _____ indenture   c.   shows the estate granted in a deed

44. _____ remainder   d.   primogeniture

45. _____ seisin   e.   follows prior estate naturally

46. _____ executory interest   f.   possibility of reverter

                                                 g.   the right to possess property

47. True or False.   Jonah conveys Greenacre to Bill on July 1. On July 15, Bill records the deed. On July 10, Jonah conveys Greenacre to Karen, a bona fide purchaser without notice of the deed to Bill. Karen records her deed on July 17. In a race-notice jurisdiction, Bill will prevail as the true owner of Greenacre.

48. True or False.   Daniel conveys Brownacre to Agnes, who registers title under the Torrens system. Joseph subsequently enters the property and remains as an adverse possessor all during the required 17-year period. On these facts, Joseph has established title to Brownacre.

49. True or False.   Tyrone has occupied a portion of the Highland Ranch as an adverse possessor for seven years. At Tyrone's death, his son (Roger) inherits all of Tyrone's property. If Roger wants to occupy the same portion of the Highland Ranch, the period of adverse possession must begin anew.

50. True or False.   Ethel and her neighbors are subject to a restriction on the use of their residential property, which provides that no fences may be higher than eight feet. Ethel's neighbor to the south has erected a privacy fence that is ten feet high. Ethel doesn't want to make the neighbor tear down the fence, but she thinks he should pay some penalty for violating the restriction. On these facts, Ethel's objective will be served best if the restriction is characterized as a restrictive covenant.

SELF-TEST ANSWER KEY

Legal Terminology

1. False
2. True
3. False
4. False
5. b
6. b
7. c
8. a
9. b
10. d
11. a
12. g
13. b
14. c
15. True
16. False
17. True
18. False
19. False
20. b
21. b
22. c
23. d
24. a
25. h
26. j
27. e
28. a
29. i
30. c
31. l
32. k
33. g
34. d
35. False
36. True
37. False
38. c
39. d
40. b
41. code
42. assignment
43. bylaws
44. devise
45. recidivist
46. relevant
47. supersedeas
48. allegation
49. pro bono
50. debenture

Communications

1. averse
2. born
3. his
4. comprises
5. nauseated
6. Regardless
7. bad
8. its
9. fewer
10. lend
11. was
12. were
13. is
14. C
15. I - among
16. I - *omit*
17. I - badly
18. C
19. I - We
20. C
21. I - were
22. I - ensure
23. I - as if
24. d
25. c
26. a
27. d
28. c
29. c
30. d
31. d
32. c
33. b

941

Communications
(cont'd)

34.	b
35.	d
36.	d
37.	a
38.	d
39.	b
40.	c
41.	a
42.	a
43.	c
44.	c
45.	d
46.	g
47.	h
48.	c
49.	f
50.	b

Ethics

1.	True
2.	True
3.	True
4.	False
5.	False
6.	True
7.	True
8.	False
9.	False
10.	False
11.	True
12.	a
13.	c
14.	c
15.	d
16.	d
17.	d
18.	c
19.	f
20.	d

21.	c
22.	False
23.	False
24.	True
25.	False
26.	False
27.	True
28.	False
29.	c
30.	f
31.	b
32.	c
33.	a
34.	b
35.	d
36.	e
37.	b
38.	False
39.	False
40.	c
41.	False
42.	True
43.	False
44.	True
45.	False
46.	True
47.	False
48.	d
49.	a
50.	b

Judgment & Analytical Ability

1.	True
2.	False
3.	False
4.	False
5.	True
6.	c
7.	d
8.	c

9.	d
10.	c
11.	a
12.	b
13.	d
14.	a
15.	b
16.	d
17.	a
18.	a
19.	c
20.	b
21.	b
22.	c
23.	c
24.	a
25.	b
26.	c
27.	c
28.	c
29.	d
30.	c
31.	b
32.	c
33.	e
34.	e
35.	b
36.	c
37.	e
38.	b
39.	c
40.	a

see sample essay answer at page 949

Legal Research

1.	c
2.	d
3.	a
4.	a
5.	b

Legal Research
(cont'd)

6.   d
7.   F. Supp.
8.   False
9.   False
10. True
11. False
12. c
13. c
14. d
15. b
16. False
17. True
18. False
19. False
20. True
21. True
22. True
23. False
24. False
25. c
26. b
27. b
28. b
29. True
30. True
31. True
32. True
33. False
34. a
35. b
36. d
37. c
38. False
39. True
40. False
41. True
42. False
43. True
44. d
45. c
46. a
47. d
48. c
49. c
50. c

Human Relations & Interviewing

1.   False
2.   True
3.   False
4.   False
5.   True
6.   b
7.   c
8.   a
9.   c
10. b
11. True
12. True
13. True
14. False
15. False
16. b
17. c
18. a
19. b
20. a
21. True
22. False
23. True
24. True
25. False
26. c
27. a
28. b
29. a
30. d
31. False
32. False
33. True
34. False
35. False
36. b
37. d
38. c
39. c
40. False
41. True
42. True
43. False
44. True
45. True
46. False
47. a
48. d
49. False
50. True

General Law

1.   a
2.   d
3.   a
4.   a
5.   False
6.   False
7.   True
8.   True
9.   False
10. False
11. False
12. False
13. a
14. c
15. b
16. a
17. False
18. True
19. False
20. False
21. b
22. c
23. b

General Law (cont'd)

24.	acknowledge-ment
25.	ad damnum
26.	nunc pro tunc
27.	witness
28.	ex post facto
29.	appellee
30.	venue
31.	chattel
32.	primary law or mandatory law
33.	writ of mandamus
34.	False
35.	True
36.	False
37.	True
38.	False
39.	a
40.	d
41.	False
42.	True
43.	False
44.	False
45.	b
46.	a
47.	c
48.	c
49.	False
50.	False

Administrative Law

1.	c
2.	b
3.	a
4.	False
5.	True
6.	False
7.	True

8.	True
9.	True
10.	False
11.	True
12.	False
13.	False
14.	False
15.	True
16.	True
17.	False
18.	True
19.	True
20.	False
21.	False
22.	d
23.	c
24.	b
25.	d
26.	False
27.	True
28.	False
29.	False
30.	True
31.	b
32.	e
33.	a
34.	c
35.	False
36.	False
37.	True
38.	False
39.	False
40.	d
41.	e
42.	a
43.	f
44.	c
45.	b
46.	True
47.	False
48.	True
49.	False
50.	True

Bankruptcy Law

1.	False
2.	False
3.	c
4.	False
5.	False
6.	b
7.	b
8.	True
9.	False
10.	True
11.	False
12.	False
13.	True
14.	True
15.	True
16.	True
17.	True
18.	False
19.	e
20.	False
21.	True
22.	False
23.	False
24.	False
25.	True
26.	c
27.	b
28.	d
29.	c
30.	a
31.	False
32.	False
33.	True
34.	False
35.	True
36.	False
37.	b
38.	b
39.	f
40.	d
41.	e

*Bankruptcy Law
(cont'd)*

42.	True
43.	False
44.	True
45.	False
46.	False
47.	True
48.	False
49.	False
50.	False

Business Organizations

1.	b
2.	c
3.	b
4.	b
5.	d
6.	False
7.	True
8.	True
9.	False
10.	c
11.	a
12.	b
13.	d
14.	False
15.	True
16.	c
17.	c
18.	d
19.	c
20.	b
21.	c
22.	b
23.	a
24.	d
25.	c
26.	b

27.	d
28.	True
29.	True
30.	True
31.	False
32.	True
33.	True
34.	False
35.	False
36.	c
37.	b
38.	c
39.	d
40.	a
41.	False
42.	False
43.	True
44.	False
45.	False
46.	b
47.	c
48.	a
49.	c
50.	d

Contract Law

1.	False
2.	False
3.	False
4.	d
5.	False
6.	True
7.	True
8.	d
9.	True
10.	d
11.	b
12.	d
13.	c
14.	False
15.	c

16.	True
17.	False
18.	False
19.	d
20.	True
21.	False
22.	True
23.	False
24.	e
25.	b
26.	c
27.	a
28.	c
29.	b
30.	b
31.	d
32.	d
33.	True
34.	False
35.	False
36.	True
37.	False
38.	False
39.	True
40.	False
41.	c
42.	b
43.	b
44.	d
45.	a
46.	True
47.	False
48.	False
49.	True
50.	False

Criminal Law

1.	False
2.	False
3.	False
4.	True

5.	False

Criminal Law
(cont'd)

6.	False
7.	False
8.	False
9.	a
10.	d
11.	a
12.	d
13.	True
14.	False
15.	False
16.	False
17.	True
18.	False
19.	True
20.	False
21.	False
22.	True
23.	True
24.	True
25.	d
26.	d
27.	b
28.	a
29.	b
30.	False
31.	True
32.	False
33.	True
34.	False
35.	False
36.	True
37.	b
38.	c
39.	b
40.	a
41.	b
42.	False
43.	True
44.	False
45.	False
46.	True
47.	False
48.	True
49.	True
50.	False

Estate Planning and Probate

1.	False
2.	True
3.	False
4.	True
5.	False
6.	False
7.	False
8.	True
9.	False
10.	False
11.	True
12.	False
13.	d
14.	f
15.	False
16.	False
17.	True
18.	False
19.	True
20.	False
21.	d
22.	d
23.	a
24.	d
25.	b
26.	True
27.	True
28.	False
29.	False
30.	False
31.	c
32.	c
33.	d
34.	b
35.	a
36.	False
37.	True
38.	False
39.	False
40.	True
41.	False
42.	False
43.	True
44.	True
45.	False
46.	False
47.	b
48.	d
49.	c
50.	d

Family Law

1.	False
2.	True
3.	False
4.	False
5.	False
6.	True
7.	b
8.	e
9.	c
10.	d
11.	b
12.	c
13.	False
14.	True
15.	False
16.	False
17.	True
18.	False
19.	d
20.	b

21. a
22. d
23. True
24. True
25. False
26. a
27. b
28. b
29. c
30. b
31. False
32. True
33. True
34. True
35. False
36. a
37. d
38. e
39. a
40. c
41. False
42. True
43. False
44. True
45. False
46. True
47. True
48. False
49. False
50. True

Litigation

1. False
2. False
3. False
4. False
5. True
6. False
7. False
8. b
9. True

10. False
11. c
12. d
13. b
14. False
15. True
16. False
17. False
18. c
19. b
20. b
21. False
22. True
23. False

Litigation (cont'd)

24. False
25. e
26. d
27. c
28. d
29. c
30. b
31. c
32. a
33. b
34. b
35. False
36. True
37. False
38. True
39. False
40. False
41. True
42. True
43. False
44. a
45. d
46. b
47. a
48. c
49. d
50. b

Real Estate Law

1. False
2. True
3. False
4. False
5. False
6. a
7. a
8. b
9. b
10. c
11. a
12. True
13. False
14. True
15. True
16. False
17. False
18. True
19. True
20. False
21. False
22. True
23. True
24. False
25. b
26. a
27. d
28. b
29. c
30. True
31. False
32. True
33. False
34. False
35. True
36. a
37. b
38. c
39. c
40. d

41.   c
42.   f
43.   a
44.   e
45.   g
46.   b
47.   True
48.   False
49.   False
50.   True

Judgment & Analytical Ability

SAMPLE ESSAY ANSWER:

MEMORANDUM

TO: Wilma Wonka, Staff Attorney
FROM: Stanley Dorite, Legal Assistant
DATE:
RE: Stewart Carr Disciplinary Proceeding

You have asked me to review existing statutes, case law, and ethics rules related to the Stewart Carr disciplinary proceedings. Mr. Tuttle has been asked to serve as special prosecutor for the Utopia State Bar Association against Carr.

<u>Facts</u>   One of Carr's clients purchased a toy chest at an estate sale and found six savings bonds in the chest. The bonds had been issued to Hans and Louise Brinker as joint tenants. When she could not cash the bonds, the client employed Carr to find the owners and to obtain a reward. The client told Carr that if she did not get a reward, she would light her fireplace with the bonds.

Carr located Dick Brinker, a grandson of the original owners (both of whom were deceased). Carr negotiated a reward of one-third for his client. However, when Brinker's attorney pointed out the Utopia statute which requires a finder to return lost property to its owner, Carr negotiated for a smaller reward. Brinker's attorney later withdrew the reward.

Gladys Watson, Dick Brinker's sister, talked to a police officer and, at the officer's suggestion, she called Carr's office and recorded her conversation. Carr's legal assistant, Jack Fehrman, relayed the client's threat to use the bonds as kindling if she did not receive a reward for them.

<u>Issues</u>   1.   Is Stewart Carr responsible for the wrongful statements made by his legal assistant?

2.   Did Stewart Carr violate any ethical rules, independent of the statements made by his legal assistant?

<u>Discussion</u>   Stewart Carr's demand on behalf of his client violated Utopia State Statute § 38-514, which states that anyone who comes into control of property he knows to have been lost or mislaid commits theft if he fails to take reasonable

steps to restore the property to its owner. Even if Carr did not know this statute existed when he made the original demand, which does not excuse him in any event, he continued in his demand after the statute was pointed out to him. The only thing that changed was that he lowered the amount of the reward sought for his client.

The Canons of Ethics require that "[a] lawyer shall not give the appearance of impropriety." Carr clearly knew the demand on behalf of his client was improper once he knew about the lost property statute. Yet, he persisted in his demand.

Although the statements made by Carr's legal assistant are superfluous given Carr's own conduct, the point should be made that Carr cannot absolve himself of the misconduct of his employees. Fehrman's wrongful statements must be attributed to Carr. A lawyer must provide management, supervision, and control of his office staff. When faced with this issue in relation to a legal secretary, the Utopia Supreme Court stated:

> such conduct does not constitute a defense to the misconduct charged. A lawyer may not avoid responsibility for misconduct by hiding behind an employee's misconduct and may not avoid a charge of unprofessional conduct by contending his employees are incompetent. *State ex rel. USBA v. Krist*, 232 Utop. 445 (1989).

Conclusion   Stewart Carr is professionally accountable for the conduct of his employee, Jack Fehrman. Independent of Fehrman, however, Carr himself appears to have violated Utopia State Statute § 38-514 and the Canons of Ethics when he made and then persisted in an improper demand on behalf of his client.

BIBLIOGRAPHY

General References

Miller/Urisko, <u>West's Paralegal Today</u>, West Publishing Company.

Miller/Urisko, <u>West's Paralegal Today Essentials</u>, West Publishing Company.

National Association of Legal Assistants, Inc., <u>NALA Manual for Legal Assistants</u>, 3rd Ed., West Publishing Company.

Statsky, <u>Essentials of Paralegalism</u>, 2nd Ed., West Publishing Company.

Statsky, <u>Introduction to Paralegalism</u>, 5th Ed., West Publishing Company.

West Publishing Company, Black Letter Series.

West Publishing Company, Nutshell Series.

Legal Terminology References and Authorities

<u>Black's Law Dictionary</u> and <u>Webster's New Collegiate Dictionary</u> are the authorities for all definitions.

Oran, <u>Law Dictionary for Non-lawyers</u>, 3rd Ed., West Publishing Company.

Oran, <u>Oran's Law Dictionary</u>, West Publishing Company.

Statsky, <u>Legal Thesaurus/Legal Dictionary</u>, West Publishing Company.

Statsky, Hussey, Diamond, and Nakamura, <u>West's Desk Reference</u>, West Publishing Company.
Weaver and Ellison, <u>West's Pocket Law Dictionary and Thesaurus</u>, West Publishing Company.

Communications References

NOTE: Strunk & White, <u>*The Elements of Style*</u> is the authority adopted by the NALA Certifying Board.

Fowler, <u>The Little, Brown Handbook</u>, 5th Ed., Little, Brown & Company.

Hurd, <u>Writing for Lawyers</u>, Journal Broadcasting and Communications, Pittsburgh, Pennsylvania.

Strunk & White, <u>The Elements of Style</u>, 3rd Ed., Macmillan Publishing Co., Inc., New York.

Vernolia, <u>Write it Right! A Desk Drawer Digest of Punctuation, Grammar, and Style</u>, Ten Speed Press, Berkeley, California.

<u>Webster's New Collegiate Dictionary</u>, 9th Ed., G. & C. Merriam Company, Springfield, Massachusetts.

Wydick, <u>Plain English for Lawyers</u>. Carolina Academic Press.

Ethics References

(The) American Bar Association, <u>Model Rules of Professional Conduct</u>.

Judd, "Beyond the Bar: Legal Assistants and the Unauthorized Practice of Law," FACTS & FINDINGS, Volume VIII, Issue VI, May-June 1982, The National Association of Legal Assistants, Inc.

Kasic, "Under the Supervision of a Lawyer," FACTS & FINDINGS, Volume IX, Issue V, March-April 1983, The National Association of Legal Assistants, Inc.

Morrison/Deciani, <u>Legal Ethics for Paralegals</u>, West Publishing Company.

(The) National Association of Legal Assistants, Inc., Code of Ethics and Professional Responsibility.

(The) National Association of Legal Assistants, Inc., Model Standards and Guidelines for Utilizaiton of Legal Assistants.

Rotunda, <u>Professional Responsibility</u>, 4th Ed. (Black Letter Series), West Publishing Company.

Statsky, <u>Essentials of Paralegalism</u>, 2nd Ed., West Publishing Company.

Statsky, <u>Introduction to Paralegalism</u>, 5th Ed., West Publishing Company.

Ulrich and Clarke, "Professional Responsibility," Working with Legal Assistants, Volume 2, page 279; 67 American Bar Association Journal 992 (August 1981).

Judgment and Analytical Ability References

Edwards, <u>Practical Case Analysis</u>, West Publishing Company.

Rombauer, <u>Legal Problem Solving</u>, 5th Ed., West Publishing Company.

Statsky, <u>Essentials of Paralegalism</u>, 2nd Ed., West Publishing Company.

Statsky, <u>Introduction to Paralegalism</u>, 5th Ed., West Publishing Company.

Statsky/Wernet, <u>Case Analysis and Fundamentals of Legal Writing</u>, 4th Ed., West Publishing Company.

Legal Research References

<u>A Uniform System of Citation</u>, 16th Ed., Harvard Law Review Association.

Cohen, <u>Legal Research in a Nutshell</u>, 5th Ed., West Publishing Company.

Cohen and Berring, <u>How to Find the Law</u>, 9th Ed., West Publishing Company.

Hein, <u>Legal Research for Paralegals</u>, West Publishing Company.

Jacobstein & Mersky, <u>Fundamentals of Legal Research</u>, 5th Ed., Foundation Press.

Rombauer, <u>Legal Problem Solving</u>, 5th Ed., West Publishing Company.

Shepard's Citations, Inc., <u>How to Use Shepard's Citations</u>, 1971.

Statsky/Wernet, <u>Case Analysis and Fundamentals of Legal Writing</u>, 4th Ed., West Publishing Company.

Walston-Dunham, <u>Practical Legal Research</u>, West Publishing Company.

<u>West Law Finder: A Legal Research Manual</u>, West Publishing Company.

Wren & Wren, <u>The Legal Research Manual</u>, 2nd Ed., A-R Editions, Inc., Madison, Wisconsin.

Human Relations References

Jongewood, <u>Everybody Wins: Transactional Analysis Applied in Organizations</u>, Addison-Wesley Publishing Co., Reading, Massachusetts.

or any general psychology book dealing with office human relations

Interviewing Techniques

Freeman and Weinhofen, <u>Clinical Law Training — Interviewing and Counseling</u>, (Chapters 2, 3, 9, and 13), West Publishing Company, 1972.

Shaffer, <u>Legal Interviewing and Counseling in a Nutshell</u>, 2nd Ed., West Publishing Company.

General Law References

Carper/Mietus/Shoemaker/West, <u>Understanding the Law</u>, 2nd Ed., West Publishing Company.

Grilliot, <u>Introduction to Law and the Legal System</u>, 6th Ed., Houghton Mifflin Company.

Walston-Dunham, <u>Introduction to Law</u>, 2nd Ed., West Publishing Company.

Administrative Law References

Cohen, <u>Practical Administrative Law for Paralegals</u>, West Publishing Company.

Gellhorn-Levin, <u>Administrative Law in a Nutshell</u>, 3rd Ed., West Publishing Company.

Hall, <u>Administrative Law</u>, Delmar Publications.

All contain at least selected text from the Administrative Procedure Act, 5 U.S.C.A.

Bankruptcy Law References

The Bankruptcy Code and Bankruptcy Rules (11 U.S.C.A.) are the authority for all questions and answers.

Frey, <u>Introduction to Bankruptcy Law</u>, 3rd Ed., West Publishing Company.

Webster, <u>Bankruptcy Law for Paralegals</u>, 2nd Ed., West Publishing Company.

Business Organizations (Corporations) References

Hamilton, <u>Corporations</u>, 3rd Ed. (Black Letter Series), West Publishing Company.

Hamilton, <u>The Law of Corporations</u>, 3rd Ed. (Nutshell), West Publishing Company.

Moye, <u>The Law of Business Organizations</u>, 4th Ed., West Publishing Company.

Most college business law texts contain excellent materials in this area.

Contract Law References

Bitting/Frey, <u>Introduction to Contracts and Restitution for Paralegals</u>, 2nd Ed., West Publishing Company.

Calamari and Perillo, <u>Contracts</u>, 2nd Ed. (Black Letter Series), West Publishing Company.

Schaber and Rohwer, <u>Contracts in a Nutshell</u>, 3rd Ed., West Publishing Company.

Thomas, <u>Contract Law for Paralegals</u>, West Publishing Company.

Weaver, <u>The Compact Guilde to Contract Law: A Civilized Approach to the Law</u>, West Publishing Company.

Most college business law texts contain excellent materials in this area.

Criminal Law References

Bacigal, <u>Criminal Law and Procedure</u>, West Publishing Company.

Bacigal, <u>Criminal Procedure: An Introduction</u>, West Publishing Company.

Israel and LaFave, <u>Criminal Procedure in a Nutshell</u>, 5th Ed., West Publishing Company.

Loewry, <u>Criminal Law in a Nutshell</u>, 2nd Ed., West Publishing Company.

Low, <u>Criminal Law</u>, Revised First Edition (Black Letter Series), West Publishing Company.

McCord/McCord, <u>Criminal Law and Procedure for the Paralegal</u>, West Publishing Company.

Estate Planning and Probate References

<u>Federal Estate & Gift Taxes Explained</u> (current issue), Commerce Clearing House.

Hower, <u>Wills, Trusts, and Estate Administration for the Paralegal</u>, 4th Ed., West Publishing Company.

Hower, <u>Wills, Trusts, and Estate Administration the Essentials</u>, West Publishing Company.

Schrader, <u>Introduction to Estates and Trusts</u>, 2nd Ed., West Publishing Company.

Averill, <u>Uniform Probate Code</u> (Nutshell), 4th Ed., West Publishing Company.

Family Law References

Krause, <u>Family Law in a Nutshell</u>, 3rd Ed., West Publishing Company.

Statsky, <u>Introduction to Paralegalism</u>, 5th Ed., West Publishing Company.

Statsky, <u>Family Law</u>, 4th Ed., West Publishing Company.

Statsky, <u>Family Law, The Essentials</u>, West Publishing Company.

Litigation References

Since procedural rules differ from state to state, all procedural questions are based on the Federal Rules of Civil Procedure and on generally accepted practice and procedure.

Blanchard, <u>Litigation and Trial Practice for the Legal Paraprofessional</u>, 4th Ed., West Publishing Company.

Bruno, <u>The Paralegal's Litigation Handbook</u>, 2nd Ed., West Publishing Company.

<u>Federal Rules of Civil Procedure</u> (paperback edition), West Publishing Company.

Kane, <u>Civil Procedure</u>, 4th Ed. (Nutshell), West Publishing Company.

McCord, <u>The Litigation Paralegal: A Systems Approach</u>, 3rd Ed., West Publishing Company.

Weinstein, <u>Introduction to Civil Litigation</u>, 3rd Ed., West Publishing Company.

Real Estate Law References

Bernhardt, <u>Property</u> (Black Letter Series), 2nd Ed., West Publishing Company.

Bernhardt, <u>Real Property</u> (Nutshell), 3rd Ed., West Publishing Company.

Dunn/Dunn/Koerselman/NALA, <u>Real Estate Law Review Manual</u>, West Publishing Company.

Flynn, <u>Introduction to Real Estate Law</u>, West Publishing Company.

Hinkel, <u>Practical Real Estate Law</u>, 2nd Ed., West Publishing Company.

Patton, <u>On Titles</u>, West Publishing Company.

Siedel, <u>Real Estate Law</u>, 3rd Ed., West Publishing Company.

INDEX

INDEX

THE COMPLETE POEMS OF
Emily Dickinson

THE COMPLETE POEMS OF

Emily Dickinson

EDITED BY

Thomas H. Johnson

LITTLE, BROWN AND COMPANY
BOSTON NEW YORK LONDON

Introduction

THERE are certain significant dates in American literary history during the nineteenth century. One was August 21, 1837, when Emerson, before the Phi Beta Kappa Society at Cambridge, Massachusetts, delivered in the presence of Thoreau's graduating class his "American Scholar" address, immediately hailed by young Oliver Wendell Holmes as "our intellectual Declaration of Independence." One was the day early in July, 1855, when Whitman "for the convenience of private reading only" began circulating printed copies of his *Leaves of Grass*. A third is surely April 15, 1862, when Thomas Wentworth Higginson received a letter from Emily Dickinson enclosing four of her poems.

Emily Dickinson, then thirty-one years old, was writing a professional man of letters to inquire whether her verses "breathed." Higginson was still living at Worcester, Massachusetts, where he had recently resigned his pastorate of a "free" church, and was beginning to establish a reputation as essayist and a lecturer in the cause of reforms. She dared bring herself to his attention because she had just read his "Letter to a Young Contributor," practical advice for those wishing to break into print, and the lead article in the current issue of the *Atlantic Monthly*. "Charge your style with life," he commented, and went on to declare that the privilege of bringing forward "new genius" was fascinating. His article happened to appear exactly at the moment that Emily Dickinson was ready to seek criticism. She knew him to be a liberal thinker, interested in the status of women in general and women writers in particular. Though the article drew responses, all of

[v]

which Higginson judged "not for publication," he sensed some quality in the enclosures of the letter posted at Amherst which elicited a reply. He asked for more verses, inquired her age, her reading and her companionships.

The importance of the correspondence with Higginson thus initiated, and continuing throughout Emily Dickinson's life, cannot be exaggerated. In the first place, the four poems she initially selected reveal that in 1862 the poet was no longer a novice but an artist whose strikingly original talent was fully developed. She enclosed "Safe in their Alabaster Chambers" (216), "I'll tell you how the Sun rose" (318), "The nearest Dream recedes – unrealized" (319), and "We play at Paste" (320). What embarrassed Higginson about the poems was his inability to classify them. In 1891 he wrote an article describing this early correspondence. "The impression of a wholly new and original poetic genius," he said, "was as distinct on my mind at the first reading of these four poems as it is now, after thirty years of further knowledge; and with it came the problem never yet solved, what place ought to be assigned in literature to what is so remarkable, yet so elusive of criticism." Higginson's problem was compounded by the fact that during Emily Dickinson's lifetime he was never convinced that she wrote poetry. As he phrased his opinion to a friend, her verses were "remarkable, though odd . . . *too delicate* — not strong enough to publish."

A representative mid-nineteenth-century traditionalist was being asked to judge the work of a "wholly new" order of craftsman. His reply to the first letter (implied in her second letter to him — his letters do not survive) must have told her that the "Alabaster" poem lacked form, that it was imperfectly rhymed and its metric beat spasmodic, a judgment which would have been shared at the time by most of the fraternity of literary appraisers. The unorthodoxy of melodic pattern controlled by key words, wherein the parts express the whole, the altering of metric beat to slow or speed the nature of time itself (the theme of the "Alabaster" poem), give it dimensions which he was not equipped to estimate. He was trying to measure a cube by the rules of plane geometry.

The first weeks of this letter exchange were critical in Emily Dickinson's literary life. Putting aside for the moment the issue whether she wished to see her poetry published (though the fact that she wrote in response to an article on how to contribute to magazines suggests